Talking about Naval History

NAVAL WAR COLLEGE HISTORICAL MONOGRAPH SERIES NO. 19

The historical monographs in this series are book-length studies of the history of naval warfare, edited historical documents, conference proceedings, and bibliographies that are based wholly or in part on source materials in the Historical Collection of the Naval War College.

The editors of the Naval War College Press express their special gratitude to all the members of the Naval War College Foundation, whose generous financial support for research projects, conferences, and printing has made possible the publication of this historical monograph.

Talking about Naval History:
A Collection of Essays

John B. Hattendorf
Ernest J. King Professor of Maritime History
Naval War College

NAVAL WAR COLLEGE PRESS
NEWPORT, RHODE ISLAND
2011

The contents of this volume represent the views of the author. His opinions are not necessarily endorsed by the Naval War College or by any other agency, organization, or command of the U.S. government.

Printed in the United States of America

Historical Monograph Series

Library of Congress Cataloging-in-Publication Data

Hattendorf, John B.
  Talking about naval history : a collection of essays / John B. Hattendorf.
     p. cm. — (Naval War College historical monograph series ; no. 19)
  Includes bibliographical references and index.
  ISBN 978-1-884733-74-1 (alk. paper)
  1. Naval history. I. Title.
  D27.H34 2010
  359.009—dc22

                              2011001541

NAVAL WAR COLLEGE PRESS
Code 32
Naval War College
686 Cushing Road
Newport, R.I. 02841-1207

TABLE OF CONTENTS

FOREWORD

I'm very honored to provide a few remarks as the foreword to this book. As a serving flag officer, I find few things as interesting as the institutional history of the U.S. Navy, and of navies generally. Arriving two years ago as President of the Naval War College, I was made painfully aware of how lacking my own knowledge was with respect to the history of not only the Naval War College but the U.S. Navy generally—and frankly, I had thought I knew a lot about it.

A well-known naval officer is said once to have remarked, "The thing I hate about historians is they are always looking at the past." Well, thank goodness, this is certainly the case with the Naval War College's Ernest J. King Chair of Maritime History, Professor John Hattendorf, and looking carefully at the past is what he has done in this masterful volume. In fact, as the faculty here in Newport will tell you, the past is the only thing we know "really happened." There may be disputes about certain facts, and historians inevitably disagree on issues arising from that most complex field of human endeavor, conflict and war—it's the nature of their chosen profession, especially for *naval* historians. In a recent edition of *Historically Speaking: The Bulletin of the Historical Society,* Professor Hattendorf and some of his esteemed colleagues engaged in a very interesting discussion about their chosen profession, a discussion that I would commend to your reading.[1] It is my view that many naval officers today lack a deep knowledge of their navy's institutional history—and by extension, its culture. There may be many reasons for this, not least of which is that we, and I include myself in this characterization, consider ourselves as people of *action,* as doers and problem solvers, content to leave the documentation of what we're doing and the study of our navy's history to others. It was, after all, civilians who wrote the first histories of the U.S. Navy—most notably, Washington Irving in the *Analectic Magazine* and James Fenimore Cooper in his two-volume *History of the Navy of the United States.*[2]

That said, some of my uniformed predecessors here at the Naval War College wrote about naval history. For example, William Ledyard Rodgers wrote *Greek and Roman Naval Warfare* (which can still be purchased at online bookstores);[3] also, William S. Sims received the Pulitzer Prize for *The Victory at Sea* in 1920, following his service during the First World War.[4] The first President here in Newport, Stephen B. Luce, was a prolific writer, as was Bradley Fiske. Also, of course, Alfred Thayer Mahan's Naval War

College lectures published as *The Influence of Seapower upon History* put the College on the map.

The point for serving professionals is that a sense of naval history is a real attribute for commanders, in terms both of understanding service identity and culture and of providing a context for the many decisions they are called upon to make during their service to the nation. This makes the role of naval historians, civilian and military, very important, as they work tirelessly to tell stories of our forebears, describe situations where things went terribly wrong, and show shining examples of solid decision and great leadership, with which, fortunately, our Navy has often been blessed. We as professionals also know that normally the truth lies somewhere in that grey area we call reality and that our naval heroes often had feet of clay. Like us today, these officers were often ordinary naval professionals trying their best to make sense out of extraordinary situations, under great pressure to take good decisions and—above all—to get the job done. The possible exceptions are officers like Horatio Nelson, whose timeless example still influences the behavior of naval officers today, over two hundred years after his death. The chapters of this book devoted to Nelson, the scholarship surrounding Nelson, and his legacy are great reading.

The chapters on naval history in the twentieth century—for example, the "lessons of Suez" and "globalization and navies"—are very relevant today, in this era of what is called the "Cooperative Strategy for 21st Century Seapower." In his *CNO Guidance for 2011,* the Chief of Naval Operations, Admiral Gary Roughead, says, "As I look to the future, I see continued disorder in the global security environment, a slow economic recovery, and an increasing demand on our Navy."[5] Even the most cursory review of international headlines tells us that CNO has this right, and frankly, it's not the first time the U.S. Navy has found itself in such a position. Naval history tells us this. That's why this book is important.

Professor John Hattendorf, a Kenyon College graduate with advanced degrees from Brown and Oxford, a naval officer brought to the Naval War College by Admiral Stansfield Turner, and an award-winning historian, has now been writing about naval history for almost fifty years, and this work is clear evidence of his mastery of the subject. In fact, in 2011 the Naval War College will award the first "Hattendorf Prize for Distinguished Original Research in Maritime History" to recognize Professor Hattendorf and his lifetime legacy of scholarship and service. Pam Ribbey, of Agoura Hills, California, a Graduate Life Patron of the Naval War College Foundation, has permanently endowed the Hattendorf Prize. Pam Ribbey's grandfather, Captain Charles Hamilton Maddox, USN (1886–1964), graduated from the Naval War College in 1935 and 1939, then served on its faculty in 1939–41.

By the terms of Pam Ribbey's endowment, the Hattendorf Prize will be made at two-year intervals and will include a minimum $10,000 cash award and the specially designed bronze Hattendorf Prize Medal. It is intended to be the most prestigious award that any scholar can receive in this field and to serve as a permanent beacon to encourage and promote new scholarship in this newly reemerging and reinvigorated field of study. Specifically, the prize is to be given for distinguished academic achievement in publishing original research that contributes to a deeper historical understanding of the broad context and interrelationships involved in the roles, contributions, limitations, and uses of the sea services in history.

These terms reflect the essence of John Hattendorf's professional values and goals for his field during his more than a quarter-century of service as the Naval War College's Ernest J. King Professor of Maritime History: to serve the Navy by improving the quality and range of scholarship in maritime history; engaging globally, with an appreciation for scholarship in different languages and from different national, cultural, and regional perspectives; and striving to see maritime history as a broad field in global history that builds on insights that cut across traditional academic and national boundaries. With these ends in view, the Hattendorf Prize will not be limited to American citizens or scholars studying within the U.S. Navy but will recognize world contributions. In so doing it will contribute to the Naval War College's academic roles in international engagement, scholarship, and service to the Navy.

This is a wonderful tribute to one of the nation's leading naval historians, and it is our hope that this award will encourage modern historians worldwide. It is absolutely in keeping with the foundations that Luce and Mahan laid here in Newport more than a century ago, when they turned to historical understanding as a fundamental element in the College's educational and research approach.

JAMES P. WISECUP
Rear Admiral, U.S. Navy
President, Naval War College

NOTES 1 Andrew D. Lambert, John Beeler, Barry Strauss, and John B. Hattendorf, "The Neglected Field of Naval History? A Forum," *Historically Speaking* 11, no. 4 (September 2010), pp. 9–19.

2 Washington Irving, "Biography of Captain James Lawrence," *Analectic Magazine* 2 (August 1813), pp. 123–39, and "Biographical Memoir of Commodore Perry," *Analectic Magazine* 2 (December 1813), pp. 494–510; James Fenimore Cooper, *History of the Navy of the United States of America* (Philadelphia: Lea and Blanchard, 1839).

3 William Ledyard Rodgers, *Greek and Roman Naval Warfare: A Study of Strategy, Tactics, and Ship Design from Salamis (480 B.C.) to Actium (31 B.C.)* (Annapolis, Md.: U.S. Naval Institute, 1937).

4 William S. Sims, *The Victory at Sea* (Garden City, N.Y.: Doubleday, Page, 1920).

5 U.S. Navy Dept., *CNO Guidance for 2011: Executing the Maritime Strategy* (Washington, D.C.: October 2010), available at www.navy.mil/.

INTRODUCTION

For an academic, talking about one's academic specialty is the bread-and-butter matter of one's craft and profession, whether done in the classroom, in tutorials one-on-one with students, in the range of public history opportunities offered by museum settings, or at academic and professional conferences. Talking about *maritime* history, especially the subspecialty of naval history within the broad field of maritime history, is the particular bread and butter of the Ernest J. King Professor of Maritime History at the Naval War College. Typically, these bread-and-butter talks go unrecorded, but one particular type does get printed and published: papers given at academic conferences. The essays in this volume constitute a selection of the papers that the current Ernest J. King Professor has written during the past decade.

Since its founding in 1884, the Naval War College has been a notable place for historical study and historical research, beginning with the pioneer historical work of the College's founder, Rear Admiral Stephen B. Luce, accompanied by his direction to Captain Alfred Thayer Mahan to begin the research and the writing for the Naval War College lectures that eventually became famous as Mahan's "Influence of Sea Power" series. A number of other naval officer historians followed Mahan at intermittent periods in Newport, including Rear Admiral Caspar Goodrich (1847–1925), who founded the Naval History Society for publishing American naval documents; Rear Admiral French E. Chadwick (1844–1919), who wrote a major work, *The Relations of the United States and Spain: The Spanish-American War* (1911); and Vice Admiral William L. Rodgers (1860–1944), who wrote *Greek and Roman Naval Warfare: A Study of Strategy, Tactics and Ship Design from Salamis (480 B.C.) to Actium* (1937) and *Naval Warfare under Oars, 4th to 16th Centuries: A Study of Strategy, Tactics and Ship Design* (1939). While these men had associations with the Naval War College and several wrote, or were inspired to write, their principal works at the College, there was no permanent academic position devoted to historical research or writing on naval history at the Naval War College during the first half of its existence, although topics in naval history have always been part of the curriculum. That changed in the wake of World War II, when the experience of that war, with all its new aspects, brought for some of the U.S. Navy's top commanders a recognition of the importance of a broader understanding of naval warfare that comes with the study of history.

As a faculty position at the Naval War College, the Ernest J. King academic chair had its immediate origins more than sixty years ago, in May 1948, when the President of the Naval War College, Admiral Raymond Spruance, recommended a plan to establish a civilian professorship of maritime history at the College. Secretary of the Navy John L. Sullivan approved the post on 29 December 1948, but it was not filled "for lack of funds" until 1951, when Thomas C. Mendenhall of Yale University became the first scholar to occupy it. In 1953, Secretary of the Navy Robert Anderson named the chair in honor of Fleet Admiral Ernest J. King, the U.S. Navy's great wartime Chief of Naval Operations. In naming this position, and with King's personal approval, Secretary Anderson not only honored King's personal interest in maritime history but underscored the particular importance that Fleet Admiral King gave to an understanding of naval history for his own professional naval career in positions of high command.

The Ernest J. King chair, so named, was first filled by Professor Clarence H. Haring, a distinguished scholar of Spanish imperial and maritime history in the seventeenth and eighteenth centuries who had come to the Naval War College for one year immediately after retiring from Harvard, where he had been the Robert Woods Bliss Professor of Latin American History for the previous thirty years. At that point, there was only one other named academic chair in the United States for the field of maritime history, namely, that held by Robert G. Albion, the Gardiner Professor of Oceanic History and Affairs, a chair established at Harvard University in 1948. The Naval War College's first permanent long-term civilian faculty member came in 1966, and its larger civilian faculty began in 1972. Between 1951 and 1973 the King chair was regularly held as a one-year visiting appointment. It became a position for a permanent faculty appointment with the tenure of Philip A. Crowl, from 1974 to 1980.

The following twenty essays were written between 2001 and 2009 and represent a wide historical perspective that ranges across nearly four centuries of maritime history. A number of these pieces have been published previously but have appeared in other languages and in other countries, where they may not have come to the attention of an American naval reading audience. This collection is divided into parts that deal with four major themes: the broad field of maritime history; general naval history, with specific focus on the classical age of sail, from the mid-seventeenth century to the end of the Napoleonic Wars in 1815; the wide scope of American naval history from 1775 to the end of the twentieth century; and finally, the realm of naval theory and its relationship to naval historical studies. They are reprinted, with only minor alterations, as they originally appeared.

As shown in the bibliographical appendix, this volume complements and continues an earlier collection of the author's work as Ernest J. King Professor, *Naval History and Maritime Strategy* (2000).

Part 1: The Field of Maritime History

I *The Uses of Maritime History in and for the Navy*

The knowledge of the past, the record of truths revealed by experience, is eminently practical, is an instrument of action, and a power that goes to the making of the future.

LORD ACTON (1832–1902)

There is an ever-present human tendency to think that all that went before is irrelevant and useless, especially in an era of transformation and change. Navies are particularly susceptible to this tendency since, in contrast to officers in other branches of service, naval officers, by and large, have tended to ignore the value of and advantages to be found in historical insight.

This negative attitude toward history within the Navy has its roots in the prevailing naval culture; it is shared widely among navies that have developed within the Anglo-American tradition. A dispassionate look at the patterns and process of innovation in the past, however, reminds us that such tendencies are to be determinedly guarded against. Maritime history is a central part of an understanding of the heritage and tradition of navies, but its value lies in more than heritage alone. Knowing what actually happened in the past is central to understanding the nature and character of naval power. It assists in knowing the limits to the usefulness of naval power as well as in understanding where we are today in the development and progression of the art of naval warfare. As every navigator understands, it is critical to know where we are and what external forces affected us on the way here if we are to lay the best course toward where we want to be.[1]

These judgments have once again been reaffirmed in the most recent study of the uses of history by, for, and in the American navy. In 2000 on the recommendation of the Secretary of the Navy's Advisory Subcommittee on Naval History, Secretary Richard Danzig commissioned an independent evaluation of the Navy's historical programs. This report, completed in October 2000, concluded that the U.S. Navy "has failed to use the rich historical information available to it in order to manage or apply effectively those resources for internal or external purposes."[2] Moreover, "while history survives in isolated pockets the use of naval heritage history is disjointed, sporadic, inconsistent, and occasionally contradictory. Without a clear service-wide mission, history in the Navy has itself become an artifact, delivering traditional products for use in a Navy seeking other types of information." Subsequent meetings in 2000 and 2002—where representatives of the perceived stakeholders of naval history throughout the Navy and supporters of naval history outside the service joined in the discussions—reviewed early drafts for a proposed strategy and a five-year plan for implementing it.

Nonetheless, despite these initiatives, at the beginning of 2003 the Navy still lacks an integrated policy for employing naval history. The recommendations and requests of Dr. David A. Rosenberg, the chairman of the Secretary of the Navy's Advisory Subcommittee on Naval History, for a strong and detailed policy statement, establishment of requirements, and the directives necessary to reverse the current trend have not yet been answered.[3]

If this situation is to be rectified, the U.S. Navy's senior leadership needs to establish clear policy guidance. The establishment at Newport of the Maritime History Department this year is but one of the first steps to be taken throughout the Navy if we are to reap the rewards from the integration of history, its lessons and its cautions, into all aspects of contemporary naval thinking, doctrine, planning, and education.

The Present Condition

The stakeholders and supporters of naval history within the U.S. Navy are few. It has been left largely to civilian specialists at the Naval Historical Center at the Washington Navy Yard and the handful of academics and administrators in the Navy's twelve museums, at the Naval Academy, and at the Naval War College. Naval history finds much more support outside the service, as can easily be seen in the keen interest in popular novels, films, and television programs with historical themes. A number of private organizations in the United States promote naval history and heritage, including the Naval Historical Foundation and the U.S. Navy Memorial Foundation in Washington, the Naval Order of the United States, the Historic Naval Ships Association, and the Center for Naval Analyses.

Perhaps the most active publisher of work on U.S. naval history outside of the Navy is another private organization, the U.S. Naval Institute, which issues not only its monthly *Proceedings* but also, since 1986, the quarterly *Naval History*. Since the 1960s, the Naval Institute Press has published an increasing number of prize-winning books on maritime history. The institute has also established an important photographic archive, available to the public. Since 1969 it has been the leader in the field in oral history, producing more than two hundred bound volumes on recent naval leaders.

For those in, or who work for, the Navy, history is not some amorphous, abstract, and intellectual creation; it happens around them all the time. What naval professionals do every day is part of our nation's history, as is the work of their predecessors. Ships and shore stations are historic sites, as well as places where important tasks are carried out today and are prepared for tomorrow. Many naval buildings and reservations are historic and even contain archaeological sites of great cultural importance. Many offices and naval stations contain valuable objects, historic documents, artwork, and books, or official records destined for permanent retention in the National Archives. The Navy and Marine Corps represent a broad cross section of American history; the safekeeping of national heritage, as reflected in its material culture, has been left to those who manage the Navy's assets. In the National Historic Preservation Act, Congress made the Navy Department responsible to the nation for the preservation of the cultural resources that it owns. It is an awesome responsibility but one easily forgotten by people struggling with immediate problems. The Navy needs to balance its management of these important cultural assets with its responsibilities for national defense, and it must do so, as the act requires, "in a spirit of stewardship" for the inspiration and benefit of present and future generations.[4]

Despite widespread interest and generous outside support, the uniformed Navy has yet to make full and effective use of maritime history as a resource. The practical challenge of implementing a Navy-wide policy for the support and practical use of maritime history in and for the Navy is a complex one. It involves promoting a range of interrelated but distinct levels of historical understanding as well as organizing and supporting a variety of responsibilities, tasks, and functions across the Navy. If such a program is to succeed, maritime history in the Navy will have to have the direct attention and the solid and continuing support of the flag officers who lead the service.

Maritime and Naval History Defined

To begin a vibrant historical program within the Navy, one needs first to understand what one means by "maritime" and "naval" history, respectively. There has long been confusion about the two terms, but in the past decade a consensus in usage has formed that clarifies the matter. Maritime history embraces naval history; it is the overarching subject that deals with the full range of mankind's relationships to the seas and oceans of the world. It is a broad theme that cuts across academic boundaries and builds linkages between disciplines to form a humanistic understanding of the many dimensions involved. Maritime history involves in particular the histories of science, technology, cartography, industry, economics, trade, politics, international affairs, imperial growth and rivalry, institutional and organizational development, communications, migration, law, social affairs, leadership, ethics, art, and literature. The range is immense, and the possible vantage points and topics are many. Yet the focus is clearly defined—ships

---

Continued on page 23

The History of History in the U.S. Navy and the Sea Services

1800	President John Adams orders the first Secretary of the Navy, Benjamin Stoddert, to gather books for a professional library, "to consist of the best writings in Dutch, Spanish, French, and especially English." This is the origin of the Navy Department Library (since 1970 it has been housed in the Washington Navy Yard).
1813	Thomas Clark publishes the first historical study of the U.S. Navy, basing it on personal communications with participants of the War of 1812.
1814	Congress establishes the Navy's first museum collection by directing that all captured naval flags be sent to Navy Department custody in Washington.
1833	Commander Matthew Perry is instrumental in establishing the U.S. Naval Lyceum, to "incite the officers of the naval service to increased diligence in the pursuit of professional and general knowledge." Following this lead, a similar institution would be established at Boston in 1842, and later another at Mare Island in California. The naval historical collections from New York and Boston will be donated to the Naval Academy Museum in 1892 and 1922.
1839	James Fenimore Cooper writes the first major history of the U.S. Navy.
1845–46	The newly established Naval Academy at Annapolis builds its first library and lyceum. Its permanent museum collection is founded three years later, with the transfer of the captured War of 1812 flags from the Navy Department.
1873	U.S. Naval Institute is founded. Two of its founders, Captain Stephen B. Luce and Commodore Foxhall Parker, will become among the earliest U.S. naval officers to advocate the professional study of naval history. James R. Soley launches the Naval Academy's curriculum first servies of lectures on naval history.
1882	The Office of Naval Records and Library is founded. Its head, James Soley, first systematically compiles the Navy's records, rare books, and other historical materials. Comprehensive publication of operational documents and dispatches relating to the Civil War begins in 1894 and the Spanish-American War operational records are published in 1899.

1884	Rear Admiral Stephen B. Luce establishes the Naval War College at Newport. Luce values historical study for learning to deal with specific situations and developing generalizations; he recruits Captain Alfred Thayer Mahan to research naval history and thereby explain to rising senior officers the art and science of high command. Mahan's pioneering historical work will establish some concepts that retain value after more than a century.
1899–1900	Captain Charles Stockton of the Naval War College faculty examines the history of international law and produces the first codification of the law of naval warfare.
1905	The remains of John Paul Jones are ceremonially removed from Paris to Annapolis, reviving widespread interest in the country's early naval history.
1917	Rear Admiral William S. Sims, Commander in Chief, U.S. Naval Forces, Europe, creates the Navy's first historical section on a major operational staff, which will continue until the end of the war. A separate historical section is also organized in Washington within the recently created Office of the Chief of Naval Operations.
1919	Major General Commandant George Barnett of the Marine Corps creates a Historical Section under the Adjutant and Inspector's Department. The first officer in charge is Major Edwin N. McClellan.
1921	Captain Dudley W. Knox becomes head of both the Historical Section in the Office of the Chief of Naval Operations and the Office of Naval Records and Library, launching a monograph series based on materials collected by the London Historical Section.
1926	The Naval Historical Foundation is founded to collect naval manuscripts and artifacts, eventually acquiring and donating to the Library of Congress the most important single collection of private naval papers in the United States.
1927	The Historical Section in the Office of the Chief of Naval Operations and the Office of Naval Records and Library in Washington merge.
1930	Dudley W. Knox assumes additional responsibility as Curator of the Navy. In 1934, in close personal cooperation with President Franklin Roosevelt, he will begin publication of a multivolume series of naval documents on the Barbary Wars and the Quasi-War with France.
1931	After overhaul, USS *Constitution* is recommissioned and sent on tour of American ports.
1938	Congress establishes Naval Academy Museum, authorizing tax-exempt gifts.
1942	Dudley W. Knox forms an Operational Archive to collect and organize wartime records. Separate from it, Samuel Eliot Morison of Harvard receives a direct commission as a lieutenant commander to prepare an operational naval history, receiving presidential carte blanche for travel and access. His fifteen-volume *History of United States Naval Operations in World War II* will appear in 1947–62.
1943	Professor Robert G. Albion of Princeton is appointed to a part-time position to oversee 150 naval officers writing some two hundred studies on the Navy's administrative history during World War II, a project that will be completed in 1950.
1944	Secretary of the Navy James Forrestal establishes the Office of Naval History within the Office of the Secretary of the Navy. Its first director is retired Admiral Edward C. Kalbfus, twice President of the Naval War College. Knox becomes deputy director of naval history under Kalbfus.

1945   The Bureau of Ships establishes the Office of Curator of Ship Models at the David Taylor Model Basin, to oversee the continuing acquisition of a collection that dated to the 1883 requirement to build and retain exhibition-quality models of the Navy's newest ships. Now sponsored by the Naval Surface Warfare Center, the Naval Sea Systems Command, and the Naval Historical Center, it currently has over 2,100 models as a three-dimensional record of naval ship and aircraft design.

1947   The Civil Engineer Corp/Seabee Museum opens at Port Hueneme, California, with a command historian and archive.

1948   At the recommendation of Admiral Raymond Spruance, the Secretary of the Navy approves establishment of an academic chair of maritime history at the Naval War College, subsequently named in 1953 in honor of Fleet Admiral Ernest J. King. USS *Texas* (BB 35) becomes a memorial and museum ship at San Jacinto State Park, in Texas.

1949   The Office of Naval History merges with the Office of Naval Records and Library to create the Naval Records and Library Division of the Office of the Chief of Naval Operations. In 1952, it will become the Naval History Division, under the Director of Naval History.

1952   The Secretary of the Navy's Advisory Committee on Naval History, an independent group of experts on naval history, is founded to advise the Navy on its historical programs. Over the years, its members will include such distinguished American historians as Samuel Flagg Bemis, Francis L. Berkeley, James Field, John Kemble, Alan Nevins, Richard Leopold, and Walter Muir Whitehill, as well as retired senior flag officers and some of the country's leading art experts, museum directors, and librarians.

1957   The Navy transfers ownership of Admiral George Dewey's flagship, USS *Olympia,* to a private organization for preservation and display.

1960   The first Marine Corps Museum is opened at the Marine Corps Base at Quantico, Virginia. It will come under the control of the newly created History and Museums Division during 1972–73 and move to the first floor of the Marine Corps Historical Center in the Washington Navy Yard during 1976–77.

1961   The U.S. Naval Historical Display Center, the forerunner of the National Museum of the U.S. Navy, is established in Washington, to open in 1963.

1963   The Naval Air Station Pensacola museum, now the National Museum of Naval Aviation, is founded.

1964   The Submarine Force Library and Museum is established at New London, Connecticut, with materials acquired from the Electric Boat Company's collection.

1967   The Coast Guard establishes a curatorial services department. The Coast Guard Academy establishes a museum at New London, Connecticut, to complement its teaching program; in 1971, it will become the U.S. Coast Guard Museum.

1970   The Naval War College creates the Naval Historical Collection for its archives, manuscript collection, and rare books.

1971   The Naval Historical Center in the Washington Navy Yard is established, replacing the Naval Historical Division. Its director (a civilian since 1986) serves on the Navy Staff as the Director of Naval History.

1972	The U.S. Naval Academy holds its first naval history symposium, which soon becomes a biennial meeting and the most important regular academic conference within the field of U.S. naval history.
1974	The Naval Supply Corps School at Athens, Georgia, establishes a museum.
1976	The private, nonprofit USS *Constitution* Museum is established.
1977	The Naval Research Laboratory establishes its historical office and develops writing, research, and oral history programs. The Marine Corps Historical Center in the Washington Navy Yard opens its doors to house the History and Museums Division of the Marine Corps, formed in 1973 under Brigadier General Edwin H. Simmons, USMC.
1978	A museum devoted to the history of aviation test and evaluation is founded at the Patuxent River Naval Air Station in Maryland. The Naval War College opens a museum in the College's first classroom building. The Marine Corps Aviation Museum is created (to be renamed the Marine Corps Air-Ground Museum in 1982–83) as a field activity of the History and Museums Division. It occupies several exhibit and storage buildings and hangars at Marine Base Quantico, Virginia, before closing to the public in anticipation of a new National Museum of the Marine Corps to be opened at Quantico in 2006.
1979	U.S. Merchant Marine Academy at Kings Point, New York, establishes a museum to complement its teaching of maritime history. The Commander, Navy Region, Mid-Atlantic establishes the Hampton Roads Naval Exhibit devoted to the naval history in the Hampton Roads, Yorktown, and Norfolk, Virginia, areas. The Marine Corps Historical Foundation is established in the Washington Navy Yard.
1980	The Bureau of Medicine and Surgery establishes historical activities as an additional duty for the editor of the Navy Medical Department's journal, *Navy Medicine*. The editor develops writing, research, and oral history programs until the Office of Historian of the Naval Medical Department is established in September 2002.
1986	The Naval Submarine Base, New London, Connecticut, acquires the deactivated USS *Nautilus* for its Submarine Force Museum.
1991	The Naval Undersea Museum at Keyport, Washington, is established, devoted to the ocean environment and the history of U.S. torpedo, mine warfare, and submarine technology.
1995	The Civil Engineering Corps Seabee Museum establishes a branch on the Gulf Coast at Gulfport, Mississippi.
2000	The Museum of Armament and Technology at the Naval Weapons Center, China Lake, California, is established to display technology and weapons that have played important roles in the previous six decades of the service's history.
2003	On 1 January 2003, the Naval War College creates a Maritime History Department, consolidating its activities and collections in the field of maritime history and establishing a research unit for basic and applied maritime history.
2005	On 1 September 2005, the U.S. Marine Corps Historical Office moves from the Washington Navy Yard to Quantico, Virginia, and becomes a component of Marine Corps University.
2006	On 13 November 2006, the National Museum of the Marine Corps opens at Quantico, Virginia. In October 2006, the Chief of Naval Operations directs consolidation of all U.S. Navy museums under the Director of Naval History.

2008   On 8 December 2008, in recognition of the increased responsibilities of the Director
            of Naval History for the Naval Historical Center and all of the Navy's museums
            across the country, the Chief of Naval Operations renames the center and its com-
            ponent museums as the Naval History and Heritage Command.

Continued from page 19

and the sailors who operate them, with specific sets of scientific understanding and technological devices, in their hostile sea environment, which covers the greater part of the globe.

Within the broad field of maritime history, there are a number of recognized major subspecialties. Among them are the history of navigational and maritime sciences; the histories of ships and their construction, the aircraft that fly over the seas, and the submarines that pass under their surface; maritime economic history; the histories of merchant shipping, fishing, and whaling; the histories of yachting and other leisure activities at sea and on the seaside; the histories of geographical exploration and cartography; social and labor history, the health of seamen; maritime law, maritime art, maritime literature; and naval history. These subspecialties are interrelated within the framework of maritime history to varying degrees, but each is tied as well to historical subject areas outside the maritime field. Characteristically, a maritime subspecialty's relationship outside the field defines its perspective on, and approach to, maritime history.

War at sea and the development of its political, technological, institutional, and financial elements is, thus, the focus of the naval history subspecialty. Within the structure of maritime history, naval history relates to the other maritime subspecialties as a special case, a particular application of the histories of ships and shipbuilding, geographical exploration, cartography, social and labor issues, health, law, art, literature, and so on. It also connects to the study of agencies and sea services that cooperate or share responsibilities with navies, such as (in the United States) the Marine Corps, Coast Guard, Revenue Service, and Coast Survey. The last three have fulfilled under a variety of organizational names critical maritime functions as hydrography, policing and safety of navigation, piloting, and the licensing of mariners. Outside the maritime sphere, naval history is closely associated with, and has adopted the broad approaches of, such fields as military studies, international affairs, politics, government, and the history of technology.

Naval history specifically involves the study and analysis of the ways in which governments have organized and employed force at sea to achieve national ends. It ranges across all periods of world history and involves a wide variety of national histories, languages, and archival sources. (Most prominent among the latter are governmental archives, supplemented by the private papers of individuals who served in or with navies.) The study of naval history involves analysis of the ways in which decisions were reached and carried out, as well as of the design, procurement, manufacture, and employment of vessels, aircraft, and weapons to achieve the ends in view. As Admiral Sir Herbert Richmond succinctly put it, naval history

> includes the "whys" of strategy in all its phases, from the political sphere to that of the minor strategy and tactics of fleets and squadrons: it includes the "hows" of the actual performances: and, not less important, the "whys" of success and failure. It embraces all those . . .

elements of foreign diplomatic relations, of economics and commerce, of international law and neutrality, of positions, of the principles of war, of administration, of the nature of the weapon, and of personality.[5]

Naval history in the machine age faces the need to explain these matters comprehensively, placing individual decisions and the collective interactions of leaders within a wide context of technological, financial, and operational issues.[6]

A traditional work in the field of naval history traces the ways in which national leaders dealt with international situations and decided upon courses of action that involved employment of ships and weapons at sea, and the reasons why. It then follows the results of those decisions and examines the actual uses of naval force at sea and its consequences, often in terms of the biographies of particular admirals, specific battles, campaigns, or accounts of the actions of fleets, squadrons, and even individual ships and aircraft.

In contrast, modern naval historians have come to understand that navies and those who serve in uniform do not exist separately from other parts of society. In addition to seeing their actions in terms of leadership, tactics, and strategy, scholars must also understand them in terms of the external environment, domestic politics, bureaucratic politics, the state of technological development and capabilities, procurement issues, organizational culture, and the capacity of naval men and women (in a profession marked by rigid hierarchical structures) for innovation, change, and alternative approaches.[7] Modern naval history looks at navies not only within their national contexts or as instruments of particular national states but also from wider international and comparative perspectives, in terms either of the chronological development of specific events or of the broad, long-term development of navies around the world.[8] Clearly the actions of one navy cannot be considered in isolation from foreign influences, whether enemies, allies, or world developments.

Naval historians, as practitioners of the wider field of maritime history, are bound by the same general requirements and standards as apply to scholars who work, research, or write in any other historical area. Any historical project requires a wide understanding of the context in which the events under study took place, a deep appreciation of the historical literature addressing the subject and its broad field, and a thorough examination of the original documents and other primary source materials that establish authoritatively what occurred, how, and why.

The Audiences for Maritime History

For the historical program to be successful, the Navy and its historians must be more strategic in their approaches, recognizing that they must appeal to a number of different audiences at once. Maritime history in the United States has four distinct audiences, each of which requires different approaches, levels of understanding, and vantage points: Congress and other government leaders, including uniformed members of the nonnaval services; the men and women of the U.S. Navy; academics; and the general public.

The first two audiences—Congress, government leaders, and uniformed men and women in all the armed services—look to a historical understanding that provides considerations and insight useful for the current and future development of the Navy. Their collective interest and approach may be described as applied history.[9] The last two audiences, the general public and academe, form a related pair; they look toward broad understanding and evaluation of maritime and naval events as fundamental and as essential for understanding world history and national life. Their interests may be described as those of basic history.

The Decision Makers: A Focused Audience

The general public's understanding of maritime and naval affairs—developed, corrected, and expanded by the academic community—provides the foundation for at least the initial understandings of the people in charge of leading, building, funding, and developing the Navy. These decision makers, leaders of government, are those who make up an important audience for applied history.

However, their needs in maritime and naval history are more detailed, specific, and technical than those of the public and academe, address professional interests beyond the scope of popular and academic interests, and typically need to be formulated and presented in different ways.

Congress and Government Leaders

Members of Congress, congressional staff members, and the uniformed men and women of services other than the Navy form a distinct audience for certain aspects of maritime history. This audience is widely varied but may include representatives from areas that have long-standing interests in maritime affairs, such as coastal states, states with traditional Navy ties, vocal groups of naval retirees or veterans, or states where assets for the Navy are produced or its bases are located. This part of the audience will have special interests in specific aspects of naval history that relate to their own state and its history, politics, or interests but may need specific information that builds on their traditional ties or broadens their regional outlook into a national perspective. Congress and government leaders also include those who do not have such built-in interests but need understandings of how and why the Navy has developed, if they are to carry out their responsibilities effectively.

A component of this audience of specific interest to the Navy comprises the Navy Department's senior civilian appointees, such as the Secretary of the Navy, the Assistant Secretaries of the Navy, and the noncareer deputy assistant secretaries. Most typically have short tenures with the Navy Department in the course of careers that take them to a variety of executive branch positions. Like many members of Congress and leaders in other services, they do not necessarily have previous exposure to naval matters. These leaders with important present responsibilities have a direct, practical need to know about the roles and functions of the Navy and when, why, and how it has been used, misused, or neglected in the past. As Sir Basil Liddell Hart once wrote, "History is a catalogue of mistakes. It is our duty to profit by them."[10]

Those who make decisions on present and future naval issues need to profit from past errors and problems. They always need a sense of the backgrounds of the difficult issues they are struggling to solve. The Navy's historians should provide historical understanding in ways that are accessible to busy leaders, who need specific information and interpretation focused on particular elements of maritime history in ways that provide insight into current debates over funding, policy making, and joint-service operational and technical planning. This type of information is likely to be precise and detailed, even quantified, pointing to specific incidents in American historical experience or drawing broad parallels to situations in American or world history.

The 2000 independent study commissioned by the Secretary of the Navy, *History and Heritage in the U. S. Navy,* found that the Navy does little to support decision makers by providing them with historical background to current issues.

What is being done is scattered informally through a variety of activities, including the Center for Naval Analyses, the Naval Historical Center, the Navy Museum, the Naval War College, and several nongovernmental organizations and museums.[11] Plainly the audience of congressional and other government leaders is a neglected audience, but one neglected at great cost. Whenever the country faces war, Congress, civilian leaders in the executive branch, the leaders of other services that cooperate with the Navy, and, above all, the nation's statesmen critically need to know and understand, in terms of actual practice and experience, the fundamental roles, limitations, and practicalities of the Navy's organization and its ability to provide mobility for military forces, project power overseas, control and protect sea and air routes, serve the objectives of foreign policy, and carry out its variety of other functions. They need to understand also the typical challenges that the Navy faces and the reasons why a number of roles that a statesman might be tempted to assign the Navy would be inadvisable, would distract it from its useful purposes. Leaders who have a broad understanding of and insight into maritime history and perceive the historical uses of and limitations upon fleets will be in a far better position to make proper decisions in regard to the present and future use of navies than those who have none.

Uniformed Men and Women in the Navy
The people who serve in uniform in the Navy provide a special audience with particular needs for history. For the uniformed Navy naval history is heritage, but at the same time professionals within the Navy need to analyze critically their profession's historical experience in ways that inform their thinking and decision making.

Understanding maritime history is part of naval professional identity. Understanding their own profession leads officers or enlisted personnel alike to feel a natural bond with other sailors, whatever their form of maritime endeavor or nationality. Today's sailors share a proud heritage that includes the world's great seamen and world explorers, such as Christopher Columbus, Ferdinand Magellan, and James Cook. Naval leaders, of course, are part of this professional maritime pantheon. Here we usually think of the great fighting commanders in the context of battles and fleet operations: Drake, Tromp, Blake, de Ruyter, Nelson, Togo, Jellicoe, and Scheer, and within our own navy, Farragut, Dewey, Nimitz, Spruance, and Halsey. But a navy, of necessity, is made up of people of many kinds of abilities. Those who specialize in one form of warfare or spend their careers in science, technology, education, and logistics offer modern sailors models of inspiration and devotion to their profession no less valuable than those of fleet commanders.

Among such other models about whom our professionals need to learn, and toward whom they should look, are the scientist and oceanographer Matthew Maury, the inventor John Ericsson, the thinker and strategist J. C. Wylie, the mathematician C. H. Davis, the salvage expert Edward Ellsberg, the gun designer John Dahlgren, the logistician Henry Eccles, the educator Stephen B. Luce, the naval engineer B. F. Isherwood, the civil engineer Ben Moreell, the intelligence officer J. J. Rochefort, the aviator William Moffett, the naval diplomatist Matthew Perry, and the submariner Charles Lockwood; Joy Bright Hancock, a pioneering advocate for women in the U.S. Navy; Grace

Murray Hopper, the brilliant developer of computer languages; Charles M. Cooke and Forrest Sherman, operational planners; H. Kent Hewitt, the amphibious innovator; Sumner Kimball, of the Life Saving and Revenue Cutter Services; Ellsworth Bertholf, of the Coast Guard; Spencer Baird, of the U.S. Fish Commission; Alexander Bache, of the Coast Survey; the many examples to be found in the history of the Marine Corps, including Holland Smith, Edson, and Puller; and a variety of people in the enlisted ranks, whose lives and services to the nation in a variety of ratings need to be discovered and made available to professionals.

There are even heroes for naval historians: Sir John Knox Laughton, Sir Julian Corbett, Sir Herbert Richmond, and Captain Stephen Roskill of Britain, alongside the Americans Alfred Thayer Mahan, Authur Marder, Robert G. Albion, and Samuel Eliot Morison.

The professional naval audience has a particular practical interest in maritime history in the context of recruiting: inculcating and maintaining service pride and tradition during the indoctrination and initial training and education of enlisted recruits, midshipmen, and officer candidates. This also plays a key role in the naming of buildings and ships, and the creation of memorials. Dr. William S. Dudley—former Director of Naval History on the staff of the Chief of Naval Operations and director of the Naval Historical Center—has reminded those in uniform who lead our sailors, "'Celebrate, commemorate, motivate,' these words suggest what history and heritage can contribute to the Navy's rich human potential."[12] With this idea in mind, Dudley suggests that the first need is to give those who serve in the Navy a ready awareness of service history, a foundation upon which to develop deeper professional understanding.

The use of history for patriotic and motivational purposes is very important and powerful. It is also, however, an approach that can be, and has been, misused by totalitarian regimes. In a democratic state, great care is required, as is particular attention to the ideals of academic history—critical analysis of documents, factual accuracy, and commitment to the truth of what actually happened. One of the principal reasons for a lack of quality in the subspecialty of naval history is the lingering suspicion that its practitioners somehow falsify it to achieve a government's political or institutional objectives.

Historians employed by governmental agencies in a democratic country have a special obligation to the historical profession in this regard. They must always bear in mind that the government belongs to the people and is, in its actions, responsible to them and to public judgment. Congress, the executive branch, and the courts have established laws and regulations mandating the freedom of public information, limiting government control over it, and laying out the responsibilities of agencies, including the National Archives, for the permanent preservation and eventual release of records. Unless lost, deliberately destroyed, or weeded out by archivists, information in government files sooner or later becomes available for public scrutiny and critical analysis. This very process requires that the government's historians serve the public interest, not varying political or institutional interest. American naval history is so rich in experience and contains so many fine examples of bravery, courage, and professional excellence that there is no need to embellish the record. Quite the contrary—an accurate relation of the historical events and their context underscores the real achievements.

Entertaining and instructive stories that define ideals and motivate professionals to achieve them is neither all that naval professionals need to know about maritime history nor all that historians can offer the Navy. As naval officers gain professional maturity and become involved in broader issues, the historical lessons they need begin to overlap with the kinds of information that government leaders use. Still, there is a professional naval dimension that differentiates their historical study from that of other users of naval history—the need to think critically about the naval past in order to deal with the problems of the present and future. To a greater degree than history used for motivational and leadership purposes, professional historical knowledge involves clear, critical, rational analysis of success and failure, in considerably more detail than the information that is normally useful or relevant to nonspecialist government leaders.

The present-mindedness of American naval culture typically leads serving professionals to consider as entirely new "bright ideas" that have in fact been tried before, in circumstances that may cast light on their applicability in a new and different context. History is particularly valuable for the insight it can bring to issues that recur only rarely, perhaps once in a generation: reorganization of the Navy Staff; the interrelationships of the offices of the secretaries of defense and the Navy, the Office of the Chief of Naval Operations; and the administration of the Navy's shore establishment by regions. Similarly, the Navy has long, useful experience in mine warfare countermeasures. Homeland harbor defense, a joint Army-Navy–Coast Guard concept that was applied in Vietnam and the Gulf Wars and is now arising again, was a "live" topic half a century ago but disappeared from view at the end of World War II.

Operational doctrine and the principles of war are attempts to distill such actual experience—historical experience, even if very recent—into "axioms" that can be readily applied to the present and future.[13] There is no doubt wisdom in them, but the idea that human conduct can be effectively reduced to axioms is doubtful. Human actions and reactions do not conform to the laws of physics, mechanics, or the natural sciences. In the nineteenth century, many thinkers thought they might, but later analysts discarded such ambitions, decades ago. Such formulations and professional axioms of the past are merely "rules of thumb"; they cannot be used blindly. They must be continually and critically tested against experiences in differing contexts. A study of the past shows what has worked and what has failed, but no two events are ever quite the same. Historical analogies do not create axioms but, more valuably, suggest the questions that need to be considered and the range of considerations that pertain.

American naval writers have been all too apt, in particular, to search the writings of Alfred Thayer Mahan for axioms of naval strategy, but he himself is a part of history, and his works need to be understood in terms of his intentions and of how they have since been used, misused, superseded, broadened, and modified.[14] Historical study provides the practical basis of, and its approaches develop the intellectual tools for, an understanding of the nature of strategy and the process it involves.[15] In this connection, historical understanding and knowledge of past events is not the object but rather one of several means to improve the ability of professionals to solve problems more wisely than arbitrary choice, pure chance, or blind intuition would allow.

The General Public

Far more than many academics are willing to grant, the general public's interest in the field of maritime history is significant and continues to grow. There is a large market for popular works across a wide range of media: biographies, narrative books and articles, heavily illustrated books and magazines, historical novels, feature films, television series on the major networks as well as such outlets as Public Broadcasting Service, the History Channel, and the Discovery Channel. This wide public audience includes former and retired members of the sea services, but it is not limited to them. A large number of people with no prior connection to the services are fascinated by naval events, are intrigued by warships, aircraft, and naval equipment, and admire and take an interest in those who go to sea and have accomplished feats of navigation or geographical exploration. This is an audience with interests that are wide and general but at the same time often focused on individual events, specific seamen, or heroic actions, ships, or weapons. The Navy meets the interests of this audience by supplying historical information; making available historical photographs, films, and other images; maintaining museums, opening its libraries and archives to the public, and making available experts who can assist in the production or editorial review of popular works and advise on their historical accuracy. The Navy also posts a great deal of information on websites, where it is easily accessible to the public. Most notable among them is that maintained by the Naval History and Heritage Command in Washington, D.C.;[16] on it can be found a wide variety of historical information, bibliographies, a guide to manuscripts located in repositories in Washington and throughout the country, and a guide to organizations, programs, and resources relating to the U.S. Navy's history. The website also includes links to numerous naval history–related sites outside the Navy.

In a democratic state, ordinary citizens need to understand why such vast sums of taxpayers' money are spent on their navy and what it achieves. They do not need to know all the technical details, but surely they need a basic sense of the importance of naval supremacy in international relations, as well as of the roles and functions of the navy in both peace and war, if they are to have a complete appreciation of the history of the nation. The wider public in the United States needs to understand the role of the sea in American history and the essential roles that mariners played in its colonization, settlement, and early national development. Among a wide range of other things, the public needs to understand the essential contribution of the French navy to the military decision at Yorktown, which won American independence. It needs to understand that nearly the entire income of the federal government in the early decades of the republic derived from tariffs on maritime trade. American citizens need to know, as a matter of their national heritage, about the role and influence of maritime power on the coasts and on rivers during the Civil War; about the terrific struggles and dramatic victories at sea in the First and Second World Wars; more recently, about how the Soviet naval threat during the Cold War was met; and about the roles and accomplishments of the Navy in the post–Cold War era, in the Caribbean, the Adriatic and Mediterranean, the Persian Gulf, and the Indian Ocean.

Moreover, to stimulate and maintain this broad audience, war monuments and veterans memorials may be found in virtually every county, if not every town, in the country. Comparatively judged, there are a large number of maritime museums in the United States. The American Council of Maritime Museums currently has some forty-two institutional members, and twenty-one other museums are affiliate members. Its membership currently includes two of the twelve museums that the U.S. Navy operates (the Navy Museum in Washington and the Naval Academy Museum) and the

Navy's Curator of Ship Models. Three of the Navy's twelve museums have been accredited by the American Association of Museums as having reached high professional standards: the Navy Museum in Washington, the National Museum of Naval Aviation in Pensacola, and the Naval Undersea Museum at Keyport, Washington.

In addition, there are more than a hundred historic ships, operated by some seventy organizations, open to the public in the United States. Moreover, a variety of other museums and libraries draw large audiences to view major permanent or temporary exhibitions in maritime and naval history.

Not everything of historical interest, of course, can or should be saved, but neither should they be inappropriately destroyed or left unmanaged. Some things are intrinsically valuable; some are useful only for the information they contain; some are both, some neither. The variety is immense. But every item worthy even of consideration for preservation has a life cycle, comprising identification, preservation, interpretation, use, and disposition—perhaps, transfer to appropriate repositories, or disposal. Every historical object needs to be taken up by an institutional infrastructure that can manage and preserve it and make it useful and accessible for professional use or public knowledge. Even tactical and administrative computer systems that process potentially historic information should be designed from the outset to preserve that information for future use.

To be a positive historical asset, an object must be placed in the context of a museum collection, an archive, a library, or some other specially formed collection with cataloging, identification, and retrieval systems.[17] In order to do this in a way that meets modern professional demands, a major naval shore command may need a trained historical officer, who is educated in maritime history, serves as a resource, advises the commander, and coordinates with guidance from the Director of Naval History in Washington, the entire range of activities relating to maritime history that the particular command is likely to face—local history, archaeology, preservation of records, archives, rare books, charts and maps, art, historical commemorations, museums, and historical objects.

The Academic Audience

By contrast, the academic audience is small and generally limited to a relatively small number of students and faculty at colleges and universities, but it is an extremely important audience, far more so than its numbers suggest. Its importance lies in the fact that the independent thinking and scholarship of these researchers create the fundamental historical understanding of maritime and naval events that serves as the basis for those of all the other audiences. Other audiences may use the products of scholarly history in ways that academics might consider fragmentary or lacking in depth, but their understandings are ultimately based upon academic perceptions, debates, and prevailing interpretations.

The most important way in which the Navy interacts with the academic world is through direct discourse—its participation in academic research, writing, and professional evaluation of academic literature. This participation is undertaken largely by the research staff at the Naval History and Heritage Command in Washington and through the research and publications of faculty members who specialize in naval history at the Naval Academy in Annapolis, the Naval War College in Newport, and the Naval Postgraduate School in Monterey, California.

The ability of historians within the Navy to publish historical studies that meet high academic standards and become part of the academic historical discourse is essential to the Navy's ability to inform the public about its contributions to national life and its role in international affairs. Additionally, the Navy makes an essential contribution to the academic audience by allowing its own academic historians to act as advocates within the service. It contributes also by publishing (on the basis of the professional knowledge and judgment of its historians) official documents on naval history and by declassifying and otherwise making available for scholarly research archival material and historical collections owned by the Navy.[18]

For a long time, the academic standard of maritime history in the United States was not of the highest quality; only a few college or university history departments in the United States provided courses in any aspect of the subject. Nonetheless, over the past decade there have been strong indications that this trend is being reversed.[19] Mystic Seaport's general history *America and the Sea: A Maritime History* (1998) has apparently been adopted as a general textbook for this purpose on several campuses where the subject was not previously offered.[20] It is certainly used at Mystic Seaport in Connecticut, where the Munson Institute of American Maritime History offers accredited, graduate-level summer courses in maritime history.[21] Today a sizeable number of individual scholars, scattered across the country in various universities, colleges, and research institutions, pursue professional research and writing interests in naval history and within the broader scope of maritime history. It is these established scholars, along with a growing number of graduate students researching master's and doctoral theses within these areas, who constitute the main academic audience within the United States. They are joined by a similar set of scholars in other countries, most recently in Australia, Britain, Canada, Denmark, France, Germany, Italy, India, Norway, the Netherlands, New Zealand, South Africa, Spain, Portugal, Sweden, and Latin America, who share interests in this field and bring to it invaluable perspectives from the vantage points of other cultures, navies, and maritime environments.

The Navy's single most important interaction with the academic historical audience is the Naval History Symposium, sponsored by the U.S. Naval Academy at regular intervals since the first was held in Annapolis in May 1972. Originally conceived as an annual event, it has been held biennially since 1973. Since the third symposium, in 1980, a volume of selected conference papers has usually been published after each conference, reflecting the new interpretations and perspectives in naval history of this forum, attended regularly by several hundred historians and graduate students.[22]

The Navy's historians, librarians, and archivists assist academic researchers in finding materials they need for research. In addition to archival guides and official naval records made available for research at the National Archives and Record Administration, the Naval Historical Center continually updates on its website a guide to manuscripts available for research in libraries and archives across the country.[23] Complementing this, the Naval War College, like other institutions, maintains on its own website a list of its manuscript and archival holdings (in its Naval Historical Collection) with a list of available research aids.[24]

Two commands within the Navy and several civilian organizations have attempted to raise the standards of naval history and promote new academic work through the establishment of prizes. Among the civilian organizations, the New York Council of the Navy League of the United States, the Theodore Roosevelt Association, and the Franklin and Eleanor Roosevelt Institute have joined forces to recognize annually the best book in U.S. naval history with the Theodore and Franklin Delano Roosevelt Prize in naval history. In 2002, this award was made a cash prize of five thousand dollars. In addition, the nation's professional organization for maritime historians, the North American Society of Oceanic Historians (NASOH), awards annually its prestigious John Lyman Book Prizes for a range of subjects in maritime history, including one in the category of U.S. naval history.

The Naval History and Heritage Command promotes new academic work through the establishment of the Rear Admiral John D. Hayes Pre-doctoral Fellowship in U.S. Naval History for civilian graduate students; Vice Admiral Edwin B. Hooper research grants for postdoctoral scholars and accomplished authors; the Samuel Eliot Morison Naval History Scholarship for active-duty naval and Marine officers engaged in graduate studies; and the Ernest M. Eller Prize, awarded annually for the best article on American naval history published in a scholarly journal.

In addition to these prizes, the Naval War College Foundation awards annually the Edward S. Miller History Prize for the best article on naval history to appear in the *Naval War College Review*. It also funds the Edward S. Miller Fellowship in Naval History, a thousand-dollar grant to assist a scholar using the College's archives and historical collections. The work of naval historians is also considered for the Samuel Eliot Morison, Victor Gondos, Moncado, and Distinguished Book Prizes awarded annually by the Society for Military History in the broad field of military history. The U.S. Commission on Military History provides two $2,500 grants to encourage and support American graduate students seeking to present the results of their research in U.S. naval history topics at the annual overseas congress of the International Commission on Military History.

Maritime History in the U.S. Navy Today

A single broad historical theme might be presented to all four audiences, but it needs to be presented to each in a different way and by different means. Some audiences and groups may acquire their general knowledge through books and articles, but others are reached most effectively through images—films, videos, and dramatizations. An academic researcher may require original documents; a teenager, an interactive game; a member of Congress, a succinct tabulation of data; a career naval professional, a technical analysis. The detailed and technical information that makes maritime history useful for the professional audience makes it opaque and useless to the general public. Government leaders seeking critical analytical insight into current problems quickly dismiss elements of celebration and commemoration. Maritime historians and those who present their work must be aware of the differing needs of their audiences and the levels and approaches to history appropriate to each. There is no "off the rack" history. No one size and style fits all—but all styles are needed if history is to become more useful in and for the Navy than it is now.

The issue, however, is more than just a question of the audiences that will benefit from historical insight, and the differing styles they need. It is far more basic than that, and the situation is much more critical. In June 1999, the chairman of the Secretary of the Navy's Advisory Subcommittee on Naval History formally reported to Secretary Danzig that the U.S. Navy as an institution needed to put a much higher priority on preserving and using history—"The Navy places a far lower priority on history than the other services measured in competitive dollars and manpower."[25] What money the Navy does receive for its current historical programs at the Naval Historical Center in Washington, it "stretches . . . very thin." The Navy employs fewer professional historians, archivists, or museum specialists than the other services and has nothing comparable to the separately funded U.S. Military History Research Institute (at the Army War College at Carlisle Barracks) or the separately funded Air Force's Historical Research Agency at the Air University, which complement the work of their Washington-based service historical offices. For the Navy, the Naval Historical Center in Washington has had the major burden, researching and writing history while also running the service's operational archive, the Navy Museum, an Underwater Archaeology branch that monitors naval ship and aircraft wrecks around the world, and the Navy's art collection. The other services have dispersed networks of historical offices to ensure that headquarters and operational history are preserved and recorded; the U.S. Navy has no similar system outside of Washington. There are no naval historians permanently attached to operational commands. The Naval Historical Center has only one naval reserve unit and a small naval reserve volunteer training unit to handle the job of gathering historical materials from deployed units to form the basis for the permanent historical record of the Navy's current operations. In the Navy today, operational history from deployed units is preserved only in summary form, through the annual ship, squadron, and unit command histories. These reports are often delegated to junior officers, who have little appreciation of the fact that they are preparing the permanent official records of their commands' activities. They sometimes treat the assignment as a public affairs exercise rather than a serious permanent record that documents commands' activities for the history of the Navy as well as for professional information and use in future decades. Unlike during World War II or the Korean and Vietnam Wars, ships and major operational commands no longer submit action reports or keep war diaries; the annual command history was designed to replace these older methods of reporting, but operational commanders often overlook this responsibility.

Today, the Navy's key operational units are the numbered fleets, with their important battle fleet experiments, carrier battle groups, and amphibious ready groups, but few, if any, of these have ever produced command histories as permanent records of their operations. These operational commanders, of course, have wars to fight and win; nonetheless, the result of neglecting their historical obligation is that the nation has no permanent record of their operations for the benefit of professionals today or of future generations. Congress, government leaders, the general public, and uniformed and civilian professionals working within the Navy will entirely lack authoritative records of the contemporary history of our times, unless some action is taken to rectify the situation.

In some cases where recent records have been created, they have been put into a microcopy or electronic formats that are not useable on a permanent basis; the information that these systems were supposed to have saved is entirely lost. Information and raw data that could be used for future historical research and retrieval appears in e-mails and the electronic formats that the Navy uses every day, yet neither operational naval commands nor shore establishments have effective systems by which electronic archives can be routinely saved and delivered to safe and permanent archival storage, and the electronic data systems themselves saved for future use and reference. The paper copies of documents that naval commands have traditionally transferred to archival storage declined by 75 percent between 1981 and 1990, and the volume of archival acquisitions declined a further 50 percent in the following decade.[26] No effective electronic or automated means of permanent record keeping has yet been created to fill this void.

In December 2001, the chairman of the Secretary of the Navy's Advisory Subcommittee on Naval History reiterated these issues to Secretary of the Navy Gordon England and noted that

> for too long the Navy as a whole has viewed history as "someone else's problem." As a result, much of our historical record over the last fifty years has been destroyed, and few of our Sailors know or appreciate our history. This mindset needs to be challenged. Every unit of the Navy shares responsibility for preserving records, understanding naval history and traditions, and drawing inspiration and wisdom from past accomplishments.[27]

As a result of these repeated reports to the Secretary of the Navy, the Vice Chief of Naval Operations, Admiral William J. Fallon, issued an instruction in August 2002 to all ships and stations to establish a policy for the development and use of historical lessons learned and of historical resources to support and inform naval operations, plans, and programs.[28] Despite this clear and positive step, much remains to be done to implement a more effective and servicewide historical program for the U.S. Navy.

The Historical Center in Washington had a nine-million-dollar budget in 2003, which includes funding for USS *Constitution,* but not the support of the museums outside of Washington and educational activities at the Naval War College and the Naval Academy. The Navy has not completely neglected maritime history, and budgets for the Naval Historical Center have not been cut to the extent that the budgets for other naval commands have been cut in recent years. At the same time, millions of dollars in the Navy's funding have gone into the review and declassification of archival records of many Navy commands. All this gives some strength and support to maritime history as it is broadly construed. The primary issue is not one of increased funding or additional manpower; the major challenge is one of changing the Navy's current mind-set and culture, which result in failure to conserve a permanent record of recent activities. They tend, specifically, to consider the Naval Historical Center as the only agency with any responsibility for the Navy's historical interest and to disregard the historical assets that are already at hand.

The historians who work for and advise the Navy can only point out, as they have repeatedly done in recent years, that the Navy and the country are in jeopardy of losing the record of a significant portion of their recent past and that the Navy is not making effective use of its historical assets and information. Only those who bear direct responsibility, the U.S. Navy's senior civilian and uniformed flag officers, can ever hope to change this mentality. Changing a servicewide attitude toward something so fundamental as history is no easy task, but it can be done if flag officers throughout the Navy actively engage themselves in the process. Even so, however, it cannot happen overnight. To understand how a professional can use history effectively requires education, reading, reflection, and knowledge.

The lack of general historical understanding within the U.S. Navy and its current inability to use history effectively are emblematic of the larger issue that the Navy faces in graduate and professional education as a whole. At least 90 percent of the general officers in the other U.S. armed services have attended both an intermediate and a senior service college, where historical understanding plays an important role in educating senior officers in policy, strategy, and the nature of warfare. In contrast, only around 30 percent of the serving flag officers in the U.S. Navy have attended even one senior service college, while less than 5 percent have attended both an intermediate and a senior service college.[29] Thus, even at the highest level, naval professionals lack education in the whole range of disciplines that provide enhanced critical thinking and decision skills for dealing with our modern world, with its increasing complexity and potential for information overload.

It is astonishing that anyone would seriously argue that historical insight is irrelevant to professional understanding, but that is a view one often finds today in the U.S. Navy. Among the many uses of historical understanding in and for the Navy, perhaps the most important is the need that our highly technological and interconnected society creates for an interdisciplinary education.[30] Precisely because our world is highly technological, education in technology and science alone is insufficient. Among all the disciplines and forms of understanding that naval professionals can and should use to broaden their outlooks and to sharpen their abilities to deal with the present and the future is history, particularly maritime history—a resource and tool with which the U.S. Navy has made limited progress. Much more could and should be done for and with maritime history.

Maritime History at the Naval War College

At its founding in 1884 and for its first half-century, the Naval War College was a major force in promoting naval historical understanding. Alfred Thayer Mahan's books, *The Influence of Sea Power upon History* and *Influence of Sea Power upon the French Revolution and Empire,* were the published versions of lectures that he delivered to Naval War College students while serving as the College's President. At Admiral Luce's instigation, Mahan returned to the College on active duty in 1910 to revise another set of his earlier college lectures for publication, as *Naval Strategy*. Thereafter the culture of present-mindedness in a faculty that was then limited to active-duty officers serving short tours of duty gradually eroded the role of innovative historical research at Newport, although the classics of military and naval history remained part of the curriculum. In 1930, the College established its first Research and Analysis Department, which in 1931 began research on the history of warship types; a study of grand strategy of World War I; studies on naval actions in that war (including Jutland and the Gallipoli campaign); translations of the official German naval history of the war; and translations of the writings of important foreign naval strategists, such as Wolfgang Wegener and Raoul Castex.

In 1948, as part of his concept to widen the education of naval officers, Admiral Raymond Spruance, President of the College, recommended that the Secretary of the Navy approve a plan to employ civilian academics to teach the social sciences, political affairs, and naval history. As the College's chief of staff explained to Spruance's successor, a professor of history was to be the "means by which we clarify our thinking on the significance of sea power and maritime transportation in modern civilization. He will be one means by which the Naval War College will regain, maintain, and exercise world leadership in naval thought." That goal remains a daunting challenge by any standard and for any academic, but in the event, the chair, authorized by the secretary on 29 December 1948, remained unfilled until 1951. In 1953, the Secretary of the Navy named the chair in honor of Fleet Admiral Ernest J. King (with the admiral's personal approval). Over the next twenty years the chair was occupied by a succession of the country's leading maritime and military historians—such prominent historians as John H. Kemble, Charles Haring, James Field, Theodore Ropp, Stephen Ambrose, and Martin Blumenson—who came to Newport on one-year visiting appointments.

This practice changed in 1972, when Vice Admiral Stansfield Turner created a large civilian faculty with longer-term appointments. Turner also explicitly revived the ideals toward which Luce and Mahan had striven nearly a century before, by making intensive use of historical scholarship a key element of the College's academic program, designed to educate midcareer officers for leadership roles in high command and as advisers to national leaders. Under his guidance, the new Strategy and Policy course carefully selected historical case studies that illustrated the recurring and major problems in the formulation of national policy and strategy.

The College's two other core courses, Joint Military Operations and National Security Decision Making, also use in-depth case studies in maritime history. In addition, a variety of optional electives have been offered in maritime history, including one-trimester courses on naval warfare in the age of sail, the Second World War in the Pacific, underwater archaeology, and the classics of naval strategy. All these form part of the curriculum for the master of arts degree program in national security and strategic studies, for which the College was accredited in 1991.

Turner also made innovations to promote the value of the history of the Navy. He established a Naval Historical Monograph series, to be published by the Naval War College Press; its first volume appeared in 1975, and a fifteenth, *The Memoirs of Admiral H. Kent Hewitt,* is being prepared for press at this writing. [This collection is the nineteenth of the series.]

Building on the initiatives of the College's archivist, Anthony S. Nicolosi, who from 1970 had begun to reconstitute the school's scattered archives and develop a rare book and manuscript collection, Turner approved a concept to establish a research center for naval history. This original plan was only partially implemented, but in 1978 the College reacquired its original building from the Newport Naval Station, arranged for it to be designated as a national historic landmark, and renovated it as the College's museum, under Nicolosi's direction.

In the first months of 2003, Rear Admiral Rodney Rempt, President of the College, revived the unfulfilled plan of his predecessor of a quarter-century earlier and established the Maritime History Department within the College's Center for Naval Warfare Studies. Chaired by the Ernest J. King Professor of Maritime History, this department is designed to include a research unit with faculty members equipped to do both basic and applied history and to coordinate all of the College's activities in maritime history—including the Naval War College Museum and the Naval Historical Collection of rare books, manuscripts, and archives of the Henry E. Eccles Library. The new Maritime History Department underscores the Naval War College's long-standing commitment, dating back to the College's conception and founding in 1884, to make effective use of maritime history for professional purposes in and for the Navy.

NOTES   This article first appeared in the *Naval War College Review* 56, no. 2 (Spring 2003), pp. 12–38. It received the Edward S. Miller prize for the best article on naval history to appear in the *Naval War College Review* in 2003.

The author acknowledges with great appreciation the constructive criticisms made on an earlier draft of this article by Dr. Christopher M. Bell, Naval War College; Dr. Philip L. Cantelon, History Associates, Inc.; Dr. Rodney Carlisle, Rutgers University; Dr. William S. Dudley, Director of Naval History and director, Naval Historical Center; Dr. Edward Marolda, Senior Historian, Naval Historical Center; Professor David A. Rosenberg, chairman, secretary of the Navy's Advisory Subcommittee on Naval History; Henry H. Gaffney and Captain Peter Swartz, USN (Ret.), Center for Strategic Studies at the CNA Corporation; and Jay Thomas, Navy Cultural Resources Officer, Naval Facilities Command. Notwithstanding their generous advice, the author alone is responsible for the views expressed herein.

1 The classical statements of the argument in this essay were written by Sir John Knox Laughton, "The Scientific Study of Naval History," *Journal of the Royal United Services Institution* 18 (1879), pp. 508–27, and Admiral Herbert W. Richmond, "The Importance of the Study of Naval History," *Naval Review* 27 (May 1939), pp. 201–18, reprinted in *Naval Review* 68 (April 1980), pp. 139–50. Their ideas are subsumed and extended herein.

2 History Associates, Inc., *History and Heritage in the U.S. Navy* (Rockville, Md.: 16 October 2000), p. 3.

3 Ibid., executive summary, p. 3.

4 As quoted from the National Historic Properties Act in H. T. Johnson, Assistant Secretary of the Navy (Installations and Environment), memo to Vice Chief of Naval Operations and Assistant Commandant of the Marine Corps, 16 November 2001.

5 Richmond, p. 201.

6 James Goldrick, "The Problems of Modern Naval History," in *Doing Naval History: Essays toward Improvement,* ed. John B. Hattendorf (Newport, R.I.: Naval War College Press, 1995), p. 11.

7 Robert Jervis, "Navies, Politics, and Political Science," in ibid., p. 46.

8 N. A. M. Rodger, "Considerations on Writing a General Naval History," in ibid., pp. 117–28.

9 For the application of the distinction between basic and applied history to naval history, I am grateful to Dr. Rodney P. Carlisle and Dr. Philip L. Cantelon and the work of History Associates, Inc., Rockville, Maryland, in the report of their independent evaluation for the under secretary of the Navy, *History and Heritage in the U.S. Navy: A Status Report,* 16 October 2000, p. 5. Some writers have used the terms "public history" and "applied history" interchangeably to describe all historical work outside academia. In this article, I argue that there is a need

to make a distinction between "public history" that is designed to inform the wider public outside academia and "applied history" that is used for highly specialized purposes with a profession. In the case of the Navy, this involves the development of professional pride as well as using the assistance of historical findings in developing policy.

10 Basil Liddell Hart, *Thoughts on War* (London: Faber and Faber, 1944), p. 138.

11 History Associates, Inc., p. iv.

12 William S. Dudley, "Reinventing Naval History," *Shipmate,* July–August 2002, p. 40.

13 See D. W. Knox, "The Rôle of Doctrine in Naval Warfare," U.S. Naval Institute *Proceedings* 41 (March–April 1915), pp. 31–75.

14 See Jon Tetsuro Sumida, *Inventing Grand Strategy and Teaching Command: The Classic Works of Alfred Thayer Mahan Reconsidered* (Baltimore: Johns Hopkins Univ. Press; and Washington, D.C.: Woodrow Wilson Center Press, 1997), and his "New Insights from Old Books: The Case of Alfred Thayer Mahan," *Naval War College Review* 54, no. 3 (Summer 2001), pp. 100–11.

15 See David A. Rosenberg, "Process the Realities of Formulating Modern Naval Strategy," in *Mahan Is Not Enough: The Proceedings of a Conference on the Works of Sir Julian Corbett and Admiral Sir Herbert Richmond,* ed. James Goldrick and John B. Hattendorf (Newport, R.I.: Naval War College Press, 1993), pp. 141–75.

16 Naval History and Heritage Command website: www.history.navy.mil.

17 Jay Thomas, Navy Cultural Resources Officer, Naval Facilities Command, e-mail to Naval Historical Center Stakeholder Working Group, 7 October 2002.

18 On making available official documents, see "Purpose and Contribution in Editing Naval Documents," in *Naval History and Maritime Strategy: Collected Essays,* ed. John B. Hattendorf (Malabar, Fla.: Krieger, 2000), pp. 91–108; and Christine Hughes in a yet to-be-published paper "Franklin D. Roosevelt, Dudley W. Knox, and Naval Documents."

19 See Benjamin W. Labaree, "The State of American Maritime History in the 1990s"; Kenneth J. Hagan and Mark R. Shulman, "Mahan Plus One Hundred: The Current State of American Naval History"; and David Alan Rosenberg, "Beyond Toddlerhood: Thoughts on the Future of Naval History"; all in *Ubi Sumus? The State of Maritime and Naval History,* ed. John B. Hattendorf (Newport, R.I.: Naval War College Press, 1994), pp. 363–419. See also Frank Broeze, ed., *Maritime History at the Crossroads: A Critical Review of Recent Historiography,* Research in Maritime History 9 (St. John's, Nfld.: International Maritime Economic History Association, 1995). For reflections on more recent developments, see Jaap R. Bruijn, "Reflections on the Recent Past of Maritime History in the Netherlands and Abroad," and Frank J. A. Broeze, "Riding the Wave: The State of Maritime History, Opportunities and Challenges," in *Frutta di Mare: Evolution and Revolution in the Maritime World in the 19th and 20th Centuries,* ed. Paul C. van Royen et al. (Amsterdam: Batavian Lion International, 1998), pp. 9–18, 195–207, and Sarah Palmer, *Seeing the Sea: The Maritime Dimension in History. An Inaugural Lecture Delivered at the University of Greenwich 11th May 2000* (Greenwich, U.K.: University of Greenwich, 2000).

20 Benjamin W. Labaree et al., *America and the Sea: A Maritime History* (Mystic, Conn.: Mystic Seaport, 1998).

21 *Mystic Seaport: The Museum of America and the Sea,* www.mysticseaport.org/.

22 Over the years, the conference proceedings have appeared under slightly different titles and from different publishers. The first published volume was Robert Love, ed., *Changing Interpretations and New Sources in Naval History* (New York: Garland, 1980). The fourth and fifth symposia papers appeared under the title *New Aspects of Naval History,* by two different publishers (Annapolis, Md.: Naval Institute Press, 1981; and Baltimore: Nautical and Aviation, 1985); the sixth and seventh appeared under the title *Naval History* (Wilmington, Del.: Scholarly Resources, 1987, 1988). From the eighth symposium (1987) to the fourteenth symposium (1999), the Naval Institute Press published the proceedings under the title *New Interpretations in Naval History.* The fifteenth symposium was planned to begin on 12 September 2001 but was canceled due to the terrorist attacks on the previous day in New York and Washington. However, many of the papers that were to have been presented there were published as the first issue of the e-journal *International Journal of Naval History* 1, no. 1 (April 2002), www .ijnhonline.org/index_apr_02.html.

23 "Sources on U.S. Naval History in the United States," Naval History and Heritage Command website: www.history.navy.mil/sources/index.htm.

24 "Naval War College Library: Naval Historical Collection," Naval War College website: www.usnwc .edu/Academics/Library/Naval-Historical -Collection.aspx.

25 This quotation and the information in this paragraph is based on Dr. David A. Rosenberg, chairman, "The Report of the Secretary of the Navy's Advisory Subcommittee on Naval History for 1998," to Secretary of the Navy Richard Danzig, 27 June 1999, quotation from p. 1.

26 Dr. David A. Rosenberg, chairman, "The Report of the Secretary of the Navy's Advisory Subcommittee on Naval History for 2001," to Secretary of the Navy Gordon R. England, 7 December 2001, p. 6.

27 Ibid., p. 1.

28 OPNAV [Navy Staff] Instruction 5750.4D of 23 August 2002.

29 "Transforming Graduate and Professional Military Education," Graduate Education Review Board briefing, 2002, p. 14 (using 1998 data).

30 Richard Suttie [Capt., USN], "The Value of Graduate Education for Corporate America," white paper for the Graduate Education Review Board, 2002, p. 4.

II *Our Naval Heritage Is in Danger*

For sea service professionals, a better understanding of naval history provides deeper insights into current and future naval problems. Despite historians' best efforts, however, the leadership has placed such little value on naval history that most of the Navy's historical activities are underfunded, and now some of its official museums are threatened with closure. Only three of the Navy's dozen museums have reached accreditation status. Even our official records are not being kept properly. Present historians have a difficult time learning what our service is doing today, and our achievements may never be known to future generations.

Our naval heritage is in danger, and our service historians have reported this repeatedly over the past five years to the Secretary of the Navy and to the Chief of Naval Operations. Most recent warnings have come through the Secretary of the Navy's Advisory Subcommittee on Naval History in April 2004 and the Naval History Stakeholders Meeting held in Washington in October 2004.[1]

Sadly, schools frequently give the false impression of history as a boring exercise that involves memorizing useless dates and learning irrelevant things. In those instances when we have accepted history, we often have seen it as just "a nice thing" and, as a result, sometimes accepted simplistic and inaccurate traditional stories about our past that lead us astray in our professional thinking.[2]

There are no alternative means for relating history except in terms of the names, dates, places, ships, planes, equipment, and people of the past. Yet, those specifics are only building blocks. A key factor for understanding history is to be aware that events take place in a particular framework of time and place. The chronological order of development has a bearing on the ultimate outcome.

One commonly hears references to early naval officers—John Paul Jones or John Barry—for example, as the "father of the Navy." Others have suggested George Washington, John Adams, Robert Morris, Silas Deane, or Thomas Truxtun. Similarly, Marblehead, Salem, and Beverly in Massachusetts have been arguing among themselves for decades, as each has lobbied to be designated the "official" birthplace of the Navy. It should be a matter of great concern that many naval professionals widely accept such an approach to history. To use metaphorical words such as "father," "birth," and "birthplace" in describing the origins of the U.S. Navy is overly simplistic and ultimately misleading.

Most important, an accurate understanding of the long and difficult process that led to the creation of the Navy is an illuminating lesson in basic national values and how the

U.S. government works. This story is not merely interesting information about a by-gone age, but a reminder to the modern professional that continuing support for the Navy, as well as its origin, reflects the complex interplay among political, economic, and bureaucratic forces. Far more than to any single individual or port town, the U.S. Navy owes its existence to Congress and the legislative process.

The Origins of the U.S. Navy

At the time of the American Revolution, the colonists were well aware of the sea as a highway of communication, a source of food, and a place for battle, if necessary.[3] Many people shared in the natural impulse to arm ships at public expense so they could further their own protection and promote their own cause in the face of British maritime power. Typical of this, the first armed action of the war at sea occurred in June 1775, when Jeremiah O'Brien and a group of fellow militiamen engaged and captured a small British armed vessel off Machias, Maine.

Meanwhile, representatives from all 13 colonies gathered in Congress. From 1775 through the 1790s, they examined and debated nearly every fundamental aspect of representative democracy and the institutions appropriate to a republic. At that time, powers and resources of the Continental Congress were limited. In one of its first discussions about naval affairs on 18 July 1775, Congress asked "that each colony, at its own expense, make such provision by armed vessels or otherwise . . . for the protection of their harbours and navigation on their sea coasts, against all unlawful invasions, attacks and depredations, from cutters and ships of war."[4]

Shortly afterward, Georgia, Maryland, Massachusetts, New Hampshire, New York, North Carolina, Pennsylvania, Rhode Island, South Carolina, and Virginia each had established a separate, tiny navy of its own, some comprising only a few flatboats and row galleys, others with substantial sea-going vessels.

An additional need soon grew to have a naval force that could operate on broader terms than just the needs of an individual colony. This became apparent when George Washington's Continental Army began to arm vessels at Beverly, Salem, and Marblehead to support land operations against British forces in Massachusetts in September 1775.

The Continental Navy

Shortly thereafter, the Rhode Island General Assembly passed a resolution "that the building and equipping of an American fleet, as soon as possible, would greatly conduce to the preservation of lives, liberty and property of the good people of these colonies."[5] The Continental Congress debated this resolution on 3 October 1775 without specific result, because some delegates felt establishment of a navy would preclude reconciliation with Britain. Two days later, Congress received intelligence that two unarmed English brigs carrying supplies to the British Army had set sail from England for Quebec with no convoy protection. On hearing this news, a congressional committee immediately recommended that Congress equip two armed vessels and order them to intercept any such supply ships. Congress delayed action until 13 October, when a letter from General Washington reported he had already acquired three schooners at Continental expense. By taking this initiative, Washington had pre-empted Congress, allowing members who had been hesitant to agree more easily to add two ships to the total.

That day, the second Continental Congress authorized the purchase and arming of two vessels "to cruize eastward, for intercepting such transports as may be laden with warlike stores and other supplies for our enemies."[6] This act created the Continental Navy. Today, the U.S. Navy recognizes 13 October as its official founding date, even though it marks only the formal beginning of its immediate predecessor, not the service that exists today.

The history of the Continental Navy was short, lasting only until 1785, when its last ship was sold. In that short period, the service had reached a reasonable size. Nearly 60 vessels served at one time or another, 18 of them frigates of 24 to 32 guns, numerous smaller craft, and at the high end, a 74-gun ship of the line.[7] As it was acquiring ships, Congress also was creating a naval administrative structure, directly copying and adapting some basic British regulations and administrative models.

Washington had famously observed to Benjamin Franklin in 1780: "Naval superiority . . . was the pivot upon which everything turned."[8] The naval superiority he had in mind was French, however, not American. With a navy appropriate to a major European power, France was the only one that could and eventually did achieve the local naval superiority that was decisive in preventing the relief of the British Army at the key Battle of Yorktown.

Under this broader strategic umbrella, which had developed at sea only since the creation of the Franco-American alliance in 1778, the tiny Continental Navy accomplished far more modest objectives. Its famous captains—such men as Esek Hopkins, Barry, Abraham Whipple, Lambert Wickes, Gustavus Conyngham, and Jones—are well remembered in U.S. naval history, but their achievements were won largely by attacking the British at the periphery of their power as well as by raiding in home waters to force the Royal Navy to divert its resources from North America. The Continental Congress did not have the resources to create either a strong naval organization or an efficient naval administration. Construction and repair were slow and inefficient, manning was difficult, supplies were scarce, and on occasion, even the authorities neglected to send timely orders for sailing. For these logistical reasons, the small naval force lost opportunities, and even war-ready ships lay idle in port for months.

Arguably, the Continental Navy's most important achievement was to maintain direct and regular diplomatic correspondence with Europe. The tiny service also proved successful in carrying another much-needed cargo: coins for currency. The fact that warships of the newly formed United States could show their flag in allied and friendly European ports demonstrated that Americans were willing and able to wield the symbols and instruments of national sovereignty. In addition, the Continental Navy joined in a larger enterprise in which more than 1,697 U.S. privateers attacked enemy trade in a way that had a much broader effect than any single action. While the direct impact was relatively small, the cumulative effect forced up the costs of shipping and maritime insurance. The occasional dramatic raid on the British coast and in European waters, such as the famous operations of John Paul Jones, underscored trends already under way, creating incidents that joined other political forces to help coalesce British public opinion against the war.[9]

Beyond these broad effects, some individual actions did have an immediate result. The ability to capture a British ship and to bring home any war supplies she was carrying benefited the meagre resources of the Continental Army and Navy. On some occasions, even a makeshift naval force, such as that created on Lake Champlain in 1776, could have a surprisingly large impact. Although British forces defeated Benedict Arnold's naval forces off Valcour Island in Lake Champlain, the defeat was a tactical one. In the broader perspective, the Americans had succeeded in delaying for many months the British Army's advance down the lake and prevented British forces from gaining control of the vital Hudson River, an element that contributed to the British defeat in the Battle at Saratoga in 1777. In Alfred Thayer Mahan's memorable phrase, the naval action on Lake Champlain was "a strife of pigmies for the prize of a continent."[10]

During its 10-year existence, the Continental Navy played a very limited, albeit important role, the maritime equivalent of peoples' and partisan warfare ashore. With the Peace of Paris and American independence secured in 1783, the Continental Navy was no longer needed. With the additional problems of finance and supply, it is not surprising the little navy was almost immediately disbanded, and few were interested in trying to revive it.

A Decade without a Navy

In the immediate postwar period, maritime commerce was clearly a fundamental interest to the new republic. In 1784, Congress developed a plan for the key issues that were to be incorporated into all the treaties of friendship and commerce the new country would soon be negotiating. Among those issues were the rights of neutrals in wartime. The main concern centered around the ideas that "free ships made free goods" and involved establishing a clear definition of what a neutral vessel was allowed to trade, what items were contraband, and what made an "effective blockade" that would prevent neutral trade in wartime.[11]

Americans only belatedly realized political independence from Britain did not bring unfettered commercial freedom at sea. In fact, the United States found it suddenly had lost the advantages and benefits of normal avenues of British imperial trade. Thus, U.S. merchants had to create new markets and work around British economic dominance at sea. In 1785, one of the Founding Fathers, James Madison, even questioned the very advantages of independence: "Our trade was never more completely monopolized by Great Britain when it was under the direction of the British Parliament than it is at this moment."[12] That fact remained commercial and strategic reality for the United States, however, throughout the next century. On one hand, this meant looking for new markets for merchant shipping, and on the other, it meant that a small U.S. Navy did not need to be concerned about the broad problems of naval supremacy or of naval competition.

The awkwardness of the Articles of Confederation, which in 1781 had created a legislative government dominated by the separate interests of its individual states and without an executive branch, soon became apparent. In 1787–88, the Constitutional Convention set about creating an improved and permanent basis for government. Whether or not the country should have a navy was not a critical issue in the debate over the Constitution, but it did arise. The discussion surrounding it began a continuing debate over what kind of a navy was most appropriate and what the roles and purposes of such a navy should be. The political sentiments revealed in this discussion have persisted throughout the nation's history. Having survived the transition to superpower status, they may even still be found on the domestic political landscape in the 21st century.[13]

The wide range of views could be seen among such key figures as Thomas Jefferson, John Adams, and Alexander Hamilton. While Jefferson preferred to have a navy operating only in wartime, Adams saw its value in dealing with pirates and protecting trade. Hamilton even more strongly saw a navy that would allow the United States to be "the arbiter of Europe in America, and to be able to incline the balance of European competitions in this part of the world as our interest may dictate."[14]

The Establishment of the U.S. Navy

Discussions in *The Federalist Papers* and in Congress were exceptionally important, as they were among the few occasions in the naval history of any country when the broad functions of a navy were examined and debated without an existing naval infrastructure and institutional bias. At the same time, however, this was all theory and debate, not action. It suggested the future and permanent scope of the nation's political views about a navy, but the country still did not have a naval force afloat. The first step toward that occurred only in December 1793, when, in response to Britain's persuasive need to develop a coalition against revolutionary France, Portugal had signed a peace treaty with Algiers. Up until that time, U.S. merchant shipping had tacitly depended on Portugal's ability to contain the activities of the Algerian corsairs. With Portugal no longer playing that role, U.S. merchants wanted protection. As if to prove the point, within a short time Algerian corsairs attacked U.S. ships.[15]

After several months of committee work and debate, Congress passed, with an 11-vote margin, "An Act to Provide a Naval Armament." Becoming law on 27 March 1794, it provided for procurement of six frigates. Taking the law one step further, President Washington decided, on the advice of naval experts such as Joshua Humphreys, not to buy ships and to convert them, but to construct three 44-gun ships and three 36-gun ships, using a new design. A contingency clause in the act provided that if peace were made with Algiers, then the plans would be put on hold. Political opponents of the act pointed out that such a force was entirely inadequate. As work proceeded, progress on construction of the ships fell behind as their costs rose steadily.

In 1796, a diplomatic arrangement with Algiers stopped work momentarily on the unfinished ships. In a political compromise, Congress eventually allowed construction to continue on three of the six ships. The first to be launched was the USS *United States* in May 1797, followed by *Constellation* in September and *Constitution* in October. Although completed, they were to be placed in reserve under the administration of the War Department until some emergency arose. At the time, many Americans believed the ships should never be allowed to be at sea in peacetime, because they might force the United States to become unnecessarily involved with a war in Europe or elsewhere.

The President at this time, John Adams, had consistently strong views in support of a navy. Eventually, he was able to oversee a change in the political climate regarding the U.S. Navy that led to its permanent establishment. "A mercantile marine and a military marine must grow up together," Adams explained at the opening of his administration; "one can not long exist without the other."[16] Adams was a man who believed in peaceful, free trade. But in the contemporary state of the world, a naval force was necessary for the protection of such trade. His point particularly was underscored by the succession of events that had occurred after Britain and France went to war in 1793, when the United States found itself caught between the two rival nations fighting in the wake of the French Revolution.

When U.S. diplomatic overtures failed to resolve issues, particularly French violations of U.S. neutral rights and attacks on trade, Adams sent a request to Congress in May 1797, asking that it create a navy that could protect commerce at sea during this crisis, along with becoming a permanent system of naval defense. As tensions increased and France even refused to recognize U.S. diplomats, Congress responded with a series of legislative acts. In April 1798, it authorized both the acquisition of a dozen small, armed vessels and the creation of the Navy Department. Shortly thereafter, the 26-gun USS *Ganges,* commanded by Captain Richard Dale, became the first U.S. Navy ship to get under way. Later congressional acts in May and June provided for additional galleys and sloops, and finally in July, Congress voted to complete the other three frigates, construction of which had been halted at the time of the peace treaty with Algiers three years earlier. On his own executive authority, Adams soon established the country's first navy yard at the capital in Washington, D.C., and others soon followed at Boston and at Norfolk.

By the time the Quasi War with France was over in 1800, the new U.S. Navy had commissioned 45 ships. Adams eloquently explained to the nation in his last address to Congress:

> While our best endeavours for the preservation of harmony with all nations will continue to be used, the experience of the world and our own experience admonish us of the insecurity of trusting too confidently to their success. We cannot, without committing a dangerous imprudence, abandon those measures of self-protection which are adapted to our situation, and to which, notwithstanding our pacific policy, the violence or injustice of others may again compel us to resort.[17]

Adams's words expressed clearly the initial basis on which Congress and the American people accepted and agreed to maintain a permanent navy. The quarter-century-long process that led to this conclusion also set the stage for the continuing discussion about the appropriate size and employment of the Navy over the coming centuries.

Simplistic vs. Full Explanations in Naval History

The contrast between the overly simplistic explanations of naval history used in naming someone such as John Paul Jones as the "father of the navy" or a place such as Marblehead or Salem as the "birthplace of the Navy" distorts beyond recognition what actually happened. In the end, such attributions are only empty titles that quickly become meaningless to the modern professional. In contrast, the complete story is full of insight into our national character, our political and governmental process, and an example of the essential interrelationships in political, military, and naval affairs. Such insights in the course of a well-rounded professional education provide an invaluable basis for understanding the process by which our Navy must necessarily work today.

NOTES   This article was originally published as "Our Naval Heritage Is in Danger," U.S. Naval Institute *Proceedings* 130, no. 12 (December 2004), pp. 64–68.

1 See Hattendorf, "The Uses of Maritime History in and for the Navy," chapter 1.

2 See John Hattendorf, ed., *Doing Naval History: Essays Toward Improvement* (Newport, R.I.: Naval War College Press, 1995).

3 Thanks to Dr. Michael Crawford, Head, Early History Branch, Naval Historical Center, Washington, D.C., for his comments on this section. See also "The U.S. Navy and the 'Freedom of the Seas,' 1775–1917," in Rolf Hobson and Tom Kristiansen, eds., *Navies in Northern Waters, 1721–2000* (London: Frank Cass, 2004), pp. 151–174.

4 William Bell Clark, ed., *Naval Documents of the American Revolution*, vol. I (Washington, D.C.: Government Printing Office, 1964—in progress), p. 916: Journal of the Continental Congress, 18 July 1775.

5 Clark, *Naval Documents*, vol. I, p. 1236: Journal of the Rhode Island General Assembly, 26 August 1775.

6 Clark, *Naval Documents*, vol. III, pp. 441–442: Journal of the Continental Congress, 13 October 1775.

7 See Howard I. Chapelle, *The History of the American Sailing Navy: The Ships and Their Development* (New York: W. W. Norton, 1949; reprinted New York: Bonanza Books, n.d.), chapter 2, pp. 52–114.

8 Washington to Franklin, 20 December 1780, quoted in Dudley W. Knox, *The Naval Genius of George Washington* (Boston: Houghton Mifflin, 1932), p. 70.

9 Gardiner W. Allen, *A Naval History of the American Revolution,* vol. 2 (1916; reprinted New York: Russell & Russell, 1969), pp. 659–668.

10 A. T. Mahan, *Major Operations of the Navies in the War of American Independence* (London: Sampson Low, 1913), p. 18.

11 Carlton Savage, ed., *Policy of the United States Toward Maritime Commerce in War,* vol. 1, *1776–1914* (Washington, D.C.: Government Printing Office, 1934), pp. 157–160: Doc. 21 "Treaty Plan of the Continental Congress, 7 May 1784."

12 Quoted in Raymond G. O'Connor, *Origins of the American Navy: Sea Power in the Colonies and the New Nation* (Lanham, Md.: University Press of America, 1994), p. 59.

13 See Craig L. Symonds, *Navalists and Antinavalists: The Naval Policy Debate in the United States, 1785–1827* (Newark: University of Delaware Press, 1980).

14 Alexander Hamilton, James Madison, and John Jay, *The Federalist Papers* (New York, 1961), p. 87.

15 See Marshall Smelser, *Congress Founds the Navy, 1787–1798* (South Bend, Ind.: Notre Dame University Press, 1959).

16 Symonds, *Navalists and Antinavalists,* p. 51.

17 Address to Congress, 22 November 1800, quoted in David McCullough, *John Adams* (New York: Simon & Schuster, 2001), p. 554.

III *Maritime History, the History of Nautical Science, and the* Oxford Encyclopedia of Maritime History

As descriptions of scholarly endeavour, the phrases "maritime history" and the "history of nautical science" in no way suggest opposing concepts, but rather recognize different planes of perspective on the same subject. Maritime history is the field of historical study that encompasses humankind's relationships to the seas and oceans of the world. It is a multidimensional, humanistic study of human activities, experiences, interactions, and reactions to the vast water-covered regions that account for more than 70 percent of the globe. A student who pursues the maritime theme may approach it from a variety of vantage points, including science, technology, cartography, industry, economics, trade, politics, art, literature, sociology and social issues, religion, military and naval affairs, international relations, comparative studies in imperial and colonial affairs, institutional and organizational development, communications, migration, intercultural relations, natural resources, sports, and recreation.

Maritime history has, in some respects, been an ignored dimension of global history. Indeed, we have become so used to thinking of our world as "earth" and as a "terrestrial orb" that we sometimes have completely forgotten that those words refer only to land and that they exclude the essence of things maritime. The subject of maritime history is a broad theme in global history that cuts across the standard boundaries of academic disciplines. In many respects it is a broad new and developing interdisciplinary field of scholarly research and writing, although it has deep roots in much older scholarship in specific and highly focused parts of the field. The study of some areas within the wider field of maritime history is a relatively recent activity. Perhaps the oldest subject area of maritime history within the English-language tradition is the history of maritime exploration that developed from the translations into English of the work of Peter Martyr.[1] In this subject area, it was Richard Hakluyt who had the greatest impact, with his compilation of early voyage accounts made during the Elizabethan age: *The Principal Navigations, Voyages, Traffiques, and Discoveries of the English Nation* (1598–1600), the work that a late-nineteenth-century Regius Professor of History at Oxford University, James Anthony Froude, called "the prose epic of the English nation." Hakluyt's collection was followed by others, as well as by the widely read firsthand accounts of the seamen of later centuries, such as George Anson and James Cook. The typical volumes in this genre were largely devoted to voyage narratives and to descriptions of distant parts of the world. Such works became so widely read that they were even parodied in the eighteenth century by writers such as Jonathan Swift in his satirical masterpiece *Gulliver's Travels* (1726).

To look at a different aspect of maritime history, Admiralty Secretary Josiah Burchett wrote the first general naval history to appear in the English language: *A Complete History of the Most Remarkable Transactions at Sea* (1720). Typical of early work on naval affairs, it was a record written by a professional whose interests in the subject were largely limited to professional matters. Equally typical, it was limited to naval operations and accounts of battles between warships, although it had the merit of using official reports as the basis for its final chapters. Studies of port cities, labor conditions, shipbuilding, fishing, and maritime business activities all came much later, as did studies of maritime art and literature. At first the focus was largely on national maritime events, and the scope only slowly widened to include a full appreciation of maritime accomplishments by other countries. Only in the late nineteenth century did historians, such as Sir John Knox Laughton, Alfred Thayer Mahan, and Sir Julian Corbett, develop the foundation for a broader, analytical approach to naval history.

In the area of the history of science, from its founding in 1846 the Hakluyt Society has played a major role in bringing to the fore many important texts. Building on as well as contributing to these works, E. G. R. Taylor brought modern British scholarship to the topic with her *Tudor Geography, 1485–1583* (London: Methuen, 1930) and *Late Tudor and early Stuart Geography 1583–1650* (London: Methuen, 1934). David W. Waters followed with his seminal work *The Art of Navigation in England in Elizabethan and Early Stuart Times* (New Haven: Yale University Press, 1958).

A quarter of a century ago maritime scholars in the English-speaking world were typically divided into small subspecialties. They rarely crossed from one subspecialty to another or made any attempt to see the whole range of the broad maritime field, with its complex interdependencies and interrelationships. Although this was not true of maritime history written in some other countries and languages, historians in the English-speaking world tended to label themselves by their subspecialties rather than by the broad field, identifying themselves as naval historians, maritime economic historians, historians of the maritime sciences, historians of nautical science and navigation, historians of hydrography, or historians of exploration. In the 1980s historians of yachting and seaside recreation, maritime art and literature, or maritime labor and social history had only just begun to make a major impact in the field. At first they, too, remained isolated within small groups that shared a focus on their own subspecialties, sometimes fiercely defending the unique characteristics of their own special topic even against others in the maritime field. In addition many subspecialists tended to define themselves by national focus, often further restricting themselves to particular periods within one national history.

In the late 1980s and 1990s this situation began to change dramatically. Some individual historians began to take a much wider view and began to make links between subspecialties, opening up new approaches and new areas for investigation. By the 1990s, it became clear that the overarching common connection behind all of these varied approaches was represented in the meaning of the adjective "maritime"—human activities relating to or involving ships, shipping, navigation, mariners, and those people bordering on, living in, or associated with activities connected to the seas and oceans.

Under the overarching label of maritime history, each of the subspecialties has a tie to a specific range of academic approaches. The maritime economic historian has a fundamental tie to the academic fields of economic and business history; the naval historian has connections to the diplomatic, military, and international history fields; the student of maritime art or maritime literature has connections to the wider fields of art history and literature; the historian of exploration has ties to the history of imperial expansion and global cultural interaction; and the historian of navigation has a fundamental tie to the history of science and technology with special interest in the histories of cosmography, astronomy, cartography, and mathematics. Each of these connections to particular academic disciplines and specialized academic fields of interest helps to define those particular subspecialties, but they are all interconnected through having the maritime element in common. It is this common maritime element, with its cross connections and relationships across the various subspecialties, that becomes a revealing and important extension of broad aspects of national and international events ashore.

To offer an example, in broad terms the study of maritime imperial and international rivalry requires a special focus that links the domestic politics of major powers to international politics and economics and includes comparative maritime technological skills and usages. Such a maritime interpretation of international relations is basic to the understanding of the interactions of the major powers in peace and in war from ancient times to the present. Even when viewed at its most basic level, a ship is built in a particular place and is a product of certain national, political, economic, social, scientific, technological, and industrial factors that are reflected in its design and construction. When that ship puts to sea, she enters a different realm. She must now utilize in a practical manner the results of investigations in the nautical and navigational sciences. At the same time, the vessel enters into the context of a wider international and global dimension that may involve her specific circumstances, such as wars, cross-cultural relations, imperial competition, scientific research, the exchange of goods, the transmission of species and information, the extraction of maritime and undersea resources, and the accumulation of capital through trade. At the same time, when that ship leaves the network of activities that created her and prepared her to cross seas and oceans, she remains a microcosm of the society that she left ashore. For much of human history sea passages were long and isolated experiences in a ship at sea, lasting for many weeks and even months out of sight of land. This created a social dimension within ships that became another determinant that affected the outcome of individual voyages and, on a larger scale, affected broad labor issues within maritime affairs.

When viewed in its full broad spectrum, maritime history has a distinct series of related themes that can be followed over long periods of world history and that are linked in various ways across the many subspecialties of maritime history. The conception behind *The Oxford Encyclopedia of Maritime History* was to present this range of historical themes and information in a readily accessible summary form, for use both by the general public and by scholars. The encyclopedia offers to its users—whether general readers, college and high school students, or scholars seeking information, definitions, ideas for research papers—an overview of recent scholarship, or an introduction to the many aspects of maritime history. Up until now this information could be gleaned only with difficulty from a wide-ranging professional library devoted to maritime affairs; there has been no single English-language scholarly reference for this field.

The first maritime encyclopedia was probably Père Georges Fournier's *Hydrographie* (Paris, 1643), but its purpose was to provide a reference for the technical and specialized aspects of maritime affairs in its own day and not to serve historical purposes—regardless of how valuable it has become for that use in more recent times. The only works of comparable scope to this are the Spanish *Enciclopedia general del mar*, edited by José Ma. Martínez-Hidalgo y Terán, 8 volumes (Madrid, 1957–1958; second edition, 1968), which is a combination dictionary and encyclopedia that includes the scientific details from the physical and biological aspects of marine science as well as historical information, the Dutch *Maritieme Encyclopedie,* 7 volumes (Bussum, 1970–1973), and the French *Dictionnaire d'histoire maritime*, edited by Michel Vergé-Franceschi, two volumes (Paris, 2002), a wide-ranging dictionary of short entries on world maritime history. In English, there have also been some important reference works on specific aspects of maritime history, such as *The British Museum Encyclopedia of Underwater and Maritime Archaeology*, edited by James P. Delgado (1997); *Ships of the World: An Historical Encyclopedia*, edited by Lincoln P. Paine (1997); *Naval Warfare: An International Encyclopedia,* edited by Spencer C. Tucker, 3 volumes (2002); and *The Oxford Companion to Ships and the Sea,* edited by Peter Kemp and I. C. B. Dear (1976; second edition, 2005). None of these, however, has sought to be a scholarly reference work for the entire field of maritime history in the way that the Oxford encyclopedia has attempted.

To compile a scholarly reference encyclopedia in the field of maritime history, which had become so fragmented into subspecialties and has only recently begun to coalesce into a larger whole, required a wide-ranging effort in scholarly collaboration. In order to bridge the various subspecialties and to build the larger view that the editorial panel members all agreed was needed, we brought together a team of subject area editors and advisory editors who each represented a subspecialty, but who were at the same time willing and able to contribute to the wider perspective that we sought. In addition we sought the advice of a wide range of advisory and consulting editors, all of whom contributed substantially to broadening the scope of the final product. Working in cooperation under the editor in chief, each individual subject-area editor had the primary responsibly of conceptualizing the scope for each of the articles in his or her area and reviewing the completed articles, passing on judgments for the editor in chief's further advice and final approval.

There are 942 articles in the *Oxford Encyclopedia of Maritime History*, arranged in alphabetical order. More than 850 contributors from 49 different countries joined in this eight-year project to write broad articles that summarize, in clearly written English, the current state of historical understanding on this global topic. The encyclopedia includes more than 425 illustrations and more than 60 maps and nautical charts.

A typical article has three parts: the narrative, end references, and bibliography. To guide readers from one article to related discussions elsewhere in the encyclopedia, end references appear right after the narrative. In addition, there are cross-references within the body of a few articles. A selective bibliography at the end of an article directs the reader who wishes to pursue a topic in greater detail to the most important scholarly works in any language plus the most useful works in English. Within the encyclopedia's main alphabetical listing, blind entries direct the user from an alternate form of an entry term to the appropriate article. While every term was not included as a blind entry, the remainder can be found in the 219 pages of index at the end of the encyclopedia. For example, under the letter A there is no article on "Astrolabe," but the subject is included in the broader article "Navigational Instruments: Measurements of Altitude" and it is mentioned in nine other articles. Similarly, under the letter B, there is no article for "Bathythermograph," but this is to be found under the larger topic "Marine Science Instruments: Measurement of Depth." These examples underscore the point that a historical encyclopedia such as this is very different in conception from a historical dictionary. While a dictionary is a comprehensive collection of entries on specific topics, an encyclopedia entry subsumes broad areas of such specifics and attempts to provide a broad, succinct analysis that links them in a broad summary of current scholarly understanding.

The experience of undertaking this exercise revealed some interesting things about the broad field of maritime history and the effects of past insularity among the separate subspecialties. On some topics the goal of the encyclopedia in providing broadly based articles and analytical summaries of global themes in maritime history stretched above and beyond the present state of scholarship in maritime history. Some topics could be put together by getting different authors to write specific pieces to create a composite article on a theme. Others topics have just not been fully researched enough to produce such an article, and in such cases we were left with no choice but to report on the current state of knowledge. Despite these acknowledged limitations and frustrations, we presented the encyclopedia as the pioneer effort in scholarship that it is. Now, we look forward to others who can now use this first stepping-stone to build upon it and to widen and further develop a global understanding for the field of maritime history.

As we look forward in the developing broader field of maritime history, I think that the problems and frustrations that we met within our collaborative process of building the encyclopedia reveal some specific challenges for all of us working in the field of maritime history. From a personal perspective, as editor in chief, I was shocked—although, on reflection, I suppose that I should not have been—by the reluctance of so many scholars to think broadly about their special historical subjects and to place their very specific research into one aspect of maritime history within the wider thematic context of the subject and in a wider context of time and place. While there was generally a laudable attention to factual accuracy and specific detail, although on a confined topic, I was concerned by repeated encounters with a variety of different potential contributors, who shrank in horror at the thought of placing a specific topic and specific period into a broader context. This was very disappointing to me, not only because of the practical issue of finding someone to produce some of the articles that I wanted and needed to have produced within a publishing deadline, but the more so because it seemed to suggest limited intellectual horizons within the field of maritime history. It strikes me as a fundamental aspect of historical scholarship that to understand one's own research in the specific one needs to be able to understand the broad development of that subject across time, as well as to place it within the context of broader understanding. I will not mention names of individual scholars or even topics here, because it is not my purpose to embarrass or complain about individuals. Rather, I point this out as a broad issue that I hope all of us can promote in current and future studies. By taking any one of the subspecialties of maritime history—the history of nautical science, in the case of most of you here—and encouraging those within your subspecialty to think about your topics not only within the traditional confines of the theme, but in relation to other subspecialties in maritime history, perhaps even using the perspectives and other academic disciplines that those subspecialties employ, we can more effectively advance contributions to knowledge in the field of maritime history as well as make a contribution to the understanding of general history.

Perhaps my point is easily lost on those who have never tried to undertake what may seem to be too daunting a task. For anyone who has not tried it, I commend to you undertaking the intellectual exercise of writing a succinct, tightly compressed summary article of a thousand words or so, on some specific broad theme in which your own detailed research is central, moving your focus from the limited time period and scope that new archival research requires and to let your mind follow the theme across centuries and range around the globe in scope. On one hand, writing an encyclopedia article would seem to be only a small and routine task. On the other hand, it is a challenging, but useful, task of communicating understanding in our field. It requires shifting focus from the minute to the general, then comparing, contrasting, and linking ideas and influences to describe the broad contour of development across long stretches of time. It has dangers in the temptations to raise minor factors to unwarranted influence. Such work requires a mastery of the topic at hand, and a balanced scholarly judgment that reflects both new and long accepted understanding. Perhaps, it may be a minor art form in itself, but I was amazed that a significant number of individuals in maritime history declined the task, not because they did not want to spend the time on it, but because they seemed overwhelmed by the broad thinking and understanding that the task required. Such work should be a necessary part and parcel of communicating our scholarly ideas and contributing to the wider body of knowledge.

In order to more effectively move forward the broad field of maritime history and advance the understanding of maritime history as part of global history, we all need to be able to place our specific research interests into a broad perspective and to see the interrelationships among the many subspecialties within maritime history.

NOTES   This paper was presented as the closing remarks for the XIVth International Reunion of the History of Nautical Science, sponsored by the International Committee for the History of Nautical Science and held in the Department of Mathematics at the University of Coimbra, Portugal, 23–25 October 2008.

1 The anglicized form of the name of Pietro Martire d'Anghiera (c. 1457–1526). Translated into English by Richard Eden, under the titles *The Decades of the New World or West India* (1555) and *The history of travayle in the West and east Indies* (1577).

IV   The Horizons of Maritime History

I n Joseph Conrad's autobiographical novel, *The Shadow-Line*, there is, as one so often finds in Conrad's work, a description that creates a memorable image of the sea and inspires deeper reflection. In search of his first command at sea, Conrad's fictional protagonist enters a harbor-master's office and is first struck by the view:

> Three lofty windows gave on the harbour. There was nothing in them but the dark-blue sparkling sea and the paler luminous blue of the sky. My eye caught in the depths and distances of these blue tones the white speck of some big ship just arrived and about to anchor in the outer roadstead. A ship from home—after, perhaps, ninety days at sea. There is something touching about a ship coming in from sea and folding her white wings for a rest.[1]

In looking for inspiration on how to capture in memorable words the essence of a theme in maritime history, it is probably natural that one literally and figuratively runs one's eyes along the spines of the books that line the library shelves where one writes. So often the titles one finds and the subjects they focus on are very specific and confined. So they should and certainly must, of necessity, be for new researchers undertaking their early work in the field. Each of the books is more likely to represent "the white speck of some big ship" and not the "depths and distances" of the blue tones that shade from the dark sea to the luminous sky in creating and embracing an horizon.

An experienced seaman like Joseph Conrad was well aware that one's height above the surface of the sea extended the distance to the horizon and the scope of what one could see. An artist would add that this also created a differing perspective from different vantage points, that is to say, a change in the viewing point resulted in a change in the mental image of size, relative importance, and shape that alters the highlights and shadows in ways that reveal different aspects. The horizon, that dividing point between sea and sky that we see from afar, is a point that moves with the level of our perceptions and always remains beyond our reach. As we sail out on a passage, it moves with us into previously unseen areas, but as we return home at the end the voyage to fold our wings, we rediscover the old horizon, but the experience of the extended horizon remains to inform our thought and perceptions of what we directly see around us. Thus, the way that horizons move and change within our perceptions at sea provides a useful metaphor in talking about the scope of maritime history as a field of study.

New researchers in any field often define their focus too narrowly. There are obvious practical temptations to do this: one does not have to work so hard, one does not have read so much, and one can circumscribe the subject at hand and one's own area of scholarship so carefully that it could exclude with considerable safety any possible academic rival. This is a temptation that befell a fellow graduate student in my own time, when I had the indiscretion to use inadvertently one of the same manuscript collections that she was using. Our topics were very different in approach, method, and purpose but overlapped in time period and involved some of the same actors. Indignantly, she formally protested to the history faculty board, declaring that since she had begun her work some months earlier than I had, I should be dismissed for poaching on "her" manuscript collections in the Public Record Office and The British Library. After a series of unpleasant situations, the little tempest was eventually resolved peacefully with logic prevailing, but not before some older male faculty members revealed their uneasiness in dealing with a tearful young woman. If nothing more, the incident was at least instructive to me and certainly suggested that the horizons of the field had not been an element in the young lady's consideration. She had employed a strategy of preemptive strike to try to define a boundary in research materials, to defend academic territory, and to carve out a safe career position. A preemptive strike is sometimes useful in war and sometimes counterproductive. Here, it certainly missed the point. It was not a question of war, but a matter of learning, contributing to mutual knowledge and understanding by making use of perspective, vantage point, and interpretation.

Perhaps the best antidote is to keep in mind the old-fashioned academic advice that the ideal piece of research should make a positive contribution to knowledge on a small, but not isolated, sector of the research front. It must be limited in its own scope in order to be manageable and comprehensible, but in its limitations it should still have a clearly discernable relationship to issues of wider significance and general interest. Put another way, for maritime history, one must ask how the speck relates to the broad horizon.

Maritime history is a field of study that is just beginning to reach maturity and we are just beginning to be able to define its scope as a major theme in general global history. As a subject for books and articles, its origins are varied and complex. Some of it had its origins in the work of professional seamen who wrote down their experiences for other working seamen and navigators to use, originally for practical use as useful guides and later, as the concept of professions grew, as a body of very specialized literature that helped to cultivate expertise and professional identity.

In terms of the English language literature, Richard Eden was among the first to contribute to the field by translating into English some accounts of the Spanish and Portuguese voyages. First in 1553 came Eden's translation of extracts from Sebastian Münster's *Cosmographiae,* titled in English *A treatyse of the newe India,*[2] followed two years later in 1555 with Peter Martyr d'Anghiera's *Decades of the New World or West India.*[3] When these books originally appeared they were at first valued primarily for the practical information that they gave to navigators who followed in the tracks of the first explorers. In fact, these books contained the only reliable information in English on these voyages and served as practical·sailing directions for seamen. Peter Martyr's work was taken to sea as the only available guide to the new Spanish and Portuguese lands.

Eventually such descriptive accounts of specific voyages formed a specific genre of English maritime history: the history of exploration. That they did so was largely the contribution of Richard Hakluyt, with his *Divers voyages*[4] in 1582 and his two collections of *The principal navigations . . . of the English nation*[5] in 1589 and in 1598–1600. But these, like the similar collection that John Harris made in the early eighteenth century,[6] were not primarily designed as history or as literature as we might think of them today, but rather as a part of a practical campaign to promote English navigation and colonization.

There has long been confusion about the two terms "naval history" and "maritime history," but in the past decade a consensus in usage has formed that clarifies the matter. Maritime history embraces naval history; it is the overarching subject that deals with the full range of mankind's relationships to the seas and oceans of the world. It is a broad theme that cuts across academic boundaries and builds linkages between disciplines to form a humanistic understanding of the many dimensions involved. Maritime history involves in particular the histories of science, technology, cartography, industry, economics, trade, politics, international affairs, imperial growth and rivalry, institutional and organizational development, communications, migration, law, social affairs, leadership, ethics, art, and literature. The range is immense and the possible vantage points and topics are many. Yet, the focus is clearly defined—ships and the sailors who operate them, with specific sets of scientific understanding and technological devices, in their hostile sea environment, which covers the greater part of the globe.

Within the broad field of maritime history, there are a number of recognized major subspecialties. Among them are the history of navigational and maritime sciences; the histories of ships and their construction, the aircraft that fly over the seas, and the submarines that pass under their surface; maritime economic history; the histories of merchant shipping, fishing, and whaling; the history of yachting and other leisure activities at sea and on the seaside; the histories of geographical exploration and cartography; social and labor history; the health of seamen; maritime law, maritime art, maritime literature; and naval history. These subspecialties are interrelated within the framework of maritime history to varying degrees, but each is tied as well to historical subject areas outside the maritime field. Characteristically, a maritime subspecialty's relationship outside the field defines its perspective on, and approach to, maritime history.

War at sea and the development of its political, technological, institutional, and financial elements are, thus, the focus of the naval history subspecialty. Within the structure of maritime history, naval history relates to the other maritime subspecialties as a special case, a particular application of the histories of ships and shipbuilding, geographical exploration, cartography, social and labor issues, health, law, art, literature, and so on. It also connects to the study of agencies and sea services that cooperate or share responsibilities with navies, such as (in the United States) the Marine Corps, Coast Guard, Revenue Service, and Geodetic Survey. The last three have fulfilled, under a variety of organizational names, critical maritime functions as hydrography, policing and safety of navigation, piloting, and licensing of mariners. Outside the maritime sphere, naval history is closely associated with, and has adopted the broad approaches of, such fields as military studies, international affairs, politics, government, and the history of technology.

Naval history specifically involves the study and analysis of the ways in which governments have organized and employed force at sea to achieve national ends. It ranges across all periods of world history and involves a wide variety of national histories, languages, and archival sources. (Most prominent among the latter are governmental archives, supplemented by the private papers of individuals who served in or with navies.)

The study of naval history involves analysis of the ways in which decisions were reached and carried out, as well as of the design, procurement, manufacture, and employment of vessels, aircraft, and weapons to achieve the ends in view. As Admiral Sir Herbert Richmond succinctly put it, naval history

> includes the "whys" of strategy in all its phases, from the political sphere to that of minor strategy and tactics of fleets and squadrons: it includes the "hows" of actual performances: and, not less important, the "whys" of success and failure. It embraces all those elements of foreign diplomatic relations, of economics and commerce, of international law and neutrality, of positions, of the principles of war, of administration, of the nature of the weapon, and of personality.[7]

Naval history in the machine age faces the need to explain these matters comprehensively, placing individual decisions and the collective interactions of leaders within a wide context of technological, financial, and operational issues.[8]

A traditional work in the field of naval history traces the ways in which national leaders dealt with international situations and decided upon courses of action that involved employment of ships and weapons at sea, and the reasons why. It then follows the results of those decisions and examines the actual uses of naval force at sea and its consequences, often in terms of the biographies of particular admirals, specific battles, campaigns, or accounts of the actions of fleets, squadrons, and even individual ships and aircraft.

In contrast, modern naval historians have come to understand that navies and those that serve in uniform do not exist separately from other parts of society. In addition to seeing their actions in terms of leadership, tactics, and strategy, scholars must also understand them in terms of the external environment, domestic politics, bureaucratic politics, the state of technological development and capabilities, procurement issues, organizational culture, and the capacity of naval men and women (in a profession marked by rigid hierarchical structures) for innovation, change, and alternative approaches.[9] Modern naval history looks at navies not only within their national contexts or as instruments of particular national states but also from wider international and comparative perspectives, in terms either of the chronological development of specific events or of the broad, long-term development of navies around the world.[10] Clearly the actions of one navy cannot be considered in isolation from foreign influences, whether enemies, allies, or world developments.

Naval historians, as practitioners of the wider field of maritime history, are bound by the same general requirements and standards as apply to scholars who work, research, or write in any other historical area. Any historical project requires a wide understanding of the context in which the events under study took place, a deep appreciation of the historical literature addressing the subject and its broad field, and a thorough examination of the original documents and other primary source materials that establish authoritatively what occurred, how, and why.

NOTES   This essay was originally delivered as the keynote address to the New Researchers Conference, held at the National Maritime Museum, Greenwich, England, on 7 March 2003. It has not previously been published.

1 Joseph Conrad, *The Shadow-Line* and *Within the Tides* (London: Folio Society, 2001), p. 48.

2 Sebastien Münster, *A treatyse of the newe India, with other new founde landes and ilandes, aswell eastwarde as westwarde, as they are knowen and found in these oure dayes, after the descripcion of Sebastian Munster in his boke of vniuersall cosmographie : wherin the diligent reader may see the good successe and rewarde of noble and honeste enterpryses, by the which not only worldly ryches are obtayned, but also God is glorified, & the Christian fayth enlarged. Translated out of Latin into Englishe. By Rycharde Eden.* (Imprinted at London, in Lombarde Strete, by Edward Sutton., 1553).

3 Pietro Martire d'Anghiera, *The decades of the Newe Worlde or West India, conteynyng the nauigations and conquestes of the Spanyardes, with the particular descripton [sic] of the moste ryche and large landes and ilandes lately founde in the West Ocean perteynyng to the inheritaunce of the kinges of Spayne. : In the which the diligent reader may not only consyder what commoditie may hereby chaunce to the hole Christian world in tyme to come, but also learne many secreates touchynge the lande, the sea, and the starres, very necessarie to be knowe[n] to al such as shal attempte any nauigations, or otherwise haue delite to beholde the strange and woonderfull woorkes of God and nature. Wrytten in the Latine tounge by Peter Martyr of Angleria, and translated into Englysshe by Rycharde Eden.* (Londini. : In αdibus Guilhelmi Powell. Imprynted at London in Lumbard streete at the signe of the Cradle by Edwarde Sutton., Anno. 1555).

4 Richard Hakluyt, *Diuers voyages touching the discouerie of America, : and the ilands adiacent vnto the same, made first of all by our Englishmen, and afterward by the French-men and Britons: and certaine notes of aduertisements for obseruations, necessarie for such as shall heereafter make the like attempt, with two mappes annexed heereunto for the plainer understanding of the whole matter.* (Imprinted at London : For Thomas VVoodcocke, dwelling in Paules Church-yard, at the signe of the blackebeare., 1582).

5 Richard Hakluyt, *The principall nauigations, voiages and discoueries of the English nation, : made by sea or ouer land, to the most remote and farthest distant quarters of the earth at any time within the compasse of these 1500. veeres: deuided into three seuerall parts, according to the positions of the regions wherunto they were directed. . . . Whereunto is added the last most renowned English nauigation, round about the whole globe of the earth.* (Imprinted at London : By George Bishop and Ralph Newberie, deputies to Christopher Barker . . . , 1589). And Richard Hakluyt, *The principal nauigations, voiages, traffiques and discoueries of the English nation, : made by sea or ouer-land, to the remote and farthest distant quarters of the earth, at any time within the compasse of these 1500. yeeres: deuided into three seuerall volumes, according to the positions of the regions, whereunto they were directed . . . : And lastly, the memorable defeate of the Spanish huge Armada, anno 1588. and the famous victorie atchieued at the citie of Cadiz, 1596. are described.* (Imprinted at London : By George Bishop, Ralph Newberie and Robert Barker., 1598–1600).

6 John Harris, *Navigantium atque itinerantium bibliotheca: or, a compleat collection of voyages and travels: consisting of above four hundred of the most authentick writers; beginning with Hackluit, Purchass, &c in English; Ramusio in Italian; Thevenot, &c in French; De Bry, and Grynaei novus orbis in Latin; the Dutch East-India Company in Dutch: and continued, with others of note, that have publish'd histories, voyages, travels, or discoveries, ih the English, Latin, French, Italian, Spanish, Portuguese, German or Dutch tongues; relating to any part of Asia, Africa, America, Europe, or the islands thereof, to this present time. With the heads of several of our most considerable sea-commanders; and a great number of excellent maps of all parts of the world, and cuts of most curious things in all the voyages. Also, an appendix, of the remarkable accidents at sea; and several of our considerable engagements: the charters, acts of Parliament, &c. about the East-India trade; and papers relating to the union of the two companies. Throughout the whole all original papers are printed at large; as the Pope's bull, to dispose of the West-Indies to the King of Spain; letters patents for establishing companies of merchants; as the Russia, East-India companies, &c. Letters from one great prince or state to another; shewing their titles, style, &c. To which is prefixed, a history of the peopling of the several parts of the world, and particularly of America. . . .* (London : Printed for Thomas Bennet, at the Half-Moon, in St. Paul's church-yard; John Nicholson, at the King's arms, in Little Britain; and Daniel Midwinter, at the Rose and Crown, in St. Paul's church-yard, MDCCV. [1705].

7 Herbert Richmond, "The Importance of the Study of Naval History," *Naval Review* vol. XXVII (May 1939), pp. 201–18.

8 Jon Tetsuro Sumida and David Alan Rosenberg, "Machines, Men, Manufacturing, Management, and Money: The Study of Navies as Complex Organizations and the Transformation of Twentieth Century Naval History," in *Doing Naval History: Essays toward Improvement*, ed. John B. Hattendorf (Newport, R.I.: Naval War College Press, 1995), pp. 25–39.

9 On these issues, see Robert Jervis, "Navies, Politics, and Political Science"; Volker Berghan, "Navies and Domestic Factors"; and Robert S. Wood, "Domestic Factors, Regime Changes, and Naval Forces," in *Doing Naval History*, ed. Hattendorf, pp. 41–71.

10 See N. A. M. Rodger, "Considerations on Writing a General Naval History," in ibid., pp. 117–28.

1652 1815 *Part 2: General Naval History*

V *Navies, Strategy, and Tactics in the Age of De Ruyter*

The quarter century that lay between 1652, when Michiel Adriaanszoon de Ruyter became a temporary flag officer in the Zeeland squadron, and 1676, when De Ruyter died as the most highly respected Dutch flag officer of the seventeenth century, was a span of years that marked a transformation in the character of European navies.[1] This period marked a change in the way navies were managed, in the weapons and ships with which they fought, and in the objectives for which they fought. These characteristics of navies that were established in this period lasted for more than 150 years, through the Napoleonic Wars and even beyond 1815. The characteristics that were established in the last half of the seventeenth century began to take another direction only in the nineteenth century with the Industrial Revolution, the introduction of mechanical propulsion, turreted guns, and metal hulled warships.

In the context of the broadest developments for war at sea in European history, these years marked the transition that brought an end to the primacy of the galley as an instrument of war and an end to the emphasis on the use of ships for raiding operations with mêlée tactics in grappling and boarding an enemy ship with hand weapons in ship-on-ship actions. While northern Europeans had set out to find a means to counter the overwhelming effectiveness of the Mediterranean galley armed with one or two forward-firing, heavy guns, they ended up with quite unexpected results.[2]

Those wide-ranging interconnected results brought the clear early beginnings of permanent national navies, the development of bureaucratic structures to support them, the gradual professionalisation of the naval officer corps, and the employment of large, heavily-gunned, purpose-built warships that became the predominant and the most potent symbols of national power. Moreover, these warships fought in a very specific, single-line-ahead tactical formation that involved using purpose-designed warships in a line of battle against warships of similar types, using similar tactics, in engagements that had the strategic object of removing the threat of a rival battle fleet in order to allow one's own merchant ships to pass safely to their destinations as part of nationally defined economic and imperial systems.

The century and a half between 1500 and 1650 had witnessed some fundamental developments in European history that set the stage for the specific naval changes that took place during the third quarter of the seventeenth century. At the beginning of the sixteenth century there had been two quite different centres of maritime technology in Europe. One was in the Mediterranean and the other in northern Europe. These two technologies slowly began to merge as merchant entrepreneurs and rulers in western

European countries began to cooperate to develop improved guns and ships that provided the technical basis for long-distance oceanic shipping. While this expansion of European dominion and trade was occurring, rulers and their states paid increasing attention to the promotion and protection of their commercial trade at sea. The Spanish and Portuguese voyages of discovery as well as state patronage for the development of nautical science in this era were part of these developments. In northern Europe, Denmark and Sweden foreshadowed future developments elsewhere as they superseded the dominance of the maritime cities of that region as they developed purpose-built, state-owned, and state-managed naval fleets to contest between them the control of foreign shipping inside the enclosed Baltic Sea.[3]

Meanwhile, the strategically located Dutch and English took over control of trade between northern and southern Europe from their positions on opposite sides of the Channel and North Sea. The Dutch were the first to successfully forge this into a European-wide supremacy in trade. When Spain had attempted to stop this development by embargoes on Dutch trade and trade warfare, Dutch business enterprise was able to offset this by successfully competing with Spain's trade monopolies overseas, thereby establishing Dutch supremacy in maritime trade. While the Dutch Republic dominated, England also shared in the subsequent shift in the balance of political and economic power from southern Europe to northern Europe.

The third quarter of the seventeenth century was marked by a number of European wars that reflected these trends and contributed further to the geostrategic situation of the maritime countries of northern and north-western Europe. Among these wars, France and Spain had fought a war between 1635 and 1659 which had as one aspect of the larger issues rivalry over control of territory in the Low Countries. From 1656, England supported France in the conflict. In the resulting peace treaty of the Pyrenees, France won control of additional fortifications in Flanders and Artois, while England acquired Jamaica in the West Indies and Dunkirk. Sweden and Denmark fought wars between 1657 and 1658 and 1658 and 1660. Sweden and Poland fought a war from 1655 to 1660, which brought Sweden and the Dutch Republic to the brink of war in 1656 due to the Swedish blockade of Danzig.

This period of conflict ended with Sweden gaining control of the eastern shore of the Kattegat through the permanent acquisition of the provinces of Halland and Bohuslän and controlling the eastern shore of the coast of the Scandinavian Peninsula with Skåne and Blekinge. During the final phase of that war, Sweden granted Dutch citizens some parity with her own subjects in customs duties on trade in 1656, but this proved to be of limited importance as the treaty made exceptions for Swedish trade through privileged Swedish companies, thereby continuing to discriminate against foreign trade. While this war was in progress, the Dutch were also engaged in a war with Portugal over the settlements that the Dutch had maintained in Brazil since the 1630s. By 1661, the Dutch had been forced to leave their claims and acknowledge Portuguese sovereignty over all of Brazil. During the War of Devolution in 1667–1668, King Louis XIV of France claimed part of the Spanish Netherlands as his wife's inheritance, she being a daughter of King Philip IV of Spain by an earlier marriage than that which produced her half brother, the current king of Spain Carlos II, and due by the laws of inheritance a division of her father's estate. The subsequent Treaty of Aix-la-Chapelle, made through English, Dutch, and Swedish mediation, allowed France to control twelve additional fortresses in Flanders.[4]

Within this broad framework of conflict, competition, and development, the series of three Dutch Naval Wars in 1652–1654, 1665–1667, and 1672–1674 that took place predominantly in the North Sea and the English Channel and its approaches were the crucial conflicts in which the new naval developments took place. Traditionally interpreted as expressions of economic and trade conflict, historians have more recently debated the additional roles of antagonistic ideology and mutual suspicion as war causes.[5] One can also justifiably add to these causal elements the extreme religious polemic that English propagandists increasingly employed across this period in characterising the Dutch as an immoral, treacherous, and ungrateful people.[6] Although these three wars have often been lumped together because of their location and relatively close occurrence in time, an overemphasis on this can obscure the differing contexts, causes, and results of the separate wars. Nevertheless, when the development of the naval elements is traced across these three wars, an observer can see a distinctive naval development that occurs during this period that differs from other wars in the period and shows De Ruyter's participation and contribution to naval development at the zenith of the Dutch Republic's economic strength.

The European Context for Dutch and English Naval Development

By the end of the Thirty Years' War in 1648, the Dutch Republic was widely recognized as Europe's leading maritime state with worldwide commercial interests that stretched from the Arctic to the Levant and from Asia to the Americas. For the maritime situations that had existed up to this point, the Dutch Republic had maintained a naval force that met their immediate needs. The Dutch Navy had played and continued to play a key role in the Republic's development and maintenance of the world's first global maritime *entrepôt* economy by using violence to open areas for trade and by keeping open the sea lanes for the safe passage of Dutch shipping. The largest navy in the world in the 1620s and 1630s was the Spanish-Portuguese navy that the Habsburgs maintained. The naval battles that the Dutch fought against the Habsburgs in the Channel in 1639 were the largest naval encounters in the first half of the seventeenth century in terms of ships and men.[7]

In this context, the outbreak of the First Anglo-Dutch War was an event that was not predicted in advance, although the outcome of the English Civil War with the overthrow of the English monarchy, the execution of King Charles I, and the establishment of the Commonwealth under Oliver Cromwell showed a volatility that had international implications. England was in a position to adopt an aggressive naval policy as an attractive tool to advance English mercantilist ideas. Yet, neither side was fully prepared for the war that occurred.

The initial advantage lay with the English Navy. Following the common practice of the time, the Dutch Navy had disbanded much of its force with the end of the war in 1648. In 1650, there was no indication of the major naval arms race that would occur within a few years. In general, the balance of naval power initially appeared to be stable across Europe. Clearly, however, the notable growth in the English Navy in the years between 1640 and 1650 was an exception, while the number of Dutch warships dropped

Comparison in Total Displacement Tonnage of Major Warships[8]

Year	England	Netherlands	France	Denmark	Sweden
1640	38,000	45,000[9]	29,000	18,000	29,000
1650	49,000	29,000	21,000	23,000	27,000
1655	90,000	64,000	18,000	21,000	28,000

Comparison in Numbers of Warships over 700 Tons Displacement[10]

Year	England	Netherlands	France	Denmark	Sweden
1650	32	2	14	8	16
1655	57	52	14	9	13

nearly in half from 120 ships to 62 ships at the same time that the English numbers rose by ten from 43 to 53 ships.[11] While Dutch naval strength had declined in the absence of any obvious external threats, it grew after 1650 in response to threat, while English strength grew as a result of the internal revolutionary situation in England.

English Naval Development

In the spring of 1649, when the English Commonwealth was established, Cromwell's New Model Army had won over Royalist opponents in England. The military men in charge had no particular love for England's naval men, who had generally been more moderate in politics and many of whom had mutinied and defected to the Royalists at Hellevoetsluis in 1648 and come under the command of Prince Rupert of the Rhine. The new English leaders understood that they were isolated and in a dangerous position, particularly while Ireland, Scotland, the islands in Home Waters, and all of England's colonies remained in Royalist hands. They believed that Royalist forces abroad were being financed and supported from other countries and there were reports that Sweden was preparing a naval expedition to support the Royalists in Scotland. In this situation, a strong naval defence was a key element to maintain their power.[12] At the same time, foreign powers had been slow to grant recognition to the new English state. Among them, France issued letters of marque against English merchant shipping. As a result, England banned trade with France and authorized her own privateers to prey on French trade. Much of French trade, however, was carried in Dutch bottoms and this led to English attacks on Dutch trade.

To deal with this array of maritime issues, the leaders of the Commonwealth immediately set out to take control of the ships and seamen close at hand and to begin a major naval construction and acquisition programme. This took place in a series of rapid ship acquisitions for the English Navy that reflected rapidly changing ideas about warship design. A key element in this was the adoption of the frigate design. It involved the adoption of some of the design elements of the ships used by Dunkirk privateers, characterised by being low-built, fast vessels with finer lines that came to have a length-to-breadth ratio of 10 to 3 in contrast to the earlier heavier warships that had a 3-to-1 ratio. Initially a single-decked, narrow, lightly-built, and fast vessel, the frigate design quickly evolved over a few years as new ships were added to the fleet. In 1649, the Parliamentary Commission for the Admiralty ordered five ships; three of them were similar to the first frigates, but two were designed to be flagships and made considerably larger with two decks. The construction of the two large ships was consigned to two brothers: the master builders Peter Pett at Deptford and Christopher Pett at Woolwich. They each built somewhat different vessels that had a major influence on ships that followed. Peter Pett's *Fairfax* included a forecastle on his two-decked ship, while Christopher Pett's *Speaker* became the direct ancestor of the two-decked ship-of-the-line that developed later with both a forecastle and a small poop deck.[13]

At the same time, the numbers of guns on ships were increased. *Speaker* was originally designed to carry 44 guns, but this was changed to 50 guns by the time she was launched in 1650, and increased to 56 by 1653. This increase in guns was paralleled by an increase in the number of men used to man guns and apparently by undocumented changes in the handling and firing of guns. The experience of the naval actions that had occurred during the English Civil War and the privateering and other actions that took place in the defence of trade from 1649 had led to a primary emphasis on speed and a secondary emphasis on a new system of using large guns firing broadsides in single-ship actions.[14] This cumulative experience had a direct influence on English warship design and on ship acquisition during this short span of years. Since the Dutch had long experience in using their ships for defending trade at sea, they had concentrated more consistently than the English in having fast, frigate-style warships. The English Navy had built its ships on the basis of different rates or classes of warships since the mid-sixteenth century. By 1652, the two navies on opposite sides of the North Sea had developed naval forces that showed a distinctive difference. The English had a strong battle fleet and a large number of smaller ships of the 4th and 5th Rates that were useful as cruisers. In contrast, the Dutch had mainly frigate-style ships comparable to the English 4th, 5th, and 6th Rates. The Dutch ships were heavily armed for their size, but the hired merchantmen that the Dutch often employed were not capable of carrying the large numbers of 18- and 20-pound cannon that the English employed.

At the same time that new English ships that were being acquired and new approaches to design instituted the naval establishment ashore had rapidly begun to change to support innovation and supervise such change with a more integrated approach than used heretofore. Improving upon earlier organizational arrangements, the Commonwealth's Council of State employed three groups that worked together under the Council to direct naval affairs: (1) The Committee for the Affairs of the Admiralty and Navy, or the Admiralty Committee, that dealt with naval policy and strategy; (2) The Commissioners of the Admiralty and the Navy, or the Navy Commissioners, responsible for the shore establishment and pay; and (3) the Commissioners to go to Sea, or the Generals at Sea.[15] This arrangement brought a basis for the coordination of policy, strategy, logistics, operations, and tactics.

By the spring of 1651, with the conquest of Ireland and Scotland completed and the risk of Royalist counter-revolution reduced, the Commonwealth could reduce military expenditure, and, despite the requirement to maintain a constabulary army in Ireland and Scotland, could reduce the army's overall strength by 30%. Financially solvent by having sold state property and having been able to obtain the English government's normal excise, customs, and assessment revenues, the Commonwealth was well positioned to pay its arrears and national debt as well as its current costs for the armed forces. This financial situation allowed enough funds to maintain the fleet to protect British commerce in Home Waters as well as in the Mediterranean and the Bay of Biscay. In January 1652, the Commonwealth planned to have 82 ships at sea, manned by 10,024 men.[16] And this continued to grow, so that by the end of the war in 1654, the Commonwealth owned more than 200 ships that required more than 30,000 sailors, and had a shore establishment of several thousand to support them.[17]

These arrays of changes for the English Navy were the innovations that provided the basis for long-term growth into a great power navy during the century that followed, but at the very outset in the First Dutch War they provided advantage over the Dutch Navy when they worked, but were a liability when they did not.

The First Dutch War, 1652–1654

When war finally erupted between the Dutch and the English in the spring of 1652, it erupted suddenly, following the breakdown of the diplomatic negotiations over England's Navigation Act and the rejection of England's proposal for a union between the English Commonwealth and the Dutch Republic. While this was in progress, the Dutch Republic ordered the mobilisation of a large fleet of 150 ships under Lieutenant-Admiral Maerten Harpertszoon Tromp to protect Dutch shipping between the Strait of Gibraltar and the Sound. At the time, the five Dutch admiralties had seventy-nine warships collectively available to them, most of which were built in the 1640s and the early 1650s. The Dutch Republic had consistently disposed of older ships and concentrated on acquiring new ships, but during periods when the Republic was at peace Dutch warships were typically maintained for protection of their own neutral trade at a time when nearby countries, such as England, France, Spain, Portugal, were at war. In the early seventeenth century, the Dutch had concentrated their peacetime naval resources by employing purpose-built warships and seldom hired merchantmen. The sudden Dutch mobilisation in 1652 brought in a variety of ships to the fleet that were essentially armed merchantmen on lease. Seeing the contrast to recent practice, the English saw this mobilisation of such a large fleet at sea as a threat. The very fact of naval mobilisation created a volatile situation.

The situation in which the conflict arose did not present opportunities for any extensive thinking about strategy, that is to say, using naval force in a comprehensive manner in order to control an enemy force for the purpose of achieving larger political objectives. Battles were largely fought as opposing fleets encountered one another. Yet, the initial tactical preference that English naval commanders had in choosing to use their warships in gunnery duels in a line of battle against opposing Dutch warships that were protecting convoys of merchant vessels and the Dutch acceptance of this challenge with a similar type of naval force created a type of operational reasoning that led eventually to a strategic rationale for naval power.

Although the Dutch fleet was numerically superior, the English Navy was in a far superior condition to fight than the Dutch. In 1652, the Dutch preferred their well tried approach in using a limited number of ships, operating from a windward position, to quickly sail down wind to attack enemy ships to immediately grapple and board them for hand to hand combat. When operating in large fleets with a wide variety of ship types, they had developed an organization of five squadrons that each sailed from the windward position in a line-ahead formation to approach the enemy, then immediately moved to attack individual ships with initial gunfire, then grappled and overwhelmed them with a large boarding party.[18]

When the English General at Sea Robert Blake encountered the Dutch fleet off Dover on 19/29 May [old style/new style dates] 1652 and demanded a salute in recognition of Britain's sovereignty of those seas,[19] gunfire was exchanged and battle ensued in which two Dutch ships were lost in an incident that marked the beginning of open conflict between the two states. This action illustrated little change in the approach from earlier practices. As a chance encounter, there is no indication of pre-planned approaches on either side, either from a strategic or a tactical point of view. The surviving accounts of subsequent engagements—including those in the Channel near Plymouth when De Ruyter had a minor victory over Sir George Ayscue in an action on 16/26 August 1652, the battle of the Kentish Knock in the Thames estuary in which Blake and Vice Admiral Sir William Penn defeated Admiral Witte de With on 28–29 September/8–9 October 1652, the battle of Dungeness in which Tromp defeated Blake on 30 November/10 December 1652—suggest that no new or distinctive tactics were being used. At Dungeness, Tromp's numerical superiority had won the day for the Dutch.

The following year, Blake and his fellow General at Sea Richard Deane were able to attack the Dutch convoy under Tromp's protection off Portland in a three-day battle that had begun on 18/28 February 1652/3. Similarly, the English defeated the Dutch at the Gabbard off the North Foreland on 2–3/12–13 June 1653, and off Terheide south of Scheveningen on 31 July–1 August/9–10 August 1653, when Tromp was killed in action. The English suffered a serious loss when Commodore Jan van Galen destroyed the four-ship English squadron at Livorno (Leghorn) in the Mediterranean on 4/14 March 1652/3.

The first minor evidence of any change taking place in tactical ideas occurred on 10/20 February 1652/3, just eight days before the battle of Portland, when Vice Admiral Sir William Penn issued instructions to his squadron directing the smaller ships to stand to windward to observe and to protect the major fighting units from an attack by enemy fire ships.[20] The major change came on 29 March/8 April 1653 at Portland, where the English were refitting after the three-day battle off that port. Preparing for the next encounter, the three English Generals at Sea—Robert Blake, Richard Deane, and George Monck—issued two complementary documents, "Instructions for the better ordering of the Fleet in Fighting"[21] and "Instructions for the better ordering of the Fleet in Sailing."[22]

While much of these were a compilation of standard and existing directives, they included some innovations. First, issued together they established a connection between cruising formations and tactical formations in battle that would be developed in the future. Despite their limitations, these documents were issued as documents to be acted upon at sea in the context of preparation for battle, giving the English fleet a degree of discipline under the control of its flag officers that it had not previously seen.

Although the evidence from surviving documents is vague, from this point forward the English fleet began to conduct itself differently than it previously had. The next major battle was at the Gabbard (or North Foreland) on 2–3/12–13 June 1653, in which Deane was killed in action. Despite that loss, both English and Dutch sources report that the English ships were under better control and that their broadside gunnery while in a line was effective in preventing the Dutch from approaching for grappling and boarding. While this is suggestive of new tactical thinking, there is no evidence that it was employed in the final major battle of the war off Terheide.

These experiences of naval warfare between 1652 and 1654 led naval leaders to think differently and to prepare for future wars. For the Dutch, the reverses at sea led to an immediate commitment to use federal funds to build a larger fleet of purpose-built warships. While the war was still in progress, the States General voted in February 1653 for the construction of thirty purpose-built warships carrying up to 54 guns. As the peace negotiations were in progress by the end of the year, thirty more similar warships were ordered, but it would require the States General to take repeated steps over the coming half century to provide the funding to maintain, man, and provision these ships as active warships.[23]

With this series of decisions, the most powerful Navy in Europe shifted to adopt the new western European standard of a large, permanent, national navy. At the same time, this led to the tacit acceptance of a strategic corollary: the protection of one's own merchant trade and the protection of one's own coast from invasion—two central functions for navies—were best achieved by fighting and defeating a similar type of enemy naval force in an engagement between warships. The presence of an undefeated enemy naval force gave the opposing nation the ability to use the seaways for either peaceful trade or for military purposes. In this, the immediate focus during these wars was on the tactical development by which large battle fleets could fight.

The Interwar Period, 1654–1665

In the dozen years that lay between the First and Second Dutch Wars, both the Dutch and English navies continued to grow and to develop, as did other navies. The displacement figures reflect not only the increase in numbers of major warships, but also the growing increase in the size of warships as the ship-of-the-line developed to carry increasing numbers of guns.

Comparison in Total Displacement Tonnage of Major Warships[24]

Year	England	Netherlands	France	Denmark	Sweden
1660	88,000	62,000	20,000	15,000	23,000
1665	102,000	81,000	36,000	24,000	31,000
1670	84,000	102,000	114,000	30,000	34,000
1675	95,000	89,000	138,000	29,000	33,000
1680	132,000	66,000	135,000	39,000	21,000

Comparison in Numbers of Warships over 700 Tons Displacement[25]

Year	England	Netherlands	France	Denmark	Sweden
1660	57	51	15	9	8
1665	69	70	25	13	16
1670	60	88	75	17	18
1675	68	73	87	19	18
1680	89	62	83	23	11

Across the two decades during which the Second and Third Dutch Wars took place, one can see a major development taking place. On the one hand is the rapid rise of the English and Dutch navies as they faced each other, but also is the sudden appearance of France as major naval power that adopted the newly emerging approaches to naval warfare and the ship of the line. While France had not entirely neglected its Navy before the institution of Colbert's reforms in 1661,[26] French naval policy dramatically changed under Louis XIV in the immediate aftermath of the First Dutch War as France moved to the front ranks of European navies and quickly adopted the new approaches to warship design, purpose-built warships, and tactics.[27]

By 1660, when King Charles II was restored to the English throne, he acquired a Navy with a total of 156 ships, of which 75 carried 40 to 64 guns. Moving to even larger ships, Peter Pett built the 80-gun *Naseby* at Woolwich in 1655, while his brother, Christopher, built the 70-gun *Richard* at Woolwich in 1658. Two years later, the 100-gun *Sovereign* was rebuilt at Chatham.[28] As war between the two maritime countries approached in the early 1660s, the Dutch also began to strengthen the fleet in a three-year period of warship construction in 1664 that brought in 60 more warships of 80 and more guns.

In the Dutch Republic, the *raadpensionaris* in Holland from 1653, Johan de Witt, reflected the commercial interests of the Amsterdam merchants and became a major political force in helping to modernize the Dutch Navy.[29] In both countries, notable naval administrators were placed to come to the fore. In Holland, the father-and-son team of David and Job de Wildt's tenure stretched from the 1640s to 1704, and, in England, the young Samuel Pepys began his notable career as a novice only in 1660.

England's Royal Navy was now under the command of the Lord High Admiral, a young and inexperienced, but strong, leader in the king's brother, the thirty-three-year-old James, Duke of York. Having seen a number of actions ashore, he had an able advisor for naval matters in the experienced Admiral Sir William Penn and his secretary Sir William Coventry.

The Second Dutch War, 1665–1667

As war approached in late 1664, the duke of York took direct command of the English fleet at Portsmouth on 9/19 November. Moving quickly on 11/21 November, he set a new tone for employing heavily armed ships by immediately organizing the fleet by dividing it into three squadrons. While the surviving documentation does not provide all the details, this seems to have been the creation of the English terminology that would last well past the age of sail with seniority given to the Red, followed by the White, and then the Blue, and with each squadron flying a flag to denote this: White in the van, Red in the centre, and Blue in the rear. In turn, each squadron had three divisions, each commanded by an admiral in the centre, with a vice-admiral in the van, and a rear admiral in the rear. This made a total of three flag officers for each squadron and a total of nine in the fleet.

Over the next two weeks, the duke of York issued separate sailing and fighting instructions that were based largely on those issued under the Commonwealth, but the fighting instructions contained two important new articles. One required the formation of a line ahead on either a starboard or larboard tack. The other required ships' captains to hold their fire until their guns came within a distance that their gunfire could have effect. Further innovations seem to have taken place between November 1664 and

1 February 1665; the duke of York issued signals that made it clear that ships were expected to take up pre-planned positions in the line of battle. Thus, a naval order of battle was established. In the coming months, several iterations of the orders were made, along with additional instructions.[30]

On the opening of the war, the English and Dutch fleets immediately took up positions from which they could aggressively use their battle fleets to protect and defend their merchant trade. In April, the duke of York moved to intercept Dutch homeward-bound convoys and to try to force a battle by luring the Dutch war fleet out to protect their commerce.

The effect of the improved English tactical dispositions showed in the battle of Lowestoft on 3/13 June 1665, when the duke of York's fleet defeated the Dutch by using line-of-battle tactics. In the course of the battle, the English flagship *Royal Charles* and the Dutch flagship *Eendracht* had engaged. During the action, *Eendracht* received a hit in the powder room and exploded killing the Dutch commander, Jacob van Wassenaer, heer van Obdam. This accident in combat led to the Dutch withdrawal from action, and was the fortuitous event that cleared the way for De Ruyter's promotion to replace Wassenaer as lieutenant-admiral of Holland and West Friesland.[31]

The actual conduct of the English ships in actual combat differed somewhat from the ideals that had been laid out on paper in the instructions issued beforehand. The plans did not work out as planned. A number of ships luffed up to windward and were in three, four, and even five ranks, instead of a single line of battle, thereby causing some casualties in English ships by friendly fire.[32]

Several months after the battle, the earl of Sandwich reflected on their actions and came up with detailed and practical recommendations for improvement in future actions.[33] The Dutch, too, reflected on their defeat in the battle of Lowestoft. But their official investigation on the defeat stressed the importance of grappling and boarding an enemy ship, while the Admiralty of Zeeland encouraged its officers to think innovatively about how to defeat the English tactics and to avoid "the long and disadvantageous gun-battle with the English and to bring about the early laying aboard at the first opportunity."[34] However, the English tactic of staying in a close-ordered line and using heavy broadside gunnery fire precluded the use of the Dutch tactics of a group attack for grappling and boarding.

Despite these official conclusions, new ideas about tactics were brewing in the minds of the Dutch admirals. After lengthy discussions with sea officers during August 1665, Johan de Witt reflected the results of those conversations in the correspondence and directives coming from the States of Holland. Their thoughts centred on several key conclusions, based on recent experience: (1) the long-acknowledged need to maintain discipline in battle with a well-ordered fleet; (2) the fighting should be done in a single line of battle, close-hauled, with three squadrons positioned to windward of an enemy; (3) the flag officers needed to be less exposed at the beginning of an action; and (4) a reserve corps was necessary. A new order to the fleet embodying these ideas was issued to the Dutch fleet under Cornelis Tromp on 15 August 1665 and had a number of variant alternatives included. One of these had the centre squadron slightly further from the enemy than the other two squadrons.[35] This became the so-called "snake-shaped line" that remained in the instructions for more than twenty years, but was rarely, if ever, used. Some further changes to the instructions were made on De Ruyter's return, after more than a year away from home waters in Africa and the West Indies, on his appointment as commander-in-chief on 11 August 1665. Yet, for the Dutch admirals, much remained to be resolved and clarified in their tactical ideas.

Meanwhile, the English victualling and shore-based naval support system had broken down. At about the same time, the overall strategic situation changed in January 1666, when both France and Denmark declared war against England. This placed even greater stress on English logistical support in the naval war, as Denmark closed the Sound, and with it access to the Baltic, to English merchant vessels, creating a further major shortage for England of the essential naval supplies from this region for shipbuilding and repair. England, as well as the Dutch Republic, faced a major shortage in seamen to man their warships. On the part of France, Louis XIV had only a peripheral interest in the war and had agreed, with growing embarrassment, to meet a 1662 treaty obligation with the Dutch. In the event, France secretly instructed her admirals to avoid battle, if possible.[36]

In the Dutch Navy, the issues concerning tactics, the numbers of squadrons, and the presence of a reserve squadron continued to remain issues of debate for some time. Finally, after extensive discussions that involved De Ruyter and de Witt as well as representatives of the States General and representatives of the five admiralties of the Dutch Republic, it was agreed that De Ruyter could have the discretion to command the fleet in battle in an arrangement of three squadrons divided into divisions under vice-admirals and rear-admirals. Just one week after this decision was made, the Dutch and English fleets met off the Thames estuary in the Four Days' Battle (1/11–4/14 June 1666).[37]

This huge, prolonged action has earned the reputation for being the largest and bloodiest battle in the age of fighting sail. The experience of the battle, although it included boarding, grappling, and the use of fire ships, showed a marked improvement in Dutch tactics and the Dutch Navy's ability to use line-of-battle tactics and to do damage with gunfire to the English with their new 70- and 80-gun ships sailing in the newly adopted line of battle. Nevertheless, the Dutch victory was not the crushing defeat of the English that many Dutch observers of the time thought that they had achieved.[38]

An equally interesting aspect of the battle was the English estimate of the strategic situation that led the English to divide their fleet. Earlier in the year, Admiral Lord Sandwich had sailed with thirty ships to protect English trade in the Mediterranean. Now, while De Ruyter was approaching with his large force of 84 ships, the English received intelligence—false intelligence, as it turned out—that the French Toulon squadron under the duke of Beaufort was approaching the Channel to join the Dutch. Leaving Albemarle with 54 English ships of the line, Prince Rupert took 20 ships and spent three of the four days of the battle guarding against the possibility of the French landing ashore in Britain or their attacking England's coastal trade. The situation illustrated England's strategic dilemma in not knowing whether to concentrate her battle force to defeat De Ruyter's fleet or to deal with the multiple smaller threats that she faced on other fronts.

After the action, the Four Days' Battle brought time for the English to reflect on tactics while repairing damage. On 16 July 1666, Prince Rupert and the duke of Albemarle issued their "Additional Instructions for Fighting," which emphasized the need to "keep up with the admiral of the fleet and to endeavour the utmost that may be the destruction of the enemy, which is always to be the chiefest care."[39] Moreover, it instructed that "all the best sailing ships are to make what way they can to engage the enemy, that so the rear of our fleet may the better come up."[40]

At the same time, the duke of York first issued one of the most important and influential English instructions of the era in July 1666, intended to ensure that the English fleet maintained the weather gage:

> In case we have the wind of the enemy, and the enemy stands toward us and we towards them, then the van of our fleet shall keep the wind, and when they are come to a convenient distance of the enemy's rear shall stay until our whole line is come up within the same distance of the enemy's van, and then our whole line is to stand along with them the same tacks on board, still keeping the enemy to leeward, and not suffering them to tack in the van, and in case the enemy tacks in the rear first, and the whole line is to follow, standing all along with the same tacks on board as the enemy does.[41]

The thought expressed here stood for more than a century as the mandatory Article XVII of the eighteenth century Royal Navy's permanent *Sailing and Fighting Instructions.* Additional points in this document expressed the importance of keeping the line and dividing an enemy's fleet by tacking through the enemy's battle line in order to gain the windward position.

Just over a week after these additional instructions appeared, the English under the duke of Albemarle, and the Dutch fleet, under De Ruyter, met again in the Two Days' Battle of St. James's Day on 25–26 July/4–5 August 1666. In this action, the two relatively equal fleets exchanged heavy gunfire, but the English maintained the advantage with a disciplined van and centre. The aftermath of this defeat for the Dutch provided the opportunity to think again about fleet tactics. In this period, De Ruyter pointed out that it was necessary for ships to keep in their assigned stations, "otherwise the train of ships would be too extended and the ships would be left unsupported."[42] In the weeks and months that followed, Johan de Witt played a key role in institutionalising further changes by establishing De Ruyter's signal to form the battle line into the general signal book, organizing the battle fleet firmly into three squadrons with three divisions each, and even established a standard diagram for the fleet, making sure that these procedures and copies of the orders were distributed for reference among all commanders afloat and shore-based authorities.[43]

By late in 1666, the English were finding serious difficulties in providing the financial resources and the supplies to keep their fleet at sea. Seamen protested and dockyard workers mutinied as peace negotiations began. In early 1667, King Charles II decided not to attempt to put the fleet to sea and opted instead to have only two small squadrons at sea to serve as coastal guard ships. This sudden weakening of England's main naval defence gave the Dutch Navy an opportunity of a completely different kind that had little to do with the tactical discussions for fleet battles. It was at this point that De Ruyter made his raid on the English coast in the Thames estuary and the Medway River, famously capturing the 86-gun ship named for the king, HMS *Royal Charles,* and towing it back as a prize to Holland.[44]

Aside from firmly establishing the line-of-battle tactics in both the Dutch and English navies, the Second Dutch War left both countries exhausted. The experience of the first two wars continued to urge on the increase in the size of warships. In ship design, stability that went toward a firm platform for gunnery had come to outweigh the importance of speed, as did a stiffness that prevented a ship from heeling too far so that its lower gun ports could not be used. The 70-gun 3rd Rate ship-of-the-line became a recognized success in the Royal Navy and the three-deck, 100-gun 1st Rates were returning to favour. Across the North Sea, consideration of the shallow waters and sandbanks led the Dutch to avoid building three-deck ships and to prefer beamy ships, but their large 60-, 70-, and 80-gun warships were fully capable of dealing with the English. Additionally, as the French began to place emphasis on their navy in the early 1660s, they initially turned to the Dutch to supply some important warships. These French ships of Dutch design were larger than their English counterparts and more stable two-deckers with their lower tier of guns higher off the water.[45]

The Third Dutch War, 1672–1674
From a strategic perspective, the Third Dutch War was significantly different from the others. The origins of the war lay in the personal enthusiasms of the young Louis XIV and not the more careful judgements of his ministers.[46] This involved a *volte-face* from previous French policy in the Second Dutch War with France's decision to invade and to overwhelm the Dutch Republic. It also involved a *volte-face* for English policymakers who had previously agreed in 1668 with Sweden and the Dutch Republic to prevent French occupation of the Spanish Netherlands.[47] As France actively sought to embroil England in the war for its own objectives, on the English side King Charles II's motives for entering into the secret Treaty of Dover and in the Third Dutch War in alliance with France against the Dutch Republic lie fundamentally in internal English politics and the king's struggle for maintaining the Crown's controlling power over Parliament.[48]

The immediate outbreak of the war resulted from the English initiative in sending out two squadrons of frigates, one under Sir Edward Spragge and the other under Robert Holmes, to contrive an incident by asserting English "sovereignty of the sea" and use this as rationale to attack the homeward-bound Dutch convoy from Smyrna. Although the Dutch forces defended themselves effectively and repulsed the English squadrons, nevertheless, the incident became the *casus belli*. On receiving the news of the incident, Charles II declared war on the Dutch Republic on 18/28 March 1671/2, followed by Louis XIV on 6 April 1672.[49]

From a naval perspective, this situation in policy and strategy created a distinctive aspect of this war that contrasted with the earlier two conflicts. In retrospect, it implied the need for the English Navy to begin to develop means to cope with a coalition naval force and also to complement military operations ashore. While the English initially anticipated a naval war, the French quickly developed plans of their own for aggressive military operations to invade the Republic. French soldiers, with troops from England, Cologne, and Münster, moved from the south and the east. Much Dutch territory was occupied, but the English were not directly part of these operations.

The naval actions were similar to the earlier wars, but showed the more mature tactical development that emerged from the experience of the first two Dutch wars. Moreover, in every one of the four major actions in this war, a French squadron joined with two English squadrons to create the line of battle. Anglo-French naval strategy was focused on blockading the Dutch coasts in order to establish a position from which an invasion from the sea could be launched. To counter this, Dutch strategy lay in flooding the polders of Holland to prevent occupation and creating a formidable naval defence to prevent any such landing.

In this war, De Ruyter had the advantage of having the Dutch fleet in an excellent state of readiness with the new warships from the 1664–1666 building programme available. In addition, De Ruyter had trained his commanding officers in procedures for meeting a superior enemy force in battle. In particular, he had finally succeeded in doing away with the earlier ideas about group tactics for grappling and boarding, concentrating on training his fleet in the effective use of the "single-line-ahead" formation that the English had pioneered and the Dutch had taken over after the battle of Lowestoft in 1665. In addition, he built further on this approach with innovative tactical thinking on how to counter the Anglo-French use of these tactics, although this was done by word of mouth and in practice rather than in formal written instructions.[50] In contrast, the duke of York, who commanded the combined Anglo-French Fleet, issued fighting instructions to the fleet that were fundamentally the same as those issued in 1666.[51]

The first fleet engagement of the war occurred on 28 May/7 June 1672, when De Ruyter with 62 ships attacked the allied fleet of 82 ships as they lay at anchor in Solebay, off Southwold, Suffolk. Although the English and French had expected an attack, they were still at anchor when De Ruyter appeared. The French squadron, under the comte d'Estrées, and the English separated and two separate actions ensued, in both of which the Dutch prevailed. De Ruyter's attack successfully served to force the English and French to postpone their plans to make a landing in Holland and, at the same time, created a major feud between d'Estrées and his second in command, Abraham Duquesne, whom d'Estrées accused of failing to support him. Similarly, the English admirals traded recriminations.[52]

Following this, the focus of events shifted ashore with the lynching of the de Witt brothers in The Hague and the military defence of Holland under the *stadhouder* Prince William III, which even utilized some guns and men taken from Dutch warships to defend the homeland. In the meantime, De Ruyter planned to make an aggressive attack on England to sink ships and block the channels to Portsmouth and London.[53] Thwarting this plan in May 1673 just as De Ruyter appeared off the Thames, the new commander of the English fleet, Prince Rupert of the Rhine,[54] forced De Ruyter's fleet back into Dutch waters. Forced to take the defensive, De Ruyter took his fleet to the Schooneveld flats off Walcheren Island, where he made brilliant use of his local knowledge of the sandbanks in two actions, the first on 28 May/7 June and the second on 4/14 June 1673.

Outnumbered 76 to 52 ships, De Ruyter used the restricted conditions to advantage. Prince Rupert expected to use his numerical superiority to deliver a decisive blow, but De Ruyter came out to windward of the shoals to gain a tactical advantage and was able to manoeuvre to avoid the advance squadron and the fire ships that the allies deployed. Instead of retreating as Rupert expected, the Dutch formed a line to defend their position. Rupert had placed the French squadron in the middle of his line to prevent the situation that had occurred at Solebay. In the van, Rupert engaged with Cornelis Tromp's squadron, while De Ruyter's and Adriaen Banckert's squadrons dealt with Spragge's and d'Estrées'. As the fleets approached a sandbank, De Ruyter tacked and broke through d'Estrées' line isolating the French rear. As the engaged fleets re-formed and separated squadrons rejoined on their new course, De Ruyter brilliantly broke through the French again and doubled it. The general action successfully prevented the allied English and French fleet from making any gains. Although neither side lost any ships, the English and French were unable to approach the Dutch ports and were baffled by the sandbanks.[55]

A week later on 4/14 June 1673, the opposing fleets met again off Schooneveld with similar results. The lack of communication between Rupert and d'Estrées caused confusion in the allied fleet and the allies withdrew to the Nore at the mouth of the Thames, concluding that they could not reach the coast by challenging De Ruyter at Schooneveld.[56]

Meanwhile, the allied fleet cruised off the Texel in order to draw De Ruyter out into open water and clear an avenue for landing. The two fleets engaged on 11/21 August in the battle off Kijkduin (Texel). With the same commanders, the fleets were slightly larger, with the Dutch outnumbered, 86 ships to 60. In the end, the battle divided into separate squadron actions, with the French taking little part. De Ruyter's manoeuvres forced the allies back to the English coast and broke their blockade of the Dutch coast.[57] The misunderstandings that had arisen in battle between d'Estrées and Rupert became recriminations after the battle and a public dispute that showed the strains within the alliance, helping to contribute to the discontinuation of allied operations and the conclusion that the war had been a failure for France and England.[58]

The Anglo-French fleet had consistently attempted to break through the Dutch naval defences, but failed in all their attempts to do so. De Ruyter's success in this was the greatest naval achievement of the era and the prevention of an enemy landing in Holland and Zeeland was the critical element for Dutch defence. In this, De Ruyter's actions in the Third Dutch War marked the firm implementation of the range of new European naval developments in the period between 1652 and 1676. Offensive and aggressive tactics with heavily gunned, large warships operating in a line of battle for major engagements dominated naval history for the remainder of the age of sail and continued in spirit for centuries.

During the three Anglo-Dutch conflicts, the navies were used primarily in home waters to fight battles with the strategic purpose of attacking and protecting trade or in breaking or enforcing blockades. The focus in the age of De Ruyter was on the development of the ships, gunnery, and tactical approaches to major battles for these purposes. The few cases during these wars in which battles were fought in America, the West Indies, and the Mediterranean were suggestions of future potential when nations in the eighteenth and nineteenth centuries also deployed their naval forces with ambitious imperial and strategic objectives in far distant seas.

NOTES   This chapter was originally published in J. R. Bruijn, ed., *Michiel de Ruyter: Dutch Admiral* (Rotterdam: Karwansary, 2011).

1 I am grateful to Jaap Bruijn and Jan Glete for their constructive critiques on an earlier draft of this chapter.

2 N. A. M. Rodger, "The Development of Broadside Gunnery, 1450–1650," in: *Mariner's Mirror, 82* (1996), 301–324; reprinted in: Jan Glete, ed., *Naval History, 1500–1680,* The International Library of Essays on Military History. Aldershot: Ashgate, 2005, 239–262.

3 Jan Glete, "Naval Power and Control of the Seas in the Baltic in the 16th Century," in: John B. Hattendorf and Richard Unger, *War at Sea in the Middle Ages and the Renaissance.* Woodbridge: Boydell Press, 2003, 217–232. For a summary of the contrasting slower naval development on the southern Baltic shore, see John B. Hattendorf, "Deutschland und die See: Historische Wurzeln deutscher Seestreitkräfte bis 1815," in: Werner Rahn, hrsg., *Deutsche Marinen im Wandel: Von Symbol nationaler Einheit zum Instument internationaler Sicherheit.* München: R. Oldenbourg Verlag, 2005, 17–40.

4 For a succinct overview, see "Chronology of War and Peace, Civil and International," in: Ragnhild Hatton, *Europe in the Age of Louis XIV.* London: Thames and Hudson, 1969 and 1979, 227–228.

5 For a summary of recent interpretations, see David Davies, "Wars, Maritime: Dutch Wars," in: John B. Hattendorf, ed., *Oxford Encyclopedia of Maritime History.* New York and Oxford: Oxford University Press, 2007, 4:325–329. See also Simon Groenveld, "The English Civil War as a Cause of the First Anglo Dutch War, 1640–1652," in: *The Historical Journal,* 30, 3 (1987), 541–566; Hans-Christoph Junge, *Flottenpolitik und Revolution.* Veröffentlichen des Deutschen Historischen Instituts London, band 6. Stuttgart: Klett-Cotta, 1980; Bernard Capp, *Cromwell's Navy: The Fleet and the English Revolution, 1648–1660.* Oxford: Clarendon Press, 1989.

6 Tony Claydon, *Europe and the Making of England, 1660–1760.* Cambridge: Cambridge University Press, 2007, 133–140, 152.

7 Jan Glete, *War and the State in Early Modern Europe: Spain, the Dutch Republic and Sweden as Fiscal-Military States, 1500–1660.* London and New York: Routledge, 2002, 162–171.

8 The statistics in Jan Glete, *Navies and Nations: Warships, Navies and State Building in Europe and America, 1500–1860.* Stockholm: Almqvist & Wiksell International, 1993, 1:179, 186, have been modified by personal communication with Jan Glete reflecting his latest research; and Martin Bellamy, *Christian IV and His Navy: A Political and Administrative History of the Danish Navy 1596–1648.* Leiden: Brill, 2006, 261–279. No reliable statistics are available for Spain.

9 This figure for Dutch warships is actually that for 1642; there is no accurate figure for 1640.

10 Glete, *Navies and Nations,* 1:204.

11 Ibid., 1:156, 130. In comparing the numbers of Dutch and English warships, the number of Dutch ships can be misleading as they were generally smaller than the English ships, as the displacement figures in the table above suggests.

12 N. A. M. Rodger, *The Command of the Ocean: A Naval History of Britain, 1649–1815.* London: Allen Lane, 2004, 2.

13 Brian Lavery, *The Ship of the Line.* Vol. 1: *The Development of the Battlefleet, 1650–1850.* Annapolis: Naval Institute Press, 1983, 1, 18–23. J. D. Davies, *Pepys's Navy: Ships, Men & Warfare 1649–1689.* Barnsley: Seaforth Publishing, 2008, 37–64. Little recent comparative study has been done of Dutch frigate designs from the 1640s and their relationship to developments in English ship design.

14 Lavery, *Ship of the Line,* 22–23; Davies, *Pepys's Navy,* 37–64.

15 James S. Wheeler, "Prelude to Power: The Crisis of 1649 and the Foundation of English Naval Power," in: *Mariner's Mirror,* 81, 2 (May 1995), 148–155; reprinted in: Glete, *Naval History,* 229–236.

16 J. S. Wheeler, "English Financial Operations during the First Dutch War, 1652–1654," in: *The Journal of European Economic History,* 23, 2 (Fall 1994), 329–343. See also James Scott Wheeler, *The Making of a World Power: War and the Military Revolution in Seventeenth Century England.* Stroud: Sutton Publishing, 1999, 43–48.

17 Wheeler, *Making of a World Power,* 46.

18 Jaap R. Bruijn, *The Dutch Navy of the Seventeenth and Eighteenth Centuries.* Columbia: University of South Carolina Press, 1993, 70–71; and J. R. Bruijn, *Varend Verleden: De Nederlandse Oorgolsvloot in de 17de en 18de Eeuw.* Amsterdam: Uitgeverij Balans, 1999, 92–93. See also "Resolution of Admiral Tromp . . . ," in: Julian S. Corbett, ed., *Fighting Instructions, 1530–1816.* Publications of the Navy Records Society, vol. 29. London: Navy Records Society, 1905; reprinted London: Conway Press, 1971; Annapolis: Naval Institute Press, 1971, 91.

19 See Thomas Wemyss Fulton, *The Sovereignty of the Sea: An Historical Account of the Claims of England to the Dominion of the British Seas, and of the Evolution of the Territorial Waters: with special reference to the Rights of Fishing and the Naval Salute.* London: William Blackwood and Sons, 1911; reprinted in facsimile, Milwood, N.Y.: Kraus Reprint, 1976.

20 Brian Tunstall, *Naval Warfare in the Age of Sail: The Evolution of Fighting Tactics, 1650–1815.* Edited by Dr. Nicholas Tracy. Annapolis: Naval Institute Press, 1990, 18.

21 Corbett, *Fighting Instructions,* 99–103; J. R. Powell, ed., *The Letters of Robert Blake Together with Supplementary Documents.* Publications of the Navy Records Society, vol. 76. London: Navy Records Society, 1937, 467–471.

22 Powell, *Blake Letters,* 471–476.

23 Bruijn, *Dutch Navy,* 73–74; Bruijn, *Varend Verleden,* 95–97.

24 Glete, *Navies and Nations,* 1:192, 195 as modified by personal communication with Jan Glete; Bellamy, *Christian IV and His Navy,* 261–279.

25 Glete, *Navies and Nations,* 204.

26 See Alan James, *Navy and Government in Early Modern France, 1572–1661.* Royal Historical Society Studies in History New Series. Woodbridge: Boydell Press, 2004; see also J. D. Davies, "The French Navy," *Pepys's Navy,* 210–213.

27 See Daniel Dessert, *La Royale: Vaisseaux et marines du Roi-Soleil.* Paris: Fayard, 1996.

28 Lavery, *Ship of the Line,* 30–32, 59–60.

29 Herbert H. Rowen, *John de Witt, Grand Pensionary of Holland, 1625–1672.* Princeton: Princeton University Press, 1978, 78–83; Bruijn, *Dutch Navy,* 75–82; Bruijn,*Varend Verleden,* 103–107.

30 Tunstall, *Naval Warfare,* 22–24; Corbett, *Fighting Instructions,* 122–130.

31 Bruijn, *Dutch Navy,* 77; Bruijn,*Varend Verleden,* 100–101; Davies, *Pepys's Navy,* 258–261.

32 R. C. Anderson, ed., *The Journal of Edward Montagu, First Earl of Sandwich, Admiral and General at Sea, 1659–1665.* Publications of the Navy Records Society, vol. 44. London: Navy Records Society, 1929, 224: 3 June 1665.

33 Ibid., 269–270: 29 August 1665.

34 R. E. J. Weber, "The Introduction of the Single Line Ahead as a Battle Formation by the Dutch, 1665–1666," in: *Mariner's Mirror,* 73 (1987), 5–19; reprinted in: Glete, *Naval History,* 313, 317, 327.

35 Ibid., 320–321.

36 Gaston Zeller, *Histoire des Relations Internationales,* publiée sous la direction de Pierre Renouvin. Tome 3: *Les Temps Modernes. Deuxième partie. De Louis XIV à 1789.* Paris: Librairie Hachette, 1955, 25.

37 See H. A. van Foreest en R. E. J. Weber med medwerking van J. F. van Dulum en J. A. van der Kooij, *De Vierdaagse Zeeslag 11–14 Juni 1666.* Verhandelingen der Koninklijke Nederlandse Akademie van Weteschapen, Afd. Letterkunde, Nieuwe Reeks, Deel 126. Werken Uitgeven door de Commissie voor Zeegeschiedenis, XVI. Amsterdam: B.V. Noord-Hollandsche Uitgevers Maatschappij, 1984; and Frank L. Fox, *A Distant Storm: The Four Days' Battle of 1666: The Greatest Sea Fight of the Age of Sail.* Rotherfield: Press of Sail Publications, 1996.

38 Rodger, *Command of the Ocean,* 75.

39 Corbett, *Fighting Instructions,* 129–130.

40 Ibid.

41 Ibid., 148–149, misdated as 1672, but 18 July 1666 as documented in: Tunstall, *Naval Warfare,* 27–30.

42 Weber, "The Single Line Ahead," 325.

43 These changes are reflected in De Ruyter's instructions of 6 August 1667 in: R. E. J. Weber, *De seinboeken voor Nederlandse oorlogsvloten en konvooien tot 1690.* Verhandelingen der Koninklijke

Nederlandse Akademie van Weteschapen, Afd. Letterkunde, Nieuwe Reeks, Deel 112. Werken Uitgeven door de Commissie voor Zeegeschiedenis, XV. Amsterdam: B.V. Noord-Hollandsche Uitgevers Maatschappij, 1984, Doc. 21; 102–114.

44 P. G. Rogers, *The Dutch in the Medway.* London: Oxford University Press, 1970.

45 Lavery, *Ship of the Line,* 32–36.

46 Paul Sonnino, *Louis XIV and the Origins of the Dutch War.* Cambridge: Cambridge University Press, 1988, 176.

47 For this agreement, see Birger Fahlborg, *Sveriges yttre politik 1664–1668.* Kungl. Vitterhets-, historie- och antikvitetsakademiens handlingar. Stockholm: Wahlström & Widstrand (ikommission), 1949, and *Sveriges yttre politik 1668–1672.* Stockholm: Almqvist & Wiksell, 1961.

48 J. R. Jones, *The Anglo-Dutch Wars of the Seventeenth Century.* London: Longman, 1996, 179–188.

49 Sonnino, *Louis XIV,* 191.

50 Bruijn, *Dutch Navy,* 88; Bruijn,*Varend Verleden,* 115.

51 Tunstall, *Naval Warfare,* 32; Corbett, *Fighting Instructions,* 133–163.

52 R. C. Anderson, ed., *Journals and Narratives of the Third Dutch War.* Publications of the Navy Records Society, vol. 86. London: Navy Records Society, 1946, 13–22, 95–101, 156–157, 164–184; Michel Vergé-Franceschi, *Abraham Duquesne: Huguenot et marin du Roi Soleil.* Paris: Éditions France-Empire, 1992, 254–260; J. D. Davies, *Gentlemen and Tarpaulins: The Officers and Men of the Restoration Navy.* Oxford: Clarendon Press, 1991, 171.

53 Rodger, *Command of the Ocean,* 83; Bruijn, *Dutch Navy,* 89; Bruijn,*Varend Verleden,* 117.

54 Frank Kitson, *Prince Rupert: Admiral and General-at-Sea.* London: Constable, 1998, 246–289.

55 J. C. M. Warnsinck, *Admiraal de Ruyter. De Zeeslag op Schooneveld, juni 1673.* 's-Gravenhage: Martinus Nijhoff, 1930, 44–59; Tunstall, *Naval Warfare,* 35; J. R. Bruijn, ed., *De Oorlogvoering ter Zee in 1673 in Journalen en Andre Stukken.* Werken uitgegeven door het Historisch Genootschap. Derde serie, no. 84. Groningen: J. B. Wolters, 1966, 55–56, 114–115; Anderson, *Third Dutch War Journals,* 32–36, 300–302, 319–320, 334, 377, 386–387.

56 Jones, *Dutch Wars,* 206; Tunstall, *Naval Warfare,* 36; Bruijn, *Oorlogvoering,* 60, 118–120; Anderson, *Third Dutch War Journals,* 37–40, 303, 322, 336, 378–379, 389.

57 Bruijn, *Oorlogvoering,* 89–90, 152–154, 184–185, 205–209; Anderson, *Third Dutch War Journals,* 46–53, 311, 355–362, 381, 386, 390–394; Davies, *Pepys's Navy,* 262–268.

58 Carl J. Ekberg, *The Failure of Louis XIV's Dutch War.* Chapel Hill: University of North Carolina Press, 1979, 161–170.

VI   *"To Aid and Assist the Other"*
Anglo-Dutch Naval Cooperation in Coalition Warfare at Sea, 1689–1714

Typical of much of the writing that has been done in naval history, the subject of combined Anglo-Dutch naval operations has usually been viewed only from the perspective of one partner or the other, stressing the tensions as seen from only one side. For the period 1689–1714, in particular, the pamphlet literature and some of the more extreme views expressed in the contemporary public press have tended to dominate later historical interpretations, instead of either the perspectives of the responsible naval commanders and officials who were actually conducting the operations or in the light of an analysis of the general conduct of the war.

Today, at the outset of the twenty-first century we are well aware of multinational naval cooperation. The most successful example of such long-term cooperation is the currently operating NATO Standing Naval Force, Atlantic, in which the Royal Netherlands Navy has played such a key role. This force is just over thirty years old. When it was established in 1968, few thought it could possibly succeed, since the complexities of such naval cooperation are so great. Yet, in a different time and context, its story reflects a resolution of many of the same professional naval issues of command, logistics, and competing national priorities that existed more than 300 years ago in the 1680s.[1]

The accession of William and Mary to the English throne created a complete turn-about in English foreign policy at the same time that it extended Dutch policy objectives to England and drew her directly into the larger issues of European power politics that William III had already been dealing with for some years. While the two countries were viewed by many in Europe as "the Maritime Powers," united in their general agreement on fundamental policy objectives through the person of William III, they were still separate and very different governments that had differing priorities and contrasting ways of doing business. This accounted for some of the strains that developed, but at the same time, they had overlapping mercantile concerns at sea, some of which were parallel and competitive. These are important, but subsidiary, issues to the larger strategic problem.

The fundamental problem that both the Dutch Republic and England faced was that France was the prevailing power in Europe, both in terms of her army and her navy. At the outset of the Nine Years' War, France had a total naval strength of 131 warships, displacing 140,500 tons, of which 89 were major warships and 32 were cruisers. In contrast, the Republic had a total naval strength that, in tonnage terms, was 48% that of France, with 74 Dutch warships displacing 67,900 tons, of which 52 were major warships and 21 were cruisers. Complementing it, England had a larger naval force than the Dutch, but still with a total strength, in terms of tonnage, that was 88% that of France, with a total of 109 vessels displacing 123,900 tons, with 83 major warships and 26 cruisers.[2]

An analysis of these general statistics shows that the English not only had more ships, but larger ships, while the Dutch had fewer, which were relatively smaller in size. To be more precise, Dutch naval forces were equal to 54% of the English in terms of total tonnage and 63% in terms of the total number of major warships. Of course, there is a well-known reason for the differences in a nation's typical ship design. The prevailing water depths in homeports and in coastal waters are the basis for local ship design. With the North Sea shallows and sand banks, Dutch ships traditionally tended to have flatter bottoms and shallower drafts in order to operate from their own ports. Since ship size is also a general indication of capabilities, this leads to the further conclusion that the characteristic vessels from one country were better suited for some types of operations than for others. Thus, smaller ships with shallower drafts were more useful for coastal patrols and protection of trade duties than serving in the main line of battle against heavy enemy ships.

The naval statistics spell out the fundamental and practical strategic problem at sea. Neither the Republic nor England could expect to reverse the general strategic balance at sea by itself, although they might be able to hold their own under limited conditions. Together, "the Maritime Powers" had clear superiority at sea. Yet, the naval issue cannot be isolated from the broader maritime picture, nor can it be isolated from the general strategic situation that the two faced. As William had long understood, the superior strength of France could only be effectively offset permanently by an alliance that could create a geo-strategic balance against France.

The Immediate Precedents for Cooperation

Navies generally tend to operate within the context of a specific nation's policy and strategy and naval officers also tend to reflect a particular national outlook. Yet, like armies, there are recurring, but relatively rare, situations in which multinational forces are useful. The great battle at Lepanto saw a variety of forces working together and Philip II's Spanish Armada of 1588 included a considerable number of Portuguese ships. French, Dutch, and English forces had operated together on occasion in various combinations on three or four occasions in the seventeenth century. More recently, a combined Anglo-French fleet had fought Dutch naval forces in the Third Anglo-Dutch War in 1672–1673.[3]

The fundamental basis for maritime cooperation between the two countries was laid following the end of the Third Anglo-Dutch War, with the completion of negotiations for a treaty of Navigation and Commerce in December 1674.[4] This agreement declared that Dutch and English armed forces and privateers would not interfere with each other's maritime trade and established the form of sea passes to be used by ships. The agreement clearly established contraband goods as limited to ammunition and weapons, while trade with the enemy in other goods and articles was allowed. Among other matters, captured goods from enemy ships had to be held safely without until an Admiralty Court could act upon the prize case. Furthermore, commanders of privateers were required to pay a security bond of 1,500 pounds or 16,500 guilders. A year later, a further agreement clarified that these provisions applied to all types of situations.[5] Together, these agreements were renewed repeatedly up through 1728.[6]

Shortly after William III's 1677 marriage to Mary, discussions had begun that touched on the specific issues of combined military and naval cooperation. These arrangements, begun more than a decade before 1689, provided the basis for the working naval relationship in this area during the Nine Years' War and in the War of the Spanish Succession. This working relationship was one, however, that was built only slowly and hesitantly in the dozen years between 1677 and 1689. As matter of precedent, as well as contrast and comparison, it is worth looking a little closer at these earlier proposals and agreements, since they were repeatedly referred to in later negotiations and there seems to be some confusion about some of them in the historical literature.

In the initial 1677 discussions, the English proposed combined Anglo-Dutch naval squadrons in the Channel, North Sea, and Mediterranean, but wished to operate independently in the Caribbean. The Dutch found this proposal too extensive and too expensive, if not a subtle comment on any recent Anglo-Dutch imperial rivalry and English reticence over both Dutch successes and losses in America.

No specific agreement was made on naval cooperation, but, shortly thereafter, a Treaty of Defensive Alliance was signed in January 1678. This agreement was created in the context of the final stages of the war then underway and specifically referred, at length, to the concrete objectives that the English and Dutch wished to achieve in the peace treaty. Articles X and XI of that agreement—even though the two articles created some confusion in meaning by dividing a sentence in half—looked to the peace beyond and stipulated that

> when peace is made between France and Spain, the King of Great Britain and the States shall be guarantees thereof, with other princes who shall think fit, and the number of troops ascertained to be used against the infringer, the said king and states do engage to defend all confederates.[7]

This defensive agreement left a decision as to troop numbers to a future negotiation and said nothing at all about naval cooperation. Discussions continued, and in February 1678, the Dutch made a very practical proposal, suggesting that since the Dutch admiralties could not fully match the financial resources needed to equal English strength in all areas at sea, the two could build on their strengths and interests in a complementary way. This meant that the English and Dutch should combine their fleets in the Mediterranean, where they were both already currently engaged in dealing with the Algerine War. At the same time, the Dutch could take responsibility in the North Sea, and by extension in the Baltic, where Dutch ships were well equipped to deal with local interests and had recently distinguished themselves in the war against France and Sweden. Complementing this distribution of Dutch naval forces, the English could concentrate their responsibility in the Channel, where their main interests lay and in waters Englishmen knew well. Although these proposals were not formally agreed upon, they are interesting in that they suggest the consistent practical strengths and recurring strategic interests of the two allies as well as the differing priorities in national maritime interests.[8]

Within a month of these discussions, a new treaty was signed in March 1678 at Westminster and formed the very general basis that was incorporated into all later naval treaties. In the Westminster agreement, the Dutch Republic and England mutually agreed to make use of all of their power by sea and land to bring France to reason.[9] In separate articles, they agreed:

> When the States are attacked, his Britannic Majesty shall assist them with 10,000 foot, and the States his Majesty with 6,000 foot well armed, and with twenty men of war well fitted, &c which auxiliaries to be maintained at the expence of him that sends them. The auxiliaries shall be subject to the commands of the party to whom they are sent.[10]

This was still not very specific, but the agreement formally laid an important foundation of understanding. A further step was taken only four months later, in July 1678, when another treaty was signed at The Hague that dealt with a potential threat that had arisen during the peace negotiations at Nijmegen. At this point, the Dutch and English sensed that the French did not intend to restore various places to Spain and to the United Provinces, as agreed upon in the Peace Treaty, until such time as the allies satisfied Sweden's diplomatic objectives. In the light of this, the English and Dutch agreed to renew the war on France, if the French attempted to delay returning any of these territories after the agreed upon date of 11 August 1678. In the event that war occurred, this new agreement between the Dutch and English specified:

> That they will so act with all their united force that the said articles may be consented to; and to this end his Majesty shall furnish one third more by sea than the States, and they one third more by land than his Majesty, til such time as the confederates engaged shall more completely unite their strength.[11]

This was a significant step toward practical Anglo-Dutch naval cooperation. In addition to establishing a specific ratio of force sizes, the agreement established the clear precedent for a proportionately higher number of English ships. Reasserting this agreement in August 1685, King James II "forever hereafter confirmed and established"[12] six treaties, including the 1668 alliance and treaty of commerce, the Peace of Nijmegen, along with the three 1677–78 agreements.

With this reconfirmation in place just three years before William III sailed for England, there was a clear general precedent and understanding about relative proportions, but still no explicit agreement on how a multinational naval command might work, although the separate article in the March 1678 treaty did specify that "the auxiliaries shall be subject to the commands of the party to whom they are sent,"[13] and it is possible that this phrase carried some indirect bearing in future discussions.

At this point, however, events intervened to create a new precedent. Prince William's choice of the Englishman Admiral Arthur Herbert as Lieutenant-Admiral-General and then as commander-in-chief of the entirely Dutch invasion fleet that sailed from Hellevoetsluis to Torbay in November 1688 was a brilliant choice, but one that had a clear political cost with Dutch naval officers. That price was resentment in the Dutch Fleet.

A distinguished Dutch officer, Cornelis Evertsen the younger, expressed more wide-spread views, when he showed that his personal and national feelings had been hurt by this appointment,[14] but, one must ask, in very practical terms, was such resentment truly justified? In this particular case, no Dutch officer could reasonably have played the role that Herbert needed to play. He was already fully recognized as one of England's most distinguished naval officers. He having been dismissed, specifically because of his principles, from the honorary position of Rear Admiral of England and as Master of the Robes at James II's court, William III's appointment of Herbert was more than just a reward for personal loyalty and being the messenger who brought William's formal invitation from England. Herbert was a key symbol. He was the senior officer whose earlier patronage had been central to the careers of some of the very best English naval officers of the period. William clearly recognized that Herbert's appointment was a key to bringing the officers of the English Navy behind the Revolution.[15]

Equally important, the expedition was heading toward England and it was an obvious advantage that the commander-in-chief knew English waters intimately. Yet, even Herbert clearly admitted that he knew the waters of the north of England far less well than he knew those of the south and west of England.[16] The expedition was not merely a naval exercise, but one that had such extensive political and military implications that an Englishman was the only one who could be readily sensitive to the subtle differences involved in transforming a foreign invasion into a domestic revolution.

In more narrowly naval terms, however, Herbert played, in many respects, more the role of a figurehead than the real commander. He was not alone, but clearly counterbalanced by Dutch flag officers. Evertsen had been the key naval figure in the practical arrangements of preparing and organizing the fleet. Appropriately, William addressed the general and the secret orders to the Fleet not just to Herbert, but also to Herbert and Evertsen together. The orders specified that the fleet was to be divided into three squadrons: one under Luitenant-Admiraal-General Herbert, one under Luitenant-Admiraal Evertsen, and one under Luitenant-Admiraal Philips Almonde.[17] Thus, in the actual functioning of the fleet at sea, Herbert was clearly and prudently counterbalanced by Dutch professional judgment. In this context, Evertsen's complaints and those of other Dutch officers, while understandable, seem overdrawn. Yet, such was the immediate precedent for Anglo-Dutch naval cooperation during the twenty-five years that followed.

The 1689 Naval Agreement

With the successful transition to the new reign of William and Mary in England, there were a variety of practical naval issues that required immediate attention, as war loomed. The issues ranged from negotiations to get the English Parliament to reimburse the Dutch admiralties for their combined £663,752 expense in sending William over to England, but, even more immediately, William needed to make practical plans for war with France.

As early as 20 December 1688, William requested that the States General send representatives to London to negotiate a detailed practical agreement. In mid-January 1689, three Dutch representatives arrived and began discussions with their three English counterparts. They soon found themselves out of their depth in technical naval issues. To deal with these matters, Dutch representatives of the five Admiralty colleges came to London to provide advice in March and April, and then returned home. The main representatives then signed a treaty on 21 May 1689, the very day that England declared war on France, but they backdated it three weeks to 29 April.[18]

This agreement was the detailed document that, with slight modification, governed Anglo-Dutch naval cooperation for the entire twenty-five-year period from 1689 to 1714. The most significant things about this agreement is that it was completed under William's watchful eye and close influence, although not with his direct participation, and that the substance of it was almost entirely based on the proposals that the Dutch representatives made. It is clear, too, that Heinsius was well aware of what was going on in connection with the treaty. Heinsius did not seem to meddle directly in the affairs of the Admiralty, but it is interesting to note that he received more letters from the secretary of the Amsterdam Admiralty, Job de Wildt, during 1689 and 1690 than he did at any other time in his life. Even then, he received only seven letters in 1689 and six in 1690, with only two more during the remaining period of the Nine Years' War.[19]

It was the Dutch who initially presented the overall assessment of French naval strength and upon which they suggested a combined allied fleet of 80 ships of the line, apportioned between the two countries with a ratio of three Dutch ships to five English ships. This, in fact, decreased the earlier Dutch proportion in the 2:3 ratio that had been established in the 1678 naval contingency agreement. Additionally, it was the Dutch representatives who initially presented the overall allocation of Anglo-Dutch naval forces: 50 ships of the line for the Channel and Irish Sea, 30 ships of the line for the Mediterranean, and 10 frigates to cruise in protection of the key lines of communication between England and Holland.

Among the matters of discussion, the English failed to accept only two significant points that the Dutch representatives proposed. First, they declined to join in a joint expedition to the West Indies and, secondly, they declined to accept the Dutch proposal on overall command. The 1678 Treaty of Westminster had allocated command to whichever of the two had received assistance after an initial attack, or, in other words, to the one who was already involved in the midst of directing combat operations. This was a practical approach under the circumstances of a surprise attack, when reinforcements came during the initial defensive action. It was a debatable matter, when one of the partners was always predominant in number. Thus, the English claimed the right of overall command by the senior English officer, in whatever rank he held, while the Dutch held that overall command should go to whatever officer had seniority, Dutch or English. In this, the Dutch had the finer sense of allied cooperation and the English, more of power control. It was the English who, in this case, prevailed. In a broader sense, however, this resolution of the issue reflected a balance between the dominant Dutch control over land forces, the Republic's primary contribution to the war, and England's control over naval forces, her primary contribution to the war.

The final agreement was a detailed document, but one worthy of some careful consideration, as it fully describes the issue at hand. In broad terms, its fifteen articles covered five major and fundamental issues for naval cooperation: (1) the allocation of ships in terms of each country's contribution and the geographical location of their operations; (2) command and management of the Joint Fleet; (3) enforcing discipline and law with officers and seamen using two differing national sets of laws, customs and regulations; (4) the procedures to use in capturing and allocating prizes; (5) the considerations involved in the protection and convoy of each nation's merchant vessels.

Allocation of Ships

Underscoring the importance of the formal agreements, the 1689 Treaty spelled out in its preamble the fact that it was specifically created to modify the agreement of March 1678 by increasing the numbers of warships involved.[20] In addition to spelling out the numbers and types of ships that each side would provide, it also established the exact number of seamen: 17,155 English and 10,572 Dutch,[21] the division into three squadrons: One in the Mediterranean, another in the Channel–Irish Sea, and six frigates along the North Sea coast of England from the Straits of Dover to Yarmouth and to Walcheren Island off the coast of Zeeland,[22] each squadron made up in the same 3:5 proportion as the overall numbers.[23] The agreement directed that the Mediterranean Squadron should be equipped and victualled for a full year, with other supplies available at Port Mahon on Minorca or Porto Perrara on Elba. The ports of Spain, Tuscany, and the Republic of Genoa were designated as friendly ports where both countries' ships would be welcome.[24]

Command and Management of the Joint Fleet

In laying out the management of the fleets, an English officer was designated to command each squadron and any detachments from that squadron.[25] The procedures for the councils of war, which met to consider actions when the fleet was deployed, were described in detail. Each squadron had its own war council, made up of all the flag officers from each country, in equal numbers. When the flag officers' votes divided equally, the captains of both the Dutch and English vessels were to join the flag officers in council. In all war councils, the English admiral or squadron commander presided, with the senior officers, and the captains of the English vessels when present, seated according to rank on the right-hand side of the table. The Dutch admiral or squadron commander with the Dutch flag officers, and their captains when present, sat on the opposite side of the table from their English equivalents. All the affairs of the war councils were determined by a plurality of votes, and anything that a council resolved upon was to be executed punctually and without delay, in the manner that the council prescribed.[26]

Discipline and Law

In legal or disciplinary cases involving only English or Dutch issues, a council restricted to the officers of the country involved resolved the issues,[27] but if a crime was committed by some of one nationality against the other, then a joint council of officers, composed in the same manner as a war council, decided the matter and the person found guilty was punished according to the laws, customs, and instructions of his own country.[28]

Taking and Disposing of Prizes

The agreement specified that all prizes taken would be divided between the Dutch and English ships in proportion to the number of vessels in each fleet, in other words, at a ratio of 3:5, and this division was to be observed even in cases where either Dutch or English vessels took a prize by themselves without assistance from the other.[29] Prize cases involving ships of war were to be adjudicated by the Admiralty courts of the vessel that took the prize, whether English or Dutch, and be divided by the 3:5 ratio. Only necessary expenses reduced the officers' portion that normally was taken in full by the Admiralty.[30] Additionally, the agreement provided that if prizes were taken by both Dutch and English vessels operating together, the Court of Admiralty was to allocate the prize to the ship with the largest number of guns.[31]

One issue that was not covered as part of this provision was the question of how to deal with Dutch and English ships that had been taken by the enemy and then recaptured, either by warships or by privateers before the enemy could take them into port and adjudicate the prize in the enemy's prize court. In October 1689, a new group of negotiators made an additional agreement on this issue in order to prevent disputes between the countries and between owners and rescuers.[32] They agreed that the value of ship and its equipment was to be returned to the captured vessel's owner, with a deduction to compensate the crew that re-took it. These deductions were different for privateers and for warships. In cases when a privateer recaptured a Dutch or English vessel that had been in enemy hands for up to 48 hours, the privateer received one-fifth of the value of the ship and equipment. For a recaptured vessel that had been in enemy hands up to 96 hours, the privateer that recaptured it received one-third of its value. When a warship took back a Dutch or English ship that the enemy vessel had captured, the one-eighth of the value normally reserved to the Crown or the States was divided between the two countries on the 3:5 ratio established in the earlier agreement and the warships' officers and men shared that portion according to the established regulation of each country.

Convoy and Protection of Trade

The longest single article of the agreement pertained to the application and interpretation of two different standard orders that the English and Dutch Admiralties normally gave their commanding officers. The English Admiralty's orders to warships to protect English merchant ships were also extended to Dutch merchant vessels, including any that happened to be following the same route as a warship and requested protection. At the same time, the instruction that the Dutch admiralties gave requiring warships to defend and protect their present and future colonies and plantations in the West Indies were also extended to English warships and the same applied to the Dutch in relation to English colonies and plantations.[33]

In August 1689, the English and the Dutch negotiated a new treaty of alliance that reaffirmed all the earlier treaties mentioned, stating that they "shall remain in their original force and vigour, as if they had been inserted here word for word."[34] In addition, two other treaties were included in this, the March 1675 convention for preventing and composing any disputes that might arise between the English and Dutch East India Companies and a convention that had been signed only two weeks before in August 1689 concerning the prohibition of commerce with France.[35] Additionally, in November 1701, a new "Particular and Perpetual Treaty of Alliance" renewed the treaties of 3 March 1678,[36] adding the Treaty of Rijswijk to the list of agreements renewed,[37] as well as the Treaty of Grand Alliance of 1701.[38] It renewed specifically the naval treaty of 1689 and the convention of 22 October 1689 regarding recapture of prizes. In doing this, the new treaty of alliance put particular emphasis on the provisions concerning prizes, the proportion of ships each provided, and operation of the war council.[39]

The Functioning of the Naval Agreement

Once the agreement had been signed, under the watchful eye of William III, the functioning of the naval agreement was largely left to the admiralties and the naval officers of both countries. In 1691, William appointed Job de Wildt, who had been secretary of the Amsterdam Admiralty since 1659, to be his personal representative with the admiralties of Holland, Zeeland, and West Friesland, thus allowing for some technical coordination at that level in addition to the work done at the States General level by its committee of naval affairs.[40] Job de Wildt remained in that role up to William's death, continuing as secretary until his own death in 1704. He later obtained the assistance of his son, David, who succeeded him. After William's death, naval representatives met annually to make plans for the forthcoming year; sometimes they met in England, sometimes in Holland. On the English side, Admiral Sir David Mitchell, an Admiralty commissioner from 1699, was they key individual who conducted negotiations until his death in 1710. Admiral Sir James Wishart, another Admiralty commissioner, succeeded him in this role.

The question as to what degree of influence and interest that Heinsius had in naval affairs is one that is not easy to answer. On the surface, Heinsius's role appears to have been minimal, but this impression is misleading. After 1691, Job de Wildt wrote, typically, only one letter a year to Heinsius. His son, David, began with only one or two, then increased to half a dozen letters in 1708 and in 1711. It is interesting to note that in all of his correspondence during the War of the Spanish Succession, there are only two surviving letters that Heinsius personally sent directly to a naval person; both were sent to the de Wildts, one in 1703 and one in 1705, and they involved an exchange of information.[41] These figures are misleading in that Heinsius would have been aware of the official correspondence and information exchanged between the Amsterdam Admiralty and the States of Holland. The relationship of those bodies within the government of Holland defined Heinsius's dealings in naval affairs as only a small part of his broader responsibilities as *raadpensionaris*.

There are no surviving letters from Heinsius to any of the major naval officers, but key admirals operating with the English at sea, such as admirals Philips Almonde, Gerard Callenburgh, Phillips van der Goes, and Anthony Pietersen, did make long and informative personal reports to Heinsius that supplemented their other official reports. Moreover, English admirals, particularly Sir David Mitchell, Sir George Rooke, and Sir James Wishart, all made contact with Heinsius on various occasions, either writing to him directly or visiting him in person, on matters of Anglo-Dutch naval relations. On a rare occasion, a more junior English naval officer might discuss a special mission in detail with Heinsius, as did Captain Edmund Halley on his secret mission to the Dalmatian Coast and the Adriatic in 1702–1703.[42]

More importantly, however, Heinsius dealt with naval affairs on a higher level and on issues that were not covered by the established naval agreement. Often, it was to deal with someone like Marlborough or Nottingham over the recurring question as to whether or not the Dutch admiralties could meet their annual naval quotas. An important example of the level on which Heinsius operated in naval affairs may be seen in the private letter that Nottingham wrote him, laying out a key statement on English grand strategy for the Mediterranean in 1703.[43] There is nothing as clear and concise as this in other English documents of the period.

There is one particular case in which Heinsius's usual detachment from the detailed issues of naval affairs changed and he became directly and deeply involved. This was the combined Anglo-Dutch naval expedition to the Sound in 1700. In that case, the strategic situation was very different from that which prevailed during the Nine Years' War and in the War of the Spanish Succession. Here was an allied expedition that required an adaptation of the previous formal agreements to use force during peacetime to try to stop hostilities between Sweden and Denmark. To work out the basic plan for this operation, Heinsius directly participated in a series of discussions in April 1700 with the English resident at The Hague, Alexander Stanhope, and the Swedish ambassador, Count Nils Lillieroot.

On this basis of these conferences, William III issued instructions to Admiral Sir George Rooke, who he appointed commander-in-chief, over his own English warships as well as Luitenant-Admiraal Philips Almonde's Dutch ships. On Rooke's arrival in May 1700, he met with Heinsius, Job de Wildt, and the Dutch admirals, at the Amsterdam Admiralty, to work out the details.[44] In this case, Heinsius needed to be on hand to help negotiate a different ratio of warships for the allied squadron. Instead of the 3:5 ratio used in the two wars against France, they eventually agreed on a nearly 1:1 ratio, with the Dutch providing thirteen to the twelve English ships. The Anglo-Dutch attempt to persuade Sweden to join their fleet to the expedition proved less successful. Admiral-General Count Hans Wachtmeister and his thirty-four-ship Swedish fleet were clearly unwilling to come under Rooke's command, although they did join in cooperative operations with the Anglo-Dutch squadron against the Danish Navy and in the bombardment of Copenhagen.[45]

In general, the strains in Anglo-Dutch naval affairs in this period were typical of those involved in any alliance. As Robert Harley commented to Buys in 1706, "You also have discovered the Factions in both countries aim at the same thing, thô they look two ways, yet like Sampson's Foxes, they carry fire in their tails."[46] As an illustration, one might look at an early proposal that the English made for Dutch naval cooperation. In July 1702, Sir David Mitchell had come across to discuss a proposed West Indian expedition,[47] which involved additional vessels from those currently involved in naval operations on the Spanish coast. The events at Cadiz and Vigo eventually also intervened in considerations about the West Indies, but Alexander Stanhope revealed how clearly he understood Dutch politics when he wrote to Secretary of State Sir Charles Hedges in August 1702:

> Sir David Mitchell has received no answer to his proposal today at noon at which he is very impatient, the truth is thô they are unwilling to own it, they are afraid of disobeying the province of Zeeland, by drawing off from them the ships we desire, there being already a high ferment in almost all the towns between the old and new magistrates, which is like to break more violently than has yet appeared and if they should fancy themselves exposed to the French by removing these ships which they look on as their safety, the Government fear they would become troublesome.[48]

In 1704, when the Dutch admiralties recalled their ships from the Mediterranean, Marlborough expressed a similar thought to Alexander Stanhope about the influence of English domestic politics on Anglo-Dutch naval relations, when he wrote:

> If any misfortune should happen to Sir George Rooke, the whole blame will be laid at their door, and there will not be those wanting at home to blow the coals, which may prove of very ill consequence.[49]

Such forces were clearly at work, as pamphleteers scribbled away, criticizing the navy of one side or the other.[50] While they had political effects, motivated by a variety of other concerns, these views did leave an indelible mark in the press that has spilled over into the history books, but it is more important to look at the actual situation at sea.

The Stresses and Strains of Allied Cooperation at Sea

Any kind of allied, international effort has its stresses and strains and the Anglo-Dutch naval alliance of 1689–1714 was no exception. At the outset in 1689, although the English contributed more to sea forces than the Dutch, the quality of English naval forces was very much open to question. England was clearly not ready to fight a naval war and there was great doubt as to whether her officers would or could fight their ships effectively against the French. It was not only a question of effective French naval forces, but of the loyalty of a number of English officers to William and the Revolution Settlement. Arthur Herbert, soon to be created earl of Torrington, had immediately set to work to remove the known Catholic naval officers from the English fleet, but such a purge could also create effects that might have unknown political consequences.

The first major fleet action of the Nine Years' War, in July 1690 off Beachy Head, marked the apogee of French naval power. The comte de Tourville's victory over Torrington's Anglo-Dutch fleet was clearly aided by the prevailing political forces in France that supported effective preparation of her naval forces.[51] At the same time, the inability of English forces to go into action effectively left the Dutch under Evertsen to take the brunt of Tourville's well-prepared fleet. Thirteen of the twenty ships in the Dutch line of battle were lost, and others suffered heavy casualties. Through this experience, the Dutch Navy clearly obtained a position of moral and professional superiority within the alliance, which was something the Dutch retained for the remainder of William's reign.[52]

Suspicion about the loyalty of English officers was an issue that emerged again in the spring of 1692, just a few days before the battle of Barfleur, but in contrast to the battle of Beachy Head, the English, this time under Russell, readily joined the twenty-six ships under Almonde and, together, they were able to help bring a less prepared French fleet to action, eventually destroying a significant number of its ships off St.-Vaast-la-Hougue.[53] Despite this success, the ability of the French to surprise and to decimate the "Smyrna Convoy" under Rooke's protection off Lagos Bay on the coast of Portugal in 1693 revealed the massive failure of the English Admiralty to provide the fleet with effective intelligence, although Rooke and the twenty-one English and Dutch warships under his overall command did a credible job in reacting to the surprise attack.[54]

In general, in this war and in the next, there were good personal relations between the naval officers and seamen of both countries. Research has yet to uncover anything that reflects either animosity between ships' companies or tensions on the order of duels between junior officers or fights between sailors that would reflect the more fundamental problems that sometimes do occur between seamen. In the absence of such data when Dutch and English ships were together, the absence of major disciplinary problems and the effective completion of their joint naval tasks lead an observer to assume that there was a fundamental, mutual respect, if not friendship, between the officers and men of the two services. Admiral Baron Wassenaer's note of sympathy in relaying the disappointing news to Sir John Leake on their joint failure to intercept the Spanish galleons entering Cadiz in March 1706 reveals much about their professional compatibility:

> I am very sorri of this great misfortune. One day sooner would have done our business. I shall not sleep all night and am afread this niews will make you verri uneasy, butt I could not forbear of letting you know of itt, as soon as I had itt and remain etc. Pray excuse my broken English.[55]

The stress that did occur was of a kind that is typical of tensions that develop in any federation or alliance situation, stemming from sensitivity to national and local honor. In such cases, it is always the smaller that either fear being overwhelmed or, in fact, are being overwhelmed by the larger. It is a common sensitivity even in a successful alliance, as the modern history of NATO attests. In the 1689–1714 period, the fundamental issue in Dutch concern over English naval officers having overall command of the combined fleet was the question of relative seniority of individual officers.

When such experienced and capable English officers as Torrington, Russell, Rooke, or Shovell, the leading English seaman of the period, held the overall command, there were not really any serious questions about individual capabilities *vis-à-vis* the seniority and capability of a Dutch admiral such as Philips Almonde. However, there was an issue when a more junior English flag officer took precedence over a substantially senior Dutch admiral. Although the 1689 treaty had clearly settled this issue, it continued to be irksome to the Dutch, who felt that the senior flag officer present afloat of whichever nation should have the command. During the Nine Years' War, there were two cases in which a junior English flag officer held overall command over a more senior Dutch flag officer. Rear-Admiral John Neville had commanded the Mediterranean squadron with Vice-Admiral Callenburgh as his second in command in 1694. When they both joined Russell in June 1694, Callenburgh remained second in command, while Neville came under them. In another case, Vice-Admiral David Mitchell commanded the Anglo-Dutch squadron at Spithead in May 1697, when two more senior Dutch officers, Luitenant-Admiraal Almonde and Vice-Admiral Callenburgh, were under him.[56]

During the War of the Spanish Succession, the issue continued to arise and it was on these grounds that Almonde and Callenburgh separated the Dutch squadron from the combined fleet when Vice-Admiral Thomas Hopsonn temporarily took command at the time that Rooke went ashore in July 1702.[57] The same issue arose also in 1706 when Luitenant-Admiraal Almonde objected to coming under Vice-Admiral Sir John Leake's command of the combined fleet in the Mediterranean.[58] Certainly Leake was a highly skilled officer, but this was not the question when so senior a figure as Almonde, who had been promoted to *schout-bij-nacht* in 1673 and held his present rank since 1692, was asked to come under an officer who had only become a post-captain in 1689 and a flag officer in 1702.

While this seems a clear breach of naval tradition, misunderstanding the different etiquette used by the two navies during war councils caused another expression of the same problem. At the outset of combined operations in 1689, the Dutch found it difficult to accept the standard English procedure of allowing the junior English officer to speak first, followed by the others in rank order. Dutch practice was the reverse, in which the most senior admiral spoke first. Moreover, not only did the most junior speak first, but also the Dutch officers were allowed to speak their opinion only after the English officers. While to the English, this may have been intended to give deference to the Dutch according to English custom, the Dutch, by their own standards, were treated as if a Dutch lieutenant-admiral were more junior than the most junior English captains.[59]

It was common in operations for the Dutch squadron to operate within a battle line as a distinct tactical unit and typically most reports of decisions taken in councils of war listed the Dutch and English officers separately.[60] Clearly both English and Dutch were aware of the relative seniority of their officers. One 1702 war council shows an interesting example, listing English and Dutch together in seniority but dividing the list in two, one side for land officers and another for sea officers.[61]

At a higher level, another type of tension occurred, in those areas that reflect differing views, competing national priorities, and alternative maritime strategies that complicated this process for both partners. It was in this area that stresses began to take place, particularly when William III was no longer alive and able to balance those views and priorities through his own influence. With the Dutch Republic's naval finances beginning to falter under the strain of the second major land war on its frontiers, the War of the Spanish Succession saw a growing inability of the Dutch to supply their share of the growing numbers of ships that England wanted to send to sea, particularly when Dutch politicians found it difficult to see the direct practical result that such naval expenses would bring to the Republic. The total number of Dutch warships at sea during the war remained relatively stable at 46–48 vessels, with peaks of 66 in 1702 and 84 in 1704, then declining to 23 in 1711–1712.[62] The number of ships that could or would be available for combined naval operations was a different matter, but they, nevertheless, represented a very high proportion of the total number of vessels that the Dutch put to sea.

The 3:5 ratio meant that the Dutch were obligated by the treaty to provide 37% of the allied fleet. In actual fact, they came short of this in every year of the War of the Spanish Succession, but the total that they did contribute averaged 37% of their own fleet and ranged in any given year from 56% to 20% of the total fleet that the Dutch had available:

Dutch Contribution to the Allied Fleet as a Percentage[63]

	of Allied Fleet	and	of Total Dutch Fleet
1702	31%		50%
1703	22%		46%
1704	18%		21%
1705	20%		41%
1706	15%		42%
1707	27%		56%
1708	25%		48%
1709	14%		20%
1710	17%		27%
1711	16%		37%

In response to the repeated English demands for more ships, Heinsius clearly spelled out the consistent Dutch view of the matter when he wrote to the duke of Marlborough in January 1703, explaining that the time for an expedition to the West Indies "had truly passed":

> Most of our ships and troops have left; thus the contribution is made, but very unnecessarily if they are undertaking a voyage that signifies nothing. I ask you, my Lord, to consider that you have desired a squadron in the Mediterranean Sea and one in Portugal, and beyond that you will be obliged to protect your coasts as well as the North Sea. Don't you think that we will have enough to do if we should have requirements either in Portugal or in Spain or some other troops as sea, or will we stretch them until they meet?[64]

In Dutch eyes, English demands could be both unreasonable and impractical. By this time, expeditions to America were less important than supporting the immediate naval needs in European waters. Part of the issue was the design character and capabilities of Dutch warships. The States General made this very clear in a 1711 resolution that spelled out the need "to aid and assist the other" but also dealt with both an issue of differing priorities as well as practicality when it declared, "The Channel according to its situation is more proper for Her Majesty's ships and the North Sea for those of the States, in regard to their harbours."[65] The inability of the Dutch to furnish their treaty quotas was not a reflection of lack of cooperation on the part of the Dutch, although it was interpreted as such in the English press. As Lord Strafford reported in 1711:

> Pensionary Heinsius made a long discourse with a great deal of warmth and with more assertion of protestations than ever I heard him before setting forth the necessity of a good correspondence & since (he said) it was not to come before the enemy he could declare their finances were in a much worse condition than ours in England could be.[66]

The problem of the high cost of the war, and of naval expenditure in particular, led to the consideration of other means by which naval force could be supplemented. The entire privateering enterprise, and the governments' encouragements of it, was, of course, one designed to bring private initiative and investment to complement naval operations at government expense. Even more radically, however, Sir David Mitchell had suggested to Heinsius in 1702 that the two governments might jointly "indulge the buccaneers, to induce them to concur in offending the enemies in the West Indies."[67] This same issue recurred in early 1711, at the very low point in the Dutch admiralties' ability to contribute ships to the allied cause. Secretary of State Henry St. John wrote to Admiral James Wishart, who was then negotiating the annual naval contribution at The Hague:

> It may not be amiss for you to propose to the Pensioner the two ways of doing this service, either on account of the Queen and the States, or in imitation of the French manner by sending ships and making a bargain with private adventurers.[68]

In the light of this remark, it is interesting to note that in 1711, there was a measurable increase in the parallel activities of both English and Dutch privateers, at least as measured by the overall financial results. However, it is nearly impossible to show a direct cause and effect relationship with diplomacy and state policy, when so many other factors were involved in privateering success at sea.[69]

Conclusion

In the light of the broad military and naval balance in Europe during both the Nine Years' War and the War of the Spanish Succession, a major coalition was the only practical way to deal with the overwhelming strength of France both on land and at sea. In that coalition, only English and the Dutch had major naval forces. The proportional naval contributions upon which the Anglo-Dutch naval agreement were laid out were those that existed at the outset, but could not reflect the changing balance of relative capabilities that developed over a twenty-five-year period. At the outset, it was the English who had more ships, but were less capable; at the end, it was the Dutch who had fewer resources to put to sea. This subtle, changing relationship created a clear strain, but the naval alliance functioned even though there were differing strategic priorities and national interests involved. Despite the public criticisms voiced at the time due to these tensions and to those that typically arise in any coalition warfare, the cooperative effort of both England and the Dutch Republic "to aid and assist the other" at sea was both necessary and successful.

NOTES   This paper was delivered at an international conference organized by the Institute of Netherlands History that was held at The Hague, Netherlands, on 29–
30 March 2001. It was subsequently published in the
conference proceedings: A. F. de Jongste and A. J.
Veenendaal, Jr., eds., *Anthonie Heinsius and the Dutch
Republic, 1688–1720: Politics, War, & Finance* (The
Hague: Institute of Netherlands History, 2002), pp.
177–198.

1 For twentieth-century experience, see John B.
Hattendorf, "International Naval Cooperation and
Admiral Richard G. Colbert: The Intertwining of a
Career with an Idea," and "NATO's Policeman on
the Beat: The First Twenty Years of the Standing
Naval Force, Atlantic, 1968–1988," in Hattendorf,
*Naval History and Maritime Strategy: Collected Es-
says* (Malabar, FL: Krieger Publishing, 2000), pp.
161–200.

2 The statistics are for 1690, based on Jan Glete, *Navies and Nations: Warships, Navies and State Building in Europe and America, 1500–1860.* Stockholm
Studies in History, vol. 48 (Stockholm: Almqvist &
Wiksell International, 1993), volume 2, pp. 551,
576, 639.

3 J. R. Bruijn, "William III and His Two Navies," *Notes Rec. R. Soc. London* 43 (1989), p. 117.

4 "Treaty of Navigation and Commerce between England and the Netherlands, signed at London 1/10 December 1674," in Clive Parry, ed., *The Consolidated Treaty Series* (Dobbs Ferry, NY: Oceana Publications, Inc., 1969), vol. 13, pp. 255–281.

5 "Declaration for the Explanation of the Marine Treaties between Great Britain and The Netherlands, signed at The Hague, 30 December 1675," in ibid., vol. 14, pp. 61–64. Although it was not specified in the 1674 agreement, this declaration also linked that agreement to the 17/27 February 1668 treaty.

6 Treaties signed 17 August 1685, 24 August 1689, 6 February 1716, and 27 May 1728 renewed the 1674 and 1675 agreements on commerce and navigation.

7 Article X and XI, "Treaty of Defensive Alliance Between England and the Netherlands, signed at The Hague, 31 December 1677 (10 January 1678)," in Parry, ed., *Consolidated Treaty Series,* pp. 277–288.

8 Bruijn, "William III and His Two Navies," pp. 117–118.

9 Articles IV, VI, VIII in "Treaty of Defensive Alliance Between England and the Netherlands, signed at Westminster, 3 March 1678," in Parry, ed., *Consolidated Treaty Series,* pp. 311–314.

10 Separate Articles I and III, in ibid.

11 Article II, in "Treaty of Alliance between Great Britain and the Netherlands, signed at The Hague, 26 July 1678," in ibid., pp. 355–363.

12 "Treaty between Great Britain and the United Provinces, signed at Windsor, 17 August 1685," in ibid., vol. 17, p. 304.

13 Separate Articles I and III in "Treaty of Defensive Alliance Between England and the Netherlands, signed at Westminster, 3 March 1678," in ibid., vol. 14, pp. 311–314.

14 J. R. Bruijn, *Varend Verleden: De Nederlandse Oorlogsvloot in de 17de en 18de Eeuw* (Amsterdam: Uitgeverij Balans, 1998), pp. 122–123.

15 Peter Le Fevre, "Arthur Herbert, Earl of Torrington, 1648–1716," in Richard Harding and Peter Le Fevre, eds., *The Precursors of Nelson: British Admirals of the Eighteenth Century* (London: Chatham Publishing, 2000), pp. 19–41.

16 N. Japikse, ed., *Correspondentie van Willem III en van Hans Willem Bentinck.* Part 1, vol. 1. RGP Kleine Serie, vol. 24 ('s-Gravenhage: Martinus Nijhoff, 1928), Doc. 567: "Memoire van Arthur Herbert, Sept. or Oct. 1688," pp. 610–613.

17 Doc. 568–569 in ibid.

18 For a detailed discussion of these negotiations, see J. C. M. Warnsinck, *De Vloot van den Koning-Stadhouder, 1689–1690* (Amsterdam: N.V. Noord-Hollandsche Uitgivermaatschappij, 1934), pp. 9–14; John Ehrman, *The Navy in the War of William III 1689–1697: Its State and Direction* (Cambridge: Cambridge University Press, 1953), pp. 251–253; Bruijn, "William III and His Two Navies," pp. 118–120. The signatories were Nottingham, Carberry, and Russell for England; N. Witsen, W. de Nassau, and de Weede for the Republic.

19 A. J. Veenendaal, Jr., *Inventaris van het Archief van Anthonie Heinsius, Raadpensionaris van Holland en West Friesland (1682) 1689–1722.* Algemeen Rijksarchief Publikatiereeks nummer 9 ('s-Gravenhage: Algemeen Rijksarchief, 2001). Incoming letters: H.A. 145 (1688), H.A. 182 (1690), H.A. 225 (1691), H.A. 302 (1693), H.A. 355 (1694), H.A. 684 (1700), H.A. 740 (1701), H.A. 803 (1703), H.A. 883 (1703), H.A. 958 (1704); outgoing letters: H.A. 223 (1691), H.A. 424 (1695), H.A. 1069 (1705). For an outgoing letter, not in the Heinsius Archief, see A. J. Veenendaal, Jr., ed., *De Briefwisseling van Anthonie Heinsius 1702–1720,* vols. 1-19 (The Hague, 1976–2001), vol. II (1703), p. 575, doc. 1454.

20 Preamble, "Treaty Between Great Britain and the Netherlands concerning the fitting out of a Fleet, signed at Whitehall, 29 April 1689" [21 May 1689], in Parry, ed., *Consolidated Treaty Series,* vol. 18, pp. 345–352.

21 Articles I and II, ibid., p. 348.

22 Article IV, ibid., pp. 348–349.

23 Article V, ibid., p. 349.

24 Article VI, ibid.

25 Article VII, ibid.

26 Article VIII, ibid., pp. 349–350.

27 Article IX, ibid., p. 350.

28 Article X, ibid.

29 Article XI, ibid., pp. 350–351.

30 Article XII, ibid.

31 Article XIII, ibid.

32 "Convention between Great Britain and the Netherlands concerning the retaking of prizes, signed at Whitehall, 22 October 1689." Not published. PRO, S.P. 108/329. The signatories were Carmarthen, Halifax, Shrewsbury, Nottingham, and T. Wharton for England; Schimmelpenninck van der Oye, N. Witsen, W. de Nassau, de Weede, and one illegible signature for the Dutch Republic.

33 Article XIV, "Treaty Between Great Britain and the Netherlands concerning the fitting out of a Fleet, signed at Whitehall, 29 April 1689" [21 May 1689], in Parry, ed., *Consolidated Treaty Series,* vol. 18, pp. 351–352.

34 "Treaty of Friendship and Alliance between Great Britain and the Netherlands, signed at Whitehall, 24 August 1689," in ibid., vol. 18, pp. 485–490.

35 "Convention between Great Britain and The Netherlands concerning the Prohibition of commerce with France, signed at London, 12/22 August 1689," in ibid., pp. 479–484.

36 Articles I and IX, "Particular and Perpetual Alliance Between Great Britain and the Netherlands, signed at The Hague, 11 November 1701," in ibid., vol. 24, pp. 55–62.

37 Article II, ibid.

38 Article V, ibid.

39 Article XI, ibid.

40 Bruijn, "William III and His Two Navies," pp. 122–123.

41 Veenendaal, *Briefwisseling*, vol. II (1703), p. 575, doc. 1454; vol. IV (1705), p. 217, doc. 620.

42 Alan Cook, *Edmond Halley: Charting the Heavens and the Seas* (Oxford: Clarendon Press, 1998), pp. 298, 299, 318.

43 Veenendaal, *Briefwisseling*, vol. II (1703), pp. 266–267.

44 See Hattendorf, ed., *Journal of Admiral Sir George Rooke, 1700–1704* (London: Navy Records Society, forthcoming); Arnout Lodewijk van Schelven, *Philips van Almonde: Admiraal in de gecombineerde vloot, 1644–1711* (Amsterdam: Drukkerij M. Lindebaum, 1947), chapter IX.

45 Gustaf Jonasson, *Karl XII och hans Rådgivare: Den utrikespolitiska maktkampen i Sverige, 1697–1702* (Stockholm: Svenska Bokförlaget, 1960), pp. 150–160.

46 PRO, S.P. 104/73, fo. 1: Harley to Buys, 19/30 April 1706.

47 Veenendaal, *Briefwisseling*, vol. I (1702), pp. 355–356.

48 British Library: Stowe MS. 244, fo. 42; A. Stanhope to Hedges, 11 August 1702.

49 Sir George Murray, ed., *The Letters and Dispatches of John Churchill, First Duke of Marlborough from 1702 to 1712* (London, 1845, reprinted New York: Greenwood Publishers, 1968), vol. 1, pp. 460–461: Marlborough to Alexander Stanhope, 11 September 1704.

50 See Douglas Coombs, *The Conduct of the Dutch: British Opinion and the Dutch Alliance during the War of the Spanish Succession* (The Hague: Martinus Nijhoff, 1958) for comments about Anglo-Dutch naval issues in the British press, pp. 35–41, 52–54, 56, 59, 80–81, 91–92, 94, 124, 129, 241–242, 274–275, 281.

51 See E. Taillemite and P. Guillaume, *Tourville et Beveziers* (Paris: Economica, 1992).

52 N. A. M. Rodger, "The British View of the Functioning of the Anglo-Dutch Alliance, 1688–1795," in G. J. A. Raven and Rodger, eds., *Navies and Armies: The Anglo-Dutch Relationship in War and Peace, 1688–1988* (Edinburgh: John Donald Publishers Ltd., 1990), p. 13.

53 See *Des Vaisseaux et des Hommes* (Saint Vaast La Hougue: Musée Maritime de l'Ile Tatihou, 1992).

54 John B. Hattendorf, "Sir George Rooke and Sir Cloudisley Shovell," in Harding and Le Fevre, eds., *Precursors of Nelson*, pp. 57–58.

55 British Library, Addit MS 5441, fo. 96. Quoted in A. D. Francis, *The Methuens and Portugal 1691–1708* (Cambridge: Cambridge University Press, 1966), p. 309.

56 "Precedents at Home and Abroad where an English Flagg Officer of an Inferior Rank has commanded a Dutch Flag Officer." Document transcribed in C. O. van der Meij, ". . . een furieus gevegt . . . " De Zeeslag bij Malaga, 1707 (unpublished M.A. thesis, Leiden University, 1995), p. 157, note 37. I am grateful to C. O. van der Meij for this information.

57 Veenendaal, *Briefwisseling*, vol. I (1702), p. 357, doc. 682: van Van Almonde, 30 July 1702. See also vol. 2 (1703), p. 568, doc. 138: van Job de Wildt, 5 December 1703; vol. 3 (1704), p. 8, doc. 18: van Job de Wildt, 6 January 1704.

58 Ibid., vol. V (1706), p. 262, doc. 493: van Van Vrijbergen, 28 May 1706; p. 514, doc. 514: van Buys, 2 June 1706.

59 Van Schelven, *Philips van Almonde*, p. 53.

60 See, for example, Brian Tunstall, ed., *The Byng Papers* (London: Navy Records Society, 1930), vol. I, p. 245: Council of War, 29 September 1707.

61 Huntington Library HM 656: Council of War 15 June 1702, but contrast this with HM 1655, Council of War 6 September 1702, involving only sea officers and divided by nationality. I am grateful to A. J. Veenendaal for this information.

62 John B. Hattendorf, *England in the War of the Spanish Succession: A Study of the English View and Conduct of Grand Strategy, 1702–1712* (New York: Garland, 1987), section "Anglo-Dutch Co-operation at Sea" pp. 155–160.

63 For the exact figures, see ibid., Tables IX and X, pp. 155, 158.

64 B. van 't Hoff, ed., *The Correspondence 1701–1711 of John Churchill First Duke of Marlborough and Anthonie Heinsius Grand Pensionary of Holland* (Utrecht: Kemink en Zoon N.V., 1951), p. 49: Doc. 83, Heinsius to Marlborough, 26 January 1703. Translated from French.

65 PRO, S.P. 84/237, fos. 41v–42: Extracts from Resolution of the States-General, 27 March 1711.

66 PRO, S.P. 84/240, fo. 16: Strafford to St. John, 26 October 1711.

67 Veenendaal, *Briefwisseling*, vol. I (1702), pp. 355–356.

68 PRO, S.P. 104/79, fo. 22: St John to Wishart, 16 February 1711.

69 The financial results are summarized in J. Th. Verhees–van Meer, *De Zeeuwse Kapvaart tijdens de Spaanse Succesieoorlog, 1702–1713* (Middelburg: Zeeuwsch Genootschap der Wetenschappen, 1986), p. 139; David J. Starkey, *British Privateering Enterprise in the Eighteenth Century* (Exeter: University of Exeter Press, 1990), p. 87. *N.B.*: So far, the published statistics on total numbers of active English and Dutch privateering ships are more suggestive than conclusive. The numbers given for Zeeland by Verhees–van Meer seem to be consistently the same for every year throughout the war, while the two English lists derive from different but complementary sources. Those in Hattendorf, *War of the Spanish Succession*, pp. 161, 323, are derived from PRO, H.C.A. 25 (Bonds), while those in Starkey, *British Privateering*, pp. 294–297, are derived from H.C.A. 26 (Declarations). As both authors note, it is extremely difficult to use these documents as a reflection of ships actually engaged in privateering, but those in Starkey have the advantage of linking a privateer's intentions to the months of the year in which he expected to be active at sea.

VII *The Caird Lecture, 2000*
The Anglo-French Naval Wars (1689–1815) in Twentieth-Century Naval Thought

As we take our first steps into the twenty-first century, it is, perhaps, worth remembering that in modern naval thought there is an intellectual link across the entire twentieth century directly to the events of the long eighteenth century. That great series of naval wars, which France and England fought between 1689 and 1815, loom large. The manner in which some professional naval officers studied those wars in the period from 1874 to 1930 has had two important effects. On the one hand, their historical study of these wars provided the intellectual basis that formed modern naval strategic theory. On the other, these same naval interpretations have sometimes had a profound and unintended effect, in a quite different field, on the manner in which academic historians have tried to think about those same wars.

Yet, for navies, today and in the future, when modern naval historians strive to raise the academic standards for the study of naval history to a level where there is no distinction between professional naval historical thought and academic history, it is important to understand that there was, at one time, a difference. Making this distinction helps us to see more clearly how earlier naval professionals thought, and to understand important phases in the navy's intellectual development. When we clearly understand what professional naval officers were attempting to do with history, we can better understand their contribution basis as we discriminate between modern standards of historical thinking and those of the past.

One of the most important strands of development in recent work on naval history has been has been the series of intellectual biographies of some of the key thinkers that have influenced modern naval thought. Beginning with Professor D. M. Schurman's pivotal volume, *The Education of a Navy,*[1] we have had, in the intervening thirty-five years, a series of important new studies on Corbett,[2] Richmond,[3] Castex,[4] Mahan,[5] and Laughton,[6] which have been paralleled by two further, multi-volume collections of books and essays on individual thinkers who contributed to the evolution of naval thought.[7] Taken together, this strand of investigation has built a much firmer basis for an analytical understanding of the development of strategic thought in naval circles. There are many fruitful directions for this work to proceed in the future, but one area that has so far been overlooked is to examine the intersections and the tensions between strategic studies and naval historical studies as they touch on the history of our understanding of the Anglo-French naval wars, a series of events which were so important to stimulating both these areas of study.

Sir John Knox Laughton

The key person within the Navy, who acted as the catalyst for this entire intellectual development, was, as Andrew Lambert has so successfully pointed out, Sir John Knox Laughton. For Laughton's generation, as well as for the generation that followed his, the Anglo-French naval wars—particularly the final phase of them, the Napoleonic Wars—represented the most recent worldwide war between major naval powers. It was not remote history, but the war, still within living memory, that his parents and their generation had fought. In his famous 1874 lecture to the Royal United Services Institution on "The Scientific Study of Naval History," Laughton spread his view widely over the whole range of naval history. Naval historians up to that time, Laughton declared, had failed to go beyond mere chronology:

> Whatever has been done by, or for, or against the Navy of any country, the manner in which its fleets have been collected, or the political system by which they have been manned or maintained, are questions of which have affected its naval power.[8]

Now this is something that sounds very modern to us and many of us may well have echoed similar views more than a century later. But, in the following sentences Laughton went on to quite a different point that overshadowed what he had just said, at least in the minds of the naval officers that heard and read his work:

> Still more important is the tactical skill which has guided those fleets to victory, or has taught them to avoid defeat; and the examination of these and many kindred subjects, approaches far more nearly to what may be called naval history, than the mere descriptions of battles and bloodshed, or the glowing eulogium of noble action.[9]

Perhaps, Laughton did not recognize the conceptual distinction that we can see today, or maybe he was merely trying to couch his approach in a way that would be attractive to naval officers, but his two consecutive sentences represent two strands that grew into two quite separate approaches, one looking at the strategic level and another at the tactical and operational levels. For his time, Laughton clearly expressed a vision that was yet to be realized. In his lifetime, he went a long way to facilitate the use of archival resources to establish the basis for a more accurate historical record that corrected the commonplace myths and legends that had grown up around various prominent events in naval memory. In doing this, however, he had an ulterior motive. "I have argued against the idea that the study of naval history is useless—is a waste of time; I have argued that the lessons it conveys are of very direct and very practical meaning."[10]

Successful naval officers are characteristically practical and want direct and useful knowledge, so Laughton's argument had some attraction. At the same, the state of historical scholarship was such that his larger, more modern and sophisticated vision for strategic understanding could not yet be realized. Thus, Laughton's contribution was necessarily limited and often focused at the tactical level.

Responding to a contemporary opinion that the new tactics for the modern steam navy needed to be individual actions of a single ship against another single ship, Laughton immediately turned to the history of tactics and argued that for nearly forty years on from the battle that Mathews and Lestock fought off Toulon in 1744, the Royal Navy had been "trammeled and bound to a false system."[11] It was wrong to conclude from this, he said, that battles between one line against another were an improper or pointless use of the fleet, even when ships were skillfully handled and well-fought. Repetitions of such battles and repeated court-martials following them all failed to reveal the true issue at hand. It was only when Rodney defeated the French at the battle of the Saintes in 1782 that the true principle became clear. While Rodney had used a tactic called "breaking the line" to achieve his victory, that was not the point; it was only a means to an end. The real end was to overwhelm part of an enemy fleet by concentrating a preponderance of force against it. Thus, Laughton concluded, history showed that ships operating together as a fleet were superior to single ships in individual combat. Even then, it was not a uniquely British insight. Off the coast of India some months before Rodney's action, Suffren had used a similar approach against Sir Edward Hughes, off Madras in February 1782 and off Providien in April that same year. On both occasions, Suffren concentrated his force against a point, rather than stretching it equally against the whole opposing force.

Laughton having instigated this very practical approach to the use of naval history from the Anglo-French Wars, the approach began to spread slowly and to develop in scope, growing first though his historical course at the Royal Naval College, Greenwich. The first major figure to carry this work forward was Laughton's own successor in teaching that course, Philip Colomb, who had just been promoted to rear-admiral on his retirement and took over teaching history and tactics at the College in 1887, later becoming a vice-admiral on the retired list.[12]

Philip Colomb

Colomb's major contribution to interpreting the Anglo-French Wars was not published until 1891, but it very clearly informed his teaching at Greenwich during the preceding four years. Like Laughton, Colomb sought to produce something of practical value for the naval service in his own time. In the absence of any other book on naval strategy, Colomb used the old and well-established histories as his sources, not rewriting them but going beyond their narration, "endeavoring always to extract the reasons for each event, and to bring out the causes which here have contributed to success, and there determined failure."[13] Putting it in more practical terms, he declared,

> I have a firm belief that the great laws of naval war, which I have endeavored to trace throughout the centuries in which England has been building up her power, would be absolutely dominant in any naval war which now arose; and that they may be depended upon for forecasting its course and preparing for it.[14]

With this in mind, Colomb looked broadly at history, searching for some broad strategic themes among historical and contemporary examples, the bulk of which were from the Anglo-French Wars. In his hefty volume that stretched to 470 large pages with notably small type, Colomb was directly carrying out the practical and applied study of history that Laughton had envisioned a quarter-century before. Because of this direct intellectual link, and equally as a contribution to the development of professional naval thought, Colomb's *Naval Warfare* deserves far more emphasis than it has heretofore been given.

In his overview of the mediaeval and renaissance eras, Colomb saw war at sea as merely a series of retaliatory raids across the sea to attack towns and ports; it was a kind of warfare that he called "cross-ravaging." Real maritime warfare, he said, did not come about until the middle of the seventeenth century and this only "when there is sufficient property at sea to make its loss of serious importance."[15] In understanding this, the principal issue that he fell upon was what he termed the "Struggle for Command of the Sea," basing his view of it on his own interpretation of the concepts that Sir William Monson and Sir Walter Raleigh had used.

About three-quarters of Colomb's long volume was devoted to the Anglo-French Wars. In dealing with them, Colomb created two major themes of professional naval interest to structure his study: The first was an examination of various attempts to gain command of the sea and the importance of doing so, not just as an end in itself, but with an ulterior purpose in mind. The second theme was a consideration of the reasons for success or failure of expeditions across the sea designed to attack territory. Both issues were of great interest to contemporary naval officers. For Colomb, the latter in particular seemed to represent the typical kind of work that the navy would undertake in the twentieth century.

Essentially, what Colomb was doing was using the factual basis of the standard eighteenth century histories and applying modern, late nineteenth century professional judgment to them. His key sources were works such as Josiah Burchett's 1720 *A Complete History of the Most Remarkable Transactions at Sea,* Thomas Lediard's 1735 *The Naval History of England,* and John Entick's *A New Naval History of 1757,* and some more recent historical studies, such Montagu Burrows's *Life of Hawke* or Laughton's Camden Society edition of *Memoirs Relating to the Lord Torrington.* Using them, Colomb categorized various tactical and operational events in history under his two major themes and interpreted them in the light of modern professional thinking.

Colomb's work had the advantage of drawing attention to historical study and building up a professional interest for naval officers in past events. In this, Colomb took a large number of events, comparing and contrasting them, in order to reach some general conclusions. While one finds in Colomb's *Naval Warfare* a mass of information about various naval events in the long eighteenth century, it is difficult, if not impossible, to find the larger political and economic context or to trace the development of events and the outside influences that affected the evolution of naval affairs. It is, in short, a dissection of the historical fabric and an analysis of disconnected parts.

Yet, Colomb's relation of events, however frustrating for the historian, was from the professional perspective of a naval officer a source of deeper understanding of what naval events were about and provided a kind of intellectual framework to guide thought. Casting it in the terms of battles and amphibious landing, Colomb spoke about history in a currency that modern naval men could readily understand and could relate to their own professional thought.

Particularly striking was his analysis of the battle of Beachy Head in 1690 and the way in which he underscored the point that a partially beaten fleet is something still to be reckoned with and something that can still prevent an invasion. In contrast, he looked at Barfleur and La Hougue in 1692 as events that demonstrated the tremendous risks involved in an attempt to obtain temporary command of the sea. In his repetitious examination of similar types of events, Colomb was pointing out that, in his view, the recurring French attempts to invade Britain were based on a false strategic principle that involved temporary command of the sea in order to carry out a particular invasion plan. In a statement that other naval strategists would subsequently make more subtle, Colomb wrote,

> I think it becomes more and more clear as we proceed, that the sea is not, and cannot be made neutral ground. For the purposes of passage it is almost always in the hands of one

side or the other in war, and if undisputed passage across it is desired by one side, it must be obtained by conquest of the water territory.[16]

Contrasting French strategic principles with those of the Dutch in the seventeenth century, Colomb felt that France was prone to wasting her energies on the dual strategic design of invading England and defeating her at sea. Because of this, in Colomb's view, "she fell more at the opening of each war, into the position of an assuredly inferior naval power."[17]

Colomb's criticism of the French habit of making preparations to invade Britain raised a corresponding point about Britain's repeated uses of overseas expeditions to attack enemy land positions. In making this point, Colomb was drawing a fine line between invasions that were dependent upon securing temporary command of the sea and attacks on overseas land positions from a position of secure command of the sea. After a detailed analysis of most of the major operations that took place in the West Indies between 1690 and 1780, Colomb concluded that attacks made over a sea that was not securely commanded was doomed to failure. On the other hand, attack over a sea that was secure against an enemy raised a variety of technical issues in regard to the relations between ships, commanders, and troops. In Colomb's view, these events illustrated all the principles that were involved in success of these operations over the entire period:

> If the strength of the land defences is properly estimated, if sufficient troops are employed, landed clear of the fortifications of the enemy, and supplied and supported from the fleet, there appears to be, so far as we have yet come, no reason to doubt the fall of any place attacked, provided relief does not come to it over the sea.[18]

Carrying on from this initial analysis, Colomb took up several sub-themes. The first of these was to study attacks from the sea that involved fortifications. Among other events, he looked at Porto Bello in 1743, Louisburg in 1758, Port Mahon in 1758, and the assaults on Gibraltar. In such situations, it was military, not naval, force that was important. The navy was very limited in making a direct attack, but powerful for an indirect attack. In his eyes, "Those that made our history for us looked to their fortifications to serve the purposes of delay only, and not really of defense."[19] In the light of the work of later writers, it is particularly interesting that Colomb placed special emphasis on Napoleon's campaign in Egypt. To Colomb, Napoleon's strategy was false to the principles of strategy and he deserved far more than the loss of the fleet and the army that followed it. The French failure to mask their landing force from the English fleet was an attempt at invasion without sufficient naval protection and, in Colomb's judgment, a foolhardy adventure. In direct contrast, he sketched Keppel's and Hodson's landing at Belle Isle in 1761 as the perfect example of an expedition. In that operation, Colomb saw that everything was done correctly in terms of principle. The result, he concluded, was a certainty. He summarized the necessary practical elements that were always needed to secure a successful attack on land from the sea: command of the area, sufficient and well-handled forces, landings away from the batteries or after their fire had been temporarily reduced, proper equipment and small vessels, well handled.[20]

Stephen B. Luce and the U.S. Naval War College
In his book *Naval Warfare*, Colomb's approach and focus was clearly that of Laughton's writ large. The same idea was equally present in the approach that Stephen B. Luce of

the U.S. Navy took with him back across the Atlantic and began to use in formulating his ideas about naval education and the ways in which naval professional thought could be stimulated and developed in the United States. Luce was unusual for an American naval officer of his time, and one who read widely, not only in British and French professional naval journals, but also kept abreast of all sorts of current literature and intellectual developments, ranging from the fad surrounding spiritualism in the mid-1870s to Max Müller's work in philology as well the principal works of the prominent historians of his day, particularly T. B. Macaulay and Thomas H. Buckle, on English history.[21] Previously aware of Laughton's published writings, Luce made contact with Laughton at the Royal United Services Institution in London, during one of Luce's several visits to England during the 1870s, while in command of two U.S. ships, the U.S.S. *Juniata* and the U.S.S. *Hartford*. Luce was the leader of the movement within the U.S. Navy to improve all levels of naval training and education, from the recruit level to the highest level of professional education for command. With much of common interest, it is not surprising that Luce found Laughton's work of direct interest.[22] In this regard, Laughton's influence combined with several other strands in Luce's thinking. Historical study was already beginning to become part of the professional discourse in the U.S. Navy with the publication of Commodore Foxhall Parker's study of ancient naval tactics in 1876, *Fleets of the World: The Galley Period,* which was to have continued on to the period of the Anglo-French Wars, but the author did not live to complete the project. Luce's own lengthy discussion of Parker's book in the pages of the recently established U.S. Naval Institute *Proceedings,* as well as his own series of articles on "Modern Navies" in the *Army and Navy Journal* that same year, began to provide an initial point of professional discussion in America.[23]

However, there were two other influences that carried equal weight in Luce's mind. One influence was a contemporary example: the great success of the German General Staff in fighting the Austro- and the Franco-Prussian Wars, with reliance on staff work and on broad concepts of operational planning. The third crucial element in Luce's thinking was the current thinking on the "comparative method" of thinking, an approach found in the writings of Buckle, Müller, and Macaulay, among others.[24]

The German Army's success, Luce concluded, was based on its educational and training institutions for operational planning and represented military methods that were easily transferable to naval operations, but, at that point, represented educational methods that were virtually unknown for navies. Of course, the German Army's success impressed everyone and its approaches stimulated military thinkers across Europe.[25] Luce was certainly not the only person to think in this way, either in America or in Britain. What was distinctive about Luce was that he saw an analytical means by which the naval profession could create its own distinctive philosophy: the use of a scientific understanding of naval history, as Laughton had advocated, along with a comparative analysis of naval history to the principles of war, as established by the great military writers.

It was these ideas that led to the establishment of the Naval War College, under Luce's direction, in the autumn of 1884. In planning the practical aspects of the College, Luce used a study that Professor James Soley of the U.S. Naval Academy had carried out in 1880 for his *Report on Foreign Systems of Naval Education.*[26] Soley covered a wide variety of institutions and countries, but there were two, in particular, which were important for the American Navy's new College. The first was the German Navy's higher level of education at its *Marine-Akademie,* founded at Kiel in 1872. The *Marine-Akademie,* with its two-year course for staff officers, paralleled the German Army's *Kriegsakademie* at Berlin, but also served to educate officers at a higher general level.[27]

Another key institution was the Royal Naval College, Greenwich, which provided the model for the first administrative structure of the U.S. Naval War College. Directly copying the example of Greenwich, Luce took for his own title the term "president," rather than commandant, of the Naval War College, wanting to signify the new institution's more academic approach.[28] Throughout, his objective was to establish a broader purpose than what these other institutions had yet achieved. He sought a College that would be "a place of original research on all questions relating to war and to the statesmanship connected with war, or the prevention of war."[29]

To reach this goal, the curriculum of the new college was founded on a study of history, military theory, international law, and the use of wargaming to test new concepts in the light of the latest technological capabilities. When Luce opened the College to its first students in 1885, he concluded his formal convocation address with the following: "Knowing ourselves to be on the road that leads to the establishment of the science of naval warfare under steam, let us confidently look for that mastermind who will lay the foundations of the science, and do for it what Jomini has done for the military sciences."[30] Fourteen years later, in July 1899, Luce wrote on a copy of the published version of this address, "He appeared in the person of Captain Alfred Thayer Mahan, U.S.N."[31]

Captain Alfred Thayer Mahan, U.S.N.

Luce had not thought of Mahan, when he first began to look for someone to take up the responsibilities of first lecturer in naval history at the newly established College. However, when Lieutenant Commander Caspar Goodrich declined the invitation, Luce turned to Mahan, who had served under him in previous assignments at the Naval Academy and at sea. Then in command of a ship on the Pacific coast of South America, Mahan had recently published his first book in 1883, a study of naval operations in the American Civil War of 1861–65, entitled *The Gulf and Inland Waters.* Luce clearly recognized Mahan's capabilities and, from his prior close association with him, also knew him as the son of Professor Dennis Hart Mahan of the U.S. Military Academy at West Point, the foremost interpreter of Jomini's works in America and the man who had educated nearly all of the country's leading military men. Elaborating on the concept that Laughton had originally suggested, Luce directed Mahan to use the comparative method as a means of breaking out of the traditional, isolated naval understanding of fleet battle tactics and naval history.

From the very beginning, Mahan envisaged a study that focused on the Anglo-French naval wars. As Mahan explained privately to his old friend, Samuel Ashe, in 1886,

> I have had assigned to me the subject of Naval Strategy and Tactics involving of course to a considerable extent Naval History as affording lessons. The subject is a very broad one, but its greatest difficulty lies in the fact that all naval history hitherto has been made by ships and weapons of a kind wholly different from those now in use. How to view the lessons of the past so as to mould them into lessons for the future, under such differing conditions, is the nut I have to crack.[32]

Lamenting that he was already 45 years old and had only a year to work this out, and not 35, with two years for the task, Mahan remarked,

> To excogitate a system of my own, on wholly *a priori* grounds, would be comparatively simple and I believe wholly useless. We are already deluged with speculations and arguments as to future naval warfare more or less well considered and plausible; but I don't see any use in my adding to the clack. I want if I can to wrest something out of the old wooden sides and 24 pounders that will throw some light on the combinations to be used ironclads, rifled guns and torpedoes; and to raise the profession in the eyes of its members by a clearer comprehension of the great part it has played in the world than I myself have hitherto had.[33]

Thus, we see that, at the very outset of Mahan's work on the Anglo-French Wars, he was combining the train of thinking that Laughton had begun and Luce's concept of the comparative method to develop a theory for practical application, adding to it the further thought of educating professional naval officers so that they could appreciate the broader role that navies have had in history.

Over the next twenty-five years, Mahan wrote more than twenty books; of them five were major works on the Anglo-French naval wars. Beginning with his one-volume study of the 1660–1783 period,[34] he wrote two-volume studies on the 1793–1812 period, and a biography of Nelson,[35] followed by a study of the War of 1812.[36] In addition, he wrote nearly half of volume three in Laird Clowes, *History of the Royal Navy,* covering the major naval operations in the period 1762 to 1783,[37] and a volume of collected biographical essays.[38] Finally, he drew upon examples from the whole period, as well as more recent contemporary events, for his collected lectures, comparing and contrasting the principles of naval and military strategy.[39]

Mahan's work has had an enormous influence that has stretched across the entire twentieth century, yet his legacy is a complex one to understand. Not everyone who used his name in justification of their own ideas had carefully read his work; not everyone who read his work understood it, and, on top of that, there were still significant groups that paid no attention to it whatsoever. In addition, a very influential group attributed to Mahan ideas that he either never believed or, after further reflection, on which he had changed his mind. In the past twenty-five years, much progress has been made in understanding Mahan's influence. Only in this very recent period have we had guides to his manuscript collections,[40] a letterpress edition of his correspondence,[41] a complete bibliography of his known works,[42] a modern biography,[43] and, most recently, an analytical study of his writing.[44]

Jon Sumida's recent analytical study is a major contribution that has rescued Mahan from the oblivion to which many had dismissed him. Sumida's book is particularly valuable in showing the complexity and subtlety in Mahan's approach and the difficulties that readers face in dealing with the changes he made, over time, in his positions on a number of major issues and his contradictory application of strategic principles.[45] Underscoring the point that Mahan had an ulterior purpose in mind for his historical study of the Anglo-French Wars, Sumida shows that Mahan had a distinctive understanding of history, one that was very different from that used by Laughton and Colomb before him and one that was often overlooked by those who followed him. Mahan dealt with two main themes: first, naval grand strategy, and, second, the art and science of command. In his understanding of the topic, naval grand strategy was interconnected with naval power, economic development, and international relations, and he focused on this issue in terms of political, political-economic, and governmental matters. Strategic and professional matters, however, fell under the second theme of the art and science of command. Initially, in Mahan's eyes, strategy was on a lower level, and directly tied to the operations of the fleet. As such, it fell within the realm of a professional naval thinking, not broad political thought, as it has since become. Each of Mahan's several volumes that deal with aspects of the Anglo-French Wars has a specific point that focused around these particular points. Many readers missed the main focus, but a reviewer for the *Manchester Guardian* commented, Mahan had a "wonderful power of exposition" but had "no skill in story telling, no power of color or of humour, no liveliness, none of that delight in detail which makes a memoir great and damns a history." As for his style, the reviewer wrote, it "is less attractive than any other writer of his eminence, it is cold, it is heavy, it is unrythmical; it is without any quality of beauty." Yet, Mahan compelled admiration, "his cold, clumsy telling phrases go home so deeply. His 'nuts of knowledge' are heavy round-shot."[46]

The heavy round shot in Mahan's first sea power book were aimed, with his governmental theme, to show that, after decades of error in its strategic stance, France's execution of a proper naval strategy during the American war finally led to victory. In his second book, Mahan emphasized that the younger Pitt's strategy of economic attrition and protracted warfare at sea allowed Britain to survive a war she might have lost without such a maritime strategy. Following this book on policy and strategy, Mahan produced his biography of Nelson and with it, turned to the underlying issues connected with the art and science of command. Casting Nelson as the personification of British naval strength, Mahan's point in this book was that it took the exceptional operational skills of a Nelson to turn the mere facts of numerical superiority at sea into functional supremacy at sea.

Carrying this same theme forward in *Types of Naval Officers,* Mahan stressed that the model of Nelson in this broad role as the embodiment of sea power was not the only type of officer that navies required, pointing to Hawke as the personification of the spirit of naval warfare in that age, to Rodney as the form, St. Vincent as disciplinarian, Saumarez as a fleet officer and division commander, Pellew as frigate captain and partisan officer, and Howe as a tactician. Finally, Mahan concluded his series on sea power with his study of the Anglo-American War of 1812. Mahan designed this volume to show that if the young American republic could have invested in a moderately larger navy, it would not have needed to be satisfied with just its minor frigate victories, but could have completely neutralized British naval supremacy in the western hemisphere, while Britain was preoccupied with the war against Napoleon.[47]

Mahan's *Naval Strategy*

In his final book that involved historical examples from the Anglo-French naval wars, Mahan very reluctantly took up the issue of the principles of naval warfare. Under great personal pressure from an 80-year-old Admiral Luce to finish the job Luce had given him a quarter-century before, Mahan returned to the Naval War College at Newport to begin revising his old lectures on the subject for publication. As Luce told Mahan in 1906, "You have made a great reputation by your work on sea power. This last work will be, in effect, the capstone, as it were of the great monument you have reared."[48] Mahan's book, *Naval Strategy,* finally appeared at the end of 1911. In its final form, it reflected

Mahan's hesitancy about the doctrinaire use of principles and the importance of historical study as the best possible means to prevent the sort of rigidity of thinking common
to military and naval officers inured to the discipline created by bureaucracy and engineering.[49] As Mahan put it,

> In this living sense, the conduct of war is an art, having its spring in the mind of man, deal-
> ing with various circumstances, admitting certain principles; but, beyond that, manifold in
> its manifestations, according to the genius of the artist and the temper of the materials with
> which he is dealing. To such an effort dogmatic prescription is unsuited: the best of rules,
> when applied to it, cannot be rigid, but must have that free play which distinguishes a prin-
> ciple from a mere rule.[50]

While he still found principles useful as themes to discuss, historical example provided the myriad ways in which any theme played itself out. As Sumida has described
Mahan's view of the historical process, it could be "likened to a game in which the dice
were loaded but not to such an extent that outcomes were preordained absolutely—
under these circumstances, determinism and contingency were complementary rather
than mutually exclusive."[51]

Thus, Mahan was looking at the Anglo-French naval wars with a very specialized
purpose and in ways that were closely attuned to the intellectual currents of the navy in
his own day that reflected some of the influences that Laughton, Colomb, and Luce
represented. We are accustomed to looking at the intellectual relationships between individuals, and certainly Mahan owed much to Luce, to whom he "gratefully acknowledged his indebtedness for guiding him into a path he would not himself have found."[52]

Yet, there was an additional central influence behind Mahan's work and that lay
with the Naval War College as an institution, where Mahan had twice served, not only
as a lecturer in history and tactics, but also as its president. Mahan, himself, was fully
aware that he would not have written the studies that he did if it had not been for the in-
structional needs of the Navy at the College. In the introduction to his second sea power
book, Mahan noted that sea officers of his time had been unduly diverted by the race for
material and mechanical development. Modestly, he wrote that any officer could have
done what he had done, given the opportunity to do so, but too few actually have the
chance during their careers to attempt such a task. That he had been able to do so, he
wrote, "is due, wholly and exclusively, to the Naval War College, which was instituted to
promote such studies."[53]

The intellectual influence of the Navy's own institutions is a matter that has yet to be
more thoroughly examined, but an influence similar to that of the Newport College on
Mahan's work was seen elsewhere and in other navies, as different navies adopted and
modified the vision that Luce had for Newport for use within other services. The widespread success that Mahan's books won led others to model their work on his and to
produce similar attempts to use history for the higher education of naval officers. In
other countries, the Anglo-French naval wars were less of a pivotal focus in historical
study, but Mahan's example helped to promote the fundamental approach in ways that
illustrate some institutional influences on naval thought.

In Japan, for example, Satō Tetsutarō first became an instructor at the Imperial
Japanese Navy's Staff College in 1902, having already written a study on Japanese maritime operations against Korea in the sixteenth century. After other assignments, he returned to the Staff College in 1906 to prepare his mammoth 900-page study on the

history of Japanese imperial defence. This was a work that ultimately had a major conceptual impact on Japanese naval strategic thinking up through World War II.[54] It is interesting to note that the German *Marine-Akademie,* whose history has yet to be systematically examined, predated the American Naval War College's focus on naval strategy. Among the key figures associated with the German college was Vice-Admiral Curt, Freiherr von Maltzahn, whose writing did touch on the Anglo-French naval wars, but he was only one of several key individuals who used an historical basis for their professional arguments.

The *Marine-Akademie:* Alfred Stenzel

The first lecturer in naval history at the *Marine-Akademie* was Alfred Stenzel, son of the professor of history at the university of Breslau, and on his mother's side, grandson of another historian. He did not devote himself on a full-time basis to the study of history and strategy, but lectured at the *Akademie* on adjunct assignment between 1875 and 1881, returning again in retirement to lecture from 1894 to 1896.[55] His lectures were not published until after his death in 1906, but they represent an independent attempt that began with a different basis, but contemporary to what Laughton was trying to do in England, as well as the first attempt to try to write a general history of world naval history in German.[56] At the same time, however, this independent approach paralleled the dual interest in broad issues as well as tactical and operational history.

Stenzel has often been hailed as the German Mahan, but as Rolf Hobson has recently argued, Stenzel's contribution may best be characterized as "one long attempt to baptize Clausewitz with salt water."[57] Stenzel is certainly a key figure in the development of the distinctive German school of naval thought that developed in the early twentieth century. At the time his lectures were first given in the 1870s and 1880s, the German Navy was small and was relatively unimportant in the thinking of German leaders. Stenzel's lectures were designed to show the importance of maritime warfare. His slim volume of lectures did not directly use examples from the Anglo-French Wars, but another work, also unfinished at his death, was a detailed six-volume study of the history of naval tactics, concentrating on selected key naval battles from ancient times to the present. Expanded to include the naval wars of Russia, Prussia, Sweden, and Denmark, Stenzel devoted several hundred pages, in two of the six volumes, to the Anglo-French Wars.[58] Here, his sources were largely the works of Mahan and Clowes. Several other officers followed Stenzel's lead and went on to produce important historical studies of their own. Among the key figures that Stenzel stimulated into doing their own historical work was Rudolph Rittmeyer, who taught at the *Marine-Akademie* from 1889 to 1893 and who eventually published a two-volume study on the development of world naval history.[59] Another was Vice-Admiral Hermann Kirchhoff, who was the officer who edited Stenzel's work for publication and who, himself, wrote a very important study on the history of sea power in the Baltic[60] that followed the lines Stenzel had laid out and devoted much space to the wars of the sixteenth through the eighteenth centuries. Including, as it did, the early origins of German participation in warfare at sea, his work played an important part in encouraging further official interest in naval history. In this group, von Maltzahn played a key role, having been a pupil of Stenzel's at the *Marine-Akademie* while taking its three, seven-month-long courses between 1879 and 1882. After a variety of other assignments, von Maltzahn taught at the *Akademie* from 1895 to 1900, and, then from 1900 to 1903, served as its director.[61] Although a boyhood friend and contemporary of Tirpitz, he became a critic of Tirpitz's thinking and, early on, suggested German investment in cruisers for commerce warfare rather than a battle fleet.[62]

The *Marine-Akademie:* Von Maltzahn

Von Maltzahn very clearly expressed his ideas in a published lecture at the *Marine-Akademie* in 1898, drawing from his study of history support for the idea of sea denial as the best course for a smaller power to use against British maritime superiority. In this he stressed conclusions from the history of the Anglo-French Wars that were quite different from those being reached about the same period in England and America. Pointing out that Trafalgar had not ended the war, von Maltzahn argued that British sea superiority was still vulnerable to attack against its trade, particularly when Britain still had to carry the main economic burden of the war effort.[63]

Building on this in 1899, von Maltzahn tried to publish a book-length study in which he used detailed historical examples from the Anglo-French naval wars to show such points as the positive value of the geographically and chronologically limited mastery of the sea that Napoleon had sought in 1805, the use of ships-of-the-line for cruiser warfare in circumstances when there was no opportunity to break an enemy's domination of the sea. Among his main points, he stressed the advantage of avoiding sea battle against overwhelming forces and suggested that the battle fleet should not dominate the fleet's resources, so as to retain the flexible use of cruiser warfare as the historically preferred weapon of a weaker power.

Tirpitz quickly saw that such heretical views were quickly muzzled and von Maltzahn, a man in a position to influence the thought of mid-career naval officers at the *Marine-Akademie,* would be unable to publish his volume that could detract from the German appreciation and interpretation of Mahan's ideas. Soon after, Tirpitz saw that von Maltzahn retired, just at the point when the *Marine-Akademie* was about to become a "greenhouse" to develop Tirpitz's theories.

In 1906, as a vice-admiral, von Maltzahn eventually did publish a small volume that contained some of his basic ideas in a series of lectures he had delivered that year, tracing the history of naval warfare from the great age of discoveries to the present. Two years later, this was translated into English and published in London.[64]

In viewing the Anglo-French Wars up through the War of the Spanish Succession, von Maltzahn concluded, "A sea state well-armed for war becomes in the eyes of its neighbors either an enemy to be feared or a friend to be desired. And the greater opportunities of contracting alliances which a state thus secures as well as the possibilities of turning every change in the political situation to advantage are increasingly noticeable in these wars."[65]

In his discussion of the Napoleonic Wars, one can find several interesting conclusions. On the one hand, he saw that the war gave no direct answer to the issue as to whether a sea power could command the land, or a land power could command the sea, but, he concluded, the issue was settled in a different way. England's naval supremacy allowed her to coerce neutral states to join in the war against Napoleon, and it was they, the formerly neutral land powers, who defeated Napoleon on land. It was French weakness at sea, von Maltzahn argued, which allowed England to play off the whole of the continent against Napoleon.[66]

In another point, von Maltzahn was influenced by the geo-political ideas of Friedrich Ratzel, whose work, at that time, was also becoming very important to political thought in Germany. With some pride, von Maltzahn claimed to be the first naval officer to quote from him. Taking up Ratzel's point about the twofold nature of sea people, marked, firstly, by a high degree of egotism that wanted control over the entire surface of the sea, and secondly, by cosmopolitanism, marked by "the meanest love of greed," and applying this formula to analyse the British way of maritime warfare, von Maltzahn concluded, "We shall understand this peculiarity aright only if we remind ourselves how incomplete a weapon naval supremacy is; for when it touches the enemy's coast line it is unable to complete the victory which the navy has won at sea by a defeat of the enemy on land, and must forge for itself indirect weapons out of the existing trade and business relationships."[67]

As von Maltzahn was writing these lines, he was becoming aware of the contributions of a new figure among naval historians, Julian Corbett. He used Corbett's work directly to correct some details in his own, but, as for many other military and naval writers in Germany, Corbett's broader, almost modern, application of Clausewitz's ideas did not fit with the German understanding of Clausewitz in this period.[68]

Julian Corbett

Unlike the other writers considered here, Corbett was never a uniformed naval officer, but he stands out, not only for his contribution to the academic study of naval history, but also for the fact that he was employed by the Royal Navy. Coming from a very different educational and intellectual background from the naval officers, he brought a dramatically different insight to the study of naval history. Interestingly, his serious contributions to understanding the Anglo-French naval wars coincide with his appointment as a lecturer at the Royal Navy's newly established Naval War Course.

In many ways, this course can be traced indirectly back to Laughton's intellectual stimulus. Certainly, its first course director was Captain W. J. May, who had succeeded Colomb in 1895 in Laughton's position as the lecturer in naval history at Greenwich, and continued those duties up through the time that Admiral Sir John Fisher established the new course at Greenwich.[69] While apparently unaware of the fact that Laughton had influenced Luce, Fisher explicitly modeled the new course on Luce's Naval War College at Newport, focusing his new course at Greenwich, like its American model, on a study of strategy, tactics, naval history, and international law.

Up to the time that May invited Corbett to become the principal lecturer on history and strategy in 1902, Corbett had concentrated on his famous studies of the Elizabethan period. Corbett's education for the law at Cambridge and his earlier career as both a novelist and a journalist were starkly different than the experience of any naval officer. Moreover, Corbett's perceptive and original investigation of the Elizabethan period gave him a far deeper understanding of history and historical studies than any other naval historian had. May's invitation to Corbett was a stroke of serendipitous genius that brought entirely new insight to the field. Like Luce's invitation to Mahan, May's invitation to Corbett not only led him to the Anglo-French Wars, but also defined his principal contribution to naval history for the future. Similar to the task that Mahan took up, Corbett's assignment was to look at the Anglo-French Wars and to present them to officers attending the Naval War Course, in a way that was "so modern that some lessons applicable to present day warfare should be deductible from it."[70]

From this beginning, Corbett produced four important studies, beginning with his study of the Mediterranean,[71] and going on to his two-volume study of the Seven Years' War,[72] and his study of Trafalgar.[73] Undergirding these studies was the constant need to educate modern naval officers in the elements of strategy. This, too, we can trace in its substantive development between 1906 and 1911, through the evolution of Corbett's early classroom definitions for the study of strategy that eventually became the "Green Pamphlet" and, then, his major book, *Some Principles of Maritime Strategy.*[74]

Like the historical work that the similar naval institutions in both the United States and Germany were encouraging, Corbett's work in connection with the Naval War Course on the Anglo-French naval wars also shows the strong tendency to link historical analysis to the very particular lens created by the military thought of Jomini or Clausewitz, who were themselves products of and participants in those very same wars. In all cases, it was the intellectual influence of a naval institution and the need to educate naval officers, paralleled by the desire to create a professional theory for the navy, which created this link.

Historians have tended to oversimplify the influences of these writers and to identify Jomini as the main direct influence on Mahan while Clausewitz is linked directly to Corbett. While there is some truth to this, a close examination shows that, in both cases, the influences were much more subtle. Mahan showed some resemblances in his thinking to Clausewitz[75] and Corbett certainly had some very serious doubts about the applicability of Clausewitz's land-bound thought to maritime situations.[76] Indeed, Corbett stood out among his contemporaries for his interpretation, particularly valuing the idea of strategy being deflected by politics rather than the typical concentration on decisive battle. With this aspect in his mind, Corbett went on to make a remarkable and original contribution to theory with his thinking about the characteristically limited nature of naval warfare.[77]

Similar to the characteristic historical work that was being done at other naval colleges in his time, Corbett also contributed some major works to the history of naval tactics. His two volumes of documents on tactics for the Navy Records Society[78] were a major contribution in historical methodology that created a remarkable contrast to the narrative description of battles that naval officers had produced up to that time. At the same time, his study of the naval tactics at Trafalgar, controversial as it may have been, was thoroughly founded in the approach of a professional historian.[79]

Corbett's work was dramatically different, in terms of both quality and approach, to that of the naval officers who had been the pioneers in the study of naval history and whose professional and practical training dominated their thinking as they approached the thicket of historical research. More than anything else, Corbett's great contribution was to bring the wider and deeper understanding of a professional historian to the Navy, in a way that officer-historians had, up to that point, been unable to do. It was not only his skill as a writer and his capacity for careful archival research, but his appreciation for the process of history and his ability to see the navy within the context of a wide understanding that defined the difference that Corbett brought to the study of naval history and to understanding the Anglo-French Wars.

In the opening lines of *England in the Seven Years' War,* Corbett explained his approach, while at the same time clarifying many conceptual issues that had troubled his predecessors. Admitting that opinions will always differ as to how far the study of history can be of practical value for those who seek insight into the higher principles of war, particularly in a period of great technological change, Corbett argued that there was one aspect of understanding that does not change. For most of his contemporaries, as it had been for Mahan, the subject of naval strategy was a professional naval matter, involving the direction of a fleet. In fact, he argued, conceived in this way, strategy was only a form of operations, best examined on a navigational chart. This was not Corbett's central focus; he stressed the importance of understanding the function of the fleet.

> In the study of the function of a fleet the chart is useless. It cuts off our vision just where the most obscure and most difficult part of the study begins. For it is behind the coastlines that are at work the dominant factors by which the functions of a fleet are determined.[80]

For Corbett, it was in comprehending the broad issue of navies in the context of international affairs where the study of history had its prime and irreplaceable value. Although it was stimulated by teaching at a naval college and expressed with reference to the classic theories of warfare, Corbett expressed an approach to the Anglo-French Wars that was similar to that developing in the academic world, which had already begun to diverge from the early ways that self-taught professional naval officers had viewed and used history.

Admiral Sir Herbert Richmond

In this regard, perhaps one of the most remarkable aspects of Corbett's intellectual legacy was the way in which Admiral Sir Herbert Richmond took up Corbett's challenge and made his own original contribution to understanding the Anglo-French Wars. His two major books on the subject make contrasting reading. Directly inspired by Corbett, Richmond began work on his study of the War of 1739–48,[81] while in command of two successive cruisers used for Torpedo School training practice. Although the volume was largely completed by 1914, the First World War delayed publication of the book until 1920.

While Richmond's professional training led him toward the same practical approach as most naval officers, this book, in particular, advanced beyond the intellectual focus that even Corbett had shown. Richmond's study was the first to look at that particular war as a whole, but, much more importantly, his careful analysis ranged over a much wider view than even Corbett had expressed. Looking deeply at the interaction between leaders, ideas, and events, Richmond produced a carefully nuanced work that had great professional relevance as well as academic value. Above all, this historical investigation was the self-directed intellectual training that provided the greatest benefit in developing his remarkable powers of analysis that he soon applied to the contemporary issues of his own day.

Apart from the role that writing the book had in helping to develop one of the Royal Navy's greatest strategic minds, there is little evidence that the book, itself, had anything close to the effect that earlier officer-writers had on professional naval thought.[82] Insights from it, however, did appear through Richmond's subsequent assignment as president of the Imperial Defence College in 1926–28. Small snippets from it appeared in the *Naval Review* and other professional journals,[83] and these may have been read more widely in the service than the book itself.

Richmond's second major book on the Navy in India in the latter part of the eighteenth century[84] arose from his own period of command on that station. In contrast to the earlier study, it is much more of a study of the lower levels of naval strategy and operations, even approaching a focus on the tactical. With the thought of examining the operations of Hughes against Suffren during the American War, Richmond was able to produce a study, based on archival sources in Europe, South Africa, and Asia, that illuminated the broad naval issues within a single maritime theatre of operations. Unlike the work of other officer-historians, or even of the civilian Corbett, Richmond's historical writings on the Anglo-French Wars had little direct effect on professional naval thought of his time. In a great part this was due to the fact that this period in history lost its immediate relevance to professional thinking in the wake of the First World War. For the creators of professional naval thinking in the late nineteenth and early twentieth centuries, these wars had been the most recent great wars.

All that changed after 1919. At that point, the naval war colleges and staff colleges were focused on recent events and the experience of the Great War and had not yet gone to the point of using the latest academic historical works for earlier periods of history. Richmond's two major historical works were much closer to professional academic history than to what the navy used and, as such, failed to enter the mainstream of professional naval thinking. One of Richmond's naval contemporaries on the other side of the Channel, Raoul Castex, had a parallel experience with some interesting differences in the French Navy.

Raoul Castex and the *École de Guerre Navale*

As other countries, France had also established a college for higher professional studies on naval warfare. First established in 1896, it had a variety of changes in name, but for forty years was known as the *École de Guerre Navale*. Like several of its sister colleges in other countries, the study of history took pride of place as one of the principal subjects of study.[85] Among its most famous instructors were Captain Gabriel Darrieus and Rear-Admiral René Daveluy. While they represented the leaders who created a renaissance of naval thinking in France in the pre–World War One period, their use of the Anglo-French Wars was highly influenced by Mahan's thinking.[86]

Like Richmond, Castex is an example of an officer whose intellectual interests in the subject of strategy developed even before he became a student at the *École de Guerre Navale*. While undergoing practical training at the *École de Pilotage*, Castex wrote his fifth book, but the first book-length historical study devoted to the eighteenth century naval wars: *Les Idées militaires de la marine du XVIIIe siècle: De Ruyter à Suffren*, which was published in 1911 and given a prize by the *Académie Française*. Castex revealed in this book his great admiration for Suffren, and through it, became the champion in France of the historical school of strategy, opposed to the materiel school.

Over the following decades, Castex continued to use examples from history, which dominate his massive five-volume study on strategic theories, particularly in volume two, published in 1930.[87] For Castex, the 1689–1815 period provided a wide array of examples to illustrate his larger theories, which reflect his advocacy for the battle fleet and his emphasis on the wide range of functions that the fleet performs in wartime. In his studies of the Anglo-French naval wars, Castex focused on the French Navy's failure to meet the British challenge, blaming, for example, in Louis XIV's reign, the two ministers, Pontchartrains, father and son. During the Napoleonic Wars, he blames Villeneuve, not Napoleon, for the failure of 1805.

One of the most distinctive aspects of his analysis is the concept of strategic manoeuvre, rather than an emphasis on battle. It is, in particular, this stress on attacks on commerce, blockade, and amphibious operations, rather than fleet battle that shows him as the preeminent exponent of the French school of strategy. Castex continued to use historical examples of the 1689–1815 period to great effect, long after naval writers in other countries had abandoned them. In doing this, however, he made an unusual innovation in his use of history. In providing an example of strategic manoeuvre, Castex referred inventively to Bruix's campaign in the Mediterranean in 1799. Rather than just relate the historical circumstances, Castex takes the outline of those events and describes them as if they involved modern warships in 1930. In his description, Nelson and Duckworth are at Minorca and Palermo as they were in 1799 and they have the same number of ships under their command, but instead of ships-of-the-line, they have 10,000-ton cruisers and they are concerned about minefields, submarines, and modern weapons. To get a sense of his approach, we can read:

> Thanks to Duckworth's aerial reconnaissance, the British know Bruix and Mazzaredo's location and heading, as of 2000 on 1 May, but they are less certain about enemy intentions. Nelson, warned by wireless, has no intention of installing himself at Marittimo with his mere nine ships, as he would have done in 1799. Thinking it prudent to barricade himself in his favorite base, Palermo, he nevertheless sends, for conscience sake, reconnaissance aircraft westward, and they discover on 2 May at 1600 the enemy force north of Bizerte.[88]

The Mid-twentieth Century and Beyond

Castex was the last major contributor to twentieth century professional naval thought who made extensive use of the Anglo-French naval wars as the fundamental material for his analysis. As the decades passed, the 1689–1815 period became more remote in professional thought, obscured by the dominant experience of the two world wars and the numerous events that followed them. In these broad trends, there were two notable exceptions. In the Royal Navy, D. W. Waters began his career as a serving officer with a prize essay on trade defence during the War of the Spanish Succession and he later continued studies on convoy operations during the Anglo-French Wars while assigned to the Admiralty Historical Office, drawing observations from them of value for current professional thinking.[89] Similarly, Captain Wayne Hughes, Jr., of the U.S. Naval Postgraduate School, examined the battle of the Nile as an important modern study of naval tactics.[90]

By the mid-twentieth century, the professional military discussion over nuclear weapons virtually obscured the use of conventional weapons, and, for many people, the traditional roles for naval and maritime forces seemed, for a short moment, irrelevant. Yet, while nuclear weapons dominated professional issues, smaller wars continued to appear, such as those in Malaya, Korea, Vietnam, and the Falklands. Fought with conventional weapons, in the context of nuclear deterrence, they began to give rise to more careful appreciation of past experience.

From very early on in the Cold War, the uses of force for political deterrence in situations short of war had become an issue. As the Cold War progressed, this gave rise to a significant literature and involved a revival of interest in the work of Karl von Clausewitz and the extension of his ideas to the maritime field in the work of Sir Julian Corbett. As a result of this, many began to rediscover older ideas about the fundamental strategic roles of maritime power and many began to show interest in older theoretical studies and in the use of history as a means to explore the dynamics of strategy.

At the close of the twentieth century, the contributions that naval officer-historians had made in the years leading up to the First World War were still very much a part of the intellectual heritage of the Navy's professional thought. In that period, naval officers tried to apply the historical understanding of their day as a means to educate naval officers in the highest aspects of their profession. Working in a period before academic historians began to examine naval history seriously with modern research techniques, the naval officers made a substantial contribution to naval education, by trying to stimulate naval officers to think about their profession through history. The history of this effort is important and fundamental to understanding the intellectual history of navies.

Yet, by the best modern standards of historical understanding, the way in which naval officers searched for "laws" and "principles" in history was fundamentally flawed and misconceived. The naval officer-historians of the past century clearly sought to use history to stimulate discussion on aspects of contemporary professional interest within the navy, but their intention was not to create a new interpretation of history or an historical explanation of the past. Yet succeeding generations have often mistaken their efforts for just that and have either mistakenly tried to sustain and to apply their "principles" to other time periods or, alternatively, have disregarded modern historical work on the 1689–1815 period as something completely misplaced for modern professional naval thought. As a result of this, we are faced with a curious situation at the opening of the 21st century, in which ideas culled from early and unsophisticated methods of historical thinking continue to have great influence, while the results of modern historical research have yet to change professional naval thought effectively.

As naval professionals and naval historians work side by side in the future, both need to understand that these older ideas were early products in growing toward a deeper sophistication and deepening perception of the past. Today, we know that it is not principles and laws that we seek, but rather an appreciation and understanding of human action over time within the process of history. With this in mind, both naval historians and naval professionals can return to the period of the Anglo-French naval wars of 1689–1815 to find a new and more balanced understanding.

NOTES On 7 December 2000, Professor Hattendorf received the Caird Medal of the National Maritime Museum, Greenwich, in the presence of the Duke of York and the other trustees of the Museum. Following the presentation of the Caird Medal, he delivered the Caird Lecture to an invited audience in the Museum's lecture theatre. The lecture was subsequently published in the Museum's on-line *Journal for Maritime Research* (June 2001).

1 D. M. Schurman, *The Education of a Navy: The Development of British Naval Strategic Thought 1867–1914* (Chicago: University of Chicago Press, 1965).

2 Donald M. Schurman, *Julian S. Corbett, 1854–1922: Historian of British Maritime Policy from Drake to Jellicoe* (London: Royal Historical Society, 1981). For Corbett and Richmond, see also James Goldrick and John B. Hattendorf, eds., *Mahan Is Not Enough: The Proceedings of a Conference on the Works of Sir Julian Corbett and Admiral Sir Herbert Richmond* (Newport: Naval War College Press, 1993).

3 Barry D. Hunt, *Sailor-Scholar: Admiral Sir Herbert Richmond, 1871–1946* (Waterloo, Ontario: Wilfrid Laurier University Press, 1982).

4 Hervé Coutau-Bégarie, *Castex: Le Stratège Inconnu* (Paris: Economica, 1985).

5 Jon Tetsuro Sumida, *Inventing Grand Strategy and Teaching Command: The Classic Works of Alfred Thayer Mahan Reconsidered* (Washington, D.C.: The Woodrow Wilson Center Press; Baltimore and London: The Johns Hopkins University Press, 1997).

6 Andrew Lambert, *The Foundations of Naval History: Sir John Knox Laughton and the Historical Profession* (London: Chatham Publishing, 1998). This will be expanded by Lambert's forthcoming selection of Laughton's papers to be published by the Navy Records Society.

7 Hervé Coutau-Bégarie, ed., *L'évolution de la Pensée Navale. I–III:* Dossier, 41, 46, 47 (Paris: Fondation pour les études de Défense Nationale, 1990, 1992, 1993); *L'évolution de la Pensée Navale IV–VI,* Hautes études Strategiques, 2, 3, 5 (Paris: Economica et l'Institut de Stratégie Comparée, 1994, 1995, 1997). Paralleling this series, see also the ten-volume series of key works on naval strategy in the Classics of Sea Power series edited by John B. Hattendorf and Wayne P. Hughes, Jr. (Annapolis: Naval Institute Press, 1988–96), each volume with its own introductory essay by an expert on the topic.

8 J. K. Laughton, "The Scientific Study of Naval History," *Journal of the Royal United Services Institution,* XVIII (1875).

9 Ibid.

10 Ibid., p. 525.

11 Ibid., p. 521.

12 Lambert, *Foundations,* p. 79; Barry M. Gough, "Introduction" to Vice Admiral P. H. Colomb, *Naval Warfare: Its Ruling Principles and Practice Historically Treated.* Classics of Sea Power Series. (Annapolis: Naval Institute Press, 1990), p. xvii.

13 Colomb, *Naval Warfare,* p. 4.

14 Ibid.

15 Ibid., p. 11.

16 Ibid., p. 182.

17 Ibid., p. 184.

18 Ibid., p. 322.

19 Ibid., p. 427.

20 Ibid., pp. 454, 492.

21 For an outline of these influences, see John D. Hayes and John B. Hattendorf, eds., *The Writings of Stephen B. Luce* (Newport: Naval War College Press, 1975) and Hattendorf, *Stephen B. Luce: Intellectual Leader of the New Navy* (Annapolis: Naval Institute Press, forthcoming).

22 Hayes and Hattendorf, *Writings of Stephen B. Luce,* pp. 71, 84, 91, 99, 178; Lambert, *Foundations,* pp. 30–46, 69, 71–72, 121, 126, 140, 231–232.

23 See "History and Technological Change: The Study of History in the U.S. Navy, 1873–1890," in Hattendorf, *Naval History and Maritime Strategy: Collected Essays* (Malabar, Florida: Krieger Publishing, 2000), pp. 1–16.

24 Hayes and Hattendorf, *Writings of Stephen B. Luce,* pp. 27, 54–57, 60, 65.

25 See Jay Luvaas, *The Education of an Army: British Military Thought, 1815–1940* (Chicago: University of Chicago Press, 1965); Brian Bond, *The Victorian Army and the Staff College, 1854–1914* (London: Eyre Methuen, 1972), and Brian Holden Reid, *War Studies at the Staff College, 1890–1930.* Occasional Paper, no. 1 (London: HMSO for the Strategic and Combat Studies Institute, 1992).

26 James Soley, *Report on Foreign Systems of Naval Education* (Washington: Government Printing Office, 1880).

27 Ibid., pp. 190–193; Rolf Hobson, *The German School of Naval Thought and the Origins of the Tirpitz Plan 1875–1900.* Forsvarsstudier 2/1996 (Oslo: Institutt for Forsvarsstudier 1996), pp. 16–22. See also "Auf der Marine-Akademie in Kiel," Errinerungen des Viceadmirals a. D. William Michaelis (1871–1948), Bundisarchiv-Militärarchiv, Nachlaß Michaelis NL 164. I am grateful to Dr. Werner Rahn for supplying me a transcript of this document.

28 Hattendorf et al., *Sailors and Scholars: The Centennial History of the U.S. Naval War College* (Newport: Naval War College Press, 1984), pp. 17–18.

29 Luce, "An Address . . . 1903," reprinted in Hayes and Hattendorf, *Writings of Stephen B. Luce,* pp. 39–40.

30 Luce, "On the Study of Naval Warfare as a Science," reprinted in Hayes and Hattendorf, *Writings of Stephen B. Luce,* p. 68.

31 Ibid.

32 Mahan to Samuel A. Ashe, 2 February 1886 in Robert Seager II and Doris D. Maguire, eds., *Letters and Papers of Alfred Thayer Mahan.* Naval Letters Series (Annapolis: Naval Institute Press, 1975), vol. 1, pp. 624–625.

33 Ibid.

34 A. T. Mahan, *The Influence of Sea Power upon History, 1660–1783* (Boston, 1890).

35 A. T. Mahan, *The Life of Nelson: The Embodiment of the Sea Power of Great Britain* (Boston, 1897; revised and corrected edition, 1899).

36 A. T. Mahan, *Sea Power in Its Relations to the War of 1812* (Boston, 1905).

37 A. T. Mahan, "Major Operations of the Royal Navy, 1762–1783," in William Laird Clowes, *A History of the Royal Navy from the Earliest Time to the Present* (London, 1898), vol. 3, ch. 31, pp. 353–564; later revised and published separately under Mahan's name as *The Major Operations of the Navies in the War of American Independence* (Boston, 1913).

38 A. T. Mahan, *Types of Naval Officers Drawn from the History of the British Navy with some account of the conditions of naval warfare at the beginning of the eighteenth century, and of its subsequent development during the sail period* (Boston, 1901).

39 A. T. Mahan, *Naval Strategy Compared and Contrasted with the Principles and Practice of Military Operations on Land. Lectures delivered at the U.S. Naval War College, Newport, R.I., between the Years 1887 and 1911* (Boston, 1911).

40 Hattendorf, *Register of the Papers of Alfred Thayer Mahan.* Manuscript Register series, no. 15 (Newport: Naval Historical Collection, Naval War College, 1987). A register of the Mahan Papers at the Library of Congress, Washington, D.C., is still wanting.

41 Robert Seager II and Doris D. Maguire, eds., *Letters and Papers of Alfred Thayer Mahan.* Naval Letters Series (Annapolis: Naval Institute Press, 1975). Three volumes.

42 John B. Hattendorf and Lynn C. Hattendorf, compilers, *A Bibliography of the Works of Alfred Thayer Mahan.* Naval War College Monograph series, no. 7 (Newport: Naval War College Press, 1986).

43 Robert Seager II, *Alfred Thayer Mahan: The Man and His Letters* (Annapolis: Naval Institute Press, 1971); updated in Robert Seager II, "Alfred Thayer Mahan" in James C. Bradford, ed., *Admirals of the New Steel Navy: Makers of the American Naval Tradition 1880–1930* (Annapolis: Naval Institute Press, 1990), pp. 24–72.

44 Sumida, *Inventing Grand Strategty.*

45 Ibid., pp. 100–107.

46 Undated and unattributed summary of a *Manchester Guardian* review in a newspaper clipping pasted into a copy of A. T. Mahan, *The Interest of America in Sea Power, Present and Future* (Boston, 1898). Author's collection.

47 Sumida, *Inventing Grand Strategy,* pp. 42–56, 100–102.

48 Luce to Mahan, 6 July 1906, quoted in Hayes and Hattendorf, *Writings of Stephen B. Luce,* pp. 19–20.

49 Sumida, *Inventing Grand Strategy,* pp. 42–56, 100–102.

50 Extract from *Naval Strategy* in John B. Hattendorf, ed., *Mahan on Naval Strategy.* Classics of Sea Power Series (Annapolis: Naval Institute Press, 1991), p. 278.

51 Sumida, *Inventing Grand Strategy,* p. 103.

52 A. T. Mahan, *The Influence of Sea Power Upon the French Revolution and Empire* (Boston, 1892), vol. 1, p. vi.

53 Ibid., p. v.

54 David C. Evans and Mark R. Peattie, *Kaigun: Strategy, Tactics and Technology in the Imperial Japanese Navy, 1887–1941* (Annapolis: Naval Institute Press, 1997), pp. 135–141.

55 "Alfred Stenzel," in Hans Hildebrand and Ernest Henriot, eds., *Deutschlands Admirale 1849–1945* (Osnabrück: Biblio Verlag, 1990), vol. 3, pp. 381–382. Hermann Kirchoff, "Alfred Stenzel's leben und Werk," in Alfred Stenzel, *Kriegführung zur See: Lehre vom Seekriege* (Hannover & Leipzig, 1913), pp. xiii–xxxi.

56 Stenzel, *Kriegführung zur See.* See also "Vortrag des Viceadmirals a.D. Eberhard v. Mantey am 30. Januar 1935," Personlicher Nachlaß Kapitän zur See a.D. Helmut v. Mantey im Besitz von Fregattenkapitän a.D Axel v. Mantey. I am grateful to Dr. Werner Rahn for providing me with a transcript.

57 Hobson, *The German School,* p. 19.

58 Alfred Stenzel, *Seekriegsgeschichte in Ihren wichtigsten Abschnitten mit Berüchsigtung der Seetaktik. Dritter Teil von 1600–1720* (Hannover and Leipzig, 1910), pp. 337–437; *Vierter Teil von 1720–1850* (Hannover and Leipzig, 1911), pp. 20–53, 143–406.

59 Rudolph Rittmeyer, *Seekriege und Seekriegswesen in Ihrer weltgeschichtlichen Entwicklung* (Berlin, 1907–1911).

60 Hermann Kirchhoff, *Seemacht in der Ostsee* (Kiel, 1907–1908).

61 Hildebrand and Henriot, *Deutschlands Admirale,* vol. 2, pp. 425–426.

62 Carl-Axel Gemzell, *Organization, Conflict, and Innovation: A Study of German Naval Strategic Planning, 1888–1940.* Lund Studies in International History, 4 (Lund: Esselte Studium, 1973), pp. 56–57, 78, 95, 114, 341–342; Ivo Nikolai Lambi, *The Navy and German Power Politics, 1862–1914* (Boston: Allen and Unwin, 1984), pp. 165–166; Wolfgang Petter et al., "Deutsche Marinegeschichte der Neuzeit," Part VIII of Militärgeschichtliches Forschungsamt, *Handbuch zur Deutsche Militärgeschichte.* Band 4 (München, 1979), pp. 227–229.

63 *Der Kampf gegen die Seeherrschaft. Vortrag gehalten am 8. Januar 1898 in der Aula der Marine-Akademie von Kapitän zur See Freiherr von Maltzahn* (Kiel: Druck von C. Schaidt, 1898), pp. 14ff.

64 Curt Freiherr von Maltzahn, *Der Seekrieg. Seine geschichtliche Entwicklung von Zeitalter der Entdeckung bis zur Gegenwart* (Leipzig, 1906); *Naval Warfare: Its Historical Development from the Age of the Great Geographical Discoveries to the Present Time.* Translated from the German by John Combe Miller (London: Longmans Green, and Co., 1908).

65 Von Maltzahn, *Naval Warfare,* p. 51.

66 Ibid., p. 72.

67 Ibid., pp. 82–83.

68 See von Maltzahn's review of Corbett "Seestrategie in ihren Beziehungen zur Landestrategie nach englisch-amerikanischem Urteil," *Marine Rundschau,* 23 (1912), pp. 869ff. Also see Uwe Dirks, "Julian S. Corbett und die britische Seekriegsführung 1914–18," *Militärgeschichtliche Mitteilungen* 1/85 (1985), pp. 35–50; Keith W. Bird, *German Naval History: A Guide to the Literature* (New York and London: Garland, 1985), p. 287; Hobson, *The German School,* pp. 19–20. For a detailed discussion of the changing interpretations of Clausewitz, see Azar Gat, *The Origins of Military Thought: From the Enlightenment to Clausewitz* (Oxford, 1989) and his *The Development of Military Thought: The Nineteenth Century* (Oxford, 1992), with Rolf Hobson, *Fra kabinettskrigen til den totale krigen. Clausewitz-tolkninger fra Moltke til Aron.* Forsvarsstudier 6/1994 (Oslo: Institutt for Forsvarsstudier, 1994).

69 Lambert, *Foundations,* pp. 157, 198–200, 220.

70 May to Corbett, 14 VIII. 1902, quoted in Schurman, *Julian S. Corbett,* p. 33.

71 Julian S. Corbett, *England in the Mediterranean: A Study in the Rise and Influence of British Power within the Straits, 1603–1714* (London, 1904).

72 Julian S. Corbett, *England in the Seven Years' War: A Study in Combined Strategy* (London, 1907).

73 Julian S. Corbett, *The Campaign of Trafalgar* (London, 1910).

74 See the definitive edition of Corbett's 1911 book, *Some Principles of Maritime Strategy with an Introduction and Notes by Eric J. Grove.* Classics of Sea Power series (Annapolis: Naval Institute Press, 1988), containing as the appendix Corbett's first 1906 version, "War Course: Strategical Terms and Definitions used in Lectures on Naval History," pp. 307–325, and the revised 1909 Green Pamphlet: "War Course: Notes on Strategy," pp. 326–345.

75 Sumida, *Inventing Grand Strategy,* pp. 110–114.

76 See "Introduction," to Julian S. Corbett, *Maritime Operations in the Russo-Japanese War, 1904–1905, With an Introduction by John B. Hattendorf and Donald M. Schurman* (Newport: Naval War College Press and Annapolis: Naval Institute Press, 1994).

77 For both Mahan and Corbett's use of Clausewitz, see Christopher Bassford, *Clausewitz in English: The Reception of Clausewitz in Britain and America, 1815–1945* (Oxford and New York, 1994), pp. 94–103.

78 Julian S. Corbett, *Fighting Instructions, 1530–1816, with elucidations from contemporary authorities.* Navy Records Society, vol. 29 (London, 1905); *Signals and Instructions, 1776–1794.* Navy Records Society, vol. 35 (London, 1908).

79 Schurman, *Julian S. Corbett,* pp. 113–130.

80 Corbett, *Seven Years' War,* vol. 1, p. 2.

81 Herbert W. Richmond, *The Navy in the War of 1739–48* (Cambridge, 1920); republished with a preface by Andrew Lambert (London, 1993).

82 Hunt, *Sailor-Scholar,* pp. 26–27.

83 See Hattendorf, "Bibliography of the Works of Admiral Sir Herbert Richmond," and James Goldrick, "Author List for the Naval Review, 1913–1930," in Goldrick and Hattendorf, eds., *Mahan Is Not Enough,* pp. 311–339, 341–405.

84 Herbert W. Richmond, *The Navy in India, 1763–1783* (London, 1931); reprinted with an introduction by Andrew Lambert (London, 1993); Hunt, *Sailor-Scholar,* pp. 136–137.

85 Contre-Amiral Rémi Monaque, *L'école de Guerre Navale* (Paris: Service Historique de la Marine, 1995), "Histoire des principales disciplines: stratégie et tactique navales," pp. 151–170, and "l'histoire," pp. 170–181.

86 Henri Darrieus and Bernard Estival, "Darrieus et la Renaissance d'une Pensée maritime en France avant la première guerre Mondiale," in Coutau-Bégarie, ed., *L'évolution de la Pensée Navale I,* pp. 89–117; Amiral Daveluy, *Réminiscences* (Paris, 1991), vol. 1, pp. 229–254.

87 Coutau-Bégarie, *Castex,* ch. 7.

88 Raoul Castex, *Strategic Theories. Selections translated and edited, with an introduction by Eugenia Kiesling.* Classics of Sea Power series (Annapolis, 1993), pp. 199–200.

89 Eric J. Grove, ed., Introduction, *The Defeat of the Enemy Attack on Shipping, 1939–1945.* Publications of the Navy Records Society, vol. 137 (Aldershot, 1997), pp. xii–xiii.

90 Wayne P. Hughes, Jr., *Fleet Tactics: Theory and Practice* (Annapolis: Naval Institute Press, 1986), pp. 16–25, 172.

VIII *Nelson's Legacy*
A Hero among the World's Navies

The legacy of Horatio Nelson is something more than just that of a fleet commander who had won a famous victory and more than just that of a distinctively British naval hero. His legacy is different from that of a Marlborough or a Wellington, who are also seen as great commanders. Beyond that, Nelson is seen as the embodiment of key professional virtues for naval leaders that provides an enduring model. Within a century after his death, Nelson had become a hero among the world's navies and an icon of naval professionalism around the globe. The applications of Nelson's name in professional naval terms are remarkable and extend to the present day and to modern navies that no longer bear any physical resemblance to those of the age of fighting sail.

If one excludes from examination here the distinctive views that may have developed in Nelson's own victorious Royal Navy and those navies that directly evolved from its traditions in British colonies and the Commonwealth and then if one adds to that number those that Nelson defeated, France, Spain, and Denmark, there are still nearly 150 of the world's navies to consider. In that wide field, one may turn to the navies of Germany, Japan, China, the Soviet Union, Latin America, and the United States as representative cases.

Turning to the United States, for example, the currently serving civilian head of the United States Navy, the Secretary of the Navy, wears as his "trademark" necktie one that features Nelson's famous flag hoist, "England expects every man will do his duty."[1] The same words are on a cast bronze plaque at the outside corridor entrance to his Pentagon office and, just inside the door, there is a framed print of Montague Dawson's painting "The Battle of Trafalgar." Until recently, another Trafalgar scene dominated the Secretary of the Navy's official dining room in the Pentagon: an anonymous Dutch painting of the French ship *Achille* exploding at the end of the battle of Trafalgar. Of course, these interconnected references in the Secretary's office to Trafalgar and "England expects" are a humorous play on words, as this Secretary of the Navy's surname is England, the Honorable Gordon R. England.[2] Yet, the application is appropriate and it is instantly recognizable to everyone who serves in the U.S. Navy as something that relates directly to the core values that the U.S. Navy emphasizes: "Honor, Courage, and Commitment."[3] These are the very values that Nelson's example as a naval warrior embodies and has come to represent as an ideal.

There are several phases in the growth of Nelson's image in navies around the world. In the history of 19th-century British culture, Nelson's image was part of a wider development of heroes which began in three stages over the century from the early development of a distinctive Victorian idea of a Christian hero, its heyday at mid-century, and then its distillation in the years leading up to World War One.[4] While the image of Nelson takes its place in Britain in these years, it was somewhat different in the context of the professional naval world, where he was, first, a professional figure noticed in his own time; secondly, a figure within recent professional memory; and thirdly, a more distant figure in history and an historical example for emulation.

Nelson as a Contemporary Naval Figure

In the broader discussion of Nelson's image in the naval profession around the world, the United States Navy provides an interesting example, not only because of its present role as a superpower navy, but also because the U.S. Navy dates only from Nelson's time and mention of Nelson's name and activities can occasionally be found in the official U.S. Navy documents of that time as well as in the centuries that have followed as Nelson gradually became a more remote professional icon.

The U.S. Navy officially recognizes 13 October 1775 as its founding date, yet following the end of the War for American Independence in the 1780s, the newly established American republic did away with its first naval force, called the Continental Navy. A decade later in 1794, Congress authorized the building of the first ships for a United States Navy, first within the War Department and from 1798 under the newly established Navy Department. While the U.S. Navy was an infant service as part of the War Department, American diplomats in Spain reported that Nelson had protected American merchant ships from the French at Malaga in March 1797.[5]

The first U.S. Navy ship went to sea in May 1798, USS *Ganges,* and she was soon followed by others. One of them was commanded by Captain James Sever, whom many had criticized for having trouble with his crew and for not chasing a privateer that had been more heavily armed than his own ship. Defending Sever's conduct to President John Adams in 1799, the first Secretary of the Navy, Benjamin Stoddert, used Nelson's reputation as an example and protested to the President that under the same circumstances Admiral Nelson, "if his understanding is equal to his bravery, would have pursued the very course that Sever did."[6]

As the ships of the United States Navy began to make overseas deployments, they were concerned first with the Quasi-War with France in 1798–1801 and nearly simultaneously, between 1800 and 1807, with protecting American trade from the depredations of the Barbary States on the North African coast. In the context of both conflicts, the operations of the Royal Navy had an indirect influence on what the small American navy was doing to protect its neutral trade. Nelson's victory at Aboukir Bay had a long-term positive influence on American interests in the Mediterranean region. Reflecting the continuing image the victory left on the North African states, the American Consul in Algiers, Tobias Lear, wrote in February 1804, "The heroic character of Lord Nelson, who commanded the fleet, forbids the idea of fear on the part of the British."[7]

One of the famous and dramatic incidents in the U.S. Navy's wars with the Barbary powers involved the U.S. frigate *Philadelphia,* which had run aground on an uncharted reef in Tripoli harbor. All the efforts failed to refloat her under gunfire from shore batteries and her officers and men surrendered and were imprisoned as hostages. *Philadelphia's*

Tripolitan captors quickly took charge of the ship and turned her guns outward to defend against the other American ships. The commander of the American squadron in the Mediterranean, Captain Edward Preble, organized a volunteer party of officers and men under Lieutenant Stephen Decatur in the ketch *Intrepid,* who boarded the captured ship on 16 February 1804 and burned her at anchor. It is often repeated in modern American naval histories that Nelson is said to have called this "the most bold and daring act of the age."[8] An entirely undocumented quotation, this is nevertheless an example of the way in which another Navy used and continues to use Nelson's approbation, real or imagined, as a means of giving some emphasis to its own naval heritage.

Nelson as a Figure within Living Memory

Within a decade after Trafalgar, Britain and the United States went to war in a conflict that occurred simultaneously with the final stages of the Napoleonic Wars in 1812–15. Even though the Royal Navy was the enemy in the War of 1812, American readers were widely interested in Robert Southey's recently published *Life of Nelson.* Several unauthorized editions of the book were printed in the United States in 1813–14[9] and these were probably the source for a growing wide-spread familiarity in America with events in Nelson's life, although these would certainly have been an event of recent memory.

Among the many events that took place during that war, Nelson's influence seems to have been clear at the battle of Lake Erie on 10 September 1813, when the American commander, the 28-year-old Captain Oliver Hazard Perry, USN, faced his 27-year-old opponent, Acting Commander Robert Heriot Barclay of the Royal Navy, who had been commended for his action at Trafalgar as a lieutenant in HMS *Swiftsure.* Perry's biographer, Alexander Mackenzie, wrote in 1843 that on the night before the battle, Perry's "last emphatic injunction with which he dismissed them was, that they could not, in the case of difficulty, advise them better than in the words of Lord Nelson, 'if you lay your enemy close alongside, you cannot be out of your place!'"[10]

A year later, one can find another prominent instance of Nelson's influence at the battle of Plattsburg Bay on Lake Champlain on 11 September 1814. There, Captain Thomas Macdonough's small squadron of U.S. naval vessels faced the squadron under Captain George Downie, R.N. Preparing for the battle that played a key role in General Provost's decision to withdraw British forces from the area, Macdonough hoisted a signal on board his anchored flagship, the 24-gun corvette *Saratoga:* "Impressed seamen call on every man to do his duty."[11] Macdonough's alteration to Nelson's signal carried with it not only a reflection of current American foreign policy in denouncing British impressment of American sailors, but it also transmitted a sense of Macdonough's caring support and concern for the ordinary seaman.

In preparing to fight British forces on Lake Champlain, Macdonough decided to fight with his squadron in a defensive formation at anchor. Clearly, Macdonough was aware of Nelson's successful tactics against an anchored enemy at the Nile in 1798 and at Copenhagen in 1801. Macdonough used descriptions of those battles to guide his defensive planning on Lake Champlain, so as to avoid the French and Danish weaknesses in those engagements and to better a British officer, whom Macdonough expected would use Nelsonian tactics.[12] Macdonough carefully guarded against having his anchored squadron doubled, as Nelson had doubled Bruey's anchored ships in Aboukir Bay. In an innovative approach, the American commander ensured that his ships could use capstans and kedge anchors with carefully submerged spring lines to their anchor cables to turn themselves and to maintain broadside fire against the attacking British.

By 1830, Southey's *Life of Nelson* was so well known that the author's name became part of the title in American editions to distinguish it from other Nelson biographical works.[13] Even before this appeared, a friend wrote to Southey to report that he had heard that the American government had produced an edition of the book for everyone in the U.S. Navy. Southey was correct to reply to his correspondent that "it is not likely that the American Government, which is as parsimonious as Mr. Hume would wish ours to be, should incur the expense."[14] No trace of such an official action has yet been found, but there is a widespread assumption that American naval officers in this era had read the book at one point or another in their early careers.

By the end of the 1850s, one begins to find the first suggestions that Southey's descriptions lacked technical accuracy. At this point, American naval professionals were beginning to wonder exactly how Nelson had won his great victories and, in this regard, much focus turned on the seamanship involved in the battle of the Nile. A one-time midshipman in the U.S. Navy and the author of the first history of the United States Navy, James Fenimore Cooper, dismissed Southey's account of the Nile. "The life of Nelson by Southey, in all that relates to this feature of the day is pure fiction, as, indeed, are other parts of the work of scarcely less importance."[15] This was, perhaps, an ironic comment coming from the creator of the American sea novel.[16] In fact, it was a point he made in a preface to his 1842 book, *The Admirals*, an early naval novel that focused, as the author described it, on the movement of fleets. Cooper's leading characters in the novel, Sir Gervaise Oates and Sir Richard Bluewater, were respectively modeled on Collingwood and Nelson and in writing it Cooper had made extensive use of the published Collingwood papers.[17] As the most widely known commentator on American naval events of his own day, Cooper went on to note, "Had Nelson led in upon an American fleet as he did upon the French at the Nile, he would have seen reason to repent the boldness of his experiment."[18]

One of the first officers in the U.S. Navy to cast a professional eye on this issue was James H. Ward. At the time that the United States Navy entered the Civil War in 1861, Commander Ward had the reputation of being the most scholarly officer in its service. As a lieutenant in 1845, he had become the first Commandant of Midshipmen at the newly established Naval Academy and one of the very first American line officers to teach a professional naval subject in the classroom. Some years later, while serving at sea on the West African coast, as he explained, "to beguile leisure and relieve the tedium of service in that horrid region," Ward wrote *A Manual of Naval Tactics* for the Academy's use that was published in 1859.[19] Two years later, he was the first combat casualty among U.S. naval officers during the Civil War, but his *Manual* continued to influence American professional thinking for a decade to come.[20]

Designing it to be a digest of the major theoretical works on naval tactics, Ward combined this work with his own insights gained from practical experience, an analysis of recent battles as well as his own understanding of how he imagined future battles might be fought. In this, an important appendix to the *Manual* was a section taken directly from Sir Howard Douglas's 1858 book *On Naval Warfare with Steam*.[21] Ward was careful to point out that he had examined some details of the historical accounts on Nelson for his volume that differed from Douglas's descriptions. Ward wrote,

> With great deference it is claimed that when the *Manual* varies from this [Douglas's] text, either as regards the distance apart of the French ships at the battle of the Nile, the length of the French line, the number of columns in which Nelson's ships approached, the mode of anchoring the ships, etc., reliable authorities or seamanship will be found to sustain the *Manual*.[22]

In the context of a broader understanding of naval tactics, Ward attempted a critical analysis of tactical usage, noting in regard to Trafalgar that "with a different sort of adversary, Nelson's tactics might have been more circumspect."[23] He concluded that the superior readiness of the British fleet was the critical factor that made Nelson's tactics successful and that they might not have been successful with a different enemy.

Between 1861 and 1865, the United States was plunged into civil war with the secession of its Southern States and the establishment of the short-lived Confederate States of America. In these years, one can find Nelson's name invoked from time to time in professional correspondence by American officers.

As an example of this in September 1861, Commander S. Phillips Lee, commanding the sailing sloop USS *Vandalia* on close blockade duty off Charleston, South Carolina, had mistaken the sleek steamer HMS *Steady* for a blockade runner and had fired a gun, the shot of which passed half a mile off *Steady*'s quarter. Promptly apologizing for the misidentification, Lee invoked British naval history when he wrote to her commanding officer to apologize for his error,

> A smart steamer moving under false colors (which we know is done, and which your great naval authorities, Admirals Nelson and Collingwood, admitted an enemy has a right to use) bent on running the blockade, can slip by a sailing vessel, lying to without steam and near the bar.[24]

Similarly three years later, Lee, now an acting rear admiral, invoked Nelson's name when he sought permission from Assistant Secretary Gustavus Vasa Fox for one of Lieutenant William Cushing's daring exploits. Cushing "thinks that the fort on Bald Hill [North Carolina] may be surprised by the blockaders," Lee wrote.

> Will you in any manner, even by a "Go it Ned" (after the fashion of the Attorney and Lord Codrington), justify the attempt? The idea is taking and the thing is possible, though Nelson failed in such an effort. But I like enterprises and have always encouraged them.[25]

Just a month before, Commander George Henry Preble, lamenting the escape of the Confederate raider CSS *Florida,* wrote in an official dispatch, "Nelson said the want of frigates in his squadron would be found impressed on his heart. I am sure the want of steam will be found engraven on mine."[26]

On the Confederate side, Secretary of the Navy Stephen R. Mallory used the measure of Nelson and a range of other British commanders to condemn the performance of the U.S. Navy under Rear Admiral S. F. DuPont in its failed attempt to take Charleston in 1863. Mallory wrote in disparagement, "If DuPont had but possessed a spark of that flame which animated Exmouth at Algiers, Nelson at Copenhagen, or Hope at the Pei-Ho, he might still have failed, but he could not have been disgraced."[27]

In a less direct way, others showed that Nelson's story had made a deep impression on their own professional conduct. Among them, Lieutenant Francis A. Roe confided in his private diary during Flag Officer David Farragut's opposed passage past the Confederate forts at the mouth of the Mississippi River in 1862. At a critical point in the operation and on the brink of battle, Roe wrote,

I look for a bloody conflict. These may be the last lines I shall ever write. But I have an un-flinching trust in God that we shall plant the Union flag upon the enemy's forts by noon to-morrow. I trust in Almighty God for the results. If I fall, I leave my darlings to the care of my country.[28]

The Civil War was a conflict that brought with it many professional innovations and developments for the U.S. Navy. One of them was the creation of the rank of admiral, a title never before used in the American service, but brought about by the practical need to divide the fleet into several operating squadrons. Initially given the title "Flag Officer," David Glasgow Farragut was the first of nine officers who were eventually commissioned as rear admirals during the war. Soon, Congress created for Farragut the rank of vice admiral in 1864, and, finally in July 1866, admiral. With his new rank, Americans quickly compared and contrasted Farragut to Nelson. At the end of the war in 1865, on the day that Farragut returned his flagship USS *Hartford* to her homeport and hauled down his flag, Assistant Secretary of the Navy Fox wrote to the hero of Mobile Bay and New Orleans, "It is a source of very great happiness to me that you have come back with the laurels of Nelson without leaving any limbs or eyes."[29] The exiled French Prince de Joinville, an erstwhile French naval officer who had come to America to observe the Civil War, wrote to Farragut, "Since the days of Nelson I don't know of any more brilliant actions, and the skill and bravery displayed is, if possible heightened by the simplicity and modesty shown by yourself and your gallant brothers in arms."[30]

A younger American officer, Winfield Scott Schley, who would become one of the leading American admirals in the Spanish-American War of 1898, had served as a lieutenant under Farragut in the Civil War and reflected in his memoirs that Nelson and Farragut were much alike. He compared them favorably in their restless energy of purpose, bravery, and self-poise. Yet, in the American's opinion, "Farragut's private life and high ideals . . . gave him preeminence over his great English compeer."[31]

From the end of the American Civil War, sixty years after Trafalgar, Nelson's image as a figure within living memory had faded. In the United States Navy, at least, mention of his name no longer carried the currency that allowed it to remain widely used in the context of general conversation, personal letters, or official correspondence. Of course, among the well-read and those who were aware of naval history, his name was never forgotten, but there seems to be a clear change by the late 1860s in the United States, coinciding with both the passing of the generations that knew of him in terms of contemporary memory and the arrival of modern naval technology and the age of naval warfare under steam.

Nelson as an Historical Naval Figure in the 19th Century

The origins of the modern study of naval history as an academic and professional naval subject may be traced to the teaching of Professor Montagu Burrows at Oxford[32] and to the work of Professor Sir John Knox Laughton at King's College London.[33] For the world's navies, Laughton's 1874 lecture, published in the *Journal of the Royal United Services Institution* as "The Scientific Study of Naval History,"[34] had direct repercussions, not only through the subsequent historical work in Britain of Vice Admiral Sir Philip Colomb, Sir Julian Corbett, and Admiral Sir Herbert Richmond, but also in foreign countries. Laughton pointed out the continuing relevance of Nelson when he commented:

It was indeed astounding; and even now, after the lapse of three-quarters of a century, to continental nations, in whose eyes an army which numbers by mere thousands is as a thing of naught, the name of Nelson is almost a synonym for England's greatness. Aboukir and Trafalgar the true epitome of England's glory.[35]

Turning to draw the attention of the modern serving naval officer, Laughton went on to say, "History, properly studied, teaches the principles on which battles have been won, or not won—have been lost or not lost."[36]

Following Laughton's 1874 initiative in Britain, naval historical studies begin to also develop for the professional use of navies, first in Germany and then in the United States. For professionals looking toward naval history in both countries, as in Britain, the Nelson era was the period of the last great worldwide, maritime war. More recent, smaller wars in Europe and in America suggested some lines of new naval technological and tactical development, but these examples had not reached the proportions that would allow their examples to answer completely all the broad issues about major wars at sea in terms of naval strategy and leadership.

In the Imperial German Navy, Kapitän zur See Alfred Stenzel began his work in 1875 as a teacher at the Marine-Akademie at Kiel—that is the higher educational institution that provided, on a voluntary basis, a three-year course of study for middle grade officers, not the Marine-Schule for cadets at the beginning of their careers. Assigned at first on a part-time basis to the Akademie from 1875 until 1881 as teacher in naval history and tactics, Stenzel later returned again to the Marine-Akademie on a full-time basis in 1894–96 to teach naval history.[37] In these years, naval history was one of the professional areas that German naval officer students could choose for one of their three major areas of concentration for their advanced studies.[38] Among those who made this choice and were taught by Stenzel, three were officers who later made their names in the early 20th century as naval historians: Vize-Admiral Curt Freiherr von Maltzahn, Kontre-Admiral Rudolph Rittmeyer, and Vize-Admiral Hermann Kirchhoff.

At the present stage of scholarship, it is difficult to assess how Stenzel's historical thinking grew and developed. His first published work was an analysis of British fleet maneuvers in 1888, which shows wide reading in English-language journals and leads one to speculate whether or not he may have read Laughton's writings as well as the works of other British and American naval historians. A further problem lies in the fact that Stenzel died in 1906, before his major work appeared posthumously in print in 1913. Although he is reported to have dealt with Nelson in his early lectures, it is difficult to ascertain with certainty what he said at the earliest stages of his lecturing and which of his thoughts he may have developed later on the basis of other influences. Nevertheless, one can get a sense of what he inculcated in his students from his conclusion:

> As the last and highest token of Nelson's esteem to consider is that, in modern times one understands his importance as entirely exceptional, [and] one must nurture the Nelsonian Spirit, and cultivate his ideas in order to achieve that greatness.[39]

In the United States Navy, the key person who directly transmitted Laughton's ideas about naval history was Rear Admiral Stephen B. Luce and it was he who first tried to institutionalize them in the U.S. Naval War College, when it was established in 1884. In creating this College to serve as the U.S. Navy's highest level of professional military education and "a place of original research on all questions relating to war and to the statesmanship connected with war, or the prevention of war,"[40] Luce placed naval history as one the principal means for studying strategy, along with international law, war gaming of future operations, and military theory.

At the opening address of the first session of the College in 1885, Luce laid out his concept for "The Study of Naval Warfare as a Science." In his concluding remarks, Luce said, "Let us confidently look for the mastermind, who will lay the foundations of that science and do for it what Jomini had done for the military sciences." Fourteen years later, Luce handwrote as a post script on a printed copy of his earlier remarks: "He appeared in the person of Alfred Thayer Mahan, U.S.N."[41]

Luce laid out for Mahan what he was to do with his historical studies and suggested to him the kinds of principles that needed to be illustrated. In doing so, Luce mentioned, among other examples, the achievements of Nelson. In particular, he stressed Nelson's use of superiority of force at the Nile and at Trafalgar[42] and the success that came through "the continuous celerity of their movements, to their great energy governed by an intelligent directive force."[43]

In another lecture in 1885 at the Naval War College, "On the Study of Naval History (Grand Tactics)," Luce contrasted Howe and Nelson, whom he considered to be the great exemplars of two different branches of tactics, Howe representing "minor, elementary or evolutionary tactics" and Nelson representing "Fighting or Grand Tactics or the Tactics of Battle."[44] Nelson, he said was also a great naval strategist, but this, Luce pointed out, is a distinct professional branch from the grand tactics of fleet fighting. The point that Luce took from his general study of British naval tactics was that Nelson's victories demonstrated to modern officers of the 1880s that success was not to be found in the old tactical concept of close action, ship to ship. This, Luce said, was "a principle directly opposite to what Nelson and his school taught. His teaching and the teachings of all great captains, both on shore and afloat, is to put two against one."[45]

Here, Luce reflected the practical application that he believed could derive from a study of naval history and this was the charge he gave to Captain Mahan, when he directed him to undertake for the Naval War College a series of lectures on naval history and tactics. Mahan, himself, was initially very skeptical of what Luce wanted to achieve from historical study. As he later admitted, "I shared the prepossession, common at that time, that the naval history of the past was wholly past; of no use at all to the present."[46] He recalled escorting a journalist through the College building at one point in 1886, a man "of magisterial condescension which the environment of the Fourth Estate nourishes in its fortunate members," who noticed a plan of Trafalgar hanging on the wall. "'Ah,' he said, with superb up-to-date pity, 'you are still talking about Trafalgar;' and I could see that Trafalgar and I were henceforth on the top shelf of fossils in the collections of his memory."[47]

Nevertheless, despite such initial reactions, Mahan went on to produce the historical study that the admiral had ordered. In the process of writing the first set of lectures delivered in the years 1886 through 1888, Mahan discovered the wisdom behind Luce's directive and went on to become Luce's immediate successor as President of the Naval War College as well as the most successful and most widely-read early promoter of the historical approach to understanding naval strategy. After publishing his first set of lectures in 1890 under the title *The Influence of Sea Power Upon History, 1660–1783,*[48]

Mahan returned to the Naval War College for his second period as College President, in 1892–93.

Even before he had completed his first *Influence* book, Mahan planned a sequel and a second series of lectures at the Naval War College to continue the theme. This volume appeared under the title *The Influence of Sea Power Upon the French Revolution and Empire, 1793–1812*,[49] a volume devoted to the Nelson era. In the preface to the new two-volume work, Mahan gave specific credit to the Naval War College as a place "instituted to promote such studies."[50] At the same time, he expressed his thanks to Admiral Luce "for guiding him to a path that he would not himself have found."[51] These references proved invaluable to the institution and they were largely responsible for saving it in the eyes of Secretary of the Navy Hilary Herbert, who had been bent on abolishing the College. On leaving an inspection visit to the College, Secretary Herbert wrote, "This book alone is worth all the money that has been spent on the Naval War College. . . . I had fully intended to abolish the college; I now intend to do all in my power to sustain it."[52]

The story of Nelson's battles were clearly a part of Mahan's second sea power book and an analysis of Nelson's strategy and tactics had, thus, played a role in the U.S. Navy's institutional history as well as a continuing role in the curriculum of its highest professional educational institution. In this volume, however, Mahan had sublimated his narrative of Nelson's detailed operations to a wider analysis that focused at the higher level of political, political-economic, and governmental issues. Here he showed how Britain was able to counter and to neutralize the maritime threats from France and Spain and to eliminate secondary threats from The Netherlands and Denmark. In this, Mahan argued that the victory at Trafalgar removed the possibility of serious maritime challenge, secured the British blockade of the Continent, and the safety of overseas commerce. Together, Mahan showed that the effect was to secure Britain's commerce and, thus, her economic foundation.[53]

In coming to these broad conclusions, Mahan could see that the pattern and results of the wars of the French Revolution and Empire had not been inevitable. Through this analysis, Mahan understood that the individual leadership and decisions by those in key naval positions of responsibility had made a real difference to the course of events. This further consideration led him five years later in 1897 to publish a biography of *Nelson: The Embodiment of the Sea Power of Great Britain*,[54] a work by a professional officer to guide other naval professionals as well as to interest the public.

In this large, two-volume biography, Mahan repeated many of the things he had already said in his similarly-sized *Influence of Sea Power* volume, but he placed these in the background as he focused at the forefront on his examination of Nelson as a naval commander. Here, most important was the message he wanted to give to naval officers. He saw in the naval officers of Nelson's time what he felt was a "too common, almost universal, weakness, which deters men from a bold initiative, from assuming responsibility, from embracing opportunity."[55] Nelson stood out from these others by his conviction in seeking a decisive victory over the French. But, Mahan underscored his fundamental professional point that battles should not be fought with blind fury and that Nelson was not merely the embodiment of an aggressive warrior. In contrast, Mahan characterized Nelson's leadership at the battle of the Nile as "an instructive combination of rapidity and caution, of quick comprehension of the situation, with an absence of all precipitation; no haste incompatible with perfect carefulness, no time lost, either by hesitation or by preparations postponed."[56] Nelson's intelligent use of what Mahan saw as military principles in fighting as well as Nelson's resolution in seeking his goals were the key attributes that made for sound military thinking. But, Mahan argued, those features also needed to be merged with another critical factor that Nelson characterized: moral courage.[57]

Five years later, in 1902, Mahan wrote another book on the same period of the Age of Sail, but this one did not become one of his famous works and it lay outside the *"Influence of Sea Power"* theme. In *Types of Naval Officers Drawn from the History of the British Navy,* Mahan's representative types were Hawke, Rodney, Howe, Jervis, Saumarez, and Pellew. Reviewing that list, "the question may naturally be asked," Mahan wrote in his preface,

> Why, among types of naval officers, is there no mention, other than casual, of the name of Nelson? The answer is simple. Among general officers, land and sea, the group to which Nelson belongs defies exposition by a type, both because it is small in aggregate numbers, and because of the eminence of the several members,—the eminence of genius,—so differentiates each from his fellows that no one among them can be said to represent the others. . . . Such do not in fact form a class, because, though a certain community of ideas and principles may be traced in their actions, their personalities and methods bear each the stamp of originality in performance; and where originality is found classification ceases to apply. There is a company, it may be, but not a class.[58]

Mahan's writings on Nelson are those of a professional naval officer interested in teaching the essential elements of high command and they reached a large range of professional naval officers as well as a much wider public readership. For years, Mahan's biography of Nelson was recognized within navies for its value as a work of professional naval importance. Through it, Mahan's interpretation had a clear influence on the way in which Nelson's image was presented in the context of American naval training and education over the next half century.[59] In a similar way, the biography had a direct effect on professional naval education in Japan[60] and in Sweden,[61] where the biography was translated for use in those navies.

Nelson's Image in the World's Navies after the Trafalgar Centenary

Mahan's sea power books influenced naval thinking about naval leadership outside Britain, but his historical information also quickly merged with the growing number of works that were appearing in Britain leading up to and following the 1905 centenary of the battle of Trafalgar. Several key books, read both in English and in translation, had a wide influence in navies outside of Britain and appeared in the years between the first edition of Mahan's *Nelson* in 1897 and the publication of Julian Corbett's *The Trafalgar Campaign* in 1910.[62]

German naval historians, beginning with Alfred Stenzel, were among the first to look at this topic, as far back as the mid-1870s, and their interest soon paralleled and was influenced by naval works published in Britain and America. Following Stenzel's work, two other German naval writers made important contributions to studies on the Anglo-French naval wars.[63] These were: Vize-Admiral Curt Freiherr von Maltzahn,[64] who had been a student of Stenzel's, and Vize-Admiral Eberhard von Mantey, who in turn had been a student of von Maltzahn's.[65] In 1906, just following the Trafalgar

Centenary, von Maltzahn published a detailed study of the battle in the professional naval journal *Marine Rundschau*[66] that summarized current understanding of the battle, while von Mantey went on to lecture to naval cadets and officers on similar subjects.[67]

In England, Joseph Conrad had clearly sensed the trend in his 1905 collection of essays, *The Mirror of the Sea,* when he wrote of the Nelsonian tradition, "Like a subtle and mysterious elixir poured into the perishable clay of successive generations, it grows in truth, splendour, and potency with the march of ages." From a narrowly British perspective, Conrad was correct in going on to say that

> in its incorruptible flow all round the globe of the earth it preserves from the decay and forgetfulness of death the greatness of our great men, and amongst them the passionate and gentle greatness of Nelson, the nature of whose genius was, on the faith of a brave seaman and distinguished Admiral, such as to "Exalt the glory of our nation."[68]

Certainly the preservation of the memory of a British hero was one effect of this, but it was not this distinctively British patriotic and sentimental attraction that interested a number of professionals serving in foreign navies around the world. For them, interest in Nelson was motivated by two overlapping approaches. On the one hand, a number of naval professionals around the world shared a desire to penetrate, to analyze, and to elucidate the characteristics that made Nelson such a successful naval leader and tactician in history and to apply these practical findings to the education and training of officers and men in their own naval services. On the other hand, there was a desire for navies to share with one another in the larger body of inspirational naval heritage. These two aspects are quite different, yet overlapping, in their applications. Both share in the distinctive and age-old belief that mariners of every nation, serving in ships under every flag, share a fundamental commonality with one other. Naval men, whether officers or ratings, deal with similar equipment, share professional competencies in navigation, gunnery, and ship handling, have similar lives, develop similar standards, and include among their highest challenges the ability to face the caprice of the basic natural elements found in the "boundless deep" of the world's oceans.

Asian Naval Views of Nelson

Research has so far found little distinctive interest in Nelson in Chinese professional naval literature during the 19th or for most of the 20th century. By contrast, there was a very large interest in the Imperial Japanese Navy,[69] which seems to arise from the personal experience of Count Heihachiro Tōgō, the Japanese admiral who had commanded the fleet in the Russo-Japanese War, bombarded Port Arthur, and defeated the Russians at Tsushima in the centenary year of Trafalgar on 29 May 1905. His initial training had been spent in England as a cadet on board the training ship HMS *Worcester* in 1871–74. On the sixty-eighth anniversary of Trafalgar in October 1873, Tōgō observed a commemorative ceremony that deeply influenced him and reputedly led him to pattern himself on Nelson.[70] Through Tōgō, Nelson became a key part of Japan's naval heritage. Most dramatically echoing in the battle of Tsushima, Tōgō ordered the "Zed" flag hoisted, meaning: "The country's fate depends upon this battle: let every man do his utmost."[71]

One of the most important theorists for the development of Japanese strategy was Satō Tetsutarō and his idea of oceanic defense.[72] Sent to Britain and the United States for research in 1899–1901, Satō studied the relevance of British maritime experience to

Japan's similar geographical position. Satō's massive, two-volume work *On the History of Imperial Defense*[73] was soon cited as a classic after its publication in 1908–10 and played a prominent role in Japanese naval thinking in the decades leading up to World War II. Although some have assumed that Satō was reflecting the ideas of Mahan in his work, a close examination of the text[74] reveals that he was most highly influenced by Vice Admiral Sir Philip Colomb and the quite different emphases in his 1891 work on *Naval Warfare*[75] and his subsequent volume of *Essays on Naval Defence.*[76] In the broad context of Satō's work, Nelson's name appears only rarely, but when it does it is in a quite different light than the British or Americans saw. In the 440 pages of the first volume, Satō makes a passing reference to Nelson, but attributes his victory at Trafalgar to the adoption of the idea that "the true national defence is not to let the enemy set foot on national territory."[77] In the second volume, Satō devotes only two pages to Nelson, where interestingly he emphasized the relative inferiority in numbers of the British fleet facing the combined Franco-Spanish fleet. With a quite different twist, the lessons that Satō interpreted here emphasized Nelson's need to do his *own* duty and for his captains to absolutely obey *his* orders.[78]

Just a year after Satō's work appeared, Ishihara Todatoshi wrote a more popular non-academic study in 1911. Entitled *Nelson and Napoleon,*[79] the book had no footnotes or bibliography, making it difficult to determine its sources, but it contained a distinctive interpretation which may have been designed to inspire those contemplating a career in the Imperial Japanese Army or Navy. Published in the wake of two victorious wars over larger opponents, China in 1894–95 and over Russia in 1904–1905, Ishihara's book emphasized some of the concepts of *bushidō* and reflected some traditional Japanese values that were being applied in a modern way to instill military values that could be useful to 19th and 20th century Japanese forces.[80] In particular, Ishihara emphasized Nelson's personal determination to overcome his many illnesses, his bravery, and his ability to stand up against an enemy alone under adversity. Most importantly, Ishihara stressed Nelson's honorable death in battle and contrasted it to the dishonor and tragedy of Napoleon's death in exile.[81] Thus, Ishihara contributed a distinctively Japanese view and interpretation of Nelson.

Continuing the tradition of British connections through today, the former Imperial Naval Academy building at Etajima, built of red-bricks imported from England, still stands and is now the Officer Candidate School for the Japanese Maritime Self-Defense Force. A 1936 building with a Doric-style portico houses the school's purpose-built museum, where one may find Nelson's portrait still in a place of honor near the entrance and a lock of Nelson's hair acquired as recently as 1981, apparently replacing an earlier lock of hair given soon after the Russo-Japanese War, and complements a similar lock of Admiral Tōgō's hair.

If Japanese interest in Nelson follows a tradition that is more than a century old, Chinese interest seems to be much more recent. Lin Hsiang-kuang published a 120-page *Nelson Biography* only in 1961;[82] based largely on the works of Robert Southey, A. T. Mahan, and Sir Geoffrey Callender, it is a fairly straightforward factual account that does not make any distinctive China-related interpretation of its own. In 1999, however, the Chinese People's Liberation Army Navy published a western-style *Chinese Naval Encyclopedia* that contained two entries relating to our subject, one on Nelson and another on Trafalgar. These both extolled Nelson for his courage in battle, trail-blazing spirit, flexible leadership, rapid concentration of forces, well-conceived tactical planning, and for breaking away from the yoke of traditional naval tactics.[83]

European and American Naval Views of Nelson in the 20th Century

When the flurry of interest in Nelson had settled following the centenary celebrations and the spate of books that appeared through 1910 had been absorbed by the reading public, views of Nelson in Europe and America settled down into the context of calmer historical study and reflection on broad historical narratives of the naval wars under sail and studies of the history of naval tactics.

In Weimar Germany, Eberhard von Mantey included the battles of St. Vincent, Aboukir, and Trafalgar in his 1928 illustrated atlas for students of naval history and tactics.[84] Similar studies looking at Nelson in the context of the broader development of naval tactics appeared in many navies, usually at the entry level of cadet or midshipman.

Typical of these were locally produced reading materials by Gaetono Bonifacio used at the Italian Naval Academy from 1930 to 1958, succeeded by a series by Emilio Francardi, in use from 1959 to 1980, and then the published books of Alberto Santoni, used since 1981.[85] Former naval cadets who studied at the Italian Naval Academy before and during the Second World War, when Mussolini's Italy was fighting against Britain, remember, despite the fascist propaganda against Britain, that their civilian and uniformed instructors in naval history taught them that Nelson was a very intelligent, audacious, courageous, charismatic leader, with an open mind for using new tactics. Similar reminiscences were expressed by former Italian cadets in the immediate post–World War II era.[86]

In the late 1920s and early 1930s, there was apparently a momentary waning of professional interest in Nelson, both in the Royal Navy and elsewhere. As the battleship HMS *Nelson* prepared for her first commission in 1927, her commander requested Admiral Mark Kerr, R.N., to prepare a series of lectures on the "godfather" of the ship for the edification of the ship's company. By 1931, a typescript copy of these lectures reached the U.S. Naval War College and came to the attention of its President, Rear Admiral Harris Laning.[87] Struck by the professional relevance of what Kerr had written, Laning apparently promised to reproduce the lectures and send them to every ship in the U.S. fleet. Although no documentary evidence has yet been found to show this actually happened, Kerr credited Laning's and the U.S. Navy's deep interest in Nelson as the key source of stimulation that led to their publication in 1932.[88]

More commonly in the United States, Nelson was dealt with in the context of the broader history of naval tactics. The U.S. Naval War College's Department of Intelligence made an early attempt to prepare a broad outline of the development of naval tactics under sail and their overview of the subject was first delivered as a series of lectures in 1927–28.[89] A more in-depth study did not appear in the U.S. Navy for many years. Finally in 1942, Admiral S. S. Robison's general history of naval tactics from the Armada to 1930[90] was published and widely used. It was superseded in 1960 by *Sea Power,* a naval history textbook for the U.S. Naval Academy, edited by E. B. Potter and Fleet Admiral Chester W. Nimitz.[91] All of these place Nelson in the context of larger developments and emphasize his importance as an innovative tactician and inspiring naval leader.

In contrast to what was going on in the United States, there was much less mention of Nelson in other navies, for example, in the Soviet Union. The old Tsarist navy had been highly influenced by the works of both Vice Admiral Philip Colomb and Mahan and had absorbed their views of Nelson in the process. The leading Soviet naval theoretician of the immediate post-1917 period, Professor Boris Gervais, continued to propound the old Mahanist theory for a battleship navy of disputing command of the sea, but these views were heavily attacked in the 1920s and '30s. Julian Corbett's views, in particular, were strongly criticized as allegedly ignoring the lessons of the Spanish-American and Russo-Japanese Wars. The new trend in Soviet naval theory was to argue that the old ideas that Nelson represented in terms of general fleet engagements and blockade were no longer valid for modern naval thought.[92] However, in the years between 1946 and 1953 Soviet naval attitudes seemed to have modified and begun to accept Corbett's understanding of a "fleet-in-being" strategy in the way that Corbett had attributed its understanding to Nelson in the Mediterranean in 1796: "an inferior fleet kept actively in being" in order to exploit its "general power of holding such command [of the sea] in dispute."[93]

Following on from these precedents in Soviet naval thinking, Admiral of the Fleet of the Soviet Union Sergei Gorshkov criticized western naval theory. In 1972–83, Gorshkov wrote a series of articles that appeared in the Soviet naval journal *Morskoi Sbornik*[94] that were eventually republished in book form under the title *The Sea Power of the State*. On a single page, Gorshkov summarized his understanding of the Wars of the French Revolution, which had been organized by "the English bourgeoisie, seeking to gain a complete hold on the colonial possessions still left to France."[95] In this struggle, the weakness of the French fleet played a fatal role for France. Napoleon's Egyptian expedition had been initially saved by Nelson's "chain of errors" that delayed his attack on the French squadron in Aboukir Bay by two and a half months. Trafalgar, Gorshkov believed, "like the role of the English fleet in the struggle with Napoleon, has been enormously exaggerated by Anglo-American ideologists." Clearly making a point that could be translated into Cold War context and the need for the Soviet Union to develop a strong navy, he noted that it was Russia's victory on land over Napoleon that had provided the most decisive effect on European politics, but at the same time:

> Trafalgar showed the total inability of France to wage war at sea against the more sophisticated English fleet consisting of better-quality ships manned by better trained crews and employing tactics new for that time. England and her colonies became practically invulnerable to strikes from the sea. This untied the hands of the English bourgeoisie to organize and finance new alliances for continuing the struggle.[96]

Contrasting with the Soviet interpretation, in a survey of the way in which Nelson has been understood and valued today in modern Latin American navies,[97] there are a number of points that can be emphasized that are shared with many other navies around the world. The Argentine Naval War College, for example, published its own evaluation of Nelson in 1940. Dealing with many aspects of Nelson's life, it became the focus for a number of student papers written by mid-career officers.[98] In Argentine naval history, the Irish-Argentine naval leader Admiral Guillermo Brown is described as having "the Nelson Touch."[99] There were direct connections, too, with Trafalgar as one of Nelson's opponents was the last Spanish Viceroy of the River Plate. The man against whom the colonists fought for their independence from Spain was Rear Admiral Balthasar Hidalgo de Cisneros, who had flown his flag in *Santissima Trinidad* at Trafalgar.

In the struggle for Chilean independence and in Chilean naval history from 1818, Lord Cochrane plays an important role. Cochrane's 1798 meeting with Nelson and Cochrane's understanding of Nelson's injunction, "Never mind the maneuvers, always go at them,"[100] had an influence in Cochrane's career and has endured in his reputation in Chile. As in other navies throughout the world, currently serving officers in the Mexican and Uruguayan navies emphasize the tradition and heritage aspects of Nelson's contribution to their navies, particularly in terms of uniforms. Typically, one may mention:

- The blue collar on a seaman's uniform that has three white stripes, reputedly commemorating the battles of the Nile, Copenhagen, and Trafalgar.
- The black tie on seamen's uniforms, believed to be a sign of mourning for Nelson's death.
- The curl on the upper stripe of the gold braid on an officer's uniform, in many navies, that is attributed to Nelson's loss of his right arm in 1797.
- The standard usage of leaving unbuttoned the upper button of the frock coat, a usage reportedly used by Nelson to hold his empty right sleeve by way of the curl.[101]

Nelson's legacy as a hero among the world's navies is a complex one that stretches not only around the globe and through a wide variety of applications and usages. It ranges from historical actions by Nelson himself that had a direct or an indirect influence on foreign navies, to the slow development over two centuries of invoking his name and attributing wide professional naval values to it. A close examination of this phenomenon shows both parallel development and tension as historical insight has developed and as traditional, heritage values have been applied as navies became increasingly professionalized during the two centuries since 1805.

Finally, there is a further dimension that has not yet been widely analyzed, but which can be seen in practice in June 2005, when ships from the world's navies participate in the International Fleet Review in the Solent at Spithead. Such an occasion is perhaps the most public culmination of what is usually a more low-key and almost imperceptible use that combines naval tradition, naval history, and naval heritage as a tool of diplomatic engagement and professional cooperation between navies. Participation and exchange of information with other navies, and the presence, displays, and exchanges of portraits of historical leaders, such as Nelson, and paintings of battles, such as Trafalgar and the Nile, join with the tradition of the annual Trafalgar Night Dinners, where one joins in drinking the toast to "the immortal memory." All these serve to create a basis for a shared naval heritage, which navies have traditionally used to create the ambiance within which to discuss and to develop the most modern and advanced multilateral or bilateral relations on issues unconstrained by the past. For the navies of the world, Nelson's legacy is that of a hero who represented the highest values of professional competence for the world and therefore a shared icon in world naval heritage. At the same time, continuing historical research goes on in naval history, reaching beyond the icons of tradition and heritage, to continue to deepen professional naval understanding of Nelson and his age.

NOTES This paper was presented in the eight-part 2004 Nelson Lectures Series "Rediscovering Nelson," sponsored by the National Maritime Museum, Greenwich, and the Institute of Historical Research, University of London. The lecture was delivered in Beveridge Hall, Senate House, University of London, on 14 October 2004 and subsequently published as "Nelson Afloat: A Hero among the World's Navies" in David Cannadine, ed., *Admiral Lord Nelson: His Context and Legacy* (London: Palgrave Macmillan, 2005), pp. 160–186.

1 Dallas–Fort Worth, Texas, *Star Telegram.* 11 August 2002. http://www.dfw.com/mld/startelegram/3841477.htm. Accessed 2 September 2004.

2 Gordon R. England (1937–), served in the administration of President George W. Bush as the 72nd Secretary of the Navy from 24 May 2001 to 23 January 2003, when he became the first Deputy Secretary of the Department of Homeland Security. After eight months in that office, he returned to the Navy Department as the 73rd Secretary of the Navy on 26 September 2003 and was serving at the time this lecture was presented on 14 October 2004. His tenure is distinctive as being only the second person in U.S. naval history to serve twice as the civilian leader of the U.S. Navy–Marine Corps team and the first to serve in two consecutive terms.

3 "Core Values of the United States Navy," http://www.chinfo.navy.mil/navpalib/traditions/html/corvalu.html. Accessed 3 September 2004.

4 C. I. Hamilton, "Naval Hagiography and the Victorian Hero," *The Historical Journal*, 23, 2 (1980), pp. 381–398.

5 Dudley W. Knox, ed., *Naval Documents Relating to the Quasi War between the United States and France* (Washington, D.C.: Government Printing Office, 1935), vol. 1, p. 26, Letter from Samuel Sewell to Secretary Timothy Pickering, 27 December 1797. Compare with Sir Nicholas Harris Nicolas, ed., *The dispatches and letters of Vice Admiral Lord Viscount Nelson, with notes* (London: H. Colburn, 1845–46), vol. II, p. 379.

6 Quoted in Michael A. Palmer, *Stoddert's War: Naval Operations during the Quasi-War with France, 1798–1801* (Columbia: University of South Carolina Press, 1987), p. 203.

7 Dudley W. Knox, ed., *Naval Documents Related to the United States Wars with the Barbary Powers* (Washington, D.C.: Government Printing Office, 1941), vol. 3, p. 434, Tobias Lear to Robert Montgomery, 19 February 1804. Other passing references to the battle of the Nile and its effect on American trade may be found in Knox, ed., *Naval Documents Relating to the Quasi War,* vol. 1, pp. 467, 480, 481, 484, 507.

8 Among recent uses of this quotation, see, for example, E. B. Potter and C. W. Nimitz, eds., *Sea Power: A Naval History* (Englewood Cliffs, N.J.: Prentice Hall, 1960), p. 202; *The Dictionary of American Naval Fighting Ships* (Washington, D.C.: Government Printing Office, 1970), vol. 5, p. 282. A detailed description of the action, without the quotation, may be found in Christopher McKee, *Edward Preble: A Naval Biography, 1761–1807* (Annapolis: Naval Institute Press, 1972), pp. 189–199.

9 Originally published in London in 1813, American editions of it were quickly published at New York by Eastburn, Kirk, & Co., and at Boston by William Wells in 1813. Another edition was published in Hartford [Conn.] by B. & J. Russell for Oliver D. Cooke in 1814; there was another printing at Boston: E. G. House, 1814; and yet another at Hartford: W. S. Marsh, 1814.

10 Alexander Slidell Mackenzie, *The Life of Commodore Oliver Hazard Perry.* 5th edition (New York: Harper & Brothers, [1858]), vol. 1, p. 222. I am grateful to Dr. David Skaggs for this reference.

11 David Curtis Skaggs, *Thomas Macdonough: Master of Command in the Early U.S. Navy* (Annapolis: Naval Institute Press, 2004), p. 127; William R. Folsom, "The battle of Plattsburg," *Vermont Quarterly,* 20 (October 1952), p. 253.

12 Skaggs, *Macdonough.* See also Charles E. Brodine, Jr., Michael J. Crawford, and Christine Hughes, *Against All Odds: U.S. Sailors in the War of 1812* (Washington, D.C.: Naval Historical Center, 2004), p. 59.

13 Beginning with the edition by Harper Brothers in their Family Library series; New York: J. & J. Harper, 1830.

14 Letter from Robert Southey to Grosvenor C. Bradford, 8 December 1828, in Rev. Charles Cuthbert Southey, ed., *The Life and Correspondence of Robert Southey* (London: Longman, Brown, Green, and Longman, 1850; facsimile reprint: St. Clair Shores, Michigan: Scholarly Press, 1969), vol. V, p. 335 and footnote.

15 James Fenimore Cooper, "Preface to the second edition [1851]," in *The Two Admirals: A Tale.* Historical Introduction by Donald A. Ringe. Text established by James A. Sapperfield and E. N. Feltskog. The Writings of James Fenimore Cooper Series (Albany: State University of New York Press, 1990), p. 8.

16 Thomas Philbrick, *James Fenimore Cooper and the Development of American Sea Fiction* (Cambridge, Mass.: Harvard University Press, 1961).

17 G. L. Newnham Collingwood, ed., *A selection from the public and private correspondence of Vice-Admiral Lord Collingwood: interspersed with memoirs of his life.* First American edition from the 4th English edition (New York: G. & C. & H. Carvill, 1829).

18 Cooper, "Preface," p. 9.

19 James H. Ward, *A manual of naval tactics: together with a brief critical analysis of the principal modern naval battles* (New York: D. Appleton & Co., 1859), p. 6.

20 Later editions of *A Manual of Naval Tactics* were published in 1865, 1867, and 1870.

21 Sir Howard Douglas, *On Naval Warfare with Steam* (London: John Murray, 1858).

22 Ward, *A manual of naval tactics,* footnote on p. 180.

23 Ibid., p. 6.

24 Letter from Commander S. Phillips Lee, USN, to Commander Henry Grant, RN, 28 September 1861. Professor Edward K. Rawson and Robert H. Woods, eds., *Official Records of the Union and Confederate Navies in the War of Rebellion* (Washington, D.C.: Government Printing Office, 1897), Series I, vol. 6, *The Atlantic Blockading Squadron,* p. 294.

25 Letter from Acting Rear Admiral S. P. Lee, USN, to Assistant Secretary of the Navy G. V. Fox, 4 April 1864. Prof Edward K. Rawson and Chares W. Stewart, eds., *Official Records of the Union and Confederate Navies in the War of Rebellion* (Washington, D.C.: Government Printing Office, 1899), Series I, vol. 9, *North Atlantic Blockading Squadron, 1863–1864,* pp. 583–584.

26 Letter from Commander George Henry Preble, USN, to Secretary of the Navy Gideon Welles, 1 March 1864. Richard Rush, ed., *Official Records of the Union and Confederate Navies in the War of Rebellion* (Washington, D.C.: Government Printing Office, 1895), Series I, vol. 2, *The Operations of the Cruisers 1863–64,* p. 622.

27 Letter from Confederate Secretary of the Navy S. R. Mallory to Commander James D. Bulloch, CSN, 7 May 1863. C. C. Marsh, ed., *Official Records of the Union and Confederate Navies in the War of Rebellion* (Washington, D.C.: Government Printing Office, 1921), Series II, vol. 2, *Navy Department Correspondence, 1861–65, with Agents Abroad,* pp. 417–419, quote from p. 418.

28 Extracts from the diary of Lieutenant Francis A. Roe, U.S. Navy. Charles W. Stewart, ed., *Official Records of the Union and Confederate Navies in the War of Rebellion* (Washington, D.C.: Government Printing Office, 1904), Series I, vol. 18, *West Gulf Blockading Squadron, 1862,* p. 768.

29 Quoted in Charles Lee Lewis, *David Glasgow Farragut: Our First Admiral* (Annapolis: Naval Institute Press, 1943), p. 315.

30 Ibid., p. 530.

31 Winfield Scott Schley, *Forty-Five Years under the Flag* (New York: D. Appleton & Co., 1904), p. 51.

32 John B. Hattendorf, "The Study of War History at Oxford," in Hattendorf and Malcolm H. Murfett, eds., *The Limitations of Military Power: Essays Presented to Norman Gibbs on His Eightieth Birthday* (New York: St Martin's Press, 1990), pp. 5–7.

33 Donald M. Schurman, *The Education of a Navy: The Development of British Naval Strategic Thought, 1867–1914* (Chicago: University of Chicago Press, 1965); Andrew Lambert, *The Foundations of Naval History: John Knox Laughton, the Royal Navy, and the Historical Profession* (London: Chatham Publishing, 1998); Andrew Lambert, ed., *Letters and Papers of Professor Sir John Knox Laughton, 1830–1915.* Publications of the Navy Records Society, vol. 143 (Aldershot, Hants; Burlington, Vt.: Published by Ashgate for the Navy Records Society, 2002).

34 J. K. Laughton, "The Scientific Study of Naval History," *Journal of the Royal United Services Institution,* XVIII (1874), pp. 508–527.

35 Ibid., p. 522.

36 Ibid., p. 523.

37 "Alfred Stenzel," in Hans H. Hildenbrand and Ernest Henriot, eds., *Deutschlands Admirale, 1849–1945*

(Osnabrück: Biblio Verlag, 1990), Band 3 *P–Z*, pp. 380–382; Hermann Kirchhoff, "Einführung: Stenzels Leben und Werke," in Alfred Stenzel, *Kriegführung zur See: Lehre vom Seekriege.* Edited by Hermann Kirchhoff (Hannover und Leipzig: Hansche Buchhandlung, 1913), pp. xiii–xxxi.

38 James Russell Soley, *Report on Foreign Systems of Naval Education.* U.S. Senate. 46th Congress. 2d Session. Ex. Doc No. 51 (Washington, D.C.: Government Printing Office, 1880), pp. 190–193.

39 "Als letzte und als höchste Ehrung Nelsons ist wohl anzusehen, daß man in der neuesten Zeit wiederum seine Bedeutung ganz besonders hervorgehoben und erkannt hat, man müsse den Nelsonchen Geist wieder aufleben lassen, ihn hegen und seine Ideen pflegen, um das Größte zu erreichen." Alfred Stenzel, *Seekriegsgeschichte in ihren wichtigsten Abschnitten mit Berüchsichtigung der Seetaktik* (Hannover und Leipzig: Hahnsche Buchhandlung, 1911), p. 344.

40 Stephen B. Luce, "An Address Delivered at the United States Naval War College . . . , 1903," reprinted in John D. Hayes and Hattendorf, eds., *The Writings of Stephen B. Luce* (Newport: Naval War College Press, 1975), pp. 39–40.

41 Quoted in editors' introduction to ibid., p. 47.

42 Ibid., pp. 61–62.

43 Ibid., p. 63.

44 Stephen B. Luce, "On the Study of Naval History (Grand Tactics)," reprinted in Hayes and Hattendorf, ed., *The Writings of Stephen B. Luce,* p. 73.

45 Ibid., p. 92.

46 A. T. Mahan, *From Sail to Steam; Recollections of a Naval Life* (New York: Harper Brothers, 1907; reprinted: New York: Da Capo Press, 1968), p. 275.

47 Ibid.

48 A. T. Mahan, *The Influence of Sea Power Upon History, 1660–1783* (Boston: Little, Brown, 1890).

49 A. T. Mahan, *The Influence of Sea Power Upon the French Revolution and Empire, 1793–1812.* Two volumes (Boston: Little, Brown, 1892).

50 Ibid., vol. 1, pp. v, vi.

51 Ibid.

52 Quoted in Hattendorf, B. Mitchell Simpson III, and John R. Wadleigh, *Sailors and Scholars: The Centennial History of the Naval War College* (Newport: Naval War College Press, 1984), p. 35.

53 Jon Tetsuro Sumida, *Inventing Grand Strategy and Teaching Command; The Classic Works of Alfred Thayer Mahan Reconsidered* (Washington, D.C.: The Woodrow Wilson Center Press; Baltimore, MD, and London: The Johns Hopkins University Press, 1997), pp. 34–35.

54 A. T. Mahan, *Nelson: The Embodiment of the Sea Power of Great Britain.* Two volumes (Boston: Little, Brown, and Company, 1897).

55 Ibid., vol. 1, p. 452.

56 Ibid., p. 347.

57 Sumida, *Inventing Grand Strategy and Teaching Command,* pp. 36–39. See also the comparison between Nelson and Farragut on this point in A. T. Mahan, *Admiral Farragut* (New York: Appleton, 1892), pp. 308–309.

58 A. T. Mahan, *Types of Naval Officers Drawn from the History of the British Navy* (London: Sampson Low, Marston & Company, 1902), pp. xiii–xiv.

59 See, for example, Lieutenant Commander Leland P. Lovette, USN, *Naval Customs, Traditions, and Usage* (Annapolis: U.S. Naval Institute, 1939), p. 15.

60 A. T. Mahan, *Eikoku Suishi Teitoku Neruson Den.* Translated by Sadamasu Oshima for Kaigun Jioiku Honbu [The Educational Headquarters of the Imperial Japanese Navy] (Tokyo: Kaubunkan, 1906).

61 A. T. Mahan, *Lord Nelson: Grundläggaren av Storbritanniens Herravälde över Haven.* Bemyndigad översättning av D. [Axel Daniel] Landquist, Underlöjnant vid K. Flottan (Stockholm: Norstedt & Söners Förlag, 1913).

62 Julian S. Corbett, *The Campaign of Trafalgar* (London: Longmans, Green, 1910)

63 See Hattendorf, "The Caird Lecture: The Anglo-French Naval Wars (1689–1815) in Twentieth Century Naval Thought," *Journal of Maritime Research* (June 2001). [See chapter 6.]

64 Hildebrand and Henriot, eds., *Deutschlands Admirale 1849–1945.* band 2, H–O: Curt Freiherr von Maltzahn (1849–1930), pp. 425–426.

65 Ibid., Dr. Phil h.c. Eberhard von Mantey (1869–1940), pp. 432–433.

66 Curt Freiherr von Maltzahn, "Nelson und die Schlacht von Trafalgar," *Marine Rundschau* (1906), pp. 259–273. See also von Maltzahn, *Der Seekrieg: Seine geschichtliche Entwicklung vom Zeitalter der Entdeckungen bis zur Gegenwart* (Leipzig: Druck und Verlag von B. G. Teubner, 1906).

67 Lectures in "Kopien aus dem Nachlass des vizeadmrials a. D. Eberhard von Mantey (1869–1940), Band 1." I am grateful to Dr. Werner Rahn for providing me with photocopies of these materials.

68 Joseph Conrad, "The Heroic Age," in *The Mirror of the Sea* (New York: Harper Brothers, 1906), pp. 328–329.

69 I am most grateful for the assistance and advice of Dr. Bruce A. Elleman, Maritime History Department, Naval War College, for his translations from Chinese and Japanese sources cited.

70 Vice-Admiral Viscount Nagayo Ogasawara, *Life of Admiral Togo* (Tokyo: The Seito Press, 1934), p. 57; Georges Blond, *Admiral Togo* (New York: The Macmillan Co., 1960), p. 48.

71 E. Stuart Kirby, "Heihachiro Togo: Japan's Nelson, (1848–1934)," in Jack Sweetman, ed., *The Great Admirals: Command at Sea, 1587–1945* (Annapolis: Naval Institute Press, 1997), pp. 327–348.

72 David C. Evans and Mark R. Peattie, *Kaigun: Strategy, Tactics, and Technology in the Imperial Japanese Navy, 1887–1941* (Annapolis: Naval Institute Press, 1997), pp. 135–141.

73 Satō Tetsaturō, *Teikoku kokubōshi ron* (two volumes, originally published 1908, 1910, reprinted Tokyo: Hara shobo, 1979).

74 For which, I thank Dr. Bruce Elleman, and also advice from Dr. Mark Peattie, Hoover Institution, Stanford University.

75 Satō refers to him throughout his work as "Co-ro-mu"; P. H. Colomb, *Naval Warfare: Its Ruling Principles and Practice Historically Treated* (originally published, London, 1891. Reprinted in The Classics of Sea Power Series, with an Introduction by Barry M. Gough; Annapolis: Naval Institute Press, 1990).

76 P. H. Colomb, *Essays on Naval Defence* (London, 1893; second edition, London, 1896).

77 Satō, *Teikoku kokubōshi ron,* vol. 1, p. 211.

78 Ibid., vol. 2, pp. 105–106.

79 Ishihara Todatoshi, *Neruson to Naporeon* (Tokyo: Keiseisha Publishers, 1911).

80 See the cautions on the use of this often misapplied term in Evans and Peattie, *Kaigun,* pp. 543 note 4, 609 note 46.

81 Ibid., pp. 2, 10, 29, 30, 419, 448.

82 Lin Xiangguang, *Na'erxun zhuan* (Taipei China Cultural Publications, 1961).

83 *Zhongquo Haijun Baike Quanshu* (Beijing: Sea Tide Publishers, 1998–99), a column and a half entry for the Naval battle of Cape Trafalgar: "Telafa'erjiajiao Haizhan," vol. 2, pages 1,673–74, and a one column entry on H. Nelson: "Na'erxun, H.," vol. 2, page 1,366. The latter includes a not altogether flattering portrait, as Nelson is shown at a slight angle with a huge nose, perhaps emphasizing the fact that the Chinese often refer to foreigners as *"Da Bizi,"* which means "Big Noses."

84 Eberhard v. Mantey, *Seeschlachten-Atlas: Eine Einführung in die Lehre vom Seekriege* (Berlin: E. G. Mittler & Sohn, 1928, second edition, 1937).

85 Gaetono Bonifacio, *Lezioni di Storia Navale* (Livorno: Tipo-Litografia R. Academia Navale, 1930); Emilio Francardi, *Appunti di Storia Navale* (Livorno: Poliigrafico dell'Accademia Navale, 1959); Alberto Santoni, *Da Lepanto ad Hampton Road* (Milano: Mursia, 1991); Alberto Santoni, *Storia e Politica navale dell'Età Moderna* (Roma: Ufficio Storico della Marina Militare, 1998). I am grateful to Dr. Marco Gemignani of the Italian Naval Academy for providing me with photocopies of the Nelson-related materials from these publications.

86 I am grateful to Dr. Marco Gemignani, who interviewed surviving former cadets from these periods, and provided me with this information, 27 August 2004.

87 Naval War College Archives. RG 28: President's File: Laning. Letter from Admiral Mark Kerr to Laning, 22 January 1931. The original typescript is in the Naval Historical Subjects file, Naval Historical Collection, Naval War College. For Laning's career, see Harris Laning, *An Admiral's Yarn.* Edited with an introduction by Mark Russell Shulman (Newport: Naval War College Press, 1999).

88 Mark Kerr, *The Sailor's Nelson* (London: Hurst & Blackett, Ltd., [1932]), p. 9. I have not yet found any evidence that Laning actually did circulate copies of the typescript to the U.S. fleet, although the published book seems to have found its way into key U.S. naval library collections ashore: Navy Department Library in Washington, Naval Academy Library in Annapolis, and two copies at the Naval War College Library in Newport, Rhode Island.

89 U.S. Naval War College. Edward C. Kalbfus, *A Review of the Naval History of the Eighteenth Century.* Two volumes reproduced for local use in typescript (Newport: Naval War College Department of Intelligence, 1929).

90 S. S. Robison, *A History of Naval Tactics from 1530 to 1930; the evolution of tactical maxims* (Annapolis: Naval Institute Press, 1942).

91 Potter and Nimitz, eds., *Sea Power.* With numerous factual historical errors, the best direct corrective was a revised edition published in German by Jürgen Rohwer, *Seemacht: Ein Seekriegsgeschichte von der Antike bis zur Gegenwart* (München: Bernard & Graefe, 1974).

92 Robert W. Herrick, *Soviet Naval Theory and Policy: Gorshkov's Inheritance* (Newport: Naval War College Press, 1988), pp. 12–13, 202–203, 206–207.

93 Ibid., p. 188, and also pp. 225, 270; Julian S. Corbett, *Some Principles of Maritime Strategy.* Edited with an introduction by Eric Grove. Classics of Sea Power series (Annapolis: Naval Institute Press, 1988), pp. 223–224. Corbett's comments are based on Nelson's letter to the Duke of Clarence, 19 August 1796. Nicolas, ed., *Letters,* vol. III, p. 246.

94 Translated and published with western commentary in Sergei G. Gorshkov, *Red Star Rising at Sea* (Annapolis: Naval Institute Press, 1974: reprinted 1978). See pp. 7–8 for comments on Nelson.

95 Sergei G. Gorshkov, *The Sea Power of the State* (Annapolis: Naval Institute Press, 1980), p. 65.

96 Ibid., pp. 65–66.

97 I am grateful to Captain Guillermo Montenegro, Argentine Navy (ret.), who provided detailed information on Argentina and coordinated additional responses for me on this subject from Captain Carlos Tromben, Chilean Navy (ret.); Lieutenant Commander Ramiro Lobato Camacho, Mexican Navy; Captain Jorge Ortiz Sotelo, Peruvian Navy (ret.); and Commander Diego Rombys, Uruguayan Navy (ret.).

98 G. J. Montenegro, "Nelson's Figure in the Argentine Navy," unpublished paper, 2004. Eloy S. Soneyra, *Ideas Estratégicas del Almirante Nelson—Trafalgar* (Buenos Aires: Escuela de Guerra Navale, 1940).

99 Felipe Bosch, *Guillermo Brown: Biografia de un Almirante* (Buenos Aires: Alborada, 1966), p. 18.

100 Thomas Alexander Cochrane, Earl of Dundonald, *The Autobiography of a Seaman* (London: Richard Bentley & Son, 1890), p. 35.

101 Captain Juan José Fernández Parés, *Hombres de Mar, un estilo de vida* (Montevideo: Liga Marítima Uruguaya, 1990). See also Kerr, *The Sailor's Nelson,* pp. 9–10; Lovette, *Naval Customs, Traditions, and Usage,* pp. 295–296.

IX Strategy, Tactics, and Leadership
The Legacy of Trafalgar in Professional Naval Thought around the World

Growth in professional understanding of naval events derives from an increasing quality of information on a topic and of improving insights and analysis brought to bear on that information. In order to understand the legacy of Trafalgar in professional naval thought one first needs to trace how information and understanding of it traveled and grew.

The First News of Trafalgar

The first detailed reports of the battle of Trafalgar reached both the public and naval professionals primarily through the special issue of *The London Gazette* published on 6 November 1805, the day that Collingwood's dispatches of 22 and 24 October from HMS *Euryalus* arrived at the Admiralty.[1] The contents of this issue were circulated even more widely through reprinting in *The Naval Chronicle*[2] as well as in newspapers and gazettes throughout the English-speaking world.

The first news reports to reach North America and the West Indies came from Liverpool, where the American ship *Neptune,* Captain Stanton, of New York sailed on or about 10 November, carrying a copy of *The London Gazette Extraordinary* and news from other London newspapers up to 8 November, which had arrived in Liverpool only a few hours before Captain Stanton sailed. Fifteen days later, on 25 November, Captain Stanton spoke the brig *Fox,* Captain Lee, in mid-Atlantic from Nantes, France, to Portland, Maine.[3] The news of Trafalgar that Captain Lee heard, shouted across the waves that day, was the first to reach North America on Friday, 13 December 1805, when the brig *Fox* reached Portland. *The Portland Gazette and Maine Advertizer* was the first in America to print and circulate the news in a handbill that same day[4] and repeated it again in its regular weekly edition on Monday, 16 December.[5]

The news from Portland was noticed and reprinted in the Boston and Newport, Rhode Island, newspapers within a week of its first appearance. It was supplemented by an additional report received by a ship that arrived on 16 December at Newburyport, Massachusetts, from Amsterdam, and had received the news by being boarded in the English Channel by an armed brig on 7 November.[6]

The most influential of the early reports that arrived in North America was that carried by the ship *Neptune.* Although Captain Stanton brought her in to New York three days after *Fox* had arrived in Portland, Stanton was the first to bring the full report in a copy of *The London Gazette Extraordinary. The London Gazette*'s report was certainly the most widely reprinted report and the most influential. It was immediately reprinted in the *New York Gazette*,[7] and from there carried overland to the South, where from that source it was copied and reprinted locally during the last two weeks of December in Pennsylvania,[8] Maryland,[9] Virginia,[10] and the District of Columbia.[11] At the same time, copies of the New York City newspapers spread north through upstate New York, and first reached Montreal, and then came down the St. Lawrence to reach Quebec from Montreal by express on 2 January 1806.[12] Through these initial reports and through the subsequent publication of a variety of early biographies of Nelson, most importantly Robert Southey's *Life of Nelson*,[13] as well as other news reports, documents, and memoirs that gradually came to light, the basic information and the initial understanding of the events came to be known to naval professionals.

Early Analysis of Naval Battles

An important aspect of professional development is to use past experience as an informative guide to aspects of future professional development. For the naval profession as a whole, this practice did not really begin to develop fully until the 1870s and 1880s, but in the context of the development of tactical ideas in the Navy, one can find an important strand of thinking that can certainly be seen in a nascent form that extends back to John Clerk of Eldin's *An Essay on Naval Tactics*,[14] if not beyond to the early beginnings of historical narratives in the English language that described naval operations: Josiah Burchett's *A Complete History of the Most Remarkable Transactions at Sea*,[15] Thomas Lediard's *Naval History of England*,[16] and John Entick's *A New Naval History*.[17]

The process by which a professional is able to study events and to learn from them is initially a process of sorting out the evidence to find out what happened, and then going on to analyze the events and reach conclusions about them that contribute to understanding. It is essentially the same process of research with which we historians are so familiar, yet it is additionally tied to in-depth professional and technical knowledge in terms of objectives and actions, and then extrapolated on to practical, future applications. Characteristically, the initial understanding of the details can be incorrect or incomplete, leading the first interpreters to reach conclusions that are faulty. We can observe that clearly in the case of Nelson and Trafalgar at the same time that service in the navy was gradually evolving from a traditional occupation into a more sophisticated profession in parallel with many other occupations in the nineteenth and twentieth centuries.

To illustrate the evolving view of Nelson's actions in professional naval thought, this paper is based on an a sampling of some key professional naval writings in the nineteenth and twentieth centuries that were devoted largely to professional naval issues of current and future naval operations and tactics and not intended as academic historical studies. Written primarily by naval officers, these studies were designed largely for the use of their fellow officers in their own navies: Britain, France, Russia, and the United States. Over this period, such works were also increasingly read, sometimes in excerpted form or in translation, by officers in navies around the world. Despite the context of the great technological changes over the past two centuries that repeatedly transformed the characteristics of ships and navies, there is a traceable strand of references throughout these works to Trafalgar and to Nelson.

One of the first professional naval books to appear following Trafalgar was compiled by Commodore Thomas Truxtun of the U.S. Navy.[18] Truxtun had been one of the original six captains that President George Washington appointed to the newly established

U.S. Navy in 1794. Truxtun had compiled the U.S. Navy's first signal book, *Instructions, Signals, and Explanations Offered for the U.S. Fleet* (1797), and, during the Quasi War with France in 1798–1801, commanded the U.S. frigate *Constellation* in some her most famous actions. He was well-known at the time for being a close observer of naval events in European waters.

In retirement in February 1806, Truxtun published a small 15-page pamphlet entitled *A Few Extracts from the Best Authors on Naval Tactics*.[19] In it, Truxtun provided extracts from the most prominent of the French theorists of the previous century, Père Hoste,[20] Bigot de Morogues,[21] Bourdé de Villehuet,[22] and Grenier,[23] as well as the only English theoretical work on tactics, Clerk of Eldin's *An Essay on Naval Tactics*. In compiling his work, Truxtun had been particularly impressed with Grenier's thoughts about preventing an enemy from doubling the van or the rear of a battle line. The French tactician had argued that a fleet commander could protect his van and rear squadrons by stationing flanking ships on a bearing opposite to the angle to the wind that was being sailed by a close-hauled line of battle. Developing Grenier's focus further, Truxtun argued that doubling could alternatively be achieved by using a curved line of battle.

Linking theory to the latest events, Truxtun commented on the tactics of Trafalgar, using the information contained in the newspaper reports with Collingwood's Trafalgar dispatch, combining it with a report from the American correspondent at Cadiz, giving the earliest official report received in the United States that had been obtained by the USS *Essex* at Malaga, Spain,[24] and additional information reported in American newspapers from *The Gibraltar Chronicle* of 9 November. Using these, the only sources then available in America, Truxtun attempted to make sense of the conflicting evidence, including Collingwood's report that Villeneuve had intentionally engaged his line in a mode of attack with an unusual structure: "a crescent convexing to leeward."[25] Modern research has made it clear that the pronounced curve in the Combined Franco-Spanish line of battle was not intentional, but the result of confusion following Villeneuve's order to his fleet, already in a loose formation, to wear together to reverse direction.[26] Nevertheless, one lesson that Truxtun took from Trafalgar was the idea that a crescent formation was as effective as the methods suggested by Grenier to prevent an enemy from doubling one's line. This, Truxtun wrote, was "the advantage to be derived from ships placed on each tack presenting their full-broadsides to the enemy's bows coming down on them, while not a ship . . . could be well-raked until their curved lines were about being broken by the impetuosity of their adversaries."[27] At the same time, Truxtun saw changing and alternative advantages to both the French tradition in preferring the lee gage and to the British preference for the windward. As an officer in a small navy, Truxtun concluded that there was "no general rule for preferring the one before the other."[28]

Truxtun's intentions in publishing his study and in drawing attention to Trafalgar were to encourage young American naval officers to study tactics and to become proficient in the art of war, just at a time when the administration of President Thomas Jefferson seemed to be favoring a navy comprised of only gunboats alone and American naval officers seemed to be ignoring tactical thinking in general.[29]

It was not until the 1870s and 1880s that the U.S. Navy began to make any extensive use of fleet tactical formations that resembled any of the traditional major battles. In general, one can correctly conclude, as Admiral Rémi Monaque has recently done, that

Trafalgar "gave the Americans confidence in their instinctive choice of commerce raiding and coastal defence, and this was the policy practiced with some success during the War of 1812."[30] Yet, there were some important exceptions.

One finds some very early examples of Nelson's legacy and of Trafalgar in the immediate applications of tactical "lessons learned" in the U.S. Navy's first official signal book, issued in mid-June 1812, which directly copied British practice and provided for fleet formations, doubling an enemy's line, and sailing in multiple columns.[31] While most of the actions in the War of 1812 were individual ship actions, there were two fleet actions in miniature that occurred on the American Lakes during the War of 1812: The American Oliver Hazard Perry's encounter with Robert Barclay's British squadron on Lake Erie, 10 September 1813, and the American Thomas Macdonough's encounter with George Downie's British flotilla on Lake Champlain in September 1814.

These small actions were fought by commanders who were fully conscious of the legacy of Nelson and of Trafalgar. As a lieutenant, Barclay had been at Trafalgar in HMS *Swiftsure,* while the Americans, Perry and Macdonough, blatantly attempted to copy Nelson's leadership style with similar signals and admonitions to their officers and men as they approached battle. Having clearly studied reports of the battle of the Nile, Macdonough had anchored his fleet for battle in a manner that would prevent the opportunity that Nelson had found with the French.[32]

In the spring of 1815, when both the War of 1812 and the Napoleonic Wars had just ended, the United States sent a squadron onto the Mediterranean to attempt to put an end to the depredations of the Barbary corsairs on American shipping. Two separate squadrons sailed, but each vessel was assigned a separate duty and operated independently. They made a show of force off the North African states and then they returned home across the Atlantic. On that return passage, the American squadron made the first recorded attempt to practice squadron evolutions and, perhaps, with Trafalgar in mind, sailed westward in parallel columns. The exercise was a notable failure and something not seriously attempted again for decades in the U.S. Navy. As one of the senior captains in command during the attempt recalled,

> It was very evident that none of our commanders were prepared to manage their vessels in a squadron which should be obliged to maneuver in the presence of the enemy, and that such knowledge was not to be acquired except by practical exercises under an officer well acquainted with the theory of tactics, and willing to devote much time and labor to their instruction.[33]

In those years, as a small navy of a neutral power, the U.S. Navy had little practical need to use such strongly disciplined tactics as those required for a fleet action, although there were certainly occasions when American warships operated together in at least a loose formation. The significance of the early reaction to Trafalgar in America is that it illustrates conclusions drawn from a partial misunderstanding of the events that took place, and, at the same, was paralleled by and interconnected with a general lack of appreciation of the broad principles of tactical theory. This situation was not unique to the little U.S. Navy, but was even paralleled to a degree in the Royal Navy.

In examining the tactical memoranda issued in the Royal Navy between 1806 and 1815, Julian Corbett concluded a century ago that the memorandum which Nelson issued to his captains just before Trafalgar[34] unsettled professional naval opinion in the years that followed the battle. On the one hand, the memorandum was widely circulated, but on the other hand, the tactical principles that motivated it were not understood. As Corbett concluded, "The failure to fathom its meaning is to be accounted for largely by the lack of theoretical training, which made the science of tactics, as distinguished from its practice, a sealed book to the majority of British officers."[35] To prove his point, Corbett examined Lord Gambier's "Order of Battle" in preparation for his attack on Copenhagen in 1807, Collingwood's General Order of 1808, and Sir Alexander Cochrane's tactical memorandum for his command of the Leeward Islands Station from 1805 to 1814. All reflected the direct influence of Nelson's practice, but of them, only Cochrane's showed a measure of in-depth insight into tactical principles. Additionally, Corbett found the same tendencies in the Royal Navy's signal book issued immediately after the war in 1816, which repeated the old instructions without significant modification, although the signals accompanying them were based on the innovations of Sir Home Popham's signal code that Nelson had used.[36] At this point, it seemed that Nelson had become an honored icon, but the majority of officers seemed to miss the substance and point of his ideas.

In his research, Corbett found a paper from a contemporary French naval officer, who had readily understood the tactical principles of Trafalgar and reached two important conclusions:

> 1. That our [the French] System of a long line of battle is worthless in face of an enemy who attacks with his ships formed in groups and told to engage a small number of ships at different points in our line.

> 2. That the only tactical system to oppose theirs [that of the British] is to have at least a double line, with reserve squadrons on the wings stationed in such a manner as to bear down most easily upon the points too vigorously attacked.[37]

In his analysis, Corbett blamed Lord Keith for excessive conservatism in adopting the old system in the 1816 Signal Book, but as Andrew Lambert has pointed out, Keith and his colleagues were fully aware that the situation at Trafalgar was unique and was based on three factors that could not be codified or even expected in a future war: "The incompetence of the enemy, the skill of the fleet, and the genius of the commander."[38] When the Signal Book and Instructions were revised again in 1826 and later, they continued to be based on the old tried and true ideas for fleet training in the fundamentals to develop fleet tactical discipline, rather than the advanced applications that Nelson had employed in going beyond the basics. The contrast that Corbett saw between Nelson's advanced methods and the practical conservatism that followed can perhaps be best explained as part of Corbett's efforts to help institutionalize higher studies in tactical and strategic theory through the recently established Naval War College course.[39]

This discussion was also being reflected in the historical accounts of the events. The historical analysis by Rear Admiral Charles Ekins, first published in 1824, was widely read and studied in navies around the world.[40] In it, Ekins quoted extensively from a commentary by "an intelligent officer" in HMS *Conqueror,* which may, in fact, reflect the views of her commanding officer, Captain Isaac Pellew, younger brother of Lord Exmouth. The author of these remarks begins by pointing out that, based on information captured during the battle, it is clear that Villeneuve's crescent formation was not the intended position, although, in fact, it would have been the most effective position to defeat Nelson, if the Combined Franco-Spanish fleet had been able to counter Nelson's attack with aggressive gunfire and disciplined maneuvering. Similarly, the author believed that the actual British attack was intended to be somewhat different than what actually occurred. The author concluded that, despite its success, there were in theory disadvantages to Nelson's mode of attack, which

> appear to consist in bringing forward the attacking force in a manner so leisurely and alternatively, that an enemy of equal spirit and equal ability in seamanship and gunnery would have annihilated the ships one after another in detail, carried slowly on as they were by a heavy swell and light airs.[41]

Historians have judged Ekins to have produced an "interesting and useful work" that "pioneered the serious study of tactical development in English, though its value was reduced by much hearsay criticism and the lack of any reference to foreign authorities. The diagrams, too, drawn from the official dispatches, which are generally vague and frequently inaccurate, are often more remarkable for their fancy than their accuracy."[42]

Ekins's volume was rapidly followed by two other works: Captain Edward Pelham Brenton's *Naval History of Great Britain*[43] and William James's similarly titled work.[44] A literary battle ensued between Brenton and James, largely based on their contrasting political outlook with Brenton, a Whig, and James, a Tory. Additionally, they came from very different professions. Brenton was the second son of a rear-admiral[45] and younger brother of a vice-admiral.[46] He had served in the Navy since 1788 and been promoted to post-captain for distinguished bravery at Martinique in 1808. Brenton's professional knowledge and training could not be matched by a civilian. In addition, he had the credibility and ready access to others in the service, who had personal knowledge of events. In contrast, James had practiced as an attorney before the supreme court of Jamaica and had been a proctor in the vice-admiralty court, between 1801 and 1813.

Brenton accused James of plagiarizing his work and making factual errors, adding that this was "but only to be expected by writers who are uninformed . . . and [from an author who is but] a mere landsman."[47] A professional naval officer's resentment of a civilian critic of naval battle tactics revealed a reaction that had been noted as early as the appearance of John Clerk of Eldin's work and is a characteristic that may be found even in modern times. James defended his intentions by noting,

> For an unprofessional writer to arraign the merits of a work on naval tactics, would seem to be a presumption equal to the highest degree of that which we have just been condemning. But tactical reasoning, like all other reasoning, must be built upon facts, or upon what are assumed as facts. Surely, then, to inquire into the reality of those alleged facts, is within the province of a writer, whose avowed purpose, to the extent of his ability, is to separate truth from fiction.[48]

James declared that Ekins had entirely misunderstood the tactical principle upon which the battle was fought, while Brenton had also committed numerous factual errors and provided a confused and inaccurate diagram. James's critical examination extended beyond Brenton's and Ekins's detailed books to the well-known pictorial representations of the battle by P. J. de Loutherbourg and J. M. W. Turner, including them among the "glaring falsehoods and palpable inconsistencies"[49] relating to Trafalgar. James even went so far as to recommend to a future artist the proper vantage point from which to attempt a correct depiction of the scene.[50]

Historians have tended to agree with James over Brenton, noting that the naval officer "seems to have been incapable of sifting his evidence, and to have been guided more by prejudice than judgement. The plan of his work is good, but the execution feeble, and its authority as to matter of fact is often slender."[51]

Up through the middle years of the nineteenth century, the professional naval discussion over Trafalgar revolved around interpretations of the opposing commanders' intentions and contrasting those intentions with the actual course of events that took place. William James's interpretation came to dominate the historical scene for nearly half a century. During that half century, navies were undergoing massive changes in gunnery, ship design, and propulsion that quickly began to give the impression to many officers that all that had gone before in the Age of Sail was irrelevant to the New Age. While this became the prevailing view among officers fully immersed in the details of the burgeoning technology, it would be some time before that view was totally accepted and, even then, there were some serious qualifications that were made.

Views of Trafalgar in the Age of Steam

As steam propulsion began to become common on the naval scene, several officers began to foresee that future warships would operate at uniform speeds and in any direction they wished. From this, they concluded that the precision by which warships could maneuver under steam propulsion meant that the old skills, dependent on the vagaries of experienced understanding of wind, tide, and weather, could now be largely replaced by adaptations of the scientific principles of movement being adopted by modern armies. In the Royal Navy, such ideas were suggested by Admiral Sir William Bowles[52] and in the United States Navy by its leading gunnery expert, Captain John A. Dahlgren.[53]

Along these lines, one of the books most widely read by naval officers in the mid-nineteenth was one by General Sir Howard Douglas. A noted expert on gunnery and the son of an admiral, Douglas had published a well-known book on naval gunnery[54] and then had gone on to examine naval tactics. In his 1857 volume, *On Naval Warfare with Steam,* Douglas gave a brief summary of naval tactics under sail, since "it will be long before sails can be entirely superseded by steam engines, if this supercession should ever take place."[55] In this volume, Douglas analyzed Nelson's actions at both Aboukir Bay and at Trafalgar. In thinking about the French position at the Nile, he concluded,

> A steam-fleet will never be caught in so helpless a position; the ships would have their steam up, get underway, and try the issue of a general action: or the ships not doubled upon in this mode of attack might rush up and double upon one or both the attacking divisions.[56]

For Douglas, Nelson's tactics were a practical exemplification of the military principle that Napoleon had used so effectively in bringing superiority of force to the attacking point. Douglas thought that doubling an enemy's battle line would continue to be an important tactic for the future, but needed to be managed in an entirely different way than practiced in the past. Under steam, Douglas concluded that the van of the fleet, not the rear, should be attacked in order to throw the enemy into confusion.

In regard to Trafalgar, Douglas agreed with French Admiral Jurien de la Gravière's analysis[57] that French gunnery was at a low point and that Nelson had taken advantage of the circumstances that allowed him to adopt a mode of attack that disregarded the established military principles in approaching an enemy. As *Victory* slowly and deliberately approached, over a period of some forty minutes, the hundreds of enemy guns with her weakest point facing the enemy and her own guns not bearing, she should have been smashed to pieces. With adequate steam power and speed, the British fleet could have run up from the rear in two columns and enveloped the enemy. Douglas believed that a battle like Trafalgar would never take place again. Nevertheless, there was a lesson to be learned from Trafalgar:

> [O]ur officers, imbued with the resources of tactical science and nautical skill, and our men able and ardent to carry out, with unflinching courage, their commands, will nevertheless find in steam warfare, ample opportunities for acting in that vigorous and audacious manner which has ever been congenial to the spirit of British seamen.[58]

In Douglas's view, an enemy fleet in the future "should never passively receive . . . an attack made upon it, but should . . . assume promptly a position in which it may, by offensive operations, actively resist and frustrate the enemy's approach."[59]

Douglas's views were adopted and elaborated on by the most influential American student of the new tactics, Commander James H. Ward, U.S. Navy, whose 1859 work informed the thinking of many American naval officers during the American Civil War of 1861–65, and in the decades immediately thereafter.[60] This war brought with it further thinking on the use of armoured steam ships, the conduct of major blockades, the use of naval warfare on rivers, and the development of tactics for torpedo flotillas. Many of these considerations went far beyond the examples set by Nelson and because of this, Nelsonian examples tended to fade into the background of professional commentary by the 1880s. As one author noted in 1883, "the kettle has emasculated seamanship."[61]

In 1884, Commander William Bainbridge-Hoff, U.S. Navy, attempted to summarize the range of worldwide tactical thinking for the U.S. Navy's recently established Office of Naval Intelligence in a slim volume of *Examples, Conclusions, and Maxims of Modern Naval Tactics*[62] as something designed to be of practical use to American naval officers. His efficiently organized and terse quotations left no room for explicit historical references, beyond mention of very recent contemporary naval events, but Nelson's example could not have been far from the minds on a few issues. At the point in tactical development when the ram was being revived as a naval weapon and it appeared momentarily that it might become the dominant naval weapon for the future, there was doubt about what position in a battle formation an admiral should occupy. To deal with this argument, Ward approvingly quoted an unidentified German author, who had written:

> The Admiral's flag belongs on the largest and most powerful vessel, which should outshine all others as a brilliant example in the heat of battle. History shows that the Admiral must himself be in the midst of the fight. If he wishes to be the vital element in his ship, and to make the best use of all the components of his command, then he must put himself in a position to see everything and to be seen of all.[63]

The kind of work that Bainbridge-Hoff was doing in America to gather the current rich and diverse opinion about naval tactics was designed to stimulate further new thinking about the effective use of new naval weapons in the hope that a more general tactical theory could evolve. Viewing the same scene from a quite different geographic and national outlook, a Russian admiral, Vice-Admiral Stepan Makarov, embarked on a project to do just that and to create a much needed tactical theory for the Imperial Russian Navy. Although his highly regarded theoretical work lost credibility outside Russia with his own defeat and death at the battle of Tsushima in 1905, Makarov's work was translated and read with great interest for a number of years by naval professionals and it retains considerable interest today.

Admiral Makarov's study, *Discussion of Questions in Naval Tactics,*[64] was one that stressed above all the importance of individual naval leadership rather than the contemporary idea of broad, overarching scientific principles that governed human actions regardless of practical and technical considerations. Makarov was one of the leading innovative minds for the Russian Navy of his time and he was thoroughly familiar with naval history. His 1898 study of tactics has been considered "as modern, concrete, practicable, and creative as can be found among any of the tactical thinkers of the turn of the century, a period distinguished by the quantity of writing on the subject."[65]

Makarov made extensive use of Nelson's example in his consideration of modern naval tactics. In doing so in the context of professional tactical discussion, Makarov widened out an understanding of Nelson in a way that paralleled what Captain A. T. Mahan had done with his 1897 biography.[66] There is no evidence that Makarov directly used Mahan's biographical work; instead, he relied on the French commentary by Admiral Jurien de la Gravière.

With the age of sailing navies now firmly in the past, Makarov looked at Nelson's example with a quite different focus than his predecessors, who had looked at it in terms of formulating improved sailing tactics. First, Makarov considered the questions of what Nelson was and why he was successful. In exploring that issue, Makarov concluded that "we turn instinctively to Nelson, for in him we find energy combined with fearlessness in war and with unusual daring as a seaman."[67] Above all, Makarov felt that Nelson's career provided "a brilliant example of the fact that true energy is indomitable."[68] But beyond this, Nelson showed a set of important characteristics. He appeared to be moderate in his requirements and expenditures,[69] took what talent he found in his fleet as it was and expressed full confidence in all who served under him,[70] was careful in his application of discipline,[71] and paid attention to health,[72] training, and education of his officers and men.[73] These attributes combined together in Nelson, "who united in himself infinite energy with rare daring." In Makarov's view, "it is even more necessary to study his energy as a seaman than his boldness in war."[74]

Nelson's capacities as a seaman complemented his quite different characteristics as a military leader. Here, Makarov attempted to explore Nelson's understanding of the concept of victory. Nelson, he found, was a leader who understood how to complete and to perfect his victories, producing results beyond a mere enemy retreat. To complete a victory one must annihilate the enemy force. Going further, Makarov declared, "By perfection of victory upon the sea we can only understand victory followed by the seizure of the enemy's transports, if he possesses them, or of his harbors, if he is protected by them."[75]

In examining the causes of Nelson's victories, Makarov followed Admiral Jurien de la Gravière's views in arguing that they were not the results of superior numbers, of wealth, nor even of the Admiralty's political influence. Rather, they were the fruits of superior preparation for battle, through better training and discipline, along with leadership that converted discipline into teamwork through "a circle of brothers and friends. His wish was that mutual love and esteem should bind together those called to fight under the same flag."[76]

Then, Makarov went further to criticize the French admiral's opinion that Nelson's tactical evolutions were mistakes of genius crowned with success and had demonstrated, particularly at Trafalgar, a clear disregard for sound tactical thinking. It was quite the opposite, Makarov argued. Nelson did not disregard the fundamental princi-ples of tactics, but acted according to them, by accomplishing his tactical purpose in us-ing unexpected methods, by massing his full force at critical point and in better position than the enemy's, and by using the existing sea conditions to greater advantage than the enemy to create a more stable platform for effective and well-aimed gunfire. "There is no reason for accusing him of neglecting tactical precautions. On the contrary, he rather took the initiative in tactics than otherwise,"[77] Makarov wrote.

Like Makarov, many professional naval commentators of the day looked to the period of the Napoleonic Wars, the last great series of worldwide naval wars, as a well for thinking about future warfare. But not everyone agreed with his approach. The exam-ples of the American Civil War and Prussian military success in the Austro- and Franco-Prussian Wars gave rise to alternative approaches to warfare and a broad range of professional reflection following on from them. On one hand, Prussian success led many countries into adopting German initiatives to apply staff procedures to prepare for war, to establish professional educational institutions to promote the profes-sionalization of the uniformed services, and to encourage the development and direct application of professional naval and military literature. In France, the effects of bitter defeat led to innovative naval thinking in the ideas of the *Jeune École.*[78]

In the United States, these trends gave rise to applications of the German approach. The German Kriegs- and Marine-Akademies were prototypes for establishing the U.S. Naval War College in 1884 and for the accompanying impetus it gave to the historical work of Alfred Thayer Mahan. Eventually, Mahan even extended his understanding of the period to include Nelson as an example of the "embodiment of sea power" in the context of education officers in an understanding of grand strategy and command.[79] In the years that followed, the establishment of a similar educational institution in Britain led its most prominent civilian lecturer, Julian Corbett, to focus his thoughts on broad strategic issues in his study of the Seven Years' War and subsequently to create his man-ual for naval strategic thinking.[80]

In the years following the huge public interest and the outpouring of books that ac-companied the centenary of Trafalgar in 1905, Corbett embarked on his two-volume study, *The Campaign of Trafalgar,* published in 1910. In undertaking this study pri-vately on the lines of a military staff study, Corbett was aiming his result at the profes-sional officer. What was needed, Corbett believed, was a coordinated professional analysis of the movements of all classes of ships engaged in major operations, with a clear understanding of the instructions and intelligence by which the operation was car-ried out. In the preface to his study of Trafalgar, Corbett modestly wrote, "No one can approach our Naval History from this point of view, even in the tentative and imperfect manner that has been attempted in the following pages without feeling how defective is the bulk of what we now possess."

> It is scarcely an exaggeration to say that the whole requires writing on Staff lines. But it is unlikely that so large and technical a task can ever be done adequately except by an Histori-cal Section at the Admiralty. The need for such a Section is crying. . . . It needs, no less than the most technical material parts of the naval art, a laboratory where civilian and naval ex-perts can work side by side to supply each others defects and ripen each others ideas.[81]

As a result of this, Corbett soon went on to be a key figure in two such organizations and to write operational naval histories of both the Russo-Japanese War and of World War

One.[82] In this way, professional thinking in Britain about Nelson, Trafalgar, and the naval operations of that time led directly to thinking about the need for more modern applications of historical analysis for professional purposes.

However, before these wider and newer applications of history could be brought to bear in the Royal Navy, official Admiralty attention was given directly to Trafalgar. The Admiralty belatedly turned its official attention to trying to settle the disputed issues of fact which had plagued studies of Trafalgar from the outset and had cast doubt on the validity of many of the conclusions that professionals had reached about the battle in the previous century. In April 1912, the Admiralty appointed a committee of investigation to determine, on the basis of thorough professional understanding and on all available documents, exactly what Nelson's tactics had been at the battle of Trafalgar. With Admiral Sir Cyprian Bridge as chairman, the committee's members consisted of Admiral Sir Reginald Custance and the Regius Professor of Modern History at Oxford University, Charles Firth, with Admiralty Librarian W. G. Perrin, as the committee's secretary.

Eighteen months later, the Admiralty published the committee's report on the eve of Trafalgar Day 1913,[83] including in it the committee's most substantial work, prepared for them by the former Assistant Hydrographer of the Navy, Captain T. H. Tizard, which the committee declared was

> the first and only plans representing any phase of the battle of Trafalgar which have been drawn to scale, and in which the positions assigned to particular ships in the British fleet have been settled in accordance with the evidence contained in the Logs and Journals.[84]

With the trauma of the Great War less than a year away, the committee's detailed work seems to have had little direct impact on subsequent professional naval thinking and, until recently, has been often overlooked by civilian scholars.[85]

In 1914, the year following the Admiralty report, one of the committee's members, Admiral Sir Reginald Custance, wrote a brief introduction to a translation of a recent study of naval battle tactics by Lieutenant Baudry of the French Navy.[86] Originally written in 1910, this volume reflected some new aspects of French naval thinking that had arisen in the previous decades and that would interest English-language audiences. Unlike the *Jeune École,* Baudry still focused on a naval battle between large warships. In this, Baudry made extensive use of Edouard Desbrière's recent study of the French side of the battle,[87] but contented himself with William James's older account of the British viewpoint. As Baudry noted, "We have no historical pretensions, either of description or research."[88] For him there were only two accounts, that of the victor and that of the vanquished; truth, he thought, oscillated between them, so it is a useless effort to try to establish detail. He felt that he knew enough about the main outline of the events to draw judgments for professional naval use. Nevertheless, "the Nelsonian battle shall be for us a beacon and a watchword," Baudry declared, going on to say that "the finest and most decisive of Nelson's manœuvres of victory is Trafalgar."[89]

Baudry reflected the views of many naval officers of his era as they expected what future naval battle might look like, as they looked back across the previous century, comparing and contrasting Trafalgar to the battles at the Nile, Lissa, and Tsushima. Baudry had examined his subject in the context of several themes: ships, gunnery, tactics, *manœuvre,* and unity in command, repeatedly using Trafalgar as his supreme example to form a set of elements for taxonomy of naval battle. In concluding his work in

1910, Baudry wrote, "We have just raised up the image of a naval battle. Is not such a battle the *decisive* battle?"

> I could wish that I had portrayed more faithfully all its passion and life; its material side, undeniabl[y] significant, but only so when multiplied by human factors—intelligence, will, energy, enthusiasm, moral ascendancy, all these summed up by discipline and loyalty to comrade in the one word MANOEVRE.[90]

In the years between the two world wars, the concept of *manœuvre* was one that Admiral Raoul Castex elaborated upon in detail in his multivolume work *Théories Stratégiques*.[91] Castex defined the word with great care: "to *manœuvre*," he wrote, "is to *move intelligently in order to create a favorable situation*."[92] For him, *manœuvre* was the pinnacle of the art of war and what he called "the divine part of the profession, that which calls upon all the treasures of spirit, intelligence, imagination, will, and knowledge."[93] Interestingly, Castex used Nelson's and Bruix's competitive *manœuvre* in the 1799 Mediterranean campaign as the historical basis to recast the same events using the ships and equipment of 1930. By this intellectual exercise, Castex wanted to illustrate for his readers the transformation in methods of executing strategic *manœuvre* over the period of a century and to suggest the repercussions that the transformation had on the conception and possibilities of the forms of *manœuvre* available in the 1930s.

As Nelson gradually had become a more remote figure in history, professional naval opinion seemed largely to settle on the battle of the Nile, rather than on Trafalgar, as Nelson's greatest battle. Here, the point was not to consider its effect on the course of history, but rather its example to emulate in the conduct of future naval warfare. As the twentieth century drew toward its close, the situation in professional naval thought was dramatically different than it had been a century earlier, when there were a wide variety of books, pamphlets, and articles on differing theories and approaches to naval tactics and strategy.

When Captain Wayne P. Hughes, Jr., of the U.S. Navy first published his book *Fleet Tactics: Theory and Practice* in 1986, it was the first book on naval tactics to be written by an American naval officer for nearly half a century and that earlier book had been a history of tactical maxims,[94] not a manual for current application. Hughes chose to open his very important book with the historical example of the battle of the Nile, but he openly warned his reader, "History is a fickle teacher who lets her opinionated and ill-disciplined students draw lessons as they will."[95] As the opening piece in Hughes's book, the account of the Nile is a dramatic one that included some considerable artistic license and use of historical imagination that borders on fiction to draw the modern naval officer into the events, but, nevertheless, Hughes does justice to the basic facts of the events. His narrative has a clear and original purpose, which is to use Nelson and the battle of the Nile to illustrate the crucial fundamentals about maritime warfare that affect naval tactics in general and in particular. These, he calls the "The Five Cornerstones" of naval tactics, all of which are illustrated by Nelson at the Nile:[96]

1. Leadership, morale, training, physical and mental conditioning, will power, and endurance are the most important elements in warfare. This cornerstone, Hughes says, appeases the reader who would rather emphasize high courage in battle over hard thinking.

2. Doctrine is the companion and instrument of good leadership. It is the basis of training and all that implies: cohesion, reliability in battle, and mutual understanding and support.

3. Tactical and technological developments are so intertwined as to be inseparable. To know tactics, you must know weapons.

4. The destruction of the enemy's fleet is the fleet's foremost immediate objective; there is always some higher goal. The set of purpose is on the land.

5. The tactical maxim of all naval battles is *Attack effectively first.* This means that the first objective is to bring the enemy under concentrated firepower while forestalling his response.

After describing these essential elements of tactical thinking, Hughes went on to comment that given the complex demands of tactics, "it has been said of C. S. Forester's greatest fictional hero, Horatio Hornblower, that had he really lived, he would have been put ashore with ulcers."[97] Nevertheless, Hughes hoped that his "vignette of the battle of the Nile . . . evoked a picture of the human element of warfare, of emotion elevated to feverish pitch, and of the way tactical plans and battlefield decisions are influenced by an environment of controlled violence and directed chaos."[98]

Finally, the current wave of publications on Nelson and his times, which has now reached tsunami proportions, has thrown up a number of very important works of historical scholarship, but few authors among them have returned to Nelson or Trafalgar in terms designed to engage modern naval officers in the context of their current professional concerns.

Rear Admiral Joseph Callo, U.S. Naval Reserve, has taken one approach to try to reach the modern uniformed officer in his small volume of excerpts from Nelson's letters, *Nelson Speaks,*[99] concentrating on selections that resonate with current military life and naval concerns. Dr. Joel Hayward, sometime instructor in strategic studies at several New Zealand military and naval colleges, has taken a very different path in his book subtitled *Lord Nelson and His Way of War.*[100]

Hayward's approach is to consider Nelson in terms of six categories of great interest to students of modern warfare, devoting a chapter to each: Nelson's conception of the enemy, his personal spiritual beliefs, his command leadership, his war fighting style, and his dealings in land warfare, and in coalition warfare. In his conclusion, Hayward defined Nelson as a man who demonstrated the strength in the human spirit that can create superiority over human frailties in warfare. In Hayward's view, "It is the triumph of Nelson's spirit as much as his tactical brilliance and physical and moral courage that places him among history's greatest warriors—that small group of exceptional humans who trusted their instincts, managed their fears, took risks, learned from mistakes, acted audaciously, and consequently proved all their foes unequal."[101]

The Legacy of Trafalgar

In conclusion, one can say that the legacy of Trafalgar in professional naval thought around the world has been a varied one over two centuries. Initially, it gave rise to immediate "lessons learned" based on an incomplete and even incorrect understanding of the events that had taken place. These initial conclusions were focused at the level of technical and practical application. Gradually, as naval warfare changed over time and as a broader understanding of the naval profession developed in the late nineteenth century, the events that took place at Trafalgar became generalized into a broader *schema* which centered on Horatio Nelson as an emblematic leader and warrior with traits that transcended his age rather than on Trafalgar as an exemplary battle in the Age of Sail.

As time passed and naval conditions changed, the attention that had been paid to Trafalgar and to Nelson's other battles helped to give impetus to the need to go beyond that period for professional purposes and to find value in studying the operational history of more recent battles, fought in different circumstances and with different equipment and weapons. Yet, these new insights from different times and places merged with the older historical examples and began to be seen as a significant part of the continuing, cumulative experience of the naval profession, ranging across the spectrum of strategy, tactics, and leadership.

NOTES This paper was delivered in Beveridge Hall, Senate House, University of London, at the "Europe at War: The Trafalgar Campaign in Context" conference, sponsored by the National Maritime Museum, Greenwich, and the Institute of Historical Research, University of London, 13–15 July 2005.

1 *The London Gazette Extraordinary* (Wednesday, 6 Nov. 1805). For the text of the original report compared to Collingwood's drafts, see Max Adams, *Admiral Collingwood: Nelson's Own Hero* (London: Weidenfeld & Nicolson, 2005), Appendix One, pp. 303–311. For the arrival of the news in England, see Derek Allen and Peter Hore, *News of Nelson: John Lapenotiere's Race from Trafalgar to London* (Brussels Belgium: SEFF Édition, 2005) and the map *The Trafalgar Way* (London: Ordnance Survey in association with Sea Britain 2005, The National Trust, and the New Trafalgar Dispatch, 2005).

2 *Naval Chronicle,* vol. 14 (1805), pp. 421–426.

3 A search for the logs of both these vessels and the papers of their masters was made in the most likely depositories in the USA, but no trace of them has yet turned up. Thus, *Neptune*'s date of sailing is conjectural and based on the reported day that *Fox* and *Neptune* met at sea.

4 No surviving copy of this handbill is known. A search was made at the Maine Historical Society, American Antiquarian Society, and the Library of Congress.

5 *Portland Gazette and Maine Advertizer,* vol. VIII, no. 35, 16 December 1805, p. 3. *Fox* arrived in Portland after a 35-day passage from Nantes.

6 *Boston Gazette,* vol. 19, no. 32, whole number 954, Thursday, 19 December 1805; *Newport Mercury,* Saturday, 21 December 1805.

7 *New York Gazette,* vol. XVIII, no. 6179, Tuesday, 17 December 1805, p. 2; printed the same day in *The New York Evening Post,* no. 1270, p. 2.

8 *Poulson's American Daily Advertiser* [Philadelphia], vol. XXXIV, no. 9059, Wednesday, 18 December 1805, p. 2.

9 *Eastern Shore General Advertiser* [Easton, Maryland], vol. 4 . . . 7, No. 18 . . . 329, Tuesday, 24 December 1805, p. 3.

10 *Alexandria Daily Advertiser* [Virginia], vol. VI, no. 1477, Friday, 20 December 1805, p. 2.

11 *National Intelligencer and Washington Advertiser* [District of Columbia], vol. VI, no. DCCCXIV, Friday, 27 December 1805, p. 3.

12 *The Quebec Gazette / La Gazette de Québec Extraordinary,* no. 2124, Thursday, 2 January 1806, p. 1; *The Quebec Mercury,* vol. II, no. 1, Monday, 6 January 1806. The brig *Good Intent,* Captain Davis, brought *The London Gazette Extraordinary* from Liverpool to Halifax, Nova Scotia, in 34 days, arriving on 19 December and Collingwood's dispatch was printed in *The Nova Scotia Royal Gazette,* vol. 1, no. 263, Thursday, 26 December 1805, through which it was transmitted to St. John, New Brunswick, and printed in the *St. John Gazette Extraordinary,* 30 December 1805.

13 Two volumes (London: Printed for John Murray, bookseller to the Admiralty and to the board of Longitude, . . . , 1813); unauthorized American editions were quickly published at New York by Eastburn, Kirk, & Co., and at Boston by William Wells in 1813. Another edition was published in Hartford [Conn.] by B. & J. Russell for Oliver D. Cooke in 1814; there was another printing at Boston: E. G. House, 1814; and yet another at Hartford: W. S. Marsh, 1814.

14 John Clerk of Eldin, *An Essay on Naval Tactics. Systematical and Historical* (London: Printed for T. Cadell, 1790–1797). See Michel Depeyre, "Clerk, John, of Eldin (1728–1812)," *Oxford Dictionary of National Biography,* Oxford University Press, 2004 [http://www.oxforddnb.com/view/article/5618] and also for a general history of tactical theory, see Michel Depeyre, *Tactiques et Stratégies Navales de la France et du Royaume-Uni de 1690 à 1815* (Paris: Economica, 1998) and limitations of abstract theory when applied in practice, explained by N. A. M. Rodger, "Image and Reality in Eighteenth-Century Naval Tactics," *Mariner's Mirror,* vol. 91 (2003), pp. 280–296.

15 A portion of which was first published as Josiah Burchett, *Memoirs of Transactions at Sea during the War with France* (London, 1703) and then included in the full book *A Complete History of the Most Remarkable Transactions at Sea* (London, 1720). See John B. Hattendorf, "Burchett, Josiah (c.1666–1746)," *Oxford Dictionary of National Biography,* Oxford University Press, 2004 [http://www.oxforddnb.com/view/article/3955].

16 Thomas Lediard, *The naval history of England, in all its branches: from the Norman Conquest in the year 1066, to the conclusion of 1734: collected from the most approved historians, English and foreign, authentick records and manuscripts, scarce tracts, original journals, &c. with many facts and observations never before made publick* (London: Printed for J. Wilcox, 1735). See J. K. Laughton, "Lediard, Thomas (1685–1743)," rev. Alexander Du Toit, *Oxford Dictionary of National Biography,* Oxford University Press, 2004 [http://www.oxforddnb.com/view/article/16269].

17 John Entick, *A new naval history: or, Compleat view of the British marine. In which the Royal navy and the merchant's service are traced through all their periods and different branches: with the lives of the admirals and navigators, who have honour'd this nation . . . Including . . . the laws and regulations for the government and oeconomy of His Majesty's navy . . . To which are added our right and title to the British colonies in North-America: and an abstract of the laws now in force for regulating our trade and commerce* (London: R. Manby, 1757). See Jennett Humphreys, "Entick, John (c.1703–1773)," rev. Penelope Wilson, *Oxford Dictionary of National Biography,* Oxford University Press, 2004 [http://www.oxforddnb.com/view/article/8824].

18 See Samuel Willard Crompton. "Truxtun, Thomas"; http://www.anb.org/articles/03/03-00502.html; *American National Biography Online* February 2000.

19 Thomas Truxtun, *A Few extracts, from the best authors, on naval tactics, to be found also in Dobson's encyclopedia the extracts selected, and some short notes made merely to show the advantages of a curve line of battle, out of the ordinary mode* (Philadelphia: Printed by A. Bartram for Thomas Dobson, 1806).

20 Père Paul Hoste, *L'art des armées navales, ou, Traité des évolutions navales : qui contient des règles utiles aux officiers Généraux & particuliers d'une Armée Navale : avec des exemples tirez de ce qui s'est passé de plus considérable sur la mer depuis cinquante ans : enrichi de figures en taille-douce.* (First edition, Lyon, 1697; Second edition, Lyon, 1727), but Truxtun may have more probably used the partial translation in English: Christopher O'Bryen, *Naval evolutions: or, A system of sea discipline; extracted from the celebrated treatise of P. L' Hoste . . . confirmed by experience; illustrated by examples from the most remarkable sea-engagements between England and Holland; embellished with eighteen copper-plates; and adapted to the use of the British navy, To which are added, An abstract of the theory of ship-building; An essay on naval discipline, by the late experienced sea-commander; A general idea of the armament of the French navy; with some practical observations* (London: Printed for W. Johnston, 1772).

21 Sébastien-François vicomte Bigot de Morogues, *Naval tactics or, A treatise of evolutions and signals, with cuts, lately published in France . . .* (Paris, 1763, translation London: W. Johnston, 1767).

22 Jacques-Pierre Bourdé de Villehuet, *The manoeuverer, or Skilful seaman: being an essay on the theory and practice of the various movements of a ship at sea, as well as of naval evolutions in general. Translated from the French of Mr. Bourdé de Villehuet, by the Chevalier de Sauseuil. Illustrated with thirteen copperplates . . .* (Paris, 1765 and 1769, translation London: Printed for S. Hooper, 1788).

23 Jacques Raymond, vicomte de Grenier, *The art of war at sea, or, Naval tactics reduced to new principles: with a new order of battle: illustrated with copper plates/translated from the French of Viscount de Grenier, Rear Admiral in the French navy, by the Chevalier de Sauseuil, Knight of the most Noble Order of St. Philip, Captain of Infantry in the French Service, late Captain and Major-Adjutant of the Legion of Tonnère, and member of the Society of Arts, &c. in London* (Paris, 1787, translation London: Printed for S. Hooper, No. 212, High Holborn, opposite Southampton-Street, Bloomsbury-Square, M.DCC.LXXXVIII [1788]).

24 U.S. National Archives and Records Administration (U.S. NARA), RG 45: Letters Received by the Secretary of the Navy from Captains, vol. 3. 1 Sept 1805–31 December 1805. NARA microfilm, no. 125, Roll T-3, reel 3, letter 31: Captain Hugh G. Campbell to Secretary of the Navy, USS *Essex* at Malaga, 30 October 1805, enclosing an account received by the U.S. Consul at Malaga, Mr. Kirkpatrick, from a correspondent at Cadiz. No date of receipt in Washington noted. This report was the first detailed report received directly by the U.S. Navy on Trafalgar. The same enclosure was printed in the *Alexandria* [Virginia] *Daily Advertiser,* vol. VI, no. 1482, 27 December 1805, p. 2. The report was reprinted from New York, where it had first arrived on 23 December in the ship *Hare,* Captain Chew, after a 49-day passage from Malaga to New York. *Hare* had departed Gibraltar on 25 October for Malaga under convoy of the U.S. brig *Vixen,* then sailed from Malaga to New York on 4 November, parting company with her escort off Cape Spartel.

25 Collingwood to Admiralty, 22 October 1805. Adams, *Collingwood,* p. 304.

26 Michèle Battesti, *Trafalgar: Les Aléas de la Stratégie Navale de Napoléon* (St. Cloud: Napoléon 1er Éditions, 2004), pp. 242–243; N. A. M. Rodger, *The Command of the Ocean: A Naval History of Britain, 1649–1815* (London: Penguin Allen Lane, 2004), p. 539.

27 Truxtun, *A Few Extracts,* p. 10, note.

28 Ibid., paragraph heading.

29 Ibid., p. 13; Eugene S. Ferguson, *Truxtun of the Constellation: The Life of Commodore Thomas Truxtun, U.S. Navy, 1755–1822* (originally published 1956, reprinted Annapolis: Naval Institute Press, 1982), p. 230.

30 Rémi Monaque, "Trafalgar 1805: Strategy, Tactics, and Results," *Mariner's Mirror,* vol. 91, no. 2 (May 2001), pp. 241–250, quote at p. 249.

31 S. S. Robison, *A History of Naval Tactics from 1530 to 1930: The Evolution of Tactical Maxims* (Annapolis: Naval Institute Press, 1942), pp. 490–493.

32 See Hattendorf, "Nelson Afloat," in David Cannadine, ed., *Admiral Lord Nelson* (London: Palgrave Macmillan, 2005), chapter 8 at pp. 169–170; David Curtis Skaggs, *Thomas Macdonough:*

Master of Command in the Early U.S. Navy (Annapolis: Naval Institute Press, 2003), p. 127.

33 J. R. Soley, ed., "Autobiography of Commodore Charles Morris," U.S. Naval Institute *Proceedings*, vol. VI (1880), pp. 111–219, and *Autobiography of Commodore Charles Morris* (Boston: A. Williams, 1880), quoted in Robison, *A History of Naval Tactics,* p. 523.

34 Memorandum, 9 October 1805, reprinted from Harris Nicolas, ed., *The dispatches and letters of Vice Admiral Lord Viscount Nelson, with notes* (London: H. Colburn, 1845–46), vol. vii, in Julian S. Corbett, ed., *Fighting Instructions, 1530–1816.* Publications of the Navy Records Society, vol. xxix (London: Navy Records Society, 1905; reprinted Conway Maritime Press, 1971), pp. 316–320.

35 Corbett, *Fighting Instructions*, p. 321.

36 Ibid., pp. 335–347; Hugh Popham, *A Damned Cunning Fellow: The Eventful Life of Rear-Admiral Sir Home Popham, KCB, KCH, KM, FRS, 1762–1820* (St. Austell: Old Ferry Press, 1991), chapter XII "Problems of Communication, 1800–12," pp. 125–132.

37 Quoted in Corbett, *Fighting Instructions,* p. 338. Corbett's bibliographical citation is incomplete; the work is Général le Comte Mathieu Dumas (1753–1837), *Précis des Événements Militaires ou essai historique sur les campagnes de 1799 à 1814, avec cartes et plans.* 19 volumes (Paris and Strasbourg: Treuttel et Würtz, 1816–1829), vol. xiv, *Pièces Justicatives,* p. 408.

38 Andrew Lambert, *The Last Sailing Battlefleet: Maintaining Naval Mastery 1815–1850* (London: Conway Maritime Press, 1991), p. 93.

39 Donald M. Schurman, *Julian S. Corbett 1854–1922: Historian of British Maritime Policy from Drake to Jellicoe.* Royal Historical Studies in History series, vol. 26 (London: Royal Historical Society, 1981), pp. 43–49.

40 Charles Ekins, *Naval Battles from 1744 to the Peace in 1814 Critically Reviewed and Illustrated* (London: Baldwin, Craddock, & Joy, 1824). The section relating to Trafalgar from pp. 271–275 is reproduced as an Appendix to Corbett, *Fighting Instructions,* pp. 351–358.

41 Ekins, *Naval Battles,* p. 274; Corbett, *Fighting Instructions,* p. 356.

42 J. K. Laughton, "Ekins, Sir Charles (1768–1855)," rev. Andrew Lambert, *Oxford Dictionary of National Biography,* Oxford University Press, 2004 [http://www.oxforddnb.com/view/article/8604].

43 E. P. Brenton, *The Naval History of Great Britain from the Year MDCCLXXXIII to MDCCCXXII.* 5 volumes (London: C. Rice, 1822–25, revised and expanded to respond to criticism in James below, 1837).

44 William James, *The Naval History of Great Britain from the Declaration of War by France in 1793 to the Accession of George IV* (London, 1822–27, reprinted and revised by various editors, 1836–37, 1847, 1859, 1864, 1886, 1898, 1902, 2002).

45 Rear-Admiral Jahleel Brenton (1729–1802).

46 Vice-Admiral Sir Jahleel Brenton, first baronet (1770–1844).

47 Quoted in Eugene L. Rasor, *English/British Naval History to 1815: A Guide to the Literature.* Bibliography and Indexes in Military History, no. 15 (Westport, Connecticut, and London: Praeger, 2004), p. 53.

48 James, *A Naval History* (London: Macmillan, 1902), vol. iii, p. 468.

49 Ibid., p. 474.

50 Ibid.

51 J. K. Laughton, "Brenton, Edward Pelham (1774–1839)," rev. Andrew Lambert, *Oxford Dictionary of National Biography,* Oxford University Press, 2004 [http://www.oxforddnb.com/view/article/3325].

52 Admiral Sir William Bowles, *Essay on Tactics* (London: Ridgeway, 1846). See Andrew Lambert, "Bowles, Sir William (1780–1869)," *Oxford Dictionary of National Biography,* Oxford University Press, 2004 [http://www.oxforddnb.com/view/article/60818].

53 John A. Dahlgren, *Shells and Shell-Guns* (Washington, 1856), p. 394. See William M. Fowler. "Dahlgren, John Adolphus Bernard"; http://www.anb.org/articles/04/04-00291.html; *American National Biography Online* February 2000.

54 General Sir Howard Douglas, *A Treatise on Naval Gunnery* (London, 1855). See H. M. Chichester, "Douglas, Sir Howard, third baronet (1776–1861)," rev. Roger T. Stearn, *Oxford Dictionary of National Biography,* Oxford University Press, 2004 [http://www.oxforddnb.com/view/article/7888]. He was the third son of Vice-Admiral Sir Charles Douglas of Carr, first baronet (d. 1789) and a defender of some of his father's naval ideas.

55 Quotations used here are from the second edition: General Sir Howard Douglas, *On Naval Warfare with Steam* (London: John Murray, 1860), p. xix.

56 Ibid., p. 129, para. 141.

57 Jean Pierre Edmond Jurien de la Gravière, *Sketches of the Last Naval War,* trans. by Captain Plunkett (London: Longman, Brown, Green, and Longmans, 1848), vol. 2, pp. 185–189.

58 Douglas, *On Naval Warfare with Steam,* p. 134, para. 147.

59 Ibid., p. 135, para. 148.

60 James H. Ward, *A Manual of Naval Tactics Together with a Brief Critical Analysis of the Principal Modern Naval Tactics* (New York: D. Appleton & Co., 1859). See William M. Fowler. "Ward, James Harmon"; http://www.anb.org/articles/04/04-01032.html; *American National Biography Online* February 2000.

61 Captain the Hon. Edmund R. Freemantle, RN, "Naval Tactics on the Open Sea with the Existing Types of Vessels and Weapons," *Ordnance Notes—No. 280, Washington, March 29, 1883,* p. 12. Reprinted from the *Journal of the Royal United Service Institution,* The Naval Prize Essay, 1880.

62 Commander William Bainbridge-Hoff, U.S. Navy, *Examples, Conclusions, and Maxims of Modern Naval Tactics.* Information from Abroad, General

Information Series, no. III (Washington: Government Printing Office, 1884).

63 Ibid., p. 88.

64 Vice Admiral S. O. Makarov, *Discussion of Questions in Naval Tactics.* Translated from the Russian by Lieutenant John B. Bernadou, U.S. Navy. Originally published by the U.S. Navy's Office of Naval Intelligence, General Information series, no. XVII (Washington: Government Printing Office, 1898), reprinted with an Introduction and Notes by Captain Robert B. Bathurst, USN (ret.), Classics of Sea Power series (Annapolis: Naval Institute Press, 1990).

65 Robert B. Bathurst, Introduction to ibid., p. xxvi.

66 A. T. Mahan, *The Life of Nelson: The Embodiment of the Sea Power of Great Britain* (Boston: Little, Brown, 1897).

67 Makarov, *Discussion of Questions in Naval Tactics,* p. 57.

68 Ibid., pp. 57–61, section 35, quote at p. 57.

69 Ibid., p. 62, section 36.

70 Ibid., p. 63, section 38.

71 Ibid., pp. 63–64, section 39.

72 Ibid., p. 64, section 40.

73 Ibid., pp. 64–65, section 41.

74 Ibid., p. 65, section 42.

75 Ibid., p. 67, section 43.

76 Ibid., p. 68.

77 Ibid., p. 78, section 47.

78 Arne Røksund, "The Jeune École: The Strategy of the Weak," in Rolf Hobson and Tom Kristiansen, eds., *Navies in Northern Waters, 1721–2000.* Cass Series: Naval Policy and Strategy, vol. 26 (London: Frank Cass, 2004), pp. 117–150.

79 Jon Tetsuro Sumida, *Inventing Grand Strategy and Teaching Command: The Classic Works of Alfred Thayer Mahan Reconsidered* (Baltimore: The Johns Hopkins University Press, 1997). See also Hattendorf, et al., *Sailors and Scholars: The Centennial History of the Naval War College* (Newport: Naval War College Press, 1984), chapter 2.

80 Schurman, *Julian S. Corbett 1854–1922.* See also Corbett, *England in the Seven Years' War: A Study in Combined Strategy* (London: Longmans, 1907) and *Some Principles of Maritime Strategy* (London: Longmans, 1911).

81 Julian S. Corbett, *The Campaign of Trafalgar* (London: Longmans, 1910), p. xii.

82 Julian S. Corbett, *Maritime Operations in the Russo-Japanese War, 1904–1905* (Annapolis: Naval Institute Press, and Newport: Naval War College Press, 1994) and Corbett, *Naval Operations. History of the Great War based on Official Documents,* vols. 1–3 (London: Longman Green, 1920–23).

83 Great Britain. Admiralty. *Report of the Committee Appointed by the Admiralty to Examine and to Consider the Evidence Relating to the Tactics Employed by Nelson at the Battle of Trafalgar Presented to Parliament by Command of his Majesty* (London: HMSO, 1913) Command 7120. Navy (Trafalgar). See also the commentary and summary of the Report by J. R. Thursfield, in *The Times,* 21 October 1913, pp. 9–10.

84 Admiralty. *Report of the Committee,* p. vii. For a note on Tizard's career, see Vice Admiral Sir Archibald Day, *The Admiralty Hydrographic Service, 1795–1919* (London: HMSO, 1967), pp. 156–157.

85 Carola Oman used it in her *Nelson* (London: Hodder & Stoughton, 1947), but see Marianne Czisnik, "Admiral Nelson's Tactics at Trafalgar," *History,* vol. 89 (2004), pp. 549–559, and Michael Duffy, " . . . 'All Was Hushed Up': The Hidden Trafalgar," *Mariner's Mirror,* vol. 91, no. 2 (May 2005), pp. 216–240.

86 Lieutenant A. Baudry (French Navy), *The Naval Battle: Studies of the Tactical Factors. Followed by Observations on the Unity of Doctrine by Captain G. Laur (French Army)* (London: Hugh Rees, 1914).

87 Edouard Desbrière, *La Campagne Maritime de 1805* (Paris, 1907); translated by Constance Eastwick as *The Trafalgar Campaign* (London: Oxford University Press, 1933).

88 Baudry, *The Naval Battle,* p. 219.

89 Ibid.

90 Ibid., pp. 320–321.

91 Raoul Castex, *Théories Stratégiques.* Five volumes (Paris: Société d'Éditions Géographiques, Maritimes, et Coloniales, 1929–35). A sixth volume was published posthumously as Raoul Castex, *Mélanges Stratégiques.* Hervé Coutau-Bégarie, ed. (Paris, 1976). See also Hervé Coutau-Bégarie, *Le Stratège inconnu* (Paris, 1985) and *La Puissance Maritime* (Paris, 1985).

92 Raoul Castex, *Strategic Theories.* Selections translated and edited with an introduction by Eugenia C. Kiesling (Annapolis: Naval Institute Press, 1994), p. 102.

93 Ibid.

94 Robison, *A History of Naval Tactics from 1530 to 1930.*

95 Captain Wayne P. Hughes, Jr., USN (Ret.), *Fleet Tactics: Theory and Practice* (Annapolis: Naval Institute Press, 1986).

96 The following points are summarized from ibid., pp. 24–25, with some further clarification from p. 14.

97 Ibid., p. 26.

98 Ibid.

99 Joseph F. Callo, *Nelson Speaks: Admiral Lord Nelson in His Own Words* (Annapolis: Naval Institute Press, 2001).

100 Joel Hayward, *For God and Glory: Lord Nelson and His Way of War* (Annapolis: Naval Institute Press, 2003). See Hattendorf's review in *The Journal of Military History,* vol. 68, no. 1 (January 2004), pp. 252–253.

101 Ibid., p. 208.

X *Whither with Nelson and Trafalgar?*
The Bicentenary Scholarship of the Nelson Era

The massive outpouring of studies on Horatio Nelson and the Battle of Trafalgar raises two questions for these themes: Where are we with this subject? And where are we going with it? Those two classic questions, "Ubi sumus?" and "Quo vadimus?" require a great deal of thought and reflection on the broad current state of scholarship in naval history, as well as on our understanding of the specific period in naval history that Nelson and Trafalgar involved.

During the course of the Trafalgar 200 commemorations, several scholars noted that the bicentenary of Trafalgar in 2005 had brought forth numerous scholarly responses, while a hundred years earlier, in 1905, the centenary had produced little new scholarly insight. While the observation struck a chord at the moment, a careful reflection shows that it was not quite true, since the Navy Records Society had published *Nelson and the Neapolitan Jacobins*[1] in 1903 and Julian Corbett's *Fighting Instructions*[2] as its 1905 volume, and followed this with Gardner's *Recollections*[3] and then the Barham papers.[4] The events of the centenary stimulated such important works as Édouard Desbrière's *Naval Campaign of 1805: Trafalgar,*[5] Julian Corbett's *Campaign of Trafalgar,*[6] Edward Fraser's narrative that used extensive translated quotations from French and Spanish eyewitness accounts,[7] the 1913 Admiralty study of the tactics at Trafalgar,[8] and the four-volume edition of the Spencer Papers.[9] The Navy Records Society provided the main impetus for the momentum that began with the centenary, continuing it well into the 1920s and beyond with the papers of St. Vincent[10] and Keith.[11]

The most significant difference between the two commemorations has been that the centenary inspired scholarship after the event, while scholars prepared for the bicentenary in advance in order to have materials readily available for the event, though some were still appearing two years later. It may be that these reactions reflected basic attitudes in these different eras. We do not yet know what sort of reflections the coming decade will bring to understanding of the Nelson era. On the one hand, there is a sense of exhaustion that suggests a secret desire to put it all aside and wait for the generation of our great-grandchildren to face the prospect of dealing with the subject again in the run-up to the tercentenary of Trafalgar in 2105. On the other hand, one recognizes that the study of history cannot be left to be dominated by commemorative events on round-numbered anniversaries. There is the nagging requirement to begin to collate the various contributions and to consolidate a cumulative understanding, particularly after so much has been published nearly simultaneously in connection with the bicentenary. In contrast to the usual sequential approach to scholarly interpretation, the appearance of so many works at nearly the same time created one of the fundamental problems for assessment of the contributions that were made, particularly as 21 October 2005 approached. But a closer analysis shows that there were significant cumulative scholarly developments upon which the final wave of publications in 2005 was founded. These initial interrelationships are important to bear in mind as one reflects on the developing interpretations.

Factionalizing the Nelson Period

The naval actions of the wars of the French Revolution and Empire have never lost their popular interest in the English-speaking world, giving rise to a wide range of widely read historical fiction, made even more popular in the late twentieth century, first by C. S. Forester's series of books featuring Horatio Hornblower, and then by Patrick O'Brian's Aubrey-Maturin series.[12] Although O'Brian first launched his series in 1969, its great popularity did not begin until 1991, when his books were reintroduced in the United States. His literary success in North America in turn stimulated the author's continuation of the series, bringing with it a growing interest and curiosity about the Nelson period. By the time of the Trafalgar bicentenary, three million copies of Aubrey-Maturin novels had been sold in twenty different languages and the series had inspired a major Hollywood film.[13] Scholars of this period of naval history, whether they welcomed the growth of this popular phenomenon as a means to educate a wider audience in their special subject, or preferred to stand clear and avoid it, benefited from this wide interest and appreciation for their period, which naval historians working in other periods did not share. The Hornblower and O'Brian factors were repeatedly made evident during the years leading up to and during the Trafalgar bicentenary, sometimes reaching an extreme when scholars made references to these fictional works as a means to explain their argument.

The first of the key scholarly foundation stones for the emerging new scholarship on Nelson and Trafalgar was undoubtedly Leonard Cowie's bibliography of Nelson, published fifteen years ahead of the bicentenary in 1990.[14] This work was inspired directly by David and Stephen Howarth's 1987 biography of Nelson,[15] which Cowie judged to be "thorough and interesting without making an original contribution to the subject" and having "no bibliography."[16] He saw, too, that it contrasted with Tom Pocock's 1987 volume, *Horatio Nelson*,[17] which Cowie found "the most-up-to-date biography to make use of newly discovered letters and information hitherto printed only in papers or historical journals."[18] The dual impact of the Howarths' and Pocock's books, which had appeared nearly simultaneously, provided the benchmark for Cowie to begin his survey of the available primary and secondary printed and manuscript sources in English. While Cowie's work may have provided the first stepping stone, it has surely been overtaken. Eugene Rasor has already taken some important first steps towards a new bibliography with the first iteration of his massive general bibliography on British naval history for this period[19] and with his bibliography on works published during the "Nelson Decade, 1995–2005."[20]

The phrase and concept of "The Nelson Decade," which soon became widely used, had its origins at the National Maritime Museum, where the staff was planning to open its new Nelson Gallery in 1995 and needed a good phrase for its opening. An informal remark from a staff member brought it about and it gained widespread usage after Dr. Roger Knight, then deputy director of the museum, started the Official Nelson Celebrations Committee with the backing of the chairman of the museum's trustees, Admiral of the Fleet Lord Lewin, to coordinate the work of the many organizations in the country that were interested in participating in the 200th anniversary events. Later called the Official Nelson Commemoration Committee, it was chaired by Colin White, 2000–2006.[21]

Nelson's Early Battles

The early recognition given to the Nelson Decade, and the series of scholarly conferences that it embraced, tied in with anniversary commemorations of the major naval events during the wars of the French Revolution and Empire and created an ongoing scholarly discussion that cumulatively developed and provided increasing depth and breadth. The first of the important conferences on the period was on the Battle of the Glorious First of June. Of course the conference had nothing directly to do with Nelson, preceding by a year the beginning of the Nelson Decade, but it established the tenor of what followed by including British and French perspectives on the action as well as consideration of the cultural context and artistic work that commemorated the event.[22] This was followed by Colin White's volume on the 1797 battles of Cape St. Vincent, in which Nelson played a major role in the British victory over the Spanish Fleet, and the abortive attack on Santa Cruz de Tenerife, in which Nelson suffered the loss of his right arm.[23] In addition, there were subsequent conference proceedings on the Battle of St. Vincent[24] and the Battle of Copenhagen.[25] Ole Feldbæck's work on the 1801 Battle of Copenhagen was translated from Danish in 2002, making a major impact on historical interpretation of this event in English and bringing to bear the author's deep knowledge of Danish history in this period and Danish manuscript sources. Thomas Munch-Petersen further complemented this with his study of the 1807 bombardment of Copenhagen.[26]

In this series of studies, Michèle Battesti's research and analysis on the Battle of the Nile[27] from the French perspective provided invaluable information and insight as well as a corrective to traditional English-language accounts with her appreciation of Nelson's role in opposing Bonaparte's strategy. Battesti's work was paralleled by Brian Lavery's work on the same subject from the British perspective.[28]

On another subject of parallel interest, the threat from the important French naval arsenal that lay close to Britain on the northwestern coast of France at Brest was a strategic issue throughout all the Anglo-French naval wars between 1689 and 1815. More than a century ago, the Navy Records Society had published two volumes of documents on the blockade of Brest, documenting Admiral Sir William Cornwallis's command in 1803–1805.[29] Roger Morriss completed the work left unfinished by Richard C. Saxby in editing a complementary set of documents for the period 1793–1801.[30] These were beautifully complemented by the contribution of Captain Michael K. Barritt, a former Hydrographer of the Royal Navy, who tapped previously unused manuscript materials for his illustrated study of the work of the naval artist J. T. Serres, who had been sent out in an inshore frigate to create views that could be employed as naval intelligence.[31]

Nelson's Fellow Naval Officers

One of the key elements in coming to an understanding of Nelson was an assessment of his place in relationship to his contemporaries and an understanding of naval officers' careers. A major tool that provided initial help in the development of research in this area was the appearance in 1994 of David Syrett's revision and correction of the list in *Commissioned Sea Officers of the Royal Navy*.[32] The Admiralty had issued it in mimeograph form in 1954, originally compiled by David Bonner-Smith. Over the following decades, a number of scholars, including C. G. Pitcairn-Jones, Commander William May and A. W. H. Pearsall, had annotated and corrected copies of this work. The work that David Syrett and Richard L. DiNardo did in updating this forty-year-old reference work was a major contribution which provided the initial basis for the new assessments that followed. It provided a key starting point for many naval historians who were drawn into the project initially known as the *New* [later, *Oxford*] *Dictionary of National Biography* project, after it began in earnest in 1992. This compilation of data was complemented for the Battle of Trafalgar with the electronic publication from 2001 of the *Ayshford Complete Trafalgar Roll*[33] that provided factual data on all 21,000 officers and ratings who served in British ships at Trafalgar. This in turn was complemented by the similar electronic publication of *The Complete Navy List,* listing the 11,000 naval officers who served in the Royal Navy between 1793 and 1815.[34] In addition, the National Archives, Kew, in an ongoing project posted on its website for genealogists, has made available details of service and some selected biographical information from the available records of officers and ratings who fought in the Royal Navy at Trafalgar.[35] Just in time for the bicentenary, Nicholas Tracy published his selection of two hundred biographical sketches of officers,[36] while Colin White and members of the 1805 Club compiled a short, but very interesting, study on the memorials and grave sites for the thirty-eight officers who had commanded ships under Nelson at Trafalgar.[37]

The first major biographical study that appeared to begin to provide a comparative perspective on Nelson was Roger Morriss's refreshing study of Admiral Sir George Cockburn;[38] it emphasized entirely different theatres of the war than those in which Nelson dominated and showed the development of a younger officer who went on to preside over the technological and political transitions faced by the Navy in the post–Napoleonic War period. This was followed with a contrasting figure in John E. Talbott's study of an older officer, Charles Middleton, who as Lord Barham served as First Lord of the Admiralty during the Trafalgar campaign.[39]

At the same time, a dozen years of collaborative scholarly work between 1992 and 2004 was going into the production of the 60-volume *Oxford Dictionary of National Biography*.[40] This work included important biographies, including the one of Nelson by N. A. M. Rodger, and numerous other biographies, including a theme article by Michael Duffy, "Trafalgar, Nelson, and the National Memory."[41] The work also bore some early fruit for naval history even before that landmark reference work appeared in print and, in stages, online in 2004, with some contributors producing early spin-off pieces for Peter Le Fevre and Richard Harding's volume *Precursors of Nelson,*[42] the first of the major new comparative biographical studies explicitly designed to provide a means to place Nelson in the general context of the tradition in which his career took place. Le Fevre and Harding's volume started at the distant opening years of the eighteenth century and ranged forward to include studies for the Nelson period with Patricia Crimmin's study of St. Vincent, Roger Morriss on Barham, and Brian Lavery on Keith. The essays collectively demonstrated that the basis for Nelson's personal achievements had developed over the preceding century and a half in the context of a flourishing maritime economy and that it was the application of money, administrative capabilities, manpower and the development of Britain's professional naval officer corps which converted the raw materials into a formidable sea power.[43] Under these broad rubrics, the fundamental developments were the evolution of institutionalized systems and procedures for manning the fleet, maintaining the health and hygiene of sailors at sea, refining the design and technology of warships, creating the effective means of directing large numbers of ships in combat and developing communications and understanding for this purpose. Moreover, the catalyst for these ingredients was applying, in appropriate measure, the complementary elements of leadership and discipline through all levels of naval organization to achieve these ends effectively. Such was the gradual and cumulative work over many generations that culminated in Nelson's unique achievements.

Le Fevre and Harding's volume was paralleled in the same year by a major biography of one of Nelson's contemporaries, Paul Krajeski's study of Sir Charles Cotton,[44] who represented a much more typical type of flag officer as opposed to the exceptional character Nelson represented. A number of other valuable studies followed in succession to provide greater range and depth, including Hilary Rubinstein's on Captain Philip Durham,[45] Brian Vale and David Cordingly on Lord Cochrane,[46] Iain Gordon on Admiral John Child Purvis,[47] Max Adams on Collingwood,[48] Victor Sharman on William Locker,[49] Kevin McCranie on Lord Keith,[50] Tim Voelcker on Saumarez,[51] and Bryan Elson on Benjamin Hallowell.[52]

While these authors provided book-length, in-depth studies of their individual subjects that give differing personal perspectives on the period, Peter Le Fevre and Richard Harding gathered a second collection of biographical essays, *British Admirals of the Napoleonic Wars: The Contemporaries of Nelson,*[53] that made a major complementary contribution, illustrating the broad range of diversity among naval officers of Nelson's time as well as identifying some of the key elements of similar outlook and experience among them. Le Fevre and Harding's choice of subjects was carefully focused on lesser known admirals whom the editors felt deserved examination. Their choices fell not on the close circle of Nelson's captains, his "band of brothers," but rather on officers whose careers spanned the same years as Nelson's and involved the same broad pattern of war and peace. While they included some leading individuals, whose lives had been examined in the older literature or whose letters had been published, such as Collingwood, Pellew, and Saumarez—the last two just a year older than Nelson—others provided entirely new perspectives: Hotham, Duncan, Orde, Rainier, Knowles, Duckworth, Calder, Warren, Troubridge, Sir Samuel Hood and Keats. Duncan, born in 1731, was the oldest of the group and twenty-seven years senior in age to Nelson, while Sir Samuel Hood, born in 1762, was just four years younger than Nelson. This collection clearly demonstrates that Nelson's career pattern was not unique for his time. Many of his contemporaries had similar experiences, having joined the Navy at about the same age, were promoted after similar periods of service, had similar sea assignments, and shared the same concerns for the health and welfare of their seamen. In addition, a naval officer rose in his profession through his abilities and his aptitude for the essential aspects of high naval command which involved attention to great administrative detail in the managerial oversight of practical, routine, logistical and operational aspects of large and complex organizations, extending even to detailed diplomatic relations with foreign powers on overseas stations. Although Nelson was not a typical individual in the naval officer corps of the time, his administrative capabilities, his views about patriotism and the importance of battle, his interest in prize money, his sensitivity to his personal honour and his insistence on certain standards of conduct for a naval officer were all views that his contemporaries typically shared. Equally important, the collection made clear the importance of a range of different types of naval actions, not just climacteric fleet battles. As Julian Corbett had pointed out so clearly in his 1911 theoretical work *Some Principles of Maritime Strategy* there is a range of naval operations to contest another naval power's ability to use the sea, among which naval battle is the traditional decisive means to achieve command of the sea over an enemy. Once command is achieved, however, there is an entirely different range of tasks if a navy is to exercise that command.[54] An officer rose in rank typically seeing only a portion of these tasks, with repeated experience of command in major fleet battle the rarest and most unusual of them all. More commonly, naval officers saw action against the enemy in a variety of circumstances, typically on blockade duty or in frigates in small operations, such as raids, single-ship actions and amphibious operations. Such operations provided relatively rare opportunities for an officer to show himself as a candidate for higher command. Richard Woodman[55] and Tom Wareham examined this range of experiences with studies of frigate captains.[56]

Building further on this range of insights, Ruddock Mackay and Michael Duffy provided an original contribution with their volume *Hawke, Nelson, and British Naval Leadership, 1747–1805.*[57] Putting Nelson into perspective with other British naval leaders in the second half of the eighteenth century, Mackay analyzed anew the qualities for successful naval leadership in this period and identified twelve key qualities. In this book, he argues that Hawke and Nelson were the outstanding naval leaders of the eighteenth century, outlining their respective careers and showing how both of them possessed, more than the other admirals, the key dozen qualities of leadership. At the same time, he shows that British fleet tactics and blockade strategy had already reached a high level in the middle of the eighteenth century that Nelson later built upon. Sam Willis's detailed and refreshingly new approach to the study of naval tactics in the period provided deeper insights into the practicalities involved in applying theoretical ideas about naval tactics and made a major contribution in this area.[58]

Making the transition between biographies of contemporaries and Nelson himself are two volumes that touch on medical practices. First, Lawrence Brockliss, John Cardwell and Michael Moss used their biography of William Beatty, the surgeon who treated the dying Nelson,[59] as a study of medical practice during the Battle of Trafalgar as well as of the general medical situation in the Royal Navy at the time. Following up on this theme, Dr. Anne-Mary E. Hills's *Nelson: A Medical Casebook*[60] served both as an examination of contemporary medical practice and as a very specialized contribution to Nelson's biography.

The Nelson Biographies

In the decades leading up to the bicentenary period, the two standard biographies by A. T. Mahan[61] and Carola Oman[62] had not been entirely superseded, with Mahan's work still holding its own after a century as the best professional naval study, and Oman's as the best personal portrait. While a number of new sources and insights had been published through the years, it took a series of biographical studies during the Nelson Decade to develop an entirely new approach built on evidence entirely independent of the older nineteenth-century traditional interpretations of the subject. Colin White's *The*

Nelson Companion[63] was the first compilation of collective scholarship that provided the basis for a new beginning in this area. The contributors to that volume in 1995 laid out the agenda for the coming decade by their thematic examination of the legend, portraits, relics, commemorations, verifiable chronology and manuscript sources, all of which suggested new perspectives and new interpretations on Nelson's life. Richard Walker followed his contribution to this volume with his book-length study on Nelson's portraits and iconography,[64] a masterful piece of art history which made a major contribution to biographical studies as well as to studies on cultural and commemorative aspects of the Trafalgar period. This was followed in 2002 with the first edition of Colin White's *Nelson Encyclopedia,*[65] a work that continued and complemented the initiatives of the *Nelson Companion,* but on a wider range of topics. As new research and insights quickly followed, both works required revision and expansion in 2005.

The first new full biography to appear was Terry Coleman's *The Nelson Touch,*[66] in which the author portrayed Nelson as "a paramount naval genius and a natural-born predator. . . . In private life, as in war, he was ruthless when he had to be, and he could be pitiless."[67] As the first to appear, Coleman's work became the spark for new and differing interpretations, leading those who followed to look for other primary sources and other aspects of Nelson's character to weigh. Coleman stressed the key importance to his work of manuscript sources, citing the edited collections in print as well as original materials at the British Library, the National Maritime Museum, the National Archives, and the Nelson Museum in Monmouth, Wales.

Joel Hayward followed with a thematic examination of Nelson's way of warfare which was constructed around themes, insights and terminology from modern naval thinking.[68] Hayward made a unique contribution to the literature with his focus on Nelson's conception of his enemies, his spiritual beliefs, his leadership, command, management and war-fighting styles. While Hayward's work was based on long published material and on the prevailing older biographical interpretations, his innovative use of modern professional thinking provided some intriguing insights for those serving in the armed forces at the opening of the twenty-first century. Nevertheless, Hayward's work was not embraced, developed or even noted by later biographers, though the use of modern insights from other professions became a thread to follow.

In 2003, Edgar Vincent published his large, vividly written biography[69] which applied a number of unusual psychological insights into Nelson's charismatic personality, utilized the insights of a range of modern medical specialists to a variety of Nelson's medical conditions, and benefited from the author's practical insights from his own career in judging the character of candidates for senior management positions and placing them in appropriate employment. Vincent's emphasis on Nelson's emotional make-up, his personal relationships and his passion for fame provided a contrasting interpretation to Coleman's judgments. In stressing his reliance on original materials, Vincent noted his pioneering use of materials at the Huntington Library as well as some seventy previously unknown Nelson letters.

In 2004, the publication of the first volume of John Sugden's proposed two-volume biography[70] came as a great surprise to many scholars working in the field. Better known to naval historians for his 1992 study of Sir Francis Drake, Sugden had completed his doctoral thesis on Lord Cochrane at Sheffield University in 1981 and had a long interest and extensive expertise in the period. Unaware of Sugden's interest in the subject until the book appeared, some critics tended to take it to task for its long and involved discussions. At the same time, it was humorously described as a "half Nelson," since it covered Nelson's life only up to 1797. Nevertheless, Sugden's book was one of the most important contributions to the scholarly discourse taking place at the time and it became a major influence on the works that followed. Most impressive was the huge range of manuscript sources that Sugden utilized. Using what his publisher described as "thousands of previously unused naval, military, diplomatic, and personal documents," Sugden listed three archival repositories in Canada, nine in the United States and twenty in the United Kingdom, making use of numerous previously untapped collections and archival series at the British Library, the National Maritime Museum and the National Archives. In addition, he listed a wide variety of published materials that had not been utilized. Sugden effectively used these widely scattered and wide-ranging materials to dissect, to analyze and to begin to refute in detail the long-accepted mythology surrounding numerous events in Nelson's early life. In doing this, Sugden's work became the most important recent research work and the key work to be superseded.

In 2004, Andrew Lambert published his study on Nelson, subtitled with Lord Byron's words as *Britannia's God of War*.[71] An important study, this book had somewhat different origins from the others and, as a result, focused on different objectives for its contribution to the literature. As Lambert explained in his preface, he had long believed that Nelson's story had been "so often told as to defy reinterpretation, but such thoughts were soon changed by the experience of trying to teach from the extant literature."[72] His students wanted to know things that the existing biographical literature did not clearly answer about Nelson's education, his views on strategy, his relations with other senior officers, his significance and the wider importance of Trafalgar. Lambert's book answers these questions while he makes the links between interpreting Nelson in context and understanding Nelson today. Lambert's most original contribution was to explain Nelson's life and achievements in terms of the part they have come to play in modern British national identity. As Lambert concluded his work, "We need to understand Nelson because he, and the culture of his age, still define the way the British see themselves in the world, and the way the world sees them."[73]

Just as Lambert's book appeared from the press in October 2004, the Institute of Historical Research and the National Maritime Museum sponsored a series of lectures at the University of London on Nelson, the context of Nelson's life and his legacy. These appeared in print the following July, edited by David Cannadine,[74] providing a range of important new insights in terms of naval leadership, quality of seamanship and fraternal relationships between officers as well as the legacy of Nelson mythology, his commemoration and his place in the national pantheon. This collection of lectures was particularly important in helping to define the range of multiple perspectives.

As the bicentennial year approached, a large number of works appeared nearly simultaneously; they fell into a variety of different categories that reflected some of the new evidence that had been unearthed and which was made use of in a number of the biographies. One of the most important discoveries occurred in 2002 when materials came to light that had belonged to Alexander Davison, Nelson's close friend and prize agent. In an attractively written popular account, Martyn Downer related these events in the dramatic style of a detective story.[75] As the head of jewelry at Sotheby's, London, Downer related his own experience in authenticating the jewelry and the other materials that provided a remarkable range of new evidence and insights into Nelson's life. This popular account directed at a wide audience put in the spotlight one of the most serious issues for scholars and researchers working on Nelson: the problem of authenticating things that had actually belonged to Nelson amidst a huge range of widely distributed reproductions, fakes, falsely identified materials, and the numerous conflicting and unsubstantiated accounts surrounding them. Following the discovery of the Davison materials, Rina Prentice, a curator at the National Maritime Museum, published a major corrective with her illustrated scholarly catalogue of all known surviving objects that Nelson had owned.[76] Prentice's work was a service to curators and collectors wrestling with questions of authenticity, and it also provided valuable insights for biographers and students of the material culture of the period.

Nelson's correspondence has always been an essential source. Sir Nicholas Harris Nicolas (1799–1848) published the standard collection in seven volumes in the mid-nineteenth century and this was republished in a paperback facsimile for the bicentenary.[77] Following on from this re-publication of a standard source, Nicholas Tracy made another very useful contribution by producing an indexed, five-volume abridgement of the forty volumes of the bi-annual *The Naval Chronicle* that originally appeared between 1799 and 1816.[78]

Roger Morriss's *Guide to British Naval Papers in North America* opened up to wider uses the often neglected manuscript material for British naval history that had migrated to the United States and Canada.[79] As a result of this and other research in Britain, a large number of additional letters began to come to light and were published in a variety of collections. Joseph F. Callo used some of these to make a selection of quotations to serve as an introduction to Nelson for American naval officers.[80] The most important work for historians and biographers was Colin White's continuing long-term effort to locate and to transcribe all Nelson's letters. His project, begun in 1999, had by August 2004 revealed 1,300 previously unpublished letters in thirty different archives. In April 2005, White published a selection of 507 of these letters, arranged thematically in a manner which directly complemented the biographies.[81] Yet, even before White published his volume, he had generously shared his findings with other scholars and reported key finds, such as his discovery of the Trafalgar battle plan,[82] in the press and through progress reports in scholarly journals.[83] Similar to Joseph Callo's earlier work but on a much larger scale, Steven E. Maffeo produced a volume of 3,000 quotations from published sources to illustrate Nelson's character and personality in his own words.[84] Yet, even while these volumes appeared and circulated, new caches of letters were still being found and the biographies continued to appear.

In 2005, Roger Knight published his major new biography, *The Pursuit of Victory*[85] Appearing after Sugden's and Lambert's works, Knight's could safely omit detailed explanations of why and how the traditional narrative about Nelson was wrong and why he did not need to feel obliged to focus on the meaning of Nelson's career for British identity. What Knight produced was notably different from all the works that preceded it. He presented an entirely new narrative picture by completely ignoring the traditional stories about Nelson and by building anew entirely from archival sources. In addition, Knight was able to place Nelson's life within the context of his times, merging the particularistic biographical approach with a more general historical explanation. To supplement this, Knight added three valuable appendices to his work that included a chronology of Nelson's life based on documentary sources, short biographical sketches of the key individuals that explained their personal relationships with Nelson, and detailed data on each of the ships in which Nelson served. All this new material was built upon the cumulative development of scholarship on this period during the preceding decade.

Two additional important biographies appeared during the bicentenary year to complete the new wave. First, Colin White published *Nelson: The Admiral,*[86] a work particularly designed to attract and inform those in the early stages of their careers as modern naval officers. In this task, White was informed by all the latest and best scholarship, but concentrated here on lucidly presenting those elements of leadership, command and naval life that might inspire and interest young serving officers. Marianne Czisnik concluded the bicentenary biographical wave with her study *Nelson: A Controversial Hero* [87] Based on her recent doctoral thesis at the University of Edinburgh, it is an unusual work, not least for the fact that its German author wrote it in English, but also for the fresh insights it offers in analyzing the controversial aspects of Nelson's life in his involvement with the Neapolitan republicans and his relationship with Lady Hamilton. In addition, she made a major original contribution to the historical literature through her study of the Nelson legend as it has been presented in French, Spanish and German history and literary works as well as in visual images.

The Ships and the Battle

While the largest outpouring of significant research and writing focused on biographical studies, other topics were certainly not ignored. They fall into two additional large categories: the ships and the tactics of the Battle of Trafalgar, and the broader context of the battle, which includes the history of the Navy and the nation in this period.

The prevailing tendency for producing volumes of data and biographical studies of naval officers extended also to ships. In the genre of books of data on ships, the first important volume to appear was David Lyon's *The Sailing Ship Navy List.*[88] A dozen years later, just in time for the bicentenary, Rif Winfield made a significant contribution when he published his even more detailed compilation of data on all British warships for the period 1793–1817.[89] This compendium included information on dates of commissions, major refit periods, changes of captain, when and on which stations vessels served and details of noteworthy actions. Between the appearance of these general works, Peter G. Goodwin published his detailed study of all the ships in which Nelson had served, making effective use of ships' logbooks.[90]

While the compilation of detailed statistics about ships has been a traditional enterprise that has benefited from the work of generations of experts, a deeper understanding of how to calculate relative naval power from such lists and how to understand the development of ship design were aspects that have long needed detailed elaboration for the sailing ship period. A number of works that appeared during the Nelson Decade benefited from the appearance in 1993 of Jan Glete's *Navies and Nations,*[91] which provided an approach that allowed a more meaningful quantification of national naval strength and linked this to the broader process of state development in Europe.

Two other important works appeared after the bicentenary that explored the subject of ship design. The first, *Technology of the Ships of Trafalgar,*[92] was the proceedings of a bicentenary conference that focused on technical issues in the history of ship design and naval engineering, such as the understanding of fluid dynamics in its relationship to ship design, the application of technology transfer through espionage, comparative hydrodynamic design, and evaluations of hull structures under sail and under gun-fire. While highly technical, this work made a key contribution in filling a major gap in understanding ships of the Trafalgar period. This volume was paralleled by a book-length study of the history of naval architecture between 1600 and 1800, by one of the editors of the conference proceedings. Larrie D. Ferreiro's *Ships and Science*[93] is a pioneering and very readable study of a hitherto neglected, but fundamental, aspect in the naval history of the period. In this work, Ferreiro describes the origin and development of the first theories in the science of explaining and predicting the physical behaviour of ships at sea, which include interrelated subjects involving the theories of manoeuvring a vessel, the use of sails, hull resistance, hydrodynamics, and stability.

A work on another under-studied technical fundamental subject related to the navigation of ships in this period was produced by a Dutch scholar, A. R. T. Jonkers, with his *Earth's Magnetism in the Age of Sail*.[94] A broad study that was not intended to be part of the Trafalgar events, it was nevertheless connected to it by its relationship to practical navigation. This volume brought together the history of geophysics and the history of ideas as well as the practical aspects of navigation in dealing with the understanding of terrestrial magnetism during the period 1600 to 1800. In terms of navigation of ships, this subject is naturally associated with the fields of hydrography and cartography. Another important study on this subject that appeared during the Trafalgar bicentenary period was the large work by Olivier Chapuis on the French aspects of the birth of modern hydrography during the eighteenth century and the first half of the nineteenth century.[95]

Less esoteric and more directly focused on the ships of Nelson's time, Brian Lavery's volume of documents *Shipboard Life and Organization*[96] gathered together an authoritative compilation that provided an essential reference to this aspect of life at sea. This was put into visual perspective with Nicholas Blake's popularly oriented volumes on daily life at sea in a ship of the line[97] and his *Illustrated Companion to Nelson's Navy,*[98] both of which were informed by early works of detailed scholarship.[99]

In addition, there were a number of other studies that focused on topics related to ships. One intriguing subject was raised by Janet Macdonald's exploratory work into the very large and complicated subject of victualling.[100] Similarly, Steven Maffeo's study of naval intelligence[101] gathered together and summarized what was already known in widely scattered secondary sources, as well as historical novels, and provided a basis upon which to begin detailed archival work. A first step towards this was taken in Elizabeth Sparrow's general study of British espionage in France[102] and elaborated upon more specifically in the naval context in Roger Knight's biography of Nelson and Jane Knight's article on Nelson's use of merchant intelligence.[103]

A further specific aspect of naval operations was developed in Richard Hill's *Prizes of War,*[104] a study of the naval prize system and a subject of major interest to Nelson and his fellow naval officers. Hill's study of the legal system and its procedures complemented and expanded on the understanding produced earlier through Henry Bourguignon's biography of Sir William Scott, the Judge of the High Court of Admiralty.[105]

Newly written accounts of the Battle of Trafalgar were central to the bicentenary. In that context, one of the first and most important appeared in French:[106] Michèle Battesti's examination of the risks that Napoleon's naval strategy against Britain involved and which resulted in the battle. Battesti successfully presented a broad strategic survey, while the first major account in English was that by Tim Clayton and Phil Craig,[107] who presented a dramatic and evocative account that made effective use of personal letters and presented views from various aspects of the battle. This was followed by Roy Adkins's *Nelson's Trafalgar*,[108] an introduction to the subject, and Adam Nicholson's *Seize the Fire*,[109] which uses a dramatic description of the Battle of Trafalgar as a means to meditate on more general ideas about heroism. Some of the most important scholarly discussion on tactics and gunnery in the battle appeared in articles by Marianne Czisnik[110] and Michael Duffy.[111]

Two additional volumes presented extended quotations from eyewitness accounts: Tom Pocock's *Trafalgar*[112] and Peter Warwick's *Voices from the Battle of Trafalgar*.[113] Both were highly readable collections of potentially important source material, but sadly neither included the references to their sources. Alexander Stilwell's *Trafalgar Companion*[114] presented a series of essays by scholars writing for a general audience.

Finally, one of the very best studies of the battle appeared in French, written by Rear-Admiral Rémi Monaque,[115] who had already published an important study on the French admiral who had successfully opposed Nelson at Boulogne: Louis-René de Latouche-Tréville.[116] Monaque's *Trafalgar* focused on the operational aspects of the battle, using extensive materials in French and Spanish archives. Based on these materials, Monaque concluded that, while Trafalgar had a massive psychological effect by inflicting irreparable humiliation on the French, in the short term the battle had little direct effect. Napoleon had already cancelled his plan to invade Britain before Trafalgar and had turned, instead, towards a strategy that would culminate with his victory at Austerlitz two months later. Monaque summarized the contents of his book in a conference that took place at Portsmouth in 2005. These papers were edited by Richard Harding and contain the most important new reconstruction of the tactics of the battle since the Admiralty study of 1913.[117]

With the battle over and Nelson dead, the final link of the event to the larger effects of the battle was made by Derek Allen and Peter Hore in their study of how the news of the battle reached Britain in HM schooner *Pickle*.[118] The Ordnance Survey further illustrated this event with a map[119] showing Lieutenant John Lapenotiere's overland route from Falmouth to London as well as other sites associated with Nelson's last visit in England.

The Context of Trafalgar: The Navy and the Nation

The high public and scholarly interest in the life of Nelson and his colleagues that created and sustained the subsequent popularity of the biographical approach to both ships and men is understandable, but this approach is neither the only nor the most effective one to understanding the broader historical context of the events. There are a variety of complementary and separate events as well as broader trends and patterns to examine. The immediate story of Trafalgar is partially linked to Britain's fear of invasion and to the viability of Napoleon's plans for it. Nelson's chase of Vice-Admiral Villeneuve and the French fleet to the West Indies is a segment that relates to Nelson, but there is a larger story for this at home in Britain that complements naval affairs. Tom Pocock dealt with Nelson's role in the story in his *The Terror before Trafalgar*.[120] J. E. Cookson examined the subject in terms of home defence and mobilization in his *The*

British Armed Nation.[121] This same subject was interpreted in visual form for the Bodleian Library's exhibition, *Napoleon and the Invasion of Britain.*[122]

Clive Wilkinson made an important contribution with his study *The British Navy and the State,*[123] documenting how the naval service as the most expensive branch of the British state created one of the major aspects in the development of public finance and bureaucratic development. Some important pioneering investigations of the social and cultural side of naval history began to appear that placed Nelson and Trafalgar in a larger view of these thematic contexts. Key among them was Margarette Lincoln's *Naval Wives & Mistresses.*[124] This is an innovative view that examines different social groups and uses a variety of sources from popular prints to legal papers to create a picture of the way in which women were forced to take on the full responsibilities at home in their husbands' absence as illustrating the cost of warfare and imperial ambition in very personal terms. Richard Blake's *Evangelicals in the Royal Navy*[125] examines the influence of religious sentiment and piety on the exercise of naval discipline. At the same time, John Byrn's volume of documents *Naval Courts Martial, 1793–1815,*[126] provides a sampling from the 122 volumes of court martial records in manuscript that are preserved in The National Archives at Kew and makes a contribution to better understanding naval jurisprudence in this period. A social historian at York University in Canada, Nicholas C. Rogers, made a key contribution with his *Press Gang: Naval Impressment and Its Opponents in Georgian Britain,*[127] which illuminated what has been a much debated and sometimes misunderstood process.

On a quite different plane, Timothy Jenks's study *Naval Engagements* is a cultural history of national identity as well as a study of naval commemoration with insights into the political struggle over patriotic symbolism. Jenks argues that, in the context of political culture, British patriotism was not something taken for granted, but rather a contested area.[128]

Nearly lost from sight are the immediate consequences of the Battle of Trafalgar in connection with Napoleon's shift of strategy away from the invasion of Britain to military operations in central Europe. One of the new strategic roles that Napoleon had set out for Villeneuve's combined fleet was to prevent an Anglo-Russian invasion of southern Italy. The Battle of Trafalgar stopped Villeneuve from carrying out that intent, an aspect that William Flayhart studied in *Counterpoint to Trafalgar.*[129] While this operation was a largely forgotten failure for both sides, it did prove to be a useful lesson for the key operations that eventually took place in Spain and Portugal. Christopher Hall examined this central aspect of the next major phase of the Napoleonic War in his *Wellington's Navy,*[130] developing themes that had appeared in his earlier work *British Strategy,*[131] a subject which Rory Muir re-evaluated in his *Britain and the Defeat of Napoleon.*[132]

Within the context of British history, Lawrence Stone's edited collection *An Imperial State at War*[133] and Jeremy Black's *The British Seaborne Empire*[134] dealt with different aspects of the broad context in which the British Empire developed through its maritime power, touching on Trafalgar as an incident and signpost within that growth. A number of other important dimensions in the Navy's relationship to and place in British culture were examined by Margarette Lincoln, first in her study on naval images and perceptions of the Navy in wider society.[135] This was an approach that informed the magnificent exhibition mounted by the National Maritime Museum for the bicentenary, "Nelson and

Napoléon."[136] Several other works examined portions of the literature and art of the period, notably Brian Southam's study of naval references in Jane Austen's novels,[137] and Nicholas Tracy's history of the community of British naval artists and their work, showing the importance of the self-employed artist for the nation.[138] The works by Lincoln and Tracy contributed substantially to a refreshing change from the predilection of most art historians to focus on a single artist working in a single medium.

The most important overarching work for the entire Nelson and Trafalgar theme was the second volume of Nicholas Rodger's projected three-volume naval history of Britain: *The Command of the Ocean: A Naval History of Britian, 1649–1815.*[139] With its first appearance in October 2004, Rodger's book built further on the approach that he had been instrumental in contributing to the Navy Records Society's centenary volume,[140] which was constructed around the five principal parallel themes in naval history: policy and strategy; tactics and operations; administration; material and weapons; and personnel. Renaming these themes as operations, administration, ships, and social history for his multi-volume history, Rodger alternated between these themes in a masterful way, producing a much more sophisticated understanding of the complex nature of naval power than had been presented in previous general histories. Indeed, Rodger summarized the story of the Trafalgar operation in a mere seven pages, illustrating the great strength of his work in placing such events and themes succinctly within a balanced perspective as part of the nation's history. One hopes that Rodger's exemplary use of foreign language sources in writing a national naval history will change forever the perception that such a task could be taken without doing so. In the context of European history, Paul Schroeder's summary of European international affairs in his *Transformation of European Politics*[141] provided a new interpretation on which to build an explanation of Trafalgar's place in history. More recently, a wide range of issues has been examined in two volumes of collaborative scholarship in Spanish by Agustín Guimerá Ravina with other scholars, one examining the context of Trafalgar and the Atlantic world[142] and another looking at the entire century from the Peace of Utrecht in 1714 up to and including the Battle of Trafalgar.[143]

In another conference sponsored by the National Maritime Museum, Greenwich, and the Institute of Historical Research in London, the participants provided a multidisciplinary approach to placing the Battle of Trafalgar in the context of fiscal issues and economics, propaganda, the balance of naval power, art, music, and heritage. This important collection concludes with Paul M. Kennedy's Caird Medal Lecture for 2005, "The Meaning of Trafalgar in World History."[144]

Whither with Nelson and Trafalgar?

The outpouring of historical studies on Nelson and Trafalgar that have appeared since the beginning of the Nelson Decade has transformed our understanding of the period as well as our understanding of many of the specific topics studied. Yet it will take some further time for this complex and widespread range of work to become absorbed into general understanding. In looking back even from this early point, it is important to see it as a cumulative conversation, discussion and exchange of views that has been gradually building towards a new consensus, but it is a conversation that is neither complete nor fully absorbed. This process will inevitably continue: the subject is not exhausted, even if some of the students of the period may be.

Looking at the body of material that has appeared, one can see two very specific tasks that need to be completed. One of them is to update Cowie's 1990 bibliography and to produce a revised and updated new bibliography on Nelson, along the same lines that Cowie established, to include all the published materials and the current known locations of the primary manuscript material; this is surely one of the most important tasks that lie ahead. The second is the great need to produce a complete edition of Nelson's letters, edited to consistent and high academic standards. Despite all the biographies that have been produced, we are still left with a hodgepodge of incomplete texts in print. Editorial work is needed of the kind that has been done at the Institute of Netherlands History for important figures in Dutch history, or in the United States for a wide variety of figures in American history, ranging from the founding fathers to presidents and authors. Such a multi-volume annotated edition of all Nelson's known letters would be the most enduring scholarly contribution that could come from the bicentenary and would serve a wide variety of scholarly purposes, as the work of Sir Nicholas Harris Nicolas did from 1845 until 2005, by which time its inadequacy for future use had been fully demonstrated. If current circumstances and trends continue, both of these great scholarly needs may possibly be best produced through databases and published with institutional support on websites that allow for continual updating and wide access.

Beyond these two fundamental steps, which would do much to advance scholarly work on this subject, the course for future work arising from the Trafalgar bicentenary should be rich and varied. The rich results that we now have in hand should be very effective in stimulating further thought and examination and they have already revealed some lacunae in the existing literature. Research work still needs to be done on such regional topics as naval operations on the Irish station and on the West Indies after Trafalgar. The follow-on from Duckworth's victory at the Battle of Santo Domingo in 1806 has remained obscure. Little work has been done to explain how the West Indian islands were recaptured from the French and how they were retained and supplied. In addition, work needs to be done on the operation of the coastal convoys around Britain and how enemy shipping from the Baltic was intercepted. More needs to be learned about shipbuilding and shipwrights in commercial yards outside the naval dockyards.

On the one hand and on a wider scope, some of the new observations and discoveries on this period need to be traced back to their origins as well as followed through into the post-Trafalgar eras. As arguably the most widely and deeply researched period of British naval history, the in-depth examination of topics relating to Nelson and the Royal Navy of his time should be a stimulus for similar work on heretofore neglected topics in other periods and on other navies. A series of such studies on nearly any particular theme should produce an understanding of trends and developments, or a lack thereof, which will lead scholars either forward or backward to this period and modify the conclusions reached during the bicentenary.

On the other hand, the emphasis on biographical studies during the bicentenary suggests there is a large range of thematic and alternative approaches that remain to be undertaken. The early work on victualling has already suggested research that is coming to fruition through a Leverhulme grant at the Greenwich Maritime Institute. It will be published under the title *Sustaining the Fleet, 1793–1815: War, the British Navy and the Contractor State* with an additional database of contactors that will appear on the National Maritime Museum's website as a result of this research. While the industrial connection to the Navy is apparent, the agrarian, financial, logistical and commercial connections have yet to be fully explored and all of them need to be seen acting together. Research on the Transport Service is underway at Greenwich University.

Beyond the subject of naval affairs strictly defined, new research work on fishing, smuggling, and other maritime activities in the Channel has suggested the possibility of a much broader and wider approach to the topic in the future, the focusing on the interactions of maritime people across national boundaries in time of war.[145] The work on cartographic history soon coming to fruition at the University of Wisconsin[146] may contribute and stimulate further insights into the history of hydrography and its relationship to the other nautical and navigational sciences. After having read through all these works, one is still left with a series of questions for which one would like more succinct and detailed answers: How do all these new insights alter our conception of the role of navies in a nation's conduct of war in the period 1660–1815? In comparative ways, how do navies function and change as institutions? What was distinctive about the Royal Navy in this regard? Daniel Baugh has pointed out that Britain was gradually losing a competitive edge over her Bourbon competitors after 1783 until revolution in France intervened. It is doubtful that British maritime power would have been completely overtaken, since Britain consistently maintained her traditional stance of actively deploying the ships of the Royal Navy at sea to safeguard her competitive economic advantage in the global marketplace created by the interconnections involved in superior manufacturing productivity, uninterrupted delivery across the world's oceans, relatively safer and more frequent maritime voyages, effective means of commercial credit and a multilateral commercial competitiveness.[147] All this needs to be further investigated in more detail.

At the same time, in our own era when joint warfare has become so central a preoccupation and so critical an element in the success of modern warfare, we want to know more about the relationships between the army and the navy in this period. Certainly, in terms of British grand strategy the military and naval relationship was fundamental to the allies' eventual victory over Napoleon. But there is a range of other levels of activity and interrelations to be further explored. The subject is not just a matter of understanding the naval elements, but rather the broad interrelations involved in the conduct of war at a variety of levels.

During the Trafalgar bicentenary, we have seen the beginnings of the application of social and cultural historical approaches to naval affairs and these are significant themes that can be followed further. The wider and deeper collection of data, some of it already in electronic formats, suggests that there are new quantitative as well as qualitative results to be garnered and applied to a broader understanding. Overall, the sub-specialty of naval history, within the broad, overarching general field of global maritime history, has increasingly benefited from interaction with a growing number of specialized approaches to history as they touch upon and illuminate aspects of mankind's relationship to the oceans of the world. One certainly expects this development to continue and to broaden and, in doing so, to contribute to scholarly understanding of war and of conflict at sea.

NOTES   This article was first published (as "Whither with Nelson and Trafalgar? A Review Article on the Bicentenary Scholarship of the Nelson Era") in the *Journal for Maritime Research* (December 2007) and is reprinted here revised and updated.

1 H. C. Gutteridge, ed., *Nelson and the Neapolitan Jacobins: Documents relating to the suppression of the Jacobin revolution at Naples, June 1799,* Publications of the Navy Records Society, vol. 25 (London: Navy Records Society, 1903).

2 Julian Corbett, *Fighting Instructions 1530–1816,* Publications of the Navy Records Society, vol. 29 (London: Navy Records Society, 1905).

3 R. Vesey Hamilton and John Knox Laughton, eds., *Recollections of James Anthony Gardner, Commander, RN, 1775–1814,* Publications of the Navy Records Society, vol. 31 (London: Navy Records Society, 1906).

4 John Knox Laughton, ed., *The Letters and Papers of Charles, Lord Barham, Admiral of the Red Squadron, 1758–1813,* Publications of the Navy Records Society, vols. 32, 38 and 39 (London: Navy Records Society, 1907–11).

5 Édouard Desbrière, *La Campagne maritime de 1805: Trafalgar* (Paris: Chapelot, 1907), translated, edited, and corrected by Constance as *The Naval Campaign of 1805: Trafalgar* (Oxford: Clarendon Press, 1933).

6 Julian S. Corbett, *The Campaign of Trafalgar* (London: Longman, 1910).

7 Edward Fraser, *The Enemy at Trafalgar; an account of the battle from eye-witnesses' narratives and letters and despatches from the French and Spanish fleet* (London: Hodder & Stoughton, 1906); republished with an introduction by Marianne Czisnik and Michael Nash (London: Chatham; Mechanicsburg, PA: Stackpole Books, 2004).

8 Great Britain, Parliament, *House of Commons Report of a committee appointed by the Admiralty to examine and consider the evidence relating to the tactics employed by Nelson at the battle of Trafalgar* (London: HMSO, 1913).

9 Julian S. Corbett and Herbert W. Richmond, eds., *Private papers of George, second earl Spencer, first lord of the Admiralty, 1794–1801* (London: Navy Records Society, 1913–24).

10 David Bonner Smith, ed., *Letters of Admiral of the Fleet, the Earl of St. Vincent: whilst the First Lord of the Admiralty, 1801–1804* (London: Printed for the Navy Records Society, 1922–27).

11 W. G. Perrin and Christopher Lloyd, eds., *The Keith Papers: selected from the papers of Admiral Viscount Keith* (London: Printed for the Navy Records Society, 1927–55).

12 John B. Hattendorf, "Fiction: Naval novel," in Hattendorf, ed., *The Oxford Encyclopedia of Maritime History* (Oxford and New York: Oxford University Press, 2007), vol. 2, pp. 7–13.

13 Dean H. King, "O'Brian, Patrick," in ibid. vol. 3, pp. 119–120.

14 Leonard W. Cowie, *Lord Nelson, 1758–1805: A Bibliography,* Meckler's Bibliographies of British Statesmen, no. 7 (London and Westport, CT, 1990), 191 pp.

15 David Howarth and Stephen Howarth, *Nelson: The Immortal Memory* (London: Dent, 1987), published in the USA as *Lord Nelson: The Immortal Memory* (New York: Viking, 1989).

16 Cowie, *op. cit.,* Item 205, p. 54.

17 Tom Pocock, *Horatio Nelson* (London: Bodley Head, 1987; New York: Alfred A. Knopf, 1988).

18 Cowie, *op. cit.,* Item 204, p. 52.

19 Eugene L. Rasor, *English/British Naval History to 1815: A Guide to the Literature,* Bibliographies and Indexes in Military Studies, no. 15 (Westport, CT and London: Præger, 2004), 875 pp., reprinted in paperback as *The Seaforth Bibliography: A Guide to more than 4,000 works on British naval history, 55 BC–1815* (Barnsley: Seaforth, 2007).

20 Eugene L. Rasor, "The Nelson Decade: A Survey of the Literature," Bicentennial edition of the *Nelson Dispatch* (December 2005), pp. 872–900.

21 Information from Dr. Roger Knight, 10 January 2010.

22 Michael Duffy and Roger Morriss, eds., *The Glorious First of June 1794: A Naval Battle and Its Aftermath* (Exeter: University of Exeter Press, 2001).

23 Colin White, *1797: Nelson's Year of Destiny: Cape St. Vincent and Santa Cruz de Tenerife* (Stroud: Sutton, 1996, 2006).

24 Stephen Howarth, ed., *The Battle of Cape St. Vincent. 200 Years: Selected Papers from the Bicentennial International Naval Conference, Portsmouth, England, 15 February 1997* (Shelton: 1805 Club in association with the Society for Nautical Research and the Nelson Society, 1998).

25 Stephen Howarth, ed., *Battle of Copenhagen 1801, 200 Years: The Bicentennial International Naval Conference, Portsmouth, England, 19 May 2001* (Shelton: 1805 Club in association with the Society for Nautical Research and the Nelson Society, 2001).

26 Thomas Munch-Petersen, Defying Napoleon: How Britain Bombarded Copenhagen and Seized the Danish Fleet in 1807. (Stroud, Gloucs.: Sutton Publishing, 2007). Ole Feldbæck, *The Battle of Copenhagen 1801: Nelson and the Danes,* translated by Tony Wedgwood (London: Leo Cooper, 2002), 270 pp.

27 Michèle Battesti, *La Bataille d'Aboukir 1798: Nelson contrarie la stratégie de Bonaparte* (Paris: Economica, 1998), 263 pp.

28 Brian Lavery, *Nelson and the Nile: The Naval War against Bonaparte, 1798* (London: Chatham, 1998), 318 pp.

29 John Ledyard, ed., *Dispatches and Letters Relating to the Blockade of Brest, 1803–1805,* Publications of the Navy Records Society, vols. 14, 21 (London: Navy Records Society, 1899, 1902).

30 Roger Morriss, ed., *The Channel fleet and the blockade of Brest, 1793–1801,* Publications of the Navy Records Society, vol. 141 (Aldershot, Hants, England; Burlington, VT: Published by Ashgate for the Navy Records Society, 2001).

31 Michael K. Barritt, *Eyes of the Admiralty: J. T. Serres, an Artist in the Channel Fleet, 1799–1800* (London: National Maritime Museum, 2008), 144 pp.

32 David Syrett and R. L. DiNardo, eds., *The Commissioned Sea Officers of the Royal Navy, 1660–1815,* vol. 1 (Aldershot: Scolar Press for the Navy Records Society, 1994).

33 Pam and Derek Ayshford, *Ayshford Complete Trafalgar Roll,* CD-Rom.

34 Patrick Marioné, *The Complete Navy List,* CD-Rom.

35 The National Archives, Kew, http://www.nationalarchives.gov.uk/trafalgarancestors/.

36 Nicholas Tracy, *Who's Who in Nelson's Navy: Two Hundred Heroes* (London: Chatham Publishing, 2005), 388 pp., £25.

37 Colin White and the 1805 Club, *The Trafalgar Captains: The Lives and Memorials* (London: Chatham Publishing, 2005), 128 pp.

38 Roger Morriss, *Cockburn and the Royal Navy in Transition: Admiral Sir George Cockburn 1772–1853* (Exeter: University of Exeter Press, 1997).

39 John E. Talbott, *The Pen & Ink Sailor: Charles Middleton and the King's Navy, 1778–1813* (London and Portland, OR: Frank Cass, 1998).

40 H. C. G. Matthew and Brian Harrison, eds., *Oxford Dictionary of National Biography: From the Earliest Times to the Year 2000* (Oxford: Oxford University Press in association with the British Academy, 2004). Also available online at www.oxforddnb.com.

41 Michael Duffy, "Trafalgar, Nelson, and the National Memory," *Oxford Dictionary of National Biography,* online ed., Oxford University Press, Oct 2009 [http://www.oxforddnb.com/view/theme/92747, accessed 18 Dec 2009].

42 Peter Le Fevre and Richard Harding, eds., *Precursors of Nelson: British Admirals of the Eighteenth Century* (London: Chatham, 2000).

43 Ibid., p. 8.

44 Paul Krajeski, *In the Shadow of Nelson: The Naval Leadership of Admiral Sir Charles Cotton, 1753–1812,* Contributions in Military Studies, no. 184 (Westport, CT: Greenwood Press, 2000), 219 pp.

45 Hilary L. Rubinstein, *Trafalgar Captain: Durham of the Defiance* (Stroud, Gloucestershire: Tempus Publishing, 2005), £17.99.

46 Brian Vale, *The Audacious Admiral Cochrane: The True Life of a Naval Legend* (London: Conway Maritime Publishing, 2004), 240 pp., £17.99; David Cordingly, *Cochrane the Dauntless: The Life and Adventures of Thomas Cochrane* (London: Bloomsbury Publishing PLC, 2007), 448 pp., £20; *Cochrane: The Real Master and Commander* (New York: Bloomsbury USA, 2007), 448 pp., $32.50.

47 Iain Gordon, *Admiral of the Blue: The Life and Times of Admiral John Child Purvis, 1747–1825* (Barnsley: Pen & Sword, 2005), 272 pp., £19.99.

48 Max Adams, *Admiral Collingwood* (London: Weidenfeld & Nicholson, 2005). Published in the USA as *Trafalgar's Lost Hero: Admiral Lord Collingwood and the Defeat of Napoleon* (Hoboken, NJ: John Wiley & Sons, 2005), 333 pp.

49 Victor T. Sharman, *Nelson's Hero: The Story of his "Sea-Daddy" Captain William Locker* (Barnsley: Pen & Sword, 2005).

50 Kevin D. McCranie, *Admiral Lord Keith and the Naval War against Napoleon* (Gainesville, FL: University Press of Florida, 2006).

51 Tim Voelcker *Admiral Saumarez versus Napoleon: The Baltic, 1807–12* (Woodbridge: Boydell Press, 2008), 288 pp.

52 Bryan Elson, *Nelson's Yankee Captain: The Life of Boston Loyalist Sir Benjamin Hallowell* (Halifax, NS: Formac, 2009), 320 pp.

53 Peter Le Fevre and Richard Harding, eds., *British Admirals of the Napoleonic Wars: The Contemporaries of Nelson* (London: Chatham Publishing, 2005), 406 pp.

54 Julian Stafford Corbett, *Some Principles of Maritime Strategy,* Classics of Sea Power Series, introduction and notes by Eric J. Grove (Annapolis, MD: Naval Institute Press, 1988), is the definitive annotated edition of this work.

55 Richard Woodman, *The Sea Warriors: The Fighting Captains and Their Ships in the Age of Nelson* (London: Constable, 2001; London: Robinson, 2002), 416 pp.

56 Tom Wareham, *The Star Captains: Frigate Command in the Napoleonic Wars* (London: Chatham Publishing, 2001), 256 pp.; and *Frigate Commander* (London: Leo Cooper, 2004), 304 pp., £19.99.

57 Ruddock Mackay and Michael Duffy, *Hawke, Nelson, and British Naval Leadership, 1747–1805* (Woodbridge: Boydell Press, 2009), 256 pp.

58 Sam Willis, *Fighting at Sea in the Eighteenth Century: The Art of Sailing Warfare* (Woodbridge: Boydell Press, 2008), 254 pp.

59 Lawrence Brockliss, John Cardwell, and Michael Moss, *Nelson's Surgeon: William Beatty, Naval Medicine, and the Battle of Trafalgar* (Oxford: Oxford University Press, 2005), £45.

60 Anne-Mary E. Hills, *Nelson: A Medical Casebook* (London: Spellmount Publishers, 2006), 320 pp., £19.

61 A. T. Mahan, *The Life of Nelson: The Embodiment of the Sea Power of Great Britain* (Boston: Little, Brown, 1897).

62 Carola Oman, *Nelson* (Garden City, NY: Doubleday, 1946; London: Hodder & Stoughton, 1947).

63 Colin White, ed., *The Nelson Companion* (Stroud: Bramley Books in association with the Royal Naval Museum; Annapolis, MD: Naval Institute Press, 1995; and Stroud: Royal Naval Museum Publications in association with Sutton, 2005).

64 Richard Walker, *The Nelson Portraits: An Iconography of Horatio, Viscount Nelson, K.B., Vice Admiral of the White* (Portsmouth: Royal Naval Museum, 1998), 316 pp. Walker published addenda and corrections in *Trafalgar Chronicle: Year Book of the 1805 Club* for 2005 and for 2006.

65 Colin White, *The Nelson Encyclopedia: People, Places, Battles, Ships, Myths, Mistresses, Memorials,*

and Memorabilia (London: Chatham Publishing; Mechanicsburg, PA: Stackpole Books, 2002; revised ed., 2005), 300 pp., £12.

66 Terry Coleman, *The Nelson Touch: The Life and Legend of Horatio Nelson* (London: Bloomsbury, 2001, 2002; New York: Oxford University Press, 2002), 424 pp.

67 Ibid., p. 1

68 Joel Hayward, *For God and Glory: Lord Nelson and His Way of War* (Annapolis, MD: Naval Institute Press, 2003), 250 pp.

69 Edgar Vincent, *Nelson: Love & Fame* (New Haven, CT, and London: Yale University Press, 2003).

70 John Sugden, *Nelson: A Dream of Glory* (London: Jonathan Cape, 2004; London: Pimlico, 2005), 943 pp., £25.

71 Andrew Lambert, *Nelson: Britannia's God of War* (London: Faber & Faber, 2004), 446 pp.

72 Ibid., p. xi.

73 Ibid., p. 361.

74 David Cannadine, ed., *Admiral Lord Nelson: Context and Legacy* (London: Palgrave Macmillan, 2005), 201 pp.

75 Martyn Downer, *Nelson's Purse: An Extraordinary Historical Detective Story Shedding Light on the Life of Britain's Greatest Naval Hero* (London: Bantam Press, 2004), 424 pp.

76 Rina Prentice, *The Authentic Nelson* (London: National Maritime Museum, 2005), 192 pp.

77 Sir Nicholas Harris Nicolas, ed., *The Dispatches and Letters of Vice Admiral Lord Viscount Nelson, with Notes, Foreword by Michael Nash* (London: Chatham, 1997–98; Elibron Classics, Boston, MA: Adamant Media Corporation, 2003).

78 *The Naval Chronicle: The Contemporary Record of the Royal Navy at War, Prepared for General Use by Nicholas Tracy,* consolidated ed., 5 vols (London: Chatham, 1998–99).

79 Roger Morriss with Peter Bursey, compilers, *Guide to British Naval Papers in North America* (London: Published by Mansell for the National Maritime Museum, 1994).

80 Joseph F. Callo, ed., *Nelson Speaks: Admiral Lord Nelson in His Own Words* (Annapolis, MD: Naval Institute Press, 2001), 216 pp., $29.95.

81 Colin White, ed., *Nelson: The New Letters* (Woodbridge: Boydell Press in association with the National Maritime Museum and the Royal Naval Museum, 2005; paperback ed., 2007), 525 pp.

82 Colin White, "Nelson's 1805 Battle Plan," *Journal for Maritime Research* (May 2002), http://www.jmr.nmm.ac.uk/server/show/conJmrArticle.32.

83 Colin White, "The Nelson Letters Project," *Mariner's Mirror,* vol. 87 (November 2001), pp. 476–478; "The New Nelson Letters: News of Remarkable Discoveries Made by the Nelson Letters Project," *Mariner's Mirror,* vol. 89 (November 2003), pp. 464–466; "'Ever with Real Esteem,' Continuing the Nelson Letters Project," *Trafalgar Chronicle: Year Book of the 1805 Club,* vol. 16 (2006), pp. 44–48.

84 Steven E. Maffeo, ed., *Seize, Burn, or Sink: The Thoughts and Words of Admiral Lord Horatio Nelson* (Lanham, MD/Toronto, ONT/Plymouth, UK: Scarecrow Press, 2007), 620 pp., $95/£62.

85 Roger Knight, *The Pursuit of Victory: The Life and Achievement of Horatio Nelson* (London: Allen Lane, 2005, and Penguin Books, 2006; New York: Basic Books, 2005, and Perseus Books Group, 2007).

86 Colin White, *Nelson: The Admiral* (Stroud: Sutton in association with the Royal Navy and the Royal Naval Museum, 2005), 240 pp., £20.

87 Marianne Czisnik, *Nelson: A Controversial Hero* (London: Hodder Arnold, 2005), 192 pp.

88 David Lyon, *The Sailing Ship Navy List: All the Ships of the Royal Navy—Built, Purchased, and Captured 1688–1860* (London: Conway Maritime Press, 1993, 1997).

89 Rif Winfield, *British Warships in the Age of Sail, 1793–1817: Design, Construction, Careers and Fates* (London: Chatham Publishing; St. Paul, MN: MBI Publishing, 2005), 418 pp., £50.

90 Peter Goodwin, *Nelson's Ships: A History of the Vessels in Which He Served 1771–1805* (London: Conway Maritime, 2002), 312 pp., £20.

91 Jan Glete, *Navies and Nations: Warships, Navies and State Building in Europe and America, 1500–1860, Acta Universitatis Stockholmiensis,* Stockholm Studies in History, vol. 48 (Stockholm: Almqvist & Wiksell International, 1993). See in particular vol. 2, pp. 375–417 and tables on pp. 554, 568–570.

92 F. Fernández-González, L. D. Ferreiro, and H. Nowacki, eds., *Technology of the Ships of Trafalgar: Proceedings of an International Congress held at the Escuela Técnica Superior de Ingenieros Navales, Madrid, and the Diputación Provincal, Cádiz, 3–5 November 2005* (Madrid: Escuela Técnica Superior de Ingenieros Navales Universidad Politécnica de Madrid, 2006), 744 pp., 150 euros.

93 Larrie D. Ferreiro, *Ships and Science: The Birth of Naval Architecture in the Scientific Revolution, 1600–1800* (Cambridge, MA, and London: MIT Press, 2007).

94 A. R. T. Jonkers, *Earth's Magnetism in the Age of Sail* (Baltimore and London: Johns Hopkins University Press, 2003).

95 Olivier Chapuis, *A la Mer comme au Ciel: Beautemps-Beaupré & la naissance de l'hydrographie moderne (1700–1850)* (Paris: Presses de l'Université de Paris-Sorbonne, 1999), 1060 pp.

96 Brian Lavery, *Shipboard Life and Organization, 1731–1815,* Publications of the Navy Records Society, vol. 138 (Aldershot, UK; Brookfield, USA; Singapore and Sydney: Ashgate for the Navy Records Society, 1998).

97 Nicholas Blake, *Steering to Glory: A Day in the Life of a Ship of the Line* (London: Chatham, 2005).

98 Nicholas Blake and Richard Lawrence, *The Illustrated Companion to Nelson's Navy* (London: Chatham Publishing, 1999; Mechanicsburg, PA: Stackpole Books, 2005).

99 E.g., Brian Lavery, *Nelson's Navy: The Ships, Men, and Organization, 1793–1815* (London: Conway Maritime, 1989); Jean Boudriot, *The Seventy-Four-Gun Ship,* 4 vols. (Paris, 1973–77; Rochester and Annapolis, 1983–88).

100 Janet Macdonald, *Feeding Nelson's Navy: The True Story of Food at Sea* (London: Chatham; Mechanicsburg, PA: Stackpole Books, 2004), 224 pp.

101 Steven E. Maffeo, *Most Secret and Confidential: Intelligence in the Age of Nelson* (Annapolis, MD: Naval Institute Press, 2000), 354 pp.

102 Elizabeth Sparrow, *Secret Service: British Agents in France, 1792–1815* (Woodbridge: Boydell Press, 1999).

103 Jane Knight, "Nelson's 'Old Lady': Merchant News as a Source of Intelligence (June to October 1796)," *Journal for Maritime Research* (May 2005).

104 Richard Hill, *The Prizes of War: The Naval Prize System in the Napoleonic Wars, 1793–1815* (Stroud: Sutton for the Royal Naval Museum, 1998).

105 Henry J. Bourguignon, *Sir William Scott, Lord Stowell: Judge of the High Court of Admiralty, 1798–1828* (Cambridge: Cambridge University Press, 1987, 2004), 310 pp.

106 Michèle Battesti, *Trafalgar: les aléas de la stratégie navale de Napoléon,* Bibliothèque Napoléonienne (Paris: Tallandier Éditions, 2004), 380 pp., 27 euros.

107 Tim Clayton and Phil Craig, *Trafalgar: The Men, the Battle, the Storm* (London: Hodder & Stoughton, 2004), 444 pp.

108 Roy Adkins, *Trafalgar: The Biography of a Battle* (London: Little, Brown, 2004; Abacus, 2005); *Nelson's Trafalgar: The Battle That Changed the World* (New York: Viking Penguin, 2005), 392 pp.

109 Adam Nicholson, *Men of Honour: Trafalgar and the Making of the English Hero* (London: HarperCollins, 2005), 341 pp., £16.99; *Seize the Fire: Heroism, Duty, and the Battle of Trafalgar* (New York: HarperCollins, 2005), 341 pp., $26.95.

110 Marianne Czisnik, "Admiral Nelson's Tactics at the Battle of Trafalgar," *History,* vol. 89, issue 4, no. 296 (October 2004), pp. 549–559.

111 Michael Duffy, "'. . . All Was Hushed Up': The Hidden Trafalgar," *Mariner's Mirror,* vol. 91 (May 2005), pp. 214–240, and "The Gunnery at Trafalgar: Training, Tactics or Temperament," *Journal for Maritime Research* (August 2005), http://www.jmr.nmm.ac.uk.

112 Tom Pocock, *Trafalgar: An Eyewitness History* (London: Folio Society and Penguin Books, 2005), 238 pp.

113 Peter Warwick, *Voices from the Battle of Trafalgar* (Newton Abbot: David & Charles, 2005), 318 pp., £19.99.

114 Alexander Stilwell, *The Trafalgar Companion* (Oxford: Osprey Publishing, 2005), 224 pp.

115 Rémi Monaque, *Trafalgar: 21 Octobre 1805,* Bibliothèque Napoléonienne (Paris: Tallandier Éditions, 2005), 393 pp., 25 euros.

116 Rémi Monaque, *Latouche-Tréville, 1745–1804: l'amiral qui défiait Nelson* (Paris: éditions SPM, 2000), 659 pp.

117 Richard Harding, ed., *A Great & Glorious Victory: The Battle of Trafalgar Conference Papers* (Barnsley: Seaforth Publishing, 2008), 128 pp.

118 Derek Allen and Peter Hore, *News of Nelson: John Lapenotiere's Race from Trafalgar to London* (Brussels: SEFF ed., 2005).

119 *The Trafalgar Way: Commemorative map of the 1805 Post Chaise from Falmouth to London* (London: Ordnance Survey, 2005), one sheet, £6.25.

120 Tom Pocock, *The Terror before Trafalgar: Nelson, Napoleon and the Secret War* (London: John Murray, 2002; New York: W. W. Norton, 2003), 225 pp.

121 J. E. Cookson, *The British Armed Nation, 1793–1815* (Oxford: Clarendon Press, 1997).

122 Alexandra Franklin and Mark Philp, *Napoleon and the Invasion of Britain* (Oxford: Bodleian Library, 2003).

123 Clive Wilkinson, *The British Navy and the State in the Eighteenth Century* (Woodbridge: Boydell Press, 2004), 246 pp.

124 Margarette Lincoln, *Naval Wives & Mistresses, 1750–1815* (London: National Maritime Museum, Greenwich, 2007), 218 pp.

125 Richard Blake, *Evangelicals in the Royal Navy, 1775–1815: Blue Lights and Psalm Singers* (Woodbridge: Boydell Press, 2008), 327 pp.

126 John D. Byrn, ed., *Naval Courts Martial, 1793–1815*, Publications of the Navy Records Society, vol. 155 (Farnham, Surrey, and Burlington, VT: Ashgate Publishing for the Navy Records Society, 2009).

127 Nicholas Rogers, *Press Gang: Naval Impressment and Its Opponents in Georgian Britain* (London and New York: Continuum, 2007).

128 Timothy Jenks, *Naval Engagements: Patriotism, Cultural Politics, and the Royal Navy, 1793–1815* (Oxford: Oxford University Press, 2008), 334 pp.

129 William Henry Flayhart III, *Counterpoint to Trafalgar: The Anglo-Russian Invasion of Naples, 1805–1806* (Columbia, SC: University of South Carolina Press, 1992; New Perspectives on Maritime History and Nautical Archaeology, Gainesville: University Press of Florida, 2004), 198 pp., $24.95.

130 Christopher D. Hall, *Wellington's Navy: Sea Power and the Peninsular War, 1807–1814* (London: Chatham; Mechanicsburg, PA: Stackpole Books, 2004), 264 pp., £25.

131 Christopher D. Hall, *British Strategy in the Napoleonic War, 1803–15* (Manchester and New York: Manchester University Press, 1992), 239 pp.

132 Rory Muir, *Britain and the Defeat of Napoleon, 1807–1815* (New Haven and London: Yale University Press, 1996), 466 pp.

133 Lawrence Stone, ed., *An Imperial State at War: Britain from 1689 to 1815* (London: Routledge, 1994), 372 pp.

134 Jeremy Black, *The British Seaborne Empire* (New Haven and London: Yale University Press, 2004), 420 pp., £25/$45. See Jeremy Black's complementary study, *Naval Power: A History of Warfare and the Sea from 1500 Onwards* (London: Palgrave Macmillan, 2009), 240 pp.

135 Margarette Lincoln, *Representing the Royal Navy: British Sea Power, 1750–1815* (Aldershot: Ashgate, 2002), 226 pp., £40.

136 Margarette Lincoln, ed., *Nelson & Napoléon,* introduction by N. A. M. Rodger (London: National Maritime Museum, 2005), 287 pp., £30.

137 B. C. Southam, *Jane Austen and the Navy* (London: Hambledon, 2000, and National Maritime Museum, 2005), 395 pp., £12.99.

138 Nicholas Tracy, *Britannia's Palette: The Arts of Naval Victory* (Montreal: McGill–Queen's University Press, 2007), 476 pp., CAN$75.

139 N. A. M. Rodger, *The Command of the Ocean: A Naval History of Britain, 1649–1815* (London: Penguin/Allen Lane in association with the National Maritime Museum, 2004; New York: W. W. Norton, 2005), 907 pp., £30/US$45/CAN$65.

140 John B. Hattendorf, R. J. B. Knight, A. W. H. Pearsall, N. A. M. Rodger, and Geoffrey Till, eds., *British Naval Documents, 1204–1960,* Publications of the Navy Records Society, vol. 131 (Aldershot: Scolar Press for the Navy Records Society, 1993).

141 Paul W. Schroeder, *The Transformation of European Politics, 1763–1848* (Oxford: Clarendon Press, 1994), 894 pp., £84.

142 Agustín Guimerá Ravina, Alberto Ramos, and Gonzalo Butrón, eds., *Trafalgar y el mundo atlántico* (Madrid: Marcel Pons Historia, 2004), 398 pp., 22 euros.

143 Agustín Guimerá Ravina and Victor Peralta, eds., *El equilibrio de los imperios: De Utrecht a Trafalgar,* Actas de la VIII Reunión Científica de la Fundación Española de Historia Moderna, Madrid, 2–6 de junio de 2004, vol. II (Madrid: Fundación Española de Historia Moderna, 2005), 856 pp., 24 euros.

144 David Cannadine, ed., *Trafalgar in History: A Battle and Its Afterlife* (London: Palgrave Macmillan, 2006), 224 pp.

145 See, for example, Gavin Daly, "English Smugglers, the Channel, and the Napoleonic Wars, 1800–1814," *The Journal of British Studies,* vol. 46, no. 1 (January 2007), pp. 30–46, and Renaud Morieux, "Diplomacy from Below and Belonging: Fishermen and Cross Channel Relations in the Eighteenth Century," *Past and Present,* no. 202 (February 2009), pp. 83–125.

146 *The History of Cartography* series: vol. 3, David Woodward, ed., *Cartography in the European Renaissance* (Chicago: University of Chicago Press, 2007); vol. 4, Matthew Edney and Mary Sponberg Pedley, eds., *Cartography in the European Enlightenment* (Chicago: University of Chicago Press, forthcoming).

147 Daniel A. Baugh, "Naval Power: What Gave the British Naval Superiority?" in Leandro Prados de la Escosura, ed., *Exceptionalism and Industrialisation: Britain and Its European Rivals, 1688–1815* (Cambridge: Cambridge University Press, 2004), pp. 235–257.

The James Ford Bell Lecture, 2008
*Fact in Fiction about Life at Sea in the 18th Century—Understanding
the Naval Novel and the World of Aubrey and Maturin*

Within the general range of historical fiction relating to the sea,[1] the subgenre of the naval novel has become one of the most popular types of historical fiction. Today, the most widely known and most widely read novels of this subgenre are the twenty-one volumes of the Aubrey-Maturin series begun by Patrick O'Brian in 1967. The Horatio Hornblower series by C. S. Forester, begun thirty years earlier in 1937, ranks as a close second to O'Brian. Both these very popular series of historical novels have their settings in the context of the Royal Navy during the Napoleonic Wars with the Aubrey-Maturin series focused largely within a narrower band of years from 1800 to 1815. There is a long tradition for such works in fiction and to understand the subgenre one first needs to understand how it developed as a whole. Once we have looked at that, we can focus more effectively on those works set in the eighteenth century, how they effectively, or otherwise, present life at sea in that period.[2]

What Is a Naval Novel?

A naval novel may be simply defined as a book-length piece of historical fiction that is set on board naval vessels or in a naval shore environment, has imaginary naval officers or naval seamen as its principal characters, or has a fictional story or plot that is true to the naval atmosphere of a particular period. Typically, naval novels are woven into the broad context of actual historical naval events of a particular period and include references to well-known naval figures and incidents in history. Most novels of this type rely on the use of period naval parlance as well as impressionistic, but often well-founded, descriptions of the prevailing naval technology in order to create a sense of authentic atmosphere.

While the literary quality varies widely, most novelists of this subgenre had served at sea in some form or another. A number of these works are of primary historical value as descriptions of their periods. In contrast to the earlier naval novel, the most widely read naval novels from the mid-twentieth century on are in series that follow a character's development across numerous volumes during the course of a particular war or historical period. Many of these authors were experienced at sea, although several successful authors were not and relied entirely on historical research.

Early Naval Novels

In general, British and American writers and subjects dominate this subgenre, whose origin is generally dated to the humorous, two-volume novel *The Adventures of Roderick Random* (1748) by Tobias Smollett (1721–1771), a major figure in the history of the early English novel. Smollett served in the Royal Navy as a surgeon's mate in

1740–1741, an experience he used in his fiction. His characters, highly original in the eighteenth-century novel, are naval caricatures, but ably portray recognizable human foibles. Smollett followed up his first success with *The Adventures of Peregrine Pickle* (1751).

Smollett had a number of imitators, but few successfully followed his model in satirically illustrating naval life. One exception is the anonymous novel *Edward and Maria*, published serially in *The London Magazine* (1774–1775) and assumed to be the work of Edward Thompson (1738?–1786), a naval officer who wrote plays, satires, and edited literary journals. A number of other minor works also appeared in the mid-eighteenth century, including such popular satiric works as Charles Johnstone's *Chrysal, or, The Adventure of a Guinea* (1760) as well as short fictional pieces in journals such as *The Naval Magazine*, *The Naval Chronicle*, and *The Britannic Magazine*.[3]

The great English novelist Jane Austen (1775–1817) included passing allusions to naval society and its characters, particularly in her books *Mansfield Park* (1814) and *Persuasion* (1817). As recent scholarship has shown, the Royal Navy was substantial and wide-ranging within the Austen family, and was important to Jane Austen personally, particularly as it involved her two naval officer brothers and their acquaintances as they interacted with the Austen family.[4] Austen's naval insights are based on a view of her two brothers, Charles and Francis, who served in the Royal Navy. Although her works are not primarily naval novels, they touch on themes relevant to the subgenre with descriptions of a naval officer's home life and characterizations of the way in which naval events at sea were followed and had an impact on naval families. This, as scholars of social history have recently stressed, is a significant dimension of a sailor's life even if it does not take place at sea.

A major new phase for naval fiction arose from the wars of the 1793–1815 period with a series of satirical works portraying institutional life in the Royal Navy. Among them were minor novels published during the course of these wars, notably, Mark Moor's *Original Anecdotes of a Naval Officer* (1795) and *The Naval Trident* (1804); John Thelwall's *The Trident of Albion* (1805); Charles Fletcher's *The Naval Guardian* (1805); and John Davis's *The Post Captain, or, The Wooden Walls Well Manned* (1805).

Major novels followed, but not until 1826, when several volumes appeared nearly simultaneously. These included the anonymous novel *The Log Book, or, Nautical Miscellany*; M. H. Barker's *Greenwich Hospital*; and Captain William Nugent Glascock's *Naval Sketch-book*. Glascock (1787?–1847) took the lead and followed with works such as *Sailors and Saints* (1829) and *Tales of a Tar* (1830). His work, along with others from this generation of writers, reached its peak between 1829 and 1841 with Glascock's *Naval Sketch-book, 2nd Series* (1834) and *Land Sharks and Sea Gulls* (1838). Soon, Jamaican planter Michael Scott (1789–1835) followed with *Tom Cringle's Log* (1829 in serial form; 1834 as a book) and *The Cruise of the Midge* (1834), as did Captain Frederick Chamier (1796–1870) with *The Life of a Sailor* (1832), *Ben Brace: The Last of Nelson's Agamemnons* (1836), *The Saucy Arethusa: A Naval Story* (1837), *Jack Adams, The Mutineer* (1838), and *Tom Bowling* (1841).[5] As the naval novel developed in the period after the Napoleonic Wars, particularly in the years between the 1820s and 1840s when many authors had known war service, novelists typically took a very gloomy attitude toward sea life and discipline that one does not find in the more direct reminiscences from the period.[6]

Captain Frederick Marryat (1792–1848) ranks as the major novelist of this early group. His book *The Naval Officer, or, Scenes and Adventures in the Life of Frank Mildmay* (1829) initiated a series of successful novels, including *The King's Own* (1830); *Jacob Faithful* and *Peter Simple* (both 1834); *Mr. Midshipman Easy* (1836); and *Percival Keene* (1842). Marryat had served under Lord Cochrane in 1806–1809 and he was the innovator who first applied Cochrane's experiences and characteristics to fictional characters, notably to Captain Savage in *Peter Simple* and Captain M in *The King's Own*. In general, Marryat created manly if comical naval characters.[7]

In the mid-nineteenth century, few British fiction writers were inspired to use recent naval experience as a setting, although the lawyer William Johnson Neale (1812–1893) wrote *Cavendish, or, The Patrician at Sea* (1831) and *The Port Admiral: A Tale of the War* (1833). Marryat's harsh reviews of these books so incensed Neale that he challenged Marryat to a duel, but Neale later went on to publish *Paul Periwinkle, or, The Pressgang* (1841) and *Pride of the Mess: A Naval Novel of the Crimean War* (1855). Additionally, the naval officer and hydrographer Sir Edward Belcher (1799–1877) published his three-volume *Horatio Howard Brenton, A Naval Novel* (1856), which interestingly used the well-known naval family name of Brenton, whose progenitors had been among the original settlers of Newport, Rhode Island, in 1639, but as loyalists had returned to Britain and contributed six naval officers to the Royal Navy, including two admirals and a naval historian of the Napoleonic War era.[8]

Cooper and Melville

As the impetus of personal experience in the Royal Navy during the Napoleonic Wars faded as a direct influence on naval fiction, another influence arose across the Atlantic. James Fenimore Cooper (1789–1851), who served for three years as a midshipman in the U.S. Navy and took part in several contentious debates about naval issues of the day, wrote the first serious narrative history of the U.S. Navy (1839) and a collection of comparative American naval biographies (1846). Although he is remembered today more for his Leatherstocking Tales about the colonial period, Cooper wrote more novels set at sea than on land. His work gave rise to the genre of American sea fiction. Unlike British naval fiction, Cooper was influenced not by Smollett and Marryat, but by the poet Lord Byron, which led him to more romantic depictions of ships and the sea. Along these lines, Cooper's *The Pilot: A Tale of the Sea* (1823) drew from his own naval service while depicting the American Revolutionary War and his research on the figure of John Paul Jones. In contrast to the romance of *The Pilot,* Cooper's novel *The Two Admirals: A Tale of the Sea* (1842) takes up more serious topics examining the relationship between Nelson and Collingwood, while also serving as an argument for the United States to organize its navy around fleets and admirals, rather than captains and individual warships. With a related theme, Cooper's *The Wing-and-Wing, or, Le Feu-Follet* (1842) depicts the controversy surrounding Admiral Francesco Caracciolo (1752–1799), who commanded the French-supported, Neapolitan fleet and was tried and executed by Horatio Nelson in 1799.[9]

Another major American writer, Herman Melville (1819–1891), wrote important naval novels.[10] *White Jacket* (1851), built on Melville's fourteen months' experience as an ordinary seaman in the frigate USS *United States* in 1843–1844, describes naval life in detail and protests the navy's harsh discipline. During his brief service in the United States Navy, Melville had witnessed 163 floggings. *White Jacket* clearly records his horror of this punishment, as does his posthumously published novella *Billy Budd, Foretopman* (1924). A complex allegorical work, *Billy Budd* tells the story of a British warship captain who is forced by institutional strictures to unjustly condemn an innocent seaman. These important literary works drew immense attention, underscoring the anomalies and tensions in naval disciplinary practices. They are tied thematically to Cooper's views on naval training as represented in the USS *Somers* affair and the resulting public outcry that led eventually to the establishment of the U.S. Naval Academy in 1845.[11]

In translation, Cooper, Melville, Marryat, and others strongly influenced the development of historical fiction in France, but there the great naval battles that inspired English-language fiction—mostly lost by the French—were passed by silently. Corsairs, adventurers, smugglers, slave-traders, and pirates dominated French sea fiction; only the rare French novelist touched on naval life. Among them, Edouard Corbière (1793–1875), who wrote *Les Aspirans de Marine* (1834), and Guillaume-Joseph-Gabriel de La Landelle (1812–1886), author of *Les épaulettes d'amiral* (1856) and *La frégate l'Introuvable* (1868), are the most notable.[12]

Collectively these early naval novels reflected a now almost forgotten romanticism about the sea, and served as a powerful force to encourage young men to go to sea in the nineteenth century. This was not lost on Richard Henry Dana (1825–1882), who noted in the preface to his factual account *Two Years Before the Mast* (1840) that he was trying to correct that image and to demystify the seagoing experience in a way that illustrated "the light and the dark together."[13] Dana was not alone in his reaction; Charles Nordhoff (1830–1901), an orphaned thirteen-year-old in Ohio who had joined the U.S. Navy in the mid-1840s, later ruefully noted in his non-fiction narrative, *Man-of-War Life* (1855):

> In common with most Western boys, I had very crude and ill-defined notions of the new existence of which I was about to embark. Marryat's and Cooper's, and other approved sea novels are delightful reading, but scarcely calculated to give one true views of the life they pretend to describe.[14]

The Twentieth Century

Much of twentieth-century naval fiction was inspired by twentieth-century events and by life amidst machinery afloat. Yet, the eighteenth century was not forgotten. In the 1930s, Charles Nordhoff (1887–1947), the grandson of the Nordhoff mentioned above, and James Norman Hall (1887–1951) returned to the eighteenth century with massive historical research for their fictional trilogy, *Mutiny on the* Bounty (1932), *Men Against the Sea,* and *Pitcairn's Island* (both 1934). This trilogy contributed substantially to the subsequent literary focus on the mutiny as a seminal event in late eighteenth-century naval life. Hall went on to write his humorous *Doctor Dogbody's Leg* (1939), about the life of a British naval surgeon in the Napoleonic Wars and his many fanciful postwar renditions of how he lost his leg. The popular author Kenneth Roberts (1885–1957) wrote novels about privateering battles during the War of 1812 in *The Lively Lady* (1931) and *Captain Caution* (1934), moving to naval affairs in *Lydia Bailey* (1947), a novel that touched tangentially on the U.S. Navy's early operations off North Africa.

The 1983 winner of the Nobel Prize for Literature, Sir William Golding (1911–1993), won the 1981 Booker-McConnell Prize with the first volume of his sea trilogy *Rites of Passage* (1980) that was followed by *Close Quarters* (1987) and *Fire Down Below* (1989). The trilogy is impressionistically set on board a British warship making a passage to Australia at the end of the Napoleonic Wars, but is more an examination of the British class system than of naval life.

Personal experience of naval operations in World War II inspired a number of other novelists. In *The Cruel Sea* (1951), Nicholas Monsarrat (1910–1979) lyrically described the bravery and selfless struggle exhibited in the treacherous North Atlantic. Herman Wouk's (1915–) Pulitzer Prize–winning *The Caine Mutiny* (1951) explores the tensions created through quirks of personality expressed through naval command.

Influence of C. S. Forester

Other widely read books in the immediate post–World War II period included *The Good Shepherd* (1955) by C. S. Forester (Cecil Scott Forester, the pen name of Cecil Lewis Troughton Smith, 1899–1966). In 1937, C. S. Forester had published *The Happy Return* (in the United States titled *Beat to Quarters*), the first in a series of eleven extremely popular novels that were published over the following thirty years. The series followed the career of Horatio Hornblower, a fictional officer in the Royal Navy during the period of the French Revolution and the Napoleonic Wars. Perhaps Forester had taken the name of his protagonist from one of Marryat's characters, called Hornblow.[15] Wherever the name came from, Forester created with Hornblower an entirely new approach to the naval novel that was widely emulated: multiple books focusing on the evolving naval career of a single character and grounded in a substantial, although romanticized, historical understanding of the period. To cap his popular series, Forester even compiled *The Hornblower Companion: An Atlas and Personal Commentary on the Writing of the Hornblower Saga* (1964).

Later, the naval historian, creator of "Parkinson's Law," and novelist C. Northcote Parkinson (1909–1993) wrote a fictional biography of Hornblower, *The Life and Times of Horatio Hornblower* (1970), so skillfully parodying the naval biographer's art that some thought it the result of archival research. Most notably a former Deputy Secretary of the U.S. Navy reviewed it for the *New York Times* and appeared to be completely taken in by the spoof and even commented on "the familiar Beechey portrait of Hornblower" that provided the book's frontispiece.[16] The anonymous reviewer in the *Times Literary Supplement* did only slightly better, concluding that the book was "certainly a tour de force of historical and biographical research," but then adding: "Yet a niggling memory recalls that Daniel Defoe was the author of a book of fiction entitled *A New Voyage Round The World,* which foxed a great many people for a great many years."[17]

Following in Forester's wake, Showell Styles (1908–2005) wrote two series on the Age of Nelson, one starting with *Midshipman Quinn* (1956) and the other with *Mr. Fitton's Commission* (1977). Forester himself personally encouraged Dudley Pope (1925–1993), who wrote *Ramage: A Novel* (1965) as the start of an eighteen-novel series about naval operations during the years 1796–1807. With *To Glory We Steer* (1968), Alexander Kent (the pen name of Douglas Reeman, 1924–, who had written twenty-four novels about World War II under his own name) launched a twenty-three-volume series about the exploits of Richard Bolitho in 1772–1814. Extending the series by creating Adam Bolitho, Richard's nephew, in *Second to None* (1999), he carries the series into the period after 1815.

The most famous and most widely read and translated series of naval novels came from Patrick O'Brian (1914–2000).[18] The twenty-one-volume series[19] chronicles the voyages of Captain Jack Aubrey and his ship's doctor, amateur naturalist, and intelligence agent, Stephen Maturin. O'Brian's series was encouraged by Forester's U.S. editor at B. J. Lippincott upon Forester's death. O'Brian, an admirer of Forester's action scenes, based his first work in the series, *Master and Commander* (1969), partly on the actions of Lord Cochrane in the Mediterranean. After a long, gradual gestation, O'Brian's work eclipsed other series on a wave of critical and popular acclaim that arose in the early 1990s. O'Brian's work captivated an unusually wide literary audience, ranging from university professors, naval professionals, and yachtsmen to general fiction readers. Despite being grounded in technical nautical vocabulary and arcane historical references, the Aubrey-Maturin series gained an audience devoted to its complex characters, rich in flaws and virtues.

While Forester inspired the approach, O'Brian's growing success added impetus to the creation of other naval fiction series. Adam Hardy (pen name of Kenneth Bulmer, 1921–) wrote fourteen short novels about George Abercrombie Fox in the years 1776–1801, starting with *The Press Gang* (1972). C. Northcote Parkinson turned to writing novels in 1973 with *The Devil to Pay,* starting a six-volume series about Richard Delancy in the years 1776–1811. With *A Fine Boy for Killing* (1979), Jan Needle (1943–) began his Sea Officer William Bentley novels dealing with some of the darker aspects of eighteenth-century naval life. A captain in Trinity House service, Richard Woodman (1944–) wrote his popular Nathaniel Drinkwater series, fourteen volumes set in the years 1779–1814, beginning with *An Eye of the Fleet* (1981). Anthony Forrest, the joint pseudonym of two writers, Antony Brown (1922–2001) and Norman Ian Mackenzie (1921–), produced three novels about secret agent John Justice in the years 1804–1807, starting with *Captain Justice* (1981). Robert Challoner (1924–1986) wrote three novels about his character Charles Oakshott in the period 1793–1801, beginning with *Run Out the Guns* (1984). Kenneth Maynard (fl. 1984–1986) wrote four novels about Matthew Lamb set in the years 1798–1801, beginning with *Lieutenant Lamb* (1984).

Branching out further, David Donachie (pen name of Tom Connery, 1944–) wrote five novels in The Privateersman Mysteries series about former naval Captain Harry Ludlow in the period 1793–1795, beginning with *The Devil's Own Luck* (1991), then wrote the Nelson and Emma trilogy, starting with *On a Making Tide* (2000), and followed these with the John Pearce novels, starting with *By the Mast Divided* (2004). Under his own name, Connery wrote three additional volumes in this period about Royal Marine George Markham, starting with *A Shred of Honour* (1996). With *The King's Coat* (1989) set in the 1780s, American-born Dewey Lambdin (1945–) began a series of a dozen volumes recounting the naval adventures of reluctant Royal Navy midshipman Alan Lewrie.

A German author, Dieter Zimmerling (1938–), planned a series of novels about Udo Graf von Krockwitz, a Prussian who had come home after serving in the Royal Navy at Trafalgar. However, the sequels to *Leutnant Krockwitz: Ein Schiff für Preußen: Roman* (1981) have not materialized. Frank Adam (the pen name of Karlheinz Ingenkamp, 1925–), a retired professor of educational research and measurement in Germany, wrote a series of fourteen novels in German between 1992 and 2005 with the central character David Winter. Set in the years 1774–1814, Frank Adam's series began with *Der Junge Seewolf: Die Abenteuer des Seekadetten David Winter in Admiral Nelsons Flotte*

(1992). In addition, Adam published a very useful general guide for readers of the genre.[20]

Julian Stockwin (1944–) began what may become an eighteen-volume series on Thomas Paine Kydd with *Kydd* (2001) that initially focused on an impressed man on the lower decks, but may now follow his career to become a tarpaulin admiral. Another author who specialized in British army fiction, Bernard Cornwell (1944–), also made contributions to the naval novel with *Sharpe's Trafalgar* (2000) and *Sharpe's Prey: Richard Sharpe and the Expedition to Copenhagen, 1807* (2002).

This entire group of novels from Forester onward is typified by works whose leading characters sail in small warships, usually operating in the Mediterranean or in the Caribbean. The British victories at Camperdown, the Nile, Copenhagen, or Trafalgar are often mentioned. Taken as a whole, the novels cover most aspects of British naval operations in the period, with notable attention to technical accuracy concerning naval operations, naval life, and language. Many readers found parallels in these books to the career of Horatio Nelson or to the adventures of Lord Cochrane, although one writer, Bryan Perrett, argued in *The Real Hornblower* (1997) that Forester really had as his model Admiral Sir James Alexander Gordon (1782–1869).

Other Approaches to Naval Fiction

Fueled by Forester, O'Brian, and other fiction writers and historians, the attraction for novelists of the Age of Nelson has continued. Authors began to think of new approaches to the period. Edwin Thomas (1977–) began a historical mystery series with *Blighted Cliffs* (2003) following the anti-hero and likable rogue Lieutenant Martin Jerrold, who had served without distinction at Trafalgar. An American, who was born into a military family and raised a Quaker, Jay Worrall (1943–) began a series featuring Royal Navy Lieutenant Charles Edgemont with *Sails on the Horizon: A Novel of the Napoleonic Wars* (2005). Very recently, British writer G. S. Beard introduced a new series featuring John Fury, beginning with *Mr. Midshipman Fury* (2006), a novel set in 1783 on a voyage in a frigate to India. Canadian author Sean Thomas Russell (1952–) began a new series beginning with *Under Enemy Colors* (2007), about British naval officer Charles Saunders Hayden, the son of an English father and a French mother, faced with the outbreak of the French Revolution.

Yet, as historical fiction continued to flourish, some authors began to turn away from the Age of Nelson and apply variations on the same approach to different navies, regions, or periods of history, as they sought a wider readership. Among those that dealt with the eighteenth century was a nine-volume series starting with *Brave Captain Kelso* (1959) by James Dillon White (pen name of Stanley White, 1913–1978), who explored the Bombay Marine in the period 1755–1760. An American attorney from Tennessee, Ellis K. Meacham (1913–) wrote a trilogy about an officer in the Bombay Marine, Captain Percival Merewether, in the period 1806–1808, opening with *The East Indiaman* (1968). Porter Hill (pen name, fl. 1985–1988) began the Captain Adam Horne series about a maritime commando unit in the Indian Ocean of the 1760s with *Bombay Marines* (1985). Canadian historian Victor Suthren (1942–) wrote two parallel series of novels on the war of 1739–1748 in American waters. The Paul Gallant novels make up the first series with a French officer, beginning with *The Black Cockade: Paul Gallant's Louisbourg Command* (1977), while the second series features a British officer, Edward Mainwaring, beginning with *Royal Yankee* (1987). London-based, Australian-born

author Peter Smalley (1943–) began a series about Captain William Rennie and Lieutenant James Hayter on a secret mission to the Pacific about 1786 in *HMS* Expedient: *A
Sea Story* (2005).

Among writers who focus on American naval topics, William Martin (1950–)
wrote *Annapolis* (1996), telling the history of the town through two rival families, the
Staffords and the Parrishes, who have someone serving in the navy in every major
American war from the Revolution through the Gulf War. James L. Nelson (1962–)
wrote the Revolution at Sea Trilogy, about Isaac Biddlecomb, beginning with *By Force
of Arms* (1996). Nicholas Nicastro (1963–) devoted a series to the life of John Paul
Jones, starting with *Eighteenth Captain* (1999). Commercial banker and yachtsman
William H. White (1942–) built a trilogy on the War of 1812 around the fictional seaman Isaac Biggs beginning with *A Press of Canvas* (2000), and began another series on
the U.S. Navy in the Barbary Wars with Midshipman Oliver Baldwin in *The Greater
the Honor* (2003). The legal counsel for an American naval shipyard, James E. Fender
(1942–), wrote a series of five novels about an American privateersman in the War of
Independence, beginning with *The Private Revolution of Geoffrey Frost* (2002). In
2005, on completion of his David Winter series about the Royal Navy during the Age
of Nelson, Frank Adam began a new German-language series featuring a Swede born
on the frontier during the American War of Independence, starting with *Sven Larsson:
Rebell unter Segeln* (2006). Another American, Broos Campbell (1957–) began a series
about the U.S. Navy in the Quasi-War with France, 1798–1801, with *No Quarter: A
Matty Graves Novel* (2006).

Within the genre of historical sea fiction, the subgenre of the naval novel became
increasingly popular in the late twentieth century, particularly novels that followed a
specific character's naval career. None of these surpassed the literary achievements of
Cooper, Melville, and Golding. In 2008, the classic series from Marryat to Forester
and O'Brian continued to dominate; among them, perhaps only O'Brian could be
considered at a level with Nordhoff and Hall and the Second World War novels of
Monsarrat, Wouk, and Buchheim. Among those writing on the eighteenth century
Kent, Reeman, and Woodman, along with Adam in Germany, have maintained a significant following. A range of new authors is still appearing, but none of them have yet
reached such a wide audience as their predecessors. The work of the new authors
seemed initially to be read largely by those interested in adventure and action novels
or the specific historical settings they presented.

Naval Novelists and Historians

Having reviewed the broad history of the naval novel and seen the broad outline of its
continuing development to date, one can turn now to think about naval novels as they
relate to the work of the naval historian. Before Patrick O'Brian's naval novels appeared,
most naval historians might not have given this subject much thought, except in terms
of writing about some of the major individual fiction writers who had also served in the
navy[21] or in examining the ways in which sailors or naval officers have been represented
in fiction.[22]

Exceptional among historians, C. Northcote Parkinson began his career as a
trained naval historian and later turned to writing naval novels set in the eighteenth
century.[23] Several other authors, who began as naval novelists, also wrote naval histories set in this same period: among them was James Fenimore Cooper, who wrote the

first historical narrative of the United States Navy,[24] collected naval biographies,[25] and recounted the oral reminiscences of a seaman who had served in the navy, but whom Cooper knew from their experiences together in the merchant ship *Stirling* in 1806–1807.[26] Cooper, himself, had served only briefly in the U.S. Navy as a midshipman in 1808–1810 and he never saw action in a warship. Nevertheless, he retained a lifelong interest in naval affairs and his histories and biographical sketches remain valuable sources as they were extensively researched and contain oral historical evidence that Cooper had obtained from key participants in naval actions.[27] While his service in the navy was important to his historical work, there is little in his novels that can be clearly traced to it. In contrast, the twentieth-century naval novelists C. S. Forester,[28] Dudley Pope,[29] and Richard Woodman[30] wrote histories based on their own research into eighteenth-century materials on naval life combined with knowledge based on their own modern experiences at sea.

One can readily observe that there are two broad categories of naval fiction. On the one hand, some novelists wrote from the inspiration of their own seagoing experience during the naval wars of the French Revolution and Empire. On the other hand, other novelists based their works to varying degrees on blending modern sea experience, historical research, and historical imagination.

In their way, the fictional works created by writers who actually lived during the period and observed the naval life of the time are documents of an era and represent a very specialized type of evidence for historians of the period to use. Like all sources, the historian must approach them critically in thinking about why and when they were created and for what purpose. No naval novel written by a person who experienced those times was written at the moment of the actions described and none is a document that can serve as a record of the moment in the way that a logbook, a letter, or an account book can.

At best, such fictional works involve reminiscences that reflect the living memory of actual experiences, but in dealing with oral histories and memoirs of any kind, historians are aware that memories are, consciously or unconsciously, selective and present only part of a picture. Moreover, the writer of fiction has no strict obligation to verisimilitude. All is there to serve the purpose of the story. Most naval novels fall into the category of light fiction, intended to be entertaining in some fashion or another, rather than to be serious works of literary art or factual representations. They may have been humorous parodies, exaggerated sea stories, ironic tales, or merely impressionistic sketches. Alternatively, works based on memory present a single viewpoint that may also have a political or personal agenda behind them. Thus, without a careful analysis and corroborating evidence, the historian takes a risk in taking such works at face value as accurate and incontrovertible descriptions of naval life. But, for those who actually experienced naval life and wrote about it in a fictional manner, their works are, at least, a human reaction of one sort or another to the actual experiences of the time.

In contrast, later works of naval fiction, written by authors who are distant in time from the periods in which they set their historical novels, must necessarily rely on research, often supplemented by the authors' resonating personal experiences at sea in their own lifetimes and in the evocative places that are described in fiction to help bridge the gaps of time and period. Such fiction is the product of informed historical imagination. To a degree, the fiction writer who writes about a period in the past shares with the historian the need to approach his subject with a sympathetic imagination about life in a different time and place. The fundamental difference between the two lies in the manner of expressing their understanding. The historian is tied to the discipline of proving his view by using and interpreting the surviving physical and written evidence from the period for the purpose of better understanding the events and actions and how they interrelate to other activities and connect to earlier or later developments in human experience over time. The historical novelist need only artfully provide an impressionistic setting of the historical setting so as to proceed with creating interesting characters involved in human interactions that resonate with the readers. Put another way, history is only a part of the problem for the historical novelist and providing documentary historical evidence is not a factor. The best historical novelists are those who master the multiple skills involved in the literary art of fiction writing. They must create and sustain narrative descriptions of the personal interactions of fascinating men and women of the writers' own creation and, at the same time, evoke a historically accurate image of a different age. They must create characters, story, and historical settings that are simultaneously attractive, interesting, and convincing to the writers' reading audience. Thus, the work of the historical novelist and the historian can overlap to a degree.

The Historiography of Naval Life at Sea

For the historical novelist, an understanding of social history is a key element. Understanding naval life at sea is fundamental to the naval novelist. Such an understanding came naturally as part of their experience to those who served at sea in warships during the Napoleonic Wars, but naval historians followed a different path and looked at quite different aspects of the Napoleonic Wars in the century that followed those wars. Naval novels were one of the few available records of daily naval life and so, in the Anglo-American tradition, they became a source of social history while the dominant historians like William James recounted the maneuvers and statistics of naval battles during those wars.[31] In the mid-1880s at the U.S. Naval War College in Newport, Rhode Island, Captain Alfred Thayer Mahan, under the guidance of Rear Admiral Stephen B. Luce, began to develop further and to popularize an approach to naval history that Sir John Knox Laughton had begun in Britain in the previous decade. Mahan's two series of Naval War College lectures were eventually published as *The Influence of Sea Power upon History, 1660–1783* (1890) and *The Influence of Sea Power upon History in the French Revolution and Empire, 1793–1805* (1892). These works and the sequels changed the course for naval historians, who from that point began to move toward an emphasis on a broader understanding of navies that emphasized strategy, policy, and higher command.[32] In this shift of focus, social history was neglected.

The pioneer book on eighteenth-century social history in the Royal Navy was a book by an experienced seaman, a *Conway* boy, and the future Poet Laureate of the United Kingdom, John Masefield (1878–1967). Masefield's *Sea Life in Nelson's Time* (1905) appeared in the context of the celebrations of the centenary of the battle of Trafalgar. It was Masefield's first historical work, but a very successful one that had a wide readership and helped to further his career.[33] Quickly written for the Trafalgar commemoration, it brought together Masefield's vivid descriptions of sea life and his reading of the already published sources. In this work, Masefield used the novels of Barker, Glascock,

Hall, Marryat, Melville, and Michael Scott. In addition, he used the range of autobiographies, memoirs, and letters from participants of the period, including Cochrane's memoirs, Collingwood's letters, works by sailors such as Jack Nasty-Face, along with other sources such as the volumes of the monthly journal *Naval Chronicle* from its inception in 1799 through 1805.

The first academic social history of the period was the study made by Professor Michael Lewis of the Royal Naval College, Greenwich: *A Social History of the Navy 1793–1815* (1960). In this work, Lewis used similar materials to those that Masefield had used, but widened the basis of research by using a few more manuscript materials. To this, Christopher Lloyd added further insight and scope in his *The British Seaman: 1260–1860: A Social Survey* (1968) and the naval novelist Dudley Pope cited significantly more manuscript source material in his *Life in Nelson's Navy* (1981).

In his deeply researched work *The Wooden World: An Anatomy of the Georgian Navy* (1986), N. A. M. Rodger challenged the picture that these earlier historians had presented. While his detailed research focused on social issues in the years 1740 to 1775, he argued that life in the Royal Navy was a reflection of contemporary British society and not an unusual exception to it, as the novels seem to suggest. Many soon noted that Rodger's view contrasted with a volume that was published the following year, Marcus Rediker's *Between the Devil and the Deep Blue Sea: Merchant Seaman, Pirates, and the Anglo-American Maritime World* (1987). For the naval social history, the subsequent research of John D. Byrn, Jr., in his *Crime and Punishment in the Royal Navy: Discipline on the Leeward Islands Station, 1784–1812* (1989) bore out Rodger's interpretation and provided a sound documentary basis for extending this view into the period of the Napoleonic Wars. In the light of these works, historians began to debate whether or not the early novels and memoirs, along with the descriptions based on them by Masefield, Lewis, Lloyd, and Dudley Pope, presented too extreme a view and to what degree naval life represented a microcosm of larger British society.

Patrick O'Brian began writing *Master and Commander,* the first of his Aubrey-Maturin series, in 1967, when the historical works of Masefield, Michael Lewis, and Christopher Lloyd were at the height of their influence and before they had begun to be seriously challenged. O'Brian continued to write the series and was halfway through it when historians began to debate the accuracy of the long-held social descriptions. At that point, knowledge on this subject based on comprehensive and detailed historical research was still fragmentary and incomplete. O'Brian's most ardent admirers point to his reputation for archival research and for his known consultation with many experts in the field. In these years, O'Brian made a contribution to understanding the subject by applying his historical imagination to the very fragmentary picture of social history that was available at that point.

O'Brian's literary merit was only slowly recognized and the Aubrey-Maturin series did not begin to sell widely until the successful re-release of the series in the United States by publisher W. W. Norton in 1990. The new paperback series featured covers with dramatic historical paintings by marine artist Geoff Hunt. By then, O'Brian had written the fourteenth book in the series, *The Nutmeg of Consolation,* and was in his mid-seventies.

In the world of naval history, the 1990s marked the beginning of a massive research focus on the period between the Battle of the Glorious First of June in 1794 and the battle of Trafalgar in 1805, in preparation for the bicentennial celebrations of Trafalgar being planned for 2005. To raise emphasis on the period, the years 1994–2005 were dubbed "the Nelson Decade" and naval historians produced a wide range of new insights and information that is only now just beginning to be digested and assessed to determine how the broad understanding of the period has been fundamentally changed.[34]

As the Nelson Decade progressed, the growing interest in O'Brian's novels paralleled and interacted with the work that historians were undertaking with their new research. O'Brian's great popularity and literary success in North America in turn stimulated the author's continuation of the series, bringing along with it a growing interest and curiosity about the Nelson period. By the time of the Trafalgar bicentenary, three million copies of the Aubrey-Maturin novels had been sold in twenty languages and the series had inspired a major Hollywood film.[35]

When the first companion to O'Brian's work, A. E. Cunningham's *Patrick O'Brian: Critical Essays and a Bibliography,* was published in 1994,[36] it carried on its dust jacket a quotation from Richard Snow's pivotal review of *The Letter of Marque* and his retrospective view of the series:

> The best historical novels ever written. . . . On every page Mr. O'Brian reminds us with subtle artistry of the most important of all historical lessons: that times change, but people don't, that the griefs and follies and victories of the men and women who were here before us are in fact the maps of our own lives.[37]

Scholars of this period of naval history, whether they welcomed this popular phenomenon or preferred to stand clear and avoid it, benefited from having a wider interest and appreciation for their subject, which naval historians working in other historical periods did not share. The Hornblower and O'Brian effects were repeatedly made evident during the lead-up to the Trafalgar bicentenary, sometimes reaching an extreme when scholars made references to these fictional works as a means to explain their argument.

The most notable historical works that wove O'Brian's works into their historical analyses were Steven E. Maffeo's *Most Secret and Confidential: Intelligence in the Age of Nelson* (1999) and Max Adams's *Admiral Collingwood: Nelson's Own Hero* (2005), both of whom cited O'Brian's novels as sources. O'Brian's skillful use of historical materials in providing the background for his novels led a number of people to provide further information to complement the novels and inform readers. The approaches to this took different paths on opposite sides of the Atlantic.

In America, Dean King, as a student of English literature, had become fascinated by O'Brian's writings, but he knew little about the technical naval background. He felt that readers would eventually want clarification of the arcane naval language and would like to have some further general historical orientation as they became increasingly enamored with the Aubrey-Maturin series. On the recommendation of a reference librarian at Mystic Seaport, Dean approached me in the spring of 1994 to be his technical naval advisor. My first inclination was to produce a map book, but Dean quite rightly argued for the need of a dictionary. Together, we recruited pharmacology professor Worth Estes of Boston University to provide the information we needed to further explain historical medical practices. In early 1995, we completed the first of three guides to the series for an American audience: the dictionary *A Sea of Words.*[38] Interestingly, we produced the entire book without ever having met in person, only working through long telephone conversations and fax exchanges between Rhode Island and New York. As we worked on the project, we eventually agreed that what we wanted was a straight-forward approach that explained matters in clear and simple terms. In this, Dean proved to be a master in his ability to simplify my overly technical and complex expla-nations. At the same time, it became clear that many Americans knew very little about the general history of this period, and it seemed that even fewer understood the ways in which the Royal Navy functioned as part of the British government. Thus, our purpose was to provide a handy primer that readers could turn to to orient themselves quickly and simply to technical terms, key people, and places.

Upon completion of the first book, we moved immediately to undertake the map book that we had initially discussed, inspired by C. S. Forester's similar work for the Hornblower series. In this, we provided an introduction to the basic facts of winds, ocean currents, and sea routes, as they related to world geography, made a summary of each of the 17 volumes in the series, and asked our cartographic colleagues to draw maps to clearly and simply orient O'Brian's readers. This work, *Harbors and High Seas,* was first published in 1996.[39] And finally, we produced a third volume that could allow O'Brian's readers to sample our choice of the well-written and engaging first-hand accounts that provided source materials for O'Brian as he wrote his series. This volume, *Every Man Will Do His Duty,* first appeared in 1997.[40]

Several other Americans joined in the effort with specialist contributions on a spe-cific theme. The mother-daughter team of Anne Chotzinoff Grossman and Lisa Grossman Thomas produced their popular volume *Lobscouse & Spotted Dog* in 1997, an explanation of the food mentioned in the series, along with modern recipes adapted to American cooking.[41] Additionally, Adam Abeshouse produced two compact disks of the works of classical music mentioned in the series.[42] More recently, Anthony Gary Brown, an Englishman living in California and Texas, produced *The Patrick O'Brian Muster Book* (1999; 2006), a descriptive catalogue and index to the 5,000 named people, animals, cannon, and ships mentioned in the series.

In contrast to what was being done in the United States by providing entertaining complementary or general, introductory-level guides to the period for an American au-dience, British authors produced much more detailed and technical historical guides. O'Brian, himself, had produced the very first companion as early as 1974 with his highly illustrated but informative 76-page *Men of War: Life in Nelson's Navy.*[43] Among British readers, the subject matter was already part of national consciousness and did not re-quire the kind of primer that the American audience needed, where many thought the period a remote historical topic. O'Brian's British readers wanted far deeper reference works. To meet this in 1989, O'Brian wrote the foreword to Brian Lavery's large format, heavily illustrated book *Nelson's Navy,* which is one of the best technical guides to the 1793–1815 period and a work that remains useful for O'Brian readers and ship buffs as well as scholars of the period. It included details of ship design, construction, and fitting-out as well as administrative and social history. As O'Brian commented about the book in his foreword, "You name it, *Nelson's Navy* has it."[44] Other books of this type included David Millar, *The World of Jack Aubrey: Twelve-Pounders, Frigates, Cutlasses, and Insignia of His Majesty's Royal Navy* (2003). To complement the release of the film *Master and Commander: The Far Side of the World,* Brian Lavery published *Jack Aubrey*

Commands: An Historical Companion to the Naval World of Patrick O'Brian (2003). Most recently, Thomas Edwards had published *O'Brian's World: A Reader's Companion* (2005). Additionally, there is also *The Marine Art of Geoff Hunt: Master Painter of the Naval World of Nelson and Patrick O'Brian* (2004), featuring details on how the artist developed his historical cover paintings for the O'Brian series in the context of the artist's other works.

Summation

By way of conclusion to this broad overview, one can say that there is, indeed, fact in fiction about life at sea in the eighteenth century. To appreciate the nuances and qualifications about the factual historical information presented in fictional contexts, one must understand the naval novel, in general, and, in particular, the world of Aubrey and Maturin as the most widely read current expression of it. First, the naval novel, like the whole literary genre of the novel itself, arose during the eighteenth century. The naval novel, as a subgenre of sea literature, began as humorous exaggeration of naval life to amuse those who knew of it first-hand. The novels from the 1820s through the 1840s, in particular, tended to stress the discomfort and brutality of life at sea, while some writers used their fiction to support political efforts to reform the social system at sea, at a time when disciplinary practices had become out of tune with the changed, liberal practices ashore. Some writers of voyage narratives, such as Richard Henry Dana and the elder Charles Nordhoff, found that the naval novels of Marryat and Cooper, which had encouraged them to go to sea, were incomplete descriptions of what they experienced. Nevertheless, the works of the early novelists continued to inspire naval novelists, including C. S. Forester and Patrick O'Brian, as well as to inform the first social historians of the Royal Navy.

One can all too easily dismiss the subject at hand by saying that fiction is simply the product of the imagination and of no interest to those interested in "real facts," but this would be to miss something worthwhile. While the naval novel has rarely risen to the level of great literature, fiction writers have used their historical imagination to craft images of the naval life in ways that are more vivid than those available to the historian. Like artists who paint historical paintings, or directors and actors of costume dramas on stage and screen, historical fiction writers provide images that help one better understand the lives of people in a distant time and place. In many ways, historical recreations are the most vivid means of doing so. The dictionaries, historical companions, and reference works that have accompanied the work of the most popular naval novelists continue to serve a worthy purpose in promoting deeper historical understanding among readers, and they may have even provided assistance to fiction writers.

Historians can and do clearly appreciate works of historical fiction, yet they are understandably critical when historical images stray too far beyond the bounds of the credible, slipping silently and seamlessly from well-grounded representation to unfounded invention. Yet fiction writers, too, are part of history. The historical images they create, as well as their popularity, say something about a writer's own time and place. Fiction, too, is grist for the historian's mill.

NOTES   This was delivered as the James Ford Bell Lecture on 1 May 2008 at the James Ford Bell Library, University of Minnesota, in Minneapolis.

1 For bibliographies, see Myron Smith and Robert Weller, *Sea Fiction Guide.* With an introduction by Rear Admiral Ernest M. Eller, USN (Ret.).

Metuchen: Scarecrow Press, 1976, with 2,525 entries, and Charles Lee Lewis, *Books of the Sea: An Introduction to Nautical Literature.* Annapolis: Naval Institute Press, 1943; Westport: Greenwood Press, 1972. See also the section entitled "Nautical Fiction," in Eugene L. Rasor, *English/British Naval*

History to 1815: A Guide to the Literature. Bibliographies and Indices in Military History, no. 15. Westport: Praeger, 2004, pp. 343–352, 355–356, and "Fiction, Films, Documentaries, Drama, Lore and War Gaming," in Eugene L. Rasor, *British Naval History since 1815: A Guide to the Literature.* Military History Bibliographies, no. 13. New York: Garland, 1990, pp. 490–497.

2 I am grateful to Dean H. King for his constructive comments on a draft of this essay, which also incorporates and further develops parts of my article "Fiction: The Naval Novel," in *The Oxford Encyclopedia of Maritime History,* John B. Hattendorf, ed. New York and Oxford: Oxford University Press, 2007, vol. 2, pp. 7–13. This work is herein cited as *OEMH.*

3 The standard work on this early period is Charles Napier Robinson, *The British Tar in Fact and Fiction: The Poetry, Pathos, and Humour of the Sailor's Life.* London and New York: Harper and Brothers, 1909, but it tends to be nostalgic rather than a critical analysis.

4 Brian Southham, *Jane Austen and the Navy.* 2 ed., revised and corrected. Greenwich: National Maritime Museum, 2005.

5 C. Northcote Parkinson, *Portsmouth Point: The Navy in Fiction, 1793–1815.* Liverpool: University of Liverpool Press; London: Hodder & Stoughton Ltd, 1948, is a thematically arranged selection of excerpts from 35 novels written between 1826 and 1848 by authors who had first-hand experience of naval life between 1793 and 1815.

6 Ibid., p. 13.

7 On Marryat, see Tom Pocock, *Captain Marryat: Seaman, Writer, and Adventurer.* London: Chatham, 2000, and Louis J. Parascandola, "Marryat, Frederick," in *OEMH,* vol. 2, pp. 479–481.

8 Rear-Admiral Jahleel Brenton (d. 1802) and his sons, Vice-Admiral Sir Jahleel Brenton, KCB, first baronet (1770–1844), and the naval historian Captain Edward Brenton (1774–1839), author of *The Naval History of Great Britain from the Year 1783 to 1836.* London: Colburn, 1822, 1823–1825, 1837. All three were born in Newport, Rhode Island.

9 Thomas Philbrick, *James Fenimore Cooper and the Development of American Sea Fiction.* Cambridge, Mass.: Harvard University Press, 1961. For a modern historical view of Caracciolo in the context of Nelson's career, see Roger Knight, *The Pursuit of Victory: The Life and Achievements of Horatio Nelson.* London: Allen Lane, 2005, pp. 177, 313, 320, 322–323, 327, 557, 627. Andrew Lambert in an appendix entitled "The Black Legend" to his *Nelson: Britannia's God of War.* London: Faber & Faber, 2004, pp. 365–373, presents the latest modern defense of Nelson's conduct. For a history of the debate, see Marianne Czisnik, "Nelson at Naples: A Review of the Events and Arguments," *Trafalgar Chronicle.* 12 (2002), pp. 84–121, and "Nelson at Naples: The Development of the Story," *Trafalgar Chronicle.* 13 (2003), pp. 35–55.

10 Mary K. Bercaw Edwards, "Melville, Herman," in *OEMH,* vol. 2, pp. 548–552.

11 See Buckner F. Melton, Jr., *A Hanging Offense: The Strange Affair of the Warship* Somers. New York: Free Press, 2003, and Harold Langley, *Social Reform in the United States Navy.* Chicago: University of Illinois Press, 1967.

12 Jean Berthou and Jean-François Détrée, *La Naissance du Roman Maritime* [Catalogue of an exhibition on display from July to December 2004]. Saint-Vaast-la-Hougue: La Manche Conseil Général, Sites et Musées Départementaux, Musée Maritime de l'Île Tatihou, 2004.

13 Thomas Philbrick, "Romanticism and the Literature of the Sea," in John B. Hattendorf, ed., *Maritime History,* vol. 2, *The Eighteenth Century and the Classic Age of Sail.* Malabar, Fla.: Krieger Publishing, 1998, pp. 274–291; this point and Dana quoted on p. 283. See also Hugh Egan, "Dana, Richard Henry, Jr.," in *OEMH,* vol. 1, pp. 545–546, and for this whole genre: Robert D. Foulke, "Literature: Voyage Narratives," in *OEMH,* vol. 2, pp. 386–393.

14 Charles Nordhoff, *Man-of-War Life: A Boy's Experience in the United States Navy, during a Voyage around the World in a Ship-of-the-Line.* With an introduction and notes by John B. Hattendorf. Annapolis: Naval Institute Press, 1985, p. 12.

15 Parascandola, "Marryat, Frederick," p. 481.

16 Thaddeus Holt, Review of *The Life and Times of Horatio Hornblower. The New York Times Book Review* (13 June 1971), p. 4.

17 "Facts of fiction," *TLS, The Times Literary Supplement* (9 July 1971), p. 812

18 On O'Brian's life, see Dean King, "O'Brian, Patrick" in *OEMH,* vol. 3, pp. 119–120; Dean King, *Patrick O'Brian: A Life Revealed.* New York: Henry Holt, 2000. Nikolai Tolstoy, *Patrick O'Brian: The Making of the Novelist, 1914–1949.* New York: Norton, 2005, was written by O'Brian's stepson and is informed by family information and more of a defense of O'Brian.

19 Patrick O'Brian, *The Complete Aubrey/Maturin Novels.* Boxed set. New York: W. W. Norton, 2004. The final and twenty-first novel was left unfinished at O'Brian's death, but the sixty-five manuscript pages were published as Patrick O'Brian, *21: The Final Unfinished Voyage of Jack Aubrey including facsimile of the manuscript.* New York: W. W. Norton, 2004.

20 Frank Adam, *Herrscherin der Meere: Die Britische Flotte zur Zeit Nelsons.* Hamburg: Koehler, 1998. An earlier version was published as *Hornblower, Bolitho & Co.: Krieg unter Segeln in Roman und Geschichte.* Berlin: Ullstein-Taschenbuch, 1987, 1992. As of 2008, none of Frank Adam's novels have been translated and published in English.

21 See, for example, the series of notes by Olaf Hartelie, "Some Notes on Marryat," *Mariner's Mirror.* I (1911), pp. 1, 48–51, 138–143, 302–305; "Note on naval novelists," *Mariner's Mirror.* III (1913), pp. 71–76; "Notes from naval novels," *Mariner's Mirror.* VI (1920), pp. 66–73, 339–343, 369–374.

22 For example, Admiral Sir Herbert Richmond, "The Naval Officer in Fiction," in *Essays and Studies by Members of the English Association.* Vol. 30 (1945), pp. 7–25. See also Harold F. Watson, *The Sailor in*

English Fiction and Drama. New York: Columbia University Press, 1931.

23 Parkinson's early historical work included his 1935 University of London Ph.D. thesis that was the basis for his *Trade in the Eastern Seas, 1793–1813.* London: Cambridge University Press, 1937, and *War in the Eastern Seas, 1793–1815.* London: Allen and Unwin, 1954. Earlier, as a student, he had written the first major biography of Edward Pellew: *Edward Pellew: Viscount Exmouth, Admiral of the Red.* London: Methuen, 1934. In addition, he edited *Samuel Walters, Lieutenant, RN.* Liverpool: Liverpool University Press, 1948, and *The Trade Winds: A Study of British Overseas Trade during the French Wars, 1793–1815.* London: Allen and Unwin, 1948.

24 James Fenimore Cooper, *The History of the Navy of the United States.* Philadelphia: Lea and Blanchard, 1839, continued with an additional third volume under the title *The History of the Navy of the United States, continued to 1853, from the Author's Notes and other Authentic Notes.* New York: Putnam, 1853.

25 James Fenimore Cooper, *The Battle of Lake Erie; or Answers to Messers. Burges, Duer, and Mackenzie.* Cooperstown, N.Y.: H. & E. Phinney, 1843; and *Lives of Distinguished American Naval Officers.* Philadelphia: Carey & Hart, 1846.

26 James Fenimore Cooper, *Ned Meyers: A Life Before the Mast.* Philadelphia: Lea and Blanchard, 1843. Classics of Naval Literature series, edited with an introduction by William S. Dudley. Annapolis: Naval Institute Press, 1989.

27 Thomas L. Philbrick, "Cooper, James Fenimore," in *OEMH,* vol. 1, pp. 496–499.

28 For example Forester wrote, as a precursor to the Hornblower novels, a biography, *Nelson.* London: Bodley Head, 1929, and later, *The Age of Fighting Sail: The Story of the Naval War of 1812.* New York: Doubleday, 1956, and *The Barbary Pirates.* London: Macdonald, 1956. In addition, he edited a naval autobiography of the period, *The Adventures of John Wetherell.* London: Penguin, 1953, 1954, 1994, 1995.

29 For example, Dudley Pope, *At Twelve Mr. Byng was Shot.* Philadelphia: Lippincott, 1962; *The Black Ship.* Philadelphia, 1963, 1964; *The Great Gamble: Nelson at Copenhagen.* London: Weidenfeld, 1972, 2001; *The Devil Himself: The Mutiny of 1800.* London: Seeker, 1987; Ithaca, N.Y.: McBooks, 2003.

30 Richard Woodman, *The Sea Warriors: Captains and Frigate Warfare in the Age of Nelson.* New York: Carroll, 2001. In addition, Woodman edited *The Victory of Seapower: Winning the Napoleonic War, 1806–1814.* Wars of the French Revolution and Napoleon, 1793–1815, vol. V. Chatham Pictorial Histories. London: Chatham; Annapolis: Naval Institute Press, 1998.

31 William James, *The Naval History of Great Britain: From the Declaration of the War by France in 1793 to the Accession of George IV.* 6 volumes. London: Macmillan, 1822–1827, 1836–1837, 1847, 1859, 1864, 1886, 1898, 1902; reprinted 2002 with an introduction by Andrew Lambert.

32 See Jon Tetsuro Sumida, *Inventing Grand Strategy and Teaching Command: The Classic Works of Alfred Thayer Mahan Reconsidered.* Baltimore: Johns Hopkins University Press, 1997, and Andrew Lambert, *The Foundations of Naval History: Sir John Knox Laughton, the Royal Navy, and the Historical Profession.* London: Chatham, 1998.

33 See Philip W. Errington, "Masefield, John," in *OEMH,* vol. 2, pp. 484–485.

34 For a summary and overview of the results of the "Nelson Decade," see John B. Hattendorf, "Whither with Nelson and Trafalgar: A Review Article on the Bicentenary Scholarship of the Nelson Era," *Journal of Maritime Research,* (5 December 2007). http://www.jmr.nmm.ac.uk/server/show/ConJmrArticle .238

35 King, "O'Brian, Patrick," pp. 119–120. The film was *Master and Commander: The Far Side of the World,* which was released by Twentieth Century Fox in November 2003; directed by Peter Weir; and starring Russell Crowe as Jack Aubrey with Paul Bettany as Stephen Maturin. The film's overall story line is original to the film, but a number of specific scenes were adapted primarily from *The Far Side of the World,* and it also included a scene each from two other novels in the Aubrey-Maturin series: *Desolation Island* and *Master and Commander.*

36 A. E. Cunningham, ed., *Patrick O'Brian: Critical Essays and a Bibliography.* London and New York: W. W. Norton, 1994.

37 Richard Snow, "An Author I'd Walk the Plank For," *New York Times Book Review* (6 January 1991), Section 7, p. 1.

38 Dean King with John B. Hattendorf and J. Worth Estes, *A Sea of Words: A Lexicon and Companion to the Complete Seafaring Tales of Patrick O'Brian.* 3d ed. New York: Owl Books, Henry Holt, 2000.

39 Dean King with John B. Hattendorf, *Harbors and High Seas: An Atlas and Geographical Guide to the Complete Aubrey-Maturin Novels of Patrick O'Brian.* 3d ed. New York: Owl Books, Henry Holt, 2000.

40 Dean King with John B. Hattendorf, eds., *Every Man Will Do His Duty: An Anthology of Firsthand Accounts from the Age of Nelson.* New York: Henry Holt, 1997; London: Conway Maritime, 2002.

41 Anne Chotzinoff Grossman and Lisa Grossman Thomas, *Lobscouse & Spotted Dog: Which It's a Gastronomic Companion to the Aubrey/Maturin Novels.* New York and London: W. W. Norton, 1997.

42 *Musical Evenings with the Captain: Music from the Aubrey-Maturin Novels of Patrick O'Brian.* Dobbs Ferry, N.Y.: Essay Recordings. S.A. Publishing Co., 1996; *Musical Evenings with the Captain, Volume II: More Music from the Aubrey-Maturin Novels of Patrick O'Brian.* Dobbs Ferry, N.Y.: Essay Recordings. S.A. Publishing Co., 1997.

43 Patrick O'Brian, *Men of War: Life in Nelson's Navy.* London: Collins, 1974; New York: W. W. Norton, 1995.

44 Brian Lavery, *Nelson's Navy: The Ships, Men and Organisation, 1793–1815.* London: Conway; Annapolis: Naval Institute Press, 1989, p. 8.

Part 3: American Naval History

XII *The Formation and the Roles of the Continental Navy, 1775–1785*

The subject of the American navy that existed for the decade between 1775 and 1785 poses three major historiographical problems: First, the focus of general interest and discussion on this period has tended to devolve into a debate over the special contributions of individuals or towns in the relation to the formation of the first American navy. Most often, it is discussion about John Paul Jones, identifying him as the "Father of the U.S. Navy."[1] Alternatively, there is a debate between the rival supporters of Beverly, Massachusetts; Gloucester, Massachusetts; Skenesboro (now Whitehall), New York; and Machias, Maine, as to which of these towns is the "Birthplace of the United States Navy."[2] Secondly, the literature on general American naval history typically looks to the period of the American Revolution for the origins of the modern United States Navy. In this, the Continental Navy is assumed to provide the basis for the steady progression and inexorable development of American naval power from 1775 to the superpower navy of 2010.[3] Thirdly, tracing this historical lineage from first establishment to the present also has led to thinking about the Continental Navy's strategy and the effect of its naval operations in terms of the standards described in the late nineteenth century by Alfred Thayer Mahan for great power navies. While there has been great progress and development in understanding the roles and functions of great power navies,[4] in general, there has been no comparable development for a theoretical understanding of the roles of small navies.[5] As part of this discussion, a subsidiary debate has arisen among historians as to whether the Continental Navy was the right type of naval force for the maritime war it fought,[6] or whether it should have been built at all.[7]

The attention paid to these three historiographical debates has often tended to draw attention away from other perspectives, including the issues of the relationship of naval developments to state formation.[8]

A navy is much more than just the presence of armed ships at sea. In modern terms, a navy is a complex bureaucratic organization within the structure of a nation that is designed to control and to maintain a monopoly over a nation's resources to fight conflicts at sea. The word "navy" implies the existence of an organization of officers and men into some type of a specialized and coherent formation of discipline for fighting at sea, along with a shore establishment to acquire, arm, and maintain armed ships and men at sea.

The relationship of warfare to state formation in the sixteenth and seventeenth centuries has been the subject of a continuing debate[9] since Michael Roberts[10] developed the idea of the "military revolution" in 1955 and Geoffrey Parker[11] elaborated further upon it in 1988. While the main focus of these important works was on military innovation in relation to European land armies, Jan Glete has more recently shown that, in this same period, the development of the complex bureaucratic fiscal-military state in relation to maritime conflict should be a major consideration.[12]

By the time of the War of the American Revolution in the late 18th century, European states were well past the formative military transformation that they had experienced one to two centuries earlier. In the context of the highly developed fiscal-military bureaucratic European states that operated navies in the late 18th century, the emergence of a tiny new American navy contrasts with those major navies. This invites modern historians to investigate the complex nature of late-18th-century navies and to consider the American example of the relationship between state formation and building a navy. The contrast illustrates both the challenges that Americans faced in trying to create their small navy and helps to illuminate the level of sophistication necessary to maintain effectively a national naval force, even at the level of a small navy.

Regional Initiatives toward Creating an American Navy

Without a well-organized state bureaucracy, the process of creating a navy in America was a slow and hesitant one.[13] As the political crisis between Britain and her American colonies grew into an open rebellion in 1774 and 1775, the Royal Navy was the superior naval power in the world, although at this point the French Navy had a potential superiority in its unmanned ships in reserve at Brest, Toulon, and Rochefort and in additional Spanish ships of the line that might come available through a Franco-Spanish alliance.[14] On opposite sides of the Atlantic, both the British and the Americans showed some reluctance to engage in an all-out naval conflict.

The opening events of the conflict began ashore at the towns of Lexington and Concord, Massachusetts, on 18 and 19 April 1775. To the British government, this initially appeared to be a fairly common type of civil unrest in which the government needed to use army troops in a police action to restore order and then to end the unrest with a political solution once order had been restored. Among the leading statesmen in the cabinet, only Lord Barrington, the Secretary at War, advocated a naval solution. His suggestion to impose a naval blockade on New England ports was quickly rejected by his cabinet colleagues as one that would tend to encourage further American opposition rather than to mollify it. With differing political and strategic views within the British government, the Cabinet eventually decided to send troops to Boston to quash the civil unrest. However, the commander on the North American Station at the opening of the rebellion, Vice Admiral Samuel Graves, began to bombard colonial ports as a means to subdue the insurrection, although the Royal Navy's principal role was to enforce the navigation acts in peacetime[15] and to carry troops and supplies in support of the British Army.[16] The naval activity that Graves sanctioned had the opposite effect to that intended and broadened resentment in America, encouraging an American maritime response to British naval activity.

Meanwhile, American representatives had gathered in the Continental Congress and were beginning the 15-year-long process during which they eventually examined and debated nearly every fundamental aspect of representative democracy and the institutions appropriate to a republic. The Continental Congress was a representative body of thirteen separate colonies with no constitutional legitimacy as a governing authority, but which, nevertheless, represented the first centralized form of government over the separate colonies. As Britain's first attempt to quell the unrest in Massachusetts failed and the rebellion grew, Congress began to slowly evolve its methods, procedures, and authority. This process was a lengthy one and, on many specific issues, reflected not a clear-sighted vision of national independence, but rather a reaction to the British use of force.

In 1774, 1775, and early 1776, the members of the Continental Congress showed no clear consensus about how to form an effective government. Bitter debates in that body often reflected differences of personality and local interests as well as disagreements on the ends and the means of handling current issues. While some expressed radical ideas about complete independence others were reluctant to take any steps that would provoke the British government into a response that might preclude an advantageous political solution for the American colonies within the British Empire. One of those steps that might be a serious disadvantage, some believed, was to create a united American naval force. Because of this, as well as the expense involved, the subject was not raised in the First Continental Congress.[17] While cost was the primary deterrent, the difficulties of manning an American navy was another issue that gave pause to some members of Congress. The British Restraining Acts had left a number of American seaman unemployed, but despite the opportunity for new employment some were not optimistic about what could be achieved against the well-trained Royal Navy.[18] As the military situation drew toward the clash at Bunker Hill, Congress voted to create a Continental Army and selected George Washington to be that Army's commander in chief.[19] The colonists were also well aware of the sea as a highway of communication, a source of food, and a place for battle, if necessary. Many shared in the natural impulse of maritime communities to arm ships in their own protection and to promote their own cause in the face of British maritime power. Interestingly, the first American maritime response to the action at Lexington and Concord was to engage a fast packet boat to sail to England with the American viewpoints.[20] This suggested what would become an important function for the new American navy in providing safe and secure maritime communications.

Meanwhile in North America, a variety of events occurred that involved the use of armed force afloat. Shortly after Lexington and Concord, a number of Americans came up with the idea of capturing the British military positions at Crown Point and Fort Ticonderoga on Lake Champlain, where the largest British supply of artillery was located. Militiamen from Massachusetts under Benedict Arnold, from Connecticut under John Brown, and from Vermont under Ethan Allen soon joined forces to undertake the project. Initially and briefly successful, Arnold's troops captured an armed loyalist's schooner on 11 May 1775 at Skenesboro, New York, named her *Liberty,* and put her to use in their attack.[21] A week or so later, on 19 May, another group of Arnold's soldiers captured an armed British supply sloop in the nearby Richelieu River, renamed her *Enterprise,* and then employed her to capture a number of bateaux.[22] This early improvised solution suggested the value that might accrue from an organized and trained naval force.

Similarly, on the New England coast between May and July 1775, a range of other incidents occurred in which local sailors made minor attacks on naval British forces using whatever arms and small craft were at hand. In late July, Americans using whaleboats attacked and burned the Boston Lighthouse, capturing the marines guarding it.[23] Throughout the war, Americans typically used whaleboats for such minor, but effective, raiding attacks that forced the British to divert their forces from other missions.[24] The frequency of these attacks rose as Americans protested attacks on their seaports as part of foraging activities to supply British forces, again suggesting uses for an organized naval force.

One of the most famous of the early attacks against the Royal Navy occurred at Machias, Maine. There local townspeople got into a dispute with a loyalist, who was bringing much needed supplies to the small lumbering community by sea with a tiny Royal Navy naval escort, and wanted to obtain firewood supplies for the British Army in Boston. After a series of altercations ashore, Jeremiah O'Brien and a group of fellow militiamen put to sea, engaged, and captured the small British naval vessel off Machias, Maine.[25] This incident is illustrative of a larger issue in which the colonists' refusals to honor British military and naval demands for colonial supplies of livestock, food supplies, and fuel were a reaction to British naval bombardments of colonial ports.[26]

With no central naval force available to call upon, the individual states had to act on their own. Almost simultaneously with the incident at Machias, the Rhode Island General Assembly voted on 12 June 1775 to charter two armed vessels, one manned with eighty men and a smaller one with thirty men in the colony's pay, to protect the colony's trade under the overall command of Captain Abraham Whipple. In response to this, Providence, Rhode Island, merchant John Brown offered to sell to the colony his sloop, *Katy,* for this purpose.[27] With this action, Rhode Island became the first of the thirteen colonies to create a naval force of its own.[28]

Meanwhile, representatives of all the American colonies had gathered in the Second Continental Congress in Philadelphia. One of South Carolina's representatives, Christopher Gadsden, who had served years before in the Royal Navy as a purser, believed that the Royal Navy was not so formidable as many feared. He suggested that the Americans could easily take some of the smaller British cutters, sloops, and schooners, then use them to take larger British warships. John Adams widely circulated Gadsden's views to legislators in the Massachusetts Provincial Congress.[29] About this same time, Massachusetts began considering the establishment of its own armed sea-going force. On 7 June, a committee was established to consider the issue[30] and on 20 June it resolved that Massachusetts should man not fewer than six vessels armed with eight to fourteen guns and a proportionate number of swivels and smaller guns. On further consideration of the resolution, the Massachusetts Provincial Congress decided that a provincial naval force initially seemed too expensive an enterprise to undertake at the moment.[31] No immediate further action was taken, but the thought remained.

While this issue was under consideration, members of Congress were beginning to understand that there was a distinctive role for American naval forces. First, they thought rather unrealistically about using small armed vessels adapted from merchant service to capture larger warships from the Royal Navy and, thereby, acquire purpose-built warships and trained sailors. Second, they saw an opportunity to force

British forces to evacuate Boston by interrupting their vital supply lines stretching across the Atlantic. Third, American seaman believed that, with armed ships, they could establish an effective system to run a British blockade of American ports in order to maintain their traditional maritime trade.[32]

While several members of the Continental Congress in Philadelphia had been involved in discussions about naval affairs, Congress had, as yet, not made any clear decisions on the subject. The first decision about naval affairs took place on 18 July 1775, after Rhode Island had established its own force and after Massachusetts had considered the issue and had temporarily laid it aside for later consideration. At this point, it was already clear that there was an important maritime dimension to the conflict and there were strategic roles that American naval forces could undertake. However, the delegates in Philadelphia agreed that the powers and resources of the Continental Congress were too limited for it to undertake any effective naval effort. After a discussion, the members of Congress delegated the matter to each of the thirteen individual colonies:

> That each colony, at their own expence make such provision by armed vessels or otherwise . . . for the protection of their harbours and navigation on their sea coasts, against all unlawful invasions, attacks and depredations, from cutters and ships of war.[33]

Soon thereafter, as events unfolded in the course of the war, additional requirements for effective fighting were revealed. An armed naval force was needed that could operate on broader terms than just those of the separate individual colonies.

Shortly after the Continental Congress had taken action to delegate naval affairs to each of the separate colonies, individuals in Massachusetts renewed their interest in the topic and, at some point between July and August 1775, John Glover, a leading fish merchant from Marblehead and the colonel of the regiment ordered to protect that port, undertook the task of obtaining and arming fishing vessels from his home port. On 24 August 1775, Glover leased to the "United Colonies of America"[34] his own fishing schooner, the 78-ton *Hannah,* having been "fitted out & equipp'd with Arms, Ammunition and Provisions, at the Continental Expence."[35]

In early September, General George Washington directed Captain Nicholas Broughton, a Marblehead fishing skipper and merchant, to take command of *Hannah* as an officer of the Continental Army in Colonel John Glover's 21st (Marblehead) Regiment. As Commander in Chief of the Army, Washington ordered him to seize "such Vessels as may be found on the High Seas or elsewhere, bound inward or outward from Boston, in the service of the ministerial Army and to take all such Vessels, laden with Soldiers, Arms, ammunition or professions for and from s[ai]d army."[36]

While Broughton and his fellow captains, in the Army-contracted Marblehead fishing vessels, put to sea and carried out their naval missions in support of Washington's Army in 1775 into 1777, other complementary initiatives were taking place that were leading toward a national naval force and the development of the central governmental apparatus that is a practical necessary in building, outfitting, manning, supplying, organizing, and directing a group of warships that can operate effectively at sea.

Bringing Regional Initiatives to Congress
In nearby Rhode Island, the General Assembly passed a resolution on 26 August 1775, recommending to the Continental Congress "that the building and equipping of an

American fleet, as soon as possible, would greatly conduce to the preservation of lives, liberty and property of the good people of these colonies."[37]

The Rhode Island delegates presented this proposition to the Continental Congress on 3 October, and scheduled a debate on it for three days later, on 6 October 1775.[38] On 5 October, the day before that discussion was scheduled to take place, Congress received intelligence that two unarmed English brigs carrying supplies to the British Army had set sail from England in August for Quebec with no convoy protection.[39] Congress immediately appointed a committee of three members, Silas Deane, John Langdon, and John Adams, to prepare a plan for intercepting these vessels. On the same day, Congress further ordered that General Washington request that Massachusetts place its two armed vessels under Washington's command and proceed immediately to capture the British supply ships.[40] At the same time, Congress requested that Rhode Island and Connecticut join the Massachusetts vessels and place their armed state vessels on Continental "risque and pay during their thus being employed."[41]

In his *Autobiography,* John Adams recalled that the opposition to these resolutions was "very loud and vehement."[42] The idea of intercepting and attacking British forces at sea was "represented as the most wild, visionary, mad project that had ever been imagined."

> It was an infant, taking a mad bull by his horns; and what was even more profound and remote, it was said it would ruin the character, and corrupt the morals of our seamen. It would make them selfish, piratical, mercenary, bent wholly upon plunder &c. &c.[43]

An ardent advocate for the motions, Adams's life experience on the Massachusetts seacoast and his career as a lawyer in dealing with legal cases in the local courts had given him much insight into maritime affairs.[44] He explained:

> I had conversed much with the gentlemen who conducted our cod and whale fisheries, as well as the other navigation of the country, and heard much of the activity, enterprise, patience, perseverance, and daring intrepidity of our seamen. I had formed a confident opinion that, if they were once let loose upon the ocean, they would contribute greatly to the relief of our wants, as well as the distress of the enemy.[45]

Without an executive branch of government, Congress inched slowly forward with the legislative process in forming the new American state. On 6 October, the committee appointed to develop a detailed plan to capture the British ships carrying arms presented its report and it was made available for members of Congress before discussion. At the same time, Congress delayed yet another day in discussing Rhode Island's resolution of 26 August to create a Continental Navy,[46] but in discussing it Samuel Chase wondered whether or not it was practical to have a naval force and whether such an order would just be "a mere Piece of Paper" and if the Committee dealing with this subject could raise and pay a naval force.[47]

Finally, on 7 October, Congress took up its first discussion of Rhode Island's resolution. As John Adams recorded in his notes on the debates, Samuel Chase of Maryland vigorously attacked the notion: "It is the maddest idea in the World to think of building an American Fleet. Its Latitude is wonderful. We should mortgage the whole Continent. Recollect the Intelligence on your table—defend N. York—fortify upon Hudson River."[48] Christopher Gadsden, from Charleston, South Carolina, one of the five largest ports in the colonies, chimed in: "I am against the Extensiveness of the Rhode Island Plan, but it is absolutely necessary that some Plan of defence by sea should be adopted."[49] After a series of further acrimonious exchanges between members, the subject was put off again for further discussion nine days later, on 16 October.

On 12 October, Washington responded directly to the letter that John Hancock had sent him on 5 October. Writing from his headquarters at Cambridge, Massachusetts, Washington explained his actions and plans at sea and sent copies of the orders he had given Captain Nicholas Broughton. In this response, Washington expressed his concern that there might be difficulties in having several naval forces with officers and men engaged on differing terms and rates of pay for similar services.

In the meantime, on 13 October 1775, General Washington's earlier letter of 5 October arrived and was read to Congress. By this letter, Congress first learned that Washington had already taken the initiative on his own and acquired three armed schooners at Continental expense. He now asked Congress to determine how the ships and sailors that he brought into service should dispose of any enemy ships and cargoes they would capture. By taking this initiative, Washington had pre-empted Congress, allowing members who had been hesitant about having a naval force to agree more easily to the proposal.

That same day, 13 October, after hearing a debate on the Committee's plan to capture the British ships carrying arms, Congress took two firm steps toward creating a navy. It authorized purchasing and arming two vessels "to cruize eastward, for intercepting such transports as may be laden with warlike stores and other supplies for our enemies."[50] This was the first congressional authorization for national warships. Paralleling this, Congress took another significant step toward centralized governmental control by appointing a committee of three men—Silas Deane, John Langdon, and Christopher Gadsden—to prepare an estimate of the expense for Congress's approval and to contract for fitting out these vessels.[51] This was the establishment of the first American governmental supervisory body for a navy. Although these were significant initial steps that would contribute toward creating a government that was more centralized than what had existed before in America, it was a faint shadow of the much more complicated fiscal-military agencies that existed to support European navies.

A week later, Congress received Washington's letter with its copy of Broughton's orders to capture British supply ships, but the debate that ensued over it focused not on naval force alone, but on its relationship to the question of whether or not America could effectively engage in maritime trade under the current circumstances. The issue of state formation lay just below the surface in the debate on this subject. Suggesting some of the functions for a central government, Samuel Chase pointed out that America must have a navy at sea to protect its trade, gain intelligence, maintain credit of American currency as well as obtain powder and shot. Without these things, Americans had no choice but to submit to Britain. American trade and commerce were the fundamental issues, Chase argued.[52]

Additional Steps in Creating a Naval Organization

It took another nine days for Congress to move ahead with further significant steps. On 30 October, the Committee brought in its estimate of the cost for the manning and fitting-out of the two warships, as directed on 13 October. In addition to looking at the financial expenses for pay and outfitting, the Committee laid out a basic structure for a navy. Its report established a system of wages, recommended that a regularized naval service was preferable to privateering, and outlined the functions for a naval committee.[53] Each of these recommendations involved giving the American government increased authority and central control over aspects of its nascent fiscal-military organization.

Congress agreed to the committee's recommendations and added to it two more larger ships: one of 36 guns and another of 24 guns. In addition, Congress immediately realized that even such a small naval force required a much larger degree of management than initially envisioned. With this in mind, Congress expanded the size of the committee from three members to seven.[54] Moving quickly to take charge, the committee procured a room in a public house to conduct its business and agreed to meet every evening at six to conduct business.[55] By taking these actions, Congress, for the first time, committed the new nation to having a navy and established the country's first organization to manage naval affairs. This step was an incremental addition to the authority of Congress as well as a contribution to the building of the new American state in adding a new agency under Congress. The earlier creation of an army and a treasury under the authority of Congress had established the fundamental elements of the American fiscal-military state and, now, the addition of a navy expanded them further. The men who were chosen as the first naval executives represented seven of the thirteen states: John Langdon of New Hampshire, John Adams of Massachusetts, Stephen Hopkins of Rhode Island, Silas Deane of Connecticut, Richard Henry Lee of Virginia, Joseph Hewes of North Carolina, and Christopher Gadsden of South Carolina.

The Congress moved in small steps to implement the various recommendations of the committee and to further develop the organizational basis for a navy. On 1 November, Congress received General Washington's report of 24 October that the 16-gun HMS *Canceaux* with three other vessels—*Halifax, Spitfire,* and *Symmetry*—had burned Falmouth, Maine.[56] The next day, 2 November, Congress reacted by authorizing the Committee to "call on the Continental treasurers, for as much cash as shall be necessary" in fitting out and manning the ships.[57] In doing this, Congress created the direct link in the formation of a fiscal-military state between the Navy, an emerging bureaucracy, and the Treasury.

On the same date, Congress formed another committee of five members, chaired by John Adams, to consider how to assist residents of Passamaquoddy, Nova Scotia, who wanted to join in with the other colonies in fighting against Britain.[58] In dealing with this question, this special committee recommended that Congress raise two battalions of Marine Infantry with ten companies apiece.[59] Congress acted on these recommendations on 10 November 1775, creating a Marine Corps.[60] This creation of a separate, specialized military organization of naval infantry to operate in cooperation with naval forces was a further incremental development, increasing the number of agencies required for the support and operation of a naval force.

Meanwhile, the Naval Committee continued to recommend to Congress further steps to create a naval organization. The Committee selected Esek Hopkins of Rhode Island, the brother of Rhode Island congressional delegate Stephen Hopkins, to be the first operational commander and commodore of the new naval squadron.[61]

In its next major decision and in response to repeated requests from George Washington to provide guidance,[62] Congress gave the government more power and took a further step in centralizing political authority when it provided instructions for dealing with ships captured from the enemy and directed that prize cases be heard in the courts of the separate colonies with the right of appeal to Congress. In addition, Congress established the proportions and entitlement for each officer and seaman involved in the capture, based on a total of 30 shares per captured vessel.[63] This act had a significant effect by allowing a monetary incentive for individual officers and men to capture enemy vessels, but it was equally important for the development of an American fiscal-military state. Depending on whether the vessel was fitted out by the Congress or by an individual state, one third of the value of the prize went to the captors, while the remaining two thirds went to Congress or the state. In the case of the capture of an enemy warship, half the value went to the captors and half to Congress or state government.[64] This process added to the further development of government, not only in creating a form of revenue, but also in relation to the development of courts to hear and to adjudicate prize claims. At this point, Congress delegated these powers to the several states, which were required to establish courts for this purpose with the right of judicial appeal to Congress. In addition, the act required that a commission from Congress was necessary for the capture of enemy ships.[65]

To provide for the basic organizational principles of a naval fleet, the Naval Committee formally laid before the full Congress a set of proposed rules and articles for the naval officers and men.[66] John Adams wrote the original draft,[67] adapting them for American use directly from the Royal Navy's *Regulations and Instructions Relating to His Majesty's Service at Sea*.[68] The full Congress then over several days debated and amended Adams's draft, paragraph by paragraph, creating the *Rules for the Regulation of the Navy of the United Colonies* that Congress formally adopted by vote on 28 November.[69] These *Rules* provided for a wide range of matters, including the conduct and authority of officers, the frequency of divine services, muster rolls, medical facilities for the care of sick seamen, victualing procedures, discipline and punishment for murder, theft, and mutiny, the composition of courts martial and the oaths to be sworn by witnesses, the pay of officers and men, and the terms of enlistment. In doing this without seeking the approval of the individual state legislatures, Congress was further contributing to the centralization of power for the management of the Navy.

Collectively, all these separate acts of Congress, involving the purchase and construction of vessels, establishing a naval committee, creating a naval infantry force, outlining the procedures for the capture of prizes at sea, and writing regulations for those in naval service, served incrementally to centralize political, military, and fiscal powers in the hands of the national government while it was creating a navy.

Building a Fleet

Finally, Congress moved to take action on the Rhode Island resolution of "furnishing these colonies with a naval armament." It had originally been voted by the Rhode Island General Assembly on 26 August and presented to the Continental Congress on 3 October. Repeatedly tabled,[70] the issue now came up for full debate and a vote. In preparation for that consideration, Congress established on 11 December a committee with twelve delegates from separate colonies to make a final report.[71] Two days later, on 13 December, this Committee made its report, recommending the construction and fitting out of thirteen new ships at a total cost of $866,666.66: five of 32 guns, five of 28 guns, and three of 24 guns. Now convinced that Britain's government wanted a military showdown instead of a negotiated settlement, the full Congress approved the plan and directed that the preparation of these vessels was to be distributed among the colonies, with four in Pennsylvania, two each in Massachusetts Bay, New York, and Rhode Island, and one each in Connecticut, New Hampshire, and Maryland.[72] The next day, Congress chose by ballot thirteen of its members representing each of the colonies to serve on the new committee. The election of committee members resulted in confirming the appointments of most of those who had been appointed on 11 December, making only three changes.[73] The election by ballot and the distribution of ship construction more widely among the colonies served to further solidify the legitimacy and national character of the Navy's management in concentrating and expanding the new Committee's responsibilities.

Soon named the Marine Committee, its purpose was to oversee the construction of the thirteen new vessels. At first, it operated alongside the previously established Naval Committee, although there is some evidence to suggest that the Marine Committee was intended to supersede the Naval Committee as soon as its accounts were rendered. Delaying this transition on 25 January 1776, Congress designated the Naval Committee to take charge of the direction of fleet operations to ensure continuity as the Continental Navy's fleet of converted merchantmen prepared to get to sea for the first time under Commodore Esek Hopkins.[74] On 11 February 1776, this fleet of five warships—*Alfred, Columbus, Andrew Doria, Cabot,* and *Providence*—put to sea from Philadelphia.[75] Two days later, on 13 February, *Wasp* and *Hornet* joined them from Baltimore off Cape Henlopen.[76] In the short time before the Marine Committee superseded it entirely, the Naval Committee continued to deal with a wide array of administrative issues including the promulgation of recruiting instructions, establishing the pay of naval personnel taken prisoner, creating rules for the distribution of prize money, and ordering officers and men to their ships.[77]

The centralization of all naval administration and operational control of the fleet under the Marine Committee of Congress soon proved to be an unwieldy solution. To try to lighten the load of central management, Congress directed the Marine Committee in April 1776 to recommend for its consideration appropriate people to be prize agents in the various ports.[78] Taking action on the recommendation, Congress appointed eleven men in different ports as prize agents.[79] Toward the end of the year, the Marine Committee recognized the need for creating three additional positions with men who were not members of Congress, but "well skilled in maritime affairs,"[80] to execute the business of the Navy under the direction of the Marine Committee. This newly created office became known as the Navy Board. This action extended the committee with employees who were not members of Congress, thereby taking the first step toward a separate bureaucracy for naval affairs. This further act of centralization increased the tension that already existed between state control of naval affairs and national control.

The thirteen ships that Congress had authorized the year before were only just begun when the Marine Committee began to develop larger ambitions for an American national navy. In late November 1776, Congress approved the Committee's recommendations for the construction of an even larger fleet by adding three 74-gun ships of the line, five 36-gun frigates, an 18-gun brig, and a packet boat.[81]

Looking for Better Administration

With these acquisition and building projects added to those already in hand, the system as established still proved an insufficient solution to managing the wide-ranging and geographically widespread business of the Continental Navy.[82] Five months later in April 1777, Congress appointed a second group of three assistants to the Marine Committee and directed that they reside in Boston, while the first group of three stayed co-located with Congress.[83] From this point onward, the first group situated at or near Philadelphia became known as the Navy Board of the Middle Department, and the newly established group at Boston was called the Navy Board of the Eastern Department. Three months later, in July, the Marine Committee laid out the new board's responsibilities by directing it "to have the superintendence of all Naval and Marine Affairs of the United States of America within the four Eastern States[84] under the direction of the Marine Committee."[85] This involved superintending the building, manning, and outfitting of warships as well as keeping registers of officers and men in the district, requiring reports from all Continental warships in the district, directing the finances of each vessel and supervising expenditures of public funds as well as ordering courts martial as needed. The Boston board, because of its distance from Congress and the higher tempo of naval activity in New England, soon became the more important of the two boards. Despite the difficulties that the various boards and officials faced in executing their responsibilities, the establishment of this new office added to the centralizing forces associated with naval expansion during the Revolution.

Even with the expanded arrangement for officials to manage naval affairs in two broad regions, the management of naval affairs became increasingly challenging to those who had undertaken it. Seeking to know more about how the Royal Navy managed its affairs, William Ellery, a Rhode Island member of the Marine Committee, wrote to a knowledgeable friend at home, William Vernon:

> I should be glad to know what is the Office of Commissioners of the Navy, and that you would point it out particularly; unless you can refer Me to some author who particularly describes. The Conduct of the Affairs of a Navy as well as those of an Army We are yet to learn. We are still unacquainted with the systematical management of them, although We have made considerable Progress in the latter.[86]

Others also assumed that the British approach to naval management would be the best to emulate, but no one among the American leaders had detailed or practical knowledge from direct experience of naval administration in London as to how the Admiralty or the Navy Board managed the Royal Navy.[87] Without this experience, there were very few clear explanations available in print to explain the complex process, even though a few Americans had some working familiarity with specific aspects of British naval administration, such as Congressman Christopher Gadsden, who had served as a ship-board purser, and others, who, as merchants, had supplied ships and supplies to the Royal Navy.[88]

Congress's early preference for defensive naval operations soon began to change. As Robert Morris, the vice-president of the Marine Committee, wrote to Captain John Paul Jones, on 1 February 1777, about a plan to attack British warships at Pensacola, Florida:

> It has long been clear to me that our infant Fleet cannot protect our own Coasts & that the only effectual relief it can afford us to attack the Enemies defenceless places & thereby oblige them to Station more of their Ships in their own Countries or to keep them employed in following ours and either way we are relieved as far as they do it.[89]

In February 1777, Morris's colleague Ellery again wrote to Vernon, now a member of the Navy Board of the Eastern Department, repeating much of what he had said earlier. Underscoring his frustration, Vernon added, "The Congress are fully sensible of the Importance of having a respectable Navy, and have endeavored to form and equip One, but through Ignorance and Neglect they have not been able to accomplish their Purpose yet. I hope however to see one afloat before long."[90]

As the operations of Continental Navy ships spread into different regions, agents were required to handle their affairs in various ports, but these were usually additional duties that devolved on another official assignment. Such was the case with William Bingham, a Commercial Agent of Congress in Martinique, who, in addition to his main assignment, did much administrative and supply work for Continental naval vessels operating in the West Indies.[91] A similar situation existed in Europe, where the American commissioners in Paris, Silas Deane, Benjamin Franklin, and Arthur Lee, dealt with a wide variety of issues in support of the Continental Navy. Also, in Spanish-held Louisiana territory, the Continental agent of the Commercial Committee at New Orleans, Oliver Pollock, armed vessels that made captures on the Mississippi and undertook some minor operations against the British in the Gulf of Mexico.

While there was considerable dissatisfaction in Congress, and even among members of the Marine Committee about their own effectiveness, it took time to make any effective reform. The Marine Committee soon found itself unable to carry out its expansive building program for 74-gun ships. It also proved difficult just to find enough members of the Committee who could take the time to meet and do its business.[92] In this, as in other areas of government, Congress was slowly learning that it could not effectively be both a legislature and an executive. To handle military affairs, Congress created a Board of War in October 1777 to try to resolve similar issues in that area and, in July 1779, Congress created a Board of Treasury.

Taking a similar approach for the Navy, John Dickinson of Delaware put forward a motion in Congress "that the management of all business relating to the Marine of these United States be vested in commissioners."[93] The motion passed, but the committee failed to make any report of its recommendations. With this failure to act, Congress directed that the Marine Committee take up the task and report back within a week. The plan that Congress adopted on 28 October 1779 was an attempt to further refine the centralization of power for the navy with a Board of Admiralty made up of five officials, each from a different state, two of whom were members of Congress and three who were paid commissioners, with an additional staff member to serve as the secretary. In order to function, the Board was required to have a minimum of three of its five members present to make a quorum.

In taking up its responsibilities, the Board of Admiralty faced a number of serious problems. First, the process of creating the Navy had been a very slow one. Of the thirteen frigates authorized to be built in 1775, only three got to sea by 1777. In that year, the Navy lost three frigates in the defence of Philadelphia,[94] one by capture and two by burning, and two other frigates were burnt on the Hudson to prevent capture,[95] while the frigate *Hancock* had been captured in July 1777. *Randolph* exploded and was destroyed in February 1778, while *Alfred* and *Virginia* had been captured shortly thereafter. These losses made Congress cautious and aware of the need to conserve scarce resources.[96] Secondly, in the face of such losses, it was difficult to find people who would willingly serve. Congress appointed the first three commissioners, but when they received notification of the selection, all three declined to accept the appointment. Finally, after three weeks, the minimum three members agreed to serve, but all had to be present to have a quorum. The next issue was for the Board to assert its authority over the two Navy Board offices in Philadelphia and Boston. When the Board of Admiralty ordered them to submit their accounts for inspection, it received no reply. Conversely, when the Navy Boards requested funds, the Board of Admiralty reported that it had none. Despite this, the Board of Admiralty was able to make some effective changes. Very importantly, it succeeded in getting Congress to adopt in May 1780 a long-needed revision to the 3 April 1776 instructions to privateers, which had made no mention of contraband or neutral rights.[97]

The arrival of the French Squadron under D'Estaing in American waters in the summer of 1778, and, later in 1780, the *Exépdition Particulière* commanded by the Chevalier de Ternay, presented some unexpected administrative issues for the Board of Admiralty. Up to that time, the tiny American fleet had been a wholly independent force, unconcerned with allied operations. In July 1778, the Marine Committee wanted to provide some of the Continental Navy's frigates to support and to assist D'Estaing.[98] Later, on 25 July 1780, the French minister to the United States, the Chevalier de La Luzerne, wrote to the President of Congress to request that American frigates be placed directly under de Ternay's command. In its response, Congress transferred the operational command of the three Continental frigates and a sloop of war to General Washington,[99] in order to maintain American control and, at the same time, to more closely adhere to the instructions that Louis XVI and Vergennes had given Lafayette for the French to act only as an auxiliary to American forces.[100] The additional support that the Navy Boards needed to provide to the French added to the burdens they already faced with the Continental Navy.[101] In the end, American warships were unable to find a way to operate effectively with the French Navy.[102]

The year 1779 became the Continental Navy's year of success and, in that year, it brought some substantial results that seemed to justify the extensive costs that had gone to produce it. The manning and equipment shortages that had plagued efforts in the previous years eased, and more ships were able to operate at sea. In March 1779, the Continental Navy's ships *Warren, Queen of France,* and *Ranger* intercepted a British convoy and captured seven transports. Four months later, in July, *Providence, Queen of France,* and *Ranger* brought eight rich prizes into Boston. The failure of the Penobscot expedition, with the loss of *Warren* and two sloops, counter-balanced some of the gain, but the frigate *Trumbull* soon got to sea to fill the gap that *Warren* had left. Across the Atlantic, John Paul Jones in *Bonhomme Richard* made his famous cruise in British waters, resulting in the loss of his own ship, but also in capturing HMS *Serapis*.

The success of 1779 was not repeated. In May 1780, when Charleston surrendered, the British took two frigates, along with *Ranger,* and American forces sank another to block the channel. This left only four frigates in service. One of them, *Confederacy,* was dismasted and immobilized in 1780, then, along with *Trumbull,* was captured in 1781, while the sloop of war *Saratoga* sank with all hands. By the time that the Yorktown campaign was beginning in mid-1781, the Continental Navy had very few ships capable of undertaking any major operations and played no part in that decisive naval and military campaign.[103]

The Decline and End of the Continental Navy

Through 1779, American naval expansion had contributed to and paralleled the tendencies toward centralizing the powers of the new American state. At the outset, the new American navy had benefitted from low prices for shipbuilding and good government credit. Inflation of the currency and rising prices increased the difficulties in building warships in America, so in 1778, Congress turned to purchases in France. By 1779, American credit was exhausted both at home and abroad, leaving captures at sea as the only viable source for increasing the Navy. Prize money proved to be an illusory source for paying the Navy's bills. The losses of American warships to the enemy made it increasingly difficult to increase the number of prize captures with the remaining vessels that carried inferior armament and had inferior capabilities.[104]

As American naval expansion faltered and the French Navy assumed the critical role in the war at sea, the centralizing forces within the American government were also weakening. This decline in both naval organization and in centralization was also one of the effects of a broader political shift, as the United States government moved under the Articles of Confederation.

With American ships dwindling in numbers, the Board of Admiralty slowly became less active and, with the reluctance of its appointed members to participate in business, the Board became entirely ineffective and inactive by the summer of 1781. Even before this, in February 1781, Congress had directed that naval affairs would be transferred to a newly established office under the Secretary of Marine.[105] But the same problem continued and no one could be found willing to accept the responsibilities of the office. With no one in sight to accept the position, Congress voted on 29 August 1781 to appoint an Agent of Marine to manage naval business temporarily until someone could be found to fill the Secretary's job. No one could be found to accept the responsibility of Agent, so, on 7 September, Congress abolished the Navy Boards in Boston and Philadelphia, and assigned the responsibility of Agent temporarily to the Superintendent of Finance, Robert Morris, who had previously served on the Marine Committee and was already well acquainted with naval affairs.[106] Morris remained to manage naval affairs through the end of the war. At the time Morris took over only two ships were then under construction, the 74-gun *America* at Portsmouth, New Hampshire, and the frigate *Bourbon* at Chatham, Connecticut. In other situations, Morris found that in the evolution of the administrative office, the instructions governing his authority had omitted some important areas. In November 1781, for example, he discovered that he did not have the power to appoint either a court of enquiry or a court martial to investigate the loss of the frigate *Hancock,* and he had to apply to Congress to obtain that authority.[107]

Robert Morris was convinced that a navy would be a necessary instrument for the United States to protect its trade in the future, but in the mid-1780s, the government of the new republic was not fully enough developed to sustain so complicated a national institution. He believed that it was premature in the fiscal condition of the new nation to maintain a navy. Writing in July 1783, Morris explained:

> Until revenues for the Purpose can be obtained it is but vain to talk of Navy or Army or any thing else. We received sounding Assurances from all Quarters and receive scarce any thing

else. Every good American must wish to see the United States possessed of a powerful fleet but perhaps the best way to obtain one is to make no Effort for the Purpose til the People are taught their feelings to call for and require it. They now give money for nothing.[108]

By 1784, it was clear that the country's finances were such that there were no funds to even repair the last two vessels in active service, *Alliance* and *General Washington.* Writing to the President of Congress, Morris reported: "As to a Marine, we must for the present give up the Idea and whenever the Situation in American Finances will permit we can certainly build better Ships than any we have yet had."[109] In totally dismantling the Continental Navy, Morris was adopting a political strategy that he hoped would force American voters into understanding the need to fund and sustain a naval force to protect American commerce. While waiting for that seed to germinate, Morris took the lead in encouraging some of the most successful of the Continental Navy's officers—such as Thomas Truxtun, Richard Dale, and John Barry—to further hone their maritime skills in preparation for the establishment of a new navy by serving in America's newly opened trade to China.[110]

The Continental Navy in Perspective

The naval force that came to be known as the Continental Navy had a relatively short history, lasting only from 1775 until it was dissolved ten years later in 1785, when its last ship was sold. In that short period, the Continental Navy had reached a reasonable size. Nearly sixty different vessels were, at one time or another, on the Navy's list, including one 74-gun ship of the line that never was commissioned, sixteen frigates built and launched for the Navy of which six never went to sea, twelve merchant ships acquired in America and converted into warships, eleven ships acquired in Europe, five prizes taken into service, and a number of local and subsidiary vessels.[111] As Congress was acquiring ships, it also tried with great difficulty to create the necessary administrative structure to manage and to support a fleet. To complicate the matter further, the Continental Navy had not had a monopoly on the use of the new nation's forces at sea. Many of the kinds of operations that, in theory, a small navy could have undertaken were more extensively and effectively done by the individual state navies and by privateers.[112] But the existence of extensive privateering was also a diversion of support for the Continental Navy and a competitor for the use of seamen, gunpowder, and other supplies.[113]

During its ten-year existence, the Continental Navy played a very limited role. Its purpose was to contribute to a civil war between American Englishmen and Englishmen at home in Britain and a revolution that brought independence to the thirteen United States of America. In this context, the Continental Navy's role was one of several maritime equivalents of the peoples' and partisan warfare ashore. While the Navy complemented the privateering activities that more precisely fit this characterization, the Navy did serve with some effectiveness during the war in undertaking some vital tasks for the nascent revolutionary government that could not effectively be given to privateers, such as showing the flag in foreign waters, carrying government funds, and delivering official diplomatic representatives. These were vital functions that underscore the Navy's role in the development of the state. Nevertheless, while there was a symbiotic relationship with the rise of an American fiscal-military state during the early growth in American naval development between 1775 and 1779, this initial development lost force. With the Peace of Paris that secured American independence, in 1783, the roles that the Continental Navy had performed were no longer needed. Given the additional problems of finance and supply, as well as the nearly complete absence of administrators willing to undertake its management, it is not surprising that the little navy was almost immediately disbanded and there was very little interest in reviving it for more than a decade. In contrast to the Europeans, with their great navies, Americans showed neither interest in nor the capability, at this point in their development, for necessary infrastructure of bureaucracy, dockyards, and industry that accompany a navy.

The necessary centralized fiscal, bureaucratic, and military control could not be fully established or sustained in the years between 1775 and 1785. It would take three more decades for the basic elements to begin to develop that would allow for the sustainment of a newly established United States Navy. In this period, the Continental Navy did leave a legacy. Reflection on its weaknesses as well as the actual experience of officers, men, and shipyards who had served the Continental Navy proved to be a resource for the new navy a decade or two later.[114] Yet, it might convincingly be argued that a full fiscal-military organization for the United States Navy, comparable to those in Europe in the late eighteenth century, did not come to fruition until the establishment of the Naval Bureaus in 1842 and their refinement during the war years of 1861–1865.

NOTES   This paper was presented at a conference organized by the Société des Cincinnati de France and the Université de Paris–Sorbonne (Paris IV), "Les Marines de la guerre de l'indépendance américaine," held at l'École Militaire in Paris, France, 11–12 June 2009. A French translation will appear in a forthcoming volume edited by Olivier Chaline, to be published in France by the Presses Universitaires de Paris–Sorbonne.

1 See, for example, Evan Thomas, *John Paul Jones: Sailor, Hero, Father of the American Navy* (New York: Simon & Schuster, 2003).

2 James L. Nelson, *George Washington's Secret Navy: How the American Revolution Went to Sea* (New York: McGraw-Hill, 2008), pp. 327–328, attempts to put a halt to this particular debate with a lucid description of the rival factual claims and a persuasive argument that only Philadelphia, as the seat of Congress, could make such a claim.

3 See, for example, Robert W. Love, *History of the U.S. Navy* (Harrisburg, PA: Stackpole, 1992) and Edward L. Beach, Jr., *The United States Navy: 200 Years* (New York: Henry Holt, 1986). In *This People's Navy: The Making of American Sea Power* (New York: The Free Press, 1991), p. 20, Kenneth J. Hagan sees the Continental Navy as a typical small navy that was complemented by privateering and designed to protect the nation's coasts. In this, he argues that it established a tradition that lasted for just one century, until the U.S. Navy began to compete for world power status in the late nineteenth century. For a more extended argument, see Kenneth J. Hagan, "The Birth of American Naval Strategy," in Donald J. Stoker, Kenneth J. Hagan, and Michael T. McMaster, eds., *Strategy in the American Revolution: A Global Approach* (London: Routledge, 2009). I am grateful to Ken Hagan for providing me with an advance copy of this chapter.

4 See, for example, John B. Hattendorf, "Recent Thinking on the Theory of Naval Strategy," in Hattendorf and Robert S. Jordan, eds., *Maritime Strategy and the Balance of Power: Britain and America in the Twentieth Century* (London: Macmillan, 1989), pp. 136–161.

5 The roles and functions of a navy opposing a great power navy are outlined in Julian S. Corbett, *Some Principles of Maritime Strategy,* edited with an introduction by Eric J. Grove. Classics of Sea Power series (Annapolis: Naval Institute Press, 1988). Some recent work that contributes to the further development of this subject includes: Rolf Hobson and Tom Kristiansen, eds., *Navies in Northern Waters, 1721–2000* (London: Frank Cass, 2004); J. R. Hill, *Maritime Strategy for Medium Powers* (Annapolis: Naval Institute Press, 1986); and Raja Menon, *Maritime Strategy and Continental Wars* (London: Frank Cass, 1968).

6 For the opposing views, see George C. Daughan, *If by Sea: The Forging of the American Navy from the Revolution to the War of 1812* (New York: Basic Books, 2008), pp. 121–123, 225, 235, 280, and Michael J. Crawford's review of Daughan's book in *The Pennsylvania Magazine of History and Biography,* vol. 133, no. 2 (April 2009), pp. 206–207.

7 For the opposing views, see Jonathan R. Dull, "Was the Continental Navy a Mistake?," *The American Neptune,* vol. 44, no. 3 (September 1984), pp. 167–170, and William S. Dudley and Michael A. Palmer, "No Mistake About It: A Response to Jonathan R. Dull," *American Neptune,* vol. 45, no. 4 (Fall 1985), pp. 167–170 and 244–48.

8 For a useful book-length narrative history, see William M. Fowler, Jr., *Rebels Under Sail: The American Navy During the Revolution* (New York: Scribner's, 1976).

9 See, for example, Steven Gunn, David Grummitt, and Hans Cools, "War and the State in Early Modern Europe: Widening the Debate," *War in History,* vol. 15, no. 4 (November 2008), pp. 371–388.

10 Michael Roberts, "The Military Revolution, 1560–1660," in *Essays in Swedish History* (Minneapolis: University of Minnesota Press, 1967), pp. 195–225.

11 Geoffrey Parker, *The Military Revolution: Military Innovation and the Rise of the West, 1500–1800* (Cambridge: Cambridge University Press, 1988; 1996); Clifford J. Rogers, ed., *The Military Revolution Debate: Readings on the Transformation of Early Modern Europe* (Boulder: Westview Press, 1995).

12 Jan Glete, *Warfare at Sea, 1500–1600: Maritime Conflicts and the Transformation of Europe* (London: Routledge, 2000); Jan Glete, *War and the State in Early Modern Europe: Spain, the Dutch Republic, and Sweden as Fiscal Military States, 1500–1660* (London: Routledge, 2002).

13 For the first studies of early American naval administration, see Charles Oscar Paullin, "The Administration of the Continental Navy of the American Revolution," U.S. Naval Institute *Proceedings* (September 1905), reprinted in *Paullin's History of Naval Administration* (Annapolis: Naval Institute, 1986); Charles Oscar Paullin, *The Navy of the American Revolution: Its Administration, Its Policy, Its Achievements* (Cleveland: Burrows Brothers, 1906); Gardner W. Allen, "Naval Administration and Organization," *A Naval History of the American Revolution* (1912, 1940, reprinted New York: Russell & Russell, Inc., 1962), chapter 2, pp. 20–58.

14 Jonathan R. Dull, *The French Navy and American Independence: A Study of Arms and Diplomacy, 1774–1787* (Princeton: Princeton University Press, 1975), p. 19.

15 See Neal R. Stout, *The Royal Navy in America, 1760–1775: A Study of Enforcement of British Colonial Policy in the Era of the American Revolution* (Annapolis: Naval Institute Press, 1973) and Thomas C. Barrow, *Trade and Empire: The British Customs Service in Colonial America, 1660–1775* (Cambridge, MA: Harvard University Press, 1967).

16 N. A. M. Rodger, *The Command of the Oceans: A Naval History of Britain, 1649–1815* (London: Allen Lane, 2004), pp. 330–333.

17 Raymond G. O'Connor, *Origins of the American Navy: Sea Power in the Colonies and the New Nation* (Lanham, MD: University Press of America, 1994), pp. 16–17.

18 Richard Buel, Jr., *In Irons: Britain's Naval Supremacy and the American Revolutionary Economy* (New Haven: Yale University Press, 1998), pp. 79–80.

19 Edward G. Lengel, *General George Washington: A Military Life* (New York: Random House, 2005), pp. 81–91. See also Don Higginbotham, *The War of American Independence: Military Attitudes, Policies, and Practice, 1764–1789* (New York: Macmillan, 1971; 2nd edition. Boston: Northeastern University Press, 1983).

20 Daughan, *If by Sea,* pp. 14–15.

21 William Bell Clark, ed., *Naval Documents of the American Revolution* [hereinafter abbreviated as *NDAR*] (Washington: GPO, 1964–in progress), vol. 1, pp. 312–313: Benedict Arnold to the Massachusetts Committee of Safety, 11 May 1775. For a thorough and modern study, see James L. Nelson, *Benedict Arnold's Navy: The Ragtag Fleet That Lost the Battle of Lake Champlain, but Won the American Revolution* (Camden, Maine: International Marine/McGraw-Hill, 2006).

22 Clark, ed., *NDAR,* vol. 1, p. 376: Extract of a letter from Crown Point, 19 May; ibid., pp. 503–504: Arnold to the Albany Committee of Safety, 22 May 1775.

23 Ibid., pp. 1022, 1027: Loose Sheets in the Narrative of Vice Admiral Samuel Graves, 31 July 1775; ibid., General Orders Issued by George Washington, 1 August 1775.

24 David Syrett, "Defeat at Sea: The Impact of American Naval Operations upon the British, 1775–1778," in *Maritime Dimensions of the American Revolution* (Washington: Naval History Division, 1977), pp. 14–15.

25 Clark, ed., *NDAR,* vol. 1, p. 759: Journal of the Massachusetts Provincial Congress, 26 June 1775; ibid., pp. 848–849: Deposition of Thomas Flinn, Master of the *Falmouth Packet,* 10 July 1775. See also Nelson, *George Washington's Secret Navy,* pp. 22–28; Daughan, *If by Sea,* pp. 24–26.

26 David C. Hsiung, "Food, Fuel, and the New England Environment in the War for Independence, 1775–1776," *The New England Quarterly,* vol. 80, no. 4 (December 2007), pp. 614–651.

27 Clark, ed., *NDAR,* vol. 1, pp. 664–665: Journal of the Rhode Island General Assembly, 12 June 1775; John Brown to Ambrose Page and Nicholas Cooke, 12 June 1775.

28 Eventually, twelve of the thirteen colonies created a naval force of their own. Only Delaware lacked a navy. See Robert L. Scheina, "A Matter of Definition: A New Jersey Navy, 1777–1783," *American Neptune,* vol. 39, no. 3 (July 1979), pp. 209–217.

29 Clark, ed., *NDAR,* vol. 1, pp. 628–629: John Adams to Elbridge Gerry, [7] June 1775. Christopher Magra, *The Fisherman's Cause: Atlantic Commerce and the Maritime Dimensions of the American Revolution* (Cambridge: Cambridge University Press, 2009), pp. 182–183.

30 Clark, ed., *NDAR,* vol. 1, pp. 621–622: Journal of the Massachusetts Provincial Congress, 7 June 1775.

31 Ibid., pp. 621–622: Journal of the Massachusetts Provincial Congress, 20 June 1775.

32 Magra, *The Fisherman's Cause,* p. 186.

33 Clark, ed., *NDAR,* vol. 1, p. 916: Journal of the Continental Congress, 18 July 1775.

34 Magra, *The Fisherman's Cause,* p. 188.

35 Clark, ed., *NDAR,* vol. 1, pp. 1287–1289: George Washington's Instructions to Captain Nicholas Broughton, 2 September 1775.

36 Ibid.

37 Clark, ed., *NDAR,* vol. 1, p. 1236: Journal of the Rhode Island General Assembly, 26 August 1775.

38 Clark, ed., *NDAR,* vol. 2, p. 285: Journal of the Continental Congress, 3 October 1775.

39 Ibid., pp. 307–315: Journal of the Continental Congress, 5 October 1775.

40 Ibid., pp. 311–312: John Hancock to George Washington, 5 October 1775.

41 Ibid., pp. 312–313: John Hancock to Nicholas Cooke, 5 October 1775.

42 Ibid., p. 308, fn 2; Journal of the Continental Congress, 5 October 1775: extract from John Adams's *Autobiography.*

43 Ibid.

44 As early as 1755, Adams had written, "We have (I may say) all the naval Stores of the Nation in our hands, it will be easy to obtain the mastery of the seas, and then the united force of all Europe, will not be able to subdue us." Robert J. Taylor, Mary-Jo Kline, and Gregg L. Lint, eds., *Papers of John Adams,* vol. 1 (1977), available online at *Founding Families: Digital Editions of the Papers of the Winthrops and the Adamses,* ed., C. James Taylor (Boston: Massachusetts Historical Society, 2007), http://www.masshist.org/ff/: John Adams to Nathan Webb, 12 October 1755, with Comments by the Writer Recorded in 1807.

45 Ibid.

46 Clark, ed., *NDAR,* vol. 2, pp. 328–329: Journal of the Continental Congress, 6 October 1775.

47 Ibid., p. 329, fn 2; John Adams's notes on the debates of 6 October 1775.

48 Ibid., p. 341, fn; John Adams' notes of debates 7 October 1775.

49 Ibid.

50 Ibid., pp. 441–442: Journal of the Continental Congress, 13 October 1775.

51 Today, the United States Navy recognizes this resolution of 13 October 1775 as marking its official "birthday."

52 Clark, ed., *NDAR,* vol. 2, pp. 554–556: John Adams's notes of debates 21 October 1775.

53 Five months later, Congress authorized privateering. See Clark, ed., *NDAR,* vol. 4, pp. 477–480: Journal of the Continental Congress, 23 March 1776.

54 Clark, ed., *NDAR,* vol. 2, p. 647: Journal of the Continental Congress, 30 October 1775.

55 Ibid., p. 647, fn 7; John Adams's notes of debates, 30 October 1775.

56 Ibid., p. 590: George Washington to John Hancock, 24 October 1775; ibid., p. 842: Journal of the Continental Congress, 1 November 1775. Falmouth was burned on 18 October 1775.

57 Ibid., p. 861: Journal of the Continental Congress, 2 November 1775.

58 Ibid.

59 Ibid., pp. 957–958, fn 2: Journal of the Continental Congress, 9 November 1775: John Adams, "Proposals."

60 Ibid., p. 972: Journal of the Continental Congress, 10 November 1775.

61 Ibid., p. 907: Stephen Hopkins to Esek Hopkins, 6 November 1775.

62 Ibid., pp. 930–931, 978–980: Letters from George Washington to Congress.

63 Ibid., p. 1133: Journal of the Continental Congress, 25 November 1775, para. 8.

64 Ibid., para. 7.

65 Ibid., paras., 3, 4, 5, 6.

66 Ibid., p. 1109: Journal of the Continental Congress, 23 November 1775.

67 Ibid., p. 1189: Autobiography of John Adams, 28 November 1775

68 First published in 1731, it has not yet been determined which edition Adams used. The most recent edition at the time was the eleventh edition, published in 1772. For a list of the editions published between 1731 and 1790, see Thomas R. Adams and David W. Waters, comps., *English Maritime Books Printed Before 1801* (Providence: John Carter Brown Library, and Greenwich: National Maritime Museum, 1995), items 1418–1429.

69 Clark, ed., *NDAR,* vol. 2, pp. 1174–1182: Journal of the Continental Congress, 28 November 1775. This important document is the basis for the U.S. Navy's current *Naval Regulations,* which retains in some places the same wording.

70 Ibid., pp. 329, 340–341, 885, 1051, 1094: Journal of the Continental Congress.

71 Clark, ed., *NDAR,* vol. 3, p. 59: Journal of the Continental Congress, 11 December 1775.

72 Ibid., p. 90: Journal of the Continental Congress, 13 December 1775.

73 Ibid., pp. 100–101: Journal of the Continental Congress, 14 December 1775. John Hancock replaced Samuel Adams; William Paca replaced Samuel Chase; and John Houston was added.

74 Ibid., p. 979, fn 2; Journal of the Continental Congress, 25 January 1776.

75 Ibid., p. 1219: Commissioned Officers of the First Fleet; ibid., p. 1236: List of Ships and Vessels fitted out by the Rebels at Philadelphia.

76 Ibid., p. 1219: *Andrew Doria* Journal

77 Ibid., pp. 162, 208, 612–613, 655–657.

78 Clark, ed., *NDAR,* vol. 4, p. 867: Journal of the Continental Congress, 17 April 1776.

79 Ibid., p. 1216: Journal of the Continental Congress, 23 April 1776. For the activities of one naval agent, see Ernest E. Rogers, ed., *Connecticut's Naval Office at New London during the American Revolution.* New London County Historical Society Collections, vol. II (New London: Ernest R. Rogers Fund, 1933).

80 William J. Morgan, ed., *NDAR,* vol. 7, p. 66: Journal of the Continental Congress, 6 November 1776.

81 Ibid., pp. 223–224: Journal of the Continental Congress, 20 November 1776.

82 Morgan, ed., *NDAR,* vol. 8, p. 282: John Adams to James Warren, 6 April 1777.

83 Ibid., p. 379: Journal of the Continental Congress, 19 April 1777.

84 The four states were Connecticut, New Hampshire, Massachusetts, and Rhode Island.

85 Morgan, ed., *NDAR,* vol. 9, pp. 256–257: Continental Marine Committee to the Continental Navy Board of the Eastern Department, 10 July 1777.

86 Morgan, ed., *NDAR,* vol. 7, p. 79: William Ellery to William Vernon, Providence, 7 November 1776.

87 For a modern historical study of British practice, see Daniel A. Baugh, *British Naval Administration in the Age of Walpole* (Princeton: Princeton University Press, 1965) and "The Eighteenth Century Navy as a National Institution, 1690–1815," in J. R. Hill, ed., *The Oxford Illustrated History of the Royal Navy* (Oxford: Oxford University Press, 1995), pp. 120–160.

88 There was at least one available source that did provide an outline of British naval administration, but no evidence has yet been found that it was used by American officials at this time. See Josiah Burchett, *A Complete History of the Most Remarkable Transactions at Sea (1720),* a facsimile reproduction with an introduction by John B. Hattendorf (Delmar, NY: Scholars' Facsimiles & Reprints for the John Carter Brown Library, 1995). Burchett provided the outline in the preface to this work.

89 Morgan, ed., *NDAR,* vol. 7, pp. 1109–1111: Robert Morris to John Paul Jones, 1 February 1777, quote at bottom of p. 1110.

90 Ibid., p. 1299: William Ellery to William Vernon, 26 February 1777.

91 See Robert C. Alberts, *The Golden Voyage: The Life and Times of William Bingham, 1752–1804* (Boston: Houghton, Mifflin, 1969), pp. 3–84.

92 See Charles Oscar Paullin, ed., *Out-Letters of the Continental Marine Committee and Board of Admiralty, August 1776–September 1780.* Naval History Society, vols. IV–V (New York: De Vinne Press for the Naval History Society, 1914).

93 Quoted in William M. Fowler, Jr., *William Ellery: A Rhode Island Politico and Lord of Admiralty* (Metuchen, NJ: The Scarecrow Press, 1973), p. 56, from Worthington Chauncey Ford, et al., eds., *Journals of the Continental Congress, 1774–1789.* 34 volumes (Washington: Government Printing Office, 1904–1936), vol. XIV, p. 708, with the debate on the issue reported on pp. 700–708 and 711–715.

94 See John W. Jackson, *The Pennsylvania Navy* (New Brunswick: Rutgers University Press, 1974).

95 See Lincoln Diamant, *Chaining the Hudson: The Fight for the River in the American Revolution* (New York: Fordham University Press, 2004).

96 Buel, *In Irons,* pp. 86–87.

97 Fowler, *Ellery,* pp. 61–62.

98 Paullin, ed., *Out-Letters of the Continental Marine Committee,* vol. I, pp. 265–274: Letters to Navy Board, Eastern Dept, 11 July, 24 July 1778 and to Count D'Estaing, 17 July 1778. See Michael J. Crawford, "The Joint Allied Operations at Rhode Island," in William R. Roberts and Jack Sweetman, eds., *New Interpretations in Naval History* (Annapolis, MD: US Naval Institute Press, 1991), pp. 236–242, and John Hattendorf, *Newport, the French Navy, and the American Revolution* (Newport: The Redwood Press, 2005), pp. 1–35.

99 Ford, et al., eds., *Journals of the Continental Congress,* vol. XVII, p. 669: 26 July 1780. For related issues, see also Paullin, ed., *Out-Letters of the Continental Marine Committee,* vol. II, p. 118: Marine Committee to Eastern Navy Board, 28 September 1779; ibid. pp. 243–244: Board of Admiralty to President of Congress, 14 August 1780.

100 Henri Doniol, *Histoire de la Participation de la France à l'Établissement des États-Unis d'Amérique. Correspondance Diplomatique et Documents* (Paris: Imprimerie Nationale, 1890), tome IV, p. 316; Jean-Pierre Bois, ed., *Deux Voyages au temps de Louis XVI, 1777–1780. La Mission du baron de Tott en Égypte en 1777–1778 et le Journal de bord de l'Hermione en 1780* (Rennes: Presses Universitaires de Rennes, 2005), pp. 123–124.

101 Buel, *In Irons,* pp. 87–88.

102 Daughan, *If by Sea,* pp. 233–234.

103 Buel, *In Irons,* p. 89.

104 Ibid., pp. 91–95.

105 E. James Ferguson, ed., *The Papers of Robert Morris, 1781–1784* (Pittsburgh: University of Pittsburgh Press, 1973–1999), vol. 1, p. 3: Diary, 7 February 1781.

106 Ferguson, ed., *Papers of Robert Morris,* vol. 2, pp. 214–219: Morris to the President of Congress, 8 September 1781.

107 Ferguson, ed., *Papers of Robert Morris,* vol. 3, pp. 202–204: Morris to the President of Congress, 17 November 1781.

108 Quoted in the heading to Elizabeth Nuxoll, "The Naval Movement of the Confederation Era," in William S. Dudley and Michael J. Crawford, eds., *The Early Republic and the Sea: Essays on the Naval and Maritime History of the Early Republic and the Sea* (Washington, D.C.: Brassey's, 2001), pp. 3–33, from Elizabeth M. Nuxoll and Mary A. Gallagher, eds., *Papers of Robert Morris,* vol. 8, p. 265: Morris to the President of Congress, 10 July 1763.

109 Nuxoll and Gallagher, eds., *Papers of Robert Morris,* vol. 9, pp. 194–195: Morris to the President of Congress, 19 March 1784.

110 Nuxoll, "Naval Movement of the Confederation Era," p. 14. On the opening of the American China trade, previously prohibited to Americans by the British Navigation Acts, see Philip Chadwick Foster Smith, *The Empress of China* (Philadelphia: Philadelphia Maritime Museum, 1984).

111 For details of the vessels, see Howard I. Chapelle, *The History of the American Sailing Navy: The Ships and Their Development* (New York: W. W. Norton, 1949; reprinted, New York: Bonanza Books, n.d.), chapter 2, pp. 52–114. For a recently researched, succinct list with ships' data, see Paul H. Silverstone, *The Sailing Navy, 1775–1854* (London: Routledge, 2006), pp. 1–16.

112 Hagan, *This People's Navy,* pp. 16–17; Daughan, *If by Sea,* p. 225.

113 William J. Morgan, "American Privateering in America's War for Independence, 1775–1783," *American Neptune,* vol. 36, no. 2 (April 1976), pp. 79–87.

114 Daughan, *If by Sea,* pp. 319–321.

XIII   *The* Expédition Particulière *of 1780–1781 as a Joint and Combined Operation*

The French expedition that left Brest bound for North America on 2 May 1780 was referred to obliquely for security reasons by the name of the *Expédition Particulière.* It was a joint expedition—that is to say, it was designed for undertaking military and naval operations in an integrated manner in which the military and naval elements were mutually supporting and of equal importance. At the same time, it was designed for combined operations—that is to say, it was designed as a French expedition that should serve cooperatively as an auxiliary to the forces of the United States of America during the last phase of the American war and independence from Great Britain. While modern defense experts have grown increasingly accustomed to thinking in terms of joint and combined warfare during the twentieth and twenty-first centuries, the novelty, challenge, and difficulty of conducting joint and combined warfare in the late eighteenth century, and even its existence in that period, have sometimes been overlooked. The purpose of this paper is to point out some key elements of the joint and combined operations as a contribution to better understanding the issues that arose in Franco-American cooperation during 1780–81.

Original Plans and Orders

As the French ministry began serious discussions about the options for sending direct assistance to North America in January 1780, the idea of emphasizing the use of a naval squadron seemed to offer the most attractive option, as it filled in resources with ships-of-the-line where the Americans had only frigates and smaller vessels. A naval presence would offer no direct conflict with American interests, while a strong and independent French military contingent could, if not handled properly, inadvertently create contention. With this in mind, the ministry decided it would be necessary to give the French military commander strict orders to act as an auxiliary under Washington's direct command and not as an independent force.[1]

To command the accompanying land forces, the war minister, the Prince de Montbarey, had to choose between several officers. The Comte de Vaux, who had commanded the forces for the planned invasion of England in 1779, seemed the logical choice, but he was 74 years old. A dozen years younger and fit, the next possibility was the Maréchal de Broglie, but he was not then in the good graces of the ministry, having refused to take the command that was then given to de Vaux for the invasion. With these considerations, Montbarey selected the 55-year-old Comte de Rochambeau, who had just come from the commanding troops that had been selected to be the first wave for the invasion of England under de Vaux.

For the naval command, Minster of the Navy Gabriel de Sartine chose the 57-year-old chevalier de Ternay, passing over Guichen and La Motte-Picquet, for whom he had other commands in mind. With forty years of naval service behind him, de Ternay had most recently served for six years, from 1771 to 1777, as commandant-général at the Île de France and Bourbon (present-day Mauritius and Réunion), key islands for French operations against the British in the Indian Ocean.

Interestingly, both commanders were highly competent, although perhaps not brilliant, and had similar traits in command: taciturn, aloof, and stern disciplinarians, with de Ternay considered by some to be proud, haughty, and approaching severity.[2] With these choices made and the basic concept of the expedition formulated, Louis XVI formally approved the secret plan on 2 February 1780, giving it the guarded name of the *Expédition Particulière.*[3]

With the news recently received in Paris that the British had voluntarily withdrawn their forces from Newport, Rhode Island, in October 1779, this defendable port with its deep bay and commodious harbor, in waters now well known to the French Navy from d'Estaing's operation there in 1778, presented an opportune first base for French operations. As the course of future events might present, joint and combined Franco-American military and naval operations could effectively be undertaken from Newport against New York, the mid-Atlantic, the southern states of Georgia and the Carolinas, or even to join with French naval forces in the Caribbean to defeat the Royal Navy in the American waters. Alternatively, the naval ministry suggested additional possible British targets at Bermuda, Newfoundland, and Hudson's Bay. Newport, if it remained unoccupied by the British, seemed to offer all such possibilities, but precise and definite plans would have to await the situation the commanders found in progress when they actually arrived in North America.

A series of implementing orders to both the army and navy quickly followed the king's approval on 2 February. In addition to the myriad problems associated with selecting troops and officers, finding sufficient transport ships and preparing them to sail from France with appropriate supplies, there was also the need to make arrangements on the other side of the Atlantic with the Americans. For that purpose, Louis XVI and Foreign Minister the comte de Vergennes sent the Marquis de Lafayette his final orders, signed on 24 February, for Lafayette to act as the principal intermediary between French and American forces and to return to the United States immediately in order to inform the Americans about the plans for the *Expédition Particulière,* commanded jointly by de Ternay and Rochambeau, and to make the practical preparations necessary to receive them. On receiving the orders on 5 March, Lafayette traveled immediately to Rochefort, where he arrived on 9 March and boarded the 36-gun frigate *Hermione* on the following day. Under her commanding officer, Louis René Levassor, Comte de Latouche-Tréville, *Hermione* proceeded to load some 4,000 uniforms for the American army and Lafayette's extensive personal baggage. Getting under weigh on the evening of 14 March, the main yard was found to be defective and the ship anchored the following day for repairs in the roads off the Île d'Aix. After making the necessary further repairs, *Hermione,* with Lafayette on board, headed westward across the Atlantic on the evening of 20 March 1780.

Six days before de Ternay and Rochambeau had even left Brest with the *Expédition Particulière, Hermione* arrived at Marblehead, Massachusetts, on 27 April after a thirty-eight day passage, then went on to Boston the next day. On 2 May, Lafayette left *Hermione* to travel over land to meet Washington. Accompanying him from Rochefort in the frigate was Colonel Ethis de Corny of the French army's commissary service, who went ahead to make advance practical logistical arrangements for the arrival of the *Expédition Particulière* at Newport, Rhode Island,[4] where it eventually safely anchored more than two months later on 11 July,[5] having spent 70 days at sea.

The initial concept for the relationship between the French and American forces was spelled out in King Louis XVI's secret instructions to Lafayette, dated 2 February 1780, the sense of which Lafayette was ordered to convey to General George Washington.

> *Le corps de troupes françoises sera purement auxiliaire et à ce titre n'agira que sous les ordres du général Was[h]ington. Le général de terre françois recevra les ordres du général en chef améri-cain pout tout ce qui ne tiendra pas à la police intérieure de son corps qui doit avoir en tout sa justice et se gouvernér par les loys de son pays. Il sera prescrit au général de mer de seconder de tout son pouvoir toutes les opérations où son concours sera reclamé. Bien entendu qu'on aura l'attention de les combinér, de les concertér avec lui et d'écoutér les objections qu'il pourroit avoir à y faire.*
>
> *Les opérations devant dépende des circonstances et des possibilités locales, nous n'en proposons aucune; c'est au général Was[h]ington et au conseil de guerre à décidér celles qui seront les plus utiles. Tout ce que le Roi désire est que les troupes qu'il envoie au secours de ses alliés les États Unis côopèrent efficacement à les delivrér une fois pour toutes du joug et de la tirannie des Anglois.*[6]

These instructions, added to Lafayette's previous experiences during the 1778 and 1779 campaigns and the reputation he gained at that time for assisting in the coordination of Franco-American operations with d'Estaing, now gave the young Lafayette a special character and enhanced role as the king's personal messenger to General Washington alongside the king's appointed envoy to the Continental Congress, the Chevalier de la Luzerne.

The Initial Crisis

With the arrival of French forces in America, both sides faced immediate difficulties. For the Americans and for Lafayette, the *Expédition Particulière* arrived at Newport, Rhode Island, with fewer large warships and fewer soldiers than they had expected. 7,500 troops had been expected, but transports to carry only 5,100 had been found and more were promised later along with additional warships.[7] This situation presented the first difficulty. On the one hand, it meant that these forces were inadequate to carry out the plans that Washington had envisaged for them in seizing the port of New York as the first step in attacking British military positions at and around New York City.[8] While Washington was disappointed in this, the French commanders, Rochambeau and de Ternay, were immediately concerned about how to secure their position safely in order to await the expected reinforcements.

The first concerns for de Ternay and Rochambeau were to put both the squadron and the troops in a mutually supporting defensive position. This was a long process, since there had been little concept of loading equipment in the transport ships to meet immediate tactical needs. First, the large warships were anchored in two lines. The first was made up from the first division: one with three ships anchored across the main en-trance of Newport Harbor, between the south tip of Goat Island and the battery at the entrance to Brenton Cove (the present site of Fort Adams). The other was made up of four ships anchored between the tip of Goat Island and stretched northward toward Coaster's Harbor Island.[9]

The transports were brought into the inner harbor. Debarkation from the ships was slowed by a lack of small boats, but among the first to be brought ashore on 13 July were about 1,500 sailors and soldiers, sick with scurvy and dysentery, who were transferred to the hospital facilities that Corny had arranged for their use at Providence and at Bristol. By 15 July, the majority of the troops came ashore on the south side of Newport Harbor and marched directly eastward up the hill to the top of the island's central ridge.[10]

In the camp, four regiments, Saintonge, Soissonnais, Royal Deux-Ponts, and Bourbonnais, occupied the left side, while the artillery held the right end of the main camp. The troops from the Legion de Lauzun occupied a defensive position slightly overlooking the Main Passage at Castle Hill. On 16 July, a further 418 troops were debarked and transferred to a large house across the Main Passage on Conanicut Island which served as a hospital.[11]

While Newport was bustling with activity as the French landed, the British were unable to respond effectively to make an immediate attack. On 8 July, Admiral Arbuthnot learned from his frigates that de Ternay was definitely en route to Newport. On the day following the French arrival in Newport Harbor, Rear Admiral Graves had sailed just south of them, without sighting the French, to arrive at Sandy Hook on 13 July with the reinforcements from England. Two days later, General Clinton urged Arbuthnot to sail directly to Newport. Turning then to his own preparations he ordered transports for 6,700 men to be loaded to attack Newport, only to be told that the transports were unavailable because they were carrying water to Arbuthnot's ships. And so things continued, with misunderstanding, lack of coordination, and delayed exchanges between the two responsible British commanders. However, Arbuthnot made an appearance off Newport. On 19 July, French lookouts reported four frigates off Point Judith and, on 21 July, the French saw eleven ships-of-the-line, five frigates, and four smaller vessels patrolling offshore.[12]

It was only a reconnaissance patrol with no intention to attack. The British presence offshore, however, was enough to spur the French forces into a frenzy of activity to better defend themselves. De Ternay revised the anchorage plans for his ships so that they better complemented each other and the land fortifications. In this new position, the two lines of heavily gunned ships created a deadly zone of crossfire between them, at the inner entrance of Narragansett Bay. The squadron retained these mooring assignments throughout its stay in Newport Harbor. At this point, Rochambeau had only managed to get a few of his artillery pieces ashore, and the arrival of Arbuthnot's squadron off shore created alarm among the French in Newport. Hurrying to offload what pieces of field artillery they could, they worked to move them to key places where they thought the British might attempt a landing.[13]

In a 24-hour period on 21–22 July, the French forces had so quickly been able to put up impressive defenses, they clearly gave Arbuthnot grounds to express caution and lead Clinton to the conclusion that the French had been able to defend themselves too well for a surprise attack to have succeeded.[14] By 25 July, all the French artillery pieces were in place and in firing condition, including a battery to fire hot shot at the British ships.

Fortifications on Goat Island, Brenton's Point, Rose Island, and Coaster's Harbor Island were all improved from existing structures.[15]

At that point, British frigates were sailing so close to the shore that the French officers in the batteries ashore could make out the dress of the British sailors.[16] After several days, Arbuthnot's ships moved further offshore, as some 4,000 American militiamen rallied to the Newport area to serve under General William Heath to defend against the threat of the British attack.

In Newport, Rochambeau had found it an extremely difficult task to divide his defensive forces between both Aquidneck and Conanicut Islands and felt uneasy about the weakness it caused. De Ternay had earlier demanded full military defense of Conanicut for the protection of the naval hospital there. De Ternay was persuaded to reconsider his position and to allow for the evacuation of Conanicut and the removal of the naval hospital to Newport.

On 29 July, the immediate crisis caused by the appearance of Arbuthnot's squadron had eased enough so that the commanders could begin to think about future planning instead of immediate defensive action. On that and the following day, Lafayette was in Newport to have meetings with Rochambeau and de Ternay to discuss Washington's proposal that French forces assist his operations in the Hudson River area by assaulting New York. De Ternay was reticent to make a move with an apparently imminent British attack on Newport, and despite urging from some of the French Army officers, de Ternay thought it inadvisable for his squadron to enter New York Harbor at Sandy Hook, remembering d'Estaing's previous experience in 1778 in finding those waters too shallow for the relatively deeper draft French 74-gun warships to enter. A movement of troops within Long Island Sound was a possibility for further consideration, but de Ternay, who still had many seamen in hospital, saw the need for additional naval forces to assure local naval supremacy and wanted the comte de Guichen's squadron to come north from the Caribbean to support him, before attempting any such major operation in New York.[17]

Commanders' Conference at Hartford

Soon after the squadron's arrival in Newport, both Rochambeau and de Ternay repeatedly expressed an urgent desire to confer personally with George Washington in order to plan operations. The discussions that Rochambeau and de Ternay had had in late July with Lafayette, as Washington's principal liaison officer, had not been in any way conclusive. Although Lafayette had Washington's full confidence and Washington had written this to Rochambeau and de Ternay, the French commanders were not impressed with Lafayette's young age and relative inexperience. A corresponding officer in French service would have nearly four decades of service behind him, while Lafayette was only in his early 20s. They soon became suspicious that Lafayette was using Washington's name to promote his own over-ambitious ideas to attack New York and therefore, they wanted to discuss the issues directly with Washington and not through Lafayette as intermediary.

Plans were laid for the commanders to meet at Hartford, Connecticut, midway between Newport and Washington's headquarters, on 20–22 September. Departing from Newport on 16 September, de Ternay appointed his next senior officer, the chevalier Destouches, commanding the 74-gun *Neptune,* to take charge of the squadron in his temporary absence, while Rochambeau appointed the baron de Vioménil to exercise authority in his absence. Shortly after their departure, British forces made menacing naval movements that led Destouches and Vioménil to take urgent action to consolidate further their defensive position.

While this work was being completed at Newport, de Ternay and Rochambeau held their important meeting at Jeremiah Wadsworth's house in Hartford, during which Lafayette served as interpreter and secretary. In concluding it on 22 September, the two French commanders formally presented to Washington in writing ten proposed principles of cooperation, to each of which Washington responded in writing. First and foremost among them was, in George Washington's words, "A constant naval superiority is essential if we are able to act in America in a decisive manner," and secondly, "New York is without doubt the first and foremost object we can have on this continent."[18] These and the additional points were all dependent on obtaining additional ships, men, and money.

The two French commanders had very clearly expressed their priorities for a joint and combined operation, underscoring that the very first consideration was to have naval superiority in North American waters before they could undertake any major operation. An attack on British positions in New York would require a military superiority about double that of the British land forces, or something very close to 30,000 effective soldiers. The two French commanders optimistically believed that a second echelon of transport ships would soon arrive that would more than double their own force and bring it up to a total of 15,000 troops for the 1781 campaign. In their present situation, Rochambeau and de Ternay believed that they had no alternative but to maintain a strictly defensive position at Newport until both military and naval reinforcements could arrive in the region.[19]

The ability to obtain local French naval superiority in North American waters was an equally, if not more, difficult matter to predict as it depended on British naval movements. They anticipated that Britain would send a proportionate number to whatever number of warships that they expected France would have on the North American coast or was in the process of sending there. Thus, much depended upon the secrecy with which warships could be dispatched from France and from which port they sailed, either Brest in the Atlantic or Toulon in the Mediterranean, and their ability or luck in avoiding interception by the British en route.

In light of the growing British naval strength, Washington concluded, "The inferiority of the fleet has forced us to take a defensive position and has directed our attention to the needs of our own security."[20] With these sentiments agreed upon, de Ternay and Rochambeau returned to Newport, where French forces soon entered winter quarters, while Washington returned to his headquarters to find the repercussions from the capture of Major André, the adjutant-general of the British Army, which revealed General Benedict Arnold's treasonous betrayal at West Point.

Sequel to the Conference

While British ships patrolled close offshore, de Ternay kept all of his in port in a defensive position and did not allow any patrols. He had made several attempts to get dispatches to France from Newport, but all had been captured by the British. The British blockade was so effective that de Ternay sent several copies of his letters to France, each by a different route. In at least one case, all four copies of one dispatch ended up in

British hands in New York. Finally, de Ternay sent the dispatches to Boston and to Salem, Massachusetts, and these managed to get through to Paris via Bilbao in Spain. Among the reports that he was trying to make was to report the urgent need for supplies. In mid-October, he wrote to the Minister of the Navy that 600 seamen were still in hospital and the squadron's men were urgently in need of flour, which was not readily available in Newport, as well as blankets, oil, and vinegar, while the ships needed sails and cordage.[21]

Finally, on 28 October, de Ternay signed orders to send ships to sea for the first time since their arrival in July. While the heavy ships remained at anchor defending the army at Newport, the orders were to the three frigates to put to sea in the heavy weather that had scattered the British blockading ships and allowed the frigates to get clear of the harbor.

Throughout, the two French commanders very clearly held to their priorities up to de Ternay's death of "putrid fever" at Newport on 15 December 1780. De Ternay had been a strict disciplinarian and had strongly held a conservative view of the mutual defensive inter-relationship of the army and navy at Newport. These views conflicted with many of his more aggressive juniors, who made little comment on his death. Rochambeau, who knew him best as a colleague and co-commander, wrote to Washington:

> I admit to you that I have been cruelly surprised to learn of his death following an illness which was so short and which turned so tragically. It is a cruel loss for our service; he was a very brave man, a very honest man and an excellent sailor, whom I infinitely regret.[22]

In the period of eleven months since Louis XVI had ordered de Ternay to take up the naval command and to join Rochambeau in the *Expédition Particulière,* the chevalier de Ternay had achieved much by safely bringing the *Expédition* across the Atlantic to Newport, effectively putting it into a defensive position, and laying the basis for the operations that would follow when time and opportunity eventually provided the appropriate moment for action.

The war had not gone well for the American cause through the autumn and early winter of 1780–81. In addition, communications between Rochambeau and Washington had abruptly ended for a time when Washington ran out of funds to pay his couriers. Then, in January 1781, a mutiny broke out in the Continental Army. In this critical situation, the French at Newport could do little but stay where they were, while ten British ships-of-the-line based at Gardiner's Island blockaded the seven French warships in their defensive anchorage at Newport.[23]

Having reports that some French frigates were at sea, Rear Admiral Thomas Graves, then with the blockading ships off Newport and at Gardiner's Island, ordered three ships-of-the-line to try to intercept them. In attempting to maintain the blockade, the 74-gun *Culloden* appeared off Newport on 21 January and seemed to be about to enter, making the soldiers ashore think she was a French ship.[24] Approaching close in, she suddenly raised her colors and fired a gun, then turned away toward the southwest. Two days later, caught in the same storm, *Culloden* went ashore and was wrecked on the east end of Long Island on 23 January 1781,[25] while the 74-gun *Bedford* lost her three masts, and 64-gun HMS *America* was seriously damaged.[26] These casualties of nature served to equalize the strength of the opposing naval forces in the Newport area, leaving the British with only the superiority of a single ship.

Thus, the storm created an opportunity for Destouches to act just as the general tide of war began to edge in favor of the Americans. In a distant area of South Carolina, Major General Daniel Morgan defeated the British at Cowpens, where they lost more than 800 of their 1,100 men. As this was going on, General Sir Henry Clinton sent Benedict Arnold, now in command of a British force, to Virginia by sea. Leaving Sandy Hook on 20 December, he had arrived at Hampton Roads on 30 December, but some of his forces were caught in the same storm that had broken *Hermione*'s bowsprit and they were delayed, but he moved on to attack Richmond and then move to a defensive position at Portsmouth, Virginia.

De Tilly's Expedition to Chesapeake Bay

Arnold's movement to the Chesapeake Bay area was the very small first step in the complicated, but fatal, process by which British commanders allowed their army to be divided into three separate groups, one in New York, one in Virginia, and one in South Carolina and Georgia.[27] At this point, Franco-American forces clearly saw Benedict Arnold's force as an isolated and tempting target for attack. While Washington ordered Lafayette to prepare to march troops toward Virginia to attack his positions, Destouches secretly organized a light squadron under the command of Captain le Gardeur de Tilly in the 64-gun *Éveillé*, accompanied by the frigates *Gentille* and *Surveillante* with the cutter *Guêpe*.

With the British blockading squadron weakened by the storm, the light squadron left Newport undetected on 9 February. De Tilly took his small squadron to the entrance to Chesapeake Bay, where they anchored and disguised themselves under British colors, ready to attack unwary merchant ships. After making several captures, they sighted a convoy of ten merchant ships approaching the bay, being escorted by the 44-gun HMS *Romulus* and an 18-gun corvette. Moving quickly, the French light squadron captured *Romulus* and eight transports without a fight. Among the other prizes taken was a ship carrying 7,000 guineas to Arnold's forces. After burning four of the prizes, de Tilly took the other four prizes into Yorktown and brought *Romulus* back to Newport, where Destouches ordered her manned and brought into French service.[28]

While de Tilly's expedition to the Chesapeake made no major impact on the British position, it was extremely successful in raising the morale of the French forces at Newport and showed capabilities for the future. The new balance of naval forces at Newport and de Tilly's success in eluding the British blockade led Destouches to plan another operation. La Pérouse had left Newport at the end of October in *Amazone,* which he had commanded since 1778, but on her arrival at Brest she was sent to be refitted and La Pérouse given command of the newly built, copper-bottomed 32-gun frigate *Astrée*. He had left Brest in her for the return voyage to North America on Christmas Day and arrived after a 64-day-long and very difficult North Atlantic passage. On his arrival, Destouches ordered him to remain for the time being in the Boston area, where plans were being laid for a possible expedition to the area near Penobscot, Maine.

Washington's Visit

As these encouraging signs of opportunity presented themselves, Rochambeau and Destouches worked out a plan to attempt a larger scale attack that would complement Lafayette's march overland to attack Benedict Arnold's forces still at Portsmouth, Virginia. British intelligence from Newport quite accurately reported that Rochambeau was about to embark 1,500 soldiers and to sail with the entire French squadron from Newport, and correctly assumed that Chesapeake Bay was their objective. The British began to make immediate preparations to thwart this, but General Sir Henry Clinton and Rear Admiral Marriott Arbuthnot continued to have the same sort of misunderstandings and miscommunications that they had experienced with each other during the previous summer. They were entirely ineffective in preventing the French move.[29] Throughout February, Destouches also watched carefully the movements of the British blockading warships based at Gardiner's Island, waiting for an opportunity to make a move.[30]

Washington wrote to Lafayette on 1 March, "I set out in the morning for Rhode Island where I hope to arrive before the fleet sails to level all difficulties and be in a way to improve circumstances."[31] There had been much rivalry among the French Army officers as to which of them would go on the expedition in command of the troops; eventually Rochambeau chose General the Baron de Vioménil over several others.

Meanwhile, the 1,120 French troops embarked on board the warships on 6 March, the very day that Washington arrived in Newport.

Destouches and Vioménil's Joint Expedition to Chesapeake Bay

With the ships about ready to leave Newport without the heavy defenses that they provided, Rochambeau took precautions and had a new battery of 36-pounders built near the town to prevent a British frigate from attempting a bombardment. In addition, he manned the redoubts with 600 American militiamen and, in the event that a British attack occurred, he ordered 1,800 more to be ready to cross over to Rhode Island (Aquidneck) from the mainland to protect Newport.

After waiting for a favorable northerly wind, Destouches weighed anchor at five o'clock in the afternoon on Thursday, 8 March. Washington and Rochambeau had gone to inspect the fortified camp on Brenton Neck and watched the departure there from the high ground overlooking the Main Passage. There, they saw the 10-ship squadron put to sea on a northwest wind. In contrast to de Tilly's four-day passage in February, Destouches took eight days to reach the Chesapeake Capes.[32]

At dawn on 16 March, Destouches and his ships were sailing through light rain and fog when they momentarily sighted a frigate at a distance of only two cannon shots away. Shortly afterwards, the lookouts sighted a formation of about a dozen warships to windward on an interception course and Destouches quickly concluded that it was Arbuthnot's squadron in pursuit of them from the British blockading station at Gardiner's Island. As these two opposing forces came together into action, Destouches came to the conclusion that he could not accomplish the original mission that he had set out from Newport to undertake. In the face of even a marginally superior British squadron actively opposing him, he could not debark his troops under fire. At this point, he came to the conclusion that his best course of action would be to make the best showing he could in fighting the British, but to preserve the troops on board.

On reflection, after receiving the initial news of the naval battle, Britain's King George III privately commented to the First Lord of the Admiralty,

> though it has not proved decisive as a naval engagement, yet it has saved the troops under the command of Arnold, and overturned the plan of operations in the south jointly undertaken by the French and the rebels. I therefore think the event very material.[33]

As the commanders had noted at the Hartford conference the previous September, the exercise of naval supremacy was the key factor that determined whether or not the land forces could achieve their objectives. In mid-March, Arbuthnot had successfully exercised that supremacy. Destouches had failed to land Vioménil's troops in Virginia, where they could have joined the small Continental Army forces that Lafayette was leading overland into Virginia, but which were forced to retreat when Destouches' expedition turned back. This was clearly a deep disappointment for the Franco-American effort, but the Continental Congress showed great insight, as well as diplomacy, when it voted a resolution of appreciation on 5 April for Destouches' efforts, describing them as "a happy presage of decisive advantages to the United States."[34] The frigate *Concorde* had arrived in Boston from France on 8 May, after a 42-day passage, and had brought with it several passengers, including the vicomte de Rochambeau, Baron Cromot Dubourg, and Comte de Barras de Saint-Laurent, who all arrived in Newport two days later on 10 May.

Baron Cromot Dubourg arrived to serve as one of Rochambeau's aides and was also a trained engineer and cartographer. The young vicomte de Rochambeau had returned after carrying out the mission that his father had sent him on from Newport to Paris and Versailles the previous October. He returned now with news that, even though no additional troops were to be sent, France was giving 6 million livres to the American cause, sending a convoy of 15 ships with supplies to Newport, and the comte de Grasse was en route to the West Indies with a squadron of 26 ships-of-the line that could be available for operations in North America in July or August. To the surprise and disappointment of Destouches, the comte de Barras had come to relieve him as *chef d'escadre*. De Barras, then 60 years old, was already familiar with Rhode Island waters, having commanded the *Zélé* under d'Estaing in 1778.

The official change of squadron command took place on 15 May, by which de Barras took overall command of the squadron in *Duc de Bourgogne* and Destouches resumed command of *Neptune* and his role as second in command of the squadron. De Barras immediately set to work preparing for operations. One of the first matters he had to deal with was the conference that Rochambeau had requested with Washington to discuss the operations for the coming campaign. The instructions that de Barras had brought from Paris had suggested that de Grasse would be available to come to Newport to support Rochambeau's army, leaving de Barras to carry out other operations that were useful for the allied cause, mentioning again the ideas that had risen a year before concerning possible operations in Canada against Halifax or Hudson's Bay. The conference was set to meet at Wethersfield, Connecticut, on 21–22 May, but with Arbuthnot's resumption of the blockade off Newport on 18 May and the imminent arrival of the convoy of supplies from France, de Barras chose not to travel to Wethersfield at the last minute.

The comte de Rochambeau and the marquis de Chastellux went from Newport for the meeting with Washington and two other Continental Army generals, Henry Knox and Louis Duportail. In order to maintain operational secrecy, Rochambeau had been instructed from Paris not to tell Washington that de Grasse was en route, but Washington had been secretly informed of it and pretended to Rochambeau during the conference that that he did not know about it. This counterproductive charade prevented serious discussion on coordinating the naval campaign; however, the commanders did agree on two important plans. First, they decided that Rochambeau's forces should march to join Washington's as soon as practicable and begin a campaign against New York City. At the same time, de Barras should move his squadron to Boston, leaving Newport to be defended by the Rhode Island militia, and then go on to undertake operations to the north.

Rochambeau and de Barras held a council of war on 30 May with all of the ships' captains and the senior army commanders. When it was over, they had unanimously agreed that de Barras' squadron should remain in Newport and not go to Boston. This surprising decision was contrary to both the agreement that Rochambeau had made with Washington, just over a week before, and the general intent of the instructions that de Barras had from Paris. While Newport Harbor remained a dangerous trap for a small fleet to be anchored in if an enemy forced its way into the harbor to attack, at the same time Newport was a strong place, when land and sea forces joined together in its defense.

In the light of these considerations of the broader strategic situation, de Barras believed that the squadron should remain at Newport until de Grasse's squadron arrived to conduct operations on the North American coast. Until then, de Barras could remain in a position that might deter the British from re-taking Newport, cover the rear of Rochambeau's march to New York, and be in an optimal position to support any operations needed in the Chesapeake Bay or New York areas. In contrast, Boston was much more difficult to use as a base for operations on the mid-Atlantic coast, although it was a safer harbor, in general, for the French and much more convenient for operations toward Canada and for communication with France.

At the urging of Rochambeau, de Barras called a second conference to confirm their earlier decision. On 8 June this council of war of naval and military commanders met on board *Neptune* and unanimously agreed that the squadron should remain in Newport.[35] On 11 June, Rochambeau's men began to leave Newport in small vessels and were ferried up Narragansett Bay to Providence, where they gathered and began their march to join Washington's army.

Sailing for Chesapeake Bay

In late July, both Rochambeau and Washington repeatedly urged de Barras to sail with the squadron from Newport, but de Barras resisted all their pleas, not wanting to leave Newport unguarded and reluctant to be at sea without having the overwhelming superiority that de Grasse's squadron would bring. Meanwhile at Cape François, de Grasse received the dispatches from Rochambeau and de Barras sent in the frigate *Concorde* on 16 July. After conferences there on Saint Domingue, de Grasse sent back his reply by the *Concorde* that he would sail for the North American coast on 13 August with 25 to 29 ships-of-the-line, 3,000 troops, and 1.2 million livres to support allied operations, but reported that he could only remain on that coast for a limited time and no later in the season than 15 October. In his dispatch, he reported that he would sail to Chesapeake Bay, as that was the place that Washington, Rochambeau, and de Barras had all mentioned as being the best place to have the optimal effect. De Grasse's letter also contained a request to de Barras to join him off the Chesapeake. *Concorde* arrived in Newport on 11 August with that dispatch and it was immediately sent on to Washington and Rochambeau by courier, arriving in their camp on 14 August.

At this point, Washington and Rochambeau were still examining the prospect of making an attack on New York. The news from de Grasse suddenly put the focus on Virginia and stressed the need to act quickly with de Grasse, during the short period that his forces would be available to directly assist allied forces in North America. However, de Barras was initially sensitive of his prestige and not inclined to serve under de Grasse, who until very recently had been junior to him. His immediate reaction was not to join with de Grasse, but to undertake his own independent expedition to Hudson's Bay, taking his own squadron and Rochambeau's troops from Newport with him.

On hearing this, both Rochambeau and Washington were deeply disturbed. Rochambeau was not able to give orders to de Barras, but Rochambeau did the next best thing by ordering the troops remaining in Newport to go nowhere other than Virginia. This had the intended effect and, along with a request from George Washington, de Barras again postponed his plans to take up La Pérouse's idea for the Hudson's Bay expedition, which eventually took place in 1782.

De Barras left Newport on 23 August 1781 with eight warships, four frigates, and eighteen transport ships loaded with the troops, military supplies, and siege equipment for the campaign in Virginia. This was only one, but an essential component, of the triple-pronged effort under way: de Grasse was bringing his forces from the West Indies, Washington and Rochambeau were marching overland with their troops from New York, and de Barras was coming from Newport with the artillery. All converged on Chesapeake Bay and British naval and military forces in that area. The particular focus was on General Lord Cornwallis's encampment on both sides of the York River, one on the Yorktown side, the other on the Gloucester side. Just to the west of them, at Williamsburg, Lafayette had made an encampment with his troops, blocking their escape by land from the Yorktown peninsula.

The details of the land battle are well known and have been carefully studied.[36] What a number of historians have not stressed is the importance of the interaction of the effects of the campaigns on land and on the sea at the strategic and operational levels. The initial idea conceived at Versailles and carried through by Rochambeau, de Ternay, Destouches, and de Barras to make certain that the *Expédition Particulière* of 1780–81 was both a joint and a combined operation was the key to its ultimate success.

NOTES This paper was presented at the "Colloque International Rochambeau" held at Vendôme, France, to
mark the bicentenary of the death of Jean-Baptiste-
Donatien de Vimeur, Comte de Rochambeau (1725–
1807). It was published in both French and English in
the *Bulletin de la Société archéologique, scientifique et
littéraire du Vendômois* (2008), pp. 66–80.

1 This paper presents a summary of the joint and
combined aspects found in John B. Hattendorf,
*Newport, the French Navy and the American Revolu-
tion* (Newport, RI: The Redwood Press, 2005).

2 Lee Kennett, *The French Forces in America, 1780–
1783* (Westport, CT: Greenwood Press, 1977), pp.
1–17.

3 Ibid.

4 Rémi Monaque, *Latouche-Tréville: L'amiral qui
défiait Nelson* (Paris: Éditions S.P.M., 2000), pp.
106–108. See also the work of Antoine Cathelineau
on editing the log of *Hermione* in Jean-Pierre Bois,
*Deux Voyages au temps de Louis XVI, 1777–1780: La
Mission du Baron de Tott en Égypte en 1777–1778 et
le Journal de bord de l'Hermione en 1780* (Rennes:
Presses Universitaires de Rennes, 2005), pp. 138–
142, 149–156.

5 Ibid., pp.178–179; Maurice Linÿer de la Barbée, *Le
Chevalier de Ternay* (Grenoble: Editions des 4
Seigneurs, 1972), vol. 2, pp. 591–592.

6 Henri Doniol, *Histoire de la Participation de la
France à l'Établissement des États-Unis d'Amérique.
Correspondance Diplomatique et Documents* (Paris:
Imprimerie Nationale, 1890), tome IV, pp. 316–317;
Bois, *Deux Voyages au temps de Louis XVI,* pp. 123–
124. The instruction reads: "The corps of French
troops will be purely auxiliary and as such will accept orders only from General Washington. The
French general on the scene will receive orders from
the American general in chief in everything not
touching upon the internal management of his
corps, which must be disciplined and governed according to the laws of its own country. It will be required of the [French] admiral to support with all
his power all operations in which his cooperation
can be claimed. It is well understood that due

attention will be paid to combining with him, concerting with him, and listening to objections that he may have.

"Operations necessarily depending on local circumstances and possibilities, we do not propose anything; it is for General Washington and his council of war to decide what will be most useful. All that the king desires is that his troops that he has sent to the aid of his allies, the United States, will cooperate effectively to deliver them once and for all from the yoke and the tyranny of the English."

7 Stanley J. Idzerda, ed., *Lafayette in the Age of the American Revolution: Selected Letters and Papers, 1776–1790* (Ithaca: Cornell University Press, 1977–1983), vol. 3, pp. 50–52: Vergennes to Lafayette, 3 June 1780.

8 Ibid., pp. 88–89: *General Washington's Memorandum for Concerting a Plan of Operations,* 15 July 1780.

9 See the map dated 12 July 1780 in Howard C. Rice, Jr., and Anne S. K. Brown, eds., *The American Campaigns of Rochambeau's Army 1780, 1781, 1782, 1783* (Providence, RI: Brown University Press, and Princeton: Princeton University Press, 1972), vol. 2, p. 125 with map 4.

10 A comparison of maps 4, 5, and 6 in ibid., with a modern street map of Newport seems to place the camp running across the island from somewhere near "The Elms," between modern Dixon Street and Parker Avenue and Narragansett Avenue. There is no known archaeological evidence that has yet clearly identified the exact location of the camp.

11 Ibid., see pp. 127–128 with map 5, and Linÿer de la Barbée, *Le Chevalier de Ternay,* vol. 2, pp. 594–595.

12 David Syrett, *The Royal Navy in American Waters, 1775–1783* (Aldershot: Scolar Press, 1989), pp. 144–149; Linÿer de la Barbée, *Le Chevalier de Ternay,* vol. 2, pp. 600–601; William B. Willcox, "Rhode Island in British Strategy, 1780–1781," *Journal of Modern History,* xvii, 4 (December 1945), pp. 304–331.

13 "Journal of Clermont-Crèvecoeur," in Rice and Brown, eds., *The American Campaigns of Rochambeau,* vol. 1, p. 18.

14 William B. Willcox, *The American Rebellion: Sir Henry Clinton's Narrative of his Campaigns, 1775–1782, with an Appendix of Documents* (New Haven: Yale University Press, 1954), p. 202.

15 Evelyn M. Acomb, ed., *The Revolutionary Journal of Baron Ludwig von Closen, 1780–1783* (Chapel Hill: The University of North Carolina Press for the Institute of Early American History and Culture at Williamsburg, Virginia, 1958), p. 31.

16 "Journal of Verger," in Rice and Brown, eds., *The American Campaigns of Rochambeau,* vol. 1, p. 120.

17 Idzerda, ed., *Lafayette in the Age of the American Revolution,* vol. 3, pp. 104–105: Rochambeau to Lafayette, 16 July 1780 and footnote 1 with excerpt from de Ternay's letter to Rochambeau of the same date; also, ibid., pp. 131–136: Lafayette to Rochambeau and de Ternay, 9 August 1780 with summary of discussions in Newport, 1–3 August.

18 "Summary of the Hartford Conference, 22 September 1780s" in Idzerda, ed., *Lafayette in the Age of the American Revolution,* vol. 3, pp. 175–176.

19 Ibid., pp. 175–178.

20 Ibid., pp. 176–177.

21 Archives Nationales, B4 183, fo. 63: de Ternay to Minister of the Navy, 18 October 1780.

22 "*[J]e vous avoue que j'ai été cruellement surpris d'y apprendre sa mort à la suite d'une maladie aussi courte et qui a tourné aussi tragiquement.*" Rochambeau to Washington, 19 December 1780 in Doniol, *Histoire,* vol. 5, p. 391.

23 Archives Nationales, Marine B4 191, fo. 184. Monaque, *Latouche-Tréville,* p. 123; Kennett, *The French Forces in America,* pp. 81, 84, 95.

24 "Verger Journal," in Rice and Brown, eds., *The American Campaigns of Rochambeau,* vol. 1, p. 126.

25 This wreck has been located and excavated.

26 Syrett, *The Royal Navy in American Waters,* p. 163.

27 Ibid. pp. 162–163.

28 Archives Nationales, Marine B4 191, fos. 13–17. Destouches to Minister of the Navy, 31 March 1781, Rice and Brown, eds., *The American Campaigns of Rochambeau,* vol. 1, pp. 23–24, 126, 240.

29 Syrett, *The Royal Navy in American Waters,* pp. 163–168.

30 Library of Congress, Miscellaneous Manuscripts: Destouches, Charles René Dominique Sochet, "Intelligence reports to Destouches on anchorage of English fleet at Gardiner's Island, with sketch charts, 1, 3, 6, and 16 February 1781."

31 Washington to Lafayette, 1 March 1781, in Idzerda, ed., *Lafayette in the Age of the American Revolution,* vol. 3, pp. 357–358.

32 Archives Nationales, Marine B4 191, fos. 13 – 17: Letter to Minister of the Navy, 31 March 1781; Kennett, *The French Forces in America,* p. 99; "Relation of the Sortie of the French Squadron," in Rice and Brown, eds., *The American Campaigns of Rochambeau,* vol. 1, pp. 126–129.

33 George R. Barnes and John Owen, eds., *The Private Papers of John, Earl of Sandwich, First Lord of the Admiralty, 1771–1782.* Publications of the Navy Records Society, vol. 78. (London: Navy Records Society, 1938), vol. 4, pp. 171-172: King George III to Sandwich, 24 April 1781.

34 Quoted in Rice and Brown, eds., *The American Campaigns of Rochambeau,* vol. 1, p. 129 footnote 33.

35 Jonathan R. Dull, *The French Navy and American Independence: A Study of Arms and Diplomacy, 1774–1787* (Princeton: Princeton University Press, 1975), p. 241; Kennett, *The French Forces in America,* p. 106.

36 Among the most recent works, see John D. Grainger, *The Battle of Yorktown, 1781: A Reassessment* (Woodbridge, UK: Boydell Press, 2005) and Richard M. Ketchum, *Victory at Yorktown: The Campaign That Won the Revolution* (Waterville, ME: Thorndike Press, 2005).

XIV Sea versus Shore
Amphibious Warfare, Theory, and the War of 1812

*A*dmirals, distinguished colleagues, ladies and gentlemen; I am honored to have been asked to deliver the closing remarks at this brilliantly organized and highly stimulating conference, "Naval Blockades and Amphibious Operations in the Wars of the Revolution and Empire (1793–1815)." My task here this evening is threefold: firstly, to provide some comments that may serve as a closing summary of the conference; secondly, to contribute to the proceedings by pointing out the experiences of blockades and amphibious assaults that occurred in North America during the Anglo-American War between 1812 and 1815; and thirdly, to try to outline the theories of blockade and amphibious assault as they may be relevant to the 1793–1815 period, particularly as they relate to the strategic level of defence against such operations. These are three large tasks that neither fit easily together nor are easily covered in the time available. Nevertheless, I shall make an attempt to carry out this assignment.*

All too often, naval historians have tended to be preoccupied by fleet battles and isolated ship-to-ship engagements rather than looking at other types of operations. In the wider range of naval operations, blockade and amphibious assault are two very important and fundamental types, yet both are among the most difficult and complicated to carry out. At the same time, when blockades and assaults are effectively carried out, they are also among the most difficult and complicated to defend against.

Naturally, these operations involve all the fundamental and typical aspects of the operational and tactical levels of any kind of warfare. In this regard, one must include such factors as leadership, training, organization, morale, and logistics as well as the capability and effectiveness of weapons and equipment. As in any naval operation, the fundamental factors surrounding capable navigation and seamanship in restricted waters, with the effects of tide, wind, weather, and sea conditions, are paramount concerns.

Beyond the fundamental range of skills needed to conduct naval operations successfully in open or restricted waters, an amphibious operation requires a range of specialized equipment, skills, and techniques applied in the context of particular types of information.[1] These include a relatively large number of boats that are suitable for transferring troops with all their weapons and equipment from large ships and safely landing them on an enemy shore. To do this successfully involves an effective organization and practiced methods for launching boats at sea to carry the men ashore. Before that can happen, however, the operation also involves accurate intelligence for selecting an enemy's relatively ineffectively defended landing areas that can be successfully approached in fully laden boats. As has also been pointed out during this conference during the discussions of the case of Sir John Moore's campaign and the subsequent withdrawal of 28,700 men from La Coruña in 1808, the reverse operation is equally important. It is not only the landing of troops that is important, but the ability and the organization to evacuate troops and their equipment from shore and to reembark them safely in ships.

Yet this is not all. In addition to studying the means, methods, and organization involved in such military and naval operations, it is also essential to understand the fundamental issues involving the capabilities of military and naval force to achieve the results that are anticipated. In some of the examples of amphibious operations discussed, there is a recurring theme, with participants in the various historical events having expectations of achieving a *"coup de main,"* making a knockout blow, or creating "shock and awe" by skillfully applying a relatively small amount of force that is expected to have a disproportionately large strategic or tactical result. However possible such effects might be, the probability and assessment of them involve calculations of risks and careful estimates of the broad situation in the context of an understanding of the limitations of military and naval power.

Blockade and Amphibious Operations in Theory

Blockade and amphibious operations are distinctive types of operations. In broad theoretical terms, blockade is an attempt to use one's armed vessels to control an opposing power's use of its warships or merchant vessels by using armed force either to immobilize an enemy's vessels in port, to restrict and police their cargos of particular commodities, or to prevent or supervise their passages to particular places. Thus, a blockade is a direct form of naval control over an opponent's maritime movements. In contrast, an amphibious assault is the use of ships to attack shore defences and, at the same time, to put ashore and sustain soldiers who are equipped to fight land battles against land defences and opposing land forces. Thus, an amphibious assault is an indirect method of operations that uses naval force to implement and facilitate military operations. It is designed to empower the use of the force that is put ashore so that it can control an opposing land force or land position.

Such enterprises are vastly different in terms of the conception, preparation, expertise, and equipment required. But despite these differences, they share some points in common. They can be separate operations, but they can also be associated and complementary in their uses. Both are naval operations that focus on relationships of naval forces to the shore. Both blockade and amphibious assault require an attacker to have local and temporary command of the sea, if not overall command, in order to maintain an effective blockade or to make and sustain an amphibious assault. In other words, the attacking or blockading naval forces need to be able to carry out these operations without substantial interference from the enemy on the open sea.

Types of Blockade in Theory

From the viewpoint of an attacking preponderant force, the imposition of a blockade on an opponent is an attempt to force that opponent to decide between two courses of action: (1) to accept the blockaders' control of passage and communication at sea or (2) to contest it by coming out to try to eliminate or evade the blockaders' control. This control by a blockading force may involve the control of passage in the local maritime area for immediate amphibious operations, or it may have broader implications in the control of trade and trade routes for the attack and defence of commerce, the control of passage and communication for distant expeditionary forces or the lines of communication for passage of an invading army.[2] In addition, blockade may be a form of control on one element of an enemy's naval forces in order to immobilize it and thus create an advantageous situation for oneself in an impending naval battle or operation against other elements of an enemy force.

As Sir Julian Corbett defined the subject, blockade can be subdivided into two broad categories: commercial blockade and naval blockade. Naval blockade can be further subcategorized into close and open blockades. The objective of close naval blockade is to close a port by immobilizing the warships within it and choking off their activity and military communications based from the port. This type of blockade is associated with securing local commands for the purpose of preventing opposing warships from operating in a particular area or undertaking particular operations, including launching a concurrent amphibious operation and conducting an invasion.

Close naval blockade has sometimes been linked with a subsidiary commercial blockade. In this connection, naval blockade has also been tied to using a subsidiary commercial blockade operation to provide a rationale for the enemy naval force to come out of port to defend its own commercial activity, and, thereby, to open itself to destruction in open battle from a preponderant blockading force. Any imposition of a close blockade involves intense naval operations in order to maintain a continuous, effective, direct, and immediate application of force that immobilizes the opposition for the period of time that the close blockade is in effect. In many cases, this means the employment of numerous heavily gunned ships in dangerous or restricted waters directly off an enemy's coast in a manner that requires high levels of risk, long periods of exhausting tension and readiness for officers and men, and extensive wear and tear on the blockading ships and their equipment. This form of blockade combines the requirements for intensity and skill in the conduct of operations with the need for a large number of ready reinforcements. Despite the dangers of exhaustion and the possibility of interruptions and dispersion of the blockading force in storms at sea, this high-level application of resources, both in terms of people and equipment, tended to produce a tactical situation that had the advantage in maintaining tough and highly skilled seamen who were ready on the spot in the most advantageous position to meet an enemy that was not tempered in such conditions of stress and strain. Close blockade is a forward and offensive operation with the negative object of preventing an enemy from taking action.[3]

The alternative form of naval blockade is traditionally called open blockade. The differences in the two forms lie both in their operational approaches and in their strategic purposes. The purpose of the open blockade is not to immobilize an enemy, but rather to lure him out of port, while watching and lying ready for the opportunity to bring heavy forces to engage and destroy the enemy force that puts to sea. The open form of blockade has the advantage of not requiring the same degree of intensity in high risk, pressure, and exhaustion. Thus, open blockade can conserve the fitness of human energy and equipment for the moment of battle, while at the same time giving an enemy opportunity to put to sea but in a position where he can be attacked advantageously before carrying out any other mission. This type of blockade has the additional advantage of the attacking fleet's occupying a more secure position, with concealed dispositions, where it may be able to use surprise with some effect.[4]

These strategic objects of naval blockade against warships need to be differentiated from that involved in commercial blockade. While the object of naval blockade is to establish initial control over and destruction of an opposing naval force, the object of commercial blockade is involved with the exercise of command of the sea after that command has been established. In controlling commercial traffic at sea, the issues revolve around how best to defend one's own trade or to attack an enemy's trade in relation to the transoceanic sea lanes—those common paths at sea that, in the age of sail, were dictated by currents, winds, and weather and were used to travel from one point on the globe to another. A commercial blockade may be undertaken as a form of economic warfare in which the strategic objective is to harm the enemy's economy to the extent that it hinders the opponent's general ability to conduct the war, affects the will of the enemy's population to support the war effort, or brings an enemy government to the negotiating table to resolve the international conflict at hand. In this dimension, the strategic effects of blockade are not direct and sequential but, rather, indirect and cumulative, requiring intense operations to put the blockade into effect but only slowly mounting in the effect created.[5]

The critical sea areas for both defence and attack of trade are those where merchant ships converge and congregate: ports of departure, ports of arrival, and the straits or narrow waters along their major routes. These areas are the places where attack can be most profitable and defence can be most easily established. These places pose the greatest risk and require greater degrees of force to attack or defend. British naval forces typically congregated in two battle squadrons for the protection of trade in the two key areas for British trade: one in the North Sea based on the Downs and, another, the "Western Squadron" based in Plymouth, supplemented with a cruiser squadron based in Cork in Ireland. The long open-transit areas in between these regions posed more uncertainty for an attacker's success but involved less risk and the use of less force to be successful. To deal with the open-ocean transit, a small number of smaller warships could safely convoy and protect merchant trade, while in the all-important coastal trades at home and overseas, smaller armed local vessels typically carried out this work. To supplement this, a system of British patrol lines was developed to connect the most important adjacent defended areas, such as that line of passage between the strategic center of gravity off Ushant and the Strait of Gibraltar, passing off French, Spanish, and Portuguese ports and the subsidiary focal sea areas off Cape Finisterre and Cape St. Vincent.[6]

The differing strategic functions involved in using warships for fleet battle, blockade, and protection of trade, as well as supporting expeditionary forces, amphibious landings, and overseas invasions, required an extensive expenditure of resources in differing regions that could produce an oscillation and imbalance in the distribution of available resources for the wide variety of purposes required and could produce an effect on British naval supremacy that an enemy could exploit. With that thought, one may turn to the other side of strategic consideration to look at the strategic issues from the point of view of an opponent and ask what options were available to a minor power trying to oppose and to defend itself against a preponderant naval power.

Opposing Defensive Strategies

Nearly a century ago, Sir Julian Corbett eloquently pointed out that "the normal condition in war is for the command of the sea to be in dispute."[7] An opposing power unable to win command of the sea through decisive operations in a fleet battle typically takes a generally defensive strategic stance; through this approach, it has the capability to hold command of the sea in dispute and is able to retain, to some extent, usage of the sea for its own purposes. A strategic defence is one that defers acquiescing to a decision over command of the sea, either temporarily or permanently, through tactically aggressive and highly mobile operations aimed at harassing the superior naval force, preventing it from attaining full control over sea passages and from achieving the full positive result it sought for its own aims. Similar to irregular guerrilla operations, this kind of defensive naval warfare is characterized by mobility, counterattack, and raids on momentary and convenient targets rather than targets of strategic gravity. It is an active hit-and-run strategy against maritime communications, whether on warships or merchant vessels.[8] And it could involve the complementary use of small squadrons of warships, individual warship actions, warships attacking trading vessels, and privateers attacking trade. A small naval force, while incapable of winning a decisive major fleet battle, could nevertheless, by remaining active and mobile, act as a "fleet in being" and retain maritime issues in dispute for as long as possible, even to the point of disputing local control of the sea to the degree that an amphibious landing could be too dangerous to undertake or a commercial blockade could be partially limited in its effect.

Defence against an amphibious landing involves a range of issues that those studying fleet naval operations may overlook. To make a successful amphibious attack, an attacking force must have a series of sequential successes before it can achieve its strategic objective in defeating an enemy's major land force. The attacking force must safely cross an ocean area to reach its landing area, have sufficient prior knowledge and intelligence about its landing area to select the appropriate site for landing, and then make the transition from ship to shore, resist all counterattacks, and move forward to achieve its strategic objective with appropriate supplies. A defending force needs to be successful against the attacker at only one of these points to achieve its objective of defence. A defending force has three basic options to consider: (1) naval defence at sea against an approaching invader; (2) defence at the water's edge where an invader is most vulnerable during the transition from ship to shore; and (3) a mobile military defence ashore against the force that has been landed.[9] These key points also apply to the defender who is attacking a withdrawing force during an opposed embarkation.

Unlike a confrontation to decide command of the sea, the key strategic element of the attacking force that a defender needs to concentrate upon is not the enemy's capital warships, but the accompanying transport ships carrying the troops of the invasion force. This may mean the interdiction of an attacking force at its place of embarkation or in the open ocean, or an attack against the ships when they are in restricted waters preparing to land, but in either case, the key target for the defensive attack is the transports, not the warships. This type of defence could be developed in cooperation with forces ashore, giving both intelligence of an impending attack and time to prepare land defences. In theory, such an arrangement allows for these two efforts to take place economically in ways that are complementary, do not compete for the same resources, and reduce the enemy's force in two separate phases. A weakness often encountered in such a defence was found in those afloat and those ashore working at cross-purposes to one another, unable to communicate in ways that allowed for detailed tactical coordination.[10]

If a naval defence is either absent or ineffective, the next strategic option for a defender is to attempt to defeat the assaulting force at the water's edge. This type of defence is one that holds an area of terrain to deny its use to the attacker. The main purpose is to defend a position, but, as a by-product of this, it could result in destroying the attacking force even though that is not the primary object to be achieved. The defenders of a shore area have the advantage of countering an amphibious assault at its most vulnerable phase in the transition from ship to shore, at a time where the shore defences can be carefully prepared and where there is less susceptibility to surprise and deception. The disadvantages to the defenders lie in the high cost of such defences and the inability to provide an equally strong defence at every possible landing point.[11]

A third option for defence is to bide one's time, allow the enemy force to land, using the time of landing to gather effective forces, and then use mobile forces to attack and destroy the invading forces after they are ashore. The advantage in this form of defence is that the defender can make the most efficient use of his soldiers and equipment by readily concentrating his forces at the decisive point while denying the attacker the ability to plan for the placement of supporting forces. However, the attacking, sea-based force has the distinct advantage of being more agile and mobile than the land-based defender and can choose its place of landing, easily making a feint to mislead the defenders into concentrating forces in the wrong place.[12]

The foregoing summation of theories about blockade and amphibious operations derives from a range of professional military and naval thinking during the later nineteenth and twentieth centuries, yet reflects on knowledge about these types of operations across a wide span of history. While the practitioners of blockade and amphibious assault would probably not have thought in these abstract terms during the years between 1793 and 1815, these thoughts still give us some starting points for coming to an interpretation of such activities in history, and they provide a framework as summary of our collaborative work in this conference.

In terms of the coverage of the conference, let me now turn from the general to the very specific. In doing so, I would like to make a small contribution toward including North American experience within the broader range of historical events mentioned here. Having looked at the range of strategic options available in theory, one is better prepared to examine and evaluate the specific strategic options available to a minor power faced with a superior naval power that was imposing a blockade and launching amphibious landings. In this, it is useful to think about the case of the United States of America in its concurrent war against the United Kingdom in 1812–1815 that overlapped with the Napoleonic Wars. In doing so, one needs to understand how the war began and what it was about.

American Strategy in the War of 1812
The War of 1812 presents the very odd situation of a minor country, largely unprepared for sustained military or naval operations, initiating a war against a major power. After considerable debate and discussion over several months, the Congress of the United States had repeatedly defeated bills to increase the size of the Navy, and its proposals to increase the American army remained largely unimplemented. Yet despite this, a majority of members of Congress proceeded to declare war against the United Kingdom on

18 June 1812. President James Madison had clearly based his recommendation for war on a series of long-standing grievances involving American neutral trade and maritime rights, as the young American republic found its commerce caught between the opposing positions of Napoléon's Berlin and Milan decrees and Britain's Orders in Council on wartime trade. In the United States, there was some discussion whether the enemy should be France or Britain, or both.[13] Congress failed to pass the bill to declare war against France by only two votes. Unaware that Britain had repealed the irritating Orders in Council, President James Madison urged war, but Congress only narrowly approved his war measure on 18 June 1812, getting support from the middle and southeastern states and strong opposition from New Jersey, New York, and the New England states. Although there had been strong words and enough political support to go to war against Britain, the country had made few practical preparations for it. Why the country went to war remains a topic of debate and involves a whole range of subsidiary issues, including American expansion into Florida.[14] In the end, the conflict was aptly characterized by one British army officer as "a species of Milito-Nautio-Guerilla-Plundering warfare."[15]

As war approached, the United States government needed to develop a strategy and to choose the weapons it had available to fight. At that point, the fledgling country had only sixteen available vessels, with five more "in ordinary," which needed repair before they could put to sea, along with 62 gunboats for local defence.[16] Meanwhile, the Royal Navy had 27 vessels assigned to the Leeward Islands station, 19 at Jamaica, and 25 on the North American station, with an additional 12 on the Newfoundland station.[17] With the United States Navy's limited resources, there is little wonder that there was no clear agreement on what sort of strategy it could or should employ.[18] The Navy's two senior naval officers disagreed; one thought that all the ships should be combined into a single squadron to search out and attack British trade, drawing ships off the American coast and evading a blockade "in a manner to astonish all Europe."[19] The other thought it wiser for the American warships to cruise against enemy commerce in pairs on distant stations as a means of relieving blockades at home by daring warships away from it.[20] In the end, the American deepwater warships were directed to protect American trade,[21] while gunboats remained the key element in naval defence—as Thomas Jefferson had suggested half a dozen years earlier, having in mind the ideas of Frederik af Chapman and Sweden's successful recent experience with gunboats to protect its coast from the Russians, and the contemporary experience of Denmark in its defence against Britain.[22]

Interestingly, a very early form of weapons innovation was rejected when in June 1812 Robert Fulton failed for the second time to interest the U.S. Navy in his invention of mines as a means to defend against blockade and amphibious assault.[23] Within a century, mines became a major means of defence against an amphibious landing as well as a means of both blockade and counterblockade.

Meanwhile, the tiny United States Navy succeeded in winning a number of single-ship encounters between frigates, which, if nothing more, provided inspiring accounts for American national morale. At the same time, it carried out a relatively successful privateering war on British trade,[24] while suffering some severe losses.

As the War of 1812 developed, it went through a series of stages. When one looks at this process today, one is reminded of the need to understand warfare as the interaction between two opponents, not merely to look at one side without noting reactions and results of actions taken. The initial British response to the American operations in November and December 1812 was to order "the most complete and vigorous Blockade of the Ports and Harbors of the Bay of the Chesapeake and of the River Delaware,"[25] focusing initially on the middle Atlantic coast of the United States and the water approaches to the national capital at Washington and the major ports of Baltimore and Philadelphia. The initial purpose was to establish a naval blockade of the American warships to prevent them from putting to sea, or, if they did venture out, to capture and destroy them completely. Unsuccessful in accomplishing this immediately, the Admiralty ordered additional reinforcements to North America, ordering the withdrawal of warships from other stations in order to build a force of 10 ships of the line, 30 frigates, and 50 sloops, as well as two battalions of Marines comprising 640 men each.[26] By March 1813, the plans for British strategy had grown from a naval blockade to a commercial blockade "of all the principal Ports in the United States to the southward of Rhode Island & Including the Mississippi."[27] Elaborating on his orders, the First Lord of the Admiralty privately wrote to Admiral Warren, declaring that "we do not intend this as a mere *paper* blockade, but as a complete stop to all trade & intercourse by Sea with those Ports, as far as wind & weather, & the continual presence of a sufficient armed Force will permit & ensure."[28] After receiving these orders, Warren publicly and formally proclaimed the blockade on 16 November 1813,[29] although he repeatedly complained that he had an inadequate force to carry out the blockade that the government in London intended.[30]

In addition to maritime blockade, British forces also initiated a policy of raiding the coast. In April 1814, an additional force of one thousand Marines was sent for this purpose, "as may be found most expedient for His Majesty's service and the annoyance of the enemy."[31] The Admiralty Secretary advised Sir Alexander Cochrane:

> Their Lordships entrust to your judgment the choice of objects on which you may employ this Force, the operations of which may be carried on against a maritime country like America with comparative ease and security, as it will rarely if ever be necessary to advance so far into the country as to risk its power of retreating to its embarkation. But it will naturally occur to you that on every account any attempts that should have the effect of crippling the Enemy's naval Force, should have a preference.[32]

By May 1814, the strategy of amphibious raiding was expanded to using the British army to make a military diversion on the coast of the United States as a means of supporting British military forces in the defence of Upper and Lower Canada. To undertake this, three infantry regiments with artillery were ordered from the Gironde, plus a company of artillery from the Mediterranean, along with an additional battalion of Marines.[33]

The effects of the British blockade on the United States have been the subject of some recent scholarly debate,[34] but for the purposes of this study the point is that Americans had few means at hand to counter directly with any significant force the blockade and amphibious raids. Blockade running was the main option, while troops ashore were often unable to concentrate quickly enough to have local superiority of force, as British forces were able to remain highly mobile, concentrating their forces to strike quickly and effectively on targets of opportunity.

One exception was the flotilla of specially designed gunboats that Captain Joshua Barney was able to organize to defend the Patuxent River estuary of Chesapeake Bay.

His force consisted of shallow-draft barges carrying oars, sails, and one long gun and, later, a carronade. Barney used his force in actions at Cedar Point and St. Leonard's Creek on the western Maryland shore, delaying and temporarily thwarting some British operations during June 1814, before it was eventually destroyed in August as British naval forces with 4,000 army troops moved on Washington and burned the capital city.[35]

Similarly, the five American gunboats under Lieutenant Thomas ap Catesby Jones were only able to momentarily delay the British landing on the shores of Lake Borgne east of New Orleans in late December 1814, while British warships on the Mississippi River fired heated cannon balls that ignited and destroyed American vessels on that approach to New Orleans. Otherwise unopposed, 5,300 British troops landed in early January 1815. Marching overland from Lake Borgne, the British force under General Sir Edward Pakenham and Major-General Sir John Lambert failed in its frontal assault on the American land defences. The British were unable to effect a coordinated movement on both banks of the river with the movement of their naval forces so that they could have flanked the American position. As a result, the British forces ashore were forced to withdraw with heavy casualties.[36]

Conclusion

The War of 1812 was in many ways "a pointless and costly war"[37] for both sides of the conflict and one that achieved little strategic effect by the clash of arms. Considering it on the basis of naval theory, the war seems to be an example in which the defenders were in no position to oppose a blockade or amphibious landings and in which the effectiveness of both types of operations was largely governed by the relative capabilities and skill of the attacking forces.

The conduct of the war did have significant and lasting side effects for the United States. Most significantly, it helped to solidify American national feeling and patriotism at a time in the early nineteenth century when those sentiments had waned. British blockade and amphibious operations played a major role in the creation of this sentiment, which arose as an American reaction against the damage to maritime trade, the loss of life, the destruction of personal property, and, in particular, the burning of Washington. The relatively minor successes of the American navy in the single-frigate actions were honored by subsequent generations as exemplary acts of naval skill and heroism and provided a solid basis of achievement upon which to construct a national naval heritage.

The experience of the War of 1812 had a direct effect on American defence policy for the next half-century and beyond. The war had exposed the failures and weaknesses of the country's defences and the need for new policies. As a result, the nation disengaged from European affairs and did not fight a major war for thirty years, focusing instead on its own economic development and westward territorial expansion. This brought a new and different role for the republic's navy. The war became a major impetus to the expansion of the United States Navy through the construction of new warships, including ships of the line, for its new peacetime roles of defending American neutral commerce, as well as to the reform of the deficiencies of internal organization and management that the war had demonstrated. In 1816, at President Madison's direction, the Navy Department established the Board of Naval Commissioners as a new reform measure to manage the Navy more effectively.[38] At the same time, the War Department established a board of officers to consider American defences in the light of recent war experiences.

While President Madison had initiated some of the new policies in his final year in office, the newly elected president of the United States, James Monroe, reaffirmed the way toward the county's future defence policy, while alluding to recent experience that all his auditors clearly understood, when he declared in his first inaugural address on 4 March 1817:

> To secure us against these dangers our coast and inland frontiers should be fortified, our Army and Navy, regulated upon just principles as to the force of each, be kept in perfect order, and our militia be placed on the best practicable footing. To put our extensive coast in such a state of defence as to secure our cities and interior from invasion will be attended with expense, but the work when finished will be permanent, and it is fair to presume that a single campaign of invasion by a naval force superior to our own, aided by a few thousand land troops, would expose us to greater expense, without taking into the estimate the loss of property and distress of our citizens, than would be sufficient for this great work. Our land and naval forces should be moderate, but adequate to the necessary purposes—the former to garrison and preserve our fortifications and to meet the first invasions of a foreign foe, and, while constituting the elements of a greater force, to preserve the science as well as all the necessary implements of war in a state to be brought into activity in the event of war; the latter, retained within the limits proper in a state of peace, might aid in maintaining the neutrality of the United States with dignity in the wars of other powers and in saving the property of their citizens from spoliation. In time of war, with the enlargement of which the great naval resources of the country render it susceptible, and which should be duly fostered in time of peace, it would contribute essentially, both as an auxiliary of defence and as a powerful engine of annoyance, to diminish the calamities of war and to bring the war to a speedy and honorable termination.[39]

Coastal fortifications to defend against amphibious landings became the key to a truly integrated system of defence, using the latest ideas that had come from European experience during the Napoleonic Wars. On the recommendation of the Marquis de Lafayette, the United States obtained the services of a French military engineer, Simon Bernard, who was a graduate of the *École Polytechnique* and had served with distinction as a brigadier under Napoléon. Commissioned as brevet brigadier in the United States Army, Bernard joined two other American military engineers, Lieutenant Colonel Joseph G. Totten and naval officer Captain J. D. Elliott, as a board on coast defence. This board reported to Congress with a detailed plan in 1821 and again in 1826; both plans were implemented. These plans for defence, which became known as the Third System, involved "first, a navy; second, fortification; third, interior communications by land and water; and fourth, a regular army and well-organized militia."[40] Under this plan, forty-two forts were newly constructed, with a series of subsidiary batteries, towers, and other works.[41]

A tangible legacy of the experience of blockade and amphibious operations during the War of 1812 and, indeed, the legacy of the general experience of these operations in European warfare during the period between 1793 and 1815 may still be seen in numerous places on the American coast in the form of the massive, still surviving but now disused, fortifications that were built on the Third System. They stand today on waterfront parks as museums; as large but silent and sometimes forgotten symbols that the effect of military and naval operations may not necessarily be confined to the professional military sphere or to the strategy of the war in which they occurred. Such experiences can have unexpected and very long-lasting effects on future national policy and the collective memory of a nation. At the same time, these structures can be interpreted as the early-nineteenth-century American application of the "lessons learned" from contemplating the theory and practice of blockade and amphibious operations between 1793 and 1815.

NOTES This paper was presented as the closing remarks and conference summary for an international conference organized by the Instituto de Historia y Cultura Naval, Madrid-Ferrol, and the Instituto de Historia, CSIC, Madrid, held at Ferrol, Spain, 4–7 July 2007 and titled "Naval Blockades and Amphibious Operations in the Wars of the Revolution and Empire (1793–1815)." It was published in Spanish as "El mar frente a la costa en la teoría y la praxis: la guerra de 1812," in A. Guimerá Ravina and Jose Mariá Blanco Núñez (coords.), *Guerra Naval en la Revolución y el Imperio: bloqueos y operaciones anfibias, 1793–1815.* (Madrid: Marcial Pons Historia, 2008), pp. 405–425.

1 For elucidation of this point, see the general works on amphibious operations, e.g., beginning with Thomas Molyneux, *Conjunct Operations, or Expeditions That Have Been Carried Out Jointly by the Fleet and the Army* (London: printed for R. and J. Dodsley, 1759); Sir Charles Callwell, *Military Operations and Maritime Preponderance: Their Relations and Interdependence,* with an Introduction and Notes by Colin S. Gray (Annapolis: Naval Institute Press, 1996); Ian Speller and Christopher Tuck, *Amphibious Warfare: Strategy and Tactics* (Staplehurst: Spellmount, 2001); T. T. A. Lovering, *Amphibious Assault: Manoeuvre from the Sea: Amphibious Operations from the Last Century* ([Great Britain]: Royal Navy, 2005).

2 Julian S. Corbett, *Some Principles of Maritime Strategy,* with an Introduction and Notes by Eric J. Grove, Classics of Sea Power series (Annapolis: Naval Institute Press, and London: Brassey's Defence, 1988), p. 165. For broad overviews of these topics, see also Eric J. Grove, "Blockade," and Richard Harding, "Amphibious Operations," in *The Oxford Encyclopedia of Maritime History,* ed. John B. Hattendorf (Oxford: Oxford University Press, 2007); e-reference edition, http://www.oxford-maritimehistory.com.

3 Corbett, pp. 184–89, 197–208.

4 Ibid.

5 For a summary of economic effect, see Lance E. Davis and Stanley L. Engerman, *Naval Blockades in Peace and War: An Economic History since 1750* (Cambridge: Cambridge University Press, 2006).

6 Corbett, pp. 261–79.

7 Corbett, p. 209.

8 Corbett, pp. 210–12.

9 Theodore L. Gatchel, *At the Water's Edge: Defending Against the Modern Amphibious Assault* (Annapolis: Naval Institute Press, 1996), pp. 2, 8.

10 Ibid, p. 3.

11 Ibid, pp. 3–4.

12 Ibid, pp. 4–6.

13 On this, see Peter P. Hill, *Napoleon's Troublesome Americans: Franco-American Relations, 1804–1815* (Washington, DC: Potomac Books, 2005), pp. 175–87.

14 See James G. Cusik, *The Other War of 1812: The Patriot War and the American Invasion of Spanish East Florida* (Gainesville: University Press of Florida, 2003).

15 Quoted by C. J. Bartlett and Gene A. Smith as the title of their essay in *Britain and America Go to War: The Impact of War and Warfare in Anglo-America, 1754–1815,* ed. Julie Flavell and Stephen Conway (Gainesville: University Press of Florida, 2004), pp. 173–204, from *The Autobiography of Lieutenant-General Sir Henry Smith,* ed. G. C. Moore (London, 1901), pp. 200–01.

16 William S. Dudley and Michael J. Crawford, eds., *The Naval War of 1812: A Documentary History* (Washington: Naval Historical Center, 1985–), vol. 1, pp. 53–62: Secretary of the Navy to Chairman, Naval Committee, 3 December 1811.

17 Ibid., pp. 180–82: Ships in Sea Pay, 1 July 1812.

18 Linda Maloney, "The War of 1812: What Role for Sea Power," in *In Peace and War: Interpretations of American Naval History, 1775–1984,* ed. Kenneth J. Hagan, 2nd ed. (Westport, CT: Greenwood Press, 1984), pp. 46–62.

19 Dudley and Crawford, eds., vol. 1, p. 120: Capt. John Rodgers to Secretary of the Navy, 3 June 1812.

20 Ibid., vol. 1, pp. 122–23: Capt. Stephen Decatur to Secretary of the Navy, 8 June 1812.

21 Ibid., vol. 1, pp. 147–49: Secretary of the Navy to Capt. John Rodgers, 22 June 1812.

22 Ibid., vol. 1, pp. 12–15: Thomas Jefferson's message to Congress, 10 February 1812. See also Gene A. Smith, *For the Purposes of Defence: The Politics of the Jeffersonian Gunboat Program* (Newark: University of Delaware Press; London and Cranbury, NJ: Associated University Presses, 1995). On Swedish experience and influence with gunboats, see Daniel H. Harris, *F. H. Chapman: The First Naval Architect and His Work* (Annapolis: Naval Institute Press, 1989), pp. 45–48; Ulf Sundberg, "Strid in skärgård," in *Skärgårdsflottan: uppbyggnad, militär användning och förankring i det svenska samhället. 1700–1824,* ed. Hans Norman (Lund: Historiska Media, 2000), pp. 117–34.

23 Dudley and Crawford, eds., vol. 1, pp. 145–47: Robert Fulton to Secretary of the Navy, 22 June 1812.

24 For a study of the motivating financial aspects behind these American operations, see the case study on Baltimore by Jerome R. Garitee, *The Republic's Private Navy: The American Privateering Business as Practiced by Baltimore during the War of 1812* (Middletown, CT: Wesleyan University Press for Mystic Seaport, 1977).

25 Dudley and Crawford, eds., vol. 1, pp. 633–34: Admiralty to Admiral Sir John Borlase Warren, 26 December 1812.

26 Dudley and Crawford, eds., *The Naval War of 1812: A Documentary History,* vol. 2, pp. 14–15: Admiralty Secretary John W. Croker to Admiral Sir John Borlase Warren, 9 January 1813.

27 Ibid., pp. 78–79: Private letter from the First Lord of the Admiralty Viscount Saunders to Admiral Sir John Borlase Warren, 26 March 1813. The separate Admiralty order of the same date specified the ports of New York, Charleston, Port Royal, Savannah, and the Mississippi River mouth.

28 Ibid.

29 Ibid., pp. 262–63: Warren to Admiralty Secretary Croker, 20 November 1813.

30 Ibid., pp. 307–08: Warren to Admiralty Secretary Croker, 30 December 1813.

31 Dudley and Crawford, eds., *The Naval War of 1812: A Documentary History,* vol. 3, pp. 70–71: Croker to Vice Admiral Sir Alexander Cochrane, 4 April 1814.

32 Ibid.

33 Ibid., pp. 72–74: Secretary of State for War Lord Bathurst to Major-General Edward Barnes, 20 May 1814.

34 See, for example, Wade G. Dudley, "The Flawed British Blockade, 1812–15," in *Naval Blockades and Seapower: Strategies and Counter-strategies, 1805–2005,* ed. Bruce A. Elleman and S. C. M. Paine (London and New York: Routledge, 2006), pp. 34–45, 275; Davis and Engerman, pp. 94–108; Brian Arthur, "The Role of the Blockade in the Anglo-American Naval War of 1812–1814" (MA thesis in Maritime History, academic year 2001–2002, Greenwich Maritime Institute, University of Greenwich, UK).

35 Christine F. Hughes, "Joshua Barney: Citizen Soldier," in *Against All Odds: U.S. Sailors in the War of 1812,* ed. Charles E. Brodine, Jr., Michael J. Crawford, and Christine Hughes (Washington, DC: Naval Historical Center, 2004), pp. 34–52. See also Louis Arthur Norton, *Joshua Barney: Hero of the Revolution and 1812* (Annapolis: Naval Institute Press, 2000), pp. 168–90; Craig L. Symonds, *The Naval Institute Historical Atlas of the U.S. Navy* (Annapolis: Naval Institute Press, 1995), pp. 50–51; Roger Morriss, *Cockburn and the British Navy in Transition: Admiral Sir George Cockburn, 1772–1853* (Exeter: University of Exeter Press, 1997), pp. 96–114.

36 Gene A. Smith, *Thomas ap Catesby Jones: Commodore of Manifest Destiny* (Annapolis: Naval Institute Press, 2000), pp. 25–32; Symonds, pp. 54–55. Gene A. Smith, ed., *A British Eyewitness at the Battle of New Orleans: The Memoir of Royal Navy Admiral Robert Aitchison, 1808–1827* (New Orleans, LA: Historic New Orleans Collection, 2004).

37 N. A. M. Rodger, *The Command of the Ocean: A Naval History of Britain, 1649–1815* (London: Allen Lane, 2004), p. 572.

38 John H. Schroeder, *Commodore John Rodgers: Paragon of the Early American Navy* (Gainesville: University Press of Florida, 2006), pp. 143–63.

39 James Monroe, First Inaugural Address, 4 March 1817, available at http://www.bartleby.com/124/pres20.html, accessed 29 June 2007.

40 Quoted in "Permanent Fortifications and Sea-Coast Defences," House of Representatives, 37th Congress, 2nd sess., 23 April 1862, Report No. 86, p. 3. The report also contains numerous references to actions in the French Revolutionary Wars and Napoleonic Wars, 1793–1815, as justification for the building of this defensive system.

41 For the overall history of American coastal defence, see Robert S. Browning III, *Two If by Sea: The Development of American Defence Policy,* Contributions in Military History, no. 33 (Westport, CT: Greenwood Press, 1983), and Emmanuel Raymond Lewis, *Seacoast Fortifications of the United States: An Introductory History* (Washington, DC: Smithsonian Institution, 1970). For a detailed history of the Third System, see John R. Weaver III, *A Legacy in Brick and Stone: American Coastal Defence Forts of the Third System, 1816–1867* (Missoula, MT: Redoubt Publishing, 2001); and for the history of one of the largest forts in the Third System, see Theodore L. Gatchel, "Fort Adams and the Defences of Narragansett Bay," *Newport History,* vol. 67, Part I, no. 230 (Summer 1995), pp. 1–35.

XV   *The U.S. Navy's Nineteenth-Century Forward Stations*

Historically, nations have had three fundamental choices in distributing ships to position a navy. First, they can keep ships in reserve, in port and in various states of readiness to go to sea and respond to situations when they may be needed. Secondly, they can maintain a substantial portion of their ships constantly in a state of operational readiness, cruising in local and home waters, but based on a domestic homeport and capable of moving to a distant area immediately on call. In this option, one does not maintain a presence beyond the endurance of a single ship or squadron. Finally, a nation can maintain ships in foreign waters on a long-term basis, using foreign or colonial overseas bases and rotating vessels to those positions. With this option, one maintains vessels in a distant region in a constant state of operational readiness. There are a variety of options between these three fundamental choices, as well as the option to use several choices simultaneously and in variable proportions. In order to evaluate the United States Navy's choices in maintaining a portion of its ships on forward stations during the nineteenth century, one needs to understand the context in which the Navy operated and what the country was trying to achieve by doing this.

Throughout the nineteenth century, the United States and its Navy could be characterized as a small power, but one that rose to medium-power status by the end of the century. The United States Navy was established in 1794 in the context of the wars of the French Revolution and Napoleon's Empire. In the 1780s, the young republic had sought to reconcile its differences with England and, after the War of Independence, the Continental Navy had been disbanded. Many Americans fervently hoped that they could live peacefully on their distant continent, without such expensive and entangling appendages as a navy or an army capable of expeditionary warfare. However, the European war that began in 1793 placed America in a difficult position. Not only were there differing interpretations between the British and American viewpoints on the terms of the peace that had created American independence, but American reconciliation with Britain created stress with America's first ally, France. As the character of French government and policy rapidly changed after 1789, America soon found that France threatened its neutral trade with Britain and British possessions, at the same time that Britain threatened American trade with France and even went further to impress seamen from vessels under the American flag. Nearly simultaneously, a new and separate threat appeared for American trade—although a long-standing one for European powers—the operations of the corsairs from North African ports.

As such threats began to become apparent at the close of the year 1793, President George Washington told Congress in his State of the Union address:

> The United States ought not to indulge a persuasion that, contrary to the order of human events, they will forever keep at a distance those painful appeals to arms with which the history of every other nation abounds. If we desire to avoid insult, we must be ready to repel it; if we desire to secure peace, one of the most powerful instruments of our rising prosperity, it must be known that we are at all times ready for war.[1]

Such steps as George Washington recommended were not to be taken lightly, or for that matter easily, but as they did develop in the following years, they were formed within the context of two broad situations. On the one hand, there was the external structure of international relations, within which America lived and which affected security at sea. On the other hand, there were the internal forces in domestic politics that created and sustained national policy and defense strategy, including those that related to the Navy.

The Structure of International Security at Sea

It has been natural enough that the conventional approach to American naval history has tended to focus on the actions of American naval officers and to look at American policy from an internal perspective. Americans have always been rightly proud of the successes their small navy had against the largest navy of the day and the role that sailors played in helping to deliver and to maintain American independence. But this focus has tended to ignore the larger fact that, despite these victories, it was Britain's Royal Navy that dominated the world's seas throughout the nineteenth century and the United States Navy, as well as the country's merchant trade, operated at sea within the structures that Britain's more powerful maritime presence created. Having said this, however, it is important to point out that British maritime dominance had its own fluctuations and changing character in that same century, which had both direct and indirect influences on the American Navy.

Most assuredly, France set out a great challenge to British maritime supremacy in the opening years of the century, at least until Trafalgar, but even in the decade of war after that great battle, the potential for French action at sea remained a serious strategic consideration.[2] This was one situation that James Madison and his administration attempted to exploit as they went to war with Britain in 1812, while the Royal Navy and the British Army were preoccupied with operations in the Iberian Peninsula. When that distraction was removed, the Royal Navy had no such restraint and America felt that change, both at sea and ashore.

The period from 1815 to the late 1840s was the central years for the period that was later named the *Pax Britannica*. At this point, the Royal Navy was the world's preeminent naval power, despite the fact that it had declined from its wartime strength of 230 major ships, including frigates, in 1814, to 49 in 1820, then rose to 54 by 1838. Of these, 99 were in commission in 1814, while there were only 23 in 1838.[3] In the same span of years, naval expenditures dropped in half from £9.5 million in 1816 to £6 million the following year, falling even further to £4.5 million in 1834, but rising in 1840 by one million from that low, but still costing only 11% of government expenditures.[4]

These years were a period when there were no major competitors at sea and Britain could afford to trim her Navy. Yet, given the situation, the Royal Navy still remained supreme at sea, seconded by a string of garrisons at colonies around the world. Despite such drastic cuts in absolute numbers, in relative terms, the Navy remained extremely effective and continued its world-wide presence. It could remain effective, with no serious adversary in sight and its largest ships in reserve, while smaller ships could carry weight to deter any minor power from interfering with trade and the Royal Navy could still appear at the right moment off shore to demonstrate the seriousness of British interest and to act as a catalyst for the diplomatic resolution of issues. In that period, any major threat to British supremacy could only come from another European power; therefore, in the event of war, the security of her empire lay in blockading or defeating any possible major enemy in European waters, thereby limiting the threats to her global interests.

British naval superiority involved an essentially deterrent strategy tied to maintaining global stability and peace. The world accepted British dominance and the Royal Navy's global policing role, while British industrial capacity remained supreme, and her government maintained a peaceful approach to global trading relations. In these years, other nations were unwilling to contest British naval supremacy.[5]

When threats of revived French power arose from the late 1840s and the European diplomatic situation became troubled after 1848, the home government in London began increasingly to encourage colonial governments to take more responsibility for their internal and regional security, bringing home both soldiers and ships from distant stations for home defense, while concentrating resources on maintaining the security of the high seas.

Twenty years later, the widespread appearance of the new technology of steam powered warships contributed to making a fundamental change to naval strategic thinking. From the 1860s, British naval policy began to change with the creation of "flying squadrons," groups of relatively larger warships that operated together on a distant station rather than the collection of small vessels that operated independently. From the 1879 Royal Commission of Colonial Defence to the end of the century, a new pattern began to emerge for British naval power, as the government in London developed a global system of imperial defense based around a system of defended coaling stations that provided comprehensive logistical support to these forward-deployed naval squadrons, whose prime goal was to maintain the safety of the sea lines of communication for a maritime trade that was truly vital to Britain.[6]

This new approach combined both colonial contributions with thoughts of centralized command that eventually and hesitantly led to the establishment of a Committee of Imperial Defence in 1902. The British system of overseas stations remained in effect through the final years of the nineteenth century, when Germany initially launched a direct challenge and until Admiral Sir John Fisher redistributed the fleet in 1904 and 1907, bringing in an entirely new approach.[7]

Throughout the nineteenth century, British maritime superiority was a political and naval fact. Its importance in considering the role of the U.S. Navy's deployments to distant stations is fundamental, for the country's tacit acceptance of it entirely removed from consideration any need for the United States to be seriously concerned with global maritime security. Unless one had the capacity and sufficient reason to challenge that regime that was a matter more prudently left to those with the capability and the interest to do so. So it was for the United States in the nineteenth century. Freed from this burden, the U.S. Navy could concentrate on a more select range of tasks. What it could and did do was bounded, by both its capabilities and interests, as well as the political compromises necessary in the creation of practical naval policy and strategy.

Domestic Politics and Naval Policy and Strategy

A casual glance at the chronology of American naval history during the nineteenth century reveals that the U.S. Navy fought in nine wars, yet that number of wars accounted for only a fifth of the century, twenty out of a hundred years. The names and dates of the naval wars are well known. The Quasi-War with France in 1798–1800 was just ending as the century began, but it was quickly followed by the First Barbary War with Tripoli in 1801–1805, the War of 1812–15 with Britian, the Second Barbary with Algeria in 1815, the Seminole War of 1839–42, the Mexican-American War of 1846–48, the Civil War of 1861–65, the Spanish-American War of 1898, and the Philippine Insurrection of 1899–1900.

The first of these wars were the ones that drew the newly formed United States Navy out into distant waters. The conflict with France was largely concentrated in the West Indies and drew American naval forces in that direction, but that region was not the only concern. On 6 January 1800, the frigate *Essex,* Captain Edward Preble, sailed from New York to convoy American ships returning from the Dutch East Indies. She was the first American man of war to double the Cape of Good Hope and she spent two months on patrol in the Sunda Strait during that cruise.[8] Returning at the end of the year, *Essex,* under her new commander, Captain William Bainbridge, was ready to sail the following year with Commodore Richard Dale's squadron to the Mediterranean.[9]

Just as Preble was sailing for the Far East, Secretary of the Navy Benjamin Stoddert reported to Congress, "It was not be expected that such a Navy as could be created in little more than a year could afford compleat protection to a foreign commerce, more extensive than that of any other Nation, one only excepted." More specifically, he said,

> The first object of the President's attention has been the security of our own Coasts, the second the protection of that portion of our trade, which is at once the most important to the whole community and most in our power to defend—and although late efforts have been made, and no doubt will be repeated to give aid to some Commercial enterprise to more distant regions, yet our trade beyond the limits of the American seas, can only receive very partial assistance from our present force.[10]

Concluding his report, Stoddert noted, "On the American Continent we cannot have an enemy to excite serious apprehensions—In this particular we have nearly all the advantages of an Island & require the same kind of defence—It is from the European World that danger must come—A Navy alone can arrest it on its passage."[11]

To those of us closely associated with the modern Navy, such remarks seem to hint at an unusual and early strategic insight, but they were not made in an academic setting, but rather in the context of political debate and in light of current resources. In 1799, with an active conflict at sea with France, the Federalists had been able to pass an act to increase the size of the Navy, but the country's resources were limited. There were severe financial limitations, but even if there had been money, there was a serious shortage of seasoned shipbuilding timber that prevented building more ships.

The political exchanges that took place over these issues clarified the differing views between political groups about the character and function of American naval force. While the exigencies of the moment favored naval growth, the political pendulum would quickly turn against it. While one side promoted the idea that a navy could protect commerce, its political opponents argued that this idea was based on fallacious reasoning and a navy was an unnecessary expense when there was no threat of a direct invasion and would merely entangle the country in European power politics.[12] While French depredations on American trade had momentarily turned the political balance, the lingering war was detrimental in the election of 1800, and John Adams narrowly lost to Thomas Jefferson. The news that Napoleon had agreed to end the war arrived in Washington in November 1800, justifying Adams's policy, but it came too late to help Adams in the election. Then, for the second time in what became a characteristic pattern in American history, the political forces declined that supported maintenance of the active Army and the Navy. Nevertheless, in a final move at the very end of John Adams's presidential term in March 1801, the outgoing Congress passed a Peace Establishment Act, generally reducing the naval force, but requiring that six frigates remain in constant service. This provision prevented the Navy from being laid up completely and provided the first and necessary step upon which forward deployment in peacetime could occur.[13] In passing this act, Congress clearly based its decision on Secretary Stoddert's January 1801 recommendations to Congress on the responsible ways in which Congress could provide for a peacetime naval establishment, keeping the most effective vessels, laying up the large ships not needed in peacetime, and selling those not designed for a long life.[14]

While naval historians have traditionally criticized Thomas Jefferson's administration for depending too much on the construction of small gunboats in coastal waters,[15] it should be pointed out that one of Jefferson's early acts as president was to send the squadron to the Mediterranean and he consistently supported its presence in operations against the North African corsairs. As recent scholarship has shown, the shallow-water capabilities that the gunboats provided were an important advantage, but they were not intended to be a substitute for a seagoing fleet, but rather only one element in a multiple-faceted and inter-linked defense system of permanent coastal fortifications, seagoing ships, various types of floating batteries, gunboats, and militia defenses.[16]

In the context of this and the passage of the Peace Establishment Act earlier in the year, the Jefferson administration first laid down the concept that was later echoed in the orders to commanders on forward-deployed stations for years to come. In this instance, the Acting Secretary of the Navy, General Samuel Smith, the brother of incoming Secretary Robert Smith, wrote to Commodore Thomas Truxtun, who was first intended to command in the Mediterranean, stressing the inter-linked points of training, protection of commerce, and rotating ships to maintain constant presence. Samuel Smith wrote:

> The object of the Squadron are Instruction to our Young officers & to carry into Execution the Law fixing the Peace Establishment of the U.S. It is conceived also that such a squadron Cruizing in view of the Barbary Powers will have a tendency to prevent them from seizing on our Commerce, when ever passion or a desire for Plunder might Intice them thereto.
>
> The Intention is to divide the Peace Establishment into 2 Squadrons the second to relieve the present squadron & thus alternately to keep a force of that kind in the Mediterranean.[17]

The orders that were repeated to Dale elaborated on this basic concept, stressing in particular the point that "one great object of the present squadron is to instruct our young officers in nautical knowledge generally, but particularly in the Shores and Coasts where you cruise."[18]

These initial plans for a forward station in peacetime were quickly obscured when it became necessary to carry out the contingency plan that was part of his orders and to be used should the Barbary powers declare war on the United States. When this happened, he was "to protect our commerce and chastise their insolence; by sinking, burning or destroying their Ships & Vessels."[19]

When the war was concluded in 1805, the American policy of maintaining a squadron forward deployed in the Mediterranean remained. The orders to Commodore James Barron in 1807 echoed the original concept:

> Being at Peace with all the world, our principal objects in sending publick vessels of War into the Mediterranean are: to protect our commerce and seamen against the predatory dispositions of the Barbary Powers; to keep them at peace with us, by a conciliatory deportment, and by displaying a force at all times prepared to protect our commerce; and to exercise our officers in the practical duties of their profession. These are justly considered interesting national objects.[20]

The War of 1812 forced withdrawal of American ships from the Mediterranean, but immediately upon its completion the American government revived its policy and laid plans to send squadrons under Decatur and Bainbridge to the Mediterranean, as another of the Barbary states, Algiers, became a threat to the safety of American commerce. The situation, however, was of such gravity that the United States alone could not deal with it during its operations in 1815. In the following year, following the failure of diplomatic negotiations to persuade Algiers to abolish Christian slavery, a combined Anglo-Dutch squadron under the command of Admiral Sir Edward Pellew bombarded the city and forced the Dey of Algiers to come to terms.[21] Even this, however, did not fully eradicate the problem. It eventually took a French expedition in 1830 to depose the Dey and to establish Algeria as a French colony, a solution that created a different, long-term problem. Up until 1830, the potential threat of attack from Algiers on American shipping remained a key motivating force for the presence of the American Squadron in the Mediterranean.

Meanwhile, the idea of having the Navy operate on forward stations began to become permanently imbedded in American naval thinking, but not without a major change in domestic politics that provided the tolls to do so. The 1816 Act for the Gradual Increase of the Navy of the United States was a complete, but temporary, reversal of previous policy and provided for the construction of major ships of the line and even such technological advanced ideas as "steam batteries." While authorizing large warships, it left the functions of those ships to the discretion of the president, a function that was never fully clarified or implemented.[22] The actions of Congress in the following decade tended to the reverse, and required the Navy to provide smaller vessels. By the end of the 1820s, it was clear that the larger warships contemplated were too expensive to build and to maintain as well as unnecessary for the country's needs. As Andrew Jackson stated in his inaugural address in 1829, the country had "need of no more ships of war than are requisite to the protection of commerce."[23]

This fundamental resolution of the issue, which remained the guiding principle of American naval policy until the very end of the century, was clearly reflected in the manner and purpose for which forward stations were established in the years that followed. In 1818, Captain John Downes in USS *Macedonian* inaugurated the Pacific station, with orders to protect American commercial interests along the western coast of South America.[24] In the decade that followed, the squadron on this station ranged in size from one to three ships. Its central achievement in this period was effectively to preserve American interests and to maintain the American policy of neutrality, keeping Americans out of the Latin American wars of independence, even though Americans privately tended to favor the South American rebels and patriots and criticized the royalists. In this, American naval forces were key to observing neutrality over a long number of years, while also liberating many Americans citizens from prison and saving American commercial property from expropriation by the warring factions.[25]

Similar in its basic rationale, a continuous naval presence was established with the designation of the West Indies station in 1822 for the specific function of serving on anti-piracy duty. To deal specifically with the threat that Cuban pirates presented, a specially designed force was necessary. Additional small forces were authorized by Congress to provide

> against every contingency that can possibly arise: for while the larger vessels, singly, will be more than a match for any force that the pirates can unite against them; the light schooners, or the steam boat and cutters when united will not only be superior to any number of piratical which it will be in the power of those lawless wretches to assemble at one point, but at the same time, from their light draft of water and peculiar construction, have it in their power to pursue them, without risk, in the most advantageous manner, into every creek and inlet, where they might attempt to seek refuge.[26]

In undertaking this duty, the Royal Navy also was involved in parallel operations dealing with the Cuban pirates, which indirectly helped to support the U.S. Navy's own operations.[27]

Similarly, protection of American trade and business required a naval presence in the South Atlantic. The immediate cause for creating a station there came in 1826, with the outbreak of war between Brazil and the United Provinces of La Plata. As both sides commissioned privateers, American merchants feared that their trade was in danger as it passed close to the seat of war. The issue was not just Brazil but the strategic location of Brazil astride the trade routes to South America, to the India Ocean and to China.[28]

By 1835, similar issues arose in the Far East. Congressional concern for the protection of America's booming maritime commerce, then second only in tonnage to that of Great Britain, led to authorization for the establishment of a new permanent station. The concern was justified when several American seamen were killed and wounded aboard the merchant ship *Eclipse,* and parts of its cargo stolen, in Sumatra. This incident led to the American warships on the station bombarding the villages of Quallah Batu and Mukkee on Sumatra, beginning on Christmas Day 1838.[29] The next concern was the series of incidents that led to the outbreak of the Anglo-Chinese Opium War in 1840, which included China's seizure of several American merchants involved in the opium trade as hostages in 1838.

Simultaneously, the U.S. Navy made one of its greatest contributions to science with the deployment of the U.S. Exploring Expedition, which cruised the world with a small squadron of ships under Lieutenant Charles Wilkes between 1838 and 1842. The rich reports that it brought back proved the existence of the Antarctic continent and provided the basis for the founding of the Smithsonian Institution and the U.S. National

Museum, the Naval Observatory, and the U.S. Botanical Garden.[30] One of its greatest accomplishments, the charting of broad areas of the Pacific, has a direct consequence a century later, when the U.S. Navy found some of those same charts essential to its operations to prevent Japanese hegemony in the Far East. While properly celebrated for these scientific accomplishments, its military significance has often been overlooked. In 1839, Wilkes brought two ships into Sydney Harbour in Australia and commented that he could have destroyed shipping, bombarded Sydney, and sailed off without any response. In the context of rising Anglo-American tensions over defining the Maine–New Brunswick border, his visit with two ships initiated the concern that led eventually to the establishment of Australia's coastal defenses.[31]

While the ships of the East Indies Squadron were largely devoted to trade protection, there were some additions and exceptions to this work as Commodore Matthew Perry negotiated treaties for the opening of Japan in 1852–54 and Commander John Rodgers commanded a detachment of ships as the U.S. Surveying Expedition to the North Pacific and charted Japanese and other adjacent waters in 1853–58.

While America's small naval force was increasingly engaged on the protection of commerce abroad, as well as on a major scientific expedition, its presence and movements were beginning to create reactions with other naval powers. In the light of this, observers noted that there was no regularly constituted naval force assigned the duty of protecting America's own coastline. In fact, there was no major threat of any serious nature to the coastline before the 1840s, when the Oregon Crisis and Maine–New Brunswick boundary dispute both led to serious tensions with Britain. In response to these situations, British forces in North America, both in the Atlantic and on the Great Lakes, were increased and the British began to build such major defensive works as Fort Henry at Kingston, Ontario, to protect the inland entrance of the St. Lawrence River with both military and naval forces. These tensions were echoed by the United States with the establishment of the Home Squadron in 1842. In this specific context, the Secretary of the Navy reported to Congress:

> While the squadrons are maintained in various parts of the world for the preservation of commerce, our own shores have been left without any adequate protection. Had a war with Great Britain been the result . . . not only would our trade have been liable to great interruption, and our merchants to great losses abroad, but a naval force comparatively small might, on our very shores, have seized our merchant ships and insulted our flag, without suitable means of resistance or retaliation being at the command of the Government. To guard against such a result . . . it is necessary that powerful squadron should be kept afloat at home.[32]

With its establishment in 1842, the Home Squadron absorbed the duties of the West Indies Squadron and its responsibilities ranged from the Grand Banks in the north to the Gulf of Mexico in the south.

The last of the forward stations to be established was the African station. Unlike the others, it was designed not for the protection of the major commercial enterprise on that coast, but for the eradication, on humanitarian grounds, of American trade in human slaves. While this objective was already stipulated in the Constitution of the United States, the origins and operations of American warships on that station were the outgrowth of both domestic politics and the rise of liberal values in Europe. The U.S. was not alone in carrying out these activities and the 1841 Treaty of London between Great

Britain, France, Austria, Prussia, and Russia complemented its participation. Slavery was not a crime *jure gentium* in international law, as was piracy, although the United States had proposed to make it such in 1823. Thus, citizens of one state engaging in it could not be arrested by another state. A tacit agreement was made between naval officers operating on this station not to board ships of one another's countries, although this often meant that some slave-traders escaped because the right country's warship was not at hand. Thus, it remained up to American warships to try to stop the continuing American commercial interest in the slave trade, unless the United States wished to compromise the sanctity of the American flag at sea by allowing foreign officers to board and search American merchant ships.[33]

Throughout the larger part of the nineteenth century, American warships on forward-deployed stations operated as single ships, not as a fleet, or a flying squadron as the Royal Navy developed at mid-century. An American naval squadron on station was not designed as a fighting force for fleet engagements, but rather for police actions, showing American interest in a region and providing recourse to American authority for American merchants abroad when faced by pirates or inappropriate regulations in the conduct of their peaceful commercial activities.

The U.S. Civil War interrupted this pattern of deployed activity. The Navy Department recalled ships on distant stations, but this order took time to carry out. In 1862 nine ships still remained on distant station. The slow progress in this served to delay the United States Navy as it concentrated its naval force to carry out a three-pronged naval strategy: blockading Southern ports, controlling the inland rivers, and deploying fast cruisers to intercept Confederate commerce raiders.

While the United States was withdrawing its own forward-deployed ships in order to meet the crisis in home waters, the Navy's concentration on its own problems brought it into sharp conflict with Great Britain and the United States found itself under threat from powerful naval forces based on Britain's forward bases in Bermuda and Halifax. When Charles Wilkes, commanding USS *San Jacinto,* stopped the Royal Mail Steamer *Trent* and seized the Confederate States' diplomatic envoys Mason and Slidell from a ship under the British flag in the international waters of the Old Bahama Channel, north of Cuba, it created a major incident and was a flagrant challenge to British maritime supremacy at the very moment that she was also facing a naval challenge from France. It was a challenge that Britain could not tolerate. Rear Admiral Sir Alexander Milne, commander-in-chief on the North America and West Indies station, immediately moved his squadron to Bermuda in preparation for a blockade of the Federal States and plans were laid to supply him with eight battleships, nine frigates, twenty-three sloops, and twenty gunboats for this purpose. The Admiralty sent a supply of 10,000 tons of coal to the station and notified commanders-in-chief around the world of impending conflict with the United States. With the ample forward-deployed forces available to him, Milne began making further plans to capture the U.S. Gulf Coast Squadron, destroy the U.S. blockading forces on the East Coast, and open Southern ports for major landings. At the same time, the War Office dispatched 11,000 troops to Canada, in a remarkably efficient demonstration of global lift capacity. Seeing this very effective example of what the world's superpower navy could do to use its forward-deployed forces and to augment them quickly and effectively with nearly overwhelming force, the Lincoln administration agreed to the proposal that Queen Victoria had personally made, offering the United States the diplomatic opportunity to disavow Captain Wilkes's action.[34]

The effectiveness of Confederate commerce raiders and the tremendous damage that had incurred on Northern shipping had a great impact on world-wide naval thinking in the late nineteenth century. Combined with the growing technological changes in navies around the world, this soon led to different ways of thinking about how to use naval vessels. Britain and other major naval powers abandoned the idea of a series of ships operating independently on distant stations and moved instead to a renewal of squadron operations. The United States was slow to follow this lead, and instead of initially following the great naval powers, reinstated the forward-deployed stations in 1865, changing only the names and making several small rationalizations.

Secretary of the Navy Gideon Welles established the European station to incorporate the old Mediterranean and African stations. The South Atlantic station took up the duties of the old Brazil station with a wider area of responsibility. The newly established North Atlantic station took up the duties of the old Home station, including the West Indies, and the Asiatic station took over the old East Indies station. Initially, the ships on station were devoted to the commerce duties that had stretched back to the beginning of the century.

As the United States embarked on a renewal of its pre–Civil War naval deployment policy, there were gradual changes taking place in the structure of world politics. Great Britain's changing naval deployment policy reflected the renewed rise of naval rivalry. While France was the center of attention, it was only part of the change as other nations began to share in the industrial revolution and to begin to challenge Britain's global empire. A number of other nations no longer tacitly accepted British maritime dominance, although Britain remained, undeniably, the world's naval superpower. In this changed environment, the old naval policies of the *Pax Britannica* were no longer effective for Britain or for others whose naval policies had provided overarching protection. The United States Navy found new types of demands on it and, eventually, opportunities to fill.

The old station system formed the basis for the United States Navy in this new period, but the changed climate as well as new national policies and ambitions began to develop as the *Pax Britannica* waned. Soon the United States Navy found itself drawn into duties that it had not previously contemplated. The new situation took time to become apparent to a nation like that of the United States that was not a direct and active participant in the forces that led to changing the strategic balance. It was not until 1873, however, that the United States found an urgent need to mobilize its individual ships into a single tactical unit. In October of that year a Spanish warship captured the steamship *Virginius,* flying the American flag, as it was attempting to take munitions to Cuban rebels. The master and a number of English and American crew members were taken ashore at Santiago and shot as pirates. HMS *Niobe* appeared to protect English citizens, while the administration of President Grant chose to collect all available naval vessels in a demonstration at Key West and laid plans to land an expeditionary force of 10,000 men within a few weeks. Rather than show themselves as a credible force, the assembled warships demonstrated their inability to operate together in the absence of any tactical fleet doctrine.

This particular incident was clearly the turning point that motivated change in American naval thinking, just at the time that other new social forces were leading toward the professionalization of the naval officer corps, and the creation of the institutions that supported it: the Naval Institute in 1873, the Naval War College in 1884, and the gradual development of uniformed, professional staff direction for the Navy from the 1880s through the turn of the century. It was a long, slow process and a major change that was not clearly apparent until after the end of the century.

Up through the 1880s, the primary objectives for naval operations remained the protection of American commerce, promoting American business interests, and protecting American citizens living abroad. This was underscored by the objectives of a wide range of activities in these decades, but it was being carried out in an increasingly interventionist way. What we are beginning to see at the end of the nineteenth century is the subtle transformation of the positioning of the fleet in deployed forward stations from a defensive, token force to a forward-deployed, offensive force.

Between 1871 and 1885, the Navy continued to place the Navy's role in relation to American commerce as its first objective, as it had since the establishment of the Navy, but with a much more aggressive stance. It was no longer a matter of protection, but of expansion. This shift can be traced beginning in 1871, when the commander of the Asiatic station, Rear Admiral John Rodgers, contemplated using force to open Korea for American commerce. Upon realizing that its opening would bring little interest among businessmen, and in the light of an attack on a hydrographic surveying flotilla, the Navy Department ordered Rodgers to make a landing in Korea and try to force the Korean government to negotiate. Using the freedom of the seas as a pretext, American minister to China Frederick F. Low, who accompanied the expedition, had explained, "The sea is a great highway of nations, which no country is at liberty to obstruct with impunity" and shipwrecked mariners and property should be returned to their rightful owners.[35] The operation went off with great efficiency, but failed to produce the diplomatic result intended. Korea refused to reach an agreement. The largest American military operation against an Asian nation in the nineteenth century ended and officials in Washington made it clear that they would not endorse Rodgers's recommendation to seize Seoul and to force the Korean king into an agreement.[36]

While less bellicose, the same thought arose again in 1878, when Secretary of the Navy Richard W. Thompson ordered Commodore Robert W. Shufeldt on a round-the-world cruise in USS *Ticonderoga* that was to last two years. In the orders drafted jointly by both the State and Navy Departments, he was directed to visit

> the unfrequented ports of Africa, Asia, the islands of the Persian Ocean and the adjacent
> seas, particularly where there are at present no American commercial representatives with a
> view to the encouragement and extension of American Commerce.[37]

This was the first indication that the United States under the administration of Rutherford B. Hayes was interested in joining the European powers in the new race for commercial influence and connections in Asia and Africa.

As Shufeldt approached Korean waters toward the end of his cruise in 1880, Secretary of the Navy Thompson responded to Shufeldt's recommendations for seizing some offshore islands in order to force Korea into agreement and telegraphed him, "Use only persuasive means with the Coreans. Avoid hostilities."[38] It too failed to achieve Shufeldt's fondest objectives and, in disappointment, he wrote, "I do not wish to see the United States use coercive measures in Corea or anywhere in the East, yet . . . America is the pioneer of the Pacific—a position which she should not only recognize but claim."[39]

The trend that Shufeldt represented was even more dramatically demonstrated five years later in Panama. This time, the operations involved neither an independently deployed squadron with a specific mission nor the ships from a single forward-deployed station, but an *ad hoc* gathering of ships from two stations, joined by a 400-man Marine landing force. A revolution in Colombia had halted international commercial transit across the Colombian province of Panama, a route that had emerged as a vital and dependable rail link connecting the Atlantic and Pacific ocean trade routes and linked the two coasts of the United States.[40] Under Admiral Jouett's command, U.S. naval forces landed at three locations in Panama and, with armed parties ashore, restored rail service across the Isthmus in the largest overseas operation undertaken by U.S. forces between 1865 and 1898.[41]

The gradual change that was taking place on the U.S. Navy's forward-deployed stations was reflected elsewhere. On the European station occured the Armenian massacres and resulting Turkish Crisis of 1895–1897. The European powers reacted to it and were deeply concerned about its implications for European affairs and the fear that Russia might seize Constantinople in order to quell disturbances on her borders. Rear Admiral Thomas Selfridge, Jr., commanding the American squadron, was quick to point out that the United States had no concern with the crisis beyond the safety of its own citizens, but the French, who opposed intervention from other European powers, publicly encouraged an American intervention, since it would not affect the European balance of power. At home, Captain Mahan and others promoted the idea of Anglo-American naval cooperation and the possibility of a maritime condominium. Yet little came of it all and American policy toward Turkey failed. Despite one of the few nineteenth-century instances of a forward-deployed squadron operating together and the visible threat it posed of a naval demonstration, the United States and the Ottoman Empire did not resolve their differences. American missionaries in the interior of the country were close to the center of the crisis, but, in the final analysis, none were injured or had property destroyed. Despite the fact that policy differences were not formally resolved, many missionaries attributed this result to the presence of American warships offshore.[42]

With the emergence of the Spanish-American War in 1898, the United States Navy made one dramatic and successful move on a forward-deployed position. Commodore George Dewey took command of the warships already on the Asiatic station and augmented them with others, as he sailed to Manila Bay in 1898. This move was clearly one further step along the trend in the changing uses for American warships that had been progressing since 1871. But, as it had been a century before, Great Britain still remained the dominant superpower at sea. Without the quiet support of Britain, in the form of the dry docks of Hong Kong, for American objectives, Dewey's Asiatic Squadron would probably not have been as effective as it was.[43]

The United States moved slowly and cautiously as it created a series of forward-deployed stations during the nineteenth century. Less than a decade after its establishment in 1794, the United States Navy began to deploy its ships to distant stations, but it took just over forty years, 1801 to 1843, to complete fully the pattern that remained in place for the reminder of the century and also provided the precedents for the entire twentieth century. Established clearly for the protection of American commerce and Americans abroad, it gradually and hesitantly grew, under that same rubric, from ships conducting a range of independent and individual operations on a distant station to units operating together as a single tactical unit.

As the twentieth century dawned, the international structure under which the United States carried out its policy remained as it had a century before. With British maritime supremacy in place, even as it was challenged during the latter part of the nineteenth century, American naval operations on distant stations were effective only to the extent that they could be tolerated and carried out under that umbrella. American diplomats and naval officers abroad tended to think, or at least to express themselves, in the narrow context of American interests and the country made few, if any, explicit agreements with the major powers that involved American participation in their global concerns. Nevertheless, the truth of the matter is that the relatively small numbers of ships that the United States deployed on distant stations could only create a broad effect when its actions harmonized with the great powers. In this period, the United States was not in any direct strategic competition with any of the great powers, despite a number of differences of opinion, and its interests were strictly limited. It was a century of stability —albeit decaying stability—in which the United States found its deployed naval forces able to achieve their goals within an implied consensus of aims and values that the world's maritime superpower was able to accept. It was a situation that soon collapsed under severe challenges of the twentieth century.

NOTES   This paper was presented at the U.S. Navy Forward Presence Bicentennial Symposium, sponsored by the CNA Center for Strategic Studies (CNA/CSS), The Naval Historical Foundation, and the Naval Historical Center. The symposium was held at CNA in Alexandria, Virginia, on 21 June 2001 and commemorated the 200th anniversary of the first United States Navy forward deployment with the arrival of the squadron under Commodore Richard Dale at Gibraltar on 1 July 1801.

1 George Washington, "Fifth Annual Address, Philadelphia, 3 December 1793," in Fred L. Israel, ed., *The State of the Union Messages of the Presidents, 1790–1966, with an Introduction by Arthur M. Schlesinger* (New York: Chelsea House–Robert Hector, 1966), vol. 1, p. 18.

2 See Piers Mackesy, *The War in the Mediterranean, 1803–1810* (London: Longmans, 1957) and Julian S. Corbett, "Napoleon and the British Navy after Trafalgar," *The Quarterly Review,* 237 (April 1922), pp. 238–255.

3 Gerald S. Graham, *Empire of the North Atlantic.* Second edition (London, 1958), p. 266.

4 Gerald S. Graham, *The Politics of Naval Supremacy: Studies in British Maritime Ascendancy. The Wiles Lectures, 1963–64* (Cambridge: Cambridge University Press, 1965), p. 110.

5 Peter Burroughs, "Defence and Imperial Disunity," in Andrew Porter, ed., *The Nineteenth Century. The Oxford History of the British Empire,* vol. 3 (Oxford: Oxford University Press, 1999), pp. 320–345, and Andrew Lambert, "The Shield of the Empire, 1815–1895," in J. R. Hill, ed., *The Oxford Illustrated History of the Royal Navy* (Oxford: Oxford University Press, 1995), pp. 161–197.

6 Donald M. Schurman, *Imperial Defence, 1868–1887,* ed. John Beeler (London: Frank Cass, 2000) and Burroughs, "Defence and Imperial Disunity," p. 335.

7 Nicholas A. Lambert, *Sir John Fisher's Naval Revolution* (Columbia: University of South Carolina Press, 1999), pp. 98–115, 157–164.

8 Michael Palmer, *Stoddert's War: Naval Operations During the Quasi-War with France 1798–1801* (Columbia: University of South Carolina Press, 1987), pp. 202–209.

9 See William S. Dudley, "The Origins of the U.S. Navy's Mediterranean Squadron, 1783–1816," in *Français et Anglais en Méditerranée de la Révolution française à l'indépendance de la Grèce (1789–1839).* IIIes Journées franco-britanniques d'histoire de la Marine. Toulon. Les 14, 15 et 16 novembre 1990 (Paris: Service Historique de la Marine, 1992), pp. 251–260.

10 Benjamin Stoddert to Josiah Parker, Chairman of the Committee on Naval Affairs, 11 January 1800, in K. Jack Bauer, ed., *The New American State Papers, Naval Affairs,* vol. 1, *General Naval Policy and Defense* (Wilmington: Scholarly Resources, 1981), Document 10, p. 19.

11 Ibid., p. 20.

12 Craig L. Symonds, *Navalists and Anti-Navalists: The Naval Policy Debate in the United States, 1785–1827* (Newark: University of Delaware Press, 1980), chapter 5.

13 Robert G. Albion, "Distant Stations," U.S. Naval Institute *Proceedings* (March 1954), p. 266.

14 Benjamin Stoddert, "Letter on the Naval Establishment, 22 January 1801" in Bauer, ed., *New American State Papers,* vol. 1, *General Naval Policy and Defense,* Document 1, pp. 27–28.

15 On the gunboats, see Spencer Tucker, *The Jeffersonian Gunboat Navy* (Columbia: University of South Carolina Press, 1993) and Gene A. Smith, *"For the Purposes of Defense": The Politics of the Jeffersonian Gunboat Program* (Newark: University of Delaware Press, 1995).

16 Smith, *"For the Purposes of Defense,"* pp. 6–21, 46–47, 56, 127.

17 Acting Secretary of the Navy Samuel Smith to Commodore Thomas Truxtun, 10 April 1801, in U.S. Navy Department, *Naval Documents Relating to the United States Wars with the Barbary Powers* (Washington: GPO, 1939), vol. 1, pp. 428–429.

18 Smith to Commodore Richard Dale, 20 May 1801, in ibid., pp. 463–464.

19 Ibid.

20 Secretary of the Navy Robert Smith to Commodore James Barron, 15 May 1807, in ibid., vol. 6, p. 523.

21 For this operation, see Roger Perkins and K. J. Douglas-Morris, *Gunfire in Barbary: Admiral Lord Exmouth's Battle with the Corsairs of Algiers in 1816: The Story of the Suppression of White Christian Slavery* (Havant, Hants: K. Mason, 1982) and C. Northcote Parkinson, *Edward Pellew* (1934).

22 Symonds, *Navalists and Anti-Navalists,* pp. 194–218.

23 Quoted in ibid., p. 235.

24 Robert Erwin Johnson, *Thence Round Cape Horn: The Story of United States Naval Forces on the Pacific Station, 1818–1923* (Annapolis: Naval Institute Press, 1963).

25 David F. Long, *Gold Braid and Foreign Relations: Diplomatic Activities of U.S. Naval Officers, 1798–1883* (Annapolis: Naval Institute Press, 1988), pp. 78–87.

26 Secretary of the Navy Smith Thompson to Chairman of the Naval Committee of the Senate, 11 December 1822, in Bauer, ed., *New American State Papers,* vol. 1, *General Naval Policy and Defense,* Document 1, p. 101.

27 [Seventh] Annual Report of the President [James Monroe, 2 December 1823], in ibid., p. 104.

28 Letters and Reports on Increasing Force off South America, in ibid., pp. 113–119.

29 Robert Erwin Johnson, *Far China Station: The U.S. Navy in Asian Waters, 1800–1898* (Annapolis: Naval Institute Press, 1979), pp. 18–19.

30 See, among several works, William Stanton, *The Great United States Exploring Expedition of 1838–1842* (Berkeley: University of California Press, 1975) and Herman J. Viola and Carolyn Margolis, eds., *Magnificent Voyagers: The U.S. Exploring Expedition, 1838–1842* (Washington: Smithsonian Press, 1985).

31 Andrew Lambert, "Australia, the Trent Crisis of 1861, and the Strategy of Imperial Defense," in David Stevens and John Reeve, eds., *Southern Trident: Strategy, History, and the Rise of Australian Naval Power* (Crows Nest, NSW: Allen & Unwin, 2001), p. 102.

32 *Senate Executive Document 1,* quoted in Robert G. Albion, *Makers of Naval Policy, 1798–1947* (Annapolis: Naval Institute Press, 1980), pp. 302–303.

33 Christopher Lloyd, *The Navy and the Slave Trade: The Suppression of the African Slave Trade in the Nineteenth Century* (London: Longmans Green, 1949), pp. 50–58.

34 Lambert, "Australia, the Trent Crisis of 1861 and the Strategy of Imperial Defence," pp. 108–113; N. B. Ferris, *The Trent Affair and Diplomatic Crisis* (Knoxville: University of Tennessee Press, 1977) and G. H. Warren, *Fountain of Discontent: The Trent Affairs and the Freedom of the Seas* (Boston: Northeastern Univ. Press, 1981).

35 Quoted in Frederick C. Drake, *The Empire of the Seas: A Biography of Rear Admiral Robert Wilson Shufeldt, USN* (Honolulu: University of Hawaii Press, 1984), p. 234.

36 Johnson, *Far China Station,* pp. 156–166.

37 Drake, *The Empire of the Seas,* p. 177.

38 Ibid., p. 244.

39 Ibid., p. 252.

40 For this development, see John H. Kemble, *The Panama Route 1848–1869* (Berkeley: University of California Press, 1943; reprinted New York: Library Editions, 1970).

41 Kenneth J. Hagan, *American Gunboat Diplomacy and the Old Navy, 1877–1899* (Westport: Greenwood Press, 1973), pp. 160–187.

42 William N. Still, Jr., *American Sea Power in the Old World: The United States Navy in European and Near Eastern Waters, 1865–1917* (Westport: Greenwood Press, 1980), pp. 113–132.

43 John B. Hattendorf, "The Battle of Manila Bay," in Jack Sweetman, ed., *Great American Naval Battles* (Annapolis: Naval Institute Press, 1998), pp. 175–197.

XVI "In a Far More Thorough Manner"
The Professionalization of the U.S. Navy at the Dawn of the Twentieth Century

Although the U.S. Navy had few ships in the decades after the Civil War, it was in these lean years that vital steps were taken toward professionalization. Two of the most important creations were the Naval War College and a professional association, the U.S. Naval Institute.

The idea of professionalism encompasses a wide range of attributes and activities. At its core, professionalism involves such things as providing high quality products and services, maintaining occupational independence in providing specialized judgments as well as embodying honor, integrity, and fair play; being truthful and candid; exhibiting diligence and punctuality; showing courtesy and respect for others; and following the rules and expectations of others who share and work in that same occupation, and understanding the broader implications that work involves.[19]

Professionalization is the process of converting a craft or occupation into a higher level of activity through the use of education and training to establish standards and to raise the general level of activity. When we speak of professionalization in a military organization, we typically think about improving its capacity to carry out its mission, to make it operate more consistently, to increase its members' discipline and accountability for their actions, to define the military's role, and to structure itself within the government in ways that make it responsive to the needs of the nation, more efficient and responsible in its uses of precious national resources, placing it under proper control and management within a democratic form of government, as well as ensuring that its members are respectful and responsive to the accepted practices of nations, the laws of war, and the established norms of society in terms of civil, legal, and human rights.[2]

Navies have been involved in improving their standards of professionalization for several centuries. Samuel Pepys's great contribution in formulating the Royal Proclamation that instituted the first formal qualifying examination for naval lieutenants in 1677, with his description of the basic requirements for the then-lowest rung of commissioned officers, specifying minimum sea time and essential experience,[3] certainly stands as a seamark in the history of the development of naval professionalization, as does the establishment of the U.S. Naval Academy, nearly 170 years later, in 1845. Between 1677 and 1845, the foundations of naval professionalization were well and surely established during the age of sail and involved some of the fundamental and enduring concepts of how a naval officer should conduct himself as an individual professional.

Paralleling and complementing these personal professional standards were equally important standards and procedures that developed for war-fighting doctrine, methods of command and control, financial management, and bureaucratic structure, which have evolved over time. Together, these are all central elements of professionalization.

In the mid-nineteenth century, the United States had one of the world's smaller navies and was by no means a great power on the world stage. Nevertheless, the rise and applications of new naval technologies was already apparent in the American Civil War and although the U.S. Navy did not permanently adopt all the new technological innovations that the Navy itself had used during that war, it was clear that technological innovation was fundamentally changing the face of the world's major navies. No longer were navies exemplified by the age-old formula of wind, wood, iron guns, and muscle. Progressive cycles of rapidly changing technological innovation brought iron, steam, and paddlewheels, then steel and propellers, and soon afterwards electricity. This continuing series of progressively more complex technological changes in the world's major navies was a fundamental stimulus that led some in uniform to begin to think about the nature and character of their profession and to ask broad questions about what new kinds of knowledge were needed, what different kinds of education and training most appropriately prepared men for the naval profession, and what revisions of administrative and command structures were needed in this new technological environment. In the United States Navy, this kind of very broad thinking was neither led nor managed nor even encouraged by the Navy Department. What initially developed was a series of scattered individual initiatives that dealt with various specific aspects of professionalization and eventually began to merge into a holistic appreciation of the naval profession.

In addition to the general growth of technological applications within navies, there were two conflicts that had an enormous impact on American naval thinking at the end of the nineteenth century. The first was the U.S. Navy's own experience during the Civil War between 1861 and 1865. The second was the perceived success that the Prussian General Staff had achieved during the wars that led to Germany's unification: the Austro-Prussian War in 1866 and the Franco-Prussian War in 1870–71.

In the late nineteenth century, the American Civil War was the most recent major war that American naval officers had actually experienced and it was one of the very first of the modern naval wars that involved improved naval gunnery and armored ships with steam propulsion. This experience, paralleled by reports of the technical advances that were rapidly taking place in the world's major navies, particularly the Royal Navy and the French Navy, led to demands within the U.S. naval officer corps for more technical knowledge, particularly in the areas of steam engineering, ship construction, and weapons. With these areas of development in their infancy, Congress and the Navy Department took some steps toward modernization, but with both fiscal and political constraints, they were initially satisfied in maintaining the Navy with sailing ships designed for the protection of trade and single ships on foreign stations to protect American interests abroad. In 1864, even while the Civil War was still in progress, Congress authorized the Naval Academy, then temporarily located at Newport, Rhode Island, to start a two-year course for educating assistant engineers, who would be selected by competitive examination among 18- to 22-year-old men with some previous experience in this area. The course was taught intermittently from 1866, after the Academy returned to Annapolis.[4]

Beyond steam engineering, the main focus for professional education toward modernization centered on the new technologies surrounding the torpedo. With the establishment of the Naval Torpedo Station on Goat Island in Narragansett Bay in 1869, this single weapon dominated much professional naval thinking, leading to a wide impact in terms of ship construction and design as well as in tactical thinking.

Thus, the initial—and, I should add, the dominant—reaction in naval professionalization was toward education and training in specific technological applications. In this, the tendency was to follow the technological imperative that incremental improvements in these technologies presented. The most famous conundrum that this presented was the incident involving the trials of the USS *Wampanoag* in 1869, in which she proved to be the fastest and most successful steamship afloat, yet she was condemned and placed out of service by a board of officers for being far too advanced a warship to build in peacetime and one that would have no technological peer in any conceivable navy for another two decades.[5] The senior officers who rejected the new technology saw it as too advanced to be effectively useable.

USS *Wampanoag* presents an interesting question for an historian of professionalization: Were the individuals who made up the board merely narrow-minded, pettifogging ultra-conservatives or were they making a sound decision? Looked at in a broader light, their rejection was based on the perception "that a machine, any machine, if left to itself, tends to establish its own conditions, to create its own environment and draw men into it."[6]

The feeling that there was something more and something bigger and more important than technology to consider motivated a, largely, different group of officers than those who led technological innovation. The first important step in this direction was taken by a group of fifteen naval officers, who met at the Naval Academy in 1873 to establish the U.S. Naval Institute. In its original conception, it was an outgrowth of a well-established approach to adult education in the United States called "the lyceum system." In this case, however, it became a professional forum for discussion about the future of the naval service. The early meetings were characterized by a member reading a paper on a subject of naval interest—the very first being a discussion of the Battle of Lepanto—and those in attendance commenting on it, much in the fashion that the Royal United Services Institution had been using in London for nearly forty years. From such meetings in Annapolis, and later from similar meetings in the chapters of the Naval Institute that were founded in Newport and elsewhere, the Institute very quickly was able to begin publishing its papers, annually at first, and on a more regular basis by 1879–80. Its *Proceedings* soon became a real professional journal.[7]

One of the things that was almost entirely lacking in the U.S. Navy of this period was a body of specialized literature that could be identified as professional literature, something that was an essential characteristic of any occupational group aspiring to become a profession. Among such bodies of professional literature, studies of the history and development of a particular profession play an essential role, alongside considerations of current and future subjects.

As recently as 1861, young Lieutenant Stephen B. Luce had told the Commandant of Midshipmen at the Academy, "Compared to the Army with their wealth of professional literature, we may be likened to the nomadic tribes of the East who are content with the vague traditions of the past."[8] As American military and naval officers watched current events in Europe in the late 1860s and early 1870s, it is not surprising that they were deeply impressed with the events that led up to German unification and, particularly, with the success of the German Army's General Staff. The Americans who admired it and wanted to adapt it to American institutions were favorably impressed with what they took to be a German system that provided progressive, professional military education, established shared common professional understanding, created effective central planning, and was able to provide the professionally informed command authority to coordinate powerful agencies and forge them into effective, mutually supporting war-fighting institutions. The vision that American proponents developed was, to a degree, an idealized view, and even a misunderstanding, that failed to appreciate the flaws in the German Army's system that became obvious in later wars: a disconnect between operational effectiveness and strategic understanding, excessive elitism, and counterproductive militarism.[9]

Nevertheless, the U.S. Army's leading proponent of German ideas, Colonel Emory Upton, had a direct influence on the U.S. Navy. The commanding general of the Army, William Tecumseh Sherman, had sent Upton on a two-year world tour in 1875 to study world military trends. He came home and took command of the Artillery School at Fort Monroe, Virginia, and began to formulate ideas and develop a plan to reform the American Army along the lines of what he had learned about German Army staff methods. Shortly after Upton's return to Norfolk in 1877, he met the commanding officer of the USS *Hartford*, Captain Stephen B. Luce. These two shared a common way of thinking and each, in his own way, was responsible for laying the intellectual foundations for professionalism within their separate services.

Captain Luce was involved in a wide variety of activities that were aimed at improving the level of professionalization of maritime affairs. As early as 1866, he had proposed the establishment of civilian nautical colleges that could provide seamen for both the Navy and the merchant marine. By 1875, this had developed into a plan with the Education Department of the City of New York to provide USS *St Mary's* as a training ship in New York, a duty the ship carried out until 1908, thereby creating the foundation for what is today known as the State University of New York Maritime College at Fort Schuyler.

By an extension of the Land Grant Act that established a number of the nation's great mid-western universities, Luce was closely involved in the movement that went to establish maritime colleges in several states and he even wrote textbooks for them as well as for the Navy. From 1877 to 1883, Luce was involved in a variety of initiatives with naval training vessels. Eventually transferred ashore at the Naval Station at Newport, Rhode Island, these activities grew to become what is today the Navy's Recruit Training Command, now located in California, Florida, and Illinois.

Following on from the educational and training reforms that were begun by individual initiatives for entry-level officers and seamen, there were other demands for wider approaches to professionalism in the realm of naval policy-making. Not surprisingly, they began with the impetus for new technology and were, at first, narrowly focused along those lines.

While Congress had neither incentive nor interest in authorizing the building of a modernized U.S. Navy in the late 1860s and '70s, naval officers saw the need to observe what was going on in other parts of the world to prepare for the day when they could build new ships. Technical information about weapons, ship-design techniques, materials for construction, and propulsion methods were all matters of great interest. Various bureaus and commands sent investigating teams in this period. Chief Engineer James King of the Bureau of Steam Engineering traveled four times to Europe to monitor progress with compound steam engines. Soon, these investigations spread into other areas. Naval Instructor James Soley of the Naval Academy surveyed European naval education in 1878–79; Lieutenant Commander Dennis Mullan was sent to observe the Latin American War in the Pacific in 1879–81; and Lieutenant Commander Caspar Goodrich observed the British bombardment of Alexandria in 1882.

At about the same time, Lieutenant Theodorus B. M. Mason had taken an extended leave of absence from active duty in 1877–79 and had gone to Europe on his own, systematically gathering information on the latest trends in naval science. On his return to active duty, Mason began to advocate the need for an office in the Navy Department that specialized in obtaining foreign information. Acting on his recommendations, Secretary of the Navy William H. Hunt established the Office of Naval Intelligence (ONI) on 23 March 1882 and ordered Lieutenant Mason as the Navy's first Chief Intelligence Officer, the precursor of the modern Director of Naval Intelligence. This new agency combined ONI with the Navy Department Library, where intelligence specialists could be supplied with the current professional naval literature from around the world and also have ready access to the archives of Navy Department offices.[10]

Closely associated with the initiative to more effectively obtain and use current information about worldwide naval affairs was the realization that there was a need to know and analyze the U.S. Navy's own experience. Little was done to promote this idea until Congress was moved on 7 July 1884 to authorize the publication of the Navy's operational records from the Civil War. The eventual result was that monumental, thirty-volume series *The Official Records of the Union and Confederate Navies in the War of the Rebellion,* which served not only as the material for officers of the day to analyze for their professional profit, but continues to be used today as the preeminent, permanent historical record of the naval aspects of war. As the Secretary of the Navy told Congress in 1888, in support of that project, "The civil war is not only the first war in which naval operations on a great scale have been conducted since the introduction of steam, but it is the only war in which those modern appliances have been used which revolutionized the art of naval warfare."[11]

With this Congressional authorization as its central focus, the Superintendent of the newly created Office of Naval Records and Library, Professor James Soley, the former head of the Naval Academy's Department of English Studies, History, and Law, used the opportunity to begin gathering the Navy's scattered official records together, and in this established the direct forerunner of today's Naval Historical Center.

One of the most unusual individuals in the U.S. Navy's Corps of Instructors, James Soley was a product of the Roxbury Latin School in Boston and Harvard, before he entered naval service. Employed at Annapolis as a uniformed instructor and then as a civilian, he had initiated the first courses in naval history at the Academy, before heading the triple-decked Department of English, History, and Law. While in recent times observers of the Navy have tended to denigrate such an odd amalgamation of disciplines, Soley, for his day, was unusual as a master and practitioner of them all. The author of a number of well-received books, he was among the early pioneer figures in developing naval history for the Navy. Yet, he also went on to earn a degree in law and to become a figure in the field of international law.

In October 1884, Secretary of the Navy William E. Chandler formally approved the recommendations of Commodore Stephen B. Luce to establish the Naval War College as a place of original research and postgraduate professional naval education:

> a place where our officers will not only be encouraged but required to study their profession proper—war—in a far more thorough manner than has ever heretofore been attempted, and to bring to the investigation of the various problems of modern naval warfare the scientific methods adopted in other professions.[12]

In Luce's thinking, the term "scientific methods" did not mean burgeoning developments of technology and science that were altering the face of the naval service, but rather he was referring to a wider rational and systematic approach to understanding the highest levels of the profession: the nature and character of war, statesmanship involved in the conduct of war, in the formulation of peace, and in the prevention of war. Intimately tied to that broad level of understanding was the need for naval officers to understand the context, purposes, uses, roles, and limitations of naval force. By defining the role of the Naval War College in this way, Luce was pointing out that all the focus on technological change and technological transformation was a focus on the means of war and not on the central issue of war itself. Luce believed that it is the phenomenon of war at sea in human experience—past, present, and future—that defines the naval profession, not merely the changing means of fighting such wars.[13]

In searching to place the naval profession and its occupational realm in perspective and in context, Luce wanted naval officers, who were fully competent in the changing means and innovative new methods of war, to see through the wider lenses that such fields as history, political science, economics, international relations, and law provided. Luce's approach brought together four interconnected approaches to form a new basis for a professional understanding of navies. To begin this process, he first turned to the more advanced situation in the Army and the contributions of both German and French military thinkers. First, he asked an army officer to teach the military approach to naval officers. For this, he chose Tasker Bliss, who would later become the first president of the Army War College and, eventually, become the Army's Chief of Staff during the First Word War. To provide the broad naval element, he chose Captain Alfred Thayer Mahan to examine the history of navies and to make a new contribution to thought by linking naval operations to the broad strands of foreign policy in a way that Luce hoped would "do for naval science what Jomini did for military science."[14]

To the comparison of armies and navies, which was designed as the first step in defining the professional domain of navies, Luce added two more elements. One of these was international law. To teach this subject, Luce turned to the versatile James Soley, who became not only the Naval War College's first faculty member in this discipline, but the college's first civilian professor. Soley's pioneering work with law at the Naval War College and with naval history at the Naval Academy and the Office of Naval Records and Library was further consolidated when he became Assistant Secretary of the Navy in 1890.

Finally, to bring all these elements together into a cohesive whole that linked these broad elements to the ever changing and constantly developing areas of technological application, Luce worked with a volunteer staff member, Lieutenant William McCarty Little, to adapt for naval use the German Army's concept of *kriegspiel* or war gaming. Through this newly developing analytical tool, naval officers could envisage how new applications of technology could actually operate, trying them in various game iterations with their varying technical capabilities and combinations, while at the same time linking these applications to likely naval situations in the context of international affairs and to the means and practice of executing naval command and control.

More than just instituting avenues of intellectual approach, Luce saw the need to draw together seasoned practitioners of the art of warfare to learn and to apply these approaches in thinking about the broad and fundamental issues to which the naval profession was devoted. For this reason, he sought a variety of experienced students. Within a decade, his initiative had successfully brought not only a wide range of naval officers from the different branches and specialties of the naval service, but also officers of the Marine Corps, the Army, the Revenue Marine (a predecessor of the Coast Guard), and even officers from foreign navies to the classrooms and war gaming boards of the Naval War College.

As the highest level of professional military education for the naval service, the Naval War College attracted students who would become the brightest and most innovative thinkers and leaders that the naval services contained at the dawn of the twentieth century. They included young officers whose names would later become well known, such as Henry Taylor, Bradley Fiske, William S. Sims, and William Veazie Pratt of the Navy, Earl Ellis of the Marine Corps, and Ellsworth Bertholf of the Coast Guard, to name but a few of those who are remembered today.

In the first thirty years of its existence, the Naval War College created a body of like-minded professionals, who began to see the Navy in terms of its larger context and began to lead the Navy toward a higher level of professionalization in its operations and command structure. Yet, there was a major roadblock in carrying through this development and the vision that Admiral Luce had for the contributions of advanced professional military education to the naval services. The problem was the knotty question of how to frame the standards for a naval career in terms of what criteria were used to determine professional advancement, how the Navy selected its leaders, and who got to the top and who did not. In short, the fundamental problem was how to define the profession of a naval officer in the context of the new technological environment for navies.[15]

The issue was primarily argued out in the context of the very bitter and deep feud between the engineers, who were technological experts, and the line officers, who were trained in the traditional methods of seamanship and navigation. This carried within it the oversimplified stereotypes of progressives versus reactionaries, tying officers' careers to either the old sailing-era propulsion technology or to the new steam propulsion technology. The argument became a very public issue in the daily and professional press and in Congress as the engineers sought to obtain status and authority for those who shared their specialist knowledge. To some, it seemed a quest of one social group against another for control of the Navy as an institution. Over several decades, this conflict reached such proportions that it created serious issues of discipline on ships at sea and internal political conflict ashore that undermined authority. In the end, the Navy was unable to resolve the professional issues by itself and it was necessary for Congress to redefine completely the naval officer personnel system and, with it, provide a new definition of the naval officers' profession.[16]

This process involved a laborious series of half steps and partial solutions over many decades. In the 1890s, serious effort was devoted to resolve these matters with the work of several boards, the investigations of Congressional subcommittees, and innumerable proposals. The most far-reaching and sweeping change occurred when Congress passed the Naval Personnel Act of 3 March 1899 that amalgamated the engineering corps with the line, established a voluntary retirement system, and created a board to select officers for involuntary retirement based on their performance.

Over the next decade and a half, these reforms were continued and refined. In 1911, Secretary of the Navy George Meyer proposed a new general approach, when he noted that all naval officers should be line officers, but "it is not the intent that each officer should take up all specialties, but that each officer should take up at least one specialty."[17] Above all, the fundamental aim was clearly to produce the sea officers best capable of commanding the country's ships and fleets.

Further acts of Congress increased the numbers of those authorized as midshipmen and junior officers in 1903, adjusted pay for sea and shore duty and for comparability with the Army's pay scales in 1906 and 1908. Additional key adjustments took place under the administration of Josephus Daniels as Secretary of the Navy. In this period, Congress established the permanent grades of admiral and vice admiral in 1915. Finally, building on its 1899 legislation, Congress passed a keystone piece of professional legislation in the Line Personnel Act of 1916, establishing a system of selecting officers for promotion to the grades of commander and above based on merit, creating lengths of sea service time for promotion, specifying the age in grade for retirement, and creating systems of graduated retirement pay based on longevity, distributing officers in different grades on the basis of ratios for each grade, and establishing the Naval Reserve.

These important progressive steps clearly established professional criteria for advancement based on a system of selection for promotion that created a flow through the officer grades. This new process placed value on the knowledge an officer acquired both through extensive practical experience and through education, as well as on the collective judgment of a panel of experienced senior officers who chose for promotion those they felt were best fit for the levels of responsibility that each grade represented.

These personnel changes were not just administrative details, but crucial parts of the process of professionalization in the Navy in the early twentieth century. They were closely tied to wider issues that involved improving the Navy's efficiency and ability to carry out its mission. As the Navy's officer personnel problems were gradually alleviated, the series of reforms that were growing out of the Navy's attention to advanced professional education could more effectively take place.

For example, the Naval Personnel Act of 1899 facilitated the further development of graduate education in established technical and scientific disciplines. In the first decade of the twentieth century, the Navy was faced with the question as to whether it was best to rely on the nation's civilian universities or to provide for its own technical and scientific education. In 1909, the issue was resolved by establishing a graduate School of Marine Engineering at Annapolis, which became the forerunner of the Naval Postgraduate

School, and by also supplementing the Postgraduate School's resident technical instruction with the use of selected civilian university programs to further and to stimulate the Navy's technological development.

Meanwhile, the focus on applied research and advanced professional education at the Naval War College had begun to bear fruit in several areas. The pioneering work done in naval history contributed to the wider understanding of the Navy's role and, with it, an increase in public support for the Navy, while actual historical experience informed professional naval thought on a wide range of subjects. The college's focus on international law produced in 1900 the world's first Code of the Law of Naval Warfare and that document quickly became the basis for international conferences and further professional standards in the twentieth century.

The early attention to the approaches used by the German General Staff had multiple professional effects for the U.S. Navy. The combined use of the approach called "The Estimate of the Situation" and war gaming were key elements in the development of the Navy's first operational contingency plans used for the Spanish-American War and then the Color Plans—War Plan Orange, Black, and others—that became famous in the twentieth century. This aspect of professionalization led to further thinking about the needs of a commander in exercising command at sea. Through this, Naval War College graduates applied their classroom thinking to create the first afloat staff for an operational commander, as Captain William S. Sims did in his Atlantic Destroyer Flotilla in 1913; promoting the first concept for the U.S. Navy's operational doctrine in 1915, as Dudley Knox did in a *Proceedings* article in 1915; and the implementation of the U.S. Navy's first major staff for a commander in chief that Admiral William S. Sims created in London in 1917–19.

The most difficult and complicated process of all was the Naval War College's effort to put in place a professional advisor to the Secretary of the Navy who could also have an effective and authoritative role as the uniformed head of the naval service and be the coordinator of the technical bureaus. The pressure from the uniformed members of the Navy to implement this change was met by strong opposition from Congress, many of whose members saw it as an erosion of civilian control. The creation of the Navy's General Board under Admiral of the Navy George Dewey in 1900 was the first successful step in this process of professionalization, and it was followed in 1909 with the establishment of a group of four, coequal rear admirals, who were responsible under the Secretary of the Navy for their respective areas. They were called, using the trend for a distinctively American spelling: Aid for Fleet Operations, Aid for Material, Aid for Personnel, and Aid for Inspections. Finally, in 1915, Congress agreed to create the Chief of Naval Operations as the service chief, with a staff to support his work, and paralleled this with the creation of the permanent grades of admiral and vice admiral, all steps which Congress had long resisted, but for which the increasing threat of war now made reasonable to adopt.

The professionalization of the naval services that came to fruition at the dawn of the twentieth century was the result of a long and drawn out process that lasted for half a century, stretching from its origins in the Civil War to its early results in the Spanish-American and First World Wars. Beginning with the uncoordinated initiatives of "young Turks" who had been stimulated by the applications of new technology to criticize the establishment, professionalization took place as innovative ideas were slowly institutionalized and widened out as their progenitors in two successive generations of naval officers rose in rank, position, and authority. The fundamental change that new technology brought to the Navy was the catalyst that created a reevaluation of the nature of the naval profession. Yet, as technologies changed and developed over this half century, it was ultimately clear that the acquisition of technological knowledge and practice was essential to a naval professional, but it was an incomplete basis upon which to ground mastery of the naval profession.

NOTES This paper was first presented at the Annapolis Naval History Symposium "Professionalization of the Naval Services," an event co-developed by the U.S. Naval Institute, Naval Historical Center, Naval Historical Foundation, Marine Corps History and Museums Division, Marine Corps Heritage Foundation, Naval Order of the United States, CNA Center for Strategic Studies, and the U.S. Naval Academy History Department, and held on 1 April 2004. The paper was subsequently published under the title "In a Far More Thorough Manner," *Naval History* 19, no. 2 (April 2005), pp. 38–43.

1 There is a large literature on the meaning of professionalism in the fields of political science, sociology, and education. See, for example, Morris L. Cogan, "Toward a Definition of Profession," *Harvard Education Review* 23 (1953), pp. 33–50, and Ernest Greenwood, "Attributes of a Profession," *Social Work* 2 (1957), pp. 44–55; Harold L. Wilensky, "The Professionalization of Everyone," *American Journal of Sociology* 70 (1964), pp. 137–145. For an example of a current statement about the attributes of professionalism in another professional domain in the United States, see the website of the Nelson Mullins Riley & Scarborough Center on Professionalism at the University of South Carolina School of Law, http://professionalism.law.sc.edu.

2 For a description of professionalization of the military in terms of modern objectives in the modernization of Third World military forces, see the website of Creative Associates International, Inc. and the discussion of military measures that contribute to internal conflict prevention and stabilization at http://www.caii-dc.org/ghai/toolbox6.thm (accessed 15 March 2004).

3 See "The first formal examination for naval officers, 1677," in Hattendorf et al., eds., *British Naval Documents, 1204–1960.* Publications of the Navy Records Society, vol. 131 (Aldershot, Hampshire: Scolar Press for the Navy Records Society, 1993), document 172, pp. 296–299.

4 Jack Sweetman, *The U.S. Naval Academy: An Illustrated History* (Annapolis: Naval Institute, 1979), pp. 90–91.

5 Elting E. Morison, *Men, Machines, and Modern Times* (Cambridge, Massachusetts: The Massachusetts Institute of Technology, 1966), pp. 98–122. See also Edward W. Sloan III, *Benjamin Franklin Isherwood, Naval Engineer: The Years as Engineer in Chief* (Annapolis: Naval Institute Press, 1965), pp. 169–188, 260–261.

6 Elting Morison, *op cit.,* p. 119.

7 For the early history of the U.S.N.I., see Lawrence Carrol Allin, *The United States Naval Institute: Intellectual Forum of the New Navy, 1873–1889* (Manhattan, Kansas: Military Historian/Aerospace Historian, 1979).

8 John D. Hayes and John B. Hattendorf, eds., *The Writings of Stephen B. Luce* (Newport: Naval War College Press, 1975), p. 162.

9 For a detailed study, see Arden Bucholz, *Moltke, Schlieffen, and Prussian War Planning* (New York and Oxford: Berg Publishing, 1991).

10 Captain Wyman H. Packard, USN (ret.), *A Century of U.S. Naval Intelligence* (Washington, D.C.: Department of the Navy, 1996).

11 "Introduction," *The Official Records of the Union and Confederate Navies in the War of the Rebellion* (Washington: Government Printing Office, 1894), vol. 1, p. viii.

12 Commodore Stephen B. Luce, "Report of a Board on a Post-Graduate Course," 13 June 1883," in 48th Cong., 2nd sess., Senate Ex. Doc No. 68, *Letter from the Secretary of the Navy Reporting . . . Steps taken by him to establish an advanced course of education for naval officers at Coaster's harbor Island . . .* (Washington: Congressional Printing Office, 1885), p. 4.

13 John B. Hattendorf, "Luce's Idea of the Naval War College," in John B. Hattendorf, ed., *Naval History and Maritime Strategy: Collected Essays* (Malabar, Florida: Robert Krieger Publishing Co., 2000), pp. 17–28.

14 S. B. Luce, "On the Study of Naval Warfare as a Science," in Hayes and Hattendorf, eds., *Writings of Stephen B. Luce,* pp. 47, 68.

15 Donald Chisholm, *Waiting for Dead Men's Shoes: Origins and Development of the U.S. Navy's Officer Personnel System, 1793–1941* (Stanford, California: Stanford University Press, 2001), p. 435.

16 Ibid., pp. 435–436.

17 Quoted in ibid., p. 541.

XVII *American Naval Bases in Europe*

I n home waters, the locations of naval bases, dockyards, and arsenals are usually tied to ports that are important for strategic defense as well as sources of industrial manpower and tied to routes of communication for providing the supplies for construction, repair, and manning.

The criteria for an overseas naval base are different. In the Age of Sail, the selection of overseas bases was based on considerations of supporting a mobile fleet in terms of geo-strategic relationships involving distance and travel patterns. These patterns were created by the prevailing favorable currents, winds, and weather that affected travel to key colonial and island possessions, shipping routes for supply within distant regions, and the locations of a country's overseas strategic interests.

This situation gave the advantage to navies that could launch a major fleet to dominate a distant area. The key strategic factor was the ability to maintain and to concentrate naval forces along key routes. The Industrial Revolution and steam warships changed this calculus, allowing speed and mobility without regard to wind and weather, and placing bases directly for operational requirements. In theory, major naval powers could reduce the size of their presence on distant stations and base themselves at home, from which they could quickly and effectively concentrate on critical distant points, shifting from one theatre of operations to another as the situation demanded. While this thinking led to repeated efforts to do without overseas basing, other practicalities intervened.

Theory was modified by the issues surrounding fuel consumption, storage, and range—a set of factors that decreased as technology advanced and more efficient fuels gradually replaced one another. At the same time, the presence of a larger and readily mobile, steam-powered war fleet close to its supply bases, which could quickly concentrate in nearby home waters, enhanced a country's ability to defy a hostile force coming from overseas. In the case of the United States, from the mid-1880s, industrial age warships provided the ability to operate outside the western hemisphere, but when comparable or superior naval forces existed, they decreased her ability to operate without the aid of allies.[1]

In our present post-industrial age, there have been significant changes in the characteristics of overseas naval basing as well as some confusion and loose usage of words in English over the differences in meaning of the ways that they have been described as a "base," a "facility," or more generically and vaguely among writers in defence issues in recent years as "access." Whatever the word or phrase used, the subject we are dealing with here involves the use of places in European countries for the support of the U.S. Navy. Their purposes and justifications have varied widely over time and sometimes one base will be used simultaneously for a variety of purposes. Generally speaking, these purposes are defined as support for naval forces (1) that are operating or expect to operate in combat operations in nearby waters; (2) that provide a presence at locations that are critical to national and overall foreign policy credibility; (3) that are part of a broad alliance structure; (4) that are designed to protect or to provide military assistance to the particular country in which they are located; or (5) that are a way station to provide support long-range or global power projection.

This last point is the one that has changed most clearly over time, as it is primarily affected by the changing needs for logistics, refueling, and communications support that are tied to changing technologies. Further categories of support can be established as subsets of these five purposes, when one narrowly defines operational and technical functions relating to such operations as protection of shipping, transport of men and materiel, submarine warfare, anti-submarine warfare, communications, surveillance, tactical air support, and so forth.[2]

From the early days of the United States Navy to 1905, the United States typically organized its overseas naval operations on a regional basis, called "stations." Sometimes only one or two ships were used to protect American trade and commercial interests abroad. In Europe, the station was first called the Mediterranean Station, and then, when American foreign policy and commercial interests grew more to the northward, the European Station.[3]

The Beginnings, 1801–1916

Ships of the U.S. Navy first appeared in European waters in 1801, when Commodore Richard Dale arrived at Gibraltar, following Tripoli's declaration of war on the United States in May 1801, in what would become known as the Barbary Wars.[4] On the invitation of the British governor at Gibraltar, Dale's three American frigates and a schooner began using the Royal Navy's facilities to support their operations along the North African coast. Since the United States did not authorize its supply vessels to pass Gibraltar, Dale established a base at Syracuse on Sicily and obtained use of a naval hospital at Pisa. On station, the American Mediterranean squadron purchased its supplies through the firm of deButts and Purviance, naval agents at Leghorn (Livorno), but these agents, in turn, were paid by the U.S. Navy through the British firm of Mackenzie and Glennie in London. At the same time, Dale used Malta occasionally as a place to water. In 1803 when one of Dale's successors, Commodore Edward Preble, obtained firm assurances that Morocco would abide by its treaty of friendship with the United States, Preble began to use Syracuse and Malta as the main bases of operations until the end of the Barbary Wars in 1807. At that point, American forces returned to Gibraltar, but retained their agents at Syracuse, Leghorn, Naples, and Malta. While these places had suited the particular needs of wartime operations, the American government looked for a more advantageous place for peacetime naval operations. As early as 1807, efforts were made to obtain an American base at Port Mahon in Spain's Balearic Islands.

The War of 1812 temporarily ended the U.S. Navy's presence in Europe, but on the conclusion of that conflict in 1815, American warships returned to the Mediterranean. The U.S. commander immediately made direct approaches to Spanish officials to try to obtain use of a base at either Cartagena, Port Mahon, or Algeciras. By 1816, the Spanish government agreed to allow temporary American use of Port Mahon, but not a more permanent arrangement while there were diplomatic differences over the American claim to West Florida as part of the Louisiana Purchase and issues related to Latin American independence. Due to this, the U.S. Navy renewed its use of Gibraltar as its principal ship repair and naval stores depôt with the use of the naval hospital at Pisa.

The U.S. Navy continued to make intermittent use of Port Mahon until 1821, when the Spanish king granted a six-month renewable right to use that port. In response to what was only a temporary grant, the United States Navy reacted strongly by sending four supply ships from the United States to Port Mahon with equipment for the new base, immediately closing the naval hospital at Pisa and moving its facilities to Port Mahon, then ordering all spare anchors, spars, and other equipment at Gibraltar to Port Mahon. Perhaps naval officials thought that this aggressive response might make it more likely that the Spanish king's grant would be renewed and, in fact, when the first renewal request was made after six months, the Spanish government answered that it would be considered while American use continued. In March 1822, however, President James Monroe proposed to Congress the recognition of Spain's former colonies in Latin America as independent states. This action brought an immediate protest from Spain and the cancellation of all basing privileges granted to the U.S. Navy at Port Mahon.

The U.S. Navy removed its supplies and equipment back to Gibraltar, but in 1825, Commodore John Rodgers was successful in his negotiations with Spain. The Spanish approved the establishment of the American depôt at Port Mahon and granted the duty-free entry of American equipment and supplies for use of the squadron. Further concessions on dutiable goods destined for the U.S. naval squadron were eventually granted, as some 2,000 officers and men circulated annually about $150,000 in the region during the 1830s and 1840s.[5]

The American position on Minorca gradually became tenuous. With the arrival of the French Navy's early steam propelled warships in the Mediterranean, American officials became concerned that France might easily seize Minorca from Spain as an increasingly important strategic point between France and Algeria. When Spain refused to give France coaling privileges on Minorca in 1843, the French government lodged a formal protest against the privileged position given to the U.S. Navy. In order to avoid further tensions, Spain promised France to take a consistent position, and in 1846 informed the United States that the privileges granted to the U.S. Navy would be terminated. At that point, the American government was preoccupied by the annexation of Texas in 1845 and the subsequent war with Mexico that forced the temporary recall of the U.S. Mediterranean Squadron for service in the Caribbean in 1846.

At the end of the Mexican War, the U.S. Navy squadron returned to the Mediterranean and proceeded to Port Mahon on Minorca to remove American supplies and to make plans for a base of operations that could accommodate future American naval needs for coal supplies. The first ship to herald the return of the squadron in September 1847 was the USS *Princeton,* the U.S. Navy's first anthracite coal–burning, screw-propeller-driven warship, which had been sent to Europe to show off her technology. These plans were soon very quickly overshadowed by events in Europe. In January 1848, *Princeton* was anchored at Messina and witnessed the first of the series of uprisings that began to spread across Europe in 1848–1849. Not uncharacteristically, many

Americans assumed that these events were the arrival in Europe of their own demo-cratic ideas.[6] Meanwhile, Commodore George C. Read dismantled the American naval base on Minorca, but not without first demonstrating to the government in Madrid the great popularity and support that Americans had won with the local people of Minorca, whose economy they had effectively supported.

Meanwhile with increased American interest in the Levant and events in Syria, Commodore Read initially thought about establishing a base at Syracuse on Sicily, but this proved impractical due to the instability of the revolutionary government there. At Genoa, the new government in the Piedmont acted quickly and gave the American squadron temporary rights to deposit its stores and equipment at La Spezia, where no duties would be imposed, and the squadron could also have the free use of a building at the *lazaretto*. Read dithered between settling the base at La Spezia, which the Pied-montese thought they might eventually use for a naval base of their own, and moving to either Syracuse or Portoferraio on Elba. In July 1848, USS *Supply*'s arrival at La Spezia with stores and equipment for the station forced Read to decide. With increasing unrest in the Italian peninsula, growing American commercial shipping in the Gulf of Genoa, and a million dollars worth of American goods that required protection ashore, Read opted for La Spezia.

From 1848 until 1861, La Spezia remained the main base for the U.S. Navy's Medi-terranean Squadron.[7] In 1861, with the secession of the southern states and the tempo-rary establishment of the Confederate States of America, the government in Washington withdrew the Mediterranean Squadron. It did not reappear until the end of the war in 1865.

Even before the end of the war, the U.S. Navy Department had decided that it needed to reestablish its presence in European waters in order to counter the threat that the Confederate raiders had posed on American merchant shipping. Before the Civil War, the focus of American naval interest had been entirely on the Mediterranean, but American officials now saw the need for a presence in both northern and southern Eu-ropean waters. With this thought in mind, the reestablished naval force became known as the European Squadron. Looking toward the need to operate in the north as well as in the south, American officials chose Lisbon to be the new base of operations, but it was to be merely an anchorage and not involve the use of property ashore. The new approach was to use mobile store ships, anchored at key rendezvous places throughout the sta-tion, to purchase fresh food and coal in local ports as needed, but to send dry stores, ma-chinery, and equipment directly from the United States. For major ship repairs, the European Squadron depended on the use of British facilities at Gibraltar.

Despite these plans made in Washington, a number of European cities were inter-ested in attracting the American squadron to the use of their port facilities and a num-ber of Americans were also making proposals for different options. These were given further impetus in May 1869, when the Navy Department decided that afloat basing was too expensive and ordered the European Squadron to move to shore-based facili-ties. At that point it also seemed clear that the main focus of future operations for the United States would remain in the Mediterranean. At the same time, the U.S. Navy found it was paying considerably more for services in Lisbon than its British counterparts.

To remedy the situation, the American squadron took up an immediate opportu-nity to use Villefranche, near Nice, as a temporary basing site, while giving thought over the next few years to a more permanent base of naval operations. Proposals were made to reestablish La Spezia as a base or a coal depôt, while others suggested the use of Crete and Cyrenaica on the North African coast.[8] A French company offered to sell a stretch of land on the Bab el-Mandeb for a coaling and watering station at the Indian Ocean entrance to the Red Sea. None of these proposals were taken up with any seriousness, and the U.S. Navy continued to rent warehouses at Villefranche for thirteen years, through 1882.

In July 1883, Secretary of the Navy William Chandler ordered the naval shore facility at Villefranche closed and its stores removed as soon as possible. At the same time, Chandler took steps to remove American family members, who had often followed officers and men stationed on board ships assigned to overseas duty. This practice had become quite common by the 1830s in the U.S. Navy, but had never been seriously challenged. Apparently motivated by what he considered to be the moral impropriety of a naval squadron wintering on the French Riviera, as well as seeing little use for American warships in European waters, Chandler threatened to dismiss any officer who did not immediately send his family members home to the United States, noting that "it is folly to deny that the presence of families does not affect the movement of the ships or the devotion to duty of the officers."[9]

Despite this, American warships continued to use Villefranche as a rendezvous. In 1889, the U.S. Navy temporarily discontinued all naval operations on its European Station. Although the new administration of President Benjamin Harrison was keenly interested in overseas expansion, there seemed little interest in European affairs, while issues surrounding Cuba, Puerto Rico, and Hawaii were beginning to develop. To counter this, the American Ambassador to France, William Whitelaw Reid, suggested that the State Department enter negotiations to obtain a coaling station in the Azores to replace the facilities at Villefranche, but neither the State nor the Navy Department approved of his recommendation.[10]

Five years later in 1894, the U.S. Navy reestablished its operations in European waters, but did not take any initiative to establish a shore base. Operations in this region over the next two decades were sporadic and, when present, the American squadron relied on the occasional supply vessel coming from the United States, supplemented by purchases in local ports. The Near Eastern crisis in the mid-1890s required U.S. naval forces to patrol the eastern Mediterranean, but no local facilities were obtained. With the outbreak of the Spanish-American War in 1898, the U.S. Navy withdrew its forces from Europe for service in the western hemisphere and on the Asiatic Station. In the course of the war, however, some thought was given to having an American base to support attacks on Spain in its home waters. In this regard, thought was given to using the Canary Islands, Morocco, or returning to Port Mahon. Nothing came of these discussions and there was apparently no attempt to acquire a base on Spanish territory as part of the peace negotiations in Paris.

In 1901, the American squadron returned to the Mediterranean, but remained only for four years without acquiring any shore-based facilities. In 1905, the system of overseas stations that the U.S. Navy had used for more than a century was abandoned. In its place, the U.S. Navy began to apply some of the strategic ideas that such officers as Stephen B. Luce and A. T. Mahan and others were beginning to recommend in terms of concentration of force for the U.S. Navy as a modern battleship navy. Three fleet groupings were established: an Asiatic Fleet, a Pacific Fleet, and the Atlantic Fleet, with the Atlantic Fleet containing all the U.S. Navy's battleships.

The recently formed United States Atlantic Fleet did deploy its Third Division to Algeciras, Spain, in 1906, as a presence to support British diplomatic efforts at the conference dealing with German aspirations in Latin America. In November and December 1910, 16 battleships, 6 cruisers, and a number of destroyers and other vessels visited England and France on a training exercise. Then, in 1911, the Second Division of the Atlantic Fleet visited the Baltic ports in an effort to improve German-American relations.

Although no U.S. naval force was permanently maintained in European waters between 1905 and 1917, the government of Montenegro initiated negotiations with the United States in 1909, offering the use of a bay and land for a U.S. naval base on the eastern shore of the southern Adriatic coast.[11] Instead, American officials decided that U.S. warships would depend on local commercial supplies or, when warranted, colliers or supply ships could be sent from the United States.

During the first, century-long period of American naval activity in Europe, the essential characteristics of the U.S. Navy's approach to basing changed little, even though the Navy itself was transformed by the Industrial Revolution. While the nature of the warships and many commodities needed for overseas use for these vessels were new—for example, coal and replacement machinery parts—the characteristics of basing in Europe between 1801 and 1916 remained much the same. All that changed in 1917.

During and after World War I, 1917–1924

The United States remained neutral during the first phase of the Great War and did not enter the war until April 1917, although American warships did visit European waters as neutrals. The battleships USS *Tennessee* and USS *North Carolina* carried relief funds to England, Holland, and France, while also protecting and evacuating refugees: Americans as well as Jews in Syria and Palestine and Armenians in Turkey. In 1915, the cruisers USS *Des Moines* and USS *Chester* relieved the two battleships. They concentrated their work in the eastern Mediterranean, joining the steam yacht USS *Scorpion* to support an international commission dealing with war refugees and displaced persons. None of these vessels used an American base ashore.

All of this changed quickly and dramatically in 1917, when President Woodrow Wilson asked Congress for a declaration of war on 2 April. During the next eighteen months the number of American ships grew, so that in November 1918 the United States Navy had a total of 354 naval vessels of all classes serving in European waters, from battleships to converted yachts, tug boats, and submarine chasers. For the first time since the American Civil War in the 1860s, the purpose for an American naval presence in Europe was active combat operations.

The new variety in ship types and the adaptation of aircraft to naval operations created new basing requirements. The first American warships to arrive in Europe were the six destroyers under the command of Commander Joseph K. Taussig that arrived at Queenstown, Ireland, on 4 May 1917. They were soon followed by a Cruiser and Transport Force that eventually comprised 45 transports and 24 cruisers that moved 911,047 troops; naval aviation units that had 500 aircraft and 16,000 officers and men, a Patrol Squadron of 38 destroyers, 16 armed yachts, plus minesweepers, tenders, and tugs; the Naval Overseas Transport Service with 450 cargo ships; and a division of five battleships.[12] While American ships delivered more than six million tons of equipment during the war, the U.S. Navy quickly discovered that mobile support needed to be complemented by shore bases[13] and each different type of operation required different facilities.

Britain, France, Portugal, and Italy provided bases, although the most important American naval forces in Europe were, with a few exceptions, under the operational command of the Royal Navy.[14] The American contribution soon began to require more permanency, so that a number of allied facilities or areas within or adjacent to allied bases were temporarily turned over to American forces to manage to provide for American forces during the war.

Entering active combat operations in the midst of the war, one of the U.S. Navy's first concerns was to find support for ships protecting its lines of communication across the Atlantic. Following the bombardment of Ponta Delgada in the Azores by a German U-boat in July 1917, the U.S. Navy took immediate steps to develop its own base there as a preemptive move to thwart any German attempt to use the islands as well as to protect American convoys. The American base eventually supported five U.S. submarines, two yachts, a tender, an oiler, two minesweepers, and a tug. In addition, the first U.S. Marine Corps aviation unit to be trained and sent overseas went to the Azores, where it used short-range aircraft of limited endurance in search of U-boats.

For convoy escort operations, an American base was developed at Queenstown in Ireland, where the destroyer tenders, USS *Melville* and USS *Dixie,* were moored to provide maintenance support. By the end of the war, some eight thousand Americans were based in the town, whose regular inhabitants numbered only six or seven thousand. Beginning with the first ships to arrive in May 1917 and remaining until the base was completely disestablished in January 1919, the U.S. base came to support 36 destroyers and 36 submarine chasers that protected the shipping lanes from the western coast of England to a meeting point some 200–300 miles west of Queenstown in the Atlantic. The American ships were credited with spending 66% of their time at sea and protecting 39% of the allied traffic on that sea route.[15]

To complement this escort work, the U.S. Navy established a base at Berehaven in Bantry Bay, Ireland, to support a squadron of coal-burning U.S. Navy battleships to serve as a back-up force for convoy protection in case the German High Seas Fleet or German cruisers eluded the British fleet. Three additional battleships were added to this squadron in August 1918. Here also, the U.S. Navy stationed seven of its L-class submarines for anti-submarine work.[16]

Similarly, Brest became a particularly important base for American naval escorts. Activities began there in June 1917 with the arrival of eight converted yachts and ended in February 1919, when the facilities were returned to the French Navy. The American presence grew rapidly from January 1918 until it was closed in February 1919. American ships here escorted 91% of all convoys in and out of France, both to Brest and to other ports, including all the ships that brought the 1,600,000 American troops to France.[17]

Brest was the main base for U.S. escorts convoying troops for France, but not all the troops debarked at Brest. Certainly, Brest was the most important debarkation point, where a total of 791,000 troops landed. The second largest number, 198,000, landed at St. Nazaire, while 50,000 landed at Bordeaux, 13,000 at Le Havre, 4,000 at La Pallice, and 1,000 at Marseilles. To support with these operations, American port officers served in each of these ports and additional American naval shore facilities were established at some of them. Lorient was the base for American minesweepers that operated between Penmarch and Fromentine with minesweeping equipment provided by the French Navy.[18]

Bordeaux provided shipbuilding, repair, and supply for American vessels at French facilities managed through the liaison of the American port officer, who also cooperated with American port officers serving at Le Verdon, Pauillac, and Bassens. Additional facilities were established at Bassens,[19] six miles below Bordeaux on the Gironde, where transport ships too large to reach Bordeaux could off-load their cargos. There, between August 1917 and April 1918, the U.S. Army Corps of Engineers built a series of wharves and extended rail lines from Bordeaux. By late 1918, a work force of some 6,000 Afro-American stevedores was employed at Bassens to unload the arriving cargo. Further to the south, a U.S. naval base was co-located with the Royal Navy to convoy shipping from the Azores, Britain, and the Mediterranean.

In Britain, additional specialized bases were established to serve American forces. In September 1918, an American naval base was established at Cardiff, Wales, to supervise the shipment of coal to France for use by American troop transports at Le Havre, Brest, and other ports on the Bay of Biscay. By November 1918, 1,758 American officers and 4,101 American seamen were working at Cardiff. During the period of its operation some 96,000 tons of coal were delivered in 53 colliers operated by the U.S. Naval Overseas Transportation Service.

More distantly, a base to support 39 American submarine chasers was built on a barren and undeveloped cove on Corfu in June 1918. Supported by the destroyer tender USS *Leonidas,* their assignment was to prevent German or Austrian submarines from passing through the Strait of Otranto, from the Adriatic to the Mediterranean. They also took part in the bombardment of Durazzo and were the subject of some unfulfilled schemes for an allied landing in the Adriatic.[20]

Two specialized American naval bases were established in Scotland to support the U.S. Naval Mine Force in 1918–1919 and its work to lay and later remove the Northern Barrage of mines across the northern part of the North Sea, between the Orkney Islands and southwestern Norway.[21] This effort required special bases in Scotland, where the predominately American manufactured mines were transferred to minelayers. Because of difficulties with the rail transport involved, two bases were developed. One was at Inverness and one at Invergordon, ports separated by thirty-five miles on the Moray Firth, and serviced by separate rail lines. Two idle distilleries were found to house 20 officers and 1,000 American sailors at each base. By the time of the armistice, the U.S. Navy had laid 56,571 of the total 70,117 mines laid in the North Sea. In 1919, the minesweeping operation was based at these same locations, with the addition of a small tract of land at Carness Point, Kirkwall, in the Orkneys.

The variety in basing requirements for specific types of operational tasks was extended even further with the appearance of naval aviation.[22] Through the initiative of Lieutenant Kenneth Whiting, the French Navy agreed to train American naval aviators at its Naval Aviation School at Horton, with further training at the main American naval air base at Moutchic on the north shore of Lake Lacanau some thirty miles north of Bordeaux. After training, American aviators served in France to protect harbor entrances and coastal shipping routes.

American naval air stations were clustered near the major ports. At Brest, a seaplane and kite balloon station was built in April 1918, with other seaplane stations directly south on Île Tudy, and on Île d'Ehre Vrach near L'Aber Vrach, twenty miles north of Brest at the entrance to the Channel. Then, an American dirigible station was built seven miles from Brest at Guipavas. Unlike others, the air station at Tréguier was a French-built facility transferred for temporary American use.

Near the mouth of the Loire River, stations were built south of the river at Fromentine and to the north of river's mouth at Le Croisic. Ten miles upstream there was a dirigible station at Paimboeuf. At La Pallice, west of La Rochelle, an air station was started, but not completed at the time of the Armistice. Kite balloons were based at La Trinité near Rochefort-sur-Mer. On the Gironde, Pauillac became the most important assembly point for American naval aircraft shipped to France. The base at St. Trojan provided air cover at the mouth of the Gironde. Rochefort was used as a supply base for dirigible parts. Near Bordeaux, construction was begun on a patrol station at Gujan and on the sand dunes at Arcachon on the eastern side of Cape Ferret, the southernmost of the American naval air stations.

American naval aviation operations began in France and soon extended to Ireland, with a cluster of stations around Bantry Bay, including kite balloon facilities at Berehaven and at nearby Castletownbere with its seaplane base at Whiddy Island. On the southern coast, there were other seaplane stations at Queenstown and at Wexford on the extreme southeast point of Ireland. On the north coast, there was a seaplane station at Lough Foyle with a kite balloon station fifteen miles to the west on Lough Swilly.

In England, Eastleigh, about fifteen miles northwest of Portsmouth and five miles north of Southampton, was used as an aircraft assembly base, while to the north in Lincolnshire, the air station at Killingholme was transferred to the U.S. Navy in March 1918 to provide naval air reconnaissance and air cover for North Sea convoys.

From 1918 American naval air stations were activated in Italy, where a seaplane station was located on Lake Bolsena, sixty miles northwest of Rome, to bomb Austrian positions at Pola across the Adriatic. For similar missions, another base was at Porto Corsini, seventy miles southwest of Venice. At Pescara, American naval aviators commanded a large base and provided the pilots and men to operate Italian aircraft.

Another specialized group of operational air facilities for land-based aircraft was organized in England and in France for the purpose of attacking the German submarine, destroyer, and minelaying bases at Ostend, Zeebrugge, and Bruges.[23] Known as the Northern Bombing Group, U.S. Navy and Marine Corps pilots, directed from their headquarters at Autingues near Ardres, operated from scattered airfields at Le Fresne, Campagne, Guînes, and St. Inglevert near Calais, and Oye near Gravelines. As German forces began to retreat, the Northern Bombing Group began to advance into Belgium with new bases at Knesselare and Maria Aalter.

Even before the Armistice, American naval forces began to dismantle and return their bases. By 1919, all the bases in Italy, France, and the British Isles were closed, with U.S. Navy equipment and men removed. Not quite all American naval forces left European waters. At Constantinople, while other bases were being closed in Western Europe, a new base was opened in early 1919. There, Rear Admiral Mark Bristol supervised U.S. naval port officers at Smyrna, Constantinople, Derindje, and Constanza, Romania, supplying the Near East Relief Program and overseeing the evacuation of Armenian and

Greek refugees during the Greek-Turkish War of 1920–1922. Following the installation of Atatürk's government in August 1923, American naval forces remained in the eastern Mediterranean for only an additional six months and closed the final bases for this phase in the spring of 1924.[24]

During and after World War II, 1941–1947

With ships and aircraft that had longer ranges, greater fuel efficiency, and enhanced underway replenishment and supply procedures, fewer shore bases were needed in Europe during the Second World War than were needed in the First World War. As in the earlier experience, American naval bases followed the operational needs of the moment. With no American bases in Europe for two decades, the U.S. Navy used whatever bases it could to meet operational demands, first to fight the Battle of the Atlantic, then to move landing forces.

Even before the United States entered the war, there was a need to maintain the lines of communication across the North Atlantic. When Iceland came within the war zone in March 1941, Britain and the United States made an agreement for its defense. Beginning with a small Marine base established in July, American facilities there grew rapidly throughout the war, complementing British facilities with a Naval Operating Base for convoy work at Reykjavík, a Construction Battalion, and a Naval Air Station at Keflavík, These and other facilities remained until American forces evacuated Iceland in 1947.

The 1940 Lend-Lease Agreement between Britain and the United States, naval staff talks in January 1941, and the March 1941 Lend-Lease Act led to the construction of four bases in the United Kingdom for the support of North Atlantic convoy work.[25] Two were operated by the U.S. Navy until 1944: the Naval Operating Bases at Londonderry, Northern Ireland, and Roseneath, Scotland, on the Firth of Clyde. For further support of the Battle of the Atlantic, Portugal granted the United States Navy the use of Terceira in the Azores as a refueling base for warships as well as merchant vessels. In June 1944, U.S. Naval Forces Azores Command was established at Santa Maria on Fayal for aircraft refueling. These facilities were returned to Portugal in May 1946.

Other American bases followed the lines of the Allied landings in the Mediterranean, initially with temporary bases first at Gibraltar, in Morocco, then Algeria, before crossing the Mediterranean to establish a naval operating base at Palermo, Sicily, six days after the capture of the city, on 28 July 1943. Palermo served as the U.S. Navy's ship repair base for the Anzio landing and support base for the landing in southern France. Even after these operations, Palermo was used to support the war in the Pacific and remained in use until March 1946.

Salerno, Italy, had been captured in September 1943 and Naples fell soon afterwards on 21 October. Following the cleanup of the damaged ports, Naples became the headquarters of Commander, U.S. Naval Forces, Northwest African Waters. In February 1944, Salerno became an Advanced Amphibious Training Base, bringing instructors and personnel from a similar base that had been established earlier in Algeria. Salerno was used for training for the landing planned for southern France. The operating base continued in service until January 1945.

The fall of Italy in September 1943 also brought the islands of Corsica and Sardinia into Allied hands. Still facing the threat of German E-boats and other enemy vessels in the region, the U.S. Navy established a number of bases for PT boats, having a limited range and endurance. The most important of these was established at La Maddalena, Sardinia, in July 1944.

Plans for a cross-Channel landing from Britain were begun as early as 1942, for which purposes amphibious training facilities were started in Cornwall and Devon. Equipment brought from the United States for the assaults was first delivered to Roseneath, Scotland, then brought to the U.S. Advanced Amphibious Base at Appledore, Devon, and to numerous other ports, such as the Royal Navy's amphibious force training bases at Fowey, Salcombe, and Teignmouth or for operations to Milford Haven, Falmouth, Plymouth, Dartmouth, and Deptford. Vicarage Barracks at Plymouth, with nearby Appledore, became the first centers for the American amphibious forces.[26] As preparations developed, numerous supporting bases and sub-bases followed as new bases opened at Portland-Weymouth, Poole, and Southampton—all of which were deactivated for U.S. Navy use in 1945. Finally, following the Normandy landings, a U.S. Naval Advanced Base was established at Cherbourg during 1944–1945, as a salvage base with a radio station, mine and bomb disposal unit, harbor control unit, and fuel office.

The final U.S. naval base to be established in Europe was the Advance Base at Bremerhaven, Germany. On 1 June 1945, this base was established under Commander, U.S. Naval Forces Germany, as nearly all U.S. naval forces left Europe. Of all the bases in Europe, Bremerhaven alone continued uninterrupted activity as a U.S. naval base into the Cold War era. The headquarters of Commander-in-Chief, U.S. Naval Forces, Europe, also remained to allow continued cooperation with the Royal Navy.[27]

Cold War, 1949–1991

The establishment of NATO brought both a new and wider structure for basing in Europe that involved reciprocal usage of national bases as required. With it came the need for even fewer bases for American naval forces in Europe,[28] but those that existed within the NATO context had a consistent structure in terms of the 1951 and 1952 Status of Forces Agreements.[29] In the first years of NATO, the U.S. Navy initially declared, in sharp contrast to its sister services, that it did not need advanced shore bases in Europe, which were both vulnerable and expensive. In particular, it declared that no base was necessary in the Mediterranean. These views slowly changed over time.

In northern Europe between 1946 and 1956, ships of the U.S. Navy operated from the Royal Navy's facilities at Plymouth. When the Peace Treaty restrictions on bases in Italy were lifted in 1950 and NATO's southern command headquarters was established at Naples in 1951, the U.S. Navy established a base there to support the Commander in Chief, Allied Forces Southern Europe, who was an American admiral. Facilities in the Naples area eventually included an Air Station with Communications, Medical, Military Sea Transportation Service, and Fleet Support Centers. Shortly thereafter a support base was established for the U.S. Sixth Fleet at Gaeta, north of Naples.

Even before this occurred, the United States saw strategic value in strengthening its relationships with Spain. Already on the Atlantic coast of North Africa, a naval air base was expanded at Port Lyautey, Morocco, for naval patrol aircraft to operate over the entrance to the Mediterranean. At the same time in 1950 and despite aversion to Franco's government, negotiations were begun to obtain U.S. air and naval bases in that country. In 1953, the Pact of Madrid was signed that allowed guest bases in Spain. The new fleet and naval air base at Rota was begun in 1955 and in operation by 1957.[30] Nearly simultaneously, Portugal agreed to the establishment of a guest U.S. Naval Air Facility in 1954 on Terceira in the Azores, which also entered service in 1957.

The growing need for long runways for land-based naval patrol aircraft engaged in intelligence collection on Warsaw Pact naval activities led in 1959 to the joint NATO and U.S. construction of the Naval Air Station, Sigonella, at Catania, Sicily, to relieve congestion at Hal Far Naval Air Facility on Malta.

Another type of highly specialized base was that established at Edzell, Scotland, between Dundee and Aberdeen on the North Sea coast. Here, from 1960, a U.S. Naval Security Group Activity provided electronic technical support for high frequency direction finding and fleet communications.

Beginning in late 1960, the base at Rota, Spain, began to support operations of American nuclear submarines in addition to its other activities. Shortly thereafter, in March 1961, the U.S. Navy opened a Fleet Ballistic Missile Submarine Base at Holy Loch, Greenock, Scotland. For this purpose, an auxiliary floating dry dock and advance base section docks were towed across the Atlantic to the Clyde, where they were joined by submarine tenders for *Polaris* and later *Poseidon* submarines. Inside the Mediterranean, American nuclear submarines used a detachment of the Naval Support Activity, Naples, in the Maddalena archipelago off the northeast coast of Sardinia. Along with the arrival of the submarine tender USS *Howard W. Gilmore* in early 1973, La Maddalena was commissioned as an independent U.S. naval station.

In July 1961, following a period when Iceland disagreed with American and NATO policies,[31] the U.S. Army and Air Force withdrew their forces and passed to the U.S. Navy the coordination of the Iceland Defense Force, moving some of its patrol aircraft from Argentia, Newfoundland, to Iceland and adding a variety of other naval units. Nearly simultaneously in 1961, a U.S. Naval Air Facility was co-located with the Royal Air Force Base at Mildenhall, Suffolk, designed to provide logistic support for U.S. naval aviation activities in the United Kingdom and in northern Europe.

In the early 1970s, the U.S. Navy increased the number of warships home ported overseas, placing nuclear submarines in Sardinia, a Carrier Task Force with a patrol gunboat squadron and tender in Italy, and destroyers at Phaleron Bay near Athens. By the end of the 1970s, the increasing range of submarine-launched ballistic missiles allowed some support to be withdrawn.[32] At the same time, U.S. naval strategy began to take a new direction, which in the 1980s would become known as the Maritime Strategy.[33] These changes made alterations in strategy, command structures, force deployment, and logistics distribution, but required no new land-based naval facilities in Europe. Throughout the Cold War period, unlike earlier peacetime periods, the point of the U.S. Navy's activity was to maintain peacetime employment strategies while at the same time supporting planned wartime employment strategies with the same vessels and from the same facilities.[34]

Summation

The history of the U.S. Navy's use of shore-based naval facilities over two centuries shows a distinct evolution in four separate phases of development in its use of advance overseas basing. During the first century, the minimal basing requirements evolved around independent, American peacetime, foreign policy activities in European waters. From the First World War onward, the U.S. Navy operated in Europe in the context of alliances and multinational arrangements, concerning both European and global issues. The short-range weapons and short-endurance ships and aircraft of the First World War era required varied types and a relatively large number of small bases clustered around key strategic positions. During the Second World War, changes in weapons and vessels and their propulsion systems required fewer bases, but, as in the previous war, they were sited where operations required. After a brief period of withdrawal from overseas basing in Europe, Cold War basing requirements returned to a very similar advanced basing policy, as part of peacetime preparation for a possible war, to deal with issues both inside and outside the structure of NATO.

NOTES   This paper was originally presented at an international colloquium, "IXèmes Journées franco-britanniques d'histoire maritime," that took place at Cherbourg, France, 2–4 December 2004. The colloquium was organized by the Service Historique de la Marine; the subject was "Les bases de la puissance: arsenaux et ports de guerre depuis la révolution industrielle" [Military Bases: Arsenals and Naval Ports since the Industrial Revolution].

1 Bernard Brodie, *Sea Power in the Industrial Age* (Princeton, N.J.: Princeton University Press; Oxford: Oxford University Press, 1941), "Chapter VII: Strategic Geography and the Fuel Problem," pp. 105–123.

2 Robert E. Harkavy, *Great Power Competition for Overseas Bases: The Geopolitics of Access Diplomacy* (New York and Oxford: Pergamon Press, 1982), chap. 2.

3 See John B. Hattendorf, "The U.S. Navy and the 'Freedom of the Seas,' 1775–1917," in R. Hobson & T. Kristiansen, eds., *Navies in Northern Waters 1721–2000*. Naval Policy and History series, no. 26 (London: Frank Cass, 2004), pp. 151–174; and Hattendorf, "19th Century Forward Stations," (see Chapter XIV in this volume).

4 The following is based on James A. Field, *America and the Mediterranean World, 1776–1882* (Princeton, N.J.: Princeton University Press, 1969) and William N. Still, Jr., *American Sea Power in the Old World: The United States Navy in European and Near Eastern Waters, 1865–1917*. Contributions in Military History, no. 24 (Westport, Conn., and London: Greenwood Press, 1980). An outline history of each base, arranged alphabetically with bibliographical references for each entry, may be found in K. Jack Bauer and Paolo Enrico Coletta, eds., *United States Navy and Marine Corps Bases, Overseas* (Westport, Conn.: Greenwood Press, 1985), and Peter M. Swartz, *Sea Changes: Transforming US Navy Deployment Strategy: 1775–2002* (Alexandria, Va.: The CNA Corporation, 2002).

5 Field, *America and the Mediterranean World*, pp. 105–112, 210–213.

6 Ibid., pp. 216–218

7 Howard R. Marraro, "Spezia: An American Naval Base, 1848–68," *Military Affairs* 7 (Winter 1943), pp. 202–208.

8 James A. Field, Jr., "A Scheme in Regard to Cyrenaica," *Mississippi Valley Historical Review* 44 (December 1957), pp. 445–468.

9 Quoted in Still, *American Sea Power in the Old World*, pp. 51–52.

10 Ibid., p. 55.

11 Richard D. Challener, "Montenegro and the United States: A Balkan Fantasy," *Journal of Central European Affairs* 17 (October 1957), pp. 236–242.

12 Statistics are based on Jack Sweetman, *American Naval History: An Illustrated Chronology of the US Navy and Marine Corps, 1775 –Present* (Annapolis: Naval Institute Press, 1984), pp. 135–139.

13 Duncan S. Ballantine, *US Naval Logistics in the Second World War* (Princeton, N.J.: Princeton University Press, 1949), p. 23.

14 Swartz, *Sea Changes*, pp. 34–35.

15 Bauer and Coletta, *United States Navy and Marine Corps Bases, Overseas*, p. 386.

16 Paul Halpern, *A Naval History of World War I* (Annapolis: Naval Instiute Press, 1994), pp. 430, 436; Bauer and Coletta, *United States Navy and Marine Corps Bases, Overseas*, p. 385.

17 Bauer and Coletta, *United States Navy and Marine Corps Bases, Overseas*, pp. 378–381.

18 Ibid., pp. 381–382.

19 Ibid., pp. 374–375.

20 Ibid., pp. 388–389; Halpern, *A Naval History of World War I*, pp. 171–172.

21 Tor Jørgen Melien, *US Navy i norske farvann under første verdenskrig*. IFS Info 4/04 (Oslo: Institutt for Forsvarsstudier, 2004); Bauer and Coletta, *Bases, Overseas*, pp. 387–388; United States Navy Department, Office of Naval Records and Library, *The Northern Barrage and Other Mining Activities*. Publication Number 2 (Washington, D.C.: GPO, 1920) and *The Northern Barrage: Taking up the Mines*. Publication Number 4 (Washington, D.C.: GPO, 1920).

22 Bauer and Coletta, *United States Navy and Marine Corps Bases, Overseas*, pp. 361–374.

23 Ibid., pp. 390–392.

24 Henry B. Beers, *US Naval Detachment in Turkish Waters, 1919–1922* (Washington, D.C.: Navy Department, 1943).

25 Ballantine, *US Naval Logistics in the Second World War*, pp. 63–66.

26 Bauer and Coletta, *United States Navy and Marine Corps Bases, Overseas*, pp. 342–347, 351–352.

27 Peter M. Swartz, "The Navy's Search for a Strategy, 1945–47," *Naval War College Review* 49 (Spring 1996), pp. 102–108; and Peter M. Swartz, *Evolution of US Navy Roles in NATO: Always an Important Part of a Larger Whole*. CIM D0010808.A1/SR 1, October 2004 (Alexandria, Va.: The CNA Corporation, 2004).

28 For studies on the relationship of the U.S. Navy to NATO, see Sean M. Maloney, *Securing Command of the Sea: NATO Naval Planning, 1948–1954* (Annapolis: Naval Institute Press, 1995); Robert S. Jordan, *Alliance Strategy and Navies: The Evolution and Scope of NATO's Naval Dimension* (New York: St. Martin's Press, 1990); and Joel L. Sokolsky, *Seapower in the Nuclear Age: The United States Navy and NATO, 1949–1980* (Annapolis: Naval Institute Press, 1991).

29 Joseph M. Snee, ed., *NATO Agreements on Status: Travaux Préparatoires*. U.S. Naval War College International Law Studies, 1961, vol. LIV (Washington, D.C.: GPO, 1961).

30 Bauer and Coletta, *United States Navy and Marine Corps Bases, Overseas*, "Rota," pp. 275–282.

31 For a survey of this period, see Thor Whitehead, *Ally Who Came in from the Cold: A Survey of Icelandic Foreign Policy, 1948–1956* (Reykjavik: University of Iceland Press, 1998).

32 Swartz, *Evolution*, p. 63.

33 For this general development, see, John B. Hattendorf, *The Evolution of the US Navy's Maritime Strategy, 1978–1986*. Newport Paper 19 (Newport: Naval War College Press, 2004). See also, Swartz, *Sea Changes*, pp. 72–74.

34 Swartz, *Sea Changes*, pp. 101–103.

XVIII *The Past as Prologue*
The Changing Roles of Sea Power during the Twentieth Century

As one looks back across the past hundred years, one can see that sea power has been employed in a variety of strategic roles during the century. Theorists have proposed an expanding range of strategic roles. Many have been put into practice; some have worked while others have been failures. In practice, there have been missed opportunities as well as close-run races. In general, however, navies have played a variety of major strategic roles that have changed in the context of different strategic situations. Over the course of the twentieth century, our abstract understanding of naval strategic roles has developed over time, as also the historical record has led us to widen further our perception of those roles. Above all, we see that the issue of strategic roles is not merely a question of abstract concepts among naval officers, but of concepts enmeshed in broader issues that range from grand strategy, bureaucracy, and finance to diplomacy and international law. On the operational level, the consideration of strategic roles must often be based on issues ranging from cooperation with other services to combat effectiveness in carrying out a strategic vision.

The State of Theory in 1900

When the twentieth century opened, the ideas of Captain Alfred Thayer Mahan were already part of the scene. In 1900, he was just beginning to work on the final volume in his famous series on sea power.[1] In that series, and in his many other writings during the previous decade, he had already firmly laid the foundation for broad thinking about the role of navies within the context of grand strategy.[2] He was already a well-known name and his ideas were already informing public policy and professional discussion. Yet, not everyone agreed with him; not everyone who read and quoted his work understood it; and not everyone listened to what he had to say.

Although historical analysis, and the theory resulting from it, is immensely valuable, it has rarely, if ever, been the initial motivating force behind the actual use of naval power. Analysis and theory do, however, help us to understand the context within which navies operate and the human, intellectual, technological, and governmental processes surrounding their use. Despite what some in the nineteenth century thought, we now know that naval theory is not a static law of the physical universe, but an ever-evolving reflection on new and changing experience, as navies are used in different ways for different purposes over the course of time.

As the U.S. Navy rapidly developed and employed new technologies in the years from the mid-1880s onwards, it was clear that there was a tension between those who were interested in employing emerging technologies, by stretching technology to its conceivable limits, and those who were trying to understand the broader strategic roles of a navy and to use such conceptions as a guideline for structuring the Navy's force. One exulted in an array of new technological developments as the other sought a finer definition in choosing the specific technologies to develop for a specific purpose. The situation, which was relatively new for navies in the nineteenth century, has become a commonplace since. An early example is revealed in Mahan's own letters.

Exactly a century ago, the U.S. Navy was in the process of designing a new class of battleships. One bureau wanted very big ships; another wanted a greater number of ships, so it wanted them to be of medium size. One wanted the greatest speed attainable, while another the largest fuel capacity. Writing about how to resolve this particular dilemma, which has had many parallels since, Mahan told Secretary of the Navy John D. Long, "The Navy does not exist for ships, but ships for the navy and correct conclusions can not be *secured* unless you call in those who think *first* what does the Navy need for war, and next what kind of ships fulfill those needs. The technologist and Bureau man necessarily thinks first of his own specialty.[3] Allowing them to prevail could create a serious error that would be difficult to reverse. The country [may] be seized with a parsimonious fit, & we be left with a few monsters, instead of a number adequate to our varied requirements."[4] In adding this point, Mahan acknowledged that navies are built through a political process that involves public finance, as well as institutional, and personal, competition for resources. In this, the roles that a navy must perform in warfare at sea may be overlooked. Even more importantly, he was suggesting that in an age when new types of vessels were emerging—battleships, cruisers, destroyers, torpedo boats, submarines—each of those types had a range of different roles to perform. Less obviously to those of Mahan's generation, those roles changed with the changing roles of sea power.

Experience and Theory between 1900 and 1914

In the first years of the twentieth century, the maritime wars that occurred were small wars in distant areas. Naval professionals followed closely the events of the Sino-Japanese War of 1894–95, the Spanish-American War of 1898, the Boer War of 1899–1902, and the Russo-Japanese War of 1904–1905. In those events, many thought they saw the pattern for the role of sea power in the foreseeable future. From the perspective of the major naval powers, these were limited wars, conducted at a distance from the home country. It was in the context of such current events that Julian Corbett began to write his analytical reflection on his research and writing into the history of British strategy, which eventually appeared in 1911 as *Some Principles of Maritime Strategy*.[5]

Corbett's book appeared nearly simultaneously with a volume of lectures entitled *Naval Strategy*[6] that Mahan had delivered at the U.S. Naval War College between 1887 and 1911, but Corbett's newer work was very different from Mahan's revised lectures, although obviously stimulated by Mahan's other writing. Both writers had found stimulus in books on military theory, but each reacted differently in an attempt to point out the differences between land and sea warfare. In *Some Principles*, Corbett established some subtle and quite original points that clearly differentiated him from Mahan. One of the most important aspects was Corbett's original thinking on maritime conflict as a form of limited warfare. In addition, he saw drawbacks to Mahan's emphasis on concentrating naval force, believing it important to remain flexible with one's force by exploiting strategic deception through the appearance of weakness, but remaining capable of quickly and unexpectedly massing one's force against an enemy.[7]

Beyond these contributions to the general understanding of the nature of naval warfare, Corbett made some very important distinctions about the specific roles of naval force. Some readers of Mahan had taken on board the impression that the *only* purpose of a fleet was to destroy a similar battle fleet in a climactic and decisive battle in the tradition of Trafalgar, and, indeed, this has been one of the oldest popular traditions among officers of both the Royal Navy and the U.S. Navy. To try to correct this view, Corbett carefully pointed out that, while the basic issue ultimately revolved around the fact that "permanent and general command of the sea is the condition of ultimate success,"[8] there were different phases, situations, and stages involved in that quest. In short, the Navy had different roles to play at different phases. Command of the sea, Corbett said, could be achieved in two ways. First, by the well-understood method of seeking out a decisive battle that destroys the enemy fleet and removes it as a threat against one's own use of the sea.[9] Secondly, a specific type of blockade—a naval blockade—designed to prevent an enemy's main naval force from even leaving its ports can achieve a similar result.[10] Lord Nelson used another type of naval blockade to try to entice an enemy to come out and to fight a battle in which it could be defeated. Through such methods, the enemy is no longer a direct threat to one's own use of the sea.

Yet, the quest for command of the sea is not what today might be called a "zero-sum game." The normal condition in a major maritime war is for the command to be in dispute between two or more powers. As Corbett put it, it is not true that "if we are unable to win the command we therefore lose it."[11] In his view, one can prevent another naval force from getting command of the sea by maintaining a force that has the potential to dispute it. If one is too weak to win command by offensive action, one can still keep command in dispute with a fleet that maintains a general defensive attitude. While such a posture does not achieve the ultimate objective, it does buy time in which one can consolidate a position and secure other objectives ashore.[12] Additionally, the new weapons that were emerging in the early twentieth century suggested an additional method that had not been successfully used earlier: the use of minor counter-attacks with a weapon, such as the torpedo, that could seriously threaten another's command of the sea.[13]

Beyond the variety of roles that naval forces played in securing and disputing command were the fundamentally different roles involved in exercising command of the sea, once it has been secured. Here, Corbett pointed out, one was involved in three major areas: (1) defense against invasion,[14] (2) attack on enemy commerce and defense of one's own commerce,[15] (3) attack, defense, and support of overseas military expeditions.[16]

At the same time that Corbett was sending the manuscript of *Some Principles* off for publication, he took up a new research project to examine *Maritime Operations in the Russo-Japanese War*.[17] In doing this study, Corbett concluded that the outcome of the Russo-Japanese War was not to be explained by the results of the old great naval wars. The role of the Imperial Japanese Navy was different than that of other navies in other wars. Its strategic function was critical to success, but its role was not to destroy the enemy force. The Japanese Navy's role was entirely defensive in firmly maintaining control over a well-defined area of the Yellow Sea and the waters including the Strait of Tsushima. In this area, its strategic role was strictly limited to protecting the Japanese Army's lines of communication as the Army annexed territory. The Japanese were successful not because they had overall command of the sea, but because they could prevent the Russians from obtaining it. "Owing to the nature of the war and its object, that was all that was required."[18] In this case, geographical position played an extremely important role. The same defensive positions and roles that the Japanese Navy took to protect the Army's lines of communication in a limited offensive operation ashore were the same that simultaneously prevented the Russian fleet from making any effective offensive counter-attack against the Japanese. Corbett, as well as other observers of the war, also noted that the Russian Navy's failure to blockade the Japanese, employing its cruisers based at Vladivostok, was a great missed opportunity.

While writers such as Mahan and Corbett were, in these ways, trying to link experience with present and future concerns, governments were acting in quite another way to make current policy. The theoretical musings of historians and analysts had some effect on them in the process, but statesmen and politicians often used such ideas only to the extent that they fit their already existing preconceptions. There were some additional considerations involved, in terms of such contrasting fields as domestic politics and international law.

International Law

The nineteenth century had seen the emergence of a law of land warfare, growing out of the experience of the American Civil War and codified for the U.S. Army's use by Dr. Francis Lieber. Until the early years of the twentieth century, there was nothing comparable for naval warfare. Up until that time, international law concerning war at sea had largely arisen from concerns about the safety and protection of commercial cargoes.[19] In response to the experience of the Spanish-American War and the initiatives taken at the Hague Convention in 1899, Captain Charles Stockton wrote the world's first "Naval War Code" at the Naval War College in 1900.[20] Almost immediately approved by both the Secretary of the Navy and the President of the United States, it became a binding restraint on American naval forces. It extended the articles of the Geneva Convention and the applicable portions of the law of land warfare to the realm of sea warfare, restricted the bombardment of undefended towns, exempted innocent coastal fishing vessels from attack, and, among other provisions, established a general classification of wartime contraband that could serve as the basis for future international discussion. At first, the Code applied only to the United States, but it soon became the basis upon which the United States sought to produce an international agreement. Stockton, as the author of the 1900 Code and as one of the American delegates to the London Naval Conference in 1908–1909, played a key role in the formulation of the Declaration of London that followed. While no country formally ratified the Declaration, it was, nevertheless, subsequently applied in several other agreements and became a basic guideline for future developments in international law. As a Chichele Professor of International Law at Oxford University, Professor D. P. O'Connell, once wrote, "The new code of blockade adopted there was totally at variance with the interests of a nation that aimed to control the seas as distinct from denying such control to others."[21] While Britain, as the leading naval power, found the rules inconvenient and overly restrictive, to say the least, "the mere fact that they existed psychologically circumscribed Great

Britain's decisions when the First World War broke out and the disparity between the rules and the direction of naval policy became manifest."[22]

Domestic Politics

In domestic politics, the actual strategic roles and functions of sea power were little understood and often ignored. The navy and its fleet, however, had a clear domestic political role to play and this role created its fundamental shape, far more than any consideration of strategic roles and functions. In Britain, for example, between 1889 and 1909, Parliament explicitly funded the Navy on the basis of the "two power standard," a long-standing idea that the Royal Navy should always be maintained at strength equal to that of the next two most powerful navies.[23] While counting particularly elements that represent power can serve as a basis to compare relative strength, roles and functions are not quantifiable. For the purposes of domestic politics and budget allocations, the relative number of battleships was the measure of strength, not the strategic roles or functions of sea power. The measure was a simple one based on something that both parliamentarians and the public could readily understand, without worrying about the niceties of strategy or the probable intentions of another state. Moreover, the system had the singular advantage of ensuring the basis for numerical superiority at sea. The traditional reliance on numerical superiority is a concept that is rarely mentioned in naval literature, but as that great naval hero Admiral Sir Cloudesley Shovell wrote as long ago as 1702:

> The misfortune and vice of our Country is to believe ourselves better than other men, which I take to be the reason that generally we send too small a force to execute our designs; but experience has taught me that where men are equally inured and disciplined to war, 'tis without a miracle, number that gains the victory.[24]

Almost exactly two centuries later in 1905, it was this point that Colonel Charles Callwell took up and extended, in his very important study on *Military Operations and Maritime Preponderance: Their Relations and Interdependence.*[25] In this analytical study, Callwell argued that numerical superiority at sea could only be converted into true command of the sea when military force was successfully turned against an enemy's fortified naval bases. In Callwell's view, "naval preponderance and warfare on land are mutually dependant, if the one is to assert itself conclusively and if the other is to be carried out with vigour and effect. There is an intimate connection between command of the sea and control of the shore."[26] This is particularly true from the point of view of an army dependent upon a vital link across the sea, but naval preponderance does not automatically bring this result alone, without the coordinated efforts of both a military and a naval force working together.

While naval superiority over a potential enemy was still an objective for many people in 1909, it no longer made sense to state it in terms of the two-power naval standard, which then required consideration of the United States Navy alongside the Imperial German Navy. More importantly, beneath this political debate, the issues of strategy, roles, and reform for the Navy were being driven, not by external diplomatic affairs and strategic issues, but by domestic financial stringency, as Nicholas Lambert has recently pointed out.[27] Admiral Sir John Fisher instituted a number of new approaches and implemented a variety of new naval technologies; in the process, he concealed his ultimate intentions from both politicians and naval officers. Only recently have historians been able to see clearly that he was trying to change the roles of naval forces, placing emphasis on different types of naval vessels in order to increase flexibility and to achieve cost savings. In reaching for these ends, however, he also tried to avoid changing the broad strategic objectives of protecting British overseas territorial and trade interests, despite political pressure to increase defense in home waters. Although never fully implemented, Fisher's concept was to have a qualitatively, rather than numerically, superior battle fleet for defense in home waters, flotillas of small torpedo boats and submarines deployed well forward to deny access to an enemy approaching home waters, with fast and powerfully armed, multi-purpose battle cruisers to provide flexible response on distant stations. In Fisher's mind, making the Channel and North Sea untenable for a fleet from either side in a conflict was an advantage for Britain. It meant that battle cruisers could be effective overseas and that an enemy could not bring invasion forces into home waters.[28] Such thinking marked a remarkable change in understanding the role of sea power.

While this evolution of thinking was occurring quietly, and sometimes secretly, within the Royal Navy, Great Britain, as the world's preeminent naval power, had an influence on nations and navies around the world. From the Renaissance period in European history onwards, navies had had a symbolic role to play, representing the power of a state or the glory of a monarch. In this regard, one need only think of Henry VIII's *Henri Grace à Dieu* in the sixteenth century, the elaborate decoration on the *Vasa* of the seventeenth century, or on the first-class ships of the line under Louis XIV. At the outset of the twentieth century, a number of leaders in a variety of countries, notably in Germany, Japan, and the United States, believed that a navy was a necessary instrument for any nation that aspired to the status of a major power. The most famous case, of course, is that of Germany, whose key naval leaders saw the role of sea power in terms of its "Risk Fleet," a naval force designed to be two-thirds the size of Britain's fleet that they believed that the British would hesitate to attack, for fear of eroding their naval strength in a major battle in the North Sea. In his planning, Tirpitz imagined that Germany should prepare for a single decisive German victory over the Royal Navy that would bring to Germany naval bases, overseas empire, and maritime trade. Such thinking provided the basis for German naval construction and war plans from 1898 to the First World War. The German Navy, however, could not fulfill its strategic role. In the July crisis of 1914, the Navy was not a deterrent factor in the diplomatic calculus.

The First World War

By early February 1915, when many in Germany began to criticize the fleet's strategic role, the admiral commanding the First Squadron circulated a document through the fleet that one of his staff officers, Korvettenkapitän Wolfgang Wegener, had prepared. In it, Wegener pointed out that Tirpitz's plan had lacked a sound strategic basis. In fact, Wegener wrote, Tirpitz's emphasis on seeking a major battle was entirely the wrong way to achieve the goals he wanted for the "Risk Fleet":

> Our strategic-political situation today is precisely the same as it was at the start of the war. The existence of our battle-ready fleet protects our Helgoland Bight, keeps the adversary out of the Baltic Sea and the trade routes open, forces the Russians into the defensive for the time being, cuts off their [maritime] resupply, and maintains Denmark's neutrality. Thus the fleet constitutes the German Empire's shield in the North and relieves the army from having to defend our coasts.

> As a result, we must avoid a decisive or even a major naval engagement in the North Sea, which would probably so weaken our fighting forces that the political significance of our fleet would disappear.[29]

When Tirpitz learned of Wegener's views, he termed them "poison for the fleet,"[30] yet Tirpitz offered no solution to the strategic problem that Wegener had identified. When Tirpitz's long-hoped-for battle finally took place off Jutland on 31 May 1916, it was not the modern-day, decisive Trafalgar that naval officers on both sides had hoped to achieve. The German gunnery fire control was better and, with their smaller guns, they did more damage and created more casualties than the British did in return. British ship design proved to be flawed when actions showed that German shells could more easily detonate British ships' magazines. Yet, the British could claim that their signal intelligence was more productive, their fuel capacity higher, their ships' propulsion plants more reliable. Such technicalities, however, meant little when the German fleet returned to harbor, unable to make a decisive impact on the course of the war. As Andrew Gordon underscored the point in his recent study of the battle,

> A rational society supports a navy for the purpose of achieving or safeguarding certain strategic ends. The Grand Fleet of 1916 had a heavy and obvious "safeguarding" task, and Jutland reaffirmed and enhanced its dominance. By contrast, the Kaiser's fleet—scarcely the product of rational strategic policy—was faced with an implausible "achieving" task.[31]

In 1917, when Germany shifted to a strategy of unrestricted submarine warfare against the Allies, it was in reprisal for the Allied economic blockade against Germany, which rested on an unreasonable definition of contraband that included virtually anything of value to Germany. On those grounds, the German government had a logical case in terms of international law that might have carried more weight than it did in diplomatic affairs. The principal problem, however, was that Germany's naval strategy was not coordinated with its diplomatic and legal positions and the stated rationale and defense for its naval action was inconsistent and constantly changed.

The German attack on the allied sea-lanes had its clear military effect, reaching a monthly average of 700,000 tons of enemy shipping sunk during the second quarter of 1917, sinking so many ships that the food supply in Britain was endangered, as Germany's had been.[32] Nevertheless, as a naval strategy designed to influence international politics as a reprisal for an unreasonable economic blockade, it was counterproductive, leading to the entry of the neutral United States into the war against Germany.[33] At the same time, the Navy's uncooperative conduct with other branches of government became the starting point for mutiny within the fleet that led to political turmoil within the country during the last days of the Reich.

The Inter-War Years

Upon the conclusion of World War One, the immediate political response to the conduct of naval warfare in the war was arms control. The resulting Washington Naval Treaty of 1921–22 was an important factor in forming relative naval strength among victorious nations in this period, but it was not the only, or even the most important, factor that created the decline in Britain's dominant position as the world's leading naval power and the subsequent rise of the Unites States Navy to assume that position. The relative change in position, while not unconnected, was neither simultaneous nor interdependent. Britain's decline as a global naval power occurred from largely internal factors before World War Two, while America's rise to fill that role was complete only after World War Two as a result of external requirements.

In the interwar period, the Royal Navy experienced four different situations in regard to its naval strength and the roles that it could play. Britain clearly maintained world maritime supremacy in the immediate post-war period from 1919 through 1921. Through the Treaty of Washington in 1922, the United States was allowed to have a naval strength equal to Britain's, but in fact did not build up to authorized limits under Calvin Coolidge's administration. Britain maintained the leading naval position through 1929. From 1930 to 1935, British maritime strength sharply declined, but, in the light of the sudden revival of the German Navy between 1936 and 1939, Britain rearmed more quickly and efficiently than any other power.[34]

The role of the Royal Navy in these years was to maintain supremacy for the protection of British interests in home waters and overseas, but such a concept was difficult to define with any precision. The Washington Treaty ended the arms race for the moment and created for Britain a "one-power standard" to measure its strength against the United States and an alternative "two-power standard" in terms of the naval strength of Japan and one European power, either Italy or France.

The treaty meant different things to different people, which showed the danger for a sea power to define its strength in terms of general numbers and words rather than in terms of its needs and its functions. Not unaware of this, British naval leaders developed a clearer rationale that argued that the worldwide British Empire was dependent upon sea communication for its well-being and existence. The security of passage from one point to another was the basis of Britain's defense system. As Admiral Sir Charles Madden defined it in Corbettian terms, "The surest method of ensuring security of sea passage is to remove, or failing removal, to render innocuous, that which threatens it."[35] To provide general strategic "cover," the main fleet was disposed geographically to points where it could concentrate its power against a major enemy fleet and thereby provide the basic security for the sea-lanes, while squadrons of cruisers could deal with sporadic attacks that might evade the basic "cover," perform economic blockades, and attack enemy trade. Direct convoy of shipping provided the third level of protection.

The economic depression that began in 1929 and the further naval limitations established by the London Naval Conference in 1930 both entered the picture as important factors, but these were not the critical factors that made for the abrupt change in British naval strength that affected its ability to carry out its planned strategic roles. By the late 1920s and early 1930s, the British government was not supplying all the resources that the Admiralty had recommended. While the general level of technology forged ahead, British ships and equipment aged, just when other powers began, once again, to invest in their navies. At the same time, the prevailing political leaders in Britain, as in the United States under Coolidge and Herbert Hoover, laid great trust in the arms control regimes that had been established. As a result, the political majority saw that the British naval armaments industry had excess capacity and could find no reasonable basis to maintain it with new orders, assuming that its traditional capacity would always be available when the demand required. These assumptions proved faulty.

Some years later, when Germany began to pose a direct threat to Britain, British shipyards responded remarkably, but the government's failure to maintain capacity had its clear effect and, along with the lack of available funds for naval rearmament, industry could not keep pace with the Admiralty's increasing requirements in the face of an expanding threat. Moreover, the Royal Navy's situation was complicated by the geostrategic fact that Nazi Germany lay directly across the North Sea, ensuring that home defense, not the defense of the empire, was the priority. To deal with this, the Royal Air Force, not the Navy, became the key institution. Additionally, when war broke out in 1939, the need to build resources for the British Army to fight on the continent with France, Britain's only major European ally, drove even more resources away from the Navy. As Chris Bell has concluded in his recently published study of the situation, "The Admiralty was in fact largely powerless to prevent the government undermining the foundations of British sea power after the First World War."[36]

For the United States, the role of sea power in the interwar years was different. It, too, was constrained by arms control treaties and political sentiment. The Navy had a contingency plan for total war against Japan in War Plan Orange, but this was not connected with contingency planning for diplomatic action or even approved at the national policy level. When war broke out in Europe, the first thought was that the role for American sea power was to maintain neutrality and prevent the war from touching the United States. In contrast to the situation in Britain, although there was little consensus and no firm concept of the role of sea power before the war, when America was drawn into the war, there had been twenty years of previous experimentation, planning, and technological implementation which could be quickly adapted and put into effective production through the nation's industrial base.[37] The American industrial base was capable of meeting the challenge.

The differences in strategic roles for the United States and for Britain were not the only differences to be found. Before moving to examine thinking about the roles of sea power in Germany and Japan, it is useful to look, momentarily, at the thinking within a neutral power in this period, Sweden, which was potentially threatened on two sides of the Baltic by the Soviet Union and by a renascent German Navy. Since the 1880s, the role of Swedish naval power was to protect the country against invasion with large, heavily gunned, armored ships. One of the problems behind this concept was that the combination of big guns on large, heavily armed ships that could be both maneuverable and fast was not something that could be successfully achieved at that time. It was a strategic vision based on an unachievable technological promise that was, fortunately, never put to the test.

Nevertheless, as an application of the same ideas that lay behind German thinking before the First World War, Swedish naval strategy was founded on the idea that an attacking nation would hesitate to take losses to engage the Swedish Navy, and, if an enemy did, it would need to commit its main battleship force if it wished to invade Sweden across the Baltic or from the North Sea in order to protect its troop transports.[38] Essentially, it was a deterrence strategy, designed not to win a war, but to make battle too costly to consider seriously.

By the late 1920s, consideration of this strategic role for the Navy began to involve a fascinating situation in which professional naval officers, professional bureaucrats, and politicians all had to compromise in order to reach a politically supportable outcome—but this is a subject somewhat beyond the realm of the discussion here. The upshot of it was, however, that the standard theoretical situation—in which elected leaders establish policy and politically neutral bureaucrats and naval professionals carry out the policy—did not work. The role conflicts that resulted within the government created a gridlock in creating a strategic role for the Navy. However, when continued attempts to preserve the role of the armored ship led to the vision of the fleet anchored in the archipelago and linked to coastal artillery batteries, the force of circumstances, the lack of funding, and lack of critical materials for building such large ships led to a reevaluation. The new development put emphasis on light and maneuverable naval forces that could operate offensively, in parallel with submarines and bomber aircraft, at a distance from the coast to protect trade and to prevent invasion. These factors eventually became the driving forces that forced the Swedish Navy to accept and to slowly begin to employ a revised strategic role for its forces.[39] While it served as a deterrent, it was never put to the test of war. If it had, this concept, too, might have been found wanting. In the light of practical experience, there has always been difficulty in getting submarines and surface ships to operate together in conjunction, while those operating Air Force bombers have generally had other visions in mind than joint operations with ships.

Meanwhile Sweden's neighbor Germany constructed a different type of force for a quite different purpose. The United States had played a key role in preventing the other allied powers from completely eliminating the German Navy after World War One and ensuring that its core competency remained. During the Weimar Republic, naval leaders had experienced difficulty in adapting to the republican form of government, but, nevertheless, saw themselves as a key element of national defense. During this period, naval leaders in the Weimar Republic began to be concerned about the rise of the Soviet Union and the defense of Germany's territory bordering the Baltic and the North Seas, but without support from the political leaders, the Navy's general strategic role was unclear.[40]

The Second World War

In the years following Hitler's rise to power in 1933, the German Navy began a rapid development and massive expansion, but its precise strategic role would not be clear until after World War Two had begun. The rapid move of the *Wehrmacht* across France to seize ports on the Bay of Biscay in 1940 and the nearly simultaneous capture of Denmark and Norway gave the *Kriegsmarine* the geo-strategic position and clear access to the Atlantic that its predecessor had lacked during World War One. But, at the time Hitler declared war, the building program had not been completed and the Navy was not yet fully prepared to fight a general war. The lack of equipment meant that Germany could not fully utilize its newly found geo-strategic position and was unable to employ its fleet for the traditional strategic purpose to command the sea. Instead, Hitler directed that the Navy launch an economic war against Britain's sea lines of communication, which soon was more closely defined as a war against the Allied capacity to protect and to use sea transportation to support their war effort.[41] It took two main forms: the use of heavy and fast surface ships and the use of submarines.

Meanwhile, on the other side of the globe, Japan also built a major navy, but with very different strategic roles in mind. The ideas behind the construction of the Imperial Japanese Navy were reflected in the writings of a contemporary of Mahan and Corbett, the Japanese Naval Staff College instructor Satō Tetsutarō. The stimulus of Satō's writing, combined with other influences within the Japanese Navy, evolved into a distinctive concept that was clearly related to Japan's earlier naval success in the Russo-Japanese War, which Corbett had so accurately analyzed for the Royal Navy. The Japanese approach was a concept of regional maritime defense, protected through an offensive naval stance.[42]

Without a clearly delineated national grand strategy to guide it, the Imperial Japanese Navy made contingency plans during the interwar period for a possible war against an isolated United States. Naval leaders envisaged a limited conflict based on the defense of a ring of advanced bases that would create an impregnable position behind which Japan could carry out its regional economic and imperial ambitions. Japanese leaders imagined that a war against the United States would be carefully controlled in stages that would lead to a negotiated peace. The first stage was designed to be a lightning blow that would immediately reduce the United States to equal footing with Japanese forces. The second stage was to prevent the intrusion of any enemy beyond a ring of widely separated, heavily defended island bastions around the Pacific, using locally deployed ships, aircraft, and garrisons. The third phase reserved the main naval fleet, including its battleships, submarines, and aircraft carriers, for a decisive battle that would eliminate the enemy's naval threat and thereby completely secure Japan for a negotiated settlement.[43]

Such a contrast in the strategic roles of the opposing navies during the Second World War created two very different naval wars in the Atlantic and in the Pacific. In both cases, the different strategic roles that Germany and Japan each chose for their navies determined the basis for the strategic roles that the Allies undertook in response. At the same time, both Japan and Germany chose strategic roles for their navies that they could not, ultimately, sustain. The Japanese concept of regional maritime defense, based on naval and air forces on widely separated island bastions, lacked depth and coverage, while the Navy's neglect of trade protection proved disastrous. The Germans held a well-chosen strategic role, but one that they were not fully equipped to maintain.

The War against Germany

In the Atlantic and in the Mediterranean, the critical strategic role of the Allied navies was to defend the merchant shipping that the German and Italian navies had targeted and which was necessary to sustain Britain at home. At the same time, the Allies also had to protect naval and military auxiliaries and naval amphibious ships, which were the keys to landing and sustaining their armies on hostile shores. Thus, in the Atlantic and Mediterranean, the Allies had dual strategic roles. The first was to protect trade and the second was to use the sea to carry out and to support its overseas military expeditions.

Despite the fact that it had a good geo-strategic position, the German Navy was unable to concentrate enough submarines in the Atlantic to cut off Allied sea communications in the open ocean. Degrading their capacity to do this even further, there were competing demands for naval resources to support German military operations on the Eastern Front, in the war against the Soviet Union, and in the Mediterranean to support operations in North Africa, Greece, the Balkans, and Italy. Adding to this, the industrial capacity of the United States was able to replace lost ships and cargoes at a rate significantly higher than Germany could sink them, much less replace its submarine losses in the face of improved Allied intelligence and innovative anti-submarine warfare procedures.

The War against Japan

In contrast, the critical strategic role of Allied navies in the Pacific was to break through the defensive maritime perimeter that Japan had established and to bring weapons to bear on Japan that would force the Japanese government to desist. Japan's naval attack on Pearl Harbor, while achieving the immediate objective that Japanese strategists sought, created a psychological and political, and, eventually, strategic, response that made the intended limited and graduated strategic use of naval power for a negotiated settlement completely impossible. Not knowing what operational strategy would ultimately be the most successful, the Allies launched four different approaches nearly simultaneously:

1. A drive from India through Burma and China toward Japan.

2. A drive from Australia and the South West Pacific to the Philippines, and on toward Japan.

3. A drive from Alaska and the Aleutians toward Japan, which was revived at the end of the war by the thought that the Soviet Union might also approach Japan through the Kurile Islands.

4. A drive across the Central Pacific to China and then to Japan.

These approaches were all part of what the American naval strategist J. C. Wylie would later call a "sequential strategy." They were strategic moves that led sequentially, from one island to another, isolating and jumping over enemy island bastions, toward the ultimate goal to bring the war directly to the Japanese home islands. The sequence involved establishing bases and moving troops, jump by jump, closer to Japan, so that the weapons of the day could get within direct range of the Japanese home islands. Whether launched by submarines, aircraft, ships, or ground forces, the idea was to have a direct military effect on targets close to home and, thereby, force the Japanese government to halt their war effort.

Alongside these four operations, there was a fifth and very different strategy, a cumulative strategy, by which the United States Navy employed its submarines in the same way that the Germans were employing theirs against the Allies: an economic war against Japan's tankers, cargo ships, and transports, defined as a war against Japan's capacity to protect and to use sea transportation to support its war effort. In contrast to the Allies' response to the Germans in the Atlantic, the Japanese gave little thought to protection of their own shipping, rarely using convoys for protection of merchant shipping. In this, the slow process of sinking one Japanese merchant ship after another ultimately had a cumulative and strangling effect on Japan's war economy as the wholesale destruction of its merchant marine ensued.[44]

As the submarine attacks on shipping in both the First and the Second World Wars showed, the limits of international law were eventually and deliberately ignored in order to achieve particular strategic or tactical objectives. Both submarines and aircraft faced the problem that they could not use their conventional weapons to their ultimate capacity if they adhered strictly to rules created for vessels of another kind and another era. Yet, violations of the law of warfare rarely occurred until the scope of the war had reached so broad a level that no major neutral powers remained outside the conflict and the military situation had become so desperate that restraint on warfare lost its practical, political, and ethical value.[45]

Yet, in the war against Japan, there was a sixth and final, strategic alternative employed: the Army Air Force's use of nuclear weapons as the direct means to achieve Japan's immediate unconditional surrender, while, incidentally, avoiding the prolonged bloodshed and high casualties that might possibly have occurred when the maritime and amphibious war reached the Japanese home islands.[46]

The Cold War, 1945–89

It is a commonplace thought that the use of nuclear weapons in 1945 revolutionized thinking about strategy in the decades that followed. As the focus turned to the variety of issues that this new weapon raised, we saw the pendulum of perception swing wildly in understanding the strategic role of maritime forces. Initially, the professionals who had experienced the Second World War saw "the bomb" as only another weapon, having seen twice in the twentieth century that what was fundamentally critical was the ability of a nation to mobilize its full resources in terms of its population, industrial and economic capacity to create, deploy, and sustain massive armed forces.[47] As the weapons spread to others beyond the hands of the United States, they proliferated to mind-boggling proportions. Only one early commentator, Bernard Brodie, saw that they could never be used, while most professional military leaders began to accept the idea that, if necessary, they could and would be used.[48] Burgeoning libraries of speculation and commentary followed the line that the professionals were accepting.

As a result of this, traditional thinking about the roles and functions of armed forces faded, particularly so for maritime forces. From the late 1940s to the early 1960s, it was largely only the committed professionals associated with navies who still talked and thought about strategic roles for the Navy. Translated to the terms of bureaucratic politics in the United States, the Navy was losing to the Air Force, because the Air Force was the only service that could effectively deploy nuclear weapons. As the Cold War developed, the Army in Europe also had a major role to play. Few beyond those in dark blue uniforms saw much of first-rate importance in the U.S. Navy taking over responsibility from the Royal Navy in the Mediterranean and its wider role within the North Atlantic Alliance as a whole. Most people who followed international events knew the name of the Supreme Allied Commander, Europe, but few understood or even knew anything about the institutionally co-equal role of the Supreme Allied Commander, Atlantic. In those decades it was not uncommon to hear even the most sophisticated defense analyst question whether a navy was needed at all. In the context of nuclear weapons, the strategic roles of navies that had been so vital and important during the first half of the century suddenly seemed irrelevant.

In the context of the Cold War, during the 1970s, three things occurred that began to reverse that perception: (1) the invention of the ballistic missile submarine and the deployment of nuclear weapons at sea, (2) the rise of the Soviet Navy, and (3) the continual appearance of small wars fought with conventional weapons.

The successful linking of the submarine to the concept of a mobile, concealed, second-strike retaliatory missile force for purposes of deterrence was a remarkable event in the history of nuclear deterrence and its theory, making a very significant contribution to it.[49] Equally, if not more, importantly for the U.S. Navy, this development was the bureaucratic and institutional victory that brought the Navy on stage for the discussion of the central issue regarding nuclear weapons and for the allocation of resources. Now that many had returned to value the Navy's strategic role, although principally for its new role in nuclear deterrence, naval leaders were able to continue their support of the traditional roles of naval power. Among other influences, the institutional value of nuclear weapons led to an increase in the number of them in the Navy's care and to an extension to naval uses beyond ballistic missile deterrence.

The rise of the Soviet Navy in the late 1960s served to revive the threat that the *Kriegsmarine* had presented to the Allies during the Second World War. Both the United States and NATO naval commanders responded in a way that emphasized the strategic role of protecting merchant shipping and military transports in the Atlantic. By the 1980s, this initial assessment of the strategic roles of sea power changed. The first writer who perceived the Soviet Navy's defensive surge was Commander Robert W. Herrick. Later intelligence assessments confirmed that the Soviet Union had a new and different thought about how to employ part of its Navy in wartime, keeping strategic missile ballistic submarines in protected bastions. In response to this changed intelligence assessment, the U.S. Navy began to formulate the Maritime Strategy of the early 1980s.[50]

Even before this took place, in thinking about naval power in the roles of navies in the Cold War period and what might happen should a third world war arise in Europe, the recent president of the Naval War College and later Commander of the Second Fleet Vice Admiral Stansfield Turner reformulated from classic maritime thinking the strategic roles and missions of the Navy and restated them in more modern terms in 1974. At this point, Turner defined them with a precision heretofore lacking as Strategic Deterrence, Sea Control, Projection of Power Ashore, and Naval Presence.[51] From this point, these particular terms entered the language of strategic maritime discussion, commonly replacing the older terms used by Mahan, Corbett, and others at the beginning of the century.

These new terms helped to elucidate the third major development in this period—the continual appearance of smaller wars, for example, those in Korea and Vietnam, fought with conventional weapons at the same time that nuclear weapons served a deterrent role in a quite different context. From very early on in the Cold War, the uses of force for political deterrence in situations short of war had become an issue. As the Cold War progressed, this gave rise to a significant literature and involved a revival of interest in the work of Carl von Clausewitz and the extension of his ideas to the maritime field in the work of Sir Julian Corbett. As a result of this, particularly in the years after the Vietnam War, many began to rediscover older ideas about the fundamental strategic roles of maritime power. This gave rise to much useful insight into the roles of maritime power in peacetime, a subject to which Mahan and Corbett had devoted little time. In this context writers such as Sir James Cable examined the recent versions of the age-old practice, long ignored by theorists, of using navies for political advantage in peacetime, or what was traditionally known as "Gunboat Diplomacy."[52] Carrying this investigation further, Ken Booth developed a sophisticated theoretical statement on navies as instruments and influences in foreign policy, seeing that the effective military roles of navies in wartime were the foundation for diplomatic and policing roles in peacetime foreign policy.[53] In the light of the kind of detailed analyses that emerged in these years, naval strategists began to see the interrelationships between strategic roles that Corbett had pointed to at the beginning of the century. Using the newly popular words, it became clear, once again, that the ability to carry out Strategic Deterrence and Projection of

Power Ashore was dependent upon Sea Control. Similarly, Naval Presence was largely a peacetime activity, most useful for the reassurance of endangered friends, but limited in its effect to deter a determined hostile state.

The Century's Last Decade, 1990–2000

In the last decade of the twentieth century, following the end of the Cold War, some additional factors have entered the discussion about strategic maritime roles. Some of the factors have been brewing for decades; others are newer, but they have resulted from maritime strategy having a new context.[54] As has so often happened in the past century, we, like our predecessors, think that everything has changed. It is true that navies, themselves, have changed, both superficially and fundamentally. Ships look different and have different propulsion systems; aircraft are faster and have a wider variety of capabilities than they did a mere fifty years ago. Naval weapons are much more accurate and more devastating in their effects. Communications have proliferated in every way imaginable to us. Yet, one could have said the same thing fifty years, one hundred years ago, and even one hundred fifty years ago and still have been right every time.

Arguably, it is only the pace of change in navies that is remarkable, but that is open to question. We sense that the speed of change and transition, noticeable even in Mahan's day, is somehow faster than it was a century ago, but it may only be our self-centered imagination that gives us this impression. Technological change is not the only issue—perhaps even more importantly navies that were once separate, autonomous entities within a government structure are no longer so today. One of the most telling lessons of the Second World War was the need to coordinate more closely the joint operations of all the armed services. Throughout the world, over the past half-century, departments of defense are slowly succeeding in merging navy departments with others. Moreover, naval officers have had to learn to talk with colleagues in other armed forces using the same terms, the same approaches to planning and budgeting, and sharing the same appropriations of tax dollars. Each of the services is increasingly becoming part of this same process, dependent upon one another and essential to one another in planning, budgeting, and operations.

At the same time that this lengthy process of unifying armed forces is occurring within nations, another process of integration is developing beyond and across national borders. While once we could think of a navy entirely in terms of one country and one country's maritime concerns, today we are learning to think of navies operating as part of United Nations forces, in terms of regional alliances, or even in terms of *ad hoc* coalitions gathered together to undertake some particular, mutually agreed-upon task. Such arrangements are not new in history, but the increased importance of international solidarity and cooperative ventures, joined with the decreased size of both naval forces and defense budgets, makes multilateral naval operations an important means for carrying out strategic roles in the future.

The range and power of naval weapons have continued to increase, as they have for centuries. Today, some equipment can detect ships and aircraft at ranges of thousands of miles and this would be merely a problem in tactical reconnaissance and communication if it had not created a conceptual problem that tends to merge strategic and tactical considerations. Once this has been clarified, however, there may possibly be a strategic role involved, if broad force can be brought to bear in a manner that controls an enemy's ability to achieve its own war objectives. This development, however, is not purely a maritime concern and the ability to deal with it effectively involves merging the capabilities found in various services. When this train of development is further combined with the factors involved in the increasing speed and intensity of operations, the emphasis shifts from the particular craft that carries weapons and the color of the uniform operating them to the effectiveness and the countering of the weapon itself.

During the last decade of the twentieth century, when there was no threat against the United States Navy's use of the sea, American military and naval leaders were able to focus on contingencies that involved the movement of overseas expeditionary forces to distant areas. With no serious threats against their safety on the high seas, the focus shifted to operations in littoral regions. Adding further emphasis to the trends that were already apparent from the general effect of increasing speed and intensity of operations, operations in coastal areas further emphasized the need for close interaction between army, air force, and amphibious landing forces.

The recent growth of naval interest in coastal regions has paralleled a change in the character and focus of contemporary naval warfare. The 1982 United Nations Convention on the Law of the Sea has now come into effect and has been ratified by the majority of the world's states, although still not the United States. This development in international law has granted coastal states specific rights and responsibilities in offshore waters. This extension of a coastal state's jurisdiction at sea has placed certain limitations on the freedom that the great naval powers have traditionally and exclusively exercised. In effect, it has enhanced the power of small- and medium-sized coastal states, just at a time when offshore resources are becoming increasingly important, both economically and politically. This situation has demanded that coastal states have the adequate power to manage their responsibilities in these areas. Combined with the capabilities of modern naval weapons to have large effects from small vessels, this has given small- and medium-sized navies the opportunity to create a major effect on a larger power. Even in the Cold War era, it was evident that small navies such as the Swedish, Norwegian, Danish, and German navies had important roles to play, but their potential importance was enhanced even further as the world's major naval powers reduced in size. In the 1990s, the strategic situation that led to emphasis on littoral warfare combined with separate developments in international law, weapons, communications, and command and control to bring attention to an area in naval affairs that major naval powers had previously disregarded: the sea power of the coastal state.[55]

The smaller states are rapidly becoming more important in an additional way: the transfer of merchant shipping from the flags of the great powers to other, often smaller, states, which have fewer hindrances and can operate ships at lower costs with more efficiency. Combined with the appearance of an increasingly global economy, made up of interdependent markets and worldwide exchange, a major naval power's own merchant marine no longer serves the key role that it once did for an economy that was defined solely by its relationships under a single national flag. To the extent that an essential exchange continues to take place and that important trade goods and supplies travel over, on, or above the seas, it is the safety of maritime passage, itself, that matters.

The Twentieth Century as Prologue

When seen from the very broadest perspective, the importance of maritime affairs ebbs and flows in relation to the context of events. Within maritime affairs, context is everything in understanding and defining maritime strategic roles, particularly when the nature of ships and aircraft forces navies to undertake a variety of missions and duties. Yet, because of the expansion of maritime interests among coastal states, as well as the very mobility of naval forces and their multidimensional capabilities and roles, the issues surrounding the strategic roles of armed force at sea continue to be important. The impact of noticeable change in so many areas—ranging from the development of a global economy, new developments in international law, and the character and effectiveness of weapons to the joint-service and multi-national employment of naval forces, as well as the organizational and technological implications coming through innovation—continues to stress the need to see conflict at sea and the strategic roles of maritime forces in a wide perspective.

As in all times when major changes are taking place, the procedures of the past superficially appear to be irrelevant and outmoded. Yet a careful look at old ideas and approaches helps to formulate new questions that need to be answered. The old answers can stimulate broad new approaches and new applications, suggesting useful insight. Even so, it is typical with navies that past answers are not the prelude that brings specific solutions for the future. A broad look at a century of experience with changing strategic roles for navies suggests that the specific strategic roles for which a navy is built are often very different from the roles it actually ends up performing. The experience of the twentieth century provides repeated evidence of this, as one contrasts the strategic roles that any major participant foresaw in a pre-war period with those actually used in the wars of 1914–19 and 1939–45. Navies have many and often unexpected uses. Strategy depends on an ever-changing context that involves what one side actually does in the calculus of what the other side wants to do and is actually able to do with effect.

At the end of the twentieth century, we can clearly see that 100 years of experience has fully borne out the fundamental distinction that both Mahan and Corbett recognized at the opening of the century, but their thoughts need to be refined to meet modern concerns. Put in the broadest terms that we use today, the fundamental strategic role for navies is to prevent any opponent from blocking the safe passage of any friendly craft on, over, or under the sea and to deny passage to any force that interferes with safe passage to its intended destination. If sea passage can be assured, an interdependent global economy, dependent on the movement of goods across the seas, can continue to grow and to sustain peaceful world development. In a twenty-first-century, global economy, the safety of sea passage can no longer be defined in terms of the strategic role of a single nation's navy. It is a multilateral role that reflects global concerns and international law.

Below that fundamental strategic role, there are secondary roles that flow from it. The strategic focus may be narrowed a step downwards and expressed in national terms, but the overriding global and international terms of reference restrict the degree to which any single nation may acceptably assume a controlling influence at sea. However, a nation that can assure safe passage for friendly commercial ships as well as for friendly naval and military vessels, preventing interference from enemy forces, is in a position to defend itself, provide and defend a secure passage for military forces, and support them on a distant shore, where they could assist allies or defend key places against the threats of the moment.

At a third level, there is a series of supporting strategic roles in wartime that allows one to gain an essential position, either sequentially or cumulatively, that facilitates the higher strategic functions. These include such roles as reconnaissance, control of information, and the creation of political or economic pressure to help friends or hinder enemies. In periods of peace, and in war during the absence of direct hostilities, a perceived capacity to carry out such strategic roles creates the basis for political perceptions in either friends or enemies.

The epilogue to the twentieth century is yet unknown, but if we read the prologue, naval forces will need the materiel and intellectual resources to meet the unexpected and be able to shift from one strategic role to another in terms of whatever context appears. If the leading naval trends of the second half of the twentieth century continue to develop, the naval history of the twenty-first century will be a story of both large nations and small, great powers and littoral states, cooperatively carrying out multilateral, joint, and combined operations at sea to maintain international order.

NOTES   Published in French under the title "Les États-Unis et les Mutations de la Puissance Maritime au XXe Siècle," in Christian Buchet, Jean Meyer, Jean-Pierre Poussou, eds., *La Puisssance Maritime* (Paris: Presses de l'Université Paris-Sorbonne, 2004), pp. 577–596.

1 Eventually published in 1905 as *Sea Power in its Relations to the War of 1812*.

2 See Jon Tetsuro Sumida, *Inventing Grand Strategy and Teaching Command: The Classic Works of Alfred Thayer Mahan Reconsidered* (Washington: The Woodrow Wilson Center Press and Baltimore: The Johns Hopkins University Press, 1997).

3 Robert Seager II and Doris D. Maguire, eds., *Letters and Papers of Alfred Thayer Mahan* (Annapolis: Naval Institute Press, 1975), vol. 2, p. 682: A. T. Mahan to John D. Long, 15 February 1900.

4 Ibid.

5 The definitive edition is Julian S. Corbett, *Some Principles of Maritime Strategy,* with an introduction and notes by Eric J. Grove. Classics of Sea Power series (Annapolis: Naval Institute Press, 1988). All following references are made to this edition.

6 A. T. Mahan, *Naval Strategy Compared and Contrasted with the Principles and Practice of Military Operations on Land* (Boston: Little, Brown, 1991). The key chapters, numbered 6, 7, 8, 9, and 10 of the original edition, are reprinted in John B. Hattendorf, ed., *Mahan on Naval Strategy: Selections from the Writings of Rear Admiral Alfred Thayer Mahan.* Classics of Sea Power series (Annapolis: Naval Institute Press, 1991) as chapters 3–7.

7 For a recent commentary on these particular points in Corbett's *Some Principles,* see Michael I. Handel, "Corbett, Clausewitz, and Sun Tzu," *Naval War College Review* 53, no. 4 (Autumn 2000), pp. 107–124.

8 Corbett, *Some Principles,* p. 167

9 Ibid., pp. 167–183.

10 Ibid., pp. 183–208.

11 Ibid., p. 209.

12 Ibid., pp. 209–227.

13 Ibid., pp. 227–232.

14 Ibid., pp. 233–261.

15 Ibid., pp. 261–279.

16 Ibid., pp. 280–304.

17 Julian S. Corbett, *Maritime Operations in the Russo-Japanese War, 1904–1905,* with an introduction by John B. Hattendorf and Donald S. Schurman (Newport: Naval War College Press and Annapolis: Naval Institute Press, 1994).

18 Ibid., vol. 2, p. 394.

19 For an overview of this subject, see John B. Hattendorf, "Maritime Conflict and the Laws of War: An Historical Outline," in Sir Michael Howard, George Andreopoulos, and Mark Shulman, eds., *Laws of War* (New Haven: Yale University Press, 1994), pp. 98–115, with notes 247–250.

20 On Stockton, see John B. Hattendorf, "Rear Admiral Charles H. Stockton, the Naval War College, and the Law of Naval Warfare," in Michael N. Schmitt

and Leslie C. Green, eds., *The Law of Armed Conflict: Into the Next Millennium*. International Law Studies, vol. 71 (Newport: Naval War College, 1998), pp. xvii–lxxii.

21 D. P. O'Connell, *The Influence of Law on Seapower* (Manchester: Manchester University Press, 1975), p. 20.

22 Ibid.

23 For the classic studies of the concept, see Arthur Marder, *The Anatomy of Sea Power: A History of British Naval Policy in the Pre-Dreadnought Era, 1880–1905* (New York, 1940; reprinted London: Frank Cass, 1972) and E. L. Woodward, *Great Britain and the German Navy* (Oxford: Clarendon Press, 1935), pp. 435–473, Appendix II, "Parliamentary History of the Two Power Standard."

24 Quoted in John B. Hattendorf, "Sir George Rooke and Sir Cloudesley Shovell, *c*1650–1709 sand 1650–1707," in Richard Harding and Peter Le Fevre, eds., *The Precursors of Nelson* (London: Chatham Publishing, 2000), p. 65.

25 C. E. Callwell, *Military Operations and Maritime Preponderance: Their Relations and Interdependence*, with an introduction and notes by Colin S. Gray. Classics of Sea Power series (Annapolis: Naval Institute Press, 1996).

26 Ibid., p. 444.

27 Nicholas Lambert, *Sir John Fisher's Naval Revolution* (Columbia: University of South Carolina Press, 1999), pp. 101–115.

28 Ibid., pp. 121–126.

29 "Reflections on Our Maritime Situation, First Squadron Memorandum, 1 February 1915," Appendix A to Vice Admiral Wolfgang Wegener, *The Naval Strategy of the World War*, translated and with an introduction and notes by Holger H. Herwig. Classics of Sea Power series (Annapolis: Naval Institute Press, 1989), pp. 133–134.

30 Quoted in Werner Rahn, "Strategische probleme der deutschen Seekriegführung 1914–1918," in Wolfgang Michalka, *Der Erste Weltkrieg: Wirking, Wahrnehmung, Analyse*. Serie Piper, Band 1927 (München: Piper Verlag, 1994), p. 351.

31 Andrew Gordon, *The Rules of the Game: Jutland and British Naval Command* (London: John Murray, 1996), p. 563.

32 Rahn, "Strategische probleme," p. 357.

33 O'Connell, *Influence of Law on Sea Power*, pp. 45–47.

34 John Ferris, "The Last Decade of British Maritime Supremacy, 1919–1929," in Greg Kennedy and Keith Neilson, eds., *Far-Flung Lines: Essays in Honour of Donald Mackenzie Schurman* (London and Portland, OR: Frank Cass, 1996), p. 126.

35 Quoted in ibid., p. 135.

36 Christopher M. Bell, *The Royal Navy. Seapower and Strategy between the Wars* (Stanford: Stanford University Press, 2000), p. 189.

37 George W. Baer, *One Hundred Years of Seapower: The United States Navy, 1890–1990* (Stanford: Stanford University Press, 1994), p. 144.

38 Anders Berge, *Sakkunskap och Politisk Rationalitet: Den Svenska flottan och pansarfrågan, 1918–1939* (Stockholm: Almqvist & Wiksell International, 1987), p. 9.

39 Bo Hugemark, "The Swedish Navy—Auxiliary Force or Strategic Factor: The Navy in Swedish Security Policy 1809–1990," in Göran Rystad, Klaus-R. Böhme, and Wilhelm M. Carlgren, eds., *In Quest of Trade and Security: The Baltic in Power Politics 1500–1990* (Lund: Lund University Press, 1995), vol. II, *1890–1990*, pp. 286–295.

40 Werner Rahn, "Kriegführung, Politik und Krisen—Die Marine des Deutschen Reiches 1914–1933," in *Die Deutsche Flotte im Spannungsfeld der Politik 1848–1985* (Hereford: Mittler, 1985), p. 100.

41 Werner Rahn, "Der Atlantic in der deutschen und allierten Strategie," in MGFA, *Das Deutsche Reich und der globale Krieg: Die Ausweitung zum Weltkrieg und der Wechsel der Initiative 1941–1943* (Stuttgart: Deutsche Verlags-Anstalt, 1990), vol. 6, *Der globale Krieg*, pp. 275–297.

42 David C. Evans and Mark R. Peattie, *Kaigun: Strategy, Tactics and Technology in the Imperial Japanese Navy, 1887–1941* (Annapolis: Naval Institute Press, 1997), pp. 135–141.

43 Ibid., pp. 492–497.

44 J. C. Wylie, "Excerpt from 'Reflections on the War in the Pacific,'" in J. C. Wylie, *Military Strategy: A General Theory of Power Control*, with an introduction by John B. Hattendorf and a postscript by J. C. Wylie. Classics of Sea Power series (Annapolis: Naval Institute Press, 1989), Appendix A, pp. 117–122.

45 O'Connell, *Influence of Law on Sea Power*, pp. 50–51.

46 John Ray Skates, *The Invasion of Japan: Alternative to the Bomb* (Columbia: University of South Carolina Press, 1994), pp. 247–257.

47 Martin van Creveld, "Through a Glass, Darkly: Some Reflections on the Future of War," *Naval War College Review* 53, no. 4 (Autumn 2000), p. 29.

48 Ibid.

49 Baer, *One Hundred Years*, pp. 352–359.

50 See John B. Hattendorf, "The Evolution of the U.S. Navy's 'Maritime Strategy,' 1977–1987," in *Naval History and Maritime Strategy: Collected Essays* (Malabar, FL: Krieger, 2000), chapter 12.

51 Stansfield Turner, "Missions of the U.S. Navy," U.S. Naval Institute *Proceedings*, 100 (December 1974), pp. 18–24.

52 Sir James Cable, *Gunboat Diplomacy, 1919–1979*, 2nd ed. (New York: St. Martins, 1981).

53 K. Booth, *Navies and Foreign Policy* (London: Croom Helm, 1977).

54 This section is adapted from chapter 15 of Hattendorf, *Naval History and Maritime Strategy*, pp. 253–266.

55 See Jacob Børresen, "The Seapower of the Coastal State," *Journal of Strategic Studies*, 17 (March 1994), pp. 148–175.

Part 4: Naval Theory and History

XIX Rear Admiral Henry E. Eccles and the "Lessons of Suez," 1956–1968

The desire to find "lessons" for practical application from the study of history has a long history in military affairs that has extended through the twentieth century, despite its increasing divergence from approaches to historical studies among university academics.[1] In the nineteenth century, it was not uncommon for military and naval historians to look at their subject in the same way that scientists looked at the physical world and to attempt to derive "laws" of warfare from historical investigations and observations. Such an approach characterized the early nineteenth century works of Henri Jomini and, in a different dimension, the works of Carl von Clausewitz. Jomini's approach was initially dominant and was carried across the Atlantic to influence military and naval thinking in North America in the nineteenth century.[2]

Naval History and the Naval Professional

In the years between 1873 and 1890, the academic study of history was just beginning in the United States with the first academic approaches being taken at the University of Michigan in 1869, Harvard University in 1871, and at the Johns Hopkins University and Columbia University in 1880. In 1884, the American Historical Society was established and first began to publish its *American Historical Review* in 1895. At the same time, a parallel, but very different, movement took place in the U.S. Navy, forming the basis for using historical study as a means in professional development. This culminated with the well-known work of Captain Alfred Thayer Mahan in his famous series of books, *The Influence of Sea Power*. Mahan's work was not isolated, but part of a lesser known effort of several naval officers in the U.S. Navy to look at naval history as a means to developing naval theory.[3] The key person in this development was Rear Admiral Stephen B. Luce, whose own thinking had been heavily influenced by Sir John Knox Laughton in Britain, and Admiral Jurien de la Gravière, some of whose works Luce had translated into English.[4] Most importantly, Admiral Luce had sought to institutionalize the study of history for professional purposes along with the development of naval theory at the U.S. Naval War College, which Luce had founded in 1884.[5]

From the first decade of the twentieth century through World War II, the Naval War College had centered its curriculum and its approach to contingency planning, naval doctrine, and to naval thinking, in general, on "the Applicatory System," a set of ideas that had been adapted for naval use from methods that the German General Staff had very successfully used in the 1870s. Known commonly within the U.S. Navy by the name of one of its component parts, "the estimate of the situation,"[6] the approach culminated in the publication of a locally produced textbook in 1942 titled *Sound Military Decision*[7] that distilled the essence of forty years of thinking about these issues.

The experience of World War II fundamentally changed ideas about military and naval education. In the late 1940s and 1950s, experienced senior military and naval leaders looked back on their own pre-war professional military education and saw that it had been characterized by what they considered to be overly rigid and impractical approaches. The huge growth in the technical, tactical, and logistical areas that occurred between 1939 and 1945 had led to the introduction of new military and naval vocabulary that made distinctions between combined and joint operations. These older works of military and naval theory became discredited. At the same time, the movement to form overarching ministries of defense to subsume the older war and naval bureaucracies led to intense inter-service controversy and debate. With the discrediting of the old approaches, previously military words and phrases came to be used in a partisan manner with particularized meanings. Adding to this, the need to simplify military ideas for the general public to gain votes for particular types of equipment and weapons programs led to competing public relations campaigns. Words tended to be used loosely rather than with rigorous care. Rear Admiral Henry Eccles of the Naval War College faculty succinctly noted, "Argument overwhelmed analysis."[8] He explained that "during the years 1946–48, the proverbial baby was thrown out with the bath water. The older more disciplined language found, for example, in *Sound Military Decision,* had been discredited—and there was no equally rigorous substitute."[9]

For thirty years, from 1947 until 1977, Rear Admiral Henry Eccles was the leading figure associated with the development of professional naval thinking at the Naval War College, both on active service from 1947 until 1951 and, from 1952 until the late 1970s, as a retired officer. Rear Admiral J. C. Wylie, ten years junior to Eccles, later complemented Eccles's work with a very important and widely read book that had an influence on American strategic thinking in the 1980s and beyond.[10] These two officers were great rarities within the U.S. Navy; they were the first since the founders of the Naval War College in the 1880s and 1890s, Stephen B. Luce and Alfred Thayer Mahan, to make original contributions to naval theory. Of the two, Eccles's work is less known today, although the Naval War College has named its library in his honor and his portrait hangs prominently in its foyer.

While Eccles and Wylie specialized in the development of theory, they were both part of a larger movement in the immediate post–World War II era during which a number of prominent officers and writers were producing histories, memoirs, and commentaries that were designed to show the importance of naval power at a time when it seemed obscured by nuclear weapons, the development of air power, and the politics surrounding service unification. From the time of the Suez Crisis, Eccles made a special point of studying it and including it as an aspect of his teaching and writing.

Rear Admiral Henry Eccles

The son of an Episcopalian priest, Henry Effingham Eccles was born in Bayside, New York, on 31 December 1898. He was initially educated privately at home by his parents and, at about the age of twelve, sent to Trinity School in New York City, where he studied from 1910 to 1916. After attending Trinity High School in 1916–17, he enrolled as an undergraduate at Columbia University in 1917. After one year at Columbia, he entered the U.S. Naval Academy in 1918, graduating with the class of 1922. After his first tours of duty in battleships, Eccles attended Submarine School. He served in two submarines before being ordered to the Naval Postgraduate School in 1928, where he earned a Master of Science degree in Mechanical Engineering through Columbia University in 1930. Following this, he commanded two submarines, served as Engineer and Repair Officer at the Submarine Base at New London, Connecticut, then spent nearly three years as Engineer in the heavy cruiser USS *Salt Lake City* (CA 25) and two years in the Design Construction Division of the Bureau of Engineering in the Navy Department, Washington, D.C. In 1940, he was ordered to command the destroyer USS *John D. Edwards* (DD 216) on the Asiatic Station, based in the Philippines. He was in command when the Japanese simultaneously attacked Pearl Harbor as well as American and British positions in Southeast Asia on 7 December 1941. He and his ship participated in the battle of the Badoeng Strait, and shortly after, while assigned to the American-British-Dutch-Australian (ABDA) Command, in the battle of the Java Sea. Wounded in action, Eccles was awarded the Navy Cross, the Silver Star, and The Netherlands Order of the Bronze Lion.

After recovering from his wounds, Eccles served in the Base Maintenance Division in the Office of the Chief of Naval Operations in 1942–43, where he helped to coordinate logistics planning for all advanced bases. After attending the Command Course at the Naval War College, he was promoted to captain and assigned as the Director, Advance Base Section, Service Force Headquarters, U.S. Pacific Fleet. In this key position, Eccles coordinated the planning, construction, and support of advance bases in the Central Pacific, a critical aspect of the American island-hopping strategy in the war against Japan. For his service in this capacity, he received the Legion of Merit, having demonstrated great foresight and organizational vision in handling key aspects of the logistics of the American naval offensive against Japan.

Immediately after the conclusion of the war, the Navy Department assigned Eccles to the Joint Operations Review Board, a group of officers from all services assigned to evaluate joint operations during World War II. From that posting, he went on to command the battleship USS *Washington* (BB 56). In 1947, the President of the Naval War College, Admiral Raymond Spruance, selected Eccles to be the first Chairman of the College's newly established Logistics Department, an area that Spruance felt had been neglected in professional naval thinking during the period between the two world wars. While in that position from 1947 to 1951, Eccles wrote his first book, *Operational Naval Logistics* (1950), a pioneering manual on the subject. He left the Naval War College in 1951 with orders to be Assistant Chief of Staff for Logistics to the Commander-in-Chief, U.S. Naval Forces, Eastern Atlantic and Mediterranean (CINCNELM), with headquarters in London and, simultaneously, Assistant Chief of Staff for Logistics to NATO's Commander-in-Chief, Allied Forces Southern Europe (CINCSOUTH), with headquarters in Naples, Italy.

Eccles retired from active duty in the Navy on 30 June 1952 and was promoted to rear admiral on the retired list. Returning to his home in Newport, Rhode Island, he was closely associated with the Naval War College, where he served in an informal capacity as a confidante and advisor to successive College presidents as well as an instructor for elective courses on military theory, principles of logistics, and international relations. Concurrently, he was a consultant to the Logistics Research Project at The George Washington University, which was closely associated with a number of U.S. military staff and war colleges, including the Naval War College.[11] Eccles became a stimulating force on the Naval War College faculty while writing his major works, often using advice and reactions from his professional Newport colleagues and academic associates: *Logistics in the National Defense* (1959, 1981, 1997); *Military Concepts and Philosophy* (1965), and *Military Power in a Free Society* (1979). After retiring from teaching in 1977, Eccles left Newport in 1985 to enter a retirement home in Needham, Massachusetts, where he died a year later on 14 May 1986.[12]

The Development of Eccles's Thinking about the Suez Crisis

During the course of events surrounding the Suez Crisis in 1956, Eccles and his colleagues at the Naval War College watched carefully, reading the variety of reports available from the press and other sources. Although he did not directly receive official documents, he benefited from off-the-record discussions and information available at the War College. During the decade, Eccles devoted much thought and effort to trying to understand and to analyze what had happened and what could be learned from those events that could be applied in the education of officers for future positions in high command. Eccles brought a valuable and unusual perspective to these issues. His advanced education in engineering was widened by his broad secondary education and his interests in music, philosophy, and history. His service assignments opened contacts and an exchange of thoughts with some key thinkers within the service and he maintained a wide correspondence and exchange of ideas with leading academics.

On 8 November 1956, the day after the Anglo-French cease fire, Naval War College staff and faculty members drafted the rough outlines of a preliminary study on the Suez operation. At noon that day, Naval War College President Rear Admiral Thomas H. Robbins, Jr., had a "Memorandum for the Files" placed on record summarizing these observations. Acknowledging that the conclusions were "by no means firm," Robbins listed three categories of results: in Category "A" were those that clearly had good effects; in Category "B" were potentially positive actions; and in Category "C" there were bad effects, any way they were regarded.[13]

In Category A, Robbins found two overarching results. First, larger powers can be pushed only up to a point by aggressive smaller powers, he observed: "Given sufficient provocation, the larger nations are bound to react with force in spite of existing moral arguments or even suggestion of power politics in opposition." Secondly, he concluded that "there is no evidence that the United Kingdom gained anything from the fact of the attack."[14]

Category B resulted in a long list. The transcending point was the indication that "the position and the effectiveness of the United Nations organization has been immeasurably strengthened."[15] The many years of hard work to build up an effective United Nations were validated in the fact that four nations ceased fire in response to a United Nations demand and that many other nations agreed to contribute troops to a UN security force. At the same time, Robbins saw the Suez Crisis as an example that could be used to better define concepts of limited war in the context of a containment strategy. He believed that Suez gave the UN a positive reputation to help deter future military aggression. In another major positive result, the Suez action drew attention to the great need to resolve and provide a long-term solution for the Suez-Egyptian-Israeli problem. The Suez Crisis underscored the breadth and depth of these issues that had not previously been widely recognized or understood.

Interestingly, Robbins looked at what seemed to be the initial effect of the Suez situation on particular nations. For the United States, he thought that the American position in the world had been strengthened by having confirmed, particularly among smaller nations not directly involved in the Suez affair, that it was firmly in favor of peaceful settlements of international disputes. For Britain, Suez provided the opportunity for its government in the future to manage its responsibilities more realistically, learning from its lack of military readiness at Suez. As a result of the United Nations' action, Canada emerged with a stronger position in NATO and within the British Commonwealth, which should also serve to improve Commonwealth relations with a number of other countries, including the United States. The crisis appeared to demonstrate to colonial powers, such as Portugal and The Netherlands, that the arbitrary use of force would not produce a satisfactory solution in the event of a future incident or rebellion. Similarly, Suez "should also point a lesson to France particularly that the use of naked force unilaterally among France's colonies will probably serve to widen rather than narrow the breach in relations between that country and her colonies."[16] In respect to the Soviet Union, the unanimity of world opinion behind the UN actions concerning Suez could conceivably be a warning to the USSR against a casual use of force. Simultaneously, the world should be aware of the Soviet Union's apparent readiness to use force unilaterally on a large scale. Aside from the possibility of the USSR starting a global war in this manner, another potential good effect flowing from Suez was the demonstration that unilateral military action would ultimately fail. It now appeared that it was possible that collective action would be a requisite for the successful use of future military force.

Robbins noted that that the United Kingdom had clearly lost its position in world affairs, since Nasser remained in power in Egypt and the Suez Canal remained under Egyptian control. Listing these under Category "C," he noted that Britain had failed completely to achieve any of its objectives during the Suez Crisis. As a result, it had lost its previously important role in the Middle East and was, perhaps, no longer considered a leader anywhere in the world except among a few Commonwealth countries. At the moment, it even appeared that the British Commonwealth might dissolve, with future rapprochement between Britain, India, Pakistan, and Ceylon seeming increasingly difficult.

The risk of global war had greatly increased as a result of Suez. The USSR's position in the Middle East had been greatly enhanced, while that of the United States diminished. "The Arab world appears together and will probably no longer be oriented to the West,"[17] Robbins wrote, while an amicable solution between France and Algeria appeared to have become more remote.[18]

In the context of the Cold War, the Suez Crisis nearly became a flashpoint. As the Soviet Union began to move troops in southwestern Russia and appeared ready to send volunteer troops to Egypt, the closing of the canal created a crisis in oil supply in Europe. Rapid action was needed to support the implementation of the UN Security Force in Egypt, while preparatory moves were now necessary to secure the NATO European area and to protect the security of the United States. Looking toward these requirements, the United States was hampered by having several hundred thousand military dependants in Germany, Britain, and France, who needed to be evacuated in case a war should develop.

In a paper that Eccles wrote on the same day, he noted that this situation "constitutes a group of interrelated problems in which Strategy, Politics, Economics and Logistics are completely intertwined. The common factor in the oil, in the U.N. police force, and in the dependants problem, is found in the logistic element of transportation."[19] As a final point to this paper, Eccles added, "From the standpoint of the study of war it would seem that much can be learned from a detailed analysis of this situation based on actual plans and discussions within the Defense Department and the National Security Council."[20]

This thought had been with Eccles for at least a decade. He later recalled, "as a member of the Joint Board of Operational Review in Washington in 1946, I heard Douglas S. Freeman state that more could be learned about war through the study of one campaign than thru the partial or superficial study of many campaigns."[21] Almost immediately, Eccles began to think about the Suez Crisis as the focus for graduate-level study relating to national security policy, seeing it in the context of seven categories of major interest: political, economic, geographic, military, scientific, sociological, and legal.[22] Viewing the crisis as an important example of the use of conventional arms in the context of the Cold War, he saw that it also involved the balance of nuclear weapons as well as being a major event that was typical of the kinds of dilemmas that faced those in high command when using military force in the modern, post–World War II era. Eccles set about writing a major study on Suez that would be instructive for mid-grade military and naval officers who were likely destined for future positions in high command or as military advisors to top-level leaders. By 1964, Eccles completed a first draft, which he partially revised in 1968. Yet he never completed the study he had intended, realizing that the ultimate answers he sought could not be reached without full access to all the relevant records of the decision makers.

Nevertheless, he continued to use the available unclassified literature on the Suez Crisis, closely following the stream of memoirs and information that became available in the first dozen years following the crisis. Eccles found much of the published literature on Suez "emotional and biased; nevertheless, there is a wide area of agreement,"[23] he noted. Many of the major lessons were unlikely to change the principles of sound military theory, even though theory was a body of thinking that was imperfect and always evolving.

While Eccles never completed or published his work, many drafts and notes remain in his extensive collections of papers. They document the ways in which a professional military thinker in the United States during the late 1950s and 1960s looked at contemporary events with an appreciation for history, attempting to draw useful information from it for professional application.

Henry Eccles's "Lessons of Suez" for the Armed Forces

After an extensive period of study, Eccles concluded that all of the leaders involved had flagrantly disregarded the fundamental principles of military planning, ignoring in particular the model of Anglo-American Allied cooperation in World War II. In addition, he found many specific faults with the concept of the operation and its execution. Most importantly, operational aspects of planning had undermined intelligence analysis preceding the operation. There had been no estimate of the situation in which all the political, economic, and military factors were brought together in a single analysis as part of the process for making major decisions. As he was working on Suez, Eccles also observed the same fault in American planning for the 1961 Cuban Crisis.[24]

What Eccles had in mind reflected a basic point in the Naval War College's ideas which had been so thoroughly examined in the years leading up to World War II in its military planning textbook *Sound Military Decision*. As Eccles explained the concept in November 1956, an estimate of the situation should include the following elements, all of which seemed to him to have been missing in the Suez Crisis:

a) A statement and thorough analysis of the objective to be achieved.

b) An appraisal of the general situation requiring decision.

c) A comparison of the forces available and the forces opposed.

d) A survey of alternative courses of action and an evaluation of each proposed course of action in relation to its suitability, its feasibility, and its consequences in terms of its cost and the acceptability of that cost.

e) An analysis of courses of action as related to enemy capabilities.[25]

Associated with the fundamental error of omitting these careful considerations during the Suez Crisis, there were serious errors in civil-military relations that took place both in France and in Britain. On one hand, Britain's civilian leaders, he concluded, ignored or disregarded the military advice they were given. On the other hand, he believed that the situation was quite the opposite in France, where "a military group whose members suffered from the frustration of years of defeat, dominated the decision."[26]

Looking across the situation, he found that none of the countries had undertaken a serious analysis of the objectives they planned to achieve through the use of military force. Eccles concluded that many of the decisions that had been made were based on dubious or false assumptions. In addition, when a plan was made, it provided no alternatives in case an assumption proved incorrect or some factor changed in the course of execution. The main faulty assumptions were:

a) British leaders wrongly assumed that Egyptians did not have the technical or administrative skills to operate the Suez Canal.

b) British leaders wrongly assumed that Egypt would not have time to block the canal.

c) American leaders wrongly assumed that economic sanctions were an effective and reliable tool to use in the context of the international alignments surrounding the Suez Crisis.

d) Both British and American leaders wrongly assumed that telephone conversations between their two leaders could bring about a clear understanding between their governments, despite the fact that the responsible governments had different interests and different concepts of their interests.

Eccles took special interest in logistics and was particularly critical of British leaders, who he felt had failed to understand the influence of logistics on the conduct of operations. Most importantly, this carried with it much wider implications, as poorly executed tactics undermine strategy, and ineffective strategy and the failure to achieve strategic aims have internal political ramifications. As Eccles pointed out, this interrelationship "can be rephrased to illustrate the principle that one should not undertake the use of force unless one has the capability and willingness to use it effectively."[27]

Eccles believed that the British could not move decisively in the Suez Crisis because they were fundamentally unprepared. No British military contingency plan had ever been formulated to occupy the Suez Canal in the case of an emergency. British airborne troops lacked both recent equipment and parachute training. In addition, the overall British logistical capabilities had been allowed to deteriorate, particularly in regard to air and sea transportation. The most useful British bases would have been located in Cyprus, but these were both incomplete and unprepared for use in 1956.

Eccles found numerous specific faults and concluded that problems of British military strategy were directly tied to failures in political policy. He found that British political leaders failed to engage their military staff on the basic and decision-making process until it became too late to achieve the political goals. This, Eccles noted, "was a specific and clear violation of one of the chief lessons of World War II."[28] At the point when decisive action to invade could have been justified in late July and August 1956, British forces were unprepared to act. In addition, it had been a major failure not to coordinate the political, economic, and military factors before the major decision to deploy military forces was taken. When the decision was taken to deploy, there was then a clear hesitancy in regard to troop movements, bombing, and propaganda in the target area. Moreover, there had been inadequate allowance in considering Egyptian capabilities for a response with guerilla warfare, sabotage, and terrorist tactics.

While acknowledging that in some issues of national policy, there will always be central issues which will contain contradictions and paradoxes, one should not be diverted by the many subsidiary problems which they cause. In broad military issues, Eccles argued, "it is the path of wisdom to concentrate on the central issues, to identify them, their inherent paradoxes and the contradictions and the forces which act in them. Many of these arise from certain fundamental concepts and assumptions which, when identified, should be challenged."[29]

Eccles grappled with broader questions of civil-military relations in considering the Suez Crisis. Eccles concluded that if Anglo-French long-term objectives had been examined carefully in the context of their assumptions and expectations, Britain and France would have recognized that the development of the Hungarian Crisis completely overshadowed their immediate objectives at Suez and in the Middle East. Eccles concluded that these factors underscored a specific lesson, that "when conceptual unity is missing, high command has the obligation to recognize its absence and either to take compensating measures or to change the course of action."[30] The Hungarian uprising that began on 23 October 1956 created a situation that was central to the Cold War and changed the relative and basic values of interests involved, but French, British, and Israeli plans had gone ahead and Britain and France were so committed that no reevaluation of interests, objectives, and strategic decisions was made.

In Eccles's view, Anthony Eden's fundamental error was to undertake a military operation without first ensuring support from the world community, particularly the United States. Regardless of whether Americans should have supported it, the national election in the United States inhibited decisive action at the very moment that Eden recognized the need for decisive action. Eden should have been aware that he could not change a situation that was a fundamental hindrance to the Americans. Eccles's lesson here was that Britain should not have intervened in Egypt unless British leaders were convinced that they clearly had both the power and the will to move swiftly and decisively without American agreement and support.[31]

In all of this, Eccles believed that the key element was the concept of control in strategy. Here he took up Herbert Rosinski's idea that "it is the element of control that is the essence of strategy: control being the element that differentiates true strategic action from a series of haphazard improvisations."[32] Strategy, in contrast to haphazard action, applies to both the offensive and the defensive. Rosinski wrote, it "is that direction of action which aims at the control of a field of activity be it military, social, or even intellectual. It must be comprehensive in order to control every possible counteraction or factor."[33] During the Suez Crisis, the Americans were surprised that they did not have control, when they assumed that they had it; at the same time, Britain and France lost their element of control and were forced into haphazard improvisation by not having the comprehensive military-economic-political power to sustain the initiative. The central lesson that Eccles took from this was that since strategy is the comprehensive direction of power to control situations and areas in order to obtain objectives, military power should never be used except to accomplish a clearly defined political purpose. Those who initiate, direct, and terminate the use of military force must have a clear idea of political purpose.[34] Eccles concluded that Western leaders had failed to understand that an effective strategic concept involves a clear statement of what the use of military force is designed to control, what the nature of that control is, and what degree of control is involved. Furthermore, Western leaders should have more carefully considered when the control was to be initiated, how long it was to have been maintained, and what methods or schemes of control would be employed to achieve their purposes.[35]

In summarizing his understanding of the Suez Crisis, Eccles criticized Anthony Eden and John Foster Dulles for failing to understand the strength of each other's commitment to opposing policies. Neither leader seemed to recognize the significance of each other's perception of their separate national interests. The use of telephone conversations to try to discuss such issues accentuated the misunderstanding, which was difficult to clarify in that form of communication. Carefully worded messages and face-to-face meetings with key staff members present had been the key to success in the two world wars. It remained a question as to what degree the thought processes and judgments of individuals, particularly Eden, Eisenhower, and Dulles, were influenced by their heavy work loads, their ill health, and the strain of extensive air travel. Ironically, the same individuals who had worked so well together during World War II failed to follow their own prior experience of good civil-military cooperation during the Suez Crisis.

In contrasting the situations of the various countries involved, Eccles saw that Britain, France, and the United States each faced extraordinarily difficult choices. Each country had complex and diverse interests and the issues seemed both uncertain and, to a degree, ambiguous. While Britain and France were dealing with frustrations involving their past power, the United States had contradictory interests that resulted from an attempt "to be all things to all people" in an election year. While contradiction and ambiguity might be expected in the face of equivocal threats and strict logic cannot govern all aspects of high-level political-military decisions, Eccles believed that logic and careful thought should have guided the commanders who planned and made decisions. The failure to do this at Suez, he thought, had "produced one of the greatest military- political disasters of our time."[36] To his mind, "Suez was a classic tragic example of what not to do and how not to do it."[37]

An Engineer's Approach to War

In approaching his study, Eccles had taken to heart a quotation from the British philosopher Alfred North Whitehead, who had once said that "one must omit much in order to get on with something."[38] What Eccles omitted in reaching his "lessons" were the details on which historians focus. Yet, interestingly, it was Eccles's immersion in this very detail that he found so enlightening and so rewarding. At the outset of his study, he felt that deep immersion in the detail of a single military action was a graduate-level education in itself. He longed to go beyond the self-serving explanations that the participants had published openly and to obtain the secret records of inner cabinet meetings and private discussions to find evidence of why a particular leader made the decisions he did. Most professional historians would appreciate Eccles's intuitive understanding and his desires on these points, but they would probably part company with him on the nature of the writing he was trying to produce and the way he was using history to create his lessons for military professionals.

It is a common situation for senior military officers and government officials to seek expedient lessons from history, while they often reject the time-consuming methodologies employed by academic historians that involve the objective study of documents with an appreciation for perspectives from the humanities, arts, and social sciences. Instructors in military colleges, such as Eccles, want to make practical use of insights that can provide their students with ready answers to use in solving present or future problems when they are in responsible positions. Such people find it particularly disconcerting that historians are uneasy about providing succinct "lessons." The practical-minded person in today's world, whether a senior military commander or someone else, may find it extremely irritating to have an historian answer such a request by saying something like: "No, I don't do lessons of history. I am trying to understand a specific and unique situation. I am reconstructing the values and outlook of a range of specific people in a specific situation in order to explain what happened and why it happened." The military professional and the layman alike are uncomfortable when historians respond that there are no lessons to be found in history. To the practical-minded, this seems to be a contrariness in historians that smacks of uselessly studying the past for the sake of drawing academic conclusions from seemingly esoteric argument and useless debate.

There is much for a military professional to learn from history. A detailed study of a particular situation can certainly provide insights for a military professional. A particular study of a series of events may reveal comparable situations that a military professional might conceivably face in the future. Alternatively, civil and military leaders studying the broad historical background to a particular situation may find useful insights that are applicable in understanding a future event or, at least, in understanding how a current situation came to be the way it is.[39] Eccles was absolutely correct when he wrote, "If anyone counters with the remark that it is not practicable to expect such leaders thus to study and meditate, that person must be prepared to accept the disastrous consequences of such ignorance and neglect."[40]

Nevertheless, the typical problem that arises when military professionals try to draw "lessons" from specific events like Suez is that they either tend to draw generalizations from a single event or, conversely, they use their historical evidence too selectively and end up shaping their facts to prove a preconceived notion.

In contrast, the professional historian is more interested in gaining the deeper understanding from the uniqueness of events and in the differences that led to the specific and unique aspects of historical events, being aware that they will never be precisely replicated at another time and place. Historians have become fond of saying that the past is a foreign land. By saying this, historians attempt to get across the point that it can be misleading to assume that people in the past are similar to us. By approaching an historical subject with the assumption that the people of that time had different attitudes and different thought processes and that the situation was unique, an historian is led to create a much more careful analysis of the past and to reach a deeper understanding, with better results for understanding human actions. The historical writing that results is more likely to be a nuanced understanding of the structure and context of historical events that examines assumptions along with the process of interacting influences and reactions that led to the events that happened. In fact, that result is what Henry Eccles was striving to achieve. The assumptions of his own education and experience were still rooted in eighteenth- and nineteenth-century approaches that stressed the creation of laws of human action similar to the laws of science. More than a century has passed since Henry Eccles was born and it has been twenty years since he died. Particularly in the sixty years since the end of World War II, we have learned the need to think differently; we have found an urgent need to understand fresh perspectives and unique points of view in a diverse world.

In 1981, Professor Sir Michael Howard at Oxford University addressed this particular problem as he was leaving one academic chair, the Chichele Professor of the History of War, to take another, to become the Regius Professor of Modern History and head of Oxford's Faculty of Modern History. In Howard's inaugural lecture for his new post, he pointed out that there were four key lessons that historians must teach:

1. Not generalizing from false premises based on inadequate evidence.

2. Understanding past beliefs and assumptions that held societies together and determined activities on the level of high politics are the most rewarding and most difficult tasks for the historian.

3. Comprehending diversity and equipping one to cope with it.

4. Appreciating the value and vulnerability of the social framework that allows the historian to ply his trade freely with intellectual and moral detachment.[41]

The contrast between Howard's lessons and Eccles's lessons is instructive. While Eccles intuitively appreciated the views that Howard represented and, to a degree, Eccles practiced what Howard advocated, Eccles's naval and engineering training led him to produce quite different results. For modern historians, an explanation of the process, interactions, and context of human interactions provides the deepest insights. Using his education and training in naval engineering, Eccles tried to avoid the time-consuming explanation of the progression and interaction of events and varied influences. Instead, he attempted to provide a shortcut and a summary of insights that was appropriate to the mechanical world. In doing so, he replaced nuanced humanistic understanding with rigid and judgmental conclusions that did not effectively transmit the full range of wisdom that he, himself, drew from his own study. For such an application, the engineering approach could not fully explain all the issues and oversimplified aspects of the problems presented.

NOTES   Originally entitled "Rear Admiral Henry E. Eccles and the 'Lessons of Suez' Gleaned at the U.S. Naval War College, 1956–1968."

1 The author acknowledges with great appreciation the constructive suggestions of Lieutenant David Kohnen, USNR, on an earlier draft of this paper.

2 For the broad context of this topic, see John B. Hattendorf, "The Conundrum of Military Education in Historical Perspective," in Gregory C. Kennedy and Keith Neilson, eds., *Military Education: Past, Present, and Future* (Westport, Connecticut: Praeger, 2002), pp. 1–12.

3 For the early history of the development of historical study in the U.S. Navy, see John B. Hattendorf, "Geschichte und technologischer Wandel: Das Studium der Marinegeschichte in der US-Marine 1873–1890," in *Seemacht und Seestrategie im 19. und 20. Jahrhundert,* im Auftrag des Militärgeschichtlichen Forschungsamtes herausgegeben von Jörg Duppler (Hamburg, Berlin, Bonn: E. S. Mittler & Sohn, 1999), pp. 105–120, translated into English, revised and republished, as "History and Technological Change: The Study of History in the U.S. Navy, 1873–1890," in John B. Hattendorf, *Naval History and Maritime Strategy: Collected Essays* (Malabar, Florida: Krieger Publishing, 2000), pp. 1–16.

4 See John D. Hayes and John B. Hattendorf, eds., *The Writings of Stephen B. Luce* (Newport: Naval War College Press, 1975).

5 John B. Hattendorf, et al., *Sailors and Scholars: The Centennial History of the U.S. Naval War College* (Newport: Naval War College Press, 1984), pp. 1–37.

6 On the use of the Applicatory System and the estimate of the situation at the Naval War College, see ibid., pp. 69–74, 76–79, 80, 86–88, 112–119, 131, 153–156, 160, 192.

7 First published for a wider audience half a century later: Naval War College, *Sound Military Decision,* edited with an introduction by Frank M. Snyder. Classics of Sea Power series (Annapolis: U.S. Naval Institute Press, 1992).

8 Henry E. Eccles, *Military Concepts and Philosophy* (New Brunswick: Rutgers University Press, 1965), p. 8.

9 Ibid., p. 7.

10 On Wylie, see "Introduction" to Rear Admiral J. C. Wylie, *Military Strategy: A General Theory of Power Control.* Classics of Sea Power series (Annapolis: Naval Institute Press, 1989), pp. ix–xxxv; John B. Hattendorf, *The Evolution of the U.S. Navy's Maritime Strategy, 1978–1986.* Newport Paper 19 (Newport: Naval War College Press, 2005), pp. 4–7.

11 On this see, Hattendorf, et. al, *Sailors and Scholars,* pp. 206, 241–244, 267, 284, 292.

12 This biographical sketch is based on the information in Evelyn Cherpak, *Register of the Papers in the Henry E. Eccles Papers.* Manuscript Register Series, no. 6. 2nd edition (Newport, Rhode Island: Naval Historical Collection, Naval War College, 1988) and Naval War College Naval Historical Collection, Manuscript Collection No. 51: Papers of Henry E. Eccles [hereafter Eccles Papers], Series 2, folder 4.

13 Eccles Papers, Series 3, Box 58, folder 1: Rear Admiral Thomas H. Robbins, Jr., "Memorandum for the Files," 8 November 1956.

14 Ibid., p. 1.

15 Ibid.

16 Ibid., p. 2.

17 Ibid., p. 3.

18 Ibid., p. 4.

19 *Loc. Cit.,* H. E. Eccles, "Notes on Strategy and Logistics," 8 November 1956, p. 2.

20 Ibid.

21 Eccles Papers, Box 58, file 4. Undated handwritten note, clipped to draft of Suez Study dated 23 June 1964. Douglas Southall Freeman (1886–1953), American journalist and author of widely read, multivolume military biographies of General George Washington (1948–57) and Confederate General Robert E. Lee (1934–35) and *Lee's Lieutenants* (1942–44).

22 *Loc. Cit.,* Box 58, file 1: "The Mid East–Suez Situation as a focus for graduate study in National Security," Nov.–Dec. 1956.

23 *Loc. Cit.,* Box 58, file 3: "Rough Orig. Suez Notes. 17 June 1964."

24 *Loc. Cit.,* Box 58, file 3. "Notes on Suez—1956," 5 January 1963, Part IV: The Lessons, p. 6.

25 *Loc. Cit.,* Box 58, folder 8. Letter to Commander Stephen King-Hall, 21 November 1956.

26 *Loc. Cit.,* Box 58, file 3. "Notes on Suez—1956," 5 January 1963, p. 6.

27 Ibid., p. 7.

28 Ibid., p. 8.

29 Ibid., p. 9.

30 *Loc. Cit.,* Series 3, Box 57, folder 39: "George Washington University Logistics Research Project. Suez 1956—Some Military Lessons" [undated, but ca. 1968], p. 7.

31 Ibid., p. 28.

32 Ibid., p. 35; Henry E. Eccles, *Military Concepts and Strategy* (New Brunswick, NJ: Rutgers University Press, 1965), pp. 36–46.

33 Rosinski quoted in Eccles, *Military Concepts and Philosophy,* pp. 46–47.

34 Eccles Papers, Series 3, Box 57, folder 39: "Suez 1956—Some Military Lessons," p. 41.

35 Eccles, *Military Concepts and Philosophy,* p. 48.

36 Eccles Papers, Series 3, Box 57, folder 39: "Suez 1956—Some Military Lessons," p. 46.

37 *Loc. Cit.,* Box 58, file 3: "Notes on Suez—1956," 5 January 1963, p. 10.

38 Quoted in the Eccles Papers in several places. E.g., Series 3, Box 57, folder 39: "Suez 1956—Some Military Lessons," p. 46. See also Eccles file of extracts from Whitehead, Box 44, file 51.

39 For an elaboration on these aspects, see John B. Hattendorf, "The Uses of Maritime History in and for the Navy," *Naval War College Review,* vol. LVI, no. 2 (Spring 2003), pp. 13–38.

40 Eccles Papers, Series 3, Box 57, folder 39: "Suez 1956—Some Military Lessons," p. 46.

41 Michael Howard, *The Lessons of History* (New Haven: Yale University Press, 1991), pp. 1–20.

XX *Globalisation and Navies*
Some Considerations for Naval Theory

The new concepts about globalisation and the traditional concept of a navy are ideas that seem, on first consideration, to be disconnected or even opposing. However, a closer analysis suggests that the broad strategic roles of navies are essential to globalisation, although globalisation presents some serious challenges to the traditional ways in which navies organize, operate, and support themselves.

On the one hand, navies are traditional expressions of an individual state, both in terms of the actual exercise of national power and as a symbolic expression of that power. On the other hand, the fundamental underlying purpose of a navy has always been to make maritime areas safe and dependable avenues for one's own use and to prevent any enemy from using them to one's detriment. For that reason, the concept of the freedom of the seas has been a major one in naval history. In this fundamental role, navies have played an essential part in global economics. One can predict that they will continue to do so, as long as there is any danger to or need to protect important maritime routes and the goods that pass on, over, or under the water-covered parts that make up the largest surface area of our planet.

It is interesting to note that in the last sixty years, since the end of World War II, the number of the world's navies has increased dramatically. Not all the new navies have remained small in this period, even if they are relatively new. At least one among them, India's navy, has made "the transition to eminence"[1] in the naval world within only half a century. Immediately after the end of World War II, the authoritative *Jane's Fighting Ships*[2] listed only 54 countries with navies. Currently, the Jane's Fighting Ships online database[3] lists three times that many: 163 countries with navies. Like India and the United States, a good number of these countries have separate armed coast guard forces in addition to their navies, and these have become increasingly important in the modern world context.

At the same time, the latest maritime trade statistics show that the seas are increasingly important to the global economy and that world shipping at sea is increasing and has already reached proportions that surpass all previous history. According to the 2005 report of the United Nations Conference on Trade and Development, more than 6.7 billion tons of merchandise was carried at sea, a rise of 4.3 percent over the previous year. Forty percent of this tonnage originated in Asia and was carried to other parts of the globe. In the same year, at the same time as the amount of cargo grew, the world's shipping fleets also grew by 4.5 percent, reaching a record-breaking total of 896 million deadweight tons.[4]

In a significant departure from past practice, today the number of merchant vessels under a particular national flag no longer expresses a direct relationship to that nation's involvement in maritime affairs. The structure and ownership of the world's merchant fleet have changed dramatically and already reflect the expansion of national business interests across the globe. For example, on the United Nations' most recent list of the world's most important maritime countries, the United States has the world's fifth largest merchant fleet, after Greece, Japan, Germany, and China. But 61 percent of the merchant vessels in which Americans have controlling interests fly a foreign flag. This same pattern is followed by the top three merchant fleets. Both Greece and Japan have about 75 percent of their merchant fleets under foreign flags, while Germany has nearly 87 percent. America's close competitor in size of merchant fleet, China, is an exception among the top five, with just 35 percent of its fleet under a foreign flag, while India, ranking fifteenth on the list, has just under 9 percent of its merchant fleet under a foreign flag.[5]

Globalisation, as many are beginning to think about it today, is all about the transformation of the way the world does business through the increasing ease and speed of global-scale communications, conductivity, commercial interdependency, collaboration, and market competition, which all converge to create for individuals, companies, and customers a cheaper, easier, more "friction-free," and more productive way of life for more people around the globe.[6] Globalisation means that industrial production, even from individual companies and traditional brand names that have long been sources of national pride, are no longer the product of just a single nation, but are produced through more economically and productively efficient cooperation and collaboration that combine local skill and concentrated specialization with competitive costs and large global markets. These are fundamentally economic and world trade issues that have transformed the production of numerous familiar products that many of us use on a daily basis. What we used to think of as an industrial product of Europe, or, more particularly, England, Germany, or Sweden, or of the United States, may now be owned by a multinational consortium of investors and businesspeople from many countries with global economic reach and may have component parts from a variety of Asian and Latin American countries that are assembled and marketed simultaneously in various other parts of the world. As this goes on around us and continues to develop, one cannot help but make the mental leap and ask what is the effect of this globalisation on a "national brand" such as a navy, and how does this bear on new naval concepts that come with the associated new security concerns and changes in procedures that we have recently come to label as "transformation."

The concepts of globalisation and transformation are closely connected. Neither idea is new and neither word is new, although one often gets the impression that they are brand-new creations. The word "transformation" in the same sense that we are using it today can be traced to the early fifteenth century, while the word "globalisation" first appeared about 1959 as a synonym for "internationalism," a word that, in turn, can be dated to the 1850s. "Globalisation" is also recognized as a synonym for "multilateralism," a word that is found from 1928 onward.[7] The aspects that are new, however, are the understandings that include the current applications of technology, the higher speeds, the growing uses, and the demonstrable commercial successes associated with these matters across the world during the past decade. Equally important is the extension of these concepts, which were once applied almost entirely to diplomacy and politics, to the economic, financial, and commercial worlds.

The Twentieth Century as Prologue

If one is to think of globalisation in terms of an explicit or tacitly agreed-upon grand strategy for the nations of the world to pursue to their mutual benefit, then the first logical conclusion to be reached is that the kind of geopolitical division that divided the globe into warring camps and dominated much of the history of the twentieth century, as well as earlier centuries, must be avoided. That sort of activity is entirely antithetical to the nature of globalisation. Such wars typically close off major parts of the globe from interactions with the other parts and serve to promote and perpetuate closed economic systems that cannot interact with one another to share in the practical and positive results that globalisation produces.

While the images of geopolitical warfare in the twentieth century and before easily tend to dominate naval thought, the twentieth century also provided the foundation upon which naval operations in a globalised world may be built. Our abstract understanding of naval strategic roles has developed and changed over the course of the twentieth century, and the historical record has led us to widen further our perception about naval roles. Above all, we see that the issue of strategic naval roles is not merely a question of abstract concepts among naval officers, but of concepts enmeshed in broader issues that range from grand strategy, bureaucracy, and finance to diplomacy and international law. On the naval operational level, the consideration of strategic roles must often be based on issues ranging from cooperation with other services to combat effectiveness in carrying out a strategic vision.[8]

When seen from the very broadest perspective, the importance of maritime affairs ebbs and flows in relation to the context of events. Within maritime affairs, context is everything in understanding and defining maritime strategic roles, particularly when the very nature of ships and aircraft forces them to undertake a variety of missions and duties. Yet, because of the expansion of maritime interests among coastal states, as well as the very mobility of naval forces and their multidimensional capabilities and roles, the issues surrounding the strategic roles of armed force at sea continue to be important ones. The impact of noticeable change in so many areas—ranging from the development of a global economy, new developments in international law, and the character and effectiveness of weapons, to the joint-service and multinational employment of naval forces, as well as the organizational and technological implications coming through innovation—continues to stress the need to see conflict at sea and the strategic roles of maritime forces in the widest perspective.

As in all times when major changes are taking place, the procedures of the past superficially appear to be irrelevant and outmoded. Yet a careful look at old ideas and approaches helps to formulate new questions that need to be answered. The old answers can stimulate broad new approaches and new applications, suggesting useful insight. A broad look at the twentieth century and its experience with changing strategic roles for navies suggests that the specific strategic roles for which a navy is built are often very different from the roles it actually ends up performing. The experience of the twentieth century provides repeated evidence of this, as one contrasts the strategic roles that any major participant foresaw in a prewar period with those actually carried out in the wars that followed. It was true of the great wars of 1914–19 and 1939–45 as well as of the smaller wars of that century. Navies have many and often unexpected uses. But this truth serves to remind us that naval strategy depends on an ever-changing context that involves what one side actually does in the calculus of what the other side wants to do and is actually able to do with effect.

At the outset of the twenty-first century, we can clearly see that just over 100 years of experience has fully borne out the fundamental distinctions that both Alfred Thayer Mahan and Julian Corbett recognized for naval forces at the opening of the last century, but their thoughts need to be refined to meet modern concerns. Put in the broadest terms that we use today, the fundamental strategic role for navies is to prevent any opponent from blocking the safe passage of any friendly craft on, over, or under the sea and to block any force that interferes with such passage. If sea passage can be assured, an interdependent global economy, dependent on the movement of goods across the seas, can continue to grow and to sustain peaceful world development. In a twenty-first-century global economy, the safety of sea passage can no longer be defined in terms of the strategic role of a single nation's navy. It is a multilateral role that reflects global concerns and the range of accepted, agreed, and customary practices among peoples and nations that form what we have come to call international law.

Below that fundamental strategic role, there are secondary roles that flow from it. The strategic focus may be narrowed a step downward and expressed in national terms, but the overriding global and international terms of reference restrict the degree to which any single nation may acceptably assume a controlling influence at sea. However, a nation that can assure safe passage for friendly commercial ships as well as for friendly naval and military vessels, preventing interference from enemy forces, is in a position to defend itself as well as to provide and defend a secure passage for military forces and support them on a distant shore, where they can assist allies or defend key places against the threats of the moment.

At a third level, there is a series of supporting strategic naval roles in wartime that allow one to gain an essential position, either sequentially or cumulatively, that facilitates the higher strategic functions. Such roles include reconnaissance, control of information, and creation of political or economic pressure to help friends or hinder enemies. In periods of peace, and in war during the absence of direct hostilities, a perceived capacity to carry out such strategic roles creates the basis for political perceptions in either friends or enemies.

The epilogue to the twentieth century is as yet unknown, but if one reads the known prologue as it played out in the twentieth century and observes the initial indications of its course in the twenty-first century, one finds that maritime forces will need the materiel and intellectual resources to meet the unexpected and be able to shift from one strategic role to another in terms of whatever context appears. If the leading naval trends that appeared in the second half of the twentieth century continue to develop, the naval history of the twenty-first century will be a story of both large nations and small, great powers and littoral states, cooperatively carrying out multilateral, joint, and combined operations at sea to maintain international order.

The realization of this broad vision would affect navies in two ways: first, in terms of an important strategic object of grand strategy toward which naval operations can contribute, and, second, in terms of the logistical and organizational means and methods through which a navy sustains its efficiency.

Globalisation as an Object of Future Grand Strategy

If globalisation were to be taken as an object of future grand strategy, its intended purpose would be to contribute to the betterment of the human condition around the globe through the latest means provided by modern communication, economic diversity, competing markets, and increased efficiency in work and production. To be successful, such a strategy must carefully nurture economic, cultural, ethnic, and national diversities, as these are the characteristics that provide for the fundamental differences in regions, markets, and workplaces that are the engines for successful globalisation.

At the same time, certain types of commonalities in business procedures and approaches must necessarily be developed and sustained to permit and promote effective and increasingly efficient economic globalisation. This move toward commonality in some areas may well be fraught with some difficulty, if it is seen as a subjugation of traditional values, work opportunities, and products to foreign ideas, labor, and means. These changes toward certain types of commonality could conceivably be limited to business procedures and to communications in ways that would not undermine the more fundamental differences that form the driving forces of globalisation. Stress of this nature, arising from economic forces and perceived ethnic and cultural values, might become a source of regional tension that could affect global economics and balance. This and other types of fragmentation of an international cooperative and collaborative market economy would become fundamental international security issues.

In thinking about the nature of security interests in a globalised world economy, the most fundamental maritime issue would clearly be to maintain the safe and free use of the seas for commerce and international economic communication and exchange. In the modern age, one can no longer think of this in terms of just the traditional uses of ocean surfaces. The undersea regions, sea bottom, and skies over waterways have now become essential and interrelated aspects. The issues are not just naval ones, although they deeply concern navies. This line of thinking reaches even beyond interservice cooperation toward international cooperation. For navies, the issues at hand lead one to think in broad terms that encompass all aspects of mankind's relationship with the world's oceans. The most proper adjective to describe that wider range of issues is the word "maritime."

One of the major developments of the late twentieth century that provides a beginning for thinking about maritime security in a global context, now and in the future, is the result of the Third United Nations Convention on the Law of the Sea in 1982. This agreement, now very widely accepted among the world's nations, lays out some key concepts. First, it lays out a geographical basis for each individual nation to understand the ocean areas for which it has responsibility in terms of its 12-mile coastal waters, the continental shelf, and waters surrounding offshore island dependencies, and beyond that, its exclusive economic zone, for the protection of offshore maritime resources. In addition, it attempts to resolve the many very specific and knotty questions involving the rights of international passage in narrow waters in which one or more countries have an interest, thus providing approaches to defuse conflicts over claims and rights within sea areas while at the same time serving to lay out the limits of national responsibility for regulation.[9] These are very helpful insofar as they take basic, practical steps toward providing some relevant fundamentals, but future practices and uses will need to develop further in the realm of the International Law of the Sea to regulate the emerging and larger issues of globalisation itself.[10] What we do have, however, helps to empower the coastal state in the role of managing its own maritime resources.

Coastal power is local, not global, but it clearly has an effect on global maritime issues. Coastal naval powers build their navies with specifically attuned equipment and training for the particular range of tasks necessary to a specific and limited geographical area. They are ready to operate and, if necessary, fight in very different circumstances and ways than naval fleets designed for distant transoceanic work.[11] Such navies may well be hard pressed to win an old-fashioned sea battle with a larger navy, but their purposes are different and focused on helping to avert a war, prevent a crisis, and stabilize national control over ports, local maritime resources, and safe passage within their own areas. At the same time, these local navies have the potential for cooperation with the world's largest navies by being able, through the varied available structures of cooperative relations and coalitions, to provide specialized naval knowledge, techniques, and equipment in times of crisis as well as long-term stabilization. Such attributes are all areas of key importance to naval roles in a globalised world economy. Thus, small and medium-size navies can have, in addition to their independent roles, new and particularly important roles to play in partnership with large and superpower navies.

Naval Roles for Globalisation

In order to support an established and growing global economy, the principal naval focus will not be on the traditional concept—one set of powers gaining command of the sea by defeating a rival or coalition fleet whose purpose is to establish a rival political and economic system for the world or a major part of it. In a globalised world, there would be no circumstances that would require a modern battle like Trafalgar (whose two-hundredth anniversary has recently been commemorated worldwide). Nevertheless, the example of Horatio Nelson's leadership, prescience, and sacrifice in that event, along with the determination, professional skill, and hardened experience that he and his sailors showed, will always remain an icon to naval professionals the world over.[12] Such epic battles are so dramatic and such towering events in naval history as we have understood it that some people may have trouble imaging what the role of a navy could possibly be if such battles cannot be envisioned as a credible potential reality. Yet the last such event occurred at Leyte Gulf in 1944, just over sixty years ago, and navies have been very profitably employed otherwise since that time, giving us pause to think further about the topic.

For the security of a global world economy, one must think somewhat differently about the central thought that emerges in classical naval theory. In that body of literature, naval battles were one means to achieve command of the sea. When Sir Julian Corbett defined command of the sea nearly a century ago, in 1911, he said that "it means nothing but the control of maritime communications, whether for commercial or military purposes."[13] In writing this, Corbett was reflecting the thought that control was a national or allied naval objective that involved removing the barriers to the use of the sea that an opposing nation's or coalition's naval power created. In a new globalised world, such control would be not just a national function, but rather a shared world function for the general good of all; it would not be viewed in the context of national or imperial rivalry. So, in terms of naval theory, we must look beyond the process of gaining command, as that is already achieved, to the concept of exercising command of the sea now that it has been gained. Here, too, one will need to think in terms of international cooperation rather than competition.

Globalisation and the Military Function of a Navy

In an ideal and completely globalised economic world, founded on the acceptance and full participation of the world's community of nations, the military role of individual national navies would focus mainly on the capability to respond to threats to the internationally recognized, global world order.

The military capabilities needed for navies to do this would be primarily (1) the capability to conduct limited wars and interventions and (2) the capability to oppose guerrilla or terrorist attacks. These two roles would supersede the previously held idea that navies existed principally to fight large-scale, general, or conventional wars and in which intervention and guerrilla warfare were lesser included tasks. The latter would now become the primary naval tasks, with general and conventional war perhaps removed entirely or placed in a lower category as a more theoretical contingency than a practical, immediate concern.[14]

The capabilities needed to perform in the extreme are those that navies very rarely use, but these same capacities that navies have for meeting their most extreme challenges are the very strengths that indirectly give them the effective power to perform other operations on a more routine basis. Thus, the peacetime roles of naval power would be the main, day-to-day, future functions of the world's navies in such a new world order.

Naval power was traditionally symbolized by a trident, its three prongs representing surface, sky, and underwater weapons. One could still use that symbol, but it may be more useful in the future to think of it in terms of the three integral categories of a navy's functions—its military, its diplomatic, and its police functions—symbolized by a single instrument. The fundamental role of a navy is found in its military capability, and this forms the basis upon which a navy may act in a diplomatic and policing function. There is much to consider in regard to globalisation and the military role of navies, but these issues first need to be seen in the light of the combined effect of the two main additional functions of naval power: policing and diplomacy.

Globalisation and the Policing Function of a Navy

The policing role of a navy is a major contribution that armed force at sea makes. It is a conceptual and practical extension of the military role of navies. On the one hand, nations need to be concerned about their coastal maritime areas and the littoral seas that surround them. These, the Law of the Sea Convention has suggested, are the specific areas for the exercise of national sovereignty. In some cases, national authorities may assign the specialized law enforcement duties in these areas to some separate armed service other than a navy—for example, a coast guard, a maritime border patrol service, or a fisheries-, undersea-, or sea-bottom-resource-protection agency. But when this is the case, it is essential that such an agency work closely and cooperatively with its associated navy in its complementary tasks.

Cumulatively, such coastal waters are central to the concept of exercising maritime power. This function maintains stability for both local and global commercial activity that passes through these areas. As such, it is a feature of the global economy. The coastal responsibility for exercising sovereignty in these maritime areas involves ensuring the good order and safe use of these areas as well as regulating the uses and harvesting of the fishing and undersea resources within them and the air space above them. All this serves to contribute to both the internal and external components of the national maritime development that, in turn, serves the individual national contribution toward cooperative, global economic growth and stability.

While these national dimensions are central in considering the concept of navies and national maritime policing power, globalisation demands that one move beyond them to look toward the international dimension and multinational cooperation. A single nation has clear responsibility within its coastal waters and exclusive economic zones. Yet there are no fences at sea, so what comes into, goes out of, or remains in those waters is, in one way or another, tied to some other part of the world's oceans. The oceans fill the center of our globe, and we, the varying peoples around the edges of the sea, look across to one another and reach toward each other through oceanic transport. International cooperation in such a globalised, interdependent world is an essential dimension, even in carrying out one's own national responsibilities in one's own local waters. Since maritime affairs are undeniably tied to the shore, even just as the origin or destination of ships and merchandise, the separate national elements are the key to international cooperation.

Thinking back to the definition of the most basic function of naval power—the idea that it is centered on the control of maritime communication, military or commercial—leads us to look at the policing function of navies in a new way. Understanding the fundamental use of naval force as maritime control leads us to ask some pertinent questions for implementation: Control of what? Control for how long? Control for what purpose? One definition of the word clarifies the point at hand and the particular use of the word: control is the "application of policies and procedures for directing, regulating, and coordinating production, administration, and other business activities in a way to achieve the objectives of the enterprise."[15] In this case, the objective of the enterprise is to protect and defend the operation of the global economy that is the engine of mutual global well-being. Put simply, this translates into directing, regulating, and coordinating shipping and other maritime activities insofar as they affect the objectives of globalisation: eliminating threats that disrupt safe global commerce and create serious problems for it. In the modern and emerging new world, these issues include such new types of perceived threats as illegal drug trafficking, illegal immigration, piracy, environmental threats, and terrorist activities.

To deal with policing these aspects of the maritime arena, intelligence and detailed information about shipping movements and cargos are essential and derive from observation and regulation in national coastal areas where shipping derives or is destined. To be effective in this context, such information needs to be shared with other nations, navies, and maritime regulatory agencies. Thus, policing is very much involved in what has recently come to be called "Maritime Domain Awareness"—that is to say, gaining an effective knowledge of all activities associated with the global maritime environment that could have an impact on the security and safety of the economy or environment. In this way, the sharing of such knowledge and awareness is linked to the diplomatic function of navies.

Globalisation and the Diplomatic Function of a Navy

The international, diplomatic function of navies is a fundamental one for globalisation. The diplomatic function in this new era is quite different from that imagined by theorists in the Cold War era, when the issues of negotiation from strength, manipulation, and prestige were seen as the characteristics of naval diplomacy. The global economy of today and of the future requires a cooperative security network if it is to function fully and effectively. No one country, not even a superpower, can begin to provide this fully. The development of such a network must be carried out through multilateral and cooperative operations. In doing this a quite different approach to naval diplomacy is required.

In the second half of the twentieth century, the world's navies cooperatively organized some important initiatives that provide for us today a viable foundation for this new kind of naval diplomacy to develop further. In the mid-1950s, new initiatives were begun with the creation of student, staff, and faculty exchanges at naval academies and staff and war colleges. This year, my own naval college and professional home, the U.S. Naval War College, celebrates the fiftieth anniversary of the 1956 establishment of its Naval Command Course. This farseeing initiative has done much to help build closer relationships between the current and future leaders of the world's navies. Its educational contribution is one of mutual understanding working toward global stability, and thus it is in itself the kind of initiative that is essential for what we may come to call the Age of Globalisation.

Following on from this first step in the professional educational field, NATO created the first viable example of an operational, multilateral naval force in its Standing Naval Force, Atlantic. At its outset in 1968, many naval leaders of that era thought it too idealistic and functionally impossible for large, medium, and small navies to work together in any sort of useful, practical, or effective way. Certainly, there were serious strains, but practice proved that it not only was possible but also has continued to be very successful. It has now been extended to other operational groups in the Channel and the Mediterranean and serves as a model outside the NATO context. The keys to this success were found in standardized logistics, standardized communication procedures and equipment, and standardized operational doctrine.[16] The cumulative insight has been shown in recent years in the multilateral naval operations in the Adriatic and in the Afghanistan and Iraq operations.

Adding another dimension that built directly on these two initiatives was the creation in 1969 of the International Seapower Symposia. These biennial meetings were the first in which chiefs of naval staff and the heads of the world's senior professional naval colleges could meet with their counterparts from around the world to discuss shared professional problems. In 2005, the seventeenth meeting of the International Seapower Symposium took place. In the thirty-six years since the beginning of this series of symposia, a number of key developments have grown from them. First is the development of regional symposia and regional cooperative initiatives that have been direct spin-offs from the International Seapower Symposium, which had first inspired the approach of using regional discussions as part of its agenda. Second is the initiative of a manual for multinational operations that could be used beyond the NATO arena.

All these initiatives in the fields of education, multinational operational art, and top-level professional discussion are strong foundations for what will need to be developed further. The very sinews of globalisation are transoceanic communication, transport, and shipping. In a truly globalised world economy, national security—most particularly the naval component involved—must be a shared effort with other nations. This observation leads us back to the point where this discourse began, globalisation and the military function of navies.

Further Thoughts on the Military Function of Navies

In the modern age, it has become important, even essential, to think about maritime forces—navy, coast guard, amphibious forces—in their joint context, alongside the other national armed forces: the army and the air force. That is a very important task, but in the course of doing this one must first understand that a navy is different from the other services, which is the very reason one needs to think of navies in complementary ways to other services rather than in identical terms. This is not to say that a navy is more important, just that it is different and performs different functions in different ways within a different medium. Of the various kinds of military forces—land, air, and maritime forces—only navies have the ready and established ability to be both weapons in war and benign elements in peace. One of the essential differences between what an army might do and what a navy might do in peacetime is that navies do not need to intrude on sovereign territory to carry out their missions effectively. This is a fundamental feature of the maritime presence of naval forces. As the great naval theorist J. C. Wylie once wrote:

> This almost indefinable quality of "maritime presence"—subtle, benign, ubiquitous presence—actual or potential presence—is the great asset of sea power in times of peace and even in times of one or another variety of tension. This quality of actual or even potential maritime presence anywhere around the world is the quality that sets navies apart from armies and air forces as employments short of war. This world-wide and benign ubiquity, this subtle evidence of naval and thus national strength is what makes viable the other normally benign elements of national strength when extended overseas.[17]

Wylie's point is fundamental in considering globalisation and the military function of navies. The military object of naval operations is to ensure some degree of effective control at sea. In this sense, the control may be economic, political, or psychological, and it may range from complete control to ranges of influence that can either be felt immediately or have a long-term effect.[18] In terms of a globalised world economy, that means that the primary role is preventing anarchy at sea, ensuring law and order for the safe passage of peaceful shipping across the open oceans, from its ports of origin, beyond coastal waters and local exclusive economic zones, to its worldwide destinations. In such a world, one can anticipate that among the most typical forms of naval operations will be the naval blockade—a primal type of naval operations, but one that has been little studied until recently[19]—conducted in the context of maritime coalitions, another fundamental dimension that has been largely ignored until recently.[20]

These kinds of core-competency naval operations on the open sea are linked to and extended from the separate and national police activities inside coastal waters. Multinational maritime coalition operations may be effectively empowered to deal with emerging military threats to economic stability and the international exchange of raw goods and manufactured products. These threats may be on the open sea, in the form of piracy or illegal maritime trade; alternatively, as military threats or actions that disrupt the equilibrium of the global economy, they may require access and intervention ashore. Such coalitions are also effective in dealing with humanitarian relief operations, as was seen following the 2005 tsunami. Such a wide range of operations may well result in more carefully defined—even mutually agreed upon—national specialization in naval roles, as vision and understanding broaden to see more clearly an individual navy's role within a global context.

This discussion has focused almost entirely on the level of grand strategy and national strategy, but globalisation has another impact for navies that, at another time and place, deserves an equal focus, to consider more closely its effects on the logistical and organizational means and methods through which a navy sustains its efficiency. Globalisation, logically extended, will put an end to the traditional national approach to defense procurement. Even naval weapons and systems will be, and in many areas already are, provided to one country from others. A truly globalised economic system will not allow defense industries to have privileged positions, and it will create many challenges to the production and industrial systems now in place.[21] This should lead to more competitive, better, and cheaper supply for navies, while at the same time helping to standardize systems around the globe for multinational cooperation and bringing home very directly the critical importance of global interchange.

In another area worthy of closer examination, globalisation, like the implementation of network-centric warfare, creates a result that empowers many more individual elements with a status that they previously did not enjoy and provides a clearer role for participation. This is as true of the small or medium-size navy that may have been overshadowed previously by the large or superpower navy as it is for the individual sailor who now with a mobile telephone can communicate directly as never before with home, family, senior officers, or even news reporters. These are both challenges to the traditional approaches among and within navies, but perhaps no more serious an adjustment than an adult makes in allowing youngsters to grow and mature. They are things to be encouraged, nurtured, and focused for mutual benefit, not denied.

To return to the broader theme, in conclusion, it is clear that the global world economy and its functioning, for which the term *globalisation* is just shorthand jargon, is a maritime economy at its base. Navies around the world have a fundamental role to play in maintaining and defending this global economy as a shared system for the peaceful enjoyment of the world's resources. Neither one nation nor any single navy, no matter how large or how powerful it may be, can achieve this purpose alone. If globalisation is to endure and to grow to its full potential in the long term, every individual navy will eventually need to define its role in terms of a maritime strategy and a wider concept of the seas for individual nations and the global community.

NOTES This paper was presented at an international seminar held 16–17 February 2006 in New Delhi, India, on "Maritime Dimensions of a New World Order," sponsored by the National Maritime Foundation. It was published in Ravi Vohra and Devbrat Chakraborty, eds., *Maritime Dimensions of a New World Order* (New Dehli: Anamaya Publishers for the National Maritime Foundation, 2007), pp. 32–51.

1 See Vice Admiral G. M. Hiranandani, *Transition to Eminence: The Indian Navy, 1976–1990* (New Delhi: Lancer Publishers, 2005).

2 *Jane's Fighting Ships, 1944–45 (Corrected to April 1946)* (New York: Macmillan, 1947).

3 Jane's Fighting Ships website, http://jfs.janes.com/public/jfs/index.shtml, accessed 13 January 2006.

4 United Nations Conference on Trade and Development, *Review of Maritime Transport, 2005,* http://www.unctad.org, accessed 13 January 2006. "World container port traffic expanded by 9.6 per cent over that of the previous year, reaching 303.1 million TEUs (20-foot equivalent units), with ports of developing countries handling 122.4 million TEUs, or 40.4 per cent of the total. The share of the developing-country fleet reached 22.6 per cent, or 202.3 million dwt (deadweight tons), at the beginning of 2005. About 77 per cent of this fleet belongs to developing countries in Asia. The net increase of developing countries' fleet was 20.9 million dwt, more than four times the net increase of the fleet of major open-registry countries, which increased by 4.5 million dwt. The worldwide merchant fleet increased by 38.8 million dwt to a record 895.8 million dwt."

5 Ibid., Chapter 2, p. 33: Table of the 35 Most Important Maritime Countries and Territories as of 1 January 2005.

6 Thomas L. Friedman, *The World Is Flat: A Brief History of the Twenty-First Century* (New York: Farrar, Straus and Giroux, 2005), p. 200.

7 See the relevant words defined in *The Oxford English Dictionary Online,* http://www.oed.com.

8 This paragraph and the following are based on my more detailed discussion in "Les États-Unis et les Mutations de la Puissance Maritime au XXe Siècle," in *La Puissance Maritime,* ed. Christian Buchet, Jean Meyer, and Jean-Pierre Poussou, Collection Histoire-Maritime (Paris: Presses de l'Université Paris-Sorbonne, 2004), pp. 577–596.

9 On this topic, see, for example, J. Ashley Roach and Robert W. Smith, *Excessive Maritime Claims,* U.S. Naval War College International Law Studies 66 (Newport: Naval War College, 1994).

10 See, for example, Daniel Moran, "The International Law of the Sea in a Globalised World," in *Globalisation and Maritime Power,* ed. Sam J. Tangredi (Washington: National Defense University, 2002), pp. 221–239.

11 Jacob Børresen, "Coastal Power: The Sea Power of the Coastal State and the Management of Maritime Resources," in *Navies in Northern Waters, 1721–2000,* ed. Rolf Hobson and Tom Kristiansen (London: Frank Cass, 2004), pp. 249–275.

12 See Hattendorf, "Nelson Afloat: A Hero to the World's Navies," in *Admiral Lord Nelson: Context and Legacy,* ed. David Cannadine (London: Palgrave Macmillan, 2005), pp. 166–192.

13 Sir Julian Corbett, *Some Principles of Maritime Strategy,* ed. Eric L. Grove, Classics of Sea Power series (Annapolis: Naval Institute Press, 1988), p. 94.

14 This and the following paragraphs are a revision and rethinking of the ideas outlined in K. Booth, *Navies and Foreign Policy* (London: Croom Helm, and New York: Carne, Russak, 1977), pp. 1–25.

15 Philip Gove, ed., *Webster's Third New International Dictionary of the English Language Unabridged* (Springfield, Mass.: Merriam-Webster, 1993), s.v. "Control."

16 "International Naval Cooperation and Admiral Richard G. Colbert: The Intertwining of a Career with an Idea" and "NATO's Policeman on the Beat: The First Twenty Years of the Standing Naval Force, Atlantic, 1968–1987" in Hattendorf, *Naval History and Maritime Strategy: Collected Essays* (Malabar, Fla.: Krieger Publishing, 2000), pp. 161–185, 187–200.

17 J. C. Wylie, "Mahan: Then and Now," in *The Influence of History on Mahan: The Proceedings of a Conference to Mark the Centenary of Alfred Thayer Mahan's* The Influence of Sea Power upon History, 1660–1783, ed. Hattendorf (Newport: Naval War College Press, 1991), pp. 41–42.

18 J. C. Wylie, "Postscript: Twenty Years Later," in *Military Strategy: A General Theory of Power Control,* with an Introduction by John B. Hattendorf, Classics of Sea Power series (Annapolis: Naval Institute Press, 1989), p. 103.

19 On this subject, see Bruce A. Elleman and S. C. M. Paine, eds., *Naval Blockades and Seapower: Strategies and Counter-Strategies, 1805–2005* (London: Routledge, 2006).

20 See Bruce A. Elleman and S. C. M. Paine, eds., *Naval Coalition Warfare: From the Napoleonic War to Operation Iraqi Freedom* (London: Routledge, forthcoming December 2007).

21 See Peter J. Dombrowski, Eugene Gholz, and Andrew L. Ross, *Military Transformation and the Defense Industry after Next: The Defense Industrial Implications of Network-Centric Warfare,* Newport Paper 18 (Newport: Naval War College Press, 2003).

APPENDIX: BIBLIOGRAPHY OF BOOKS AND ARTICLES BY JOHN B. HATTENDORF, 1960–2011

1960

"Prize Winning Essay: 'My True Security—The American Way.'" *Western Springs Citizen* (28 April 1960), part 2 [unpaginated p. 13].

1964

A Dusty Path: A Pictorial History of Kenyon College. Gambier, Ohio: Kenyon College Reveille, 1964.

1966

"*O'Brien*'s Odyssey: One Destroyer's Duty in the Seventh Fleet." By Cdr. C. S. Christensen and Ens. J. B. Hattendorf. Photography by Ens. M. R. Hamilton. *Our Navy: The Navyman's Magazine* 61, no. 9 (September 1966), pp. 2–4, 60.

1971

"Research in the Mahan Library: A Long Lost Farragut Letter Is Rediscovered." *Naval War College Review* 24, no. 4 (December 1971), pp. 97–99.

"Sir Julian Corbett on the Significance of Naval History." *American Neptune* 31, no. 4 (October 1971), pp. 275–85. Revised and reprinted in *Naval History and Maritime Strategy: Collected Essays* [hereafter *Naval History and Maritime Strategy*; see entry for 2000], pp. 77–89.

"Technology and Strategy: A Study in the Professional Thought of the U.S. Navy, 1900–1916." *Naval War College Review* 24, no. 3 (November 1971), pp. 25–48. Reprinted in B. M. Simpson, ed., *War, Strategy, and Maritime Power.* New Brunswick, N.J.: Rutgers Univ. Press, 1977, pp. 111–38. Revised and reprinted in *Naval History and Maritime Strategy*, pp. 29–57.

1975

The Writings of Stephen B. Luce. Edited with Rear Admiral John D. Hayes, USN. Naval War College Historical Monograph 1. Newport, R.I.: Naval War College Press, 1975. Reprinted 1977, 1993.

1976

"The American Navy in the World of Franklin and Jefferson, 1775–1826." In *War and Society,* edited by Brian Bond and Ian Roy. Vol. 2. London: Croom-Helm, 1976. [This is the text of a lecture given at the British Museum, London, on 17

October 1975 in connection with the exhibition "The World of Franklin and Jefferson."]

1980

"The Machinery for the Planning and Execution of English Grand Strategy in the War of the Spanish Succession." In *Changing Interpretations and New Sources in Naval History: Papers from the Third Naval Academy History Symposium,* edited by R. W. Love, Jr. New York: Garland, 1980.

"The Rakoczi Insurrection in English War Policy, 1703–1711." *Canadian-American Review of Hungarian Studies* 7, no. 2 (Fall 1980), pp. 91–102.

Register of the William L. Mullin Papers. Newport, R.I.: Naval War College, Naval Historical Collection, 1980.

"The Naval Defense of Sweden in the 1980s." *Naval War College Review* 33, no. 1 (January–February 1980), pp. 22–34.

1981

Register of the William McCarty Little Papers. Newport, R.I.: Naval War College, Naval Historical Collection, 1981.

1982

"American Thinking on the Theory of Naval Strategy, 1945–1980." In *Naval Strategy in the Nuclear Age,* edited by Geoffrey Till. London: Macmillan, 1982.

"Note: Some British and American Sailors' Tombstones in Penang, Malaysia." *Mariner's Mirror* 68, no. 3 (August 1982), pp. 325–26.

"Notes for a Guide to Western Historical Manuscripts in Singapore." *Journal of the History Society National University of Singapore* (1982/83), pp. 69–78.

"Some Concepts in American Naval Strategic Thought, 1940–1970." In *The Yankee Mariner and Sea Power,* edited by J. J. Bartell. Los Angeles: Univ. of Southern California Press, 1982, pp. 93–108.

1983

"English Grand Strategy and the Blenheim Campaign, 1704." *International History Review* 5, no. 1 (February 1983), pp. 3–19.

"Note: H.M.S. *Redpole* at Christmas Island." *Mariner's Mirror* 69, no. 2 (May 1983), p. 199.

On His Majesty's Service: Observations of the British Home Fleet from the Diary, Reports, and Letters of Joseph H. Wellings, Assistant U.S. Naval Attaché, London, 1940–1941. Naval War College Historical Monograph 5. Newport, R.I.: Naval War College Press, 1983. Reprinted 1993.

1984

"Benbow's Last Fight: Documents Relating to the Battle of Cape Santa Marta, August 1702." In *Naval Miscellany,* edited by N. A. M. Rodger. Vol. 5. London: Naval Records Society, 1984.

"Luce's Idea of the Naval War College." *Naval War College Review* 37, no. 5 (September–October 1984), pp. 35–43. Revised and reprinted in *Naval History and Maritime Strategy,* pp. 17–28.

"Purpose and Contribution in Editing Naval Documents: A General Appreciation." In *Editing Naval Documents: An Historical Appreciation.* Washington, D.C.: Naval

Historical Center, Department of the Navy, 1984, pp. 43–61. Revised and re-printed in *Naval History and Maritime Strategy,* pp. 91–108.

Sailors and Scholars: The Centennial History of the Naval War College. With B. Mitch-ell Simpson III and John R. Wadleigh. Newport, R.I.: Naval War College Press, 1984. Chinese translation, Taipei: Operations and Planning Advisory Committee, Republic of China Navy, 1994.

Two Beginnings: A History of St. George's Church, Tanglin. Singapore: St. George's Church, 1984.

1985

"Editor's Introduction" and notes to Charles Nordhoff, *Man-of-War Life.* Classics of Naval Literature. Annapolis, Md.: Naval Institute Press, 1985.

"English Governmental Machinery and the Conduct of War, 1702–1713." *War and Society* 3, no. 2 (September 1985), pp. 1–22.

"Stephen B. Luce." In *Dictionary of American Military Biography,* edited by Roger J. Spiller. Vol. 2. New York: Greenwood, 1985, pp. 668–70.

1986

A Bibliography of the Works of Alfred Thayer Mahan. Compiled with sister-in-law Lynn C. Hattendorf. Naval War College Historical Monograph 7. Newport, R.I.: Naval War College Press, 1986. Reprinted 1990, 1993.

"Med sjövinden till Newport." *Forum Navale,* no. 41 (1986), pp. 30–75. [In Swedish, jointly authored with father-in-law Gunnar Sundell on the first Swedish naval of-ficers to come to the Naval War College.]

"Note: A Special Relationship: The Royal Navy and the U.S. Naval War College." *Mariner's Mirror* 72, no. 2 (1986), pp. 200–201.

"Note: Naval Memorials in Singapore Cathedral." *Mariner's Mirror* 72, no. 2 (May 1986), pp. 150–51.

1987

England in the War of the Spanish Succession: A Study of the English View and Conduct of Grand Strategy, 1702–1712. Outstanding Dissertations in Modern European History Series, edited by William H. McNeill and Peter Stansky. New York: Gar-land, 1987.

Register of the Alfred Thayer Mahan Papers. Newport, R.I.: Naval War College, Naval Historical Collection, 1987.

1988

"Admiral Sir George Byng and the Cape Passaro Incident, 1718: A Case Study in the Use of the Royal Navy as a Deterrent." In *Guerre et Paix 1660–1815.* Vincennes: Service Historique de la Marine, 1988, pp. 19–38.

"The Evolution of the Maritime Strategy: 1977 to 1987." *Naval War College Review* 41, no. 3 (Summer 1988), pp. 7–28. Revised and reprinted in *Naval History and Maritime Strategy,* pp. 201–28.

"International Naval Co-operation and Admiral Richard G. Colbert: The Intertwin-ing of a Career with an Idea." In *The RCN in Transition: Challenge and Response, 1910–1985,* edited by W. A. B. Douglas. Vancouver: Univ. of British Columbia Press, 1988, chap. 12. Revised and reprinted in *Naval History and Maritime*

Strategy, pp. 161–85. Further revised and reprinted as "Admiral Richard G. Colbert: Pioneer in Building Global Maritime Partnerships." *Naval War College Review* 61, no. 3 (Summer 2008), pp. 109–30.

"NATO's Policeman on the Beat: The Standing Naval Force, Atlantic, 1968–1988." With Commander Stan Weeks. U.S. Naval Institute *Proceedings* (September 1988), pp. 66–71. Revised and reprinted in *Naval History and Maritime Strategy,* pp. 187–200.

"The Protestant Wind." *Cruising Association Bulletin* 27, no. 4 (December 1988), pp. 150–51.

"Résumé of the Eighth International Seapower Symposium." In *Ninth International Seapower Symposium: Report of the Proceedings of the Conference: 26–28 October 1987.* Newport, R.I.: Naval War College, [1988], pp. 6–10.

1989

"The English Royal Navy." In *The Age of William III and Mary II: Power, Politics and Patronage 1688–1702: A Reference Encyclopedia and Exhibition Catalogue,* edited by Robert P. Maccubbin and Martha Hamilton-Phillips. Williamsburg: College of William and Mary, 1989, pp. 127–32.

The Evolution of the U.S. Navy's Maritime Strategy, 1977–1987. Newport Papers (classified series), no. 6. Newport, R.I.: Naval War College, 1989.

"The Hattendorf-Jarvis Family." In *A Place Called Portage: A Collection of Memories by Those Who Experienced the Development of a Place Called Portage from 1912–1989,* compiled and edited by Bill Smythe. Manistee, Michigan: J.B. Publications, 1989, pp. 109–12.

"Introduction" to J. C. Wylie, *Military Strategy: A General Theory of Power Control.* Classics of Sea Power. Annapolis, Md.: Naval Institute Press, 1989. Revised and reprinted in *Naval History and Maritime Strategy,* pp. 137–59.

Maritime Strategy and the Balance of Power: Britain and America in the 20th Century. Coedited with Robert S. Jordan. London: Macmillan in association with St. Antony's College, Oxford; New York: St Martin's, 1989. Chinese translation, Taipei: Operations and Planning Advisory Committee, Republic of China Navy, 1994.

"An Outline of Recent Thinking on the Theory of Naval Strategy." *Tidskrift i Sjöväsendet,* no. 1 (1989), pp. 55–65.

"War at Sea." In *The Encyclopedia of Twentieth Century Warfare,* edited by Noble Frankland. London: Mitchell Beazley, 1989, pp. 129–42.

1990

"The Anglo-American Way in Maritime Strategy." *Naval War College Review* 43, no. 1 (Winter 1990), pp. 90–99. Revised and reprinted in *Naval History and Maritime Strategy,* pp. 109–20.

"The Bombardment of Acre, 1840: A Case Study in the Use of Naval Force for Deterence." In *Les Empires en Guerre et Paix, 1793–1860: Journées franco-anglaises d'histoire de la Marine, Portsmouth, 23–26 mars 1988,* edited by Edward Freeman. Vincennes: Service Historique de la Marine, 1990, pp. 205–23.

The Limitations of Military Power: Essays Presented to Norman Gibbs on His 80th Birthday. Coedited with Malcolm H. Murfett. London: Macmillan; New York: St. Martin's, 1990.

"My Parents, Rear Admiral and Mrs. Alfred Thayer Mahan." By Lyle Mahan, edited by John B. Hattendorf. *Naval War College Review* 43, no. 4 (Autumn 1990), pp. 81–97.

"Stephen B. Luce." In *Admirals of the New Steel Navy: Makers of American Naval Tradition,* edited by James Bradford. Annapolis, Md.: Naval Institute Press, 1990, pp. 3–23.

1991

"Alliance, Encirclement, and Attrition: British Grand Strategy in the War of the Spanish Succession." In *Grand Strategies in War and Peace,* edited by Paul M. Kennedy. New Haven: Yale Univ. Press, 1991, pp. 11–29, with notes on pp. 186–88.

The Influence of History on Mahan: The Proceedings of a Conference Marking the Centenary of Alfred Thayer Mahan's The Influence of Sea Power upon History, 1660–1783. Edited by John B. Hattendorf. Naval War College Historical Monograph 9. Newport, R.I.: Naval War College Press, 1991. Reprinted 1993. Chinese translation, Taipei: Operations and Planning Advisory Committee, Republic of China Navy, 1994.

Mahan on Naval Strategy: A Selection of Essays by Alfred Thayer Mahan. Edited by John B. Hattendorf. Classics of Sea Power. Annapolis, Md.: Naval Institute Press, 1991.

1992

Contributed to the revision of C. P. B. Jefferys, *Newport, R.I.: A Short History.* Newport, R.I.: Newport Historical Society, 1992. With further revisions published as *Newport, R.I.: A Concise History.* Newport, R.I.: Newport Historical Society, 2008.

Eleventh International Seapower Symposium: Report of the Proceedings of the Conference: 6–9 October 1991. Edited by John B. Hattendorf. Newport, R.I.: Naval War College, 1992.

"Introduction" to *England's Way to Win Wealth and to Employ Ships and Mariners,* by Tobias Gentleman (1614); *The Trade's Increase,* by Robert Kayll (1615); *The Defence of Trade,* by Dudley Digges (1615); and *Britaines Bussse,* by Edward Sharpe (1615). John Carter Brown Library Maritime History Series. Delmar, N.Y.: Scholars' Facsimiles and Reprints, 1992.

"Résumé of the Tenth International Sea Power Symposium." In *Eleventh International Seapower Symposium: Report of the Proceedings of the Conference: 6–9 October 1991.* Newport, R.I.: Naval War College, 1992.

"Sea Power as Control: Britain's Defensive Naval Strategy in the Mediterranean, 1793–1815." In *Français et Anglais en Méditerranée de la Révolution française à l'indépendance de la Grèce (1789–1830).* Vincennes: Service Historique de la Marine, 1992, pp. 203–20.

1993

British Naval Documents 1204–1960. Edited by John B. Hattendorf, R. J. B. Knight, A. W. H. Pearsall, N. A. M. Rodger, and Geoffrey Till. Publications of the Navy Records Society. Vol. 131. London: Navy Records Society, 1993.

"The Decision to Close Rhode Island Bases in 1973." In *What a Difference a Bay Makes.* Providence, R.I.: Rhode Island Historical Society, 1993, pp. 104–106. Revised and reprinted in *Newport History* 79, no. 262 (Spring 2010), pp. 54–65.

Mahan Is Not Enough: Proceedings of the Corbett-Richmond Conference. Edited with James Goldrick. Newport, R.I.: Naval War College Press, 1993.

"Sea Battle." *Gunji Shigaku* 29, no. 3 (December 1993), p. 1 [In Japanese, a one-page introduction to a special number on this theme.]

"Seapower." In *International Military and Defense Encyclopedia,* edited by Trevor N. Dupuy. Vol. 5. Washington and New York: Brassey's (US), 1993, pp. 2378–83.

"'We Have Met the Enemy and They Are Ours': The Naval War of 1812." *Documentary Editing* 15 (September 1993), pp. 57–60. [A review article on William S. Dudley et al., eds., *The Naval War of 1812.*]

1994

"Introduction" to *St Barthélemy and the Swedish West India Company: A Collection of Printed Documents, 1783–1823.* Delmar, N.Y.: Scholars' Facsimiles and Reprints, 1994.

"Introduction" with D. M. Schurman to Sir Julian Corbett, *Maritime Operations in the Russo-Japanese War.* Annapolis, Md.: Naval Institute Press, 1994, pp. v–xiv.

"Maritime Conflict and the Laws of War: An Historical Outline." In *Laws of War,* edited by Sir Michael Howard, George Andreopoulos, and Mark Shulman. New Haven, Conn.: Yale Univ. Press, 1994, pp. 98–115, with notes pp. 247–50.

"Résumé of Eleventh International Sea Power Symposium." In *Twelfth International Seapower Symposium: Report of the Proceedings of the Conference: 7–10 November 1993.* Newport, R.I.: Naval War College, 1994, pp. 7–10.

Twelfth International Seapower Symposium: Report of the Proceedings of the Conference: 7–10 November 1993. Edited by John B. Hattendorf. Newport, R.I.: Naval War College, 1994.

Ubi Sumus? The State of Naval and Maritime History. Edited by John B. Hattendorf. Newport, R.I.: Naval War College Press, 1994.

1995

"Alfred Thayer Mahan and American Naval Theory." In *Navies and Global Defence: Theories and Strategy,* edited by Keith Neilson and Jane Errington. Westport, Conn.: Praeger, 1995, chap. 3, pp. 52–67. Revised and reprinted in *Naval History and Maritime Strategy,* pp. 59–75.

"The Battle off Cape Passaro, 1718." In *Great Battles of the Royal Navy,* edited by Eric Grove. London: Arms and Armour, 1995, pp. 64–70.

Doing Naval History: Essays toward Improvement. Edited by John B. Hattendorf. Newport, R.I.: Naval War College Press, 1995.

"Introduction" to Josiah Burchett, *A Complete History of the Most Remarkable Transactions at Sea (1720).* Delmar, N.Y.: Scholars' Facsimiles and Reprints, 1995.

"Maritime Strategy for the 21st Century." In *Maritime Strategy for Developing Countries,* edited by Greg Mills. Johannesburg: South African Institute of International Affairs; and Lancaster, U.K.: Univ. of Lancaster Centre for Defence and International Security Studies, 1995, chap. 2, pp. 38–48.

"Prince Louis of Battenberg." In *The First Sea Lords and British Naval Policy: From Fisher to Mountbatten,* edited by Malcolm Murfett. New York: Praeger, 1995, pp. 75–90.

A Sea of Words: A Companion to the Seafaring Novels of Patrick O'Brian. With Dean H. King and Worth Estes. New York: Henry Holt, 1995; second edition (revised and expanded), 1997; third edition (revised and expanded), 2000.

"The Struggle with France, 1689–1815." In *The Oxford Illustrated History of the Royal Navy,* edited by J. R. Hill. Oxford, U.K.: Oxford Univ. Press, 1995, chap. 4, pp. 80–119. Reprinted with corrections in paperback, Oxford Univ. Press, 2002.

"Toulon," "Malaga," "Vigo." In *The Treaties of the War of the Spanish Succession: An Historical and Critical Dictionary,* edited by Linda and Marsha Frey. Westport, Conn.: Greenwood, 1995, pp. 261–63, 437–40, 473–76.

1996

"Admiral Spruance as War College President." Naval War College *Foundation Notes,* no. 27 (Spring 1996), pp. 8–9.

Harbors and High Seas: A Map Book and Geographical Guide to the Aubrey-Maturin Novels of Patrick O'Brian. By Dean H. King, with John B. Hattendorf. New York: Henry Holt, 1996; second edition (revised and expanded), 1999; third edition (revised and expanded), 2000.

Maritime History. Vol. 1, *The Age of Discovery.* Edited by John B. Hattendorf. Malabar, Fla.: Krieger, 1996.

"Review Essay: The War Diary of the German Naval Staff, 1939–1945." *Documentary Editing* 18 (September 1996), pp. 58–62. [A review article on Werner Rahn et al., eds., *Kriegstagebuch der Seekriegsleitung, 1939–1945.*]

"Stephen B. Luce: Intellectual Leader of the New Navy." In *Quarterdeck, Bridge and Pentagon: Two Centuries of American Naval Leadership,* edited by James Bradford. Annapolis, Md.: Naval Institute Press, 1996, pp. 203–18.

Thirteenth International Seapower Symposium: Report of the Proceedings of the Conference: 5–8 November 1995. Edited by John B. Hattendorf. Newport, R.I.: Naval War College Press, 1996.

1997

Every Man Will Do His Duty: An Anthology of Firsthand Accounts from the Age of Nelson. Edited by Dean H. King, with John B. Hattendorf. New York: Henry Holt, 1997.

"From the Hill" [remarks on receiving an honorary degree]. *Kenyon College Alumni Bulletin* 20, no. 1 (Summer/Fall 1997), pp. 12–13, 55.

"Great Ships and Grand Strategy: England, 1400–1700." In *L'Invention du vaisseau de ligne, 1450–1700,* edited by Martine Acerra. Collection Kronos 24. Paris: S.P.M., 1997, pp. 167–81.

Maritime History. Vol. 2, *The Eighteenth Century and the Classic Age of Sail.* Edited by John B. Hattendorf. Malabar, Fla.: Krieger, 1997.

"Review Essay: A Dutch Door to Europe, 1702–1720." *Documentary Editing* 19 (September 1997), pp. 57–61. [A review article on A. J. Veenendaal, ed., *De Briefwisseling van Anthonie Heinsius, 1702–1720.*]

"Sea Power and Sea Control in Contemporary Times." *Journal of the Australian Naval Institute* 23 (April–June 1997), pp. 15–20. Revised and reprinted in *Naval History and Maritime Strategy,* pp. 253–65.

"Sea Warfare." In *The Oxford Illustrated History of Modern Warfare,* edited by Charles Townshend. Oxford Univ. Press, 1997, pp. 213–27. Republished in paperback under the title *The Oxford History of Modern War.* Oxford, U.K.: Oxford Univ. Press, 2000, pp. 245–61. New updated edition, Oxford, U.K.: Oxford Univ. Press, 2005, pp. 245–61.

"What Is a Maritime Strategy?" In *In Search of a Maritime Strategy: The Maritime Element in Australian Defence Planning since 1901,* edited by David Stevens. Canberra Papers on Strategy and Defence, no. 119. Canberra: Strategic and Defence Studies Centre, Australian National Univ., 1997, pp. 5–18. Revised and reprinted in *Naval History and Maritime Strategy,* pp. 229–40.

1998

"The Admirals." In *The Greatest Thing We Have Ever Attempted: Historical Perspectives on the Normandy Campaign,* edited by Steven Weingartener. Cantigny Military History Series. Wheaton, Ill.: Cantigny First Division Foundation, 1998, pp. 106–11.

America and the Sea: A Maritime History, by Benjamin W. Labaree, Edward W. Sloan, John B. Hattendorf, William M. Fowler, Jr., Jeffrey Safford, and Andrew German. Mystic, Conn.: Mystic Seaport Museum, 1998. John Lyman Book Award for the Best Book in U.S. Maritime History, 1998.

"The American Friends of the Hakluyt Society: Annual Report 1997–8." *The Hakluyt Society: Annual Report and Statement of Accounts for 1997.* London: Hakluyt Society, 1998, pp. 11–12.

"The Battle of Manila Bay." In *Great American Naval Battles,* edited by Jack Sweetman. Annapolis, Md.: Naval Institute Press, 1998, pp. 175–97. John Lyman Book Award for the Best Book in U.S. Naval History, 1998.

"Forget the *Maine:* Navies in the Modern World." *Culturefront: A Magazine of the Humanities* 7 (Spring 1998), pp. 83–86.

Fourteenth International Seapower Symposium: Report of the Proceedings, 2–5 November 1997. Edited by John B. Hattendorf. Newport, R.I.: Naval War College, 1998.

"Introduction" to Christopher Lloyd, *Lord Cochrane: Seaman-Radical-Liberator.* Heart of Oak Sea Classics. New York: Henry Holt, 1998.

John Robinson's Account of Sweden, 1688. Karolinska Förbundets Årsbok, 1996. Stockholm: Karolinska Förbundet, 1998.

"Joshua Slocum: The First Solo Circumnavigator." *Log of Mystic Seaport* 50, no. 1 (Summer 1998), pp. 23–25. [Vignette reprinted from *America and the Sea.*]

"Rear Admiral Charles H. Stockton, the Naval War College, and the Law of Naval Warfare." In *The Law of Armed Conflict: Into the Next Millennium,* edited by Leslie C. Green and Michael N. Schmitt. International Law Studies, vol. 71. Newport, R.I.: Naval War College, 1998, pp. xvii–lxxii.

"Résumé of the Thirteenth International Seapower Symposium." In *Fourteenth International Seapower Symposium: Report of the Proceedings, 2–5 November 1997.* Edited by John B. Hattendorf. Newport, R.I.: Naval War College, 1998, pp. 5–12.

"U.S. Navy, 1941–1993." In *A Guide to the Sources of U.S. Military History: Supplement IV,* edited by Robin Higham and Donald J. Mrozek. North Haven, Conn.: Archon Books, 1998, pp. 378–90.

1999

"The American Friends of the Hakluyt Society: Annual Report 1997–8 [1998–99]." *The Hakluyt Society: Annual Report and Statement of Accounts for 1998.* London: Hakluyt Society, 1999, pp. 19–20.

"Foreword" to Alexander Boyd Hawes, *Off Soundings: Aspects of the Maritime History of Rhode Island.* Chevy Chase, Md.: Posterity, 1999, pp. ix–xi. Honorable Mention: John Lyman Book Award for U.S. Naval and Maritime History, 1999.

"Geschichte und technologischer Wandel: Das Studium der Marinegeschichte in der US-Marine 1873–1890." In *Seemacht und Seestrategie im 19. und 20. Jahrhundert. Im Auftrag des Militärgeschichtlichen Forschungsamtes herausgegeben von Jörg Duppler.* Hamburg, Berlin, Bonn: E. S. Mittler and Sohn, 1999, pp. 105–20 [in German]. Revised and published in English in *Naval History and Maritime Strategy,* pp. 1–16.

"Introduction" to Joseph Conrad, *The Rover: A Novel.* Heart of Oak Sea Classics. New York: Henry Holt, 1999, pp. xi–xvii.

Naval Policy and Strategy in the Mediterranean: Past, Present, and Future. Edited by John B. Hattendorf. London: Frank Cass, 1999.

"Theodorus Bailey," "William Caperton," "Napoleon Collins," "Stephen B. Luce," "Silas Stringham." In *American National Biography,* edited by John A. Garraty and Mark C. Carnes. Oxford and New York: Oxford Univ. Press, 1999, vol. 1, pp. 899–900; vol. 4, pp. 357–58; vol. 5, pp. 255–56; vol. 14, pp. 94–96; vol. 21, pp. 30–31.

"The U.S. Naval War College, Newport, Rhode Island." *Oxford, U.K.: The Journal of the Oxford Society* 51, no. 2 (November 1999), pp. 18–20.

2000

"American Strategies in the Pacific War." In *Kia Kaha: New Zealand in the Second World War,* edited by John Crawford. Auckland: Oxford Univ. Press, 2000; paperback edition, 2002, pp. 36–48. Reprinted in *Naval History and Maritime Strategy,* pp. 121–35.

"A Contribution to the Discussion about NASOH." *NASOH Newsletter* 24, no. 2 (Fall 2000), pp. 4–5.

"Foreword" to William H. White, *A Press of Canvas: A Novel.* "War of 1812" Trilogy, vol. 1. St. Michaels, Md.: Tiller, 2000, pp. 8–11.

"Horatio Bridge," "*Monitor* and *Merrimack,*" and "Charles Nordhoff the Elder." In *An Encyclopedia of American Literature of the Sea and the Great Lakes,* edited by Gil Gidmark. Westport, Conn.: Greenwood, 2000, pp. 51–52, 297–98, 326–27.

Naval History and Maritime Strategy: Collected Essays. Malabar, Fla.: Robert Krieger, 2000.

"Sir George Rooke and Sir Cloudesley Shovell, *c*1650–1709 and 1650–1707." In *The Precursors of Nelson: Admirals and the Development of the Royal Navy,* edited by Richard Harding and Peter Le Fevre. London: Chatham, 2000, pp. 48–78.

"Stephen B. Luce" and "Sea Power." In *Professional Military Education in the United States: A Historical Dictionary,* edited by William E. Simons. Westport, Conn.: Greenwood, 2000, pp. 176–79, 289–91.

"Die Ursprünge des Spanischen Erbfolgekrieges [The Origins of the War of the Spanish Succession]." In *Wie Kriege entstehen: Zum historischen Hintergrund von Staatenkonflikten,* edited by Bernd Wegner. Krieg in der Geschichte, Band 4.

Paderborn: Verlag Ferdinand Schöningh Gmbh, 2000; second edition, 2003, pp. 109–44 [in German].

2001

"The Caird Lecture, 2000: The Anglo-French Naval Wars (1689–1815) in Twentieth Century Naval Thought." *Journal for Maritime Research* (June 2001). Available at www.jmr.nmm.ac.uk/jmr_new_articles.htm#caird2000. Reprinted in *Talking about Naval History,* pp. 97–117.

"Charles XII" and "United States: Armed Forces: Navy." In *Reader's Guide to Military History,* edited by Charles Messenger. London and Chicago: Fitzroy Dearborn, 2001, pp. 90–91, 604–605.

"The Experience of the Spanish-American War and Its Impact on Professional Naval Thought." In *Theodore Roosevelt, the U.S. Navy, and the Spanish-American War,* edited by Edward J. Marolda. London and New York: Palgrave, 2001, pp. 61–80.

"Review Essay: Closing the Dutch Door." *Documentary Editing* 23 (September 2001), p. 59. [Review of A. J. Veenendaal, ed., *De Briefwisseling van Anthonie Heinsius,* vol. 19.]

Semper Eadem: A History of Trinity Church in Newport, 1698–1998. Newport, R.I.: Trinity Church, 2001.

2002

"The Conundrum of Military Education in Historical Perspective." *In Military Education: Past, Present, and Future,* edited by Gregory C. Kennedy and Keith Neilson. Westport, Conn., and London: Praeger, 2002, pp. 1–12.

Dictionnaire d'Histoire maritime. Edited by Michel Vergé-Franceschi. Collection Bouquins. Paris: Editions Robert Laffont, 2002. 15 entries:
Burke, Arleigh, p. 258
Dewey, George, p. 482
Dupont, Samuel F., p. 516
Farragut, David Glasgow, p. 595
Halsey, William F., Jr., p. 723
Hewitt, H. Kent, p. 741
Jones, John Paul, pp. 803–804
King, Ernest J., p. 814
Luce, Stephen B., pp. 890–91
Maury, Matthew Fontaine, pp. 954–55
Perry, Oliver Hazard, p. 1123
Porter, David Dixon, p. 1173
Rickover, Hyman, pp. 1246–47
Sims, William S., p. 1337
Spruance, Raymond, p. 1353.

Naval Warfare: An International Encyclopedia. Edited by Spencer Tucker. New York: ABC-Clio, 2002. 38 articles, totaling 17,500 words:
Albion, Robert G. (1896–1983), vol. 1, pp. 18–19
Association (British Navy, Ship of the Line, 1697), vol. 1, pp. 60–61
Benbow, John (1653–1702), vol. 1, p. 114

Burrows, Montagu (1819–1905), vol. 1, p. 166

Byng, Sir George (1663–1733), vol. 1, pp. 168–69

Cape Passaro, Battle of (11 August 1718), vol. 1, p. 186

Cartagena, Battle of (28 May 1708), vol. 1, p. 196

Chappell, Howard I. (1901–1975), vol. 1, pp. 203–204

Colbert, Richard C. (1915–1973), vol. 1, pp. 234–35

Cooper, James Fenimore (1789–1851), vol. 1, p. 255

Corbett, Sir Julian (1854–1922), vol. 1, pp. 258–59

Eccles, Henry E. (1898–1986), vol. 1, p. 348

Gambier, James, First Baron Gambier (1756–1833), vol. 2, p. 422

Goodrich, Caspar Fredrick (1847–1925), vol. 2, pp. 441–42

Hayes, John D. (1902–1991), vol. 2, pp. 484–85

Knox, Dudley W. (1877–1960), vol. 2, pp. 584–85

Laughton, Sir John Knox (1830–1915), vol. 2, pp. 613–14

Leake, Sir John (1656–1720), vol. 2, pp. 616–17

Luce, Stephen B. (1827–1917), vol. 2, p. 640

McCarty Little, William (1845–1914), vol. 2, p. 666

Morison, Samuel E. (1887–1976), vol. 2, p. 710

Mountbatten, Prince Louis of Battenberg (1854–1921), vol. 2, pp. 716–17

Naval War College, vol. 2, p. 737

Oppenheim, Michael (1853–1915), vol. 2, p. 773

Paullin, Oscar (1868–1944), vol. 2, pp. 788–89

Richmond, Sir Herbert (1871–1946), vol. 3, p. 854

Rooke, Sir George (1650–1709), vol. 3, p. 860

Rosinski, Herbert (1903–1962), vol. 3, p. 862

Santa Marta, Battle of (19–24 August 1702), vol. 3, p. 886

Shovell, Sir C. (1650–1707), vol. 3, pp. 923–24

Spanish Succession, War of the (1702–1714), vol. 3, pp. 951–53

Stockdale, James (1923–), vol. 3, pp. 971–72

Stockton, Charles Herbert (1845–1924), vol. 3, p. 972

Taylor, Henry Clay (1845–1904), vol. 3, pp. 1004–1005

Turner, Stansfield (1923–), vol. 3, pp. 1045–46

Vélez-Málaga, Battle of (13 August 1704), vol. 3, pp. 1070–71

Vigo Bay, Battle of (12 October 1702), vol. 3, pp. 1080–81

Wylie, J. C. (1911–1993), vol. 3, pp. 1121–22.

"The Origins of Aquidneck's Anglican Parishes." St. John the Evangelist Church *Evangelist,* Newport, Rhode Island (December 2002), pp. 6–7.

"'To Aid and Assist the Other': Anglo-Dutch Cooperation in Coalition Warfare at Sea, 1688–1714." In *Anthonie Heinsius and the Dutch Republic, 1688–1720: Politics, War, & Finance,* edited by Jan A. F. de Jongste and A. J. Veenendaal, Jr. The Hague: Institute of Netherlands History, 2002, pp. 177–98. Reprinted in *Talking about Naval History,* pp. 79–95.

War at Sea in the Middle Ages and the Renaissance. Edited by John B. Hattendorf and Richard W. Unger. Woodbridge, Suffolk, and Rochester, N.Y.: Boydell and Brewer, 2002.

2003

The Boundless Deep: The European Conquest of the Seas, ca. 1450–ca. 1830: Catalogue of an Exhibition of Original Sources on Maritime History from the John Carter Brown Library. Providence, R.I.: John Carter Brown Library, 2003.

"The Englishmen Abroad: Professor John Hattendorf Charts the Emergence of the Maritime Book from Its Earliest Origins in the 15th Century." *Antiquarian Book Review* 30, no. 3, issue 337 (April 2003), pp. 24–28.

"Foreword" to *Naval Mutiny in the Twentieth Century,* edited by Christopher M. Bell and Bruce Elleman, London: Frank Cass, 2003, pp. xv–xviii.

"The French Connection in Newport during the American Revolution: An Overview." *Newport History* 72–73, nos. 249–50 (Fall 2003–Spring 2004), pp. 5–11.

"L'Histoire Maritime et son Enseignement à l'Étranger: 4. Aux États-Unis." *Chronique d'histoire maritime* 50 (avril 2003), pp. 19–22 [in French].

"Luce, Mahan, and the Founding of the Naval War College." In *U.S. Navy: A Complete History,* edited by M. Hill Goodspeed. Washington: Naval Historical Foundation, 2003, pp. 256–57.

"The Uses of Maritime History in and for the Navy," *Naval War College Review* 56, no. 2 (Spring 2003), pp. 13–38. Edward S. Miller History Prize, Naval War College Press, for the 2003 publishing year. Reprinted in the *International Journal of Naval History* 2, no. 2 (August 2003). Available at ijnhonline.org/volume2_number1 _Apr03/article_hattendorf_uses_apr03.htm. Reprinted in Andrew Lambert, ed. *Naval History, 1850–Present.* Vol. 2. International Library of Essays on Military History. London, U.K., and Burlington, Vt.: Ashgate, 2007. Reprinted in *Talking about Naval History,* pp. 17–38.

2004

"Anglo-Dutch Naval Wars." In *Europe 1450–1789: Encyclopedia of the Early Modern World,* edited by Jonathan Dewald. Vol. 1. New York: Charles Scribner's Sons, 2004, pp. 63–66.

"Les États-Unis et les Mutations de la Puissance Maritime au XXe Siècle." In *La Puissance maritime,* edited by Christian Buchet, Jean Meyer, and Jean-Pierre Poussou. Collection Histoire-Maritime. Paris: Presses de l'Université Paris-Sorbonne, 2004, pp. 577–96 [in French]. English text in *Talking about Naval History,* pp. 283–301.

The Evolution of the U.S. Navy's Maritime Strategy, 1977–1987. Newport Paper 19. Newport, R.I.: Naval War College Press, 2004.

"Halsey, William Frederick, Jr. (1882–1959)." In *The World Book.* Vol. 9. New York, 2004, p. 28. Reprinted in editions 2005 and after, vol. 9, pp. 27–28.

Newport, the French Navy, and American Independence. Newport, R.I.: Redwood, 2004. Revised and corrected edition, Newport, R.I.: Redwood, 2005.

Oxford Dictionary of National Biography, edited by H. C. G. Matthew and Brian Harrison. Oxford, U.K.: Oxford Univ. Press, 2004. Research Associate of the *Oxford DNB.* 22 articles:

Benbow, John (1653–1702), vol. 5, pp. 52–58

Berkeley, James, third earl of Berkeley (1680–1736), vol. 5, pp. 379–80

Burchett, Josiah (1666?–1746), vol. 8, pp. 728–30

Byng, George, Viscount Torrington (1663–1733), vol. 9, pp. 309–13

Churchill, George (1654–1710), vol. 11, pp. 601–603

Churchill, John, first duke of Marlborough (1650–1723), vol. 11, 607–33

Cutts, John, Baron Cutts of Gowran, Ireland (1661–1707), vol. 14, pp. 850–54

Griffith, Richard (d. 1719), vol. 23, pp. 973–74

Herbert, Arthur, earl of Torrington (1647–1716), vol. 26, pp. 654–58

Jennings, Sir John (1664–1743), vol. 30, pp. 19–20

Leake, Sir John (1656–1720), vol. 32, pp. 973–78

Mitchell, Sir David (1650–1710), vol. 38, pp. 397–98

Mordaunt, Charles, third earl of Peterborough (1658–1735), vol. 39, pp. 13–21

Robinson, John (1650–1723), vol. 47, pp. 360–64

Rooke, Sir George (1650–1709), vol. 47, pp. 689–94

Savage, Richard, fourth Earl Rivers (1660–1712), vol. 49, pp. 78–81

Sergison, Charles (1654–1732), vol. 49, pp. 777–78

Shovell, Sir Clowdesley (1650–1707), vol. 50, pp. 441–46

Smith, Thomas (d. 1708), vol. 51, pp. 337–38

Walton, Sir George (1665–1739), vol. 57, p. 201

Webb, John Richmond (1667–1724), vol. 57, pp. 842–45

Wright, Lawrence (d. 1713), vol. 60, pp. 468–70.

"The Sea as an Arena for Conflict." In *Maritime History as World History,* edited by Daniel Finamore. Gainesville: Univ. Press of Florida, 2004, pp. 130–39.

Sixteenth International Seapower Symposium: Report of the Proceedings, 26–29 October to 2003. Edited by John B. Hattendorf. Newport, R.I.: Naval War College, 2004.

"The US Navy and the 'Freedom of the Seas,' 1775–1917." In *Navies in Northern Waters 1721–2000,* edited by R. Hobson and T. Kristiansen. Naval Policy and History series, no. 26. London: Frank Cass, 2004, pp. 151–74.

2005

"The Cold War at Sea: An International History." Guest editors, Lyle Goldstein, John Hattendorf, and Yuri Zhukov. *Journal of Strategic Studies* 28, no. 2 (April 2005), pp. 151–439.

"Deutschland und die See: Historische Wurzeln deutscher Seestreitkräfte bis 1815." In *Deutsche Marinen im Wandel: Vom Symbol nationaler Einheit zum Instrument internationaler Sicherheit,* edited by Werner Rahn. Beiträge zur Militärgeschichte, Band 63. München: R. Oldenbourg Verlag, 2005, pp. 17–40 [in German].

"'In a Far More Thorough Manner.'" *Naval History* 19, no. 2 (April 2005), pp. 38–43. Revised and reprinted in *Talking about Naval History,* pp. 259–268.

"In Memoriam John Allen Gable, 1943–2005: Some Memories from Four Decades of Friendship." *Theodore Roosevelt Association Journal* 26, no. 2 (2005), pp. 14–15.

"Introduction" to *The Trafalgar Companion,* edited by Alexander Stillwell. Oxford, U.K.: Osprey, 2005, pp. 8–35, with footnotes p. 213.

"Letters from Overseas: From Our Correspondent in the USA." *Newsletter of the Society for Nautical Research,* no. 57 (February 2005), pp. 13–14.

"Le livre maritime dans le monde anglophone, 1750–1850." In *Le Livre maritime au siècle des Lumières: Édition et diffusion des connaissances maritimes (1750–1850),* edited by Annie Charon, Thierry Claerr, and François Moureau. Paris: Presses de l'Université Paris-Sorbonne, 2005, pp. 59–68 [in French].

"The Naval War College Museum in Founder's Hall, at Fort Adams, and in the Navy" and "Battle of Trafalgar." *Naval War College Foundation: Members Only Newsletter* 14 (November 2005), pp. 7, 12.

"Nelson Afloat: A Hero among the World's Navies." In *Admiral Lord Nelson: His Context and Legacy,* edited by David Cannadine. London: Palgrave Macmillan, 2005, pp. 160–86. Reprinted in *Talking about Naval History,* pp. 119–137.

"Our Naval Heritage Is in Danger." U.S. Naval Institute *Proceedings* 130, no. 12, issue 1,222 (December 2005), pp. 64–68. Reprinted in *Talking about Naval History,* pp. 39–45.

"Stephen B. Luce: Scholarship" and "Alfred Thayer Mahan: Professionalism." In *Leadership Embodied: The Secrets of Success of the Most Effective Navy and Marine Corps Leaders,* edited by Lt. Col. Joseph J. Thomas. Annapolis, Md.: Naval Institute Press, 2005, pp. 35–38, 51–54.

2006

"Foreword" to *Naval Blockades and Seapower: Strategies and Counterstrategies, 1805–2005,* edited by Bruce A. Elleman and S. C. M. Paine. London and New York: Routledge, 2006, pp. viii–xx.

Register of the Schlie Family Papers. Register 36. Newport, R.I.: Naval War College, Naval Historical Collection, 2006.

Seventeenth International Seapower Symposium: Report of the Proceedings 20–23 September 2005. Newport, R.I.: Naval War College, 2006.

Trafalgar and Nelson 200: Catalogue of an Exhibition of Rare Books, Maps, Charts, Prints, Models, and Signal Flags Relating to Events and Influences of the Battle of Trafalgar and Lord Nelson. Newport, R.I.: Naval War College Museum, 2006. Printed in a limited edition of thirty numbered and signed copies; published on the internet at www.usnwc.edu/About/NWC-Museum.aspx.

U.S. Naval Strategy in the 1990s: Selected Documents. Edited by John B. Hattendorf. Newport Paper 27. Newport, R.I.: Naval War College Press, 2006.

2007

"Globalization and Navies: Some Considerations for Naval Theory." In *Maritime Dimensions of a New World Order,* edited by Ravi Vohra and Devbrat Chakraborty. New Delhi, India: Anamaya Publishers on behalf of the National Maritime Foundation, 2007, pp. 32–51. Reprinted in *Talking about Naval History,* pp. 319–330.

The Oxford Encyclopedia of Maritime History. Four volumes. Oxford and New York: Oxford Univ. Press, 2007. John B. Hattendorf, editor-in-chief and author of "Introduction" and the articles on: Astronomers and Cosmographers; Atlantic Ocean: North Atlantic: North Atlantic Navies; Constable, John; Chartered Companies: Northern Europe; Discipline and Punishment: Galley Discipline and Punishment; Fiction: Naval Novel; Fishing Vessels; Gibraltar, Strait of; Mahan, Alfred T.; Naval Logistics before 1850; Newport, Rhode Island; Rivers, Canals, and Inland Waterways; Stockton, Charles H.; Suez Canal. American Library Association— Dartmouth Medal, 2008; North American Society for Ocean History—John Lyman Book Award for Reference Works; Association of American Publishers Professional and Scholars' Publishing Division Award for Excellence in

Multivolume Reference/Humanities and Social Sciences—Honorable Mention; *Library Journal* Best Reference of 2007.

U.S. Naval Strategy in the 1970s: Selected Documents. Edited by John B. Hattendorf. Newport Paper 30. Newport, R.I.: Naval War College Press, 2007.

"Whither with Nelson and Trafalgar? A Review Article on the Bicentenary Scholarship of the Nelson Era." *Journal for Maritime Research* (December 2007). Reprinted with revisions and additions in *Talking about Naval History,* pp. 157–177.

2008

"Les Américans et la Guerre sur Mer (1775–1783)." In *La France et l'Indépendance Américaine,* edited by Olivier Chaline, Philippe Bonnichon, and Charles-Philippe de Vergennes. Paris: Presses de l'Université Paris-Sorbonne, 2008, pp. 131–51 [in French].

Command of the Sea: Catalogue of an Exhibition of American Naval Art from the U.S. Naval Academy Museum, the U.S. Navy Art Collection, and the U.S. Naval War College Museum Displayed at the Newport Art Museum, Newport, Rhode Island, 6 June–12 August 2007. Newport, R.I.: Naval War College Museum, 2008. Printed in a limited edition of thirty numbered and signed copies; published on the internet at www.usnwc.edu/About/NWC-Museum.aspx.

"*L'Expédition Particulière*' de 1780–1781, 'une opération jointe et combinée.'" *Bulletin de la Société Archéologique du Vendômois* (2008), pp. 66–73 [in French].

"*L'Expédition Particulière* of 1780–1781 'as a Joint and Combined Operation.'" *Bulletin de la Société Archéologique du Vendômois* (2008), pp. 74–80. Reprinted in *Talking about Naval History,* pp. 219–232.

"Foreword" to *Naval Coalition Warfare: From the Napoleonic War to Operation Iraqi Freedom,* edited by Bruce A. Elleman and S. C. M. Paine. London: Routledge, 2008, pp. xvi–xviii.

"El mar frente a la costa en la teoría y la praxis: la guerra de 1812." In *Guerra Naval en la Revolución y el Imperio: bloqueos y operaciones anfibias, 1793–1815,* coordinated by A. Guimerá Ravina and Jose Mariá Blanco Núñez. Madrid: Marcial Pons Historia, 2008, pp. 405–25 [in Spanish]. English text published in *Talking about Naval History,* pp. 233–244.

Register of the Papers of Admiral of the Fleet Sir James Hawkins Whitshed, Bart., G.C.B., Royal Navy. Register 34, Manuscript Collection 279. Newport, R.I.: Naval War College, Naval Historical Collection, 2008.

"Silas Duncan," "William Lynch," and "James Spotts." In *Dictionary of Falklands Biography (Including South Georgia),* edited by David Tatham. Ledbury, Hereford: ABC Print, 2008, pp. 203, 347–48, 512–13.

"The Sinking of the Galleon *San José* on 8 June 1708: An Exercise in Historical Detective Work." By Carla Rahn Phillips, John B. Hattendorf, Thomas R. Beall. *Mariner's Mirror* 94, no. 2 (May 2008), pp. 176–87.

U.S. Naval Strategy in the 1980s: Selected Documents. Edited by John B. Hattendorf and Peter M. Swartz. Newport Paper 33. Newport, R.I.: Naval War College Press, 2008.

2009

Eighteenth International Seapower Symposium: Report of the Proceedings, 17–19 October 2007. Edited by John B. Hattendorf with John W. Kennedy. Newport, R.I.: Naval War College, 2009.

Faces of the Naval War College: An Illustrated Catalogue of the U.S. Naval War College's Collection of Portrait Paintings and Busts. Newport, R.I.: Naval War College, 2009. Available on the internet in pdf format at www.usnwc.edu/About/NWC -Museum.aspx.

"Foreword" to Gary J. Ohls, *Somalia . . . From the Sea.* Newport Paper 34. Newport, R.I.: Naval War College Press, 2009.

"Foreword" to *Three Splendid Little Wars: The Diary of Joseph K. Taussig, 1898–1901,* edited by Evelyn Cherpak. Naval War College Historical Monograph 16. Newport, R.I.: Naval War College Press, 2009.

2010

"Foreword" to Albert A. Nofi, *To Train the Fleet for War: The U.S. Navy Fleet Problems, 1923–1940.* Naval War College Historical Monograph 18. Newport: Naval War College Press, 2010, pp. ix–x.

"Foreword" to Hal M. Friedman, *Digesting History: The U.S. Naval War College, the Lessons of World War Two, and Future Naval Warfare, 1945–1947.* Naval War College Historical Monograph 17. Newport: Naval War College Press, 2010, pp. ix–x.

"Here's for a Coriolis Effect in Maritime History." *Coriolis: An Interdisciplinary Journal of Maritime History* 1, no. 2 (April 2010). Available on the internet at http:// ijms.nmdl.org/index

"The Neglected Field of Naval History? A Forum." By Andrew D. Lambert, John Beeler, Barry Strauss, and John B. Hattendorf. *Historically Speaking* 11, no. 4 (September 2010), pp. 9–19.

Nineteen-Gun Salute: Case Studies of Operational, Strategic, and Diplomatic Naval Leadership during the 20th and Early 21st Centuries. Edited by John B. Hattendorf and Bruce A. Elleman. Newport, R.I.: Naval War College Press; and Washington, D.C.: U.S. Government Printing Office, 2010.

Nineteenth International Seapower Symposium: Report of the Proceedings, 6–9 October 2009. Edited by John B. Hattendorf and John W. Kennedy. Newport: Naval War College, 2010.

2011

"Foreword" to Bruce A. Elleman and S. C. M. Paine, *Naval Power and Expeditionary Warfare: Peripheral Campaigns and New Theatres of Naval Warfare.* London: Routledge, 2011, pp. xii–xiii.

"Introduction" to Lawrence Wroth, *The Way of a Ship and Some American Contributions to Navigation.* Edited by John B. Hattendorf. Revised edition, Providence, R.I.: The John Carter Brown Library, 2011.

"Navies, Strategy, and Tactics in the Age of de Ruyter." In *Michiel de Ruyter: Dutch Admiral,* edited by J. R. Bruijn. Rotterdam: Karawansary, 2011. Reprinted in *Talking about Naval History,* pp. 61–77.

Talking about Naval History: A Collection of Essays. Naval War College Historical Monograph 19. Newport, R.I.: Naval War College Press, 2011.

"The United States Navy in the Twenty-First Century: Thoughts on Naval Theory, Strategic Constraints and Opportunities," *Mariner's Mirror* 97, no. 1 (February 2011), pp. 265–277.

NOTE   This list does not include some 140 book reviews published in thirty different journals. Also, except where an individual volume has been edited by Hattendorf, his work as a book-series editor is not included: senior series editor with Wayne P. Hughes, Jr., of the *Classics of Sea Power,* eleven volumes (Annapolis, Md.: Naval Institute Press, 1989–98), each volume of which has a half-page "series editors" note; and work as general editor, *Maritime History 1475–1815,* a series of facsimile rare books from the collections of the John Carter Brown Library, twenty-one volumes (Delmar, N.Y.: Scholars' Facsimiles and Reprints, 1993–99).

ABOUT THE AUTHOR

John B. Hattendorf is the Ernest J. King Professor of Maritime History at the U.S. Naval War College, Newport, Rhode Island, a position he has held since 1984, where he has additionally been Chairman of the Maritime History Department and Director of the Naval War College Museum since 2003.

He holds degrees in history from Kenyon College (1964), Brown University (1971), and the University of Oxford, where he completed his D.Phil. in war history at Pembroke College in 1979. A graduate of the Munson Institute of American Maritime History at Mystic Seaport in 1970, he has served as an adjunct faculty member of the Institute since 1990 and was its adjunct director from 1996 to 2001.

A U.S. naval officer during the Vietnam War era (1965–73), he served at sea in three destroyers, earning a commendation from the Commander, U.S. Seventh Fleet, for his combat service. Ashore, he served as an officer at the Naval History Division, Office of the Chief of Naval Operations, and on the uniformed faculty of the Naval War College.

As a civilian academic, he has been visiting professor at the National University of Singapore 1981–83, a visiting scholar at the German Armed Forces Military History Research Office 1990–91, and a visiting fellow at Pembroke College, Oxford University, in 2001–2002. He is author, editor, coauthor, or coeditor of more than forty books and numerous articles in the field of maritime history, including being editor-in-chief of the multivolume *Oxford Encyclopedia of Maritime History* (2007), which was awarded the Dartmouth Medal of the American Library Association in 2008. His scholarship has been recognized with the award of an honorary doctorate of humane letters; the Caird Medal of the National Maritime Museum, Greenwich, in the United Kingdom; the K. Jack Bauer Award of the North American Society for Oceanic History; the Samuel Eliot Morison Award from the USS *Constitution* Museum; and the Alfred Thayer Mahan Award from the Navy League of the United States. For his service as Chairman, Secretary of the Navy's Advisory Subcommittee on Naval History in 2006–2008, he was awarded the Department of the Navy Superior Civilian Service Award. In 2011, the Naval War College named in his honor the endowed Hattendorf Prize for Distinguished Original Research in Maritime History.

He is a past president of the North American Society for Oceanic History (NASOH), the national organization for historians and museum, archives, and library professionals in the broad field of maritime history. He has served on the Board of Advisors of the

Canadian Forces College and is a Fellow of the Royal Historical Society in the United Kingdom. He has been a member of the Council of the Navy Records Society in the UK, a corresponding member in the United States for the Society of Nautical Research (UK), vice president of the Hakluyt Society, founding president of the American Friends of the Hakluyt Society, and an honorary corresponding member of the Royal Swedish Society for Nautical Sciences, the Académie du Var in France, and the Portuguese Navy's Academia de Marinha.

INDEX